BERTOLT BRECHT:
CRITICAL AND PRIMARY SOURCES

VOLUME III

BERTOLT BRECHT:
CRITICAL AND PRIMARY SOURCES

PRACTICE

VOLUME III

Edited by David Barnett

BLOOMSBURY ACADEMIC
LONDON • NEW YORK • OXFORD • NEW DELHI • SYDNEY

BLOOMSBURY ACADEMIC
Bloomsbury Publishing Plc
50 Bedford Square, London, WC1B 3DP, UK
1385 Broadway, New York, NY 10018, USA

BLOOMSBURY, BLOOMSBURY ACADEMIC and the Diana logo are trademarks
of Bloomsbury Publishing Plc

First published in Great Britain 2020

Introductions and editorial content copyright © David Barnett, 2020

English language translations copyright © Romy Fursland, 2020 (unless otherwise stated)

David Barnett has asserted his right under the Copyright, Designs and
Patents Act, 1988, to be identified as the Editor of this work.

For legal purposes the Permissions Acknowledgements on pp. 375–6 constitute an extension
of this copyright page.

All rights reserved. No part of this publication may be reproduced or transmitted in any
form or by any means, electronic or mechanical, including photocopying, recording, or
any information storage or retrieval system, without prior permission in writing
from the publishers.

Bloomsbury Publishing Plc does not have any control over, or responsibility for, any
third-party websites referred to or in this book. All internet addresses given in this book
were correct at the time of going to press. The author and publisher regret any
inconvenience caused if addresses have changed or sites have ceased to exist,
but can accept no responsibility for any such changes.

A catalogue record for this book is available from the British Library.

A catalog record for this book is available from the Library of Congress.

ISBN: HB: 978-1-4742-9947-3
HB set: 978-1-4742-9949-7

Series: Critical and Primary Sources

Typeset by Deanta Global Publishing Services, Chennai, India
Printed and bound in Great Britain

To find out more about our authors and books visit www.bloomsbury.com and
sign up for our newsletters.

CONTENTS

VOLUME III
PRACTICE

Note on the Text and Common Abbreviations   ix

Introduction   1

Part One   Brecht as Theatre Director and Documenter

Weimar Republic

1   Brecht's Formative Years   9
  Edward Braun

Switzerland/GDR/Berliner Ensemble

2   Rhythm and Structure: Brecht's *Antigone* in Performance   27
  Bruno C. Duarte

3   Original Interpretations of Brecht Plays   45
  Bertolt Brecht

4   Undogmatic Marxism: Brecht Rehearses at the Berliner Ensemble   46
  David Barnett

Brecht and the Actor

5   Instructions to Actors   63
  Bertolt Brecht

6   Brecht and the Contradictory Actor   65
  John Rouse

Brecht and Documentation

Modelbooks

7   *Couragemodell*: Detail and Arrangement of a Model Book   83
  Kristopher Imbrigotta

Photography/the Image

8   'Was besagt eine Fotografie?' Early Brechtian Perspectives on Photography   91
Tom Kuhn

PART TWO   BRECHT'S RELATIONSHIPS WITH PRACTITIONERS

Caspar Neher

9   Stylistic Devices of a Set Designed by Caspar Neher for Brecht's Epic Theatre   109
Susanne de Ponte

Helene Weigel

10   Helene Weigel   119
Bertolt Brecht

11   Weigel's Figuration and Defiguration in Brecht's Texts   120
Patrick Primavesi

Karl Korsch

12   Brecht's Marxist Aesthetic: The Korsch Connection   137
Douglas Kellner

Walter Benjamin

13   Walter Benjamin and Bertolt Brecht: Account of a Constellation   149
Erdmut Wizisla

Kurt Weill

14   'Suiting the Action to the Word': Some Observations on *Gestus* and
Gestische Musik   161
Michael Morley

Hanns Eisler

15   Eisler/Brecht or Brecht/Eisler? Perspectives, Forms and Limits
of their Collaboration   179
Albrecht Dümling

Paul Dessau

16   Composing for BB: Some Comments   193
Paul Dessau

Brecht's Female Collaborators

17 Victimhood or Camouflage? The Modesty of Elisabeth Hauptmann 201
    Sabine Kebir

18 '... Now I've Gone and Put Ideas in His Head Again': Notes on Margarete
    Steffin, Brecht's 'Personal Editor' 210
    Wolfgang Jeske

19 Berlau Photographs Brecht's Life and Work – a Collaboration (More or Less) 224
    Grischa Meyer

Brecht's Assistants in the Theatre

20 Notice [3]: *To the Members of the Berliner Ensemble* 241
    Bertolt Brecht

21 Interviews with Claus and Wera Küchenmeister and with Egon Monk
    Joachim Lang and Jürgen Hillesheim 242

PART THREE GLOBAL BRECHT

Europe

22 The Politics of the Body: Pina Bausch's *Tanztheater* 267
    David W. Price

23 Theatre for the People: The Impact of Brechtian Theory on the Production
    and Performance of *1789* by Ariane Mnouchkine's Théâtre du Soleil 276
    Agnieszka Karch

Asia

24 Brecht's East Asia: A Conspectus 287
    Antony Tatlow

25 Brecht: A Participant in the Process of Nation-Building 299
    Amal Allana

Africa

26 African Brecht 315
    Brian Crow

North America

27 New Measures for Brecht in America 333
    Peter W. Ferran

South America

28 Brecht and Latin America's 'Theatre of Revolution' 347
    Diana Taylor

29 Activist Theater: From Brecht through Boal 358
    Steven K. Smith

PERMISSIONS ACKNOWLEDGEMENTS 375
INDEX 377

NOTE ON THE TEXT AND COMMON ABBREVIATIONS

Texts first published in English have been reproduced as they were first printed, with any extracts in German, or other languages, retained as per the originals.

- **BBA**   Bertolt-Brecht-Archive
- **BE**   Berliner Ensemble
- **BFA**   See GBA
- **BH**   *Brecht Handbook*, 5 volumes
- **GBA**   Brecht, *Grosse Berliner und Frankfurter Ausgabe*, 30 volumes and an index volume
- **GDR**   German Democratic Republic
- **GW**   Brecht, *Gesammelte Werke*, 20 volumes
- **HUAC**   House on Un-American Activities Committee
- **IBS**   International Brecht Society
- **SED**   Socialist Unity Party of Germany
- **SPD**   Social Democratic Party

Introduction

While it was necessary to differentiate this volume ('Practice') from the previous one ('Theory') for the sake of clarity, the distinction is perhaps a little misleading when considering the way that Bertolt Brecht himself treated the two categories. Before assessing this relationship, however, it might be worth examining the terms themselves. Practice, in Brecht's case, frequently confronts particular problems in the theatre with particular responses: no two plays, scenes or actors are the same, and thus all practice has to focus on the reality of specific issues and contexts as they arise. Theory, on the other hand, is not reality; rather, it attempts to construct more generally applicable ideas to drama, theatre and performance as a whole, sometimes in a systematic, sometimes in a less organized fashion.

These brief definitions prompt a chicken-and-egg question: What comes first? Does observing practice produce theoretical accounts of that reality or does theory try to influence practice by challenging it with new ideas? Both questions could be answered in the affirmative in different contexts. For Brecht, the observation of theatrical practice was crucial for constructing ideas for representing reality. On the other hand, Brecht's theoretical innovations for the theatre were, especially during his period of exile from 1933 to 1947, articulated without concrete reference to experiences in the theatre because he had little access to that institution at the time. As should be clear, the relationship between theory and practice for someone like Brecht, who was both a theorist *and* a practitioner, was complex.

One need look no further than Brecht in rehearsal to understand how theory and practice mutually informed each other. Having founded his own theatre company together with his wife, Helene Weigel, in 1949, Brecht mostly led the early productions of the Berliner Ensemble. Here his directing practice was profoundly influenced by the theoretical approaches he had developed to making theatre while in exile. He experimented with practical ways of realizing these ideas. In this case, theory was derived from observation of reality *and* speculation on potentially productive ways of making theatre to influence that reality. However, while he set about directing or co-directing, that is, leading by example, he assembled a team of assistants, whom he hoped would go on to direct or lead dramaturgical teams themselves in due course. The assistants took special rehearsal notes, called 'Notate' (rather than the usual German word 'Notizen'). The *Notate* were not merely a descriptive record of rehearsal but also an analytical and reflective exercise, designed to feed back into the rehearsal process itself.

What emerges from this example is the complex interplay of theory and practice for Brecht. His direction tried to embody, to turn into practice, certain theoretical positions concerning the representation of reality on a stage. The practice itself, however, was continually being modified by the theoretical input of his assistants, who then continued to speculate on the efficacy of that practice. By the time of the production's premiere, Brecht would continue to reflect on the work done in order to look back on one process and prepare for the next. Theory and practice were in a perpetual dialogue with each other. This is evidenced by more than 350 printed pages of writings, written between

1949 and the year of his death, 1956, as collected in the standard German edition of Brecht's work. He never stopped theorizing, yet he was nonetheless most active in the practice of making theatre.

While the focus of this volume is 'practice', readers should not forget that it is difficult to talk of a firm division between theory and practice for Brecht. Rather, the two are actually different ways of approaching the same thing: the construction of a theatre that can activate an audience to intervene in the workings of the world through its own representations of that world.

This volume opens with a consideration of Brecht's work as a practising theatre director. The essays chart his journey from a disastrous start in the Weimar Republic through the development of a number of key directorial strategies to their later revision and articulation when Brecht served as the lead director at the Berliner Ensemble. At each point, new practices were deployed and interrogated, and the results of the work, in the form of productions themselves, were evaluated. Brecht the practitioner was continually stepping back from his work in order to reflect on it.

This section also includes a short but important reflection on the concept of 'originality' in theatre production, written by Brecht and published here in English for the first time. The single paragraph offers a challenge to contemporary directors who may believe that their aim is to offer an audience something novel. Brecht counters that originality is not an end in itself and implies that directors have a greater obligation to representing reality accurately. Again, implicit here is the position that the rehearsal process discovers the unexpected and the surprising in the represented actions, and these are the 'original' elements of the production.

Closely associated with Brecht's directing practices are his understanding of and relationships with his actors. A classic essay, which has lost none of its insight or relevance, addresses this in detail. It is preceded by a list of important aspects for actors to consider when performing in Brecht's theatre. The list that Brecht wrote while in exile in the early 1940s summarizes ideas he articulated earlier and includes some new ones for good measure. The list of 'instructions' presents a neat checklist in a remarkably compact form that can still benefit actors seeking to show the processes that lead to the actions they perform on stage.

The following two essays consider how Brecht documented his theatrical work. Again, it is clear that the practical endeavour of setting out a record of a production already included a great deal of theoretical conceptualization. The harmony of theory and practice can be appreciated not only in the care taken to set out the processes Brecht employed in rehearsal and the effects he sought to achieve but also in the pedagogical desire to pass his practices on to other theatre-makers.

The major section 'Brecht's relationships with practitioners' covers three areas, yet all are concerned with a central facet of Brecht's creative life: collaboration. Much has been written about the nature of this relationship, with Brecht sometimes positioned as exploitative or failing to credit the work of others appropriately. The essays in this section take a nuanced approach to Brecht's collaborative working practices and point to mutuality, interactivity and respect in the mechanisms of the creative process. This is perhaps best understood in the subsection on Brecht's work with his assistants. Here, the husband-and-wife team of Claus and Wera Küchenmeister, and the director Egon Monk reflect on their formative experiences with Brecht, with several decades' hindsight. While the work was not easy, and Brecht could make great demands on their time, talents and efforts, there is the sense that they greatly benefited from his attempts to engage them in making new kinds of theatre. And the claim that Brecht did not acknowledge the input of his collaborators is queried by the short notice to the members of the Berliner Ensemble he composed in September 1955, translated into English for the first time, too. Here he clearly announces to the company that he wants to correct the unfair impression that the 'work of the young directors' is in some way eclipsed by his own.

The opening subsection deals with Brecht's collaborations with a major designer, two influential philosophers, the Berliner Ensemble's principal actor, Helen Weigel, and some of his most important musical collaborators. The following subsection focuses on three of Brecht's female collaborators, all of whom were also his lovers at various junctures (unlike Weigel who was his wife). These women have been especially targeted as Brecht's exploited victims over the years, a relationship that immediately fails to acknowledge their substantial, active contributions to Brecht's projects. This is not to say that Brecht treated these women well on an interpersonal level all the time. Ruth Berlau, for example, had mental-health and alcohol-dependency problems that were almost certainly exacerbated by Brecht's rejection of her as a lover, yet she also developed the concept of the 'modelbook', an innovation that Brecht relied on and acknowledged as her invention to disseminate his work.

The 'Global Brecht' section that concludes this volume considers Brecht's practical legacy across the world's continents. In the 'Europe' subsection, the essays focus on two particular practitioners whose work registers a clear Brechtian influence. Yet neither of the featured directors should be understood as epigones. In a dialectical process, one does not acquire something by blindly accepting it. On the contrary, rejection already implies an understanding of the thing being discarded – one has to know what one is rejecting for that decision to be sensible. There is thus a contradiction at the heart of the process in which the creative artist *both* accepts and rejects the influence of another to arrive at their own reception. This contradictory process can be understood in all the essays in this section. Influence is not something that artists or theatres simply absorb; instead, it is something that is negotiated. Brecht himself was absolutely clear on the subject of copying: he called it an 'art'.[1] That is, a great deal of effort goes into copying anything if the copy is to have any value. Copying theatrical practice involves understanding where that practice came from, which ends it was trying to pursue and how it sought to achieve them. Copying is a process and its results are the product of close study. Consequently, all the discussions in 'Global Brecht' acknowledge the manifold processes, the trial and the error, inherent in the transmission of cultural practices between places and times.

Brecht's reception outside of Europe is discussed against the backdrop of national and international traditions. The essays pick out particularly interesting instances of how Brecht's ideas and practices have been taken up and understood against a broad backdrop of contexts. The example of North America is particularly telling. Brecht's play *The Measures Taken* (also known in this set of volumes as *The Decision*) arrives in a society in which its content is understood as inimical to the nation's values, which are themselves inflected by the Cold War. Yet the essay reveals how the content, the apparent justification of political murder, is framed by a revolutionary form in which the performance of the

---

[1] Brecht, 'Does the Use of the Model Restrict Artistic Freedom?', in Brecht, *Brecht on Performance: Messingkauf and Modelbooks*, ed. Steve Giles, Tom Kuhn and Marc Silberman (London: Bloomsbury, 2014), pp. 238–41, here p. 340.

play before an audience is actually secondary to its status as a performative exercise in complex thinking for those participating in the process.

As should be evident from this volume as a whole, 'practice' is never free from theoretical input; it does not exist as a 'thing in itself'. And while Brecht was fond of quoting the English maxim that the proof of the pudding was in the eating,[2] this does not imply that practice was in some way an autonomous measure of success or failure. This is because the criteria that lead to a judgement are themselves already informed by a wide range of theoretical considerations: values do not simply appear from nowhere. It would thus be sensible to understand this volume and the previous one on 'theory' as dialogical – they are always talking to each other.

---

[2] For one example, written in English rather than German in the original, see journal entry for 30 June 1940, in Brecht, *Journals 1934-1955* (London: Methuen, 1993), p. 73.

PART ONE

BRECHT AS THEATRE DIRECTOR AND DOCUMENTER

Weimar Republic

CHAPTER ONE

Brecht's Formative Years

EDWARD BRAUN

More than one critic has observed that whereas Piscator, the director, has made his most lasting impression in the field of dramatic writing, the lessons of Brecht, Germany's greatest modern playwright, have been most deeply absorbed by directors, designers and actors. Partly, this is explained by the fact that the past fifty years have seen a merging of the roles of dramatist and director, with Brecht the ultimate example of the two in one; but equally it is because both men, in their striving for a theatre that would reflect society in its totality, needed to master all the resources at the stage's command. In the years from 1922, when his first play reached the stage, up to his death in 1956 Brecht usually took some active part in any production of his play that was within reach. Of them, some twenty can be ascribed to him personally as director, usually working in collaboration with others.

Towards the end of 1921 Brecht, at the age of twenty-three, was gaining recognition as a dramatist: his first play *Baal* was due shortly to appear in print and his second, *Drums in the Night*, had been accepted for performance by the Munich avant-garde theatre, Die Kammerspiele. But with the publication *of Baal* deferred for fear of censorship and the production *of Drums in the Night* slow to materialise, Brecht decided to force his luck by abandoning his university studies in Munich and moving to Berlin. By the time he returned to his home-town of Augsburg the following Easter he had little to show for his initiative: no Berlin management had made a firm commitment to stage any of his plays, and his first venture as a director, Arnolt Bronnen's expressionist drama *Vatermord* (*Patricide*) for the Junge Bühne, had ended abruptly when two of the leading performers left a rehearsal in protest at Brecht's caustic comments.[1]

However, Brecht left Berlin with many invaluable contacts established and the first draft of a third play, *In the Jungle*, completed. Back in Munich it was accepted by the Residenztheater, and then on 29 September 1922 *Drums in the Night* was finally presented by Otto Falckenberg at the Kammerspiele. Brecht had persuaded Herbert Ihering, drama critic of the *Berliner Börsen-Courier*, to attend and a few days later he wrote: 'The twenty-four year-old writer Bert Brecht has transformed the literary face of Germany overnight. With Bert Brecht a new tone, a new melody, a new vision have come into being. ... No dramatist since Wedekind has afforded such a soul-shattering experience.'[2] A month later, Brecht was awarded the Kleist Prize as that year's outstanding new

---

Edward Braun, 'Brecht's Formative Years', in Braun, *The Director and the Stage* (London: Methuen, 1982), pp. 162–79.

[1] For an account of the incident by Arnolt Bronnen see Hubert Witt (ed.). *Brecht As They Knew Him* (London, 1975), pp. 32–34.
[2] Reprinted in Monika Wyss (ed.), *Brecht in der Kritik* (Munich, 1977), pp. 5–6.

dramatist, Ihering being the judge. As a result, other productions of *Drums in the Night* soon followed, including one at the Deutsches Theater in Berlin, again by Falckenberg. Then in May 1923 *In the Jungle* (later retitled *In the Jungle of Cities*) was staged by Erich Engel at the Residenztheater, with designs by Brecht's boyhood friend and close collaborator, Caspar Neher. Much as the critics admired the acting, they could make little of this most enigmatic of Brecht's plays, their task being made even more difficult by attempts to disrupt the performances by members of the newly-formed Nazi Party. After six nights it had to be taken off, and the theatre's dramaturg was dismissed.

By now, though, Brecht was well established, having been appointed to the dramaturgical and directing staff of the Kammerspiele immediately following the premiere of *Drums in the Night*. He was not slow to make his presence felt; as Arnolt Bronnen recalls, 'Even before he had been performed anywhere, he was the terror of the mediocre stage director, the absolute horror of the manager. He dictated the casting from the first to the twenty-second role; he fought with a never tiring tenacity for the actor and the actress whom he had built into his scenes.'[3]

Originally, it was intended that Brecht's first production for the Kammerspiele should be a Shakespeare, probably *Macbeth*. However, he argued that a lesser known work would be a safer choice for his debut, and proposed Marlowe's tragedy *Edward the Second*. It was agreed that Brecht would adapt it in collaboration with his friend and mentor, the successful writer Lion Feuchtwanger, who also worked as a dramaturg for the company and had a good command of English. Apart from the possible appeal of the play's homosexual theme (which had already figured in *Baal* and *In the Jungle*), Brecht was attracted by its loose chronicle form with rapidly shifting scenes and discontinuity of mood and action. Thirty years later he recalled: 'We wanted to make possible a production which would break with the Shakespearian tradition common to German theatres; that lumpy monumental style beloved of middle-class philistines.'[4]

The adaptation took the greater part of 1923 to complete and finally contained no more than one-sixth of Marlowe's original lines. Entitled *The Life of Edward the Second of England*, the new version was altogether swifter moving and sacrificed much of Marlowe's sensuous rhetoric for the sake of a harsher mode of expression and jerky, irregular speech rhythms. It also introduced a number of dramaturgical devices that were later to become familiar features of Brecht's style, notably the interpolated sardonic street ballad or 'Moritat', and titles announcing the date, location and content of the scene to come.[5]

Brecht's work as adaptor by no means ended when rehearsals began in January 1924. Bernhard Reich, the Kammerspiele's artistic director at the time, writes:

> The rehearsals directed by Brecht took a curious course. Brecht as director liked one of the actors: ergo he must be shown off to better advantage. Brecht as dramatist took a piece of paper from his pocket and wrote new lines for the actor. Director Brecht discovered that the intentions of the author could not be implemented stagewise. Next morning Dramatist Brecht brought altered and more suitable lines. The final

---

[3] Quoted in Klaus Völker, *Brecht Chronicle* (New York, 1975), p. 35.
[4] 'On looking through my first plays (iv)' in *Bertolt Brecht Collected Plays*, Vol. 1, ed. J. Willett and R. Manheim (London, 1970), p. 454.
[5] Brecht and Feuchtwanger also made fundamental changes in the action and characterisation. For a discussion by Eric Bentley of their version see Bertolt Brecht, *Edward II – A Chronicle Play* (trans. Eric Bentley, New York, 1966), pp. vii–xxviii.

rehearsal drew ever nearer, and Brecht grew ever more active, handing to the actors over the footlights whole rolls of new lines. If one of them protested, Brecht looked at him with such unconcealed honest amazement that he took the manuscript and got down to the job of learning the new text.[6]

Edward the Second took eight weeks to rehearse, the longest period in the company's history, partly due to the delays caused by Brecht's rewriting of the text, but equally because of the demands for precision and clarity that he made of his actors. He insisted on making the story of the play plain in order that the audience should understand precisely what the characters were doing and what was happening to them. 'Pedantically' – says Reich – 'he exposed at the rehearsals the plot of the drama, the basic events of each single scene, the chain of events.' Henceforth, nothing in the theatre was more important for Brecht than the story (*Die Fabel*), and to ensure its clarity every physical action was made as concrete as possible. Hence, when rehearsing the scene in *Edward the Second* where Baldock surrenders his friend Edward to enemy soldiers (Scene 10) by handing him a handkerchief, Brecht objected to the haste and the insignificance of the gesture, and explained:

> Baldock is a traitor ... You must demonstrate the behaviour of a traitor. Baldock goes about the betrayal with friendly outstretched arms, tenderly and submissively handing [Edward] the cloth with broad, projecting gestures. ... The public should note the behaviour of a traitor and thereby pay attention![7]

Similarly, he insisted that the hanging of Gaveston be carried out with the same attention to detail – 'professionally', as he put it:

> Brecht stopped the actors and told them to do it properly, to tie the noose and make it fast to the cross-beam. Shrugging their shoulders, the actors did their best to follow the director's unexpected instructions. Brecht stopped them again and, refusing to give way, insisted relentlessly that they repeat the hanging, but do it like experts. The audience had to get pleasure from seeing them put the noose round the fellow's neck.[8]

As models of this demonstrative style of acting Brecht held up the players in the popular fairground booths, and invited the celebrated clown Karl Valentin to sit in on rehearsals. It was Valentin who supplied the solution to the portrayal of the soldiers in the long battle scene. 'What's the truth about these soldiers? What *about* them?' – asked Brecht, at his wits' end. 'They're pale, they're scared, that's what!' – replied Valentin. 'They're tired,' added Brecht, and it was straightway decided to make up the soldiers' faces thickly with white chalk. Brecht regarded this as the point at which the production's style was determined, and in latter years quoted it as the moment when the idea of Epic theatre first came into his head.[9]

To some degree this precision of style was dictated by the small stage of the Kammerspiele and the proximity of the audience. Brecht and Caspar Neher made a virtue of the enforced simplicity in the production's decor: 'Brecht primitivised the settings: a room was a room, and a king's chair was a chair, but the rooms and the chairs were kept in the style of the old German masters in their simple, merely suggested style. The costumes of the king

---

[6] *Brecht As They Knew Him*, p. 40.
[7] W. Stuart McDowell, 'Actors on Brecht: The Munich Years' in *The Drams Review*, Vol. 20, No. 3 (T 71), p. 113.
[8] Bernhard Reich, quoted in Klaus Völker, *Brecht: A Biography* (London, 1979), p. 72.
[9] 'Conversations with Brecht' in Walter Benjamin, *Understanding Brecht* (London, 1973), p. 115. The incident is also mentioned by Brecht in *The Messingkauf Dialogues* (London, 1965), pp. 69–70.

and the barons were made of coarse dyed material: the spear-carriers wore sacks.'[10] The collaboration between Brecht and Neher, though interrupted by exile between 1933 and 1947, formed the basis for Brecht's work in the theatre. Neher's remarkable approach precisely suited Brecht's perception of man's behaviour, his social relationships and his environment; his design sketches did much to concretise Brecht's imagery. As Brecht wrote in 1951:

> His sets are significant statements about reality. He takes a bold sweep, never letting inessential detail or decoration distract from the statement, which is an artistic and intellectual one. At the same time everything has beauty, and the essential detail is most lovingly carried out. ... And there is no building of his, no yard or workshop or garden, that does not also bear the fingerprints, as it were of the people who built it or who lived there. He makes visible the manual skills and knowledge of the builders and the ways of living of the inhabitants. In his designs our friend always starts with 'the people themselves' and 'what is happening to or through them'. He provides no 'decor', frames or backgrounds, but constructs the space for 'people' to experience something in. ... He is a great painter. But above all he is an ingenious story-teller. He knows better than anyone that what does not further the narrative harms it.[11]

In insisting on concreteness and narrative clarity in *Edward the Second* Brecht and his collaborators were reacting on the one hand against the operatic monumentality with which the classics were habitually staged in the German theatre, and on the other against the idealised abstractions of Expressionism. Erwin Faber describes the style as 'naturalistic'; but far from meaning the creation of a lifelike illusion, he has in mind the emphasising of significant detail, of cause and effect, as typified by the examples quoted of the betrayal of Edward and the execution of Gaveston. In this sense, Brecht was never other than 'naturalistic', both aesthetically and philosophically.

Thus *Edward the Second* was of enormous importance in Brecht's development, containing many of the seeds of what was his particular conception of Epic theatre. The premiere took place on 18 March 1924, just over two months before *Fahnen*, Piscator's first major production in Berlin. Hence, although Brecht learnt much from Piscator subsequently, he owed little to him at this point.

Despite the fact that the future film star, Oskar Homolka, who played Mortimer, was incoherent from drink by the end of the first performance, the production was warmly received and by a few critics at least it was recognised as a significant advance in staging technique. Whereas Julius Bab objected to the sensation of 'the fair-barker Brecht ... with his invisible pointer' standing on the sidelines, Ihering saluted his capacity to respond to the public of 'the streets, the sports arenas, the six-day cycle races, the boxing matches', and to treat history as 'a medium for human communication, a ballad or a broadsheet (*Moritat*)'.[12] Looking back in 1948, Ihering wrote:

> Brecht substituted for the concept of greatness that of *distance*. ... He did not reduce the human being. Nor did he anatomize him. He 'removed' him. ... This production in Munich was the turning point of the classical theatre.[13]

---

[10]*Brecht As They Knew Him*, pp. 41–42.
[11]John Willett (ed. & trans.), *Brecht on Theatre* (London, 1964), pp. 231–232.
[12]Reprinted in Günther Rühle (ed.), *Theater für die Republik* cit., pp. 509–10.
[13]Quoted in Frederic Ewen, *Bertolt Brecht* (London, 1970), p. 130.

Ihering was not being merely wise after the event; two years before he staged *Edward the Second* Brecht had written in his diary:

> There is one common artistic error which I hope I've avoided in *Baal* and *Jungle*, that of trying to carry people away. Instinctively I've kept my distance and ensured that the stage realisation of my (poetical and philosophical) effects remains within bounds. The spectator's 'splendid isolation' is left intact, it is not *sua res quae agitur*, he is not fobbed off with an invitation to feel sympathetically, to fuse with the hero and cut a meaningful and indestructible figure while watching himself in two simultaneous versions. There is a higher type of interest to be got from making comparisons, from whatever is different, amazing, impossible to take in as a whole.[14]

In September 1924 Brecht moved to Berlin to become a dramaturg at Reinhardt's Deutsches Theater, though he did little there but observe productions and draw his pay. By December both *In the Jungle* and *Edward the Second* had been given their premieres in the capital, and Brecht was working on his next play, *Man equals Man*, which took the best part of a year to complete in the first of its several drafts.

Despite the promise he had shown with *Edward the Second* Brecht had to wait nearly two years for another opportunity to direct. The play was a considerably shortened version of *Baal*, retitled *Life Story of the Man Baal*, purged of its expressionistic timelessness and set in the period 1904–1912 against a background of developing technology. Baal was now a garage mechanic-turned-poet from Augsburg instead of the 'simple clerk' of the original version.

Introduced by Brecht himself singing the 'Hymn of Baal the Great', the production, described as 'a dramatic biography', was given an 'epic' framework of 'factual' scene titles, announcing date, location and event, all designed to confer documentary authenticity on the action. With Oskar Homolka as Baal, the production was given a single Sunday matinee in February 1926 at the Deutsches Theater under the auspices of the 'Junge Bühne'. The performance provoked the now predictable scenes in the auditorium and was covered extensively by the Berlin critics. It was a clear sign of the times that Johannes Harnisch of the right-wing paper *Der Montag* saw the play as proof of the degeneracy of German culture and called on the Prussian authorities to put a stop to the theatre being used as an 'institution for public pollution'.[15]

Brecht, however, saw little prospect in exploiting the established theatre as it then functioned. A few days before the premiere of *Baal* he published an article in the *Berliner Börsen-Courier* entitled 'More Good Sport', in which he wrote:

> There is no theatre today that could invite one or two of those persons who are alleged to find fun in writing plays to one of its performances and expect them to feel an urge to write a play for it. They can see at a glance that there is no possible way of getting any *fun* out of this. No wind will go into anyone's sails here. There is no 'sport'. ... A play is simply unrecognizable once it has passed through this sausage machine. If we come along and say that both we and the public had imagined things differently – that we are in favour, for instance, of elegance, lightness, dryness, objectivity – then the

---

[14]Diary entry for 10 February 1922 in *Bertolt Brecht Diaries 1920–1922* (trans. John Willett, London, 1979), p. 130.
[15]G. Rühle, op. cit., pp. 689–90.

theatre replies innocently: Those passions which you have singled out, my dear sir, do not beat beneath any dinner jacket's manly chest.[16]

Brecht was constantly in search of ways to overcome the numbing effect of theatrical convention. In December 1926 he persuaded the director of his one-act comedy *The Wedding* (later retitled *A Respectable Wedding*) in Frankfurt am Main to stage it in a boxing ring. The following summer he collaborated for the first time with the composer Kurt Weill to produce a work for the Baden-Baden chamber music festival called *Mahagonny*. Subtitled as a 'Songspiel', it was a dramatised setting of six poems from Brecht's recently published collection *Devotions for the Home* (*Hauspostille*). Described in a programme note as 'a short epic play which simply draws conclusions from the irresistible decline of our existing social classes', *Mahagonny* was performed, once again in a boxing ring, in front of projections of drawings by Caspar Neher. Weill's music – said Brecht – 'precisely because it behaved in a purely emotional way and eschewed none of the usual narcotic stimuli ... played its part in exposing the bourgeois ideologies'.[17]

By now Brecht had been engaged for several months in a systematic study of Marxism. His collaborator Elisabeth Hauptmann says that this was prompted by the need to elucidate the workings of the stock exchange whilst working on a play called *Joe P. Fleischhacker from Chicago*. The play was never completed, but Brecht's enquiries led him to the realisation that the only dramatic means adequate for the elucidation of the complex workings of capitalist society was the Epic theatre, which he now formulated as 'acting from memory (quoting gestures and attitudes)'.[18] The inference of this is that the actors tell a story with foreknowledge of its outcome, and use the characters to 'illustrate' the narrative, rather than 'live' their roles. As we have seen, Brecht had gone a long way towards realising this style intuitively in his work on *Edward the Second*, but at that time it had no political underpinning. By 1927, he had had the chance to observe Piscator's work and to explore the prospects revealed by such productions as *Revue Roter Rummel*, *Trotz Alledem!*, and *Sturmflut*. In autumn 1927 Brecht joined Piscator's dramaturgical collective and worked on adaptations of *Rasputin* and *Schwejk* as well as the rewriting of Lania's *Konjunktur*. Thus, for nearly a year he was in a position to assimilate Piscator's methods at close quarters.

The extent of Piscator's influence on the development of Brecht's Epic theatre has been discussed by a number of critics in recent years, and numerous references in Brecht's own writings acknowledge the extent of his debt to Piscator.[19] However, there remain fundamental differences between the two men that help to explain why none of Piscator's plans for staging Brecht's work ever materialised,[20] and why they never actually got round to collaborating in the 1950's when they were both back in Germany. Piscator summarised their differences in a note in his diary in 1955:

B.'s starting point is episodic succession
P.'s is political fatality

---

[16]*Brecht on Theatre*, pp. 7–8.
[17]Quoted in K. Völker, *Brecht: A Biography*, cit., p. 126.
[18]See Elisabeth Hauptmann, 'Notes on Brecht's Work' in *Brecht As They Knew Him*, pp. 52–53. For a discussion or Brecht's conception of Epic Theatre see John Willett, *The Theatre of Bertolt Brecht* (London 1959), 167ff.
[19]Among others see F. Ewen, op cit., pp. 148 ff; Christopher Innes, *Erwin Piscator's Political Theatre* (Cambridge, 1972), pp. 189–200; John Willett, *The Theatre of Erwin Piscator*, cit. (numerous references: see Index). For Brecht's comments on Piscator see *Brecht on Theatre*, in particular, pp. 77 ff, 130 ff.
[20]Except *Mother Courage*, staged in Kassel in 1960, after Brecht's death.

> B. demonstrates it in miniature
> P. on the big scale. I wanted to comprehend fate as a *whole*, showing how it is made by men and then spreads beyond them. (Hence the machinery, film etc.)[21]

Also, having once written to Brecht, 'I believe for my part, that no writer came closer to the conception I had of the theatre than you',[22] Piscator later commented in an interview:

> Brecht is my brother, but our views of totality differ. Brecht unveils significant details of human life while I attempt to give a conspectus of political matters as a whole. In a sense you can say that his Mother Courage is a timeless figure. I'd have tried to portray her more historically by showing the Thirty Years' War.[23]

Readily as Brecht acknowledged Piscator as his forerunner in the field of political theatre, and deeply as he respected his credentials as a Communist, he was not convinced that the mechanisation of the stage carried out by the Piscatorbühne was the right means for the revolutionising of the theatre. In essence, he argued, it remained anti-revolutionary, because it was passive and reproductive. All Piscator's technological innovations 'merely created an active atmosphere', whilst failing to show individual characters in the process of change. What was needed, he said, were new principles of dramatic construction and a new approach to acting. In his view, Piscator was relatively little interested in the actor, and hence stood no chance of fundamentally changing the nature of the communication between performer and spectator.[24] Piscator was only too aware of the need to develop a more 'scientific', politically conscious attitude towards acting, but he was never able to tackle this problem systematically. On the other hand, he was as anxious as Brecht to achieve a new, active relationship with the audience, as his efforts with §218 and *Tai Yang erwacht* demonstrate. Nevertheless, Brecht owed a vast debt to Piscator which only recently has been fully acknowledged; around 1940 Brecht wrote in *The Messingkauf Dialogues*: 'Above all, the theatre's conversion to politics was Piscator's achievement, without which the Augsburger's [his own] would hardly be conceivable.'[25]

Piscator had announced the premiere of *Joe P. Fleischhacker* (now titled *Wheat*) for the 1927/28 season at the Theater am Nollendorfplatz, but in spring 1928 *The Threepenny Opera*, Brecht and Weill's free adaptation of John Gay's *Beggar's Opera*, was commissioned for the reopening of the disused Theater am Schiffbauerdamm. Lotte Lenya, Weill's wife and the play's original Jenny, has described the hectic and acrimonious months that culminated in the totally unanticipated triumph of the first night on 31 August 1928.[26] The production ran for over a year to become by far the most celebrated work in the German repertoire of the 1920's. It made an international reputation for Brecht and Weill, not to mention the director, Erich Engel, Caspar Neher, again Brecht's designer, and a number of the cast, most notably Lotte Lenya. How far the fashionable public who flocked to *The Threepenny Opera* recognised it as an oblique attack on the political corruption of Weimar Germany is questionable: Ernst Josef Aufricht, the fortunate impresario who commissioned it, called it 'a literary operetta with flashes of social criticism', whilst the

---

[21]Quoted in John Willett, *The Theatre of Erwin Piscator*, cit., p. 187.
[22]Quoted in C. Innes, op. cit. p. 200.
[23]Quoted in *The Theatre of Erwin Piscator*, cit., p. 188.
[24]See K. Völker, *Brecht: A Biography*, cit., pp. 115–116.
[25]*The Messingkauf Dialogues*, cit. p. 69.
[26]See *Brecht As They Knew Him*, pp. 54–62.

Communist Party organ *Die Rote Fahne* commented: 'Not a trace of modern social or political satire, but all in all, a lively and entertaining hotch-potch.'[27]

However, what nobody doubted was the theatrical significance of the production, on which Brecht, Weill, Engel and Neher worked closely together. Both in terms of the music's function and of the staging, it represented a significant advance in the direction of what Brecht was later to term '*Verfremdung*', the 'alienation' or 'distancing' of the audience from the action that Brecht had sought in his early years in Munich. Although in terms of dramatic structure *The Threepenny Opera* is far closer to being 'well-made' than anything else Brecht ever wrote, he and Weill conceived the songs as a means of interrupting and commenting on the narrative. In 1931 Brecht wrote in his 'Notes to *The Threepenny Opera*'.

> Nothing is more revolting than when the actor pretends not to notice that he has left the level of plain speech and started to sing. The three levels – plain speech, heightened speech and singing – must always remain distinct, and in no case should heightened speech represent an intensification of plain speech, or singing of heightened speech. In no case therefore should singing take place where words are prevented by excess of feeling. The actor must not only sing but show a man singing. ... As for the melody, he must not follow it blindly: there is a kind of speaking-against-the-music which can have strong effects, the results of a stubborn, incorruptible sobriety which is independent of music and rhythm.[28]

The separation of the music from all the other elements of the play was emphasised by the production:

> ... the small orchestra was installed visibly on stage. For the singing of the *songs* a special change of lighting was arranged; the orchestra was lit up; the titles of the various numbers were projected on the screens at the back, for instance 'Song concerning the Insufficiency of Human Endeavour' or 'A short song allows Miss Polly Peachum to confess to her Horrified Parents that she is wedded to the Murderer Macheath'; and the actors changed their positions before the number began.[29]

As regards the setting, Siegfried Melchinger writes: 'Neher erected a giant circus calliope [steam organ] at the back of the stage and illuminated it for the moritat. He painted the [projected] scene titles on blotting paper in a child's scrawl, and threw in a cannibal's head whose derivation from Klee could be overlooked only by the innocent. Pieces of scenery were rolled on stage, raised from below, or lowered from above.'[30] In fact, there were two screens upstage flanking the steam organ and a white half-curtain downstage on a visible steel wire, eight-foot high so that the audience could glimpse something of the preparations for the scene to come. The scene titles in child's scrawl were projected on to the front curtain, which then parted to disclose the action, whilst the upstage screens were used to display a synopsis of the events in the scene to come ('*Die Fabel*', or story) and the titles and texts of songs as they were sung. Both the white half-curtain and the screens now became regular features of Brecht's production style.

---

[27] Quoted in *Brecht: A Biography*, cit., p. 131 and M. Wyss, op. cit., p. 83.
[28] *Brecht on Theatre*, pp. 44–45.
[29] Ibid., p. 85.
[30] 'Neher and Brecht' in *The Drama Review*, Vol. 12, No. 2 (T-38), p. 140.

The debt to Piscator did not escape the critics, but, as Brecht pointed out some years later, there was an important difference:

> In Piscator's productions or in *The Threepenny Opera* the educative elements were so to speak *built in*: they were not an organic consequence of the whole, but stood in contradiction to it. ... [*The Threepenny Opera*] *has a double nature. Instruction and entertainment conflict openly. With Piscator it was the actor and the machinery that openly conflicted.* [my italics, E.B.][31]

The success of *The Threepenny Opera* placed Brecht financially in a position to pursue his studies in Marxism more intensively and systematically. As a consequence he came into closer contact with workers, labour leaders and Communist Party members. Like Piscator, Brecht recognised that the rapidly growing power of the extreme Right called for a form of drama that was politically useful. This need was brought home to him forcefully on May Day 1929 when he saw the police open fire on a prohibited workers' demonstration, killing twenty-five and severely wounding thirty-six. In contrast to Piscator and his Collective, whose touring production of Credé's pro-abortion play *§218* in November 1929 was a highly effective reversion to the agit-prop style, Brecht responded by developing the *Lehrstück* or learning play, 'meant' – as he said – 'not so much for the spectator as for those who were engaged in the performance ... art for the producer, not art for the consumer'.[32] This was not to say that his learning plays were written regardless of audience requirements, but their analytical style was intended to provoke the debate of specific issues raised by Communism rather than mobilise the audience to action, which was more the aim of Piscator and the workers' theatre movement at large.

Altogether, Brecht completed seven *Lehrstücke*, four of which he staged himself between 1929 and 1930. They took the form of concert performances with orchestra, singers, performers, and sometimes the director, sharing the same platform. The action was further clarified by the use of placards and projected titles. Mostly, these plays were devised for performance by school children, but *The Measures Taken* (*Die Massnahme*) was performed in December 1930 at the Grosses Schauspielhaus with a chorus of four hundred of the Greater Berlin Workers' Choir and Brecht's leading actors, Helene Weigel (his wife since 1929), Alexander Granach, Ernst Busch, plus a tenor from the Berlin State Opera, as the four soloist-performers. The score was by Hanns Eisler, a noted Communist composer with whom Brecht was collaborating for the first time. It was the beginning of a long partnership; as John Willett says, Eisler was ideally suited to the style that Brecht was now developing:

> He had none of the faintly cheap nostalgia that haunts much of the work of Weill: he is an even more skilled (and in many ways highbrow) composer, who used his gifts like Brecht himself to make the meaning simple and clear. Like Brecht he used ecclesiastical (the Lutheran chorale) and popular models (folksong, popular ballads and jazz), and made of them something in no way imitative or spiced-up but recognizably his own.[33]

---

[31] Lecture delivered by Brecht in 1939, *Brecht on Theatre*, p. 132.
[32] Ibid., p. 80.
[33] John Willett, *The Theatre of Bertolt Brecht* (London, 1959), p. 138.

Many of the Party comrades who saw *The Measures Taken* disliked the play, and *Die Linkskurve*, the organ of the Proletarian-Revolutionary Writers League, took him to task for his evident lack of revolutionary experience:

> One feels that he does not draw his knowledge from practice, that he is merely deducing from theory. ... The unreal analysis of the premises leads to a false synthesis of their political and artistic consequences. All this mirrors an abstract attitude towards the manifold and complicated store of knowledge, derived from experience, which the Party possesses.[34]

Brecht was to answer his critics resoundingly a year later with his adaptation of Gorky's novel *The Mother*. But meanwhile he continued to pursue the parable form, set in exotic never-never lands of his own imagining, which confronted his audience on an aesthetic rather than an ideological plane. *Happy End*, his unlikely fantasy of gangsters and the Salvation Army set in 'modern Chicago', was a fiasco when he staged it as a follow-up to *The Threepenny Opera* at the Theater am Schiffbauerdamm in August 1929, and he immediately disowned it. However, *The Rise and Fall of the City of Mahagonny*, also written in collaboration with Kurt Weill and with the no less bizarre setting of a Wild West boom-town, was a wild success if judged by the offence it caused at its premiere in Leipzig and at subsequent performances in other provincial opera houses. Mindful of the innocent enjoyment that *The Threepenny Opera* had afforded Aufricht's patrons in Berlin, Brecht was determined to allow no escape from the implications of *Mahagonny*. Thus, at the play's climax when the hero is condemned to the electric chair for the capital crime of running short of money, the projected inscription reads (in Auden and Kallman's translation):

> Execution of Jimmy Gallaher. Many of you, perhaps, will be shocked at what you are about to see. But, Ladies and Gentlemen, ask yourselves this question: 'Would I have paid Jimmy Gallaher's debts?' Would you? Are you sure?

Brecht regarded *Mahagonny* as a programmatic statement of his notion of Epic theatre, now refined in the light of his early experience of the *Lehrstück*. In a lengthy series of notes appended to the published text he attempted to demonstrate how the opera could be developed from 'the means of pleasure into an object of instruction' by dismantling all the components of Wagner's *Gesamtkunstwerk* ('integrated work of art'):

> Once the content becomes, technically speaking, an independent component, to which text, music and setting 'adopt attitudes'; once illusion is sacrificed to free discussion, and once the spectator, instead of being enabled to have an experience, is forced as it were to cast his vote; then a change has been launched which goes far beyond formal matters and begins for the first time to affect the theatre's social function.[35]

But Left critics remained sceptical towards Brecht's emphasis on theatrical form as the primary means of alerting the audience. After the Leipzig premiere, Kurt Tucholsky wrote in *Die Weltbühne*:

---

[34]Quoted in Martin Esslin, *Brecht: A Choice of Evils* (London, 1959; 3rd edition, 1981), p. 139.
[35]*Brecht on Theatre*, p. 39.

Life is not like that, not even in the Klondike of yesteryear, certainly not in the America of today; and the relevance of it all to the Germany of 1930 is very thin. This is stylized Bavaria. ...[36]

In February 1931 Brecht launched his most violent assault on what he termed 'the culinary theatre' (because it catered to the audience's sensual gratification) when the Berlin Staatstheater incautiously allowed him to direct a much revised version of his earlier play *Man equals Man*. Consistent with the work's thesis that human personality can be dismantled and reassembled like a motor-car, the production adopted a radically different approach to the portrayal of character. The vague location of 'Kilkoa Barracks' in India under the British Raj (in 1925 with Queen Victoria on the throne) was rendered by Brecht and Neher in their familiar style with fragmented setting, projected titles (plus a huge caricature of the soldier Galy Gay) and exposed half-curtain – only as much as was necessary to tell the story. It was the depiction of the British Army that was startlingly different; the visiting Soviet dramatist Sergei Tretyakov wrote: 'Across the stage strode giant soldiers, holding on to a rope [probably the wire for the half-curtain] so as not to fall from the stilts concealed in their trousers. They were hung about with rifles and wore tunics smeared with lime, blood and excrement.'[37] In fact, only two of the soldiers were on stilts, the third being massively padded, whilst Helene Weigel as the canteen proprietress Begbick, the young Peter Lorre as Galy Gay, and the rest were normal size.

What particularly puzzled and exasperated the audience and critics was Lorre's manner of delivery: in order to convey the conflicts and contradictions in the character of Galy Gay, Brecht made him speak in a broken and disjointed manner, heavily stressing some phrases and withholding others. As Brecht explained to his critics soon after the performance,[38] the aim was to bring out the underlying meaning or *'gestus'* of each fragment of Galy Gay's behaviour. This concept of *'gestus'* was to become a cardinal feature of Brecht's theatre practice; in John Willett's definition 'It is at once gesture and gist, attitude and point: one aspect of the relation between two people, studied singly, cut to essentials and physically or verbally expressed. It excludes the psychological, the sub-conscious, the metaphysical unless they can be conveyed in concrete terms.'[39]

This is closely akin to the style of acting already developed by Meyerhold out of his training system of 'Biomechanics'; but although Meyerhold's company had performed in Berlin in 1930 there is no particular reason for presuming a direct influence on Brecht, the idea of *gestus* being a logical extension of his earlier work. Willett draws attention to its close affinity with Behaviourism, the doctrine that psychological theories should be based on outwardly observable data of human actions without reference to the products of introspection. It is here that the obvious link with Meyerhold can be traced, Behaviourism being one of the acknowledged sources of Biomechanics.

The failure of *Man equals Man*, which ran for only six performances, was not necessarily due to its daunting formal innovations; much as it had been revised, it remained a work from Brecht's early years, laden with bizarre absurdities that did little to advance the central, important, argument concerning personality. But this should not detract from the production's importance for Brecht: for the first time he had applied the principle of

---

[36] Quoted in Martin Esslin, op. cit., p. 45.
[37] Quoted in *Brecht As They Knew Him*, p. 72.
[38] See *Brecht on Theatre*, pp. 53–56.
[39] *The Theatre of Bertolt Brecht*, cit., p. 175.

Epic theatre systematically to the elements of acting. He was not to use the actual term *'Verfremdung'* to describe this technique until 1935 when he visited Moscow,[40] but with *Man equals Man* the technique was developed in all but name and ready for refinement in his post-war productions.

Later in 1931 Brecht embarked on two projects that were a total contrast to *Man equals Man* in the concreteness of their style and subject matter. The first was the script (written with Ernst Ottwalt) for the film *Kuhle Wampe*, a semi-documentary account of Berlin working-class life, directed by Slatan Dudow and released in May 1932. The second was his play *The Mother*, describing the growth to revolutionary consciousness and activism of a working-class woman in the context of events in Russia between 1905 and 1917. Loosely derived from Gorky's novel, completed in 1906, the play was written in collaboration with Slatan Dudow, Günther Weisenborn, and Hanns Eisler.

The Mother was the most fully developed of Brecht's *Lerhstücke*; its aim, he said, 'was to teach certain forms of political struggle'; addressed mainly to women, it was 'a demonstration of illegal revolutionary struggle'. Such a demonstration could not have been more timely: by 1932 there were six million unemployed in Germany and in the July elections the Nazis were by far the largest party in the Reichstag with 230 seats against the KPD's 89; with no overall majority, further elections were held in November at which the Nazis lost 34 seats and the KPD gained eleven.

Originally the dramatisation of *The Mother* had been commissioned by the Volksbühne, but cancelled when Brecht's involvement was discovered, as he was no longer considered politically acceptable there. Instead, it was taken over by the 'Group of Young Actors', a company born of the Piscator Studio, which since 1928 had staged a sequence of challenging left-wing plays. The twenty-seven-strong cast for *The Mother* included such notable professional actors as Helen Weigel (then thirty-one) as Pelagea Vlasova, and Ernst Busch as Pavel Vlasov, but the majority were young amateurs. Under the auspices of the Junge Volksbühne, it was given its premiere at the Komödienhaus am Schiffbauerdamm on 17 January 1932 to mark the thirteenth anniversary of Rosa Luxemburg's murder. On the five preceding days the production had been previewed at the Wallner Theater before invited audiences of trade unionists and extensively modified in the light of their comments. Whilst Emil Burri was named as the director, it was a collective undertaking closely involving Brecht, Hanns Eisler and Caspar Neher.[41]

The run of *The Mother* in the centre of Berlin was due largely to the unlikely backing of Aufricht, the impresario for *The Threepenny Opera*, but after thirty or so performances the production was taken out to halls in the working-class district of Moabit. Caspar Neher's setting was designed with this in mind: a simple booth was created from white material stretched on metal frames with a half-curtain in front; the furniture was minimal and purely functional, with locations indicated by small suspended placards; behind the acting area a single screen was suspended for the projection of quotations (mostly from Lenin) and occasional photographs, which remained throughout the scenes 'to show the great movement of ideas in which the events were taking place'.[42] Once again, there were

---

[40]On the origins of the term *'Verfremdung'* see *Brecht on Theatre*, pp. 91–99; Katherine *Eaton*, 'Brecht's Contacts With the Theatre of Meyerhold', *Comparative Drama*, Vol. 11, No.1 (Spring, 1977), pp. 12–13.
[41]The production is fully documented in Werner Hecht (ed.), *Materialen zu Bertolt Brechts 'Die Mutter'* (Frankfurt am Main, 1973) and Friedrich W. Knellessen, *Agitation auf der Bühne* (Emsdetten, 1970), pp. 192–201.
[42]Brecht, 'Notes to *Die Mutter' Brecht on Theatre*, p. 58.

obvious similarities to Piscator's recent work (*Tai Yang erwacht* having been staged twelve months earlier), not to mention the workers' theatre groups. As Brecht wrote:

> The production showed some features of the agit-prop theatre of those days: the pointed, sketch-like situations, the songs and choruses directed at the audience, the threadlike dramaturgy, loosely linking scenes and songs. But although both play and production owed much to the agit-prop theatre they none the less remained distinct from it. Whereas the agit-prop theatre's task was to stimulate immediate action (e.g. a strike against a wage-cut) and was liable to be overtaken by changes in the political situation, *The Mother* was meant to go further and teach the tactics of the class war. Moreover play and production showed real people together with a process of development, a genuine story running through the play, such as the agit-prop theatre normally lacks.[43]

Thus, the style of *The Mother* combined the cool, expository delivery and the direct address to the audience of the earlier *Lehrstücke* with three-dimensional characters who were seen to develop through the episodic sequence of the action. At the same time, care was taken to make the characters universal 'types' who could be seen as directly relevant to the audience's own experience; hence, no attempt was made to 'russify' them, and their clothes merely conveyed their social positions. Similarly, the typical was emphasised in the use of simple groupings: 'No more "casual", "like-like", "unforced" grouping' – said Brecht – 'the stage no longer reflects the "natural" disorder of things. The opposite of natural disorder is aimed at: natural order. This order is determined from a social-historical point of view.'[44] The actor, he added, needed 'to make himself observed standing between the spectator and the event'. One example of this was the opening scene in which Vlasova shows the audience her incapacity to feed her son properly and the consequent growing gulf between them:

> In the first scene the actress stood in a particular characteristic attitude in the centre of the stage, and spoke the sentences as if they were in the third person; and so she not only refrained from pretending in fact to be or to claim to be Vlasova (the Mother), and in fact to be speaking those sentences, but actually prevented the spectator from transferring himself to a particular room, as habit and indifference might demand, and imagining himself to be the invisible eyewitness and eavesdropper of a unique intimate occasion. Instead what she did was openly to introduce the spectator to the person whom he would be watching acting and being acted upon for some hours.[45]

Another was Scene Five, the 'Report on 1st May 1905' in which a worker Smilgin is shot down by the police when leading a demonstration:

> The May Day demonstration was spoken as if the participants were before a police-court, but at the end the actor playing Smilgin indicated his collapse by going down on his knees; the actress playing the Mother then stooped during her final words and picked up the flag that had slipped from his hands.[46]

---

[43]Ibid., pp. 66–62.
[44]Ibid., p. 58.
[45]Loc. cit.
[46]Ibid., p. 59.

Eisler's music played a crucial part in the production. There were ten songs, scored for chorus, soloists and a band comprising trumpet, trombone, piano and drums (seated this time in front of the stage). As Brecht says, the style, designed to induce in the spectator a critical attitude, was careful to keep 'well clear of the general drug-traffic conducted by bourgeois show business':

> Eisler's music can by no means be called simple. Qua music it is relatively complicated, and I cannot think of any that is more serious. In a remarkable manner it makes possible a certain simplification of the toughest political problems, whose solution is a life and death matter for the working class. In the short piece which counters the accusation that Communism leads to chaos the friendly and explanatory gest of the music wins a hearing, as it were, for the voice of reason. The piece 'In Praise of Learning', which links the problem of learning with that of the working class's accession to power, is infected by the music with a heroic yet naturally cheerful gest. Similarly the final chorus 'In Praise of Dialectics', which might easily give the effect of a purely emotional song of triumph, has been kept in the realm of the rational by the music. (It is a frequently recurring mistake to suppose that this – epic – kind of production simply does without all emotional effects: actually, emotions are only clarified in it, steering clear of subconscious origins and carrying nobody away.)[47]

Repeated attempts were made by the authorities to obstruct the production. Originally, it was planned to project documentary film of the October Revolution after Vlasova's closing lines, but this was banned by the censor. Later, when the production was taken to Moabit, the police first used fire regulations as a pretext to stop it, and then argued that 'there was no demand for the performance' – despite the fact that the hall had only recently been used for theatrical purposes and was now sold out for *The Mother*. The performance went ahead regardless, without setting, props and costumes – whereupon the police declared even the use of the curtain illegal. Finally, the performers sat in a semi-circle on stage and recited their lines. As Herbert Ihering reported in the *Börsen Courier* of 29 February, 'Even in this abbreviated and limited form, the question of the need for the performance was answered by the audience in the affirmative'.[48] By their intervention, the police had unwittingly lent a whole new dimension of *Verfremdung* to the performance, thereby endorsing Brecht's argument that characters can be more effectively 'demonstrated' than impersonated.

Brecht remarked on the contrasting reactions to the production:

> ... Since the audience for some of the performances was almost entirely bourgeois, while that for others (the bulk) was purely working-class, we were able to get an exact idea of the difference between their respective reactions. It was very wide. Where the workers reacted immediately to the subtlest twists in the dialogue and fell in with the most complicated assumptions without fuss, the bourgeois audience found the course of the story hard to follow and quite missed its essence. The worker – it was the working-class women who reacted with particular liveliness – was not at all put off by the extreme dryness and compression with which the various situations were sketched, but at once concentrated on the essential, on how the characters behaved in them.

---

[47]Ibid., p. 88.
[48]See Herbert Ihering, *Von Reinhardt bis Brecht* (Hamburg, 1967), pp. 358–359.

His reaction was in fact a political one from the first. The West-ender sat with so bored and stupid a smile as to seem positively comic; he missed the emotional embroidery and embellishment he was used to ... [49]

On this occasion Brecht was successful in winning the approval of the Left, though some critics still had reservations about his interpretation of events in Russia. *Die Rote Fahne* announced:

This is a new Bert Brecht. He has escaped from the desert of bourgeois theatre business; he is fighting for the revolutionary working class. As yet he has not torn off all the shackles that bind him to his past. But he will. He must – soon.[50]

In little more than a year Brecht was forced to tear off those shackles in the most literal sense. On 30 January 1933 Hitler became Chancellor; on 27 February the Nazis engineered the burning of the Reichstag building, and within twenty-four hours the Communist Party was declared an illegal organisation. That day Brecht, who was in hospital recuperating from an operation, escaped to Prague with his wife Helene Weigel and their son Stefan. *The Mother* proved to be the last production of Brecht to be staged in Berlin for seventeen years.

Brecht's exile took him through Scandinavia, the Soviet Union, America and finally Switzerland. Throughout this entire period his only large-scale productions were the celebrated *Life of Galileo* with Charles Laughton in Los Angeles in 1947,[51] and his adaptation of *Antigone* the following year in Switzerland. However, this period of exile saw the writing of virtually all his major plays, a number of important theoretical works, and numerous poems. By the time he returned with Helene Weigel to Berlin in October 1948, he had a clear view of the kind of theatre he wanted to establish, thanks mainly to the experience he had gained before 1933. Not that he saw his method as finalised: as numerous accounts testify, each production continued to be a learning process, with Brecht seeming (or affecting) to know less about the script than anyone, and with suggestions welcome from any quarter, artistic or otherwise.[52] When the Berliner Ensemble was founded at the Deutsches Theater in 1949 [it moved to the Theater am Schiffbauerdamm in 1954] rehearsals were open to all comers and Brecht placed absolute reliance on audience reaction, mercilessly cutting and rewriting his own scripts to avoid boredom or obscurity. 'The word of the writer' – he argued – 'is only as sacred as it is true.' With massive support from the state (75% of the company's total budget in 1959),[53] the Ensemble could afford to devote as much as a year to preparation and rehearsal of each new production, the great proportion of this time being taken up with clarifying the narrative and making the action concrete and true, 'cleaning the stage' – as Carl Weber says – 'of the "sweet lies" which keep man from recognising the world as it is'.[54]

---

[49] *Brecht on Theatre*, p. 62.
[50] *Die Rote Fahne*, 19 January 1932. Quoted in M. Esslin, op. cit., p. 142.
[51] Admirably documented in James K. Lyon, *Bertolt Brecht in America* (Princeton, 1980).
[52] See especially Carl Weber, 'Brecht as Director' in *The Drama Review*, Vol. 12, No. 1 (T-37), pp. 101–107.
[53] See Michael Mellinger, 'Goodbye to East Berlin' in *Encore*, Vol. 7, No. 5 (September–October, 1960), pp. 11–18.
[54] The notes to Brecht's *Collected Works*, edited by John Willett and Ralph Manheim contain extensive material relating to the work of the Berliner Ensemble. See also Part Four of Willett's *Brecht on Theatre*, and *Theaterarbeit* (ed. Brecht and others, Dresden, 1952), a large illustrated volume covering the Ensemble's work 1949–1951. Jan Needle and Peter Thomson's *Brecht* (Oxford, 1981) contains a chapter on Brecht's 1949 production of *Mother Courage*.

With the Swiss production of *Antigone* in 1948 Brecht initiated the practice of documenting his work in so-called 'model books', a number of which have since been published. He emphasised that the model was intended only as a starting point, one of many possible solutions to the play: 'They are intended' – he said – 'not to render thought unnecessary but to provoke it: not as a substitute for artistic creation but as its stimulus.'[55] Unfortunately, since his death in 1956 this caution has not prevented a great deal of dull and imitative 'Brechtian' orthodoxy by directors totally unaware of the fun ('*Spass*') that Brecht never ceased to demand of himself, his designers, his musicians and his actors, and incapable of applying his simple maxim: 'the proof of the pudding is in the eating'.

---

[55] *Brecht on Theatre*, p. 216.

Switzerland/GDR/Berliner Ensemble

CHAPTER TWO

Rhythm and Structure: Brecht's *Antigone* in Performance

BRUNO C. DUARTE

Brecht's adaptation of Sophocles' *Antigone* in 1948 was openly a political gesture that aspired to the complete rationalization of Greek Tragedy. From the beginning, Brecht made it his task to wrench ancient tragic poetry out of its 'ideological haze', and proceeded to dismantle and eliminate what he named the 'element of fate', the crucial substance of tragic myth itself. However, his encounter with Hölderlin's unorthodox translation of *Antigone*, the main source for his appropriation and rewriting of the play, led him to engage in a radical experiment in theatrical practice. From the isolated first performance of *Antigone*, a model was created – the *Antigonemodell* – that demanded a direct confrontation with the many obstacles brought about by the foreign *structure* of Greek tragedy as a whole. In turn, such difficulties brought to light the problem of *rhythm* in its relation to Brecht's own ideas of how to perform ancient poetry in a modern setting, as exemplified by the originally alienating figure of the tragic chorus. More importantly, such obstacles put into question his ideas of performance in general, as well as the way they can still resonate in our own understanding of what performance is or might be in a broader sense.

1947–1948: SWABIAN INFLECTIONS

It is known that upon returning from his American exile, at the end of 1947, Bertolt Brecht began to work on *Antigone*, the tragic poem by Sophocles. Brecht's own *Antigone* premiered in the Swiss city of Chur on February 1948. This event is widely documented (Hecht 1988, Wüthrich 2015, Wüthrich 2003, De Ponte 2006), and, owing to the radical experiment that it was or was claimed to be, as well as to the relevance it had for Brecht's subsequent involvement with theatre, it eventually became a milestone of theatre history.

In a note from December 1947 referring directly to his adaptation of *Antigone* (which he had just finished, he says, in less than two weeks), Brecht recounts that, on the advice of his friend and collaborator the scenographer Caspar Neher, he had decided to make use of:

> the Hölderlinian translation, which is rarely or never performed, since it is considered to be too obscure. I detect Swabian intonations and grammar school Latin constructions, and I feel at home. There's also something Hegelian about it. It's probably the return to the German language space that compels me in this undertaking.
>
> (BFA 27:225)

In a reference to Swabia, the region where Hölderlin was born and raised, Brecht speaks of '*schwäbische Tonfälle*', a word one can translate as intonations, but also as inflections, or, more properly speaking, cadences – to all effects a property of rhythm. The 'Hegelian' element, on the other hand, may seem somewhat less evident, but is no less vivid. On the one hand, it invokes a concrete biographical background – Hegel, a close friend and fellow student of Hölderlin at the *Stift* in Tübingen, was himself originally from Swabia, just like Brecht. On the other hand, the Hegelian tone anticipates Brecht's vision of history and dialectical materialism as heir to countless prominent readers of Hegel through Marx.

In a way, the physical space (the homesickness of language in the aftermath of World War II) introduces the political as constricted by time (the regenerative force of language in the face of destruction). The social function brought about by artistic consciousness would be expected to do the rest.[1] However, Brecht will admit from the start that the 'analogies to the present' (BFA 24:350), no matter how evident they appear, can only be exploited to a certain degree. His change of mind on how the play was to begin somehow clarifies this issue. In its first version, Brecht's *Antigone* starts off with a Prelude [*Vorspiel*] that takes place at the end of the war, in April 1945 in Berlin, presenting as the main cast two sisters, their brother as a deserter, and an officer of the SS (BFA 8:195–199). For the production at Greiz in 1951, Brecht removed this overture and replaced it with a New Prologue [*Prolog*] in which Tiresias, the seer, addresses the audience in a didactic tone, presenting the characters standing beside him, Antigone and Creon, along with a brief narrative of the action. This speech is key to understanding what it means to deal with form through content. Tiresias starts by warning the audience that the 'elevated language' of the poem they are about to hear may be 'unfamiliar' [*ungewohnt*] to them. Their ignorance of the plot, in turn, justifies the need to introduce them to the characters: 'Unknown / to you is the subject of the poem which was / intimately familiar to its former listeners.' After which the plot is summarized in a few lines: Creon, the 'tyrant of the city of Thebes', engages in a 'predatory war against the remote Argos [...] But his war, now called inhuman / causes him to succumb.' Hence the plea to the audience: 'We ask you / To look into your souls for similar deeds / In the recent past or for the absence / Of similar deeds' (BFA 8:242).

In the Remarks to the adaptation, Brecht will once more highlight the contrast between the 'representation of the Ancients' [*Vorstellung der Alten*], that is, their very own perception of man as subjected to the laws of fate, and the conviction, based on a 'practical knowledge of humankind and political experience', according to which 'the fate of man is man himself' (BFA 24:350). Thus the greatness of *Antigone* as a poem is not to be accepted in its own terms, but rather raises the question 'if it is still

---

[1] For a political and historical overview of the adaptation, see Philipsen (1998), Rehbein (1962), Bunge (1957).

understandable to an audience who today lives with completely different beliefs [*in ganz anderen Vorstellungen*]' (BFA 24:350). Noticeably, the word *Vorstellung*, here used in the sense of the notion, the idea or the conception one might have of a given reality, is often rendered as representation, in a philosophical context, or as performance, in the sense of a theatrical performance. This many-sided concept stalls Brecht's propensity to overestimate the correlation between 'the fall of the ruling house of Oedipus' and the 'gruesome ravenous war' (BFA 24:350) led by Creon on the one hand, and 'the role of the use of violence in the downfall of the head of state' (BFA 25:74) and the fall of the Nazi regime led by Hitler, on the other – so that, following the battle, 'Argos becomes today's Stalingrad'. Brecht's intentions were clear: 'war between Thebes and Argos is presented realistically' (BFA 24:350–351). But in order to arrive at this 'objective depiction' of the events and draw on the 'elements of the epic kind' recognizable in the 'ancient play', a concession had to be made with regards to the 'subjective problem' (BFA 25:74–75) of representation, in its passive (a mental image or picture of the play) as well as in its dynamic (a real process or a scene) state.

In his rewriting and staging of *Antigone*, Brecht was faced with the intricate and perplexing *structure* of Greek tragedy as a whole. Moreover, such difficulties were highlighted by the emphasis put on the question of *rhythm* in its relation to Brecht's own ideas of how to perform ancient poetry in a modern framework, as exemplified by the originally alienating figure of the tragic chorus. It is only fair to say that all of these aspects inevitably have a resonance in his ideas of performance in general, and play a significant role in our own understanding of what performance is or might be in a much broader sense.

HÖLDERLIN'S 'LANGUAGE OF *ANTIGONE*'

Friedrich Hölderlin published his translations of Sophocles' *Antigone* and *King Oedipus* in 1804, not without some hope that they would eventually be accepted at the Weimar Theater. Instead, they became the object of a heated controversy among poets, scholars and literary critics. Accused of philological inaccuracy and seen as severely flawed in terms of their understanding of Greek prosody and metrics, they were ultimately judged incomprehensible. This level of critical derision was then fueled by the association of these works with Hölderlin's retreat into the state of isolation and apathy that was to characterize the second half of his life. The myth of the mad poet both overshadowed and tarnished the translations of Sophocles as the mere symptoms of the inevitable downfall of poetic genius. In time, however, this logic became inverted: the tendency to romantic subjectivity and psychological narrative was overrun by the objective body of the text. That being said, it was only in the 20th century that the recognition of the aesthetic value and inner autonomy of these translations fully came to light – and it is no coincidence that this mostly happened on stage, as the question of their performance became central.

This late recognition notwithstanding, it remains a curious fact that the initial response to Hölderlin's translations somehow still resonates today as a complex side effect within a more academic environment. Next to the experts in Ancient Studies and Greek Tragedy, who maintain that Hölderlin made unforgivable mistakes as a translator of Sophocles, stands the highly institutionalized realm of Hölderlin scholarship, intent on justifying and redeeming Hölderlin's errors by seeing in them a deliberate action that would be impossible to differentiate from his own creative path as a lyric poet. Both have to critically bow before the authority that the name 'Hölderlin' has become in world literature. Accordingly, they tend to act with extreme caution. Whilst admitting that the poet might well have erred as a translator, they suggest that he did so for his own legitimate reasons, aiming at the reconstruction of Greek prosody in ways that undermine every conventional understanding of what the translation of ancient dramatic poetry is or should be. From here onwards, all variations are possible.[2]

Brecht's position in regard to Hölderlin was a peculiar one. He seems to have sensed immediately the physical violence of the latter's translations. In a letter from late December 1947, not far from the premiere of the play, he writes: 'Hölderlin's language of Antigone ['*Antigone*'-*Sprache*] would be worthy of a deeper study than the one I was able to devote to it. It is of an astounding radical nature' (BFA 27:258). A devoted analysis of the materiality of Hölderlin's language was therefore postponed, or rather cast aside in favor of what was seen as a more urgent task: its performability. Whereas Hölderlin's major ambition as a translator was deeply rooted in achieving an ancient modern form of tragic poetry within the conflation of the historical and the metaphysical, Brecht's adaptation was effectively based on a deliberate disregard for the original Greek (Sophocles) as much as on a fully conscious and meticulous desecration of the original German (Hölderlin). Neither the original nor its translation were among his concerns when handling tragedy as raw material.

As the receiver of the foreign Greek original in the form of a foreign German translation, Brecht cuts through the text as if it was originally a spontaneous unity of some kind. His revision of Sophocles' play through Hölderlin's rendering of it displays a process of formal reduction that necessarily brings about the distortion of meaning. In this respect, the title 'The Antigone of Sophocles according to Hölderlin's transposition, adapted to the stage' is as long and descriptive as it was insidious and artful. These would presumably be the premises for the practice of *Nachdichtung* – commonly rendered by the term 'free adaptation', but actually embodying an obscured second chamber in the making of poetry through extreme compression. Brecht's functionalist conception of tragic form as a whole reveals itself as much more complex than it may seem at first sight. In the face of the 'material and spiritual collapse' of post-war Germany, he asks himself how it is still possible to 'make progressive art [...] in a period of reconstruction' (BFA 25:73–74). It is significant that he justifies his decision to replay Antigone by bluntly equating form with content:

> The *Antigone* drama was chosen for the present theatrical undertaking because it could attain a certain present relevance from the standpoint of content, and because formally it sets interesting tasks.
>
> (BFA 25:74)

Tragedy is a spatial form that can only be acknowledged as such through the experience of time. Brecht was well aware of this, and acted accordingly. In the best tradition of a Marxist critique of tragic heroism and the humanist tradition, he was determined to show Greek tragedy as immune and hostile to all sense of transcendence. In order to detach *Antigone* from its original mythical foundation, the substance of which tragic poetry itself is made of, the linguistic texture of tragic form had to be intertwined with the semantic progression woven by history. The complete and utter rationalizing of tragedy – '*Durchrationalisierung*' (BFA 25:74; see also Barner 1987) – was the first and major step to arrive at such a process of eradication.

---

[2] See as examples: Binder (1992), Beaufret (1965), Benn (1959), Harrison (1975), Beissner ([1933] 1961), Schadewalt (1960), Berman (1987), Bernofsky (2001), Böschenstein (2004), Louth (1998).

A truly secularized view of tragedy will not seek to modify or correct the supposed misconceptions of its content, but rather begin by dismantling and suppressing its core. Brecht's adaptation of *Antigone* was built on an understanding of dramaturgy that is not identical with the simple transposition of the mythical into the political. It relates more directly to their abrupt clash in a single act of coarse effacement. If the formal task of adapting the tragic poem is performed correctly in this sense, it will bring its object to a state of self-corrosion where the one thing that matters is the effect itself of the text in anticipation of its performance, regardless of the defacing of everything it stood for. In Brecht's own words:

> As to the dramaturgic, 'fate' eliminates itself by itself, so to speak, as it goes along. Of all the gods, only the local saint of the people remains, the god of joy. Step by step, with the progressive adaptation of the scenes, the supremely realistic popular legend emerges out of the ideological haze.
>
> (BFA 27:255)

There is nothing surprising in such rhetoric of secular (or individualized) godliness against the mere acceptance of pure (plural) deification. The image of realism – the folk-tale coupled with its main character, the people – emerging from the ground by way of the strict demolition of ideology that itself moves ideologically can be seen as a general feature of Brecht's discourse overall. In fact though, the dramatic action which he is attempting to describe here, as utterly self-determined, still depended on a tense interaction with text as matter. In order to instrumentalize tragedy, one first needs to get close to it.

As so often proved to be the case, Brecht resorted to the strategic manipulation of material to retain and revive ambivalence. His art of crafting tragic poetry anew with the aim of setting forth his own political stance constantly plays with the need for historical or dialectical materialism to exert pressure on ancient matter. But at the same time, it takes pride in not letting itself be reduced to such key-words, remains wary of definitive programmatic methodologies, or at least engages in such procedures only provisionally, without ever relinquishing its mastery of ambiguity. Even the alleged shaping of modern tragedy under the sign of epic theatre should not be viewed in straightforward terms. The contention that he would presumably be looking for the 'epic moment' in the composition of the tragic poem ought to be read with much caution. With such density of dissimulation, one is forced to ask how all of this reflects on the handling of *Antigone* in performance.

A PERFORMANCE MODEL

Not long after the event at Chur, Brecht published a theoretical and practical treatise, titled the *Antigonemodell*, intended to serve as a manual of sorts in stage direction. Brecht himself described it as a 'mandatory performance model [...] made visible through a collection of photographs alongside explanatory instructions', something that must be shown or demonstrated in order for it to be 'successfully imitated', so that whenever it is put to good use it becomes 'a mixture of the exemplary and the unparalleled' (BFA 25:75). Such a beneficial usage of the model essentially depended upon two things: a 'collective creative process' delineating 'a continuum of a dialectical kind', and the ability of the actor to 'come up with modifications to the model, such that the image of reality it has to offer will be made more faithful to truth and more insightful, or artistically more satisfactory'. If such demands are to be met fittingly, Brecht continues, they will themselves acquire an 'exemplary character', and, as a consequence, 'the learner turns into the teacher, the model modifies itself'. For the model is not immovable, but rather grounded on evolution and progression: 'it is to be considered as unfinished from the very start' (BFA 25:76–77).

It is sometimes noted that one of the reasons Brecht chose Hölderlin's translation of *Antigone* – the model before the model, so to speak – was the latter's implicit resistance to a classicist view of tragedy. This might not be untrue to some degree, but does not do justice to that which at once separates and brings together these two authors. By contrast to Hölderlin's reading and translation of *Antigone*, which were the result of a lifelong process of rethinking the scission between the Ancient and the Modern, Brecht's dilemma – to what extent or in what way could *Antigone* be made 'understandable' to a modern audience – chiefly consisted of trying to deal with the possibility or impossibility of overcoming a given 'representation of the Ancients' (BFA 24:350) on stage. Hence the insistence on the political by way of a demythologisation of tragedy based on the historicisation of myth.

To be sure, Brecht's look from a distance over Antiquity and Greek civilization was anything but non-reflective. It simply relied too heavily on politics to acknowledge the autonomy of its object in its completeness. As always, he was more than eager to explain himself in advance:

> It can no longer be about highlighting culture within Hellenism, as if it was the highest measure; that which the classics of the bourgeoisie accomplished is only aesthetically of some interest. (Even in democracy only aesthetically of interest). The whole *Antigone* belongs to the barbarian horse skull shrine.
>
> (BFA 27:265)

In this particular utterance, historical insight, in the form of a rash judgement, provides the means for theatrical practice. The horse skull shrine alludes to a fundamental device used in the 1948 staging of the play, namely four sticks, with a horse skull standing on top of each of them. The entrances and movements of the actors were then determined according to the position they came to occupy in relation to these four marks on the stage. The 'whole Antigone' thus refers not to the classical world, in the sense of a theological-political geometry of Antiquity, but to something that has yet to be understood and explained in its particular terms. In the Prelude to the *Antigonemodell*, Brecht noted:

> Incidentally, the point is not in any way to 'summon the spirit of the Ancients' – for instance through the *Antigone* drama, or in favor of that same drama – philological interests could not be served. Even if one felt obligated to do something for a work such as *Antigone*, we would only be able to do that by letting the work do something for us.
>
> (BFA 25:75)

In between the pedagogical and manipulative quality of Brecht's model, the first of all talents appears to be that of a rather twisted logic: 'even if' one was compelled to bring *Antigone* to life, for instance by reworking a given translation, such an endeavor would 'only' be made possible by inquiring if the already existing work could be of some use to us, prior even to any intention to adapt it, or additionally presenting itself as the requirement for such an intention. Every (philological) desire for accuracy in reconstructing the Ancient – and every (spiritual) expression of reverence for it as well – have to be put aside in order to respond to the urgency of the present. Conversely, in the name of what appears to be a recognition of the work's self-activity, causing its instrumentalization to become imminent or necessary, political interests alone are to be served, safeguarded as that 'something' which the work will potentially 'do' for us, once we learn how to make use of it.

THE CAESURA: RHYTHM AND STRUCTURE

Side by side with its assemblage of photographic documentation, the *Antigonemodell* uses a recurrent device that reflects on the performance of Greek tragedy in practical dialogical terms. The book is punctuated by segments where Brecht creates an exchange between two nameless characters, something one could easily interpret as a conversation piece of sorts between the author and his head dramaturg, who take turns in incorporating question and answer. In one of those occurrences, the dialogue reads as follows:

> Question: How were the verses spoken?
> Answer: Above all else, the deplorable habit was avoided according to which the actors, when standing before larger units of verse, overinflate themselves, so to speak, with an emotion that roughly covers up the whole. There should be no 'fervor' before or after speaking and agitating. The pacing happens from verse to verse, and each of them is brought out of the *Gestus* of the figure.
>
> Question: How about the technical?
> Answer: There should be a caesura at the point where the verse lines come to an end, or an accentuation of the next beginning of each verse should then take place.
>
> Question: How is the rhythm to be dealt with?
> Answer: Through the use of the syncope in Jazz, through which something contradictory will come about in the flow of verse, and the regularity will prevail over that which is irregular.
>
> (BFA 25:124)

It is more than likely that the word 'caesura', commonly described as a pause or an interruption in metrical succession – was here brought to mind through Hölderlin, who emphasizes this same term in his *Remarks on Oedipus* and the *Remarks on Antigone* that accompanied the publication of his translations of both tragedies. Near the beginning of the *Remarks on Oedipus*, Hölderlin describes in detail how he conceives of tragic poetry as the reciprocity of its strict formal laws as a genre and its individual specific content. He comes to consider the relation between what he names the 'calculable law' or the 'lawful calculation' of poetry, on the one hand, and its 'living meaning, which cannot be calculated', on the other. The key concept guiding these considerations is rhythm.

> The law, the calculation [...] is, in the tragic, more a balance than mere sequence. [...] Thus, in the rhythmic sequence of representations, wherein transport presents itself, that which in poetic meter is called caesura, the pure word, the counter-rhythmic interruption, becomes necessary; namely in order to meet the raging alternation of representations, at its summit, in such a way that thereupon – what appears it is no longer the alternation of the representation, but the representation itself. [...] Thereby the sequence of the calculation and the rhythm are divided, and in its two halves refer to one another in such a manner that they appear of equal weight. (Hölderlin 1992, 309–310)

This same law is then to be applied to each of the tragedies, *Oedipus* and *Antigone*, in accordance with what Hölderlin saw as the relation between the 'specific content' (related to each tragic cycle) of each tragedy and the 'general calculation'. The 'calculable law' of tragic poetry is founded upon the dynamics of what Hölderlin calls 'the rhythm of the representation'. Depending on the pace determining the action of each play, and on the length of each of the two halves it consists of, the caesura acts as the 'counterrhythmic rupture' or the 'counteracting' figure in the course of the action. It will appear in different time frames, at different moments, thereby determining the structure of the whole.[3]

Unsurprisingly, Brecht did not care to delve into the complexity of Hölderlin's understanding of rhythm, which stands at the core of his poetics.[4] Brecht's appropriation of the word 'caesura' was as plain and literal as could be. Prompted by a need for immediacy in the process of eliminating, dividing or cutting entire verses and strophes, his rudimentary practice of calculated caesura did not contemplate the need to articulate the metaphysical with the physical slopes within language that configure Hölderlin's conception of a 'poetic logic'. To Brecht, the balance or imbalance between form and meaning were subordinated to the underlying induction process that was to guide much of his theatrical writing in the time to come. In reading tragedy through a logic of political causality that eschews every ahistorical element from the start, he had only to enforce its measure on Hölderlin's text to arrive at the demonstration of such a causal nexus within the text and beyond it. Only so could the contradiction implied in the reference to the syncopated rhythm as the allegory of Jazz music be equated with a 'regularity' able to overcome every potentially uneven pattern 'in the flow of verse'.

Hölderlin's considerations of rhythm were bound not to resonate with Brecht's abrupt examination and treatment of *Antigone*. By stressing the full-scale reciprocity between rhythm and the structure of the play, Hölderlin was in search of the general laws of the construction of an individual poetic work. This would allow him to arrive at a sound general definition of 'tragic presentation'. His commentary stood alongside his translation as the pivotal point sustaining his treatment of language. Similarly, Brecht's *Antigonemodell* contained a commentary to *Antigone*, with the significant difference that it now revolved around the *performance* of language. This becomes particularly clear when one considers more closely Brecht's handling of the chorus.

'RIDDLES THAT DEMAND SOLUTIONS': THE CHORUS

Recalling the 'Hegelian' tone of Hölderlin's translation, Brecht insists on seeing in the latter a 'swabian popular gesture', to which he adds the following: 'the "people's grammar" goes as far as the highly artistic choruses!' In the same letter to Stefan Brecht, from December 1947, he writes:

> The changes that forced me to write whole new passages are made with the aim of cutting out the greek 'moira' (the element of fate); which means that I am trying to push forward the underlying popular legend. You can best appreciate the experiment when you see what has been done with the choruses.
>
> (BFA 29:440)

---

[3]Hölderlin's 'poetics of tragedy' have been the subject of numerous essays. See for instance Kasper (2000), Fynsk (1999), Häny (1946), Krell (2004), Kurz (1988), Lacoue-Labarthe (1986).
[4]The majority of studies on the connection between Brecht and Hölderlin tend to interpret form through content. See for example: Flashar (1988), Doering (2010–2011), Weisstein (1973).

What has in fact been done with the choruses? Brecht's verdict on this much discussed and long-standing issue surrounding Greek Tragedy – the reconstitution of what the original 'Greek chorus' was or might have been – was seemingly devoid of any hesitation, and as programmatic as one might expect it to be:

> These choruses, just like many other passages of the poem, can barely be entirely understood by listening to them one single time. Parts of the choruses sound like riddles that demand solutions. But the exquisite thing about them is that, once they start to be analyzed for a while, they bring out more and more things of beauty. The adaptation didn't want to simply get rid of this difficulty, the overcoming of which is the source of so much joy – all the more considering that the work 'Antigone' had the bliss to have as its translator one of the greatest masters of the German language, Hölderlin.

(BFA 24:115)

Brecht starts by paying tribute to Hölderlin as the superior maker or sculptor [*Gestalter*] of the German language, thereby revising or at least polishing his earlier judgement where Hölderlin was portrayed as the representative of the 'entirely pontifical line' of German literature, in contrast with the 'entirely profane line' led by Heine, and following the decay of the 'beautiful contradictory unity' that had taken place 'after Goethe' (BFA 26:416).

It is certainly not without irony to notice how Brecht comes to discover the beauty of his own language in a language that was not meant to be spoken, but rather sung – and whose tone was often none other than pontifical, in the sense of a word that had its roots in an ancient divinatory world, with all its religious ritualistic overtones. In many ways, the mention of a 'contradictory unity' that would have come first in the line of descent of German poetry represents Brecht's inadvertent recognition of all that which he didn't care – or simply was not prepared – to explore.

As a translator, Hölderlin spoke of the chorus in extremely visceral terms, seeing in it the '*suffering organs* of the divinely struggling body' (Hölderlin 1992, 374). This body exudes the body to body experience with the Greek text by Sophocles. As for Brecht, he limited himself to retrieving Hölderlin's German Greek, molding its matter in line with his own purposes. As far as Brecht was concerned, the 'language of *Antigone*' was indeed Hölderlin's, that is, a language *a priori* alienated of Hölderlin's confrontation with the language of Sophocles. This limitation was not only left unrecognized by Brecht's crudity in approaching his object, but protracted as something to take advantage of. To him, the recognition of the chorus as something that constitutes an obstacle to any modern theatrical dimension immediately demands the suppression of the said obstacle as such. This is the reasoning behind the image of 'riddles that demand solutions', and the stringent imperative to go beyond (or below) the merely beautiful character of language by working through it. In Brecht's view, something had to be done in order to re-master the 'highly artistic' character of the choruses: the answer to their incomprehensibility and obscurity could only be delayed for so long.

The need to pause for a moment, as if struck by the awareness of the artistry of the German language, also marks the point where a supposed classicism had to come to terms with realism in its many forms and shapes. The lyric element within tragedy only brings out this limitation that shapes the radical approach to epic intentness. Likewise, Brecht's hasty condemnation of Greek culture through Greek tragedy was politically founded upon a confusing refusal of what he believed to be the origins of barbarism and ideology. Furthermore, his lack of knowledge of the Greek language placed him in a position where he could only sense the double nature of Greek tragedy and diction by means of his own homemade antinomy of the artistic vs. the realistic, which did include the possibility of their fleeting encounter, but never that of their actual coalescence. All of this is shown in the warping and wavering of the choruses, by way of a processual reduction, variation, or mutation.

MUSIC AND ACROBATICS

Significantly, the awareness of the theatrical imperative that occupied Brecht seems to have been directed, at least in part, to the emergence of music and the treatment of sound. Admitting to not having found an effective 'aesthetic solution' that would allow him to show 'the instrument in the middle of the background' (BFA 25:120), Brecht nonetheless goes to great lengths to recount what would have been his conception of music within the play. He describes in detail the way the music was created and executed at Chur, partly by transcribing the part of the musical score that determines the 'rhythm' to be achieved, partly by naming the instruments and objects used in the process, the intensity of the sound level, what each player was expected to do, and so on.

Brecht's version of the song to Eros that composes the third stasimon is made in stark contrast to Hölderlin's. As Antigone is taken away to a remote place where she is to be buried alive under a rockbed, following the King's decree, Creon doesn't simply exit the scene: he heads 'towards the city' to reestablish his power. The Elders then speak of a city that, in its thirst for joy and oblivion, chooses to reject the mourning for its sons and 'hastens to the orgy of Bacchus, in the search of exhaustion' (vv. 723–731). After which *The Elders grab the sticks of Bacchus* from the stage floor 'and place themselves in the middle of the acting space' (BFA 25:120), ready to speak their lines.

> Spirit of the pleasures of the flesh, and yet always
> Triumphant, in conflict! He throws even those related by blood
> amongst themselves, the one who mightily pleads.
> Never will he be wrecked, and he
> Who partakes in it is not at one with himself.
>
> (BFA 8:224)

A passage in the *Antigonemodell* book explicitly refers to this hymn in a very precise manner. The verses are placed like captions under the photographs taken by Ruth Berlau of the production at Chur. The chorus consists of four figures in long vestures, each holding a stick with a square-shaped mask hiding their faces, eyes and mouth carved upon each mask as in archaic fashion. The instructions as to the disposition and division (see BFA 25:96,121) of the lines spoken are clear: to each member of the chorus is attributed a set of two verses; accordingly, they speak in line, individually, in undisturbed succession. The directions can be seen on the left side:

> As they speak the chorus song 'Spirit of the pleasures of the flesh', the Elders beat their sticks quietly against the ground, in time with the music. While speaking, each of them shows his face, and at the start of the respective first verses he spins the crook in such a way that the red side of it becomes visible.
>
> (BFA 25:120)

At the sight of Antigone's suffering as she walks toward her grave, the chorus is brought to a state of great affliction. The difference in formulating the identification becomes apparent at the very beginning of the strophe. Whereas Hölderlin stresses Antigone's tragic fault by bringing together the language of Right and that of the Gods, Brecht chooses the objectified over the metaphorical. In Hölderlin: 'But now I myself step / outside of the law' (Hölderlin 1992, 830–831). In Brecht: 'But now I myself am / out of step' (BFA 8:224). The law of men embroidered within the law of the Gods becomes, in Brecht's adaptation, a matter of non-synchronicity. The Elders no longer react intensely to transgression, but rather lose their sense of time and rhythm: they get out of step, *aus dem Takt*. The choice of words clearly reflects the terminology – the demands – of performance.

A few moments before the fifth chorus, the *Elders* are said to hear 'the music of the roundel of Bacchus as it begins' (BFA 25:120). And in yet another reference to that same chorus, Brecht writes:

> After verse 1192, one of the Elders goes toward the alarm panel and beats against it with his flat hand during the chorus song 'Spirit of Joy, you who from the waters'. / The music of the roundel of Bacchus comes to an end.
>
> (BFA 25:152)

This instantly recalls the instructions in the *Modell*, as described above, regarding the third stasimon: a rhythmic instance of performance is introduced that in many ways contradicts Brecht's one-sided interpretation of the 'ancient form of theatre' (BFA 25:110). With its archaic connotations, the beating of the stick against the ground cannot help but collide with the purpose of a realistic actualization of the play.

After such insistence on music and sound as evident sources of rhythm, one would be justified in expecting any sort of recognition of the chorus as a primary instance of song merging with movement, as established by most studies dealing with the reconstruction of Greek tragedy. And yet, again there is no mention of singing and dancing in Brecht's adaptation, but only of speaking. The words of the Elders are spoken, not sung. The actors are instructed to speak and move in a certain way, instructions are given as to the tone of their pronouncements (BFA 25:112) as well as their placement on stage interweaved with the acoustics of the theatrical space, but nothing explicit is said about the performance of song and dance.

This is all the more intriguing when one thinks of how Brecht notes that, exactly because of its 'immense subject-matter', *Antigone* demands not so much a 'more ponderous presentation', but rather the 'lightest' one of all. The answer to the overwhelming character of Greek tragedy, to the vastness of its theme, would then be its opposite: the loosening of the heavy disposition, its dissolution in poise and levity. The *Darstellung* 'as a whole', he says, 'should have something of a flight', and continues: 'The actors should display some of the effortlessness that is acquired through great effort by acrobats. It's precisely the separation of the parts that can cause the action to keep on moving further' (BFA 25:130).

As with the individual characters, who are expected to maintain the 'flow of the presentation' (BFA 25:92), the members of the chorus also have strict orders to follow concerning their movement in space. The mental disposition of the Elders is treated as the correlate of their posture, and the latter functions as the *analogon* to the position they come to occupy on stage. The stirrings and oscillations of the chorus are turned into the technical positioning of its physical body, in such a way that a specific articulation of its pacing within the stage produces what Brecht calls the regular, planned or scheduled 'position for the chorus song' (BFA 25:94).

THE COMMENTATOR AND THE PERFORMER AS ONE

It comes as no surprise that the choruses pose the major obstacle and the greatest difficulty to every attempt at a modern adaptation of Greek tragedy. Since they presuppose and embody the indeterminate space between dramatic and lyric poetry, between the universal and the particular, they are bound to stand at the heels of the self-appointed and multi-layered modern poet, dramaturg and stage director. Given the inseparable nature of history and myth in ancient tragic poetry, the choruses of *Antigone* are historical figures in their own right, necessarily unaware or unconsciously disdainful, one might say, of any adaptation bent on their historicization through a revised scaffolding of the socio-political approach. This was clearly and knowingly overlooked by Brecht, whose first measure was to dismiss Greek culture and art as being the 'highest measure' of all, by tearing down the idea of its greatness and excellence and replacing it with the theatrical syllogism of modern rationality: analysis, demonstration, showing.

This being said, the main question lies not so much in how the Greek choruses come to confirm or contradict Brecht's 'model' of tragic poetry on stage, or in the way they relate to his varying notion of 'epic style' (BFA 25:152), but rather, in a broader sense, in their identification as 'riddles that demand solutions' (BFA 24:115). If nothing else, the fact that their pronouncements as riddles need to be clarified and thoroughly rationalized at all is enough to qualify the chorus, in its singularity, as a riddle by definition, a cryptogram of magnified proportions.

As the *Bearbeiter*, in this particular case the one who adapts a translation that he could only behold and approach as an original work, and is therefore forced to adapt himself to the origin he so recklessly wanted to destroy, Brecht had to be as unrelenting with the choruses of *Antigone* as he was inexorable in his handling of the play as a whole. In this context, his comments on the ambivalent function of the Greek chorus, who acts simultaneously as the interpreter and the performer of the action, are worthy of some attention.

> One must not make a big fuss about the double function of the chorus (commentator and performer). One can think that the chorus simply lends itself to the presentation of the Theban Greats in the action. But this is not even something one needs to think about, since wisdom in knowledge and baseness in conduct are commonly found together. – For that matter, one has renounced to show the Elders as old men, since neither wisdom nor poetry are predominantly to be found in old men, and given that in order to make war, one does not need to be old, but rather belong to the dominant class.
>
> (BFA 25:102)

For something that is said to be not worth much thinking about, this seems to have occupied Brecht's cogitations considerably. In itself, his dismissal of the question follows the same line of reasoning as before. It goes without saying that the chorus is as contradictory a figure as can be: being identical with the Elders of Thebes, it seems obvious that its faltering behavior and judgement goes from one extreme to the other in very little time. One is therefore left with the problem of their presentation [*Darstellung*]. This is rapidly solved by the tactics of estrangement: to present the Elders as elderly men imbued with the wisdom of old age would signify an effort to be truthful to the image of the Ancients as the source of such wisdom and nobleness of character. Brecht's contention seems to be that there is no need for such concessions. In fact, as he explicitly points out, one needn't think too much about these matters: political reason teaches us that both virtues and flaws are socially determined. Ergo, the Elders have good expectations to grow young before they appear on stage.

There is yet another way to read Brecht's note. On the one hand, the final version of *Antigone* has the chorus stand effectively in the midst of the action, a fact no political rhetoric would be able to erase. On the other hand, the chorus resonates throughout the whole play as Brecht's own mouthpiece, commenting upon the events, and acting as the mirror image of the stage director, who not only is caught overseeing or overruling the action, but actually performing its conception and realization – as shown in the *Antigonemodell*. And this is something one needs to think about, since sagacity in theory and corruption in practice are commonly found together.

Referring to the 'last chorus' of the play, Brecht clarifies its division: it shall be separated in four parts, each spoken by a member of the group. Only then comes the dramaturgical inference: 'After speaking his verses, each of the Elders walks away' (BFA 25:158). It is worthy of note that just a few pages before he had returned to his invocation of acrobatics as the way to counter the metaphysical weight and thickness of Greek drama:

> In the last scene, it is especially important that the performers will approach the limits of the acting space in a loose posture, at the spot where they form the planned group, and that, when leaving the acting space, they exit in a loose posture.
>
> (BFA 25:154)

Reading these instructions from the *Antigonemodell*, the performer who might have been chosen to form part of the chorus will know precisely how he is expected to proceed. At which point though, one could ask, is the writer of this model supposed to exit his own acting space? If Brecht, the eternal dramaturg and director of his own plays, demanded acrobatic skills from the performers of *Antigone*, skinned of its solemn tone and deprived of its poetic and cultural authority, it is not inopportune to ask if that same dramaturg and stage director isn't himself, after a certain time, the subject of the performance he sought to accomplish.

IDEAS ON PERFORMANCE

Somewhat unwillingly, the expression 'Greek Tragedy in action' (Taplin 1978) or 'on stage' marks the point where Greek Drama ultimately has to come to terms not only with the way it is to be performed, in a traditional, scholarly or 'theatrical' understanding of the term, but rather with the ever-changing and not as easily tamable concept of performance. Brecht did violence to a text that was not his own – Hölderlin's translation – by moving and redistributing its parts, using it largely to his own ends and causing the deflection of its core. This act of breaking in, however, came at the price of its gradual disappearance.

There is nothing extraordinary or unexpected in the will to historicize tragedy by making it fiercely political. All things considered, Brecht's *Antigone*-experiment, conceived as a deliberately invasive adaptation of an 'ancient form of theatre' with the aim of formulating a performance model for the future, achieved little more than a political statement, while the object of its appropriation was surprisingly left intact. Other 'models' were still to emerge in a more convincing way, such as *Life of Galileo* (also from 1947–1948), *Mother Courage and Her Children* (1949–1951) or the *Katzgraben Notes 1953*, but the *Antigonemodell* quickly subsided and fell into stagnation. Brecht himself saw *Antigone* as routine work or an experimental preamble to that which was yet to come in the years after. Its relevance within Brecht's body of work is anything but clear. One can always speak of 'modernist Hellenism', the role of experimentation and critique, or wish for the 'efficacy of tragedy in modernity' (Taxidou 2008, 256–257), but the fact remains that soon enough Brecht abandoned any plans to restage the play. After the small-scale symbolic production at Chur, *Antigone* would be staged only twice during Brecht's lifetime, in Zurich in March 1948 and in Greiz in November 1951. That, by itself, should be telling enough. Brecht's depiction of fate as something that immediately becomes self-destructive, once it is confronted with its methodical rationalization, seems appropriate to characterize his own endeavors with *Antigone*. And yet, it is *Antigone* that, despite all its encumbrances and inconsistencies, challenges more profoundly the notion itself of performance.

Brecht's idea of performance was inevitably tied to his manifold ways of exploring the innumerable implications of theatrical practice by way of its fusion with theory. While it may seem more than likely that the intersection of philosophy and performance eventually crossed his mind at one point or another, it is not clear to what extent he regarded it as a problematic or pressing issue. This does not mean, however, that he disregarded such a connection altogether. When he did try to consider that relation in a more immediate manner, it prompted him – as in the *Messingkauf* texts (1939–1955) – to devise a dialogical and figurative script where one character (the philosopher) is keen to confront its estranged double (the dramaturg), not forgetting of course the omnipresence of the actor and the director pertaining to the endless discussion on the subject of proximity or distance: from actor to spectator, from the audience to the play-text.

Throughout the 1950s up until his death in 1956, Brecht scrutinized and reignited this question in every possible way, both in theory and in practice. This ensured him a large following of both disciples and detractors, and a continuing dissemination of his work either through repudiation or enthusiasm, so that, in accordance with the shifting wind between revolutionary procedures and dubious indoctrination that is so typical of the preparation of his plays, controversy about his theories and working methods has been kept very much alive to this day.

In spite of all its complexity and its many contradictions, the by now traditional dichotomies associated with Brecht's teachings fueled the need for their constant reexamination in such a way that, however outdated its background might appear, such inquiry continues to thrive and renew itself. One need only look at their almost organic unfolding, via the balance (or the lack thereof) between the performer and his role, the actor and his character: the epic vs. the naturalistic, the socio-political vs. the psychological, objectivity vs. subjective involvement, analysis vs. identification, distance vs. empathy, observation vs. pathos, dispassion vs. warmth.

One could argue that the impact of Brecht's work and thought is grounded first and foremost in its ambiguity and all the loose ends it left behind, rather than in the consistency that it spells out so assertively. As a playwright who himself deliberately acted as a dramaturg, and a dramaturg who was adamant about playing his role as the stage director, Brecht was harsh but masterful when it came to reflecting and acting upon the performance of his plays. In this sense, even though his role as a theatre practitioner by far overshadows all others, he may be seen as a philosopher of sorts as regards the concept of performance, understood as the staging or enactment of a play, but equally in the free fall condition of the performing mind, meticulously premeditated while apparently devoid of a score or a script. This is why, more often than not, he can be said to have stolen the performance altogether – again, both in theory and in practice.

Surely, what one might call Brecht's 'ideas on performance' cannot claim to be something distinct from 'Brecht's ideas about the business of acting' – both join hands from the beginning as 'Brecht's ideas on the function of theatre and dramatic performance' (Eddershaw 2002, 8, 36, 1). One can certainly alienate the text, but not the context: here, the performer still equals the actor, acting equals playing a role, and playing a role equals theatrical art. The latter, however, is not that which precedes performance as a somewhat ill-defined notion, but the persistent questioning of its realization. Moreover, for Brecht as an author who so strongly emphasized the role of thinking, and was so demanding of the performer in terms of his or her ability to be conscious of the act of performance itself, surely philosophy, seen as an indefinite or loose notion, would seem to be only a step away from the never-ending, inexhaustible concept of performance. Nonetheless, given that such linearity remains faint and unconfirmed, one is left with tentative conclusions such as these: 'Brecht himself, even in the late stages of his career, was still trying to find an effective formulation of the immediacy of performance, on the one hand, and the achieving of an objective understanding on the part of the spectator on the other' (Eddershaw 2002, 17). In turn, it is no doubt legitimate to discuss Brecht's work and legacy as a whole in terms of the 'possibilities of performing theory', or to digress on the 'many different forms of performative writing' (Barnett 2015, 40, 51) that it entails. However, that still won't be enough to conceal the fact that philosophy remains unseen or unheard of as a substantive category of performance, just as the self-awareness of philosophy as performance cannot be equated with that which it stood for in Western philosophy at large, despite the several historically proven resemblances between the two.

In light of this, it is not surprising that Brecht's brief encounter with ancient tragic poetry comes to partially subsume the shortcomings of his plan for a theatre practice based on models. Such a project simply falls short of its ambition as soon as it is faced with that which no modern subjective or objective consciousness can truly assimilate: Greek Tragedy, as incorporated by the Greek chorus, shrouded in the mystery of its performance through song and dance. Just as Brecht had sensed the 'historical other-worldliness' of Sophocles' *Antigone* – 'the ancient play', so he calls it – as the obstacle to every possible 'identification with the main figure', he was the first to recognize that the several 'incisions for the chorus' as alienating instances proper to the 'Hellenic dramaturgy' (BFA 25:75), were ultimately impervious to a modern audience. The chorus therefore tends to appear in the guise of a pre-existing *Verfremdungseffekt*, something that, rather than being caused by the will to rationalize and push Greek drama to its limits, is really the first and the last hurdle of performance in itself. One example would suffice to make this clear: in the English translation of the Foreword to the *Antigonemodell*, 'performance' is the word chosen to translate Brecht's German term *Spielweise*, literally the way or the mode of acting or playing a role (Brecht 2014, 165,167; see also BFA 25:73, 75) However, rather than criticizing such choices on account of their inaccuracy, one could instead see them as the point of departure toward something else.

The stumbling of the Brechtian concept of theatre at the very beginning of the performing arts as such was perhaps a misadventure and a false step, but not a barren one. As it comes to a halt, *Antigone* points to that interim space where all seems possible. As a self-sufficient entity, the poem that by definition encapsulates both tragedy as philosophy and a philosophy of tragedy of its own, it breaks new ground by positing a different view on how to approach tragic drama in performance. As a failed attempt at wrenching a new model (a modern Organon) out of the master model (Ancient Tragic Poetry), it summons the 'aesthetics of interruption' (Brecht 2014, xii) and change that many are tempted to see as Brecht's most significant contribution to keep thinking about performance by keeping track of its many ramifications, its recurring deflection, or its constant displacement.

WORKS CITED

All references to Brecht's writings are to the following edition, quoted as BFA, followed by the respective volume and page number: *Werke, Große kommentierte Berliner und Frankfurter Ausgabe*, edited by Werner Hecht, Jan Knopf, Werner Mittenzwei, and Klaus-Detlef Müller. 30 vols. Berlin and Weimar: Aufbau-Verlag; Frankfurt a.M.: Suhrkamp. All translations are my own, except when otherwise noted. An English translation of Brecht's *The Antigone of Sophocles*, along with several texts directly related to it, are included in Vol. 8 of the *Collected Plays* (Brecht 2003). The translations of Hölderlin's *Antigone* as they appear in this essay differ significantly from the extant version in English (Hölderlin 2001).

BFA 8. 1992. *Die Antigone des Sophokles. Nach der Hölderlinschen Übertragung für die Bühne bearbeitet, Stücke* 8. In *Werke*, Große *kommentierte* Berliner *und* Frankfurter Ausgabe, 8: 193–242.

BFA 24. 1991. *Zu «Die Antigone des Sophokles»* (*Vorwort, Anmerkungen zur Bearbeitung*), *Schriften 4. Texte zu Stücken*. In *Werke*, Große *kommentierte Berliner und Frankfurter Ausgabe*, 24: 349–353.

BFA 25. 1994. *Antigonemodell 1948, Schriften 5. Theatermodelle. «Katzgraben»-Notate*. In *Werke*, Große *kommentierte Berliner und Frankfurter Ausgabe*, 25.

BFA 26. 1994. *Journale I. 1913–1941*. In *Werke*, Große *kommentierte Berliner und Frankfurter Ausgabe*, 26.

BFA 27. 1995. *Journale 2. 1941–1955*. In *Werke*, Große *kommentierte Berliner und Frankfurter Ausgabe*, 27.

BFA 29. 1998. *Briefe 2. Briefe 1937–1949*. In *Werke*, Große *kommentierte Berliner und Frankfurter Ausgabe*, 29.

Barner, Winfried. 1987. «Durchrationalisierung» des Mythos? *Zu Bertolt Brechts «Antigonemodell 1948»*. In *Zeitgenossenschaft. Zur deutssprachigen Literatur im 20. Jahrhundert*, edited by P. M. Lützeler, H. Lehnert, and G. S. Williams, 191–210. Frankfurt a.M.: Festschrift für Egon Schwarz.

Barnett, David. 2015. *Brecht in Practice: Theatre, Theory and Performance*. London: Bloomsbury.

Beaufret, Jean. 1965. Hölderlin et Sophocle. In *Hölderlin, Remarques sur Oedipe/Remarques sur Antigone*, 7–42. Paris: Union générale d'éditions.

Benn, M. B. 1959. 'Hölderlin and Sophocles'. *German Life & Letters* 12 (3): 161–173. https://doi.org/10.1111/j.1468-0483.1959.tb00563.x

Beißner, Friedrich. (1933) 1961. *Hölderlins Übersetzungen aus dem Griechischen*. Stuttgart: Metzler.

Berman, Anotine.1987. Hölderlin, ou la traduction comme manifestation. In *Hölderlin vu de France*, edited by B. Böschenstein and J. Le Rider, 129–44. Tübingen: Gunter Narr.

Bernofsky Susan. 2001. 'Hölderlin as translator: The perils of interpretation'. *The Germanic Review* 76 (3): 215–233. https://doi.org/10.1080/00168890109597436

Binder, Wolfgang. 1992. *Hölderlin und Sophokles*. Tübingen: Turm-Vorträge.

Böschenstein, Bernhard. 2004. '«du scheinst ein rotes Wort zu färben?». Hölderlin als Übersetzer des Sophokles. Ein Berliner Vortrag'. In *«...auf klassischem Boden begeistert». Antike-Rezeption in der deutschen Literatur*, edited by O. Hildebrand, and Th. Pittrof. 265–81. Rombach, Freiburg i. Br.

Brecht, Bertolt. 2003. *The Antigone of Sophocles*. In *Collected Plays*, vol. 8, edited by Tom Kuhn and David Constantine. Translated by David Constantine. London: Methuen.

———. 2014. *Brecht on Performance. Messingkauf and Modelbooks*. Edited by Tom Kuhn, Steve Giles and Marc Silberman. London: Bloomsbury.

Bunge, Hans-Joachim. 1957. *Antigonemodell 1948 von Bertolt Brecht und Caspar Neher. Zur Praxis und Theorie des epischen (dialektischen) Theaters Bertolt Brechts*. PhD diss., Greifswald.

De Ponte, Susanne. 2006. *Caspar Neher – Bertolt Brecht. Eine Bühne für das epische Theater*. Berlin; Henschel Verlag.

Doering, Sabine. 2010–2011. 'Vom Mythos zum Modell. Brechts *Die Antigone des Sophokles. Nach der Hölderlinschen Übertragung für die Bühne bearbeitet*'. Hölderlin-Jahrbuch 37, 141–169.

Eddershaw, Margaret. 2002. *Performing Brecht: Forty Years of British Performances*. London and New York: Routledge.

Flashar, Hellmut. 1988. 'Durchrationalisieren oder provozieren? Brechts 'Antigone', Hölderlin und Sophokles'. In *Das fremde Wort. Studien zur Interdependenz von Texten*, edited by Ilse Nolting-Hauff and Joachim Schulze, 394–410. Amsterdam: B.R. Grüner.

Fynsk, Christopher. 1999. 'Reading the *Poetics* after the "Remarks"'. In *The Solid Letter: Readings of Friedrich Hölderlin*, edited by Aris Fioretos, 237–246. Stanford: Stanford University Press.

Häny, A. 1946. 'Aus dem Motivkreis von Hölderlins Anmerkungen'. *Trivium* 4, 262–86. Reprinted 1978. Harrison, Robin B. 1975. *Hölderlin and Greek Literature*. Oxford: Clarendon Press.

Hecht, Werner (ed). 1988. *Brechts Antigone des Sophokles*. Frankfurt a. M.: Suhrkamp.

Hölderlin, Friedrich. 1992. *Die Trauerspiele des Sophokles. Oedipus der Tyrann – Anmerkungen zum Oedipus. Antigonae – Anmerkungen zur Antigonä*. In Friedrich Hölderlin, *Sämtliche Werke und Briefe*, edited by Michael Knaupp, vol. 2. Munich: Carl Hanser.

Kasper, Monika. 2000. *«Das Gesetz von allen der König». Hölderlins Anmerkungen zum Oedipus und zur Antigonä*, Würzburg: Köningshausen & Neumann.

Krell, David. 2004. 'A Small Number of Houses in the Tragic Universe. A Second Look at Hölderlin's "Anmerkung on Sophocles" Against the Backdrop of Aristotle's *Poetics*'. In *'Es bleibet aber eine Spur/ Doch eines Wortes'. Zur späten Hymnik und Tragödientheorie Friedrich Hölderlins*, edited by Christophe Jamme, and Anja Lemke, 345–378. Munich: Wilhelm Fink.

Kurz, Gerhard. 1988. 'Poetische Logik. Zu Hölderlins «Anmerkungen» zu «Oedipus» und «Antigonä»'. In *Jenseits des Idealismus. Hölderlins letzte Homburger Jahre*, vol. 5, edited by Christoph Jamme, and Otto Pöggeler. Bonn: Bouvier.

Lacoue-Labarthe, Philippe. 1986. 'La césure du spéculatif'. In Philippe Lacoue-Labarthe, *L'imitation des modernes (Typographies II)*, 39–70. Paris: Galilée.

Louth, Charlie. 1998. *Hölderlin and the Dynamics of Translation*. Oxford: Legenda.

Philipsen, Bart. 1998. 'Das Zaudern der Macht. Tragödie und Demokratie in Brechts 'Antigonemodell 1948'''. *Germanische Mitteilungen* 48, 52–67.

Rehbein, Antje. 1962. *Brechts ,Antigonemodell 1948'. Ein Beitrag zu Brechts Antikerezeption*. Rostock.

Schadewalt, Wolfgang. 1960. 'Hölderlins Übersetzung des Sophokles'. In *Hellas und Hesperien. Gesammelte Schriften zur Antike und zur neueren Literatur*, 767–824. Zurich: Artemis.

Taplin, Oliver. 1978. *Greek Tragedy in Action*. Oxford: Oxford University Press. https://doi.org/10.4324/9780203324301

Taxidou, Olga. 2008. 'Machines and Models for Modern Tragedy: Brecht/Berlau, Antigone-Model 1948'. In *Rethinking Tragedy*, edited by Rita Felski, 256–257. Baltimore: Johns Hopkins University Press.

Weisstein, Ulrich. 1973. 'Imitation, Stylization and Adaptation. The Language of Brecht's "Antigone" and its relation to Hölderlin's Version of Sophocles'. *The German Quarterly* 46: 581–604. https://doi.org/10.2307/403404

Wüthrich, Werner. 2015. *Die Antigone des Bertolt Brecht. Eine experimentelle Theaterarbeit, Chur 1948*. Zürich: Chronos.

——. 2003. *Bertolt Brecht und die Schweiz*. Zürich: Unter Mitarbeit von Stefan Hulfeld.

CHAPTER THREE

Original Interpretations of Brecht Plays

BERTOLT BRECHT
TRANSLATED BY ROMY FURSLAND

If I chose my arguments like Bernard Shaw, I would say that allowing directors to come up with original interpretations would cost me, as the author, too much money. Even taking into account the fact that if I allowed their original interpretations, the directors would be more likely to encourage the theatres to buy the rights to my plays, I would worry about the inevitable failures. And the more original a director's talents, the more worried I would be.

Brecht, '[Originale Auffassungen zu Brechtstücken]', in Brecht, *Schriften*, vol. 3 (Berlin and Frankfurt/Main: Aufbau and Suhrkamp, 1993), p. 127.

CHAPTER FOUR

Undogmatic Marxism: Brecht Rehearses at the Berliner Ensemble

DAVID BARNETT

The foundation of the Berliner Ensemble (BE) on 1 September 1949 in East Berlin gave Brecht the resources he needed to develop approaches to making theater: approaches that, for the most part, it had only been possible to theorize during his fifteen years in exile. According to the contract between the Soviet occupying authorities and Brecht's wife Helene Weigel, the BE was to receive just over one and a quarter million marks in its first year, despite the fact that the BE was a theater company that did not have its own theater building.[1] Initially, the BE was only a guest at the Deutsches Theater (DT) and had to wait until 1954 to gain full control over its means of production when it finally moved to the Theater am Schiffbauerdamm. The financial security guaranteed by the state, however, gave Brecht the freedom to experiment, not only with production aesthetics but also with the very way that a theater could be organized. This essay is concerned with the ways in which Brecht realized his ideas with the BE. Some critics have been keen to suggest that Brecht's managerial and directorial work owed nothing to his theories of theater. John Fuegi writes that for Brecht theory 'had a valuable place outside the theatre but almost none in actual day-to-day staging practice'.[2] The curious basis for this assertion is that Brecht rarely used the term *Verfremdung*[3] in rehearsal, a point W. Stuart McDowell also makes. McDowell goes on to claim that 'theories such as *Verfremdung* and *Gestus*

David Barnett, 'Undogmatic Marxism. Brecht as Director at the Berliner Ensemble', in Laura Bradley and Karen Leeder (eds.), *Brecht and the GDR. Politics, Culture, Posterity* (Rochester NY: Camden House, 2011), pp. 25–43.

I should like to thank the British Academy for its Research Development Award and the Humboldt Foundation for supporting the research for this essay.

[1] Contract between Helene Weigel and the Verwaltung für Volksbildung (Office for Education), 24 September 1949, in BBA, uncatalogued file 'Aktuelles'. The contract, as the date of signing shows, actually came into effect after the BE had been founded.
[2] John Fuegi, *Bertolt Brecht: Chaos according to Plan* (Cambridge: Cambridge UP, 1987), xiii.
[3] The term for 'making the familiar strange', to which I shall return, is often mistranslated as 'alienation'. While 'defamiliarization' is a closer rendition, I shall retain the untranslatable German. It is well documented that Brecht rarely used the term in rehearsal.

become academic exercises and not effective processes to realize the text [...]'.[4] At the heart of both commentators' arguments is a determination to de-politicize Brecht the theater practitioner by suggesting that his productions tell us more about the richness of a timeless human condition than the political realities of the moment. Brecht refuted this formulation in a text published posthumously that describes the work at the BE as focused on showing human nature as both changeable and dependent on social position.[5] On one of the last pages of Fuegi's book, he writes with respect to the productions of *Edward II* in 1924 and *Galileo* in 1957: 'from first to last, essentially Brecht had remained the same' (185). This simplistic, convenient, and ahistorical conclusion, which classes Brecht as an unchangingly great director, will be challenged in this essay. I shall be examining how Marxist theory suffused Brecht's approaches to staging at the BE, and how its tenets could produce quite varied results while ultimately remaining close to a dialectically materialist understanding of the world. First, however, I shall consider the ways in which Brecht sought to realize his politicized practice by radicalizing the organization of the BE along more democratic lines.

From the very beginning of the enterprise, Brecht was keen to turn the BE into an institution that empowered as many of its workers as possible to make positive contributions to the rehearsal process. This extended all the way from the creative staff via the actors to the technicians and even more tangential figures, like Brecht's driver.[6] While Brecht's word was usually final, it was important to him to allow constructive debate that would influence the way productions took shape. This attempt to undermine traditional hierarchies, or at least to open them up, had ideological roots whose benefits were twofold: cultural workers could become less alienated, in the Marxist sense, from the production process; and their contribution could ultimately lead to a better quality in production. That is, the ideological drive to empower as many as possible had the practical advantage of serving the theater in a virtuous circle.

The desire to enfranchise the company's creative staff can be seen clearly in a document circulated barely two weeks after the first rehearsals began at the BE. The young assistant directors and dramaturges were required to attend special lectures and to make active contributions to the company. Further suggestions were 'erwartet [...], die [...] das theoretische Handwerkzeug der Einzelnen bereichern und gebrauchsfähig machen' (expected [...], which [...] enrich the individuals' theoretical 'toolkit' and make it serviceable).[7] This short quotation shows how important the dynamic and reciprocal relationship between theory and practice was at the company. The pedagogical thrust casts Brecht more as a teacher than a theater-maker determined willfully to push through his ideas and monopolize the limelight. Instead he sought to expose his practice to other influences and to discuss it with other people in a bid to test its efficacy and, if necessary, modify or adapt it. The impulse to let others take charge was realized remarkably early, too. Brecht was quick to promote his protégés, entrusting Egon Monk, who was just twenty-three at the time, with directing what was only the company's sixth production,

---

[4] W. Stuart McDowell, '*Verfremdung* be Damned! Putting an End to the Myth of Brechtian Acting', *Communications from the International Brecht Society* 38 (2009): 158–68, here 160–61 and 165.

[5] See Brecht, '[Die Eigenarten des Berliner Ensembles I]', *BFA* 23:311.

[6] See the report of the driver, Werner L., that Brecht encouraged him to attend rehearsals and offer opinions, in *Erinnerungen an Brecht*, ed. Hubert Witt (Leipzig: Reclam, 1964), 228–29.

[7] Anon., 'Pflichtbesuch', 25 September 1949, Berliner-Ensemble-Archiv (hence forth BEA), File 2. All translations from the German are mine unless otherwise acknowledged.

Biberpelz und roter Hahn (The Beaver Coat and the Red Hen) in 1951. However, often without taking credit directly, Brecht supervised almost all BE productions and so his imprint was always clearly visible.[8]

Brecht's own directorial practices, bolstered by the input from and debate among his collaborators, demonstrate how a common approach to making theater politically can produce divergent results. As will be shown, Brecht's Marxist aesthetics did not make for propagandistic productions but were concerned with opening up the dramas in question to dialectical investigation. I have chosen two contrasting productions for analysis in this essay, *Herr Puntila und sein Knecht Matti* (Mr. Puntila and His Man Matti) of 1949 and *Winterschlacht* (Battle in Winter) of 1955. They are taken from the beginning and the end of Brecht's short directorial career at the BE, not only to understand a sense of development in his practice, but also to examine how two contrasting genres were treated.

Puntila was the very first production by the BE and is subtitled 'ein Volksstück', a genre for which there is no adequate translation in English. This term, meaning roughly 'play of/for the people', was a nineteenth-century coinage and it was primarily intended to entertain. In an essay, Brecht associated the 'krudes und anspruchsloses Theater' (crude and unambitious theater) of the *Volksstück* with a similar view of the common people handed down by the ruling classes.[9] His aim was to write a play that represented the spectrum of social classes in such a way that entertainment could be combined with class analysis and the study of social contradiction. The play itself can equally be called a comedy, due to the humor evinced by the conflicts. *Puntila* was directed by Brecht and Erich Engel. Engel staged the world premiere of *Die Dreigroschenoper* (The Threepenny Opera) at the Theater am Schiffbauerdamm in 1928, the production that would make the play an international hit. It should be noted here that although Engel co-directed the production, he was responsible more for the delivery of the lines than the innovative visual practices that Brecht sought to introduce.[10]

Winterschlacht by Johannes R. Becher, on the other hand, is unmistakably a tragedy. It is set during the battle of Moscow (1941–42) and follows Johannes Hörder, a middle-class soldier whose experiences of Nazi aggression finally drive him to disobey a barbaric order to bury pro-Soviet partisans alive and to shoot himself dead instead. Tragedy was, in a way, an illusory genre for Brecht, as can be seen from the following extract from the *Messingkauf* (The Messingkauf Dialogues, 1939–55):

> Philosoph: Die Ursachen sehr vieler Tragödien liegen außerhalb des Machtbereichs derer, die sie erleiden, wie es scheint.
> Dramaturg: Wie es scheint?

---

[8]The one exception was the BE's second production, which was directed by Brecht's friend Berthold Viertel, Even the two productions credited to actors Therese Giehse – Heinrich von Kleist's *Der zerbrochene Krug* (The Broken Urn, premiered 23 January 1952) – and Ernst Busch – Nikolai Pogodin's *Das Glockenspiel des Kreml* (The Kremlin Chimes, premiered 28 March 1952) involved much input from Brecht.
[9]Brecht, 'Anmerkungen zum Volksstück', BFA 24:293.
[10]Helene Weigel said that she could not have played Mother Courage in the production of 1949 if Brecht had not co-directed with Engel. Quoted in Werner Hecht, *Helene Weigel: Eine große Frau des 20. Jahrhunderts* (Frankfurt a.M.: Suhrkamp, 2000), 28–29. This is not to deny the importance of Engel's contribution, something Weigel affirmed: see 77–78.

Philosoph: Natürlich nur wie es scheint. Menschliches kann nicht außerhalb des Machtbereichs der Menschen liegen, und die Ursachen dieser Tragödien sind menschliche. [11]

[Philosopher: The causes of a lot of tragedies lie outside the power of those who suffer them, so it seems.

Dramaturge: So it seems?

Philosopher: Of course it only seems. Nothing human can possibly lie outside the powers of humanity, and such tragedies have human causes.]

The tragic therefore requires qualification and relativization in a theater concerned with the potential for change rather than the inevitability of disaster. *Winterschlacht* was staged by Brecht and Manfred Wekwerth in 1955, a year and a half before Brecht's death. It should be noted that Wekwerth played the role of the apprentice here, as evidenced by the production's rehearsal records. And while he certainly was not a silent partner, Brecht was the main creative force in the relationship.

I shall be exploring Brecht's approaches to staging these contrasting plays with a view to showing how a common theoretical position might generate very different types of performance while nonetheless adhering to a Marxist understanding of reality.

UNDOGMATIC MARXISM

It is worth understanding an important distinction in terminology from the outset: Meg Mumford notes that while 'contradiction was a vital feature of Brecht's theatre […], as he became increasingly familiar with Marxism he came to view the idea of contradiction in accordance with the philosophy of dialectical materialism.'[12] This distinction moves Brecht the director away from a broad notion of conflict, common to all productions of drama, to a more nuanced understanding of contradiction. The dialectic is a specific form that articulates contradiction and is Hegel's model of how change occurs: a thesis meets its contradiction in an antithesis; when the tension between the two becomes too great, elements of both sides form a new entity, the synthesis. This process never stops, as the synthesis in turn becomes a thesis itself, against which a new antithesis will emerge, and so on in perpetuity. While the process may appear mechanical or deterministic, this is not the case at all. If one considers how complex each aspect of a dialectical tension may be, it is impossible to predict which elements will combine to form a synthesis. The classical Marxist dialectic concerns the contradiction between labor and capital, yet syntheses of this tension were quite different in different parts of the world where different conditions dominated. In Russia, for example, a revolution took place, whereas in Britain the tension led to the establishment of a welfare state. Brecht was clear about the non-deterministic nature of the dialectic in a note: 'zu der ent. idealisierung [*sic*] der dialektik gehört es auch, dass der Versuchung, ein system zu bilden, widerstanden wird' (part of the de-idealization of the dialectic involves resisting the temptation to create a system).[13] Here the 'system' is the attempt to predict the outcome of the dialectic, since its productive

---

[11]Brecht, '[*Messingkauf.* Fragment B 13],' *BFA* 22:711; *The Messingkauf Dialogues*, trans. John Willett (London: Methuen, 1965), 32.
[12]Meg Mumford, *Bertolt Brecht* (Abingdon: Routledge, 2009), 85.
[13]Brecht, '[Notizbuch 48–50],' BBA 814/52.

strength, according to Brecht, lies in presenting contradictory material on stage without pointing to a definite synthesis. That task was passed on to the audience and made them co-producers of meaning.

The dialectic is also, in Marxism, materialist, which effectively means that what happens on stage cannot flout the laws of society or history at any given time. In Brecht's theater, materialism was guaranteed by a concept of realism that departs from the more common one in theatrical aesthetics and that may broadly be described as an accurate copy of what one finds in everyday life. The prerequisite for Brecht's writing and directing practice was an idea of realism that is defined in *Theaterarbeit* (1952), the book that documents the first six productions at the Berliner Ensemble, in a quotation from Friedrich Engels, as 'die Wiedergabe typischer Menschen unter typischen Umständen' (the representation of typical people under typical circumstances).[14] This postulate is placed in contradistinction to an unashamedly partisan definition of naturalism as a 'Kunstrichtung, die bei der Wiedergabe der Naturerscheinungen nach peinlichster Genauigkeit strebt, jedoch bei der pedantischen Anhäufung zufälliger Details oft alle Sinnzusammenhänge zudeckt' (an artistic direction that strives for the most painstaking accuracy in the reproduction of natural appearances but that often smothers any meaningful connections by pedantically accumulating arbitrary details).[15] It is clear from the two definitions that realism has a special meaning in Brecht's theater because it includes a generalizing principle that goes beyond the superficial imitation of reality. It is a philosophical rather than a purely aesthetic category. Realism here is something that applies to a given society as a whole because it reproduces the laws under which the dialectic works, regardless of apparent differences between individuals.

Human beings are in constant dialogue with their environment, which means that they, too, are always in dialogue with the dialectic. They have the power to make decisions but not to stand outside the dialectical process. Consequently, characters on stage have to show their connection with greater social, political, or historical formations, and this is where Brecht's powerful tools for performance play a central role.

What connects bodies on stage to their fictional but materialist society is the untranslatable term *Gestus*, which is a central part of Brecht's theatrical arsenal. As Laura Bradley writes, *Gestus* 'is best understood as a physical action or a spatial configuration which reveals the ideological, social and economic relations between two or more characters'.[16] While one might want to expand this definition to include the relationship between one person and his or her sociopolitical context, the term nonetheless articulates how actors' physicalities can be used to go beyond the individual and connect him or her to the social. That contexts change suggests that the actor also changes between and/or during the scenes themselves at particular turning points. *Gestus* thus becomes a readable index of a character's status at any given time. And *Gestus*, unlike *Verfremdung*, was a term that was frequently used in rehearsal and concretely tied Brecht's practices to dialectical materialism.

The undogmatic quality of Brecht's direction, as we shall see, is rooted in the non-determinism he identified in the processes of dialectical materialism. There was no

---

[14]Ruth Berlau, Bertolt Brecht, Claus Hubalek, Peter Palirzsch, and Käthe Rülicke, eds., *Theaterarbeit: 6 Aufführungen des Berliner Ensembles*(Dresden: VVV Dresdner Verlag, 1952), 434.
[15]*Theaterarbeit*, 433.
[16]Laura Bradley, *Brecht and Political Theatre: 'The Mather' on Stage* (Oxford: Oxford UP, 2006), 6.

definitive solution to staging the dialectic; it was more a question of how contradictions could best be articulated from a complex set of theses and antitheses. As Brecht put it in another note: 'es handelt sich nicht darum, [...] die aufführung zu fixieren – sondern im gegenteil darum, änderungen zu provozieren, die eine entwicklung der spielweise bewirken und wahrnehmbar machen können' (it isn't a question of turning the production into something fixed – on the contrary, it's about provoking changes that can influence the development of the mode of performance and make it perceptible).[17] The idea, then, of a 'finished' production was profoundly undialectical, and Brecht was keen to play with the different aspects of the dialectical elements in a bid to make them as striking and effective as possible. While he viewed the dialectic in partisan terms and clearly loaded it in the favor of the proletariat, he sought any dialectical means necessary to effect a richness of contrast that would astonish and galvanize the audience into seeing the relations on stage with fresh eyes.

PUNTILA AS THE COMIC RAISING OF CLASS CONSCIOUSNESS

Brecht had already directed *Puntila* in Zurich in 1948, although for legal reasons he was not allowed to be credited as director at the time.[18] He was therefore very familiar with the play in performance and decided to open the BE's tenure at the DT with a new production. He was able to persuade Leonard Steckel, who played Puntila, to reprise the role in Berlin, although, as Steckel was to discover, important changes were to be made in order to improve the dialectical impact of the character.

Puntila deals with the tensions between the property-owning middle class and the working class in a variety of ways, because the *Volksstück* form allows for the inclusion of characters from all walks of life. The central tension, however, is focused, as the title suggests, on Puntila, the landowner, and his chauffeur Matti. The central conceit of the play is that Puntila is a brutal exploiter when sober but a perfectly reasonable person when drunk, which he is for much of the play. From this simple contrast, Brecht explored the very question of what it meant to be a human being in a class society. In the opening scenes of the play, production notes establish how 'merkwürdig' (strange) Puntila is in that he becomes a 'Mensch' (human being) when drunk. In addition, Eva, Puntila's daughter, makes 'die merkwürdige Entdeckung' (the strange discovery) in the second scene that Matti is also 'ein Mann' (a man) and not just a servant.[19] These apparently self-evident qualities required special theatrical measures to reveal that the definition of what it means to be human varies between different social classes. As a result, the first meeting between Matti and Puntila was to suggest a 'Begegnung zweier Patrouillen, Erkundung im fremden Gebiet' (meeting of two patrols, reconnaissance on *terra incognita*).[20] Brecht was fond of using analogies to suggest the gestic situation; this image evokes mutual suspicion and asks the actors to investigate each other, rather than to treat the first encounter as something self-evident. This *Verfremdung* of the

---

[17]Brecht, '[Notizbuch 48–49],' BBA 811/32.
[18]See Werner Hecht, *Brecht Chronik* (Frankfurt a.M.: Suhrkamp, 1997), 823. Brecht did not possess a Swiss work permit.
[19]Anon., untitled, undated, BBA File 2.
[20]Anon., '*Puntila* – Stellprobe – 1. Bild, 19. 9. 49', undated, BEA File 2.

meeting is also comic; the put-upon worker does not merely accept his employer's humanity but treats it as a remarkable trait.

Brecht had discovered from the Zurich production that Puntila ran the risk of being perceived as a mainly sympathetic character 'mit einigen üblen Anwandlungen im Zustand der Nüchternheit' (with some nasty traits when sober) and thus set about keeping the character in check through the application of dialectical tension.[21] His humanity when drunk could thus be rendered not as in some way natural but as a particular behavior that worked to his advantage. Steckel wore a bald cap in the BE production and this allowed him, an actor who was well known to the theatergoing public, to appear more grotesque, with a hint of 'Genghis Khan'.[22] His drunken self, while ostensibly friendly, took on the qualities 'eines Krokodils' (of a crocodile) charming its prey.[23] Steckel consciously performed pleasantness for the BE production; here the characteristic was no longer merely humanizing but suggested invitation and threat, a dialectic that the audience could then trace back to Puntila's social position. In other words, the friendliness was subjected to *Verfremdung*, and the familiar became strange, as a way of suggesting that drunkenness was a refuge from Puntila's viciousness rather than a state of natural affability.

Matti, on the other hand, was presented as a likeable working man, but this, too, could simply have offered the audience an undialectical presentation, ignoring the fact that a proletarian is also a social being. Matti was not constructed in the same grotesque fashion as Puntila, although Brecht had also experimented with furnishing him with a prosthesis. Erwin Geschonneck, who played Matti, reports that a large ear was tried but discarded during rehearsals.[24] Instead, Matti was dialectically integrated into the production through *Gestus*, best understood in the scene in which he is offered Eva's hand in marriage. Here Matti takes from Eva a platter of herrings that are meant to be served to other guests. His contemplation of one herring among the many connects him to the fish in an unexpected way: 'wie in der griechischen Tragödie, Matti erkennt den Hering. Einer hat den anderen immer für einen fremden Mann gehalten, nun erkennt er: er ist ein naher Verwandter' (as in Greek tragedy, Matti recognizes the herring. One who has always considered the other a stranger recognizes: he's a close relative).[25] The unexpectedness of the *anagnorisis*, in which two previously unequal parties are revealed as exploited equals, is funny. Having established the equivalence, Matti then serves the fish to the other guests, who come from different social classes. Their gestic response to the fish, which is now a symbol of the downtrodden, tells the audience more about social attitudes, Puntila, for example, eats the fish with great curiosity, reminding the audience of his attitude to Matti in his drunken state; Laina the cook shows how familiar she is with the fish after years of service in the kitchen. All the characters betray something about their social position and thus suggest the ways in which their society has affected them. Matti, who experiences the epiphany, examines the responses as a transformed man in possession of new knowledge.

---

[21] Brecht, 'Steckels zwei Puntilas', *BFA* 24:310.
[22] See Anon., '*Puntila* – Stellprobe – 1. Bild, 19. 9. 49', undated, BEA File 2.
[23] Anon., '*Puntila* – Stellprobe – 1. Bild, 19. 9. 49'.
[24] See Geschonneck in '*Denken heißt verändern...*' *Erinnerungen an Brecht*, ed. Joachim Lang and Jürgen Hillesheim (Augsburg: Maro, 1998), 51. The ear was supposed to signify Matti's sensitive perception of situations but was considered crass and was rejected.
[25] Anon., 'Freitag 28. Oktober 1949. BB EE CN. VIII', undated, BEA File 2.

The scenes themselves were divided up into sections to help the actors negotiate their turning points. For Brecht, a lack of clarity spelled doom for a sequence – he had no problem with complexity, but that complexity had to be broken down into its constituent parts in order for the audience to follow the dialectical unfolding of events. The scene in which Eva initially toys with Matti, for example, was plotted precisely, based on the contradictions of social interaction between the classes. Here Eva becomes bored with Puntila and decides to amuse herself with Matti as someone she assumes she can net with ease. Matti recognizes the maneuver and puts her off; the rebuttal leaves her nonplussed. She has intended to embark upon a romantic adventure but is not prepared for the resistance she encounters. Each section of the story was told as an image and changed only when the situation demanded it. Every movement had to serve the social development of the action and visually the scene unfolded with the utmost clarity. Similarly, in the scene in which Puntila sobers up before dismissing the four women to whom he has previously proposed marriage, the stages of his sobriety had to be clearly shown in order for the audience to note his gradual change from kindness to nastiness.

As is clear from the above descriptions and analyses, actors found that characteristics stemmed from situations, from action, and not vice versa. This is typical of the *Fabel* in Brecht's directorial work. The *Fabel* is the term Brecht favored as a paraphrase for 'the action', but it suggests more than this. The *Fabel* is the control element in the analysis of a play; it reveals the rules under which a particular society functions and how they affect the characters. In an early note on the rehearsals, an anonymous assistant quotes Brecht's instruction: 'wir wollen jetzt nur den Text lesen und uns bemühen seinen Sinn zu erfassen' (at present we only want to read the lines and try to discover their meaning). The assistant explained that the aim was to find out 'wie die Sätze am einfachsten, am natürlichsten klingen, noch nicht auf die Charakterisierung der Person eingehend' (how the words sound simplest, most natural, not yet considering how to portray the character).[26] The quotation tells much about the inductive approach Brecht took. The rehearsal itself was a 'Stellprobe', literally a 'placement rehearsal'. Actors were positioned on stage so as to make their relationships, in response to the *Fabel*, as clear as possible. The lines were a tool in this process, and Brecht, despite being the author of the text, had no monopoly on interpretation; the process of realization was open to all involved.

The quest for clarity pervaded every aspect of the production. A suggestion from Geschonneck, for example, was turned down 'weil die gewünschte Wirkung durch ein Zuviel von Nebenbedeutungen verwischt worden wäre' (because the desired effect would have been blurred by too many secondary meanings).[27] The opposing sides of the dialectic had to be clearly articulated and a muddling of the terms would obscure its mechanism for the actors and the audience. The kind of input Brecht welcomed can be seen in a suggestion by Engel that was adopted. He wondered whether a fence could be placed on stage as 'Zeichen des begrenzten Besitzes' (a sign of the limits of wealth), that is, that despite his onstage dominance, Puntila's power was not unbounded and there were others like him abroad.[28]

---

[26]Anon., '*Puntila* VIII. Bild, Stellprobe, 23.9. BB und Assistenten. P/K', undated, BEA File 2.
[27]Anon., '*Puntila* Donnerstag, 22. September 1949. BB EE + Assistenten', undated, BEA File 2.
[28]Anon., 'Stellprobe 4. Bild *Puntila* 21. 9. 1949 (B. E. N.)', undated, BEA File 2,

The production was a great success. A typical response may be found in a comment from Susanne Hess-Wyneken, who wrote:

> es [gibt] keine Vernebelung der Gesinnungen; deutlich und streng trennt [Brecht] die Schichten, die sozialen und die menschlichen. In grossartige Breite baut Brecht kein Drama, sondern eine Zustandsschilderung, in der ein scharf beobachteter Realismus zur Kritik wird und aus übersteigerter Groteske alle Humore blitzen.[29]

> [there is no confusion in the politics; Brecht clearly and strictly divides the classes, both social and human. With wonderful breadth, Brecht constructs not a drama, but a depiction of conditions in which a sharply observed realism is treated critically and heightened grotesquery gives rise to all manner of humor.]

The primacy of social conditions over human drama noted here is a tribute to Brecht's attempts to emphasize the process and not the end point of the scenes, social mechanisms rather than their localized vicissitudes. The reviewer identifies a distinction between the clarity of the action and questions it left open. While other reviews drew attention to the occasional caricatures of some of the characters, the production nonetheless achieved many of its aims by moving away from character-based theater into one firmly rooted in the social context and the actions it brought forth.[30]

HISTORICIZING *WINTERSCHLACHT* AWAY FROM TRAGEDY

Johannes R. Becher had been a member of communist organizations since 1917, and fled the Nazis in 1933. On returning to the Soviet-occupied sector after the Second World War, he began to play a major role in the cultural life of the sector and, after 1949, the GDR itself. He co-founded the influential literary magazine *Sinn und Form*, and became the GDR's first Minister of Culture upon the formation of the Ministry in 1954. Becher's play offered something of a contrast to the critical mirth of *Puntila*. Initially, though, Brecht had not planned to direct it at all and had invited the Czech Emil Burian to restage the play, which Burian had successfully produced in Prague in November 1952. Burian was a committed communist, yet his approach to directing the play demonstrated the differences between a director who emphasized the inherent political qualities of the characters and one who, like Brecht, derived these qualities from the characters' social contexts.

In a rehearsal on 1 November 1954, Burian instructed: 'der Schauspieler muss tief in die Person eindringen, wenn er sie begreifen will' (the actor has to plumb the depths of the character if he is to understand it).[31] The problem with this point of departure was that it led to a number of imputations that did not correspond to the material reality of the play. One of the smaller characters in the play is a Russian Prince who had gone into exile in Paris but is now enlisted in the German army in a bid to regain the rank and privileges lost after the Russian Civil War. Burian was reported to have imputed

---

[29]Susanne Hess-Wyneken, 'Bert Brechts *Herr Puntila und sein Knecht*', *Berlin's* [sic] *Modenblatt* 1 (1950): 22.
[30]See, for example, Hans-Ulrich Eylau, '*Herr Puntila und sein Knecht Matti*,' *Berliner Zeitung*, 13 November 1949.
[31]Anon, 'Notate *Winterschlacht*', undated, 15 pages, here p. 7, BEA File 18.

a 'Dostojewski'sche Emigranten-Sentimentalität' (Dostoevskian sentimentality of an émigré) to the Prince when he remembered his time working as a chauffeur in France.[32] The notes from Brecht's production include the following one by Heinz Kahlau:

> Der Fürst hat ein stärkeres Klassenbewusstsein als die deutschen Offiziere. [...] Wenn er auch in Paris als Chauffeur war, dann gerade deshalb. Er hatte diese revolutionären Leute kennen gelernt [sic], denen man nichts nachweisen kann, [sic] und die so gefährlich sind.[33]
>
> [the Prince has a stronger class consciousness than the German officers. [...] Even if he's been a chauffeur in Paris, then precisely because of this. He's seen these revolutionaries up close, who won't be told anything and who are therefore dangerous.]

In Brecht's production, the Prince's characteristics are located more concretely in his bitter experiences. In addition, the Prince was positioned relationally to the action, as notes of a rehearsal on 20 November 1954 report: 'Der Fürst will die Deutschen benutzen, damit er seinen Grundbesitz wieder bekommt. Die Deutschen wollten den Fürsten benutzen, um in der Heimat Stimmung zu machen. Jeder will jeden für sich benutzen' (the Prince wants to use the Germans to regain his estates. The Germans want to use the Prince to blow their trumpet in his homeland. Everyone wants to use everyone else for their own ends).[34] In this way, a dialectical relationship was established in which competing political objectives could be shown in tension on stage, something that clearly contrasts with Burian's speculative psychologism. It is also worth noting just how much care was taken with such a minor character.

The move from Burian to Brecht was not simply a case of rejecting everything that had gone before. Brecht observed: 'Jede unserer Neuerungen soll man nach der Burian'schen Anlage auswerten und ihr gegenüberstellen' (each one of our new ideas is to be evaluated and compared with Burian's plans).[35] Even here one notes how the team proceeded dialectically by adopting the productive material and rejecting the rest.

Becher often uses monologues in his play but these presented Brecht with an ideological and aesthetic problem. While Brecht was used to writing direct addresses to the audience in his plays as a way of either moving the action forward or articulating social pressures affecting a character, Becher's monologues ran the risk of entering the realms of the naturalism criticized above. The danger of straying into the private, something that could exclude the social dimension, was addressed in a rehearsal note entitled 'Vorschläge, [...] den Monolog aufzumachen' (suggestions to open up the monologue ...).[36] One suggestion that won out here was for an actor to imagine he was in dialogue with his image of Germany's grandeur itself. In his reflections on the production after its premiere, Brecht noted: 'Das Monologisieren [...] zeigt die Zerrissenheit der Gesellschaft, die Isolierung des Einzelnen' (the monologues show the shattered society, the isolation of the individual).[37] By contextualizing the potentially private moment, Brecht was able to give the speeches

---

[32] Anon., 'Notate', 4.
[33] Heinz Kahlau, 'Notate *Winterschlacht*' undated, 35 pages, here p. 29, BEA File 18.
[34] Anon., 'Notate *Winterschlacht*', undated, 14 pages, here p. 2, BEA File 18.
[35] Kahlau, 'Notate', 30.
[36] See BBA 940/11.
[37] Brecht, 'Zur Aufführung der *Winterschlacht* beim Berliner Ensemble', *BFA* 24:444.

a social dimension rather than allow them to stand as individual contemplations divorced from the outside world.

While *Puntila* played in a version of the present, *Winterschlacht* had a concrete historical frame and this allowed Brecht to shift the emphasis from tragedy to history. He called the play 'die ideologische Abrechnung mit der Nazizeit' (the ideological reckoning with the Nazi period).[38] This meant that the action and characters portrayed could be faced with insoluble contradictions because their circumstances, rather than innate character flaws, were to blame for the catastrophes that run through the play. The ideological dimension could be found at all turns and was not merely restricted to the Nazis on the battlefield. Much action takes place on the home front where a socialist alternative, as represented by working-class soldiers and partisans, is not present. In a scene between Hörder's father and mother, Brecht worked on presenting a clash of rigid Prussian morality in the mother and a more pragmatic Nazi morality in the father, 'die bequemer und nützlicher ist' (which is more convenient and useful).[39] The two ways of thinking helped to define the two characters in dialectical fashion, but because neither offered a solution, the production's suggestive techniques were able to indict both positions.

Brecht pointed to his protagonist's historical constriction and lack of agency in the following metaphorical sketch of his character's arc: 'Hörder ist zu Anfang des Stückes blind, als er sehen [sic] wird, werden ihm die Augen gewaltsam geschlossen' (at the beginning of the play, Hörder is blind; when he does start to see, his eyes are violently closed).[40] The short description traces a line of development that is progressive, born of experience, but that is prematurely cut short by the brutality of his situation. The tragedy is therefore one of its time; Hörder is unable to realize his insights because of historical circumstances that need to be changed.

The relativization of the characters' agency was brought about by a constant play of individual and society, something encapsulated in another telling line from Brecht: 'wir können keinen Klassenkampf darstellen, ohne die Sitten und Gebräuche der Klassen zu zeigen' (we can't depict the class struggle without showing the customs and habits of the classes).[41] Customs and habits are developed over time, and betray an interdependency between people and their social environment. Brecht differentiated the social from the apparently natural in instructions given to the Nazi officers when they got drunk, for example. On the surface, actors playing characters under the influence might see this as a purely physiological transformation, but Brecht insisted that officers got drunk in a different way from the rank and file, in that they tended to stiffen up with more drink as a way of showing their discipline.[42]

Brecht also saw the necessity of depicting the soldiers in such a way that put across their commitment to the Nazi cause. Originally, the actors, pursuing a most Brechtian impulse, ironized the fascist and militarist lines as a way of opening them up to criticism. However, this lessened their realistic force. It was only when Wekwerth directed the actors to drown out the sound of their vehicles' engines on stage by barking their lines that they achieved

---

[38]Brecht, *BFA* 24:444.
[39]Kahlau, 'Notate', 13.
[40]Kahlau, 'Notate', 8.
[41]Anon., 'Notate', 4.
[42]See Kahlau, 'Notate',14.

'den überzeugten Ton' (the tone of conviction) for which the production was striving.[43] Thus, rather than exacting a critique on stage through irony, the directors confronted the audience with realistic fanaticism, against which Hörder's drama took place.

A key to unlocking the historicized tragedy was to be found in the actors themselves. Possibly the greatest virtue a Brechtian actor could demonstrate was the difference between him- or herself and the role. (For example, at Regine Lutz's audition, Brecht asked her to recite a poem but was more interested in her ability to recite it as if she had never seen a poem before.[44]) Brecht emphasized the quality of difference in an exchange with the actress Carola Braunbock:

> B[recht]: Sie müssen eine feine Dame spielen.
> Braunbock: Dann bin ich falsch besetzt.
> B[recht]: Gerade Sie können das besser als die wirklich feinen Leute.'[45]
> [B[recht]: You're to play a well-heeled lady.
> Braunbock: Then I'm the wrong person for the role.
> B[recht]: You of all people can play her better than the real upper crust.]

Showing social construction by contrasting the actor with the role was a crucial way of de-naturalizing what was seen on stage. This could also, however, be achieved by the careful contrast of attitudes as a way of opening up the contradictory forces acting upon a character. In a letter of praise to Ekkehard Schall, who played Hörder, Brecht wrote that he enjoyed 'das widerspruchsvolle Entsetzen zur Eingrabung der Partisanen [...]: Entsetzen über die Barbarei und über die eigene Insubordination zugleich' (the contradictory horror at burying the partisans alive [...]: horror at the barbarity and at his own insubordination at the same time).[46] The split showed Hörder at the point of traditional tragedy, just before he takes his own life. He was torn between a revulsion at what he had been asked to carry out, which would denote a very human response, and the social anxiety that he was disobeying an order. Hörder's death was a tragedy, but a political one – he had been put in an impossible position from which, under the prevailing circumstances, there was no escape.

THE POSSIBILITIES OF DIALECTICAL PERFORMANCE

Brecht's rehearsal practices were materialist and dialectical; without either of these he felt that he would be offering unrealistic theater that would have no political function for his audience because the performances would be removed from its experiences of the world. Reality, however, was something he acknowledged as complex and contradictory, and he claimed no sovereign right to play its flawless interpreter. Rehearsals, conducted in an air of constructive criticism, were concerned with identifying dialectical conflicts, firstly by constructing a text's *Fabel*, and then by articulating its terms on stage. This process was not a science but a series of attempts at understanding how characters related to their circumstances. There was nothing mechanical about the procedure, as different aspects of the dialectic were teased out, emphasized or sidelined over the whole rehearsal period.

---

[43]Heinz Kahlau, '*Winterschlacht* Notate', undated, n.p., BEA File 18.
[44]See Monika Buschey, *Wege zu Brecht* (Berlin: Dittrich, 2007), 37–38.
[45]Anon., 'Notate', 3.
[46]Brecht, 'Brief an den Darsteller des jungen Hörder in der *Winterschlacht*' BFA 23:408.

The 'virtuous circle,' mentioned earlier, in which ideological imperatives concerning democracy in the workplace led to an actively open invitation for input from those involved in the productions themselves, was a crucial prerequisite for the development of the BE's stagecraft. The perspectives offered by the creative team the actors, and the technical staff called existing theatrical solutions into question and provoked new approaches to staging the dialectic. While critics often praised BE productions for their ensemble playing, they were unable to observe just how collective the realization process was, and how the productions they lauded owed so much to the formal organization of the company.

Neither production discussed above was considered finished once it had been premiered, and both were given new productions in the years that followed their respective premieres. Leonard Steckel, who played Puntila in 1949, departed, for example, and was replaced by the popular comic actor Curt Bois. The difference between the two was great in terms of their physicality: Steckel was a large man, while Bois was slight and wiry. The association of Steckel with a well-fed landowner was relatively straightforward but Bois had to develop his own way of fleshing out the character and establishing its authority. As a result, all the scenes needed to be rethought and restaged to integrate a very different human being into the dialectics of the production. The problem with Bois was that his lean body often brought an unwelcome haste to the scenes, something that Brecht's famous rehearsal technique, in which actors play their parts in the third person and in the past tense, sought to correct.[47] Bois's nervousness disappeared when the actor concentrated on the actions that drove the scene forward, and when it was replayed in the present, gestural clarity trumped nervous energy. That said, the majority of reviews reproached Bois for weakening the contrasts between the drunk and the sober Puntila, arguing that he was not able to go beyond his own well-developed physical comedy.[48]

The complexity of the components of the dialectic meant that the search for contradictory representations could produce a variety of solutions. Brecht and his team sought contrasts that would provoke the audience to produce meaning from the open questions articulated on stage. As a result, the productions, with their orthodox Marxist inflection, cannot be called propaganda; they are dialectical explorations of a complex of problems. By the end of *Puntila* and *Winterschlacht*, the contradictions that force Matti to leave his master's service and Hörder to take his own life remain. And while a socialist revolution may well seem to be suggested as the implicit answer to the global problems of the plays, the complexity of the relationships in the productions themselves show that this is no simple matter. Brecht was aware that the GDR's socialism was imposed from 'above' and that there had been no popular workers' movement in the wake of the Second World War. (Indeed, the BE's third production, an adaptation of J. M. R. Lenz's 1774 play *Der Hofmeister* [The Tutor] was a critique of the failure of Germans to carry off a revolution of their own.)

The BE's productions, aside from their specificities, were attempts at offering spectators a dialectical view of the world. Brecht's method had the effect of shifting plays away from their original genres into presentations of situations, opened up for the dialectical insights they could produce. *Puntila* lost some of its drama in favor of the

---

[47]See Brecht, 'Kurze Beschreibung einer neuen Technik der Schauspielkunst, die einen Verfremdungseffekt hervorbringt', *BFA* 22:644; BT 138.
[48]See, for example, Lothar Kutsche, 'Ein entschärfter *Herr Puntila*' *Die Weltbühne*, 30 January 1952.

depiction of dialectically constructed characters whose contradictions were humorous; *Winterschlacht* lost some of its emotional bleakness in favor of a historical analysis of Hörder's position as soldier on the 'wrong' side. Yet both productions attained a liveliness drawn from the well-honed and precisely presented contradictions of the plays. The shift from un-reflected emotional effects (mindless laughter or humanist pity) to considered examinations of the comic and the tragic marks the Brechtian turn in performance. This turn, however, cannot be pinned down to any specific individual effects in isolation: Brecht's undogmatic pursuit of his own method continually sought new insights into the workings of the stage and the world.

Brecht and the Actor

CHAPTER FIVE

Instructions to Actors

BERTOLT BRECHT
TRANSLATED BY ROMY FURSLAND

The *Not/But*. On all essential points the actor should, in everything he does, also identify something he is *not* doing and make this thing identifiable and visible to the audience. For example, he does not say 'I forgive you' but 'I'll make you pay for that'. He does not fall in a faint, but comes to life. He does not love his children, but hates them. He does not walk to the back right-hand corner, but to the front left-hand corner. In other words: the actor acts what lies behind the *But*; he should act it in such a way that the audience also perceives what lies behind the *Not*.

Memorising first impressions. Actors should read their roles in an attitude of astonishment and dissent. Before they memorise the words, they should memorise the moments where they were astonished and the moments where they dissented. If they can preserve these moments in their performance, they will (as they should) enable the audience to experience astonishment and dissent too.

Making up stage directions and speaking them aloud. The actor should come up with instructions and comments about what he says and does, and speak these aloud during rehearsals. He should preface the line he has to say, for example, with the words: 'To which I replied crossly, because I hadn't eaten yet ...' Or: 'I didn't know anything about the situation at the time, so I said ...' It is also good for the actor to read his role once in the first person and once in the third person. If the actor imagines the 'he or she' speaking in the third person to be a particular character in the play – an adversary, for example – then he can learn how to assert his way of speaking against the commentary and the stage directions. An example: in the first person the actor says: 'I told him what I really thought; I said ...' In the third person, the actor says: 'He got angry and tried to think of something that would hurt me, and eventually said ...' And now what was said in the tone of the person who said it can be spoken in the tone of the person who heard it. Key to the performance, of course, is the third person, in which the speaker is the actor, meaning that the stage directions and comments reflect the actor's opinion of the character.

Swapping roles. Actors should swap roles with their partners, first copying their partners and then demonstrating their own acting style to them.

Quoting. Instead of trying to give the impression that they are improvising, actors should show what the truth is: they should quote.

Brecht, 'Anweisungen an die Schauspieler', in Brecht, *Schriften*, vol. 2 (Berlin and Frankfurt/Main: Aufbau and Suhrkamp, 1993), pp. 667–8.

Composition is a skill actors need to learn. They need to be able to appropriate any style – in other words, to improvise in the tone of the writer. It is beneficial, however, if they learn to write down their improvisations, ideally before speaking them aloud.

Being agreeable is one of the actor's principal tasks. Actors must perform everything – even terrible things – with pleasure, and must show their pleasure. An actor who cannot educate in an entertaining way and entertain in an educational way has no business in the theatre.

CHAPTER SIX

Brecht and the Contradictory Actor

JOHN ROUSE

Much scholarly material has been written on the subject of Brecht and the actor. The vast majority of this material, however, has focused on Brecht's various theoretical statements about acting, absolutizing them into an inviolate theory of so-called Epic performance and getting caught up in vaguely generalized comparisons between Brecht's 'system' of acting and Stanislavski's.[1] I would not want to deny the partial validity of these discussions or impugn the assistance they have given several generations of theatre people in understanding and making use of Brecht's accomplishments. Such discussions tend, however, to undervalue the fact that Brecht was not primarily a theoretician who sometimes directed in order to exemplify his principles, but rather a director who continually modified or reconstituted his theories on the basis of what he learned from his practice; as Brecht told a group of students in 1954, 'one mustn't think of it as if there were someone with a specific conception of theatre that he wants to impose at all costs'.[2] The *Short Organon* (1948), for example, is not Brecht's ultimate statement either about theatre in general or acting in particular. Rather, it is a position paper summarizing Brecht's thinking about his theatre work up to around 1947. During the remaining nine years of his life, Brecht constantly modified this thinking on the basis of his directorial and dramaturgical work at his Berliner Ensemble – as the many and varied amendments, clarifications, and counter-statements to the *Organon* collected in Volume 16 of the *Gesammelte Werke* make perfectly clear.

I am not attempting to insinuate that we should replace an absolutized characterization labeled 'Brecht the theoretician' with an equally absolutized characterization that could be labeled 'Brecht the director'. Rather, I am suggesting that we cannot adequately

---

John Rouse, 'Brecht and the Contradictory Actor', *Theatre Journal*, 36: 1 (1984), pp. 25–42.

[1] For a recent example of this absolutizing tendency, see Timothy J. Wiles's discussion of Brecht in his *The Theater Event: Modern Theories of Performance* (Chicago: University of Chicago Press, 1980). The tendency towards generalized comparisons with Stanislavski mars one of the most recent contributions to the discussion on Brecht and the actor, Margaret Eddershaw's otherwise frequently interesting examination, 'Acting Methods: Brecht and Stanislavski', in *Brecht in Perspective*, ed. Graham Bartram and Anthony Waine (New York: Longman, 1982), pp. 128–44.

[2] Brecht, in a discussion with students and professors at the Universität Greifswald, 1954, 'Über die Arbeit am Berliner Ensemble', in *Brecht im Gespräch, Diskussionen, Dialoge, Interviews*, ed. Werner Hecht, edition suhrkamp No. 771 (Frankfurt/Main: Suhrkamp, 1975), p. 123. All translations in this essay are the author's.

understand Brecht's thinking about the theatre in general, and certainly not his thinking about acting, until we complement consideration of his theoretical perspectives with consideration of his practical work. This is hardly a task that can be accomplished in a single essay. Consequently, I should like here to sketch an overview of Brecht's work with his actors, or, more precisely, an overview of what Brecht expected the actor to contribute to the total complex of a theatrical production and how he worked with the actor to fulfill this requirement. I should point out that this discussion will itself be fairly theoretical; only a pure description of Brecht's day-to-day work with his actors could hope to be anything else.[3] I shall hope at least, however, to indicate the value of reconsidering the theoretical concepts Brecht develops in the *Organon* and the *Messingkauf Dialogues* in the light of his theatre practice.

My discussion will concentrate on only one phase of Brecht's practical work. Since Brecht was able to work concretely for an extended period of time with a carefully selected ensemble only during his postwar years at the Berliner Ensemble, this period can rightly be given priority for our discussion. Besides, it was the results of this work, as exemplified in the Ensemble's guest performances in Paris and London, that influenced practical theatre men like Giorgio Strehler, Roger Planchon, William Gaskill, and Peter Brook – and through them the entire European theatre of the mid-twentieth century.[4]

Even more significantly for our purposes, an overview of Brecht's work with his actors at the Ensemble underlines with particular clarity both the shift of emphasis that results when we consider Brecht's theory in light of his practice and some of the consequences of that shift. Brecht's theoretical writings abound with references to acting methods, both particular and general. As we shall see, however, Brecht was far less concerned with acting method than he was with the interpretive basis of the actor's work. In fact, as Brecht once told Peter Palitzsch during a discussion on Stanislavski, his theatrical activity was not centered around the actor

> as a point of departure. Stanislavski directs primarily as an actor, I direct primarily as a playwright. ... He begins with the actor. ... [You] can also hear me say that everything depends on the actor, but I nevertheless begin completely with the play, its requirements and demands.[5]

This begins as a statement defining the relationship between director and actor and ends up as a statement defining the relationship between director and text. The abrupt transition is instructive: Brecht reveals himself as a director who gives the text (or rather, as we shall see, his interpretation of the text) absolute priority. The actor's work, and the director's work with the actor, may be critically important, but they are important only in

---

[3]Today, twenty-seven years after Brecht's death, such invaluable discussion based on rehearsal observation is virtually impossible to come by. However, a monograph now being prepared by John Fuegi for Cambridge University Press's Directors in Perspective series promises to provide us with further detailed accounts of Brecht's work with his actors. Fuegi has had access to Brecht's co-workers, to tape recordings and notes of rehearsals, and to his own vast knowledge and experience of Brecht's theatre.

[4]On the other hand, concentration on Brecht's work with actors at the Ensemble precludes consideration of such aspects of his work as the interrelationship of theory and practice during the late 1920s when Brecht was evolving his theory of the *Lehrstücke*, the Learning Plays.

[5]Brecht, *Gesammelte Werke in 20 Bänden*, ed. Werner Hecht (Frankfurt / Main: Suhrkamp, 1967), Vol. 16, p. 865. Hereafter, the *Gesammelte Werke* will be cited in the text as *GW*.

so far as they serve to realize the director's interpretational ends.[6] If we are to understand what is unique about Brecht's work with the actor, therefore, we must first examine his directorial goals in terms of his work on the text. Only then can we adequately discuss the actor's particular contribution to the fulfillment of these goals and the particular kind of rehearsal process through which the actor develops this contribution.

The Brechtian theatre's most fundamental principle is its commitment to social change. The dramaturgical principle most basic to fulfilling this commitment is, in turn, that the theatre must attempt to present society and human nature as changeable. Theatre does not, however, depict either society or human nature directly, but rather through interpretive examples. As Brecht defines it, theatre 'consists of the production of living illustrations of historical or imagined occurrences between people' (GW 16, 663). This definition serves as the foundation both for Brecht's general theatre theory and for his directorial work on individual dramatic texts. Using Brecht's general perspective, the core of any text may be examined as a total composition, a structuring together in time of all the individual occurrences that take place between the play's characters (see GW 16, 693). The original author's interpretation of his historical experience becomes visible in the character of the occurrences he chooses to illustrate and in the way in which he structures these occurrences together. Directorial interpretation, in turn, proceeds through the reworking of the occurrences illustrated and the restructuring of their relationship to each other. Brecht uses a special term to describe both the original composition of incidents and its interpretational re-composition, calling both 'fables'. He also emphasizes the predominant role of the interpretational fable in production work: 'Everything depends on the fable; it is the heart of the theatrical production' (GW 16, 693).

The first question such an interpretive approach must answer is whether one stresses the occurrences between characters or the characters themselves. Brecht is quite specific in his demand that production must shift focus away from the characters themselves to what happens between them. As he puts it, 'from what happens *between* them, people get everything that can be discussed, criticized, changed' (GW 16, 693).

This shift already carries with it a shift from the individual to the group and from the psychological to the sociological. In themselves, however, these shifts are not sufficient. Brecht sets two further requirements that clarify the ideological framework within which interpretation must take place. First, both the fable's occurrences and the relationship between them must be examined dialectically. As Brecht notes, the dialectical approach treats

> social conditions as processes and pursues these in their contradictions. Everything exists to this perspective only inasmuch as it transforms itself. ... This is also true for the feelings, opinions, and behavior of men, through which the contemporary mode of their social life together expresses itself.
>
> [GW 16, 682]

Brecht's theatre, then, concentrates on 'the contradictions in people and their relationships.' At the same time, however, a dialectical theatre must also reveal the 'determinants

---

[6] Given the fairly widespread misconception represented by Eddershaw's statement that Brecht founded the Berliner Ensemble 'primarily to facilitate the perfect staging of Brecht's own plays' (p. 137), it should be stressed that Brecht and his actors developed their interpretational techniques for the full range of the world's dramatic literature, from Sophocles' *Antigone* to Synge's *Playboy of the Western World*. Of the Ensemble's fifteen most important productions during Brecht's lifetime, only four were of plays by Brecht.

under which [these contradictions] develop' (GW 19, 547); further, it must reveal these determinants critically. Both these requirements are essentially part of the same concern – the depiction of the contradictory process through which men structure and restructure their lives and the critical examination of the ways in which these structures are used by men to repress other men. Historical determinants – the economic, political, and social factors that influence the social conditions of any historical period – must not simply be made recognizable. They must be made recognizable as constitutive elements in the individual occurrences between human beings:

> One clearly must not think of *historical determinants* as dark powers (backgrounds); rather, they are made and maintained by men (and will be changed by them): they are constituted by what is being done right now.
>
> [GW 16,679]

Brecht is speaking here not about reality, but about the theatrical illustration of reality. The theatre is for him precisely the place best suited to examine the social conditions in any historical period as constitutive elements in human relationships. This examination is what the director undertakes together with the actors as they structure out the fable's examples of the moment-by-moment occurrences between people.

The first step in applying this general interpretational framework to a specific text involves the pre-rehearsal work of the director and his dramaturgical colleagues. The text is treated as an historical document. The background of the text and its author are painstakingly researched in order to identify both the historical character of the social life being illustrated and the determinants that influence it. The text is then subjected to a dialectical analysis that reads its structures back into the historical experiences they mediate. Finally, the text's fable is recomposed in brief sentences that describe the fundamental action of each individual occurrence. Or rather, the sentences describe each occurrence as the production will elaborate it; Brecht's theatre is true to its interpretation of the text, not necessarily to the text itself, which may be left relatively untouched or drastically restructured.

The precision with which this dramaturgical approach focuses on each separate interaction between the play's characters is well illustrated by Brecht's directorial breakdown of the first scene of his own *Mother Courage:*

- Recruiters roam the country looking for cannon-fodder.
- Courage presents her family, acquired in various theatres of war, to a sergeant.
- The market woman defends her sons with a knife against the recruiters.
- She discovers that her sons are succumbing to the recruiters, and prophesies an early soldier's death for the sergeant.
- In order to scare them away from the war, she also lets her children draw the black mark.
- As a result of a small bit of bargaining, she ends up losing her brave son anyway.
- The sergeant prophesies something for Courage: he who would live off the war must also give it something.[7]

---

[7]'Anmerkungen zur Aufführung 1949'; rpt. in *Materialien zu Brechts Mutter Courage und ihre Kinder*, ed. Werner Hecht, edition suhrkamp No. 50, 10th ed., 1976 (Frankfurt / Main: Suhrkamp, 1964), pp. 19–20. I have altered

As in the Stanislavski approach, this scene is broken down into its 'beats'; indeed, the American-Stanislavskian term is an excellent equivalent to Brecht's 'individual occurrence' (*Einzelgeschehnis*). From a Stanislavskian perspective, however, Brecht's breakdown remains a director's description of the fable rather than an actor's. The basic actions and relationships between all the characters in each beat have been sketched in, but the description does not center on any individual character's objectives, nor has a throughline of motivation been developed to link the various beats together. The concentration of effort at the level of the beat allows an assimilation of Stanislavski's acting methods to Brechtian interpretational ends.

Brecht's actors were not encouraged to structure the separate beats smoothly together. On the contrary, Brecht considered the transitions between beats as significant as the beats themselves, and he demanded that these transitions occur dialectically. Each beat can be examined as a self-contained entity in which a particular interaction takes place or a particular situation arises. As Manfred Wekwerth points out, the personal and social forces that determine these relationships can change in respect to each other, bringing about an alteration in the situation; this change is marked by the evolving of one beat into another. On the other hand, each determining factor can suddenly pass over into its opposite, bringing about a completely new situation, marked by a sudden leap from one beat to the next.[8] There need be no more unity either of character or of action between the beats than there is between the self-contained scenes around which Brecht's dramaturgy is structured on a larger scale. Indeed, Brecht made extensive use of all the possibilities inherent in a disunity of action in order to present the 'development of characters, conditions, and events as discontinuous (in leaps)' (*GW* 16, 724).

The director's paramount task in rehearsals is to structure out the dialectical transitions between beats and the historically determined interactions between characters in the beats themselves. The descriptive reconstitution of the fable is already a first step in the development of a theatrical interpretation, but the fable still needs, of course, to be elaborated using all the means of the theatre. Most importantly, the fable depends on the actors, since they physically enact the events out of which the fable is composed. Consequently, their activities need themselves to be structured to achieve what appear, at first glance anyway, to be fundamentally directorial results. We shall, therefore, move from our consideration of Brecht's pre-rehearsal work to a consideration of the actor's contribution to his finished theatrical interpretation, putting aside for a moment the rather surprising process through which the actor perfected this contribution.

As Brecht states, the most important procedure by which the fable is presented to the audience is 'the blocking, that is, the placing of the characters, the determination of their position regarding each other [there is a pun here in the German: "*Stellung*" refers both to physical and attitudinal position], changes in this position, entrances and exits. The blocking must tell the story intelligently' (*GW* 16, 755).

---

the format of this list, which is printed in paragraph form, the individual sentences being separated by ellipsis points.
[8]Manfred Wekwerth, *Schriften: Arbeit mit Brecht* (Berlin [East]: Henschel, 1975), p. 119. Roland Barthes provides an excellent discussion of the dialectical development of beats in the first scene of *Mother Courage*, using photographic illustrations, in his 'Seven Photo Models of *Mother Courage*', trans. Hella Freud Bernays, *The Drama Review*, T37 (Fall 1967), 44–55.

The pun in the midst of what seems otherwise a fairly straightforward description of blocking should alert us that Brecht is talking here about something quite different from traffic directing. The German term for '*Arrangement*' perhaps comes closer to what Brecht is aiming for – an absolutely transparent physical elucidation of the fable. As Peter Palitzsch puts it, 'the blocking and the *Gestus* of the actors tell the fable in such a way that one could discover what is happening even if one couldn't hear anything. Transformations in the dialectic are marked on stage through transformations in the blocking.'[9]

The importance of this kind of physical elaboration of the fable is reflected in the term '*Gestus*', a word Brecht made up based on the German for 'gesture' (*Geste*) and which he somewhat confusingly defined in several different ways. Each of the fable's individual occurrences has what Brecht calls a '*Grundgestus*' (GW 16, 693). On one level, this *Grundgestus* is simply the production staff's interpretation of each textual beat. Underlying this *Grundgestus*, however, is the '*gesellschaftliche*' or 'social' *Gestus*: 'the mimetic and gestural expression of the social relationships in which the people of a particular epoch stand to each other' (GW 15, 346). The notion of *Gestus* is thus, as Giorgio Strehler has pointed out, at bottom not an aesthetic but a sociological one – sociological in that it allows historical determinants to be concretely manifested in the physical elaboration of the motivated actions that move the characters from beat to beat.[10]

This notion of the physical manifestation of historical determinants goes beyond the use of blocking to include the actor's smallest physical gesture. As Hans Curjel noted while observing Brecht rehearsing his 1948 *Antigone*, 'The directorial method was based on investigation and varied experimentation that could extend to the smallest gestures – eyes, fingers. ... Brecht worked like a sculptor on and with the actor.'[11] Curjel was also impressed by the ability of this approach to clarify and enliven the transitions between beats: 'Certain pregnant behavioral motifs were extended over long passages of text and situation, to then be transformed into new gestures, basic behavior, or movement structures as if on hinges.'[12]

The second beat in the first scene of Brecht's 1950 adaptation of Lenz's *Der Hofmeister* (*The Private Tutor*) provides an excellent example of this kind of detailed physical interpretive work. Having just told the audience in the Prologue that he intends to sell himself as a private tutor, Läuffer approaches and bows to the Major (his prospective employer) and to his brother the Privy Councilor, who are discussing the terrible state of the economy. The two ignore Läuffer, even when he repeats his bow three more times. In the middle of the fourth bow, he curses them under his breath. He then exits.

The beat is a brief one, but as staged it provided its audiences with some essential interpretive information about the relationship between the play's characters. In the first place, the 'bow' that the actor Hans Gaugler developed for his character was a highly stylized, highly exaggerated, very funny bit of actor technique. It was also far more elaborate than the 'natural' bows of the period (Lenz's play takes place around 1774), and it went lower to the ground – or to the feet of the Major, as the case may be.

---

[9]Peter Palitzsch, in an interview with Artur Joseph for his *Theater unter vier Augen: Gespräche mit Prominenten* (Köln: Kiepenheuer und Witsch, 1969), p. 178.
[10]Giorgio Strehler, *Für ein menschlicheres Theater*, trans. and ed. Sinah Kessler (Berlin [East]: Henschel, 1977), pp. 87–88.
[11]Hans Curjel, 'Brechts *Antigone*-Inszenierung in Chur 1948'; rpt. in *Die Antigone des Sophokles: Materialien zur 'Antigone,'* ed. Werner Hecht, edition suhrkamp No. 134 (Frankfurt/Main: Suhrkamp, 1967), pp. 137–38.
[12]Curjel, p. 138.

First established in this beat, it was used as a 'quotable' gestural leitmotiv for Läuffer throughout the production.[13]

As performed by Gaugler, Läuffer's bow also became a fine example of Brecht's concept of *'Verfremdung'*. Despite all the critical blood that has been spilled over it, the term's basic definition is quite simple: 'A defamiliarized illustration is one that, while allowing the object to be recognized, at the same time makes it appear unfamiliar' (*GW* 16, 680). Brecht's definition will, I hope, clarify why I have rejected either 'alienation' or 'distancing' in favor of 'defamiliarization' as a translation of the term; Brecht's ultimate point is that a spectator will not think about anything happening on stage if clichéd conventions or a mistaken naturalism make what is happening appear familiar to him. Everyone knows, for example, that people bowed to each other in the eighteenth century, so why should a bow be the stimulus for a critical social examination of an interpretation of occurrences between people? As Gaugler executed it, Läuffer's bow became a *Gestus* that defamiliarized itself, forestalling any possibility of its being accepted as simply a customary greeting rather than the conscious action of a man who wants something from another man with more economic power.

This meaning is not, of course, explicit in the bow itself. Rather, it is a significance the audience could be led to recognize within the context both of Läuffer's expressed intentions in the Prologue (written by Brecht, not Lenz), and of the discussion on economic matters which the bow interrupts (by directorial design). The audience could, however, work through to this recognition only if instructed to examine the bow as an object of analysis.

Partly for this reason, the bow was emphasized twice over in performance. First, it was repeated four times, each bow more aggressively fawning than the last. The Major's and Privy Councilor's repeated ignoring of Läuffer's greeting thus became clearly the result of a conscious choice. Second, the bow was defamiliarized by the text itself.[14] As Läuffer executes his last, most fawning bow, he curses his two 'betters' under his breath: 'Der Teufel hol Euch, Flegel' [Go to the devil, louts] (*GW* 6, 2335). Läuffer's language here (especially the choice of *'Flegel'*) recalls the way during this period people like the Major talked to their servants, and not vice versa.

Läuffer's bow, its conscious rejection by the Major and Privy Councilor, and Läuffer's response to this rejection all provide the audience not simply with information about Läuffer but about the character of the play's social relationships. Even as he grovels before them, Läuffer holds his interlocutors in contempt; and they return the favor. The dialogue in the beat following Läuffer's exit underlines this: the Major discusses his intention to hire this 'lickspittle', as the Privy Councilor calls him (*GW* 6, 2335), because he comes cheap. Established in the bow and the reaction to it, the scene's underlying social *Gestus* is developed after Läuffer's exit.

Läuffer's bow illustrates the degree to which the dramaturgical and directorial interpretation of the script depends not only on the actor's gestural work on his characterization but on his gestural work in interaction with his fellow actors. Gaugler's exaggeration of his character's 'natural' behavior is also as good a practical example as we

---

[13]For further discussion on Brecht's use of 'quoted' gestures throughout a production, see Walter Benjamin, *Versuche über Brecht*, edition suhrkamp No. 172, 2nd ed., 1967 (Frankfurt / Main: Suhrkamp, 1966), pp. 26–27.
[14]Käthe Rülicke-Weiler points this out in *Die Dramaturgie Brechts: Theater als Mittel der Veränderung*, 2nd ed. (Berlin [East]: Henschel, 1968), p. 206.

are likely to get of Brecht's concept of the actor standing beside his role in performance, at once demonstrating and commenting on his character's behavior.

Our example from the *Hofmeister* is particularly clear in part because the beat's *Grundgestus* is focused in a single character *Gestus*, in part because this *Gestus* is so highly exaggerated. Such exaggerations are, however, better suited to comic texts than to straight dramatic ones. Indeed, Brecht once mentioned to Giorgio Strehler that his defamiliarizing acting style was much easier to achieve in comedies, since the comic form tends itself to defamiliarize its characters and events.[15] This is one reason why the Ensemble tended to use a much less gesturally over-elaborated style in its productions of serious texts, including such Brecht texts as *Mother Courage*.

This difference was, however, primarily one of degree. Brecht and his actors used stylization and exaggeration of gesture, intonation, or tempo in some of their most serious productions, although with a different emotional emphasis and a different balance between playing the role and demonstrating it. One of the best known 'emotional' moments in Brecht's theatre work, for example, is Helene Weigel's silent scream in the 1951 *Courage* (an Ensemble revival of a production originally staged in 1949). As she hears the salvo that signals the execution of her son Swiss Cheese, Weigel's Courage is seated on a low stool with her hands in her lap. She clenches her rough skirt, leaning forward with a straight, tense back as if shot in the stomach. At the same time, she thrusts her head straight back against her shoulders; her mouth tears open until it seems that her jaw will break, but no sound comes forth. For a moment, her whole physicality has the impossible, angular contortion of one of Picasso's screaming horses in *Guernica*. Then she snaps her mouth shut, brings her torso and head back into alignment, and collapses the tension in her torso, slumping in on herself.

The moment is justifiably famous, both as an example of Weigel's unmatched skill as an actress and as an example of the type of carefully elaborated physicality the Ensemble's actors were expected to develop in fulfilling their responsibility to the production interpretation. It is also an unabashedly emotional moment – an emotionality, however, carefully controlled and used both by Weigel and by the production developing around her. In the first place, the very physicality of the moment moves it beyond the level of naturalistic grief with which an audience can empathize. We are shocked, stunned, shaken by Courage's grief, but we are not allowed to share it on the plane of petty emotional titilation. The technically accomplished extremity of Weigel's acting, in short, defamiliarizes Courage's grief through the very demonstration of that grief.

Moreover, both Brecht's play and his production allow Courage this intensely human moment in order to illustrate for the audience the basic social contradiction out of which the character is built. Courage is both businesswoman and mother. Or rather, she tries to be both; the social realities of the total war from which she tries to profit as businesswoman prevent her from fulfilling her responsibilities as mother. She has been confronted with a nearly impossible economic choice – either she lose her son or she pay a sum that will cost her the wagon, her only means of supporting herself and her daughter. But she has tried to avoid making this choice in attempting to deal her way out. Just prior to the execution,

---

[15]Brecht, as reported by Hans Joachim Bunge, 'Über eine Neuinszenierung der *Dreigroschenoper*: Ein Gespräch zwischen Brecht und Giorgio Strehler am 15.10.1955 über die bevorstehende Mailänder Inszenierung', in *Bertolt Brechts Dreigroschenbuch: Texte, Materialien, Dokumente*, ed. Siegfried Unseld (Frankfurt/Main: Suhrkamp, 1960), p. 134.

Courage has sent the prostitute Yvette offstage to bribe the soldiers holding Swiss Cheese. She is unwilling, however, to pay the ruinous sum demanded, and sends Yvette back again and again to bargain. Just before the salvo, she turns to the army chaplain whom she is hiding from his so-called religious enemies and comments haltingly that perhaps she has haggled too long. Sounds of gunfire teach both her and the audience that her delay is indeed costly. Courage bears responsibility for her own extreme moment of grief – a lesson underlined in performance by the simple expedient of having the chaplain, who is seated on a stool next to Courage, get up and walk away from her in the middle of her scream. Brecht allows Courage her grief, but he also uses it to provide his audience with the necessary data for a dialectical analysis of his play's social relationships.

Weigel's scream, although unusual in its degree of technical accomplishment, illustrates the way in which Brecht combined the actor's gestural elaboration of role with the careful elaboration of emotive and textual contexts. The characters' reactions to the scream provide Brecht's audiences insight into the social contradictions affecting even the most seemingly personal, emotional behavior. As with Läuffer's bow, this gestural elaboration could extend to the development of a basic physical *Gestus*, centered on one or a series of quoted gestures, even for a straight dramatic character. *Courage* provides several examples of such a *Gestus*, modified to suit the development of a dramatic character. One of the better known is Weigel's treatment of money. Every time she received payment in the course of her play's performance, Weigel's Courage would 'mistrustfully' bite the coin to make sure it was real.[16] Now, this kind of gesture is certainly something any creative director or actor might invent while working on the play – assuming they understand the play's dialectics properly.

Still, Brecht's productions developed their fables so clearly, not because of any special magic, but because Brecht and his actors went to the trouble to understand and outline in performance vocabulary the story they were telling. Without the aid of Brecht's *Modellbuch* (a photographic and descriptive record of an Ensemble production intended to guide interpretation elsewhere), for example, it is doubtful that a director working within the conventions of the German theater of 1949 would have thought through to the telling variation of Courage's treatment of money Brecht and Weigel used at the very end of the play. Courage's daughter Kattrin has been shot trying to alert the city of Halle to an impending enemy attack. Courage is now alone. She must drag her wagon herself back into the war, back into the train of the army that feeds her. She cannot afford to wait to bury Kattrin herself, so she pays a peasant family to bury her daughter for her. She fishes a handful of coins from the leather purse at her waist, starts to hand them to the peasants, looks at the coins, hesitates, slowly puts one coin back in her purse, then gives the rest over in payment. Even as she displays her character's total personal collapse, Weigel demonstrates once again the basic contradiction between businesswoman and mother that has led to that collapse.[17]

This last example, like the others we have examined, illustrates both the degree to which Brecht expected his actors to serve directorial interpretation and, at the same time, the degree to which this interpretation depended on the actor's contributions. On the other hand, the examples do not reveal the dominance of any single all-powerful acting

---

[16]Ruth Berlau, Bertolt Brecht, et al., *Theaterarbeit: 6 Aufführungen des Berliner Ensembles* (Dresden: VVV Dresdner Verlag, 1952), p. 264.
[17]See Brecht's description, 'Anmerkungen zur Aufführung 1949', *Materialien*, p. 76.

technique, let alone the dominance of a global acting methodology, over either the actor's work or the director's demands. On the contrary, the examples reveal the application of virtually the full range of customary actor technique, from vocal and physical flexibility to precise emotional control. This fact, in turn, has a significant corollary: 'There is *no* technique that *cannot* be used in the Brecht-theater, so long as it serves to expose the contradictions in processes in such a way that they can be pleasurably recognized by the spectator and lead to his own transformation.'[18] In fact, Brecht not only encouraged the use of a wide variety of performance techniques, he structured his rehearsal process in a way that allowed these techniques to be subsumed in the service of his interpretational ends. Since the nature of this process has a great deal to do with the strengths of performances like Hans Gaugler's or Helene Weigel's, we will profit by turning back to it here.

Our examples from the *Hofmeister* and *Mother Courage* have underlined the degree to which the detailed '*Fabelbau*' – the building up of the fable – is the principal goal not simply of pre-rehearsal analysis but of rehearsal itself. The kind of detailed analysis of beats we saw in Brecht's *Courage* breakdown provides an anchor-point in rehearsals; when problems arise, one can check to see whether the fable is being told in the most effective way, or whether the right fable is being told. At the same time, the concrete discoveries made by the actors, director, and dramaturgs during rehearsals are used to tighten and fine-tune the analysis of the fable as its concrete theatrical elaboration is developed. The precise choreographic effect of Läuffer's repeated bows, for example, is not something a directorial team can plan beforehand.

Or, at least, this effect is not something Brecht and his coworkers planned beforehand. Although Brecht went into rehearsals with a detailed description of the text and concrete plans for initial blocking to provide a structure for the exploration of character relationships, he did not begin rehearsals with a specific scheme of the final physical production. He knew what his goals were, but not the concrete measures necessary to achieve them. Consequently, he could maintain that 'we develop pretty much from nothing, exploring the most varied possibilities. We speak the text, move around within the situations. Slowly we try to find out what is interesting. That is then kept, other things are let fall. We then develop the characterizations, and also the blocking.'[19]

This kind of leisurely approach to the building up of the concrete production is clearly an essential safeguard against the impatient tendency to impose directorial decisions on the actor from outside – to treat the actor like a puppet. Consequently, Brecht took this approach seriously. Carl Weber remembers the first time he watched the Ensemble at work: Brecht, his assistants, and the actors stood around, smoked, talked, laughed. Every so often an actor would go up on stage and try one of thirty ways of falling off a table. Weber thought everyone was taking a break, until the horseplay went on long enough to make him realize he was watching the rehearsal[20] – a rehearsal, one suspects, devoted to the serious business of discovering the one way of falling off a table that will illuminate concretely its historical determinants.

---

[18] Manfred Wekwerth, 'Brecht-Theater in der Gegenwart' (Stockholmer Seminar 1978), in *Aktualisierung Brechts*, ed. Wolfgang Fritz Haug, Klaus Pierwoß, und Karen Ruoff. Argument Sonderband No. 50 (Berlin: Argument-Verlag, 1980), p. 108.
[19] Brecht, 'Über die Arbeit am Berliner Ensemble', p. 125.
[20] Carl Weber, 'Brecht as Director', *The Drama Review*, T37 (Fall 1967), 102–3.

Brecht's actors were encouraged to make their own discoveries – subject only to Brecht's dramaturgic principle that the fable retain dominance over its characters. Brecht suggested that this process of discovery and elaboration takes place in three broad and overlapping phases. The first of these extends through reading rehearsals and the early blocking rehearsals. It involves making a first acquaintance with the character by continually asking why he does what he does: 'you look assiduously for contradictions, for deviations from type, for the ugly in the beautiful and the beautiful in the ugly' (*GW* 16, 843). This is also the phase during which the actor most intensely fulfills a specifically dramaturgical responsibility, studying the fable and familiarizing himself with the results of the production staff's background work: 'The study of the role is at the same time a study of the fable; more precisely, it should at first be a [study] of the fable. ... For this, the actor must mobilize his knowledge of the world and of people, and he must ask his questions as a dialectician' (*GW* 16, 704).[21] An actress playing Mother Courage, for example, would be expected to note that in one beat she attempts to protect her children by rigging the business of drawing for the black spot, while in the very next beat she ignores her children completely in order to swing a deal over a belt buckle, thereby letting Eilif get stolen out from under her nose. She would not, however, be asked to bridge this contradiction by developing a complex character conception; rather, this contradiction is the element to be explored in rehearsal. Clearly, this first phase is crucial – if the actor is not able to think along the same lines as the directorial staff, he will not be able later to teach his directors what they need to learn.

The second phase continues the work already done, but in an antithetical direction – one in which more than a few theoretical purists have assumed Brecht was not interested. As Brecht describes it, 'the second phase is that of identification with the character [*Einfühlung*], the search for the character's truth in a subjective sense, you let it do what *it* wants to do, to hell with criticism as long as society provides what you need' (*GW* 16, 843). The actor must explore his character in all the detail demanded by the most naturalistic director, but the criterion for selection among his discoveries remains the character's social behavior. Brecht never denied that there were character elements outside the realm of social determination, but he frequently pointed out that such aspects 'hardly belong to the constitutive elements of the illustration of reality' (*GW* 15, 282). Indeed, as Werner Hecht puts it, 'we don't want characters' in the literal sense of the word on our stage, that is, people with engraved, unchangeable peculiarities that at best unfold themselves monadically. What interests us about people is their way of behaving, the historically conditioned reactions.'[22] With this orientation, it is hardly surprising that 'Brecht in fact almost never spoke about the character of the stage figure during rehearsals, but rather about his way of behaving; he said virtually nothing about what a man *is*, but rather what he *does*. And when he did say anything about character, he related it not to the psychological but the sociological.'[23]

---

[21] The *Gesammelte Werke* misprints '*Stadium*' (stage) for '*Studium*' (study).
[22] Werner Hecht, *Sieben Studien über Brecht*, edition suhrkamp No. 570 (Frankfurt / Main: Suhrkamp, 1972), p. 151.
[23] Käthe Rülicke-Weiler, in *Sinn und Form*, 2nd Special Brecht Issue, 1956, as quoted by Albrecht Schöne, 'Bertolt Brecht: Theatertheorie und dramatische Dichtung', in *Zu Bertolt Brecht: Parabel und episches Theater*, ed. Theo Buck, LGW Interpretation No. 41 (Stuttgart: Klett-Cotta, 1979), p. 39.

In fact, Brecht rarely spoke about individual characters in isolation. Rather, he exhorted his actors to create their characters dialectically with each other, to react rather than act: 'The smallest social unit is not the individual; but two people. We create each other in life, too' (GW 16, 688). Hence, Brecht could describe his second phase as one in which the actor lets the character react to the other characters, to the milieu, to the fable. As Brecht rather un-epically puts it, 'this collecting process proceeds slowly until it then nevertheless takes a leap – until you leap into the final character, unite yourself with it' (GW 16, 843).

Only when the work of this 'naturalistic' or 'Stanislavskian' phase has been completed can the third, antithetical, more properly 'Brechtian' phase begin.[24] During this phase the actor, having come to identify with his character, to know it from the inside, examines it once again 'from outside, from the point of view of society', and attempts to recapture the 'mistrust and astonishment of the first phase' (GW 16, 843-844). It is primarily during this phase that the actors and director, using the insights won from a critical reexamination of the social behavior of the characters they have come to know intimately, structure out the final composition of gestures and positions that will elaborate the fable concretely in performance. The actor's goal during this phase is not, however, to reject everything he has learned during the second phase lest the audience be contaminated by un-epic playing. Rather, as Brecht points out clearly in one of his 1954 appendixes to the *Organon*, the actor's ultimate goal in performance is to achieve a dialectical unity between the gestural presentation of the character in his social relationships and a realistic emotional foundation won through identification:

> Ignorant heads interpret the contradiction between playing (demonstration) and experiencing (identification) as if only the one or the other appeared in the actor's work (or as if according to the *Short Organon* one only plays, according to the old technique one only experiences). In reality it is, of course, a matter of two competing processes that unite in the work of the actor. ... Out of the struggle and the tension between the two antipodes ... the actor draws his real impact.
>
> [GW 16, 703]

Brecht, of course, did develop and discuss a number of his own techniques intended to enforce the dialectic between 'playing' and 'experiencing'. Most of these techniques were, strictly speaking, rehearsal exercises, such as having the actor speak the character's lines in the third person or speak the stage directions along with his lines. Many of these exercises were, in fact, used at the Ensemble, particularly during the early productions, most notably the *Hofmeister*. They were, however, included when useful during the second and third stages of the actor's work and without theoretical discussion about their epic purpose. Brecht knew that the practical workshop is not the place for theoretical discourse.[25]

Indeed, Herbert Blau is quite correct when he maintains that Brecht's approach to acting is 'more a matter of the environment created around the actor than a methodology

---

[24]This labeling of Brecht's second and third phases is Peter Palitzsch's, as quoted by Hans Daiber, *Deutsches Theater seit 1945* (Stuttgart: Reklam, 1976), p. 218.

[25]See Herbert Blau, 'The Popular, the Absurd, and the *Entente Cordiale*', *Tulane Drama Review*. 5, No. 3 (Spring 1961), 121.

of acting itself'.[26] The concentration of communal effort on the interpretation of dramatic texts may be seen as one element of this environment, the use of a leisurely approach to building up a production is another, the time committed to this approach a third.[27] Underlying all of these, however, is the creation of true ensemble working methods. Only when directors, designers, dramaturgs, and actors work continuously together using a shared dramaturgical approach and developing group methods to explore a number of productions treating texts from different historical periods and different genres can they create the common vocabulary necessary to allow the ensemble members to use their particular training, experience, and techniques towards the creation of a production that bears the stamp not just of individuals but of a recognizable whole. That is something we should keep in mind when we try to characterize the distinctive quality of Brecht's work with the actor, and certainly if we try to make practical use of it.

---

[26]Blau, p. 121.
[27]Brecht's productions are, of course, famous for rehearsal periods lasting six months or longer. As Peter Palitzsch has pointed out in a personal interview (3 March 1979), however, Brecht's early productions at the Ensemble were often worked up relatively quickly; the *Hofmeister* had only about nine weeks of rehearsal, for example. Brecht began to indulge in long rehearsal periods during his last years, when he was both very ill and intent on developing his young directors and actors. The issue is not whether a Brechtian approach needs six months of rehearsals, but that it needs as long as necessary to proceed effectively through Brecht's three phases

Brecht and Documentation

Modelbooks

CHAPTER SEVEN

Couragemodell: Detail and Arrangement of a Model Book

KRISTOPHER IMBRIGOTTA

What exactly is a 'model book'? Described literally, it is a play text amplified by explanatory and illustrative materials – especially production notes and hundreds of production photographs – that interpret and particularize the play's actions, characters stage settings, and ideas. The *Couragemodell 1949*, the published model book for Brecht's staging of *Mutter Courage und ihre Kinder*, is less a 'book' per se than an amalgamation or package of elements that fit together. The original publication consists of three separate, paperbound volumes: play script, photographs of the Berlin (November 1948-January 1949, with Helene Weigel as Courage) and Munich production (October 1950, with Therese Giehse as Courage), and notes.[1] The script is not a special version of *Mutter Courage* but the published text of the play in the version found in the 'Versuche'.[2] The photography volume begins with 106 pages meticulously depicting the play's action scene by scene. The first set of photographs is comprised of 'live shots' from each scene, combined with 'Bildlegenden'[3] or short captions. Next come photographs of the figure of Mother Courage, 55 photos of 'Sequenzen', 14 photos labeled 'Gestisches', three on 'Beschäftigungen', five of 'Bewegte Vorgänge', and a final 40 or so variant photos of the Berlin and Munich productions of *Mutter Courage*. The volume of notes is arranged by

---

Kristopher Imbrigotta, '*Couragemodell*: Detail and Arrangement of a Model Book', in Imbrigotta, *Framing Brecht: Photography and Experiment in the Modellbücher, 'Arbeitsjournale', and 'Kriegsfibel'*, unpublished PhD thesis, University of Madison, Wisconsin, pp. 100–111.

[1] Subsequent editions and publications of the *Couragemodell* also included production photographs from other performances. The final constellation of photographic images included in the *Couragemodell* dates to 1956 along with textual revisions. The complete 'Modellbuchmappe' appeared posthumously in 1958 from Henschelverlag (GDR).

[2] The text ('Versuch' number 20) was included in the first printing of the ninth volume of 'Versuche', textual and sociological 'experiments' from Brecht's plays. Accompanying the *Courage* play text in this volume was Brecht's seminal essay 'Fünf Schwierigkeiten beim Schreiben der Wahrheit'. See Brecht, *Versuche 20/21*, Vol. 9 (Frankfurt am Main: Suhrkamp, 1948).

[3] See editorial commentary in BFA 25: 533.

scene, which usually begins with dissecting the basics followed by a few lines detailing problems or issues pertaining to the scene in question. Taken together, the books in the *Couragemodell* demonstrate how and why *Mutter Courage* might be comprehensibly and artistically staged.

A model book is by nature explicitly intended for other theaters' copying use, something Brecht not only encourages with his *Couragemodell* but also personally practiced during his career. In a fabricated 'exchange' with Erich Winds, theater manager of the Städtische Bühnen Wuppertal about the dangers of such practices for the theater as a whole, Brecht muses:

> Man muß sich frei machen von der landläufigen Verachtung des Kopierens. Es ist nicht das 'Leichtere'. Es ist nicht eine Schande, sondern eine Kunst. Das heißt, es muß zur Kunst entwickelt werden, und zwar dazu, daß keine Schablonisierung und Erstarrung eintritt.[4]

Brecht's stance on copying is that it is not something criminal per se, but rather to be cultivated; copying for purposes of reactivating a theater piece, when done correctly, can be an art form unto itself. The act of re-appropriating a text, dramaturgical conception, or performance can be seen as a productive step towards expanding the original in the same vein of his 'Bearbeitungen' taking into account Brecht's many stage adaptations or his use of Chinese philosophy, etc.

Brecht also repeatedly warned against the persuasiveness of model books. They are to serve as a starting point and guide for rehearsals, not as a blueprint for a definitive production. The director should not use the *Couragemodell* to excess: 'Man muß das Modell nicht so sehr pressen.'[5] Brecht argued for 'practical copying', or following the exemplary, towards creating innovative theater, saying: One has to start somewhere, and it might as well be with something that has been well thought out. The model books offer clues and photographic examples of how he intended to stage his plays; however, they were not intended to substitute or replace the requisite thought processes and creativity of a director's vision. Defending the model books against those even within the Berliner Ensemble who criticized them as 'Diktatur auf dem Theater', Brecht offered this brief letter titled 'Über die Arbeit der Dramaturgen, Regisseure, Assistenten und Schüler des Berliner Ensemble':

> Sogar die schon selbstständigen Regisseure studieren die Modellbücher nicht und zeigen wenig Kenntnis und Schätzung des Neuen und Guten. Niemand scheint verstanden zu haben, daß die Herstellung der Modellbücher eine außerordentliche Gelegenheit eröffnet, das Regieführen und Kritisieren zu erlernen.[6]

Brecht was never one to shy away from polemic. His riposte was hung on the bulletin board at the Berliner Ensemble in 1952 for all to see, which led to much debate among his colleagues and actors. The model's value is mainly pedagogical. Using it, the theater practitioner is invited to focus directly on *problems* with theater production rather than

---

[4]Brecht, *Couragemodell*, BFA 25: 388.
[5]Ibid., 172.
[6]Brecht, 'Über die Arbeit der Dramaturgen, Regisseure, Assistenten und Schüler des Berliner Ensemble' (1952), BFA 23: 221.

the solutions and/or suggestions presented in the model book.⁷ This is the dialectical modus operandi inherent in much of Brecht's work:⁸ examination of different perspectives leading to conscious, deliberate decisions; to present what has come before in another way; and to instruct in the ability to 'work backwards' in a sense, beginning with the representations in the model book which one then traces back to its root cause, how to stage such a scene or event.

Model books were a response to theatrical disputes about the epic theater and also conformed to Brecht's collectivist vision of art in general:

> Wo bleibt, werden [andere] fragen, bei Modellbenutzung das Schöpferische? Die Antwort ist, daß die moderne Arbeitsteilung auf vielen wichtigen Gebieten das Schöpferische umgeformt hat. Der Schöpfungsakt ist ein kollektiver Schöpfungsprozeß, ein Kontinuum dialektischer Art, so daß die isolierte ursprüngliche Erfindung an Bedeutung verloren hat.⁹

In many ways, Brecht's model books seek to engage these very questions: how do we find meaning in art in our technologically advancing world? His answer, at least within the specific context of the model books, is to find meaning in contextualizing details – specifically in details that simultaneously show the exemplary and the unique, and seek to redefine how we interpret, look at, and interact with theater.

The epic theater presents one thing after another. This characterization comes to the fore in the *Couragemodell* and was exactly how Brecht directed his plays, carefully taking up one detail 'eins nach dem andern',¹⁰ as if performing an autopsy. Of the 103 notes in the *Couragemodell*, more than ten percent are titled 'Detail' or some variant thereof. Many of these details are miniscule (some just one sentence long!),¹¹ but integral nonetheless in shaping the scene and its message. Directing in detail means insisting that small elements are important enough to warrant detailed attention and emphasis. Brecht makes this point clear in Scene I of the *Couragemodell*: 'Das Detail, auch das kleinste, muß natürlich bei der strahlend hell erleuchteten Bühne voll ausgespielt werden. Besonders gilt das für Vorgänge, die auf unserer Bühne nahezu grundsätzlich übergangen werden, wie das Bezahlen bei einem Handel.'¹² A central principle of such an approach to directing is to avoid carelessness with regard to seemingly minor matters on stage. Without explicit direction, actors might hurry through significant actions which should last long enough to mean something to the scene, e.g., how actors exit the stage, how long one shows his/her finger, making sure that when Mother Courage's leather purse shuts the audience can hear the click, etc. Brecht's approach is demonstrative and incremental rather than psychological or emotional; he comments on how the particulars of such directing by necessity serve to slow the process: 'Das Tempo bei den Proben sei langsam, schon der Herausarbeitung des Details wegen; das Tempo der Aufführung zu bestimmen, ist ein eigener, späterer Prozeß.'¹³

---

⁷Brecht, *Couragemodell*, BFA 25: 172.
⁸Notice the related motivation of the Lehrstücke such as *Jasager/Neinsager* or *Die Maßnahme*, which involve working through an episode from the same starting point but considering different outcomes.
⁹Brecht, *Antigonemodell*, BFA 25: 76.
¹⁰Brecht, *Couragemodell*, BFA 25: 186.
¹¹See Brecht, *Couragemodell*, BFA 25: 233.
¹²Ibid., 185.
¹³Ibid., 186.

The *Couragemodell* shows Brecht's thought process and attention to detail. The notes and accompanying production photographs demonstrate both textually and visually that his plays were not finished even when on stage because some thing, action, or event could always be different and could mean more. Especially when approaching a character, Brecht sought to analyze the problematic details. For example, the *Couragemodell*'s single longest note, 'Das Alter spielen,' relays how Brecht taught a young, relatively inexperienced actress how to play the Peasant Woman in Scene 11. This note describes a common problem in the theater: how a younger actress playing an older woman on stage might try to generalize her display of the character's age, using unrealistic posturing. In this case Brecht employed a different approach. He made the peasant woman not just 'old' but 'zumindest vierzigjährig[ ], wohl aber ihrer Klasse entsprechend früh gealtert[ ]'.[14] The age was created by the actor who practiced playing the role, working out from the text 'Tonfall um Tonfall und Haltung um Haltung,' or one detail after another, until in the end the image of a prematurely aged forty-year-old woman emerged by virtue of this inductive approach. When the actress had to kneel and whine, she did not kneel and whine simultaneously, but knelt and then whined. Detailed parsing of actions shows how they were part of a deliberate, well-rehearsed sequence. In this scene the woman leads Kattrin in prayer, and by doing so, she must show the gestural act of teaching by demonstrating how 'die Bäuerin lehrt die Fremde das Beten': first the kneeling, then folding one's hands at the stomach, finding the right cadence and sound for one's chanting, etc. The act of teaching Kattrin how to pray contributes to the 'aging' effect of the woman. Brecht adds: '[G]egen Ende des Gebets schien sie [Kattrin] in 'echtes' Beten hineinzukommen: Sie wurde durch das Beten sozusagen frömmer.'[15] From beginning to end, these issues were framed as specifically as possible.

This instance provides an example of the approach that informed Brecht's ideas of gestic (or gestural) acting. 'Was ist die Haltung?' is indicative of Brecht's perspectives on truth and class relations, for which he sought to provide a physical response while acting. How could actors make a detailed point regarding human behavior so that it would become apparent or visible on stage? Brecht's basic intention becomes clear when we see how actors display their character's attitude toward another, especially one that is socially significant, by developing and making visible the characters' physical relations. Such gestures are often complicated and usually contradictory; they are not attitudes describable in one single word, but rather through a constellation of images.

As previously stated, the model book's notes to the individual scenes are organized into two main parts: *Grundarrangements* and *Details*. The beginning of every scene in the *Couragemodell* contains these foundational remarks, coinciding with the 106 'Szenenfotos' of the adjoining picture volume that were meant to be read/viewed together. One should also note that this textual 'arrangement' was illustrative of how Brecht operated: first the fundamentals, then the particulars; first isolation, then elaboration. The *Grundarrangements* lay the groundwork for the visual division of the actions, whereas the detailed notes that follow problematize and seek to develop the slight movements on stage. *Grundarrangements* is a polysemous term. As in English, the German word *Grund* has both a material/physical meaning (earth, foundation, ground) as well as an analytical sense (reason, basis, cause). Brecht used *Arrangements* to convey duality, in

---

[14]Ibid., 233.
[15]Ibid., 234.

terms of character positioning as well as examination of the textual sequencing itself. These 'basic arrangements' are crucial to the director because they serve as a foundation to all articulations in the play, e.g., rhythm, tempo, character.[16]

The *Grundarrangements* in the *Couragemodell*, like the published version of *Mutter Courage* and the scenes on stage, begin with titles. The titles in the *Couragemodell* are pithier and often condensed, reducing the scene's content to the simplest statement possible. They are all thematically consistent and reduce each scene describing Mother Courage in relation to three main points: war, business, and family. After the titles come italicized sentences that parse a scene into constitutive elements. Following the titles and parsing comes the actual *Grundarrangements* where Brecht subsequently restates the italicized sentences and expands each with commentary. Most frequently the stress is on the visual. In the expanded commentary for Scene 3, for example, Brecht describes this image of the attack on the camp where Mother Courage is stationed: '*Der Überfall*. Der feste Punkt in dem Gelaufe und Gerufe ist der Feldprediger, der allen im Weg stehend nicht vom Platze weicht. Das übrige Arrangement ergibt sich aus dem Buch.'[17] Here we get a glimpse of how the action on stage revolves around a single stationary vantage point in the figure of the preacher, who serves also as point of contrast to the chaos around him. Brecht visually situates the scene's layout and arrangement in another note to Scene 3: 'Der Planwagen [der Courage] steht während der ganzen Szene links, mit dem Deichselende gegen den Zuschauer, so daß die links von ihm Stehenden von denen rechts nicht gesehen werden.'[18]

With these *Grundarrangements* Brecht indicates the play's *Drehpunkte*, places where the scene's dynamic or structure shifts or is redirected by some type of discovery or motivational change. One such pivotal point is found early in the play in the second scene's arrangement, in an exchange between the Cook and Mother Courage: 'Die Szene hat ihre Bewegung am Drehpunkt ("Sehen Sie, was ich mach?"). Der Koch beendet sein Rübchenschälen, fischt aus der Kehrichttonne das verfaulte Fischstück und trägt es zum Hackblock. Die Erpressung der Courage ist mißlungen.'[19] Here, as the commentary points out, the extortion has failed. These *Drehpunkte* often seem coincidental but have thematic importance. In Scene 1 of the play, Mother Courage asks the Feldwebel and the Werber whether one could use a 'nice pistol or a belt buckle', seeking to turn an unfortunate encounter with two representatives of military power into a business opportunity. The Feldwebel answers provocatively: 'I need something else' and motions to her eldest son, the sturdy but unsuspecting Eilif. With this exchange Brecht introduces the audience to a central thematic issue in the play, the needs of business in contrast to the needs of war. Later in Scene 1, other pivotal moments echo this one, resulting in the successful sale of the buckle. However, Courage discovers that her commercial transaction has cost her one of her sons.

The following briefly suggests other practical examples of how the production photographs in Brecht's *Couragemodell* relate to the epic theater. In Scene 10 in *Mutter Courage*, Mother Courage and Kattrin pull their wagon on a road past a farmhouse when

---

[16]Brecht scholars and translators John Willett and Ralph Manheim called these *Grundarrangements* 'overall arrangements'.
[17]Brecht, *Couragemodell*, BFA 25: 195.
[18]Ibid., 194.
[19]Ibid., 189.

they hear a voice singing the song 'Das Lied von der Bleibe'. The words they hear are directly juxtaposed with their own situation: wandering Europe for years following in the footsteps of the Thirty Years' War and its destruction. In contrast, the voice from the farmhouse sings the virtues of the rose in the garden, the farmer working his land, and the comfort and protection of a permanent roof over one's head. Brecht's short note detailing Scene 10 in the *Couragemodell*, titled 'Ausdruck unerwünscht,' reads as follows: 'Die beiden Frauen kommen, den Wagen ziehend. Sie hören die Stimme aus dem Bauernhaus, bleiben stehen, horchen, setzen sich mit ihrem Wagen wieder in Bewegung. Was in ihnen vorgeht, soll nicht gezeigt werden; das Publikum kann es sich denken.'[20] This note reveals a rather unique moment for Brecht, who usually insists that epic actors show not only their relation to others, both in the form of *Menschenverhalten* and *Schauspielerverhalten*, but also the act of showing itself ('1 Zeigende, 2 Gezeigte').[21] For instance, the actor does not need to cry on stage; instead, the actor should show *how* one cries and perhaps that his/her sleeve is wet afterward.[22] In the above example the inner contradiction when Mother Courage realizes her plight yet again (even for just a moment) should not be signaled to the audience. The actors show that they have stopped to listen, but not that they realize the consequences of their actions during the war. This comprises the entirety of Scene 10 on stage: entrance of wagon, the song, and then the exit of the wagon.

The audience is not meant to see Mother Courage and Kattrin outwardly express this realization, but with the aid of the production photograph we can study the situation on stage in detail. The photograph from Scene 10 included in the *Couragemodell* isolates this moment of realization for the reader and simultaneously allows each individual element in the scene to be scrutinized for analysis.[23] This photograph becomes the visual representation of another *Drehpunkt* in the play: we see how Mother Courage and Kattrin have been visually detached from the scene and exposed on stage. In this case, simply viewing the actors' pause while the scene continues is enough for Brecht, to the extent that showing nothing else but their internalization also carries meaning.[24] Mother Courage and Kattrin stand physically in opposition to the progression of the scene.

---

[20]Ibid., 228.
[21]Brecht, 'Über das Theater der Chinesen,' BFA 22.1: 126.
[22]See the conversation between Herbert Jhering and Marcel Marceau in a book found in Brecht's *Nachlassbibliothek* [BBA call number A 10/27]: *Die Weltkunst der Pantomime* (Berlin: Aufbau, 1956), 15 ff. Here, Marceau echoes this sentiment of making something invisible visible to the spectator: 'Der Wind ist zum Beispiel unsichtbar. Wir müssen ihn sichtbar machen.' Here, the actor places importance on body movements ('das mimische Theater') that carry meaning, not in actually reproducing real-life actions.
[23]See *Couragemodell*, BFA 25: 290.
[24]This instance from Scene 10 is only one example; one could find any number throughout the play. At this point the audience has been prepared by prior examples of this contradictory behavior on Courage's part to 'read' or 'see' the consequences on their own.

Photography/the Image

CHAPTER EIGHT

'Was besagt eine Fotografie?' Early Brechtian Perspectives on Photography[1]

TOM KUHN

Brecht's interest in modern technologies and media (radio, film and so on) is generally so well documented and so much commented upon, it is at least surprising that extremely little has been said about his interest in photography and its uses. In the first place this must have to do with the fragmentary nature of this engagement, over several decades during which his point of approach kept changing. It also has to do with the fact that he wrote nothing in the way of sustained reflections about this technology, means of reproduction, technique of record, medium of documentary, art-form – however we choose to understand it – about which other contemporaries, notably Siegfried Kracauer, Franz Roh, and Walter Benjamin, were producing a substantial theoretical literature. In a broader context, it has to do with the fact that we have as yet, as Jan Knopf has recently remarked,[2] hardly begun to consider the importance of the visual and the visual arts for Brecht. Insofar as there is a consensus at all about Brecht's own position, it is that his thoughts on photography are unexciting.[3] That view is, however, easily problematized by a consideration of the context of the so-called new German photography of the 1920s. Gradually it becomes possible to piece together, from photographs of the period, occasional remarks and notes, quite distinctively Brechtian perspectives on photography, especially in relation to notions of *Gestik* and of a cognitive realism.

Although he was not much of a photographer himself, photography is a recurrent issue in Brecht's work, whether as an object of his theoretical writings or as a practice which clearly held some fascination for him: from the wonderfully self-conscious poses which he

---

Tom Kuhn, '"Was besagt eine Fotografie?" Early Brechtian Perspectives on Photography', *Brecht Yearbook*, 31 (2006), pp. 260–83.

[1] A line from a Brecht poem of 1926, *Große kommentierte Berliner und Frankfurter Ausgabe*, ed. Werner Hecht, Jan Knopf, Werner Mittenzwei *et al*, in 30 vols. (Berlin and Weimar: Aufbau, and Frankfurt a.M.: Suhrkamp, 1987-2000) (henceforth BFA), 13: p. 335.
[2] *Dreigroschenheft*, 3/2004, p. 8.
[3] The case for the lack of interest in Brecht's remarks about photography is made by Michael Koetzle in his afterword to *Brecht beim Photographen* (Munich: Gina Keyahoff Verlag, 1998), esp. pp. 87-8.

struck as a young man for private and public portraits, through to the use of projections in the theater, the mixed media work of the *Kriegsfibel* (1944) and the *Journal* (1938 to 1952), and the contentious records of theatrical practice, the *Modellbücher* (compiled in the 1950s). One of his closest collaborators from the 1930s, Ruth Berlau, distinguished herself as a photographer and contributed to all these later projects.[4] It is a very broad field. For the time being, however, I want to stay in the 1920s: to see how photography figured in the period of Brecht's most intense development towards a social theory of art, and to sketch as it were the prehistory for those later enterprises.[5]

1.

In July 1924 Brecht noted '*Fotografieren*' in a list of skills he wanted to learn (others include 'Moderne Jamben ... Schifahren ... Jiu-Jitsu') and put a camera on his shopping list. The immediate use his first camera seems to have found was taking photographs of his children, the only thing children are good for, he suggests.[6] Brecht's first interest in these early mentions of photography seems to be in portraits, or photographs of people. I have mentioned his own poses. In 1927 he undertook the now famous photo-session in his leather coat in the Augsburg studio of Konrad Reßler, and in the same year set up his Berlin flat for the often reproduced group portrait of 'Der Dichter Bert Brecht' in the *Uhu* magazine, on which he commented archly, 'unsere unnatürliche Haltung [beruht] auf unserem Entschluß, ausnahmsweise so zu tun, als wüßten wir, daß wir photographiert werden.'[7] In one poem, of about the same date, he adds the portrait-photograph to his catalogue of images of ephemeral identity:

> Willst Du sie vergessen
> Zerreiß ihre Fotografie
> Da wirst Du sie schon vergessen.
> Aber ihre Wörter nie.[8]

The idea that words mean more than images, or that images may mean little without words, will become important later.

The interest in portraiture and in the nature of what may be revealed or obscured in a photograph of a person is echoed in the contemporary work of August Sander, Erich Salomon, and other practitioners, as well as of other writers on photography. Siegfried Kracauer's 1927 essay for the *Frankfurter Zeitung*, 'Die Photographie', sets out from

---

[4] A collection of her own photographs and writings has recently appeared as *Ruth Berlau: Fotografin an Brechts Seite*, ed. Grischa Meyer (Berlin: Propyläen, 2003).
[5] I hope to follow this essay with two further articles: one on the *Journal* and the *Kriegsfibel* (photography and poetry), and one on photography and the theater (from *Gestus* to *Modellbuch*).
[6] BFA 26: pp. 279-80; and 26: p. 285; cf. 28: p. 294.
[7] The photo-session now published as *Brecht beim Photographen*, ed. Michael Koetzle (see note 3); the group portrait originally in *Uhu* 1927, vol. 11 : pp. 38-9. Despite Brecht's group portrait, the *Uhu* series is somewhat comically entitled 'Bei der Arbeit: Künstler und Werk mit sich allein', The other images are conventional artist-portraits: Otto Dix sketching at a canvas, Rudolf Belling working on a bust, Max Reinhardt looking up from his director's desk. The accompanying article is also inappropriate to Brecht: it is concerned with the artist's struggle with his material to achieve immortality. The idea that one should be aware of the camera of course accords nicely with Brecht's idea that the spectator should be fully aware of the mechanisms of the theater.
[8] BFA 13: p. 325, dated 'um 1925/26'.

a portrait-photograph of a film diva; and Walter Benjamin's 1931 'Kleine Geschichte der Photographie' discusses portraits above all other genres.[9] It is unsurprising, given Brecht's anthropological, behaviorist interests, that his attention should be drawn first to photographs of people. However, already we can discern a more complex attitude. Brecht's comment on the *Uhu* group portrait – 'Ein Bild zustandezukriegen aus dem zu ersehen ist, wie man arbeitet, ist nicht leicht'[10] – demonstrates a clear awareness of the 'constructed' nature of the photograph. It is not the case that the camera always 'naturally' reveals something; on the contrary, the image can be manipulated to say what we want it to say. In this instance it is constructed as a document of a collective process of artistic creation, that is, of an important principle for Brecht. In the case of the Reßler portraits, on the other hand, the confident pose, the poet as a 'hard-boiled' American-style investigator with his notebook and cigar, is a self-conscious irony. The pose can conceal, the *Gestus* should reveal. Photography can be good for both.

A page of notes headed 'Fotografie', possibly from about 1928 (BFA 21: p. 265), tries to draw a distinction between 'essentielle Bildnisse' – images which do relatively simply disclose something about subjects and circumstances – and 'funktionelle Bildnisse' – developing the idea of photography as a potential instrument for the analysis of social behavior:

> Beispiel für funktionelle Bildnisse:
> Hände, Hände von Arbeitern, die Hämmer, Sensen,
> Maschinenteile halten, von Kopfarbeitern, die Bleistifte,
> Zeichnungen usw. halten (Kontobücher!), von Arbeitern,
> die Kontobücher, Bleistifte usw. halten, von Kopfarbeitern,
> die Hämmer, Maschinenteile halten. Dasselbe bei Frauen.

This is the sort of approach we find in the collections of material for a number of his later plays, as indeed also in his acting theory and practice of rehearsal. Brecht's folders of notes and sketches often contain photographs which seemed to him to capture a typical or illustrative *Gestik* which he sought to investigate in a dramatic scene (for example, newspaper images of the 'masses' in the *Johanna* file or pictures of Hitler amongst the material for *Die Rundköpfe und die Spitzköpfe*). The photographs of the *Journal* and the *Kriegsfibel* seem likewise largely to have been chosen for their human and 'gestural' subjects. The point was to 'discover' a gesture, not as the expression of the psychology of the individual, but as a symptom of social relations.

As well as people, however, Brecht's early writings also contain a number of reflections about photographs of cities or of buildings; and it is here that we get a little more of a view on the general problems of the contradictory (not simply revealing) representational function and analytical potential of photography.

---

[9]'Die Photographie' in *Frankfurter Zeitung*, 28 October 1927, reprinted in Kracauer, *Das Ornament der Masse* (Frankfurt a.M.: Suhrkamp, 1963, pb 1977), pp. 21-39; 'Kleine Geschichte der Photographie' in *Die literarische Welt*, September/October, 1931, reprinted in Benjamin, *Gesammelte Schriften, ed.* Rolf Tiedemann and Hermann Schweppenhäuser (Frankfurt a.M.: Suhrkamp, 1972-89) II, pp. 368-85. This is one of a number of instances where Benjamin's ideas on technological progress in photography are consonant with Brecht's own remarks, in this case in the *Dreigroschenprozeß* (BFA 21: pp. 480-1, also 1931/32).
[10]In the caption beneath the portrait, as note 7.

In his 1927 'Kurzer Bericht über vierhundert (400) junge Lyriker' Brecht makes a first remark, in passing, about the photograph's lack of political effect:

> Was nützt es, aus Propagandagründen für uns, die Photographien großer Städte zu veröffentlichen, wenn sich in unserer unmittelbaren Umgebung ein bourgeoiser Nachwuchs sehen läßt, der allein durch diese Photographien vollgültig widerlegt werden kann?
>
> (BFA 21: p. 192)

Thrust a city photograph in the face of some feeble Rilke-epigone, and his whole aesthetics should surely fall apart ... but, laments Brecht (contradicting, by the way, the confidence of many other contemporaries in the documentary potency of the photographic medium), it doesn't work like that. The flood of sentiment and wilful ignorance of social conditions, which Brecht sees evidenced in the entries for the poetry competition he has been asked to judge, appears so powerful that it may overwhelm even the starkest documents of the real reality (the industrialized cities) which lies outside the bourgeoisie's degraded, dreamy imaginations. Not for the last time in Brecht's writings, photography stands in for the sort of surface realism which permits no analysis. Three years later, Brecht appears to be still saying much the same thing: 'Die Fotografie ist die Möglichkeit einer *Wiedergabe*, die den Zusammenhang wegschminkt' (21: p. 443); and then the famous remark from the writings of the *Dreigroschenprozeß*, 'Eine Fotografie der Kruppwerke oder der AEG ergibt beinahe nichts über diese Institute. Die eigentliche Realität ist in die Funktionale gerutscht' (21: p. 468). This view of photography as nothing more than a model of impotent mimetic realism features in the writing of other contemporaries too. Siegfried Kracauer's essay argues that because photography fixes reality in a superficial way it impedes the viewer from understanding that reality historically or conceptually. And the remark about a photograph of a factory started off, it would seem, as a comment by the Marxist sociologist Fritz Sternberg (there it is a Ford factory) and subsequently migrated, now as an explicit quotation from Brecht (from the unpublished typescript of the *Dreigroschenprozeß*), to Benjamin's 'Kleine Geschichte'.[11] Brecht anyway goes on to conclude that representing reality is not enough, 'es ist also ... tatsächlich Kunst nötig' if we are to intervene in social processes.

I have been looking at remarks over a period of some four or five years, and they are significant years for Brecht, but it is not possible to establish any very clear development in his thinking about this medium. 'Was besagt eine Fotografie?' Brecht asks in a poem of 1926. Not necessarily very much, would seem – notwithstanding a cautious interest in the analytical potential of photographs of people – to be the answer, so far.

2.

It is striking that Brecht's apparent dismissal of photography as a sort of inadequate documentary realism should have coincided with a general explosion of interest in more experimental, abstract, and 'art'-photography, in what was widely dubbed 'die neue Photographie' at the time, and has since been identified as one of the important areas of

---

[11] Cf BFA 21: pp. 443-4; and Benjamin, *Gesammelte Schriften* II, pp. 833-4. There was clearly a regular exchange between Brecht and Benjamin on this subject. Compare Steve Giles, *Bertolt Brecht and Critical Theory* (Bern: Peter Lang, 1998), pp. 133-6; and, for the larger context of this relationship, Erdmut Wizisla, *Benjamin und Brecht: Die Geschichte einer Freundschaft* (Frankfurt a.M.: Suhrkamp 2004), and esp. pp. 168, 170, 173 and 252.

technological-artistic experiment in the Weimar Republic.[12] The debate about whether photography was just a technology of reproduction or a potential medium for artistic expression began right back at the origins, in the mid-nineteenth century; but, beginning in the 1900s, and more especially after the First World War, a whole range of photographers began to question photographic practice, in the context of the development of a modernist aesthetics in other media. For them, the photograph was not to be concerned with mirroring the literal world and trotting after the mirage of verisimilitude. Instead, it was to be developed as the site of a new aesthetic, whether psychological or social, crucially beyond the reach of outmoded media like painting, and essentially critical of dominant ideologies and traditions. Much of this development took place in Revolutionary Russia and in 1920s Germany, where the assumptions of representational art were aligned with a discredited bourgeois ideology. Photographers such as Lissitzky, Rodchenko, Moholy-Nagy and Man Ray drew on notions of 'constructivism' and 'estrangement' to disrupt received ideas about how we structure a supposedly 'natural' world, and to exploit the camera as a radically new means of perception.

It is not clear how far Brecht was conscious of these new spirits – in his published writings he nowhere mentions their photographic work. László Moholy-Nagy is mentioned in the mid-1930s for his stage design of Mehring's *Der Kaufmann von Berlin* (1929), and Constructivism in painting gets a brief mention only in the context of his reflections on Formalism in the 1950s.[13] Perhaps Brecht's engagement with the more radical experimenters did not begin until after their experiments were over. On the other hand, one of his closer associates, George Grosz, had also worked in photography, alongside John Heartfield, whose work Brecht also most certainly knew. Brecht's interest in Heartfield again really begins with his stage design (and late), but he presumably knew the photomontages as well, from posters, Malik book-jackets and the covers of the *Rote Fahne*.[14] As for Grosz, he first encountered his work in 1918, and knew him well and worked closely with him after 1927. Besides, personal contacts are not necessary to establish that Brecht had more than an inkling of what was going on in the world of photography. The print media were full of examples and discussions of the work of the new photographers. By the time of the *Film und Foto* exhibition of the Deutsche Werkbund in Stuttgart in June 1929 (visiting Berlin in October and November), with work by Moholy-Nagy, Helmar Lerski, Renger-Patzsch, Andreas Feininger, Werner Gräff, Hanna Höch, Man Ray and many others, feuilleton interest had reached a peak. Of course, not all of these exponents were so radical in their visions for their art, and a softer version of the new visual style was everywhere: in advertisements, posters and illustrated magazines, as well as in the widely promoted photographic art of such popular publications as Albert Renger-Ratzsch's *Die Welt ist schön* and Karl Blossfeldt's *Urformen der Kunst*, both published in 1928, the latter reviewed quite favourably in the same year by Benjamin, the former derided in both the 'Kleine Geschichte' and 'Der Autor als Produzent'.[15]

---

[12]Some of the classic documents and manifestos associated with the trend are collected in *Germany: The New Photography 1927-33*, ed. David Mellor (London: Arts Council of Great Britain, 1978).
[13]BFA 22:p. 165 and 233; and 23: p. 143.
[14]Heartfield only began providing covers for the *Arbeiter-Illustrierte-Zeitung* (to which Brecht also contributed literary texts) from 1930.
[15]Renger-Patzsch, *Die Welt ist schön: Einhundert photographische Aufnahmen* (Munich: Kurt Wolff, 1928); Blossfeldt, *Urformen der Kunst: Photographische Pflanzenbilder* (Berlin: Ernst Wasmuth, 1928). The latter was

However far he was getting to know this varied oeuvre, there is of course anyway little to suggest that Brecht would have been all that impressed by the aesthetics of most of the representatives of the new photography. Just because he had a lifelong mistrust of the literal and simple documentary, did not mean that he was about wholeheartedly to embrace Dadaism or any playfully abstract avant-garde. Nor could it possibly imply that he was seeking the kinds of metaphysical moment of transcendence which Renger-Patzsch hoped to reveal in his transfigured 'schöne Welt'.[16] In this sort of fashionable 'modishness', according to Benjamin, 'entlarvt sich die Haltung einer Photographie, die jede Konservenbüchse ins All montiert, aber nicht einen der menschlichen Zusammenhänge fassen kann, in denen sie auftritt.'[17] In the same year that Benjamin wrote that, 1931, Brecht wrote a very short piece for the celebration of the ten-year anniversary of the *Arbeiter-Illustrierte-Zeitung*. As well as providing more evidence that Brecht had been watching the development of modern photography with alert and critical eyes, his piece gives us some sense of the resistance which he felt in the face of the bourgeois fetishism of the 'truths' which could supposedly be revealed by placing objects before a camera lens.

> Die ungeheure Entwicklung der Bildreportage ist für die *Wahrheit* über die Zustände, die auf der Welt herrschen, kaum ein Gewinn gewesen: die Photographie ist in den Händen der Bourgeoisie zu einer furchtbaren Waffe *gegen* die Wahrheit geworden. Das riesige Bildmaterial, das tagtäglich von den Druckerpressen ausgespien wird und das doch den Charakter der Wahrheit zu haben scheint, dient in Wirklichkeit nur der Verdunkelung der Tatbestände. Der Photographenapparat kann lügen ebenso wie die Setzmaschine.

Or, as Siegfried Kracauer had earlier put it, 'In den Illustrierten sieht das Publikum die Welt, an deren Wahrnehmung es die Illustrierten hindern.'[18]

Brecht's more familiar early remarks on photography seemed at first sight, out of context, just an expression of his repudiation of mimetic literalism, where the medium is made to stand in, almost lazily, for the 'mirror' aesthetic. To a certain extent, photography does indeed have that function in Brecht's critique of realism in the later 1920s. Now however – in close dialogue, not to say chorus, with Benjamin and Kracauer – his scattered comments begin to coalesce as a more sophisticated critique, not of the medium for itself, but of a particular aesthetic and a particular fashionable practice of photographic art. In fact the clearest statement of his scepticism comes not in 1931, but back in 1928, and in direct response, we must presume, to Renger-Patzsch's picture book. In a short sketch, unpublished at the time (BFA 21: pp. 264–5), Brecht observes that the time when a photograph had true documentary force has passed:[19]

---

reviewed by Walter Benjamin in *Die literarische Welt*, November 1928 (= *Gesammelte Schriften* III, pp. 151-3); the mentions of the former are in *Gesammelte Schriften* II, pp. 383 and 693.

[16]Renger-Patzsch's book was promoted with a comment by Thomas Mann, perhaps another reason for Brecht to disdain it (see *Germany: The New Photography*, p. 8).

[17]'Kleine Geschichte', p. 383.

[18]*A-I-Z*, Berlin, No.41, October 1931 (BFA 21: p. 515); and Kracauer, 'Die Photographie', p. 34.

[19]He refers to 'das herrliche St Cloud 1871' and must be thinking of photographs of the ruins around Paris following the siege and destruction of the Commune. An example of such an image is at www.library.northwestern.edu/spec/siege/images/PAR00272.JPG. The originals are located in the Charles Deering McCormick Special Collections in the Deering Library at Northwestern University. (There is an intriguing contrast between these documents and Eugène Atget's photographs, a generation later, of the park at St Cloud

> Ich meine nicht nur die Auswahl der Objekte, obwohl ich auch die meine, sondern vor allem jenen Ausdruck von Einmaligkeit, Besonderheit in der Zeit, den Künstler ihren Bildern verleihen können, die wissen, was ein Dokument ist. Aber dazu gehört Interesse für die Dinge und genügt nicht Interesse für die Beleuchtung.[20]

He goes on – taking the example of an 'artistic' photograph of a woman's bottom – to bewail the fascination of contemporary photography with its own 'art', at the expense of its objects: 'Es handelt sich hauptsächlich wohl darum, zu zeigen, daß "das Leben doch schön ist."' And the piece ends with a typically profane turn to the social and *gestisch*:

> Die Fotografie hat noch dazu den Nachteil, da sie selten die besten, nicht einmal die teuersten Hintern vor die Lupe bekommt. Berufsmäßige Modelle sind auch zuwenig durch den Apparat irritiert, sie präsentieren sich dem Apparat anders, als sie sich dem nachmaligen Beschauer präsentieren würden, es entsteht eine abgeschmackt harmlose Atmosphäre. Etwas aufzuhelfen wäre dem vielleicht nur durch den Titel

The text breaks off here, at the end of a page, before developing this tantalizing reference to the importance of a caption for the photographic image.

Given the almost unbounded enthusiasm for the 'new' photography manifested at the time in countless illustrated publications and exhibitions, Brecht's skepticism seems at least healthy: 'Der Photographenapparat kann lügen ebenso wie die Setzmaschine.' The objects of all this 'new' photographic practice appear, not as transfigured, nor yet even revealed as themselves, but rather under a spell which both freezes and withdraws them from our understanding, in an effect which Herbert Molderings calls 'reified sight, the content of which is no longer the real world so much as the camera's artistic technique'. As another contemporary commentator put it, 'was an Augenbotschaft übermittelt wird, starrt uns an wie ein Fetisch.'[21]

At this point, and as an aside, it is worth pointing out that Brecht first contemplated using photographs in the theater as early as *Jae Fleischhacker* and *Im Dickicht*, in 1926 and 1927;[22] and Karl Ebert did indeed use film projections for the 1927 production of the latter. Brecht himself was still using paintings by Caspar Neher for the back-projections for the first production of *Mahagonny* in 1930 (which might have been a nice occasion

---

in all its monumental (timeless) splendour. It is not unreasonable to speculate that Brecht may have known these too, given Benjamin's interest in Atget.)

[20]One recalls the contemporary exhortation that poems should aspire to this same documentary force – 'Alle großen Gedichte haben den Wert von Dokumenten' – in the 'Kurzer Bericht', BFA 21: p. 191.

[21]Herbert Molderings, 'Urbanism and Technological Utopianism: Thoughts on the photography of Neue Sachlichkeit and the Bauhaus', in *Germany: The New Photography*, p. 94. Carl Linfert, another of the in fact very few commentators who resisted the photographic euphoria of those years, remarked on the occasion of the exhibition *Das Lichtbild* in Essen, also in 1931: 'Denn wie selten sagen Photos etwas aus über das, was sie vermitteln! Aber was an Augenbotschaft übermittelt wird, starrt uns an wie ein Fetisch. Seit Renger-Patzsch nämlich können Photos erschrecken. ... Die Sucht des Anschauens, vielmehr des Aufnehmens ist so fieberhaft, daß alles gesammelt, aber schließlich nichts mehr erfaßt wird, ... Das Ding selbst, so knapp und gelreu der Apparat es auch sieht, wird stumm, wie es noch nie gewesen ist.' (Linfert, 'Das moderne Lichtbild', in *Frankfurter Zeitung*, no. 742/3, 8 October 1931.)

[22]See BFA 10: p. 281; and 24: p.29: 'Praktisch gesprochen, würde es mir ausreichen, wenn die Theater Amerika als gewöhnliche Fotografie auf den Prospekt würfen ... .'

for a photographic backdrop), and did not, as director, employ photographs until *Die Mutter* in 1932.[23]

Anyway, we can discern a growing confidence in the usefulness of some photography at least, which coincides both with his aggressive critique of the fetishistic and un-analytic character of contemporary magazine and 'art' photography, and with the development of his notions of cognitive realism (especially in the *Dreigroschenprozeß*).

3.

It is fascinating now to come to two contemporary works of photography which Brecht certainly did know, and about which he was notably (and at first sight surprisingly) enthusiastic, at a very early date. They may have helped to inform his ideas about an alternative, 'useful' photography. In December 1926 (so somewhat earlier than the other remarks I've quoted so far) Brecht responded to a questionnaire by *Das Tage-Buch* and recommended six 'beste Bücher des Jahres 1926'. Two were collections of photographs: namely Ernst Friedrich's compilation of war photographs, *Krieg dem Kriege!* and Erich Mendelsohn's collection of images of the cities of the United States, *Amerika: Bilderbuch eines Architekten*.[24] One a book of photographs of people (destroyed by war), the other of buildings (erected by capitalism).

Ernst Friedrich (1894–1967) was by this time already a well-known anarchist and pacifist. He had refused to serve in the First World War and had spent several periods in asylums and prisons. In 1919 he founded the anti-authoritarian breakaway group from the Freie Sozialistische Jugend, the Freie Jugend, under which name he published a journal and founded, in 1925, an 'international anti-war museum' in Berlin.[25] He was a friend of Ernst Toller and Erich Mühsam. Friedrich's book, with commentary and captions in four languages, was the first widely distributed collection of photographic

---

[23]In the text of *Die Mutter*, in the 'Lied vom Flicken und vom Rock' (1931; BFA 14: p. 125), Brecht also develops a refrain derived from a Kurt Tucholsky text, 'Wohltätigkeit' which appeared originally in Tucholsky's and Heartfield's innovative satirical book of photographs and texts, *Deutschland, Deutschland über alles* (Berlin: Neuer Deutscher Verlag, 1929) (here p. 224). Although he nowhere mentions it, we may presume Brecht knew this book too.

[24]Ernst Friedrich, *Krieg dem Kriege* (Berlin: Freie Jugend, originally 1924 and 1926 – in 1926 a second volume was issued and the first re-issued); and Erich Mendelsohn, *Amerika: Bilderbuch eines Architekten* (Berlin: Mosse, 1926 – in fact the very end of 1925). Friedrich's book went through at least ten editions before 1930, with only small changes to the copyright notice and 'Nachwort', and to the 'fourth' language (the first edition was in German, French, English and Dutch). It seems that the 1926 edition was more efficiently distributed and made a particular impact (Tucholsky reviewed it then). More recent editions have been launched in the 1980s by Zwettausendeins and Journeyman Press, *and* the book has just appeared in a new edition with an introduction by Gerd Krumeich (Munich; Deutsche Verlagsanstalt, 2004). Some editions have some of the pictures or text in slightly different orders (or languages), but they all contain much the same material. My quotations are of the original German text (i.e. not the sometimes misleading original English), and from the recent dva edition, which follows the same pagination as the first editions of the 1920s. Of Mendelsohn's book there are also numerous reprints, extended editions and translations. Again, my quotations refer to the original German text, but the page references to the Mendelsohn are to the widely available American edition (New York: Dover, 1993). Brecht recommends the books in *Das Tage-Buch*, Berlin, 4 December 1926, p. 1799 (BFA 21:p. 176).

[25]Already a victim of judicial and SA harassment long before 1933, Friedrich then managed to escape, eventually to France, where he continued his pacifist endeavors until his death. The Anti-Kriegs-Museum became an SA-Sturmlokal. Today, however, Friedrich's grandson maintains a successor pacifist museum in Berlin-Mitte, at Brüsseler Straße 21.

images of the atrocities of the recent war, an explicit anti-war protest, ironically dedicated to 'den Schlachtendenkern, den Schlachtenlenkern, den Kriegsbegeisterten aller Länder' (p. 2). It contains some 200 pages, mostly of truly horrific photos – of the war dead and injured, of atrocities, of incomplete operations on the wounded, and so on. They are presented, in an apparently straightforward documentary style, as 'das nüchtern-wahre, das gemein-naturgetreue Bild des Krieges ... von der unerbittlich, unbestechlich photographischen Linse erfaßt' (pp. 5-6). The text argues simply and insistently that schooling and the church, in alliance with big business, the state and other institutions of bourgeois society, prepare children for a militarized society and ultimately for war.

Not, then, immediately what one would expect to appeal to Brecht, or no longer what he thought possible for the camera. But the deeply felt, bitter sarcasm of the text reveals the photographs as rather more than just documentary realism. At one point Friedrich calls the book a 'Kriegs-Bibel' (p. 6), perhaps foreshadowing Brecht's equally bitterly ironic subversion of genre in his *Kriegsfibel*. The photographs themselves are presented in significant juxtapositions, many of them in pairs. A photograph of a posing recruit ('der Stolz der Familie') is followed by a picture of a corpse ('der Stolz der Familie ... einige Wochen später') (pp. 94 and 95). The captions provide a laconic commentary, or repeatedly juxtapose the official propaganda and rhetoric of the war-mongers and political leaders with the horror – in a sort of 'Wiederherstellung der Wahrheit', as Brecht was later to call one of his own exercises of the 1930s.[26] One photograph of skulls on the battlefield (p. 77) is accompanied by Kaiser Wilhelm's famous slogan (also memorably lampooned by John Heartfield), 'Ich führe euch herrlichen Zeiten entgegen'. Other captions are appeals or rhetorical questions, some of them reminiscent of Goya's series of 'Disasters of War';[27] under one picture Friedrich asks, 'Mütter! ... warum habt ihr das geduldet???' (p. 103).

This is not the 'neue Photographie' at all. Indeed, it is neither abstract 'art' nor objective documentary, but rather an uneasy mixture of emotional rhetoric and photographic 'evidence', a model which perhaps ties in with Brecht's own anti-war protests and with the later *War Primer*. But that goes beyond the scope of this essay.

Brecht's other recommendation in *Das Tage-Buch*, Erich Mendelsohn's images of *Amerika*, recalls those 'photographs of big cities' which Brecht writes about in the 1927 piece on the new generation of poets. Indeed, given the closeness in time, it seems highly likely that he was thinking of Mendelsohn, perhaps amongst others, when he wrote that remark. Mendelsohn (1887-1953) was at the time a prominent architect and on his way to becoming an important theorist of modernity and functionalism in architecture. Ironically, Walter Benjamin, whose interest was more in the old architecture of the great European cities, mentions Mendelsohn in one of his pieces on the *flâneur* as one of the authors of the destruction of 'die alte Wohnkultur'.[28] He is famous as the architect of, amongst many other buildings, the Einstein Tower in Potsdam (1924, one of the few of his works in Germany to survive the successive ravages of the Nazis, the Allied bombing raids, and

---

[26]BFA 22: pp. 89-96.
[27]Which Brecht appears to have got to know as a very young man, cf letter to Caspar Neher, October 1917, BFA 28: p. 34.
[28]'Giedion, Mendelsohn [sic], Corbusier machen den Aufenthaltsort von Menschen vor allem zum Durchgangsraum aller erdenklichen Kräfte und Wellen von Licht und Luft.' Review of Franz Hessel, *Spazieren in Berlin*, in *Die literarische Welt*, October 1929 (=*Gesammelte Schriften* III, pp. 196-7).

the conservative post-war restoration), and the De La Warr Pavilion at Bexhill-on-Sea in Sussex (1935).[29] He had also been responsible for the sensational re-conception of the Mosse Verlagshaus in the Kochstraße, after its extensive destruction during the Spartakus Uprising in 1919, and had engaged on commissions for department stores, office blocks and villas in Berlin and all over Germany. Mendelsohn's trip to America, in 1924, was financed by the *Berliner Tageblatt* (published by Mosse), for which he wrote occasional diary-like contributions, and then put together this book on his return. The moment of his arrival in New York harbor, standing at the railing of the ocean liner *Deutschland* next to Fritz Lang, has been mythologized by Lang as the moment of conception of the film *Metropolis*.[30] For Mendelsohn, however, the excitement very soon gave way to disappointment and stern critique. This was not, after all, a 'new world', but an exaggerated parody of aspects of the old, disfigured by its obsession with production and consumption, and without tradition or substance: 'Land zu jung und ungewiß, triebhaft, ausbeuterisch, Recorddelirium, unkonsolidiert, traditionslos.'[31]

Mendelsohn's book of photographs, nearly all taken by himself,[32] is a part-documentary account of the new architecture, part-subjective polemic against this unregulated capitalist America. Although Mendelsohn travelled hundreds of miles by car (often sleeping in a tent) and visited Frank Lloyd Wright on his estate in Wisconsin,[33] his *Bilderbuch eines Architekten* contains nearly only pictures of the big cities: New York especially, Detroit, Chicago and Buffalo (where he was fascinated by the huge wheat silos). The over eighty photographs, divided into six thematic 'chapters', are mostly of skyscrapers and new buildings, some of building sites, taken mostly from below, from street level, with several longer street perspectives. They are not technically 'good' photographs: the focus is sometimes blurred and the composition jumbled. Some remain nonetheless striking images, and have considerable documentary force; their 'snapshot quality' reinforces their aura of facticity, helps to lift the veil of reification so as to suggest real social and economic relations – in a way that one might have expected to appeal to Brecht. But these are documentary records of buildings, not of people. Mendelsohn is concerned above all with those vertical views, and with skyscrapers – both as architectural designs and as metonymic images of capitalism. Because the photos are all taken from below, however, the buildings appear to lean – into the street or away from the observer, and the concrete of this city is revealed as startlingly precarious. The images are often in extreme vertical formats and often awkwardly cropped. The perspectives are forced and deliberate, the views crammed, as if it was almost impossible to shove a photographer into the narrow chasms of the city, to achieve a perspective on these cities at all. Some of the buildings (Broadway, the Woolworth Building, the Chicago Tribune Building) are familiar, but the

---

[29]Mendelsohn was also forced into exile, first to England, then Palestine, and finally the USA.
[30]Interview with Peter Bogdanovich in Bogdanovich, *Fritz Lang in America* (London: Studio Vista, 1967), p. 15. And compare Lang, 'Was ich in Amerika sah', in *Film-Kurier*, 292, 11 December 1924; and Mendelsohn's letter to Luise Mendelsohn, on board, 11 October 1924, in Oskar Beyer, *Erich Mendelsohn: Briefe eines Architekten* (Munich: Prestel, 1961), p. 56. Some of these letters home to his wife were subsequently exploited as the basis for his *Berliner Tageblatt* articles.
[31]Letter to Luise, Pittsburgh, 22 October 1924. Extracts from the letters are also quoted by Ita Heinze-Greenberg in *Erich Mendelsohn: Architekt 1887-1953 – Gebaute Wetten*, ed. Regina Stephan (Ostfildern-Ruit: Verlag Gerd Hatje, 1998), p. 88 for this quotation.
[32]Sixteen were by Knud Lonberg-Holm and one by Fritz Lang. In the later 1928 edition, Mendelsohn replaced some of the old photographs with new pictures by Erich Karweik.
[33]Lloyd Wright's buildings were the only ones he really admired in America, although the three images of them in the *Bilderbuch* are not attributed and are partially misidentified.

perspectives have changed and multiplied, so that they do not retain their fixed, familiar appearance. Juxtaposed with the traditional sights are new street fronts, especially chosen by Mendelsohn to illustrate the messy unregulated growth of the American cities, as well as building sites and rear elevations too (with blank walls, staircases and fire-escapes), which Mendelsohn admired for their logical structures and their capacity to unmask the street facades as clumsy and pretentious. The focus on the buildings dwarfs the people, or they are absent entirely. Mendelsohn gives us statistics – how many storeys, how many meters, how many offices, how many people – but there is only an engineer's perception of how they could all fit into these mismatched geometric designs. Recommending the book, Brecht commented, 'ausgezeichnete Photos, die man eigentlich fast alle einzeln an die Wand heften kann und die den (bestimmt trügerischen) Anschein erwecken, als seien die großen Städte bewohnbar' (BFA 21: p. 176). That parenthetical 'bestimmt trügerisch' is, I would argue, already contained in the images themselves. These streets are not so much comfortably habitable as almost perversely, by necessity, inhabited. The heights of the skyscrapers are generally over-exposed in brilliant sunshine, and it is always dark at street level, the faces of the men on the streets lost in shadow or turned away. It is the grim balance-sheet of a city necessarily both constituted by and constitutive of the ways of these people's lives. Most city photography gives us either frozen views of the bustle of street-life or monumental images of the architectural structures. But Mendelsohn manages to historicize the bustle of the architecture. With his emphasis on building and building sites, he shows us a dynamic city in a process of expansion. A photograph of a skyscraper under construction permits a moment of analysis, not only for the architect but also for the sociologist. It may unmask what Brecht elsewhere called the 'bösartige steinerne Konsistenz' of the modern city (BFA 26: p. 236). In his early writings Brecht was wont to imagine the apocalyptic destruction of the cities (in 'Vom armen B.B.', to cite the most famous example), but clearly Mendelsohn's 'eruptive Aufbau' (p. 10) excited his imagination too.[34] These are photographs of a city and a society in headlong movement.

But one of the key things which undoubtedly attracted Brecht to Mendelsohn's book is again – as in the previous volume – the extraordinary accompanying text. Some of this has the function of an architect's captions, commenting on the forms and proportions of the buildings, but other passages are judgments on American society, formulated in emotive, rhythmic, again almost expressionist language by a European radical of the old school. Mendelsohn was in the Workers' Council for Art in 1919, although he was never a member of a political party, and on his American journey he enjoyed exchanges with that great American critic of the modern city, Lewis Mumford. The Preface to Amerika (pp. ix–xi) sets the unmistakable tone, 'Amerika heute zu sehen, ist […] ein perspektivischer Rausch. Erst hier erkennen wir die ganze Ungeheuerlichkeit der verneinenden Zivilisation'; or, in phrasing which recalls *Mahagonny* or Brecht's other portrayals of the city around this time:[35]

> Seine Bevölkerung, eine aus allen Erdteilen zusammengewirbelte Masse, bildet den Unterwind dieses babylonischen Kessels. Vakuum, das ansaugt, immer von neuem,

---

[34] One recalls lines from a contemporary Brecht poem: 'Drum haltet nicht ein / Mit dem Bau eurer Stadt nimmermehr …' (BFA 13: p. 372).

[35] There are repeated references, especially in the play sketches of these years – *Jae Fleischhacker, Dan Drew, Sintflut*, even *Fatzer* to a marginal extent, to 'die großen Städte' (an often repeated formulation, e.g. BFA 10: p. 330) in an apparently violent dynamic of building and destruction. E.g. in dramatic fragments, BFA 10: pp. 289, 293-5, 299; 324, 332-3; 335, 380-1, 391; 536-8, 540-42; and in poems, BFA 11 : p. 170, and 12: pp. 336 and 372.

immer die kühnsten, den Auswurf und die Abenteurer, das Glücksrittertum und die spekulativen Naturen ...

They are all driven by 'eine sich überstürzende und somit völlig ungeordnete Glücksucht'. 'Denn was ist verboten, was erlaubt, wo die Dimension sich selbst jede Freiheit genehmigt und vor überkommener Begriffsweite keinen Respekt kennt.'

In some respects the texts simply reinforce the impressions already provided by the pictures, of cities in a process of swift, unregulated expansion, but they also exaggerate and speed up that sense: now it becomes a frenzied, unbridled chaos. Mendelsohn's metaphors are of biological growth: buildings 'aufblühen' in 'wildes Wachstum' (pp. 68, 58 and 59), and (this is again interesting in relation to *Mahagonny*) of natural disaster: whirlwinds, eruptions and so forth. Of course, the captions also heighten that sense of a particular perspective and purpose in the presentation of the photographs.

4.

Most of Brecht's literary works of these years try to imagine human life in a city that dwarfs the human, human activity in the context of vast and inscrutable market forces. One might even say that his two greatest themes in the 1920s were the inhumanity of war and the militarism of society on the one hand, and, on the other, the perverse 'Unbewohnbarkeit' of the cities and their power to draw human life into the vortex of their economies. Pursuing the connections suggested by Brecht's recommendations of Friedrich's and Mendelsohn's books makes Brecht a more interesting commentator on capitalism, war and the modern city.

It makes him a more interesting commentator on photography too. Photography, despite the remarks about surface realism and the antipathy to contemporary fashions in photographic art, was perhaps, already in 1926, on its way to becoming an opportunity for, or a component of, that sort of 'complex seeing' which Brecht (and Benjamin and Kracauer) saw as a way forward for a socially critical aesthetic practice, a combination of making 'sichtbar' and making 'fremd', of which we can already see the first shadowy trace in his responses to both Friedrich's *Krieg dem Kriege!* and Mendelsohn's *Amerika*. Free-floating contemplation of these photographs, such as was encouraged by the 'art' photography of the period, is clearly no longer sufficient. The images are presented to us, by engaged social critics, as evidence – this time the 'Zusammenhang' is by no means 'weggeschminkt' (BFA 21: p. 443) – and we are compelled to participate in a political interpretation of the historical process. From Brecht's point of view, here was a use of image and text which could avoid both naturalist realism and abstraction. And it is, crucially, the accompanying texts which support this process of engaged reflection.[36] We recall how easily images become meaningless or fetishistic without the help of words. The interplay between text and image was to become immensely important to Brecht in his later work, for example in the *Kriegsfibel* (not to mention his whole work in the theater). We see a picture, we hear or look down to a text which tells us something perhaps unexpected, and

---

[36] A third *Tage-Buch* recommendation was René Fülöp Miller's polemic against Soviet Russia, *Geist und Gesicht des Bolschewismus* (Zürich: Almathea-Verlag 1926) for the enjoyment of which Brecht wrily recommended, 'den Text mit einer Schere herauszuschneiden: das Bildmaterial ist ausgezeichnet ...' Mendelsohn's book is then described as 'eine Art Ergänzung dazu' (BFA 21: p. 176).

we look back to the picture with new eyes and a new understanding.[37] The relationship between texts and images may work in many ways, but for Brecht the point was always, whether by contradiction or affirmation, to press further towards that understanding. So a caption may help us to tease out the *gestisch* implications of an image, which without this help might be passive at best.

By these strategies photography may even acquire anew some of its old documentary force. The first editions of both *Mann ist Mann* and *Im Dickicht der Städte* (*Berlin*: Propyläen, 1926 and 1927) exploit photographs, rather unexpectedly perhaps, to support their radically *verfremdet* views of modern society. The end-papers of *Mann ist Mann* depict (at the front) a huge crowd of men, their faces all turned to the bottom right, and (at the back) an equally boundless array of motor-cars, all parked facing the bottom left. The cover of *Im Dickicht* is adorned with a montage of skyscrapers (seen this time from above) and the book has, most significantly in this context, four plates at the end, introduced as 'Städte- und Menschentypen aus den ersten Jahrzehnten des Jahrhunderts' – cities and people again. These are unaccredited photographs of a street scene and an aerial view of a city of skyscrapers (both Chicago, I presume), and portraits of an unidentified seated youth and of Brecht's wife Marianne (the dedicatee of the book). The photographs themselves have no captions, but they are of course preceded by the text of the play itself. A photograph of a city on its own has lamentably little force, Brecht commented in his 'Kurzer Bericht', but here, juxtaposed with images of the people who might have to live in it and with Brecht's extraordinary fable of abstracted struggle, it forces us to confront a social reality. Brecht's *Verfremdung* demands not only estrangement and distanciation, but also that anchor in the real; and his aesthetic as it develops comes to depend more and more on an oscillation of responses: between a perception of distance and of the proximate real, of high emotion, pathos even, and yet immeasurable strangeness. Here, the photographs give us a quick documentary fix of the real and the human, after the strange and remote story which has preceded them.

I have tried in this essay to outline Brecht's very great interest in photography and to register the emergence – against the contexts of contemporary 'new' photography, the theories of Benjamin, Kracauer and others, and Brecht's own other work – of distinctly Brechtian perspectives on the medium, which were, moreover, to dominate his subsequent use of photographs in the multi-media work of the *Journal* and the *Kriegsfibel*. After 1931 Brecht does not write *about* photography again, but he does *use* photography in his writings, and he most emphatically returns to these questions of *Verfremdung*, realism and abstraction. Obviously, one might just leave it at that: the engagement with photography simply parallels and reflects Brecht's interests in other media. But I would go further: there is evidence to suggest that the encounter with the contemporary practice and glimpsed potential of photography provided another impulse, amongst the many, for the development in the later 1920s of Brecht's characteristic, socially engaged aesthetic of cognitive realism, and of those key notions of *Gestus* and *Verfremdung*.

---

[37]Rather as Brecht later, in another reflection on the construction of the cities and the destruction of humanity, described the response to the caption 'Steel stood' beneath a photograph of the devastation of the earthquake in Tokyo, in *Fünf Schwierigkeiten beim Schreiben der Wahrheit* (BFA 22: p. 79)

PART TWO

BRECHT'S RELATIONSHIPS WITH PRACTITIONERS

Caspar Neher

CHAPTER NINE

Stylistic Devices of a Set Designed by Caspar Neher for Brecht's Epic Theatre

SUSANNE DE PONTE
TRANSLATED BY ROMY FURSLAND

Even if Caspar Neher does not formulate any explicit theory of Brecht's epic theatre, he and Brecht do develop, over the course of many years of shared theatre practice, a distinct design vocabulary for epic theatre which is still relevant today. Their joint theatrical projects give rise to a repertoire of set design devices that are stylistically characteristic of epic theatre (just like its typical acting style, by which they are conditioned).

The devices used by Neher are by no means his own inventions, however. Their pioneering novelty lies, rather, in the way already-existing methods are combined and used in new and different ways. It seems that Neher – just as Brecht did when it came to world literature – made use of existing set design possibilities in world theatre. By extending or altering their traditional use, and having them interact in new ways with other devices, he endows them with new significance for the theatre.

The stylistic elements developed by Neher are characterised not by elaborate technology or craftsmanship but by the meticulous and purposeful way in which each individual device is put to use and assigned its own dramaturgical task. The development of these stylistic elements of set design originates in the collaboration between Brecht and Neher. It is of a collectivist nature and no longer based on a clear-cut divide between different spheres of activity. The creation of a design which gives the dramatic text a framework and a form on stage is conceived as a collaborative undertaking. The set designer, ideally, plays a major role in shaping language, gestus, composition and even the text. The stage space and the set do not emerge from the set designer's ideas in isolation, but are developed hand in hand with the work the actors are doing in rehearsals. In practice, the set designer Neher has a decisive influence over questions of blocking. These questions, which are traditionally part of the director's remit, relate to the spatial treatment of the text. The collaborative work on staging which Brecht and Neher undertake goes beyond the set designer simply advising the director, and takes the form of a discursive exchange. Based on the pros and cons to be considered in terms of the characters in the space, Brecht

---

Susanne de Ponte, 'Stilmittel einer Bühne Caspar Nehers für das epische Theater von Brecht', in de Ponte, *Caspar Neher. Bertolt Brecht. Eine Bühne für das epische Theater* (Munich: Henschel, 2006), pp. 48–53.

and Neher experiment with possibilities in order to find solutions. This process seems to be so decisively bound up with Neher's set design for Brecht's stage that the process itself becomes one of the characteristic stylistic features. The design of epic theatre also developed in this way because the experimental working method, in which consensus was very important, created the right climate for certain possibilities.

At the beginning of the 1920s, Neher systematically built upon the system of the split stage which had already been introduced in Expressionist theatre, and developed it further. In the front section of the stage, a special set is built using half-height walls. In the rear section, a higher-up background is created using large painted backdrops or projection screens. This creates a clear contrast between two-dimensional painted or projected backdrops and the area of three-dimensional structures in the foreground where the characters are. With this design principle Neher introduces a counter-concept to the traditional illusionistic proscenium stage. By placing two different or even irreconcilably contrasting spaces within a single (stage) framework, he breaks the rules of the unity of space and undermines the spatial illusion.

The set in the front part of the stage tends to be reduced to a few important elements. The space and the things in it are not portrayed in their entirety. Individual components stand for the whole. They do not come across as fragments, however, but as summaries – essences distilled to a relevant formula. The focus is on the overarching idea of the performance, and only the essential elements of the stage set are included. All decorative embellishments are done away with in favour of sparse clarity. Fundamentally, the simplification of the stage set and the minimal props are guided by the pursuit of the essential but also of the universal.

In addition to this anti-illusionistic method, Neher's use of scene-painting also serves the purposes of abstraction. His surface designs only hint at the things they depict, and his paintings are not intended to create an illusionistic effect but to open up space for reflection within the set. Neher is indebted to the aesthetic experiments of the avant-garde for the way he designs his stage sets not only to express things in a simplified way (in order to show the imperfect and the unfinished) but also to reflect roughness, squalidness and rawness as appropriate expressive qualities for the play, translated into imagery. The early sets of *In the Jungle* and *The Life of Edward II* are characterised by a visual language which points directly and ruthlessly to that which is destructive, discordant and melancholy. Neher practises showing things overtly. He gives form to dramatic qualities in surface and object. These experiments in extracting the inner expressive qualities of a drama lead, with growing experience, to a concentrated visual language which is charged with meaning in a precise and purposeful way. This design style does not overload the spectator with information but provides visual cornerstones in the 'theatre of showing, of demonstrating', in which fractures and deviations prevent a uniform picture from forming. Neher's visual language aims to create an interaction between producer and recipient, and gives no complete answers; instead it demands active, alert participation from the spectator who is willing to question what he or she is being shown.

Both the simple nature of the foreground and the elevated backdrops or projections in the background help to ensure a stage set that is highly flexible and mobile. Thin partition walls or covered frames of a light and flexible construction mean that the stage set can undergo rapid transformations.

The fact that Neher's stage set can be quickly modified according to the demands of the plot is another way in which it fulfils not a traditional, decorative function but its own dramaturgical one. It can comment and paraphrase, and thus functions almost like another actor. The dramaturgical purpose and the targeted functionalisation of the split stage, in combination with various anti-illusionistic processes such as scenic sparseness and abstract design techniques, were used again and again in Neher's set designs for Brecht's plays, and thus became increasingly established as integral elements of the stage of epic theatre.

Neher designs props with great care and precision. Both the detailed and historically accurate nature of his props and their used, worn-out look are crucial. Through the sparing use of props, the few objects that do feature in the play attract greater attention and symbolise something more than simply what they appear to be. The elements which characterise the milieu can consist of documentary material. They are real used objects, not imitation props made from cardboard or wood. Neher sets great store by material authenticity. This concern for authenticity does not spring from a desire on his part to create a naturalistic stage, however, but from the need to make objects more striking. The way actors handle authentic material can also be a key factor in its use.

The furniture is not stage furniture but real furniture that shows signs of wear and tear. The significance of these used objects goes beyond their purpose and their design; Neher has them tell us about their history and how they were used. The former use of the prop, its own historicity, serves as a statement by that prop and becomes part of the play.

Props are also used by Neher to structure space. Characters' gestures or gaits which are conditioned by the use of props influence the constructed set. The dimensions of props are sometimes made to correspond to their relative importance. And so, if necessary, Neher will alter their overall size in relation to other components. Changing the proportions of props (such as the legs of chairs or tables) changes the use of the prop, and thus also changes the play. This 'Neher height' can make any given prop seem to be a strange size, creating a V-effect. Thus the spectator also gains a new perspective on the furnishings, which should be low enough for the spectator to see over them. This usually means that Neher will lower tables and chairs to assist with certain attitudes adopted by the actors in the play. In this way, the furnishings intervene in the performance and change it. The 'Neher height' is five to ten centimetres below normal height and subjects the 'normal dimensions' of furniture (relative to human dimensions) to *Verfremdung*, not drastically but perceptibly. The height of the furniture directs the spectator's attention to the (now so necessary) way in which it is being used by the actor. The set designer's art plays a key role in what happens on stage. In 'The Playwright's Speech about the Theatre of the Set Designer Caspar Neher', Brecht refers to Neher's use of non-standard heights for furniture and doors as a helpful process for more clearly emphasising certain incidents in the play.[1]

Although Neher puts costumes completely at the service of the actors and does not envisage them functioning in an independent or a showy way, he does attach a great deal of importance to them. Costumes play many roles: they identify the character in a historical, social and personal sense. They serve to illustrate the character's personality. They can, in Neher's view, embody the inner attitude of the character. Following Brecht, Neher himself calls this the 'basic gestus' of the character. Costumes also have the task of illustrating the gestic actions of the character. In many cases this also means amplifying the gestures the character performs, augmenting them through the particular design of the costume. Neher's costumes, therefore, often have a distorted, exaggerated, caricaturing quality.

---

[1] See BFA 22.2, Schriften 2, 854.

They include wigs and masks; from the earliest experimental phase of epic theatre, Neher uses half- and three-quarter masks, as well as white face makeup, in a targeted way. Using masks, a character's facial expression can be partially fixed. By standardising a character's physiognomy in this way, Neher defines that character via an associative facet and commits them to it in a powerful way. He designs costumes the same way he designs props. Fabric quality and cut are meticulously planned and the end result carefully checked. Clothing also communicates through its use, its second-hand condition and its history. Neher's main focus is on generating a historical, social meaning for a fabric or a piece of clothing, not on ensuring that the cut or the fabric is completely historically accurate. The colour and condition of the costume – it may be faded, washed-out, ripped etc. – give a voice to associative characteristics within the play. Neher sets out these special costume designs at the draft stage. When the costumes are produced, these details have to be taken into account. For Puntila's costume, for example (German premiere: 12 November 1949), Neher chooses felt, because it doesn't stretch and therefore provides 'outlines' very strongly.[2]

As an overall design technique for the entire set, Neher uses colour with great restraint. In the costumes and in the stage set, it serves to create aesthetic unity. A colour always has a meaning and does not appear in any given place by chance. Here Neher draws on his knowledge of colour iconography in art history. He exploits opportunities to use colour to convey a great deal of information: through the way in which it is applied, the clarity of its tone, how dirty or translucent it is. The nature of this information goes far beyond the unambiguous statement of a colour value and opens up an associative space. By using colour in the most sparing way, Neher gives the colour scheme a voice within the play too. It is used for emphasis, as a dramaturgical element which highlights or ironizes the personality or function of a character or setting. In places where it is not dramaturgically important, it vanishes into an insignificant hue – the 'non-colour' grey.

The costumes form an aesthetic unit with the stage set. The material and the nature of the performance are usually tailored to each other. For *The Life of Edward II of England* (Munich, 1924), Neher draws the hessian costumes on the performers' bodies in the same way as the partition walls of the foreground in a kind of wash technique which makes them look dirty. In *Antigone* (Chur, 1948) the costumes, like the covered partition walls, are made of hessian to emphasize the archaic character of the material.

Caspar Neher gives new meaning to the use of projections in epic theatre. He himself starts experimenting with projections in the context of set design in 1925.[3] Whilst Piscator, Meyerhold and Tairov before him had all used projections on the stage much earlier (since 1915), mainly for documentary purposes, in Neher's work projections acquire the status of an independent, artistically designed image area within the stage space. It is Neher's drawings and passages of handwritten text which are transposed 1:1 onto glass plates, to appear via front or rear projection on flexible, lightweight projection screens on the stage. The projections of these drawings play very different roles throughout the play. Using the drawings, Neher can alternate the location or the time of day at which the action is taking place. Projections can thus take the place of the constructed stage set. But Neher transports the projections, through the use of his drawings, into a reality that has been subjected to artistic V-effects. It is not supposed to be a reflection of reality

---

[2]*Theaterarbeit*, 363.
[3]For the first time in 1925 for Klabund's *Der Kreidekreis* [*The Chalk Circle*] at the Deutsches Theater in Berlin, directed by Max Reinhardt.

but a commentary on reality. The demonstrated discrepancy between real scenery on the stage and a projected drawing becomes an element of 'productive disruption' or a V-effect of the stage set. The projections are independent components of the performance alongside the text and the music. The dramaturgically functionalised drawings are projected onto backdrops, partition walls, curtains and other parts of the stage. With the help of projections, elements can be integrated into the scene which it would be difficult or impossible to include or to realise using constructed three-dimensional scenery. The predominant use of projections as a dramaturgical device serves to intervene in what is happening on stage in the form of a projected drawn image or text, explaining and commenting, paraphrasing or contrasting, structuring or lending rhythm.

Quite unlike Piscator, who was interested in the documentary function of photographic projection and film, in the monumental effect of typographically composed slogans and in the constructional elements of stage design that were necessary for projection, and wanted to use these things for propaganda purposes, for Brecht's epic theatre Neher contrasts his pictorial and graphic inventions with scenic realities. From this contrast, tensions are generated which break up the unity that sometimes arises over the course of the performance. The model for a series of images shown on the stage as a way of commenting on a narrative is familiar, of course, from the world of the fairground: the *Moritatentafel* (a series of illustrations displayed on a board as a visual accompaniment to a ballad or moral tale).

The title of the play, the titles of the scenes, place names and song lyrics are also projected as handwritten text alongside the drawings. During the literarization that took place in the early days of epic theatre, passages of text were written on solid boards which were displayed and alternated manually; later, this role was taken over by image projection. Text as diagram is an integral part of the stage design and appears completely separately, as well as in the form of captions within the projected drawings. The font – whether old German script or a more functional standard typeface – also seems to aim at a characteristic quality.

After the young Neher encountered the lighting of the Expressionist stage, in which the dramaturgical use of light plays a major role, he does not attach any great importance to spotlighting in his collaboration with Brecht. The light on the stage does not take on any symbolic or illusionistic function here. Lighting effects which create certain moods or atmospheres using spotlights (which are invisible to the audience) have no dramaturgically significant function, at least on the epic stage, so they seem not to have been an explicit design element.[4] In the mid-1920s, Neher starts using exposed overhead lighting on the stage. Regardless of the play he is designing for, he always tends to use a kind of large, plain lamp with a metal shade. These lamps seem to represent the epitome of the mass-produced, simple and functional factory lighting used to illuminate the production process day and night. These ceiling lamps appear within the stage set – as a component of it, in other words – and are not concealed as part of the stage equipment. In a few productions around 1930, Neher leaves the apparatus of lighting bridges or towers visible. The hanging lamps mainly light the front part of the stage. They seem to

---

[4]When designing sets for other authors' plays, however, Neher certainly does use lighting in a scenic way and as an atmospheric tool. He also works with coloured light on these occasions. Colours are changed and thus set in motion. He uses not only spotlights but also multiple coloured projection plates to create light zones. These methods are not documented in his designs for Brecht plays.

constitute constant lighting of a uniform brightness. Even if Brecht stipulates that the epic stage should be evenly lit,[5] in practice this is not actually possible. With his unconcealed, functional light sources, however, Neher emphasises certain areas of the stage with a continuous, noticeably brighter light. To allow for the frequent projections shown in the front and rear parts of the stage, the light – at least in the upper stage area – needs to be kept dim. At best, then, the stage of the epic theatre is lit by a dull, sallow light punctuated by brighter spots in certain places (where the projections are shown or where the hanging lamps are installed).

The more or less overt scene changes, the introduction into the open performance space of hanging projection screens or boards with location details, the extension of the performance space onto the podium or into the auditorium, and the visible integration of the musicians on the stage, all reflect the demonstrative inversion of traditional space boundaries which ensure that everything used to create illusions in the theatre is hidden from the audience's gaze. The process by which stage equipment is made visible in epic theatre follows the highlighting and appreciation of these theatrical devices as artistic ones, and emphasises their presence on the stage. The technical apparatus itself is not stylised in a constructivist or abstracting sense, but it manages, precisely by being used overtly within the stage context – in the 1920s, at least – to disrupt the conventions of the theatre.[6]

Very early on, Neher starts to open up the performance space to the auditorium. He ignores the large stage curtain which usually marks out the proscenium by separating the stage from the auditorium. As well as dividing the stage into the lower foreground and the higher background areas, he separates the stage space from the auditorium using only a light, half-height curtain, which he positions on the front half of the stage in such a way that the forestage is still easily accessible. The low curtain, which is hung across the stage by a wire rope, can be easily moved and when it is closed does not completely shut off the performance space from the auditorium. Higher up, it leaves scene changes visible. It also gives the opportunity for interludes, which can be performed in front of the curtain. The curtain also acts as a projection surface for titles or images so that projections can be used in the front part of the stage.

The 'little Neher curtain', as Brecht himself described it in 1936 in his 'Notes on Plays and Performances',[7] is, again, not Neher's own invention. Simple curtains that were quick and easy to set up, like those used on the temporary stages of popular theatres or by showmen at fairgrounds, were similar in their design and use to the half-height

---

[5] In the text 'Set Design in Non-Aristotelian Drama', written in 1937/38, Brecht states, in the section entitled 'The visibility of the light sources': 'The fact that the lamp apparatus is put on display is significant, because it can be one of the means by which undesirable illusions can be prevented. [...] If we illuminate the actors' acting in such a way that the lighting equipment is visible to the spectators, then we destroy some of the illusion they may be under that they are witnessing a momentary, spontaneous, unrehearsed real event. [...]' (BFA 22.1, Schriften 2, 239). And he goes on to say, in the section entitled 'The lighting': 'The normal state is full light. [...]' (BFA 22.1, Schriften 2, 240). See also in the section 'Bright, even lighting': 'Plays in which the aim is to give the audience the pleasure of seeing the social contexts in everything the characters on stage do, will benefit from bright, even lighting. This way the audience is not as likely to daydream as they would be in dim light; they stay awake and indeed alert. The set designer can create colour and contrasts without relying on coloured light' (BFA 23, Schriften 3, 115).
[6] Carl Zuckmayer admired Neher's daring in flouting theatrical conventions – by not concealing the stage machinery, for example – during his time as set designer at the Deutsches Theater.
[7] See BFA 24, Schriften 4, 216.

curtain in epic theatre, and undoubtedly served as a model for it. In the theatre, the appearance of the half-height stage curtain is documented in 1916, having been used by Knut Ströhm for a production of *Hamlet*.[8] Neher experiments with the half-height curtain from 1923 onwards, and his drafts show that he plans to use it at the premiere of *In the Jungle* (Munich, 1923). The realities of the revolving stage at Munich's Residenztheater, however, lead him to opt for completely exposed scene changes. Only afterwards does he develop the curtain into a regular stylistic device of epic theatre. For Brecht, Neher uses the half-height curtain on the stage for the first time at the premiere of *Man Equals Man*, at the Landestheater in Darmstadt in 1926. The half-height curtain appears as a step on the way to the curtainless, completely open semi-circular stage Neher designs for the *Antigone* production, on which – inspired by the presence of the chorus on stage – all the actors can be seen even before they make their entrances.

---

[8]See Monika Wyss, *Brecht in der Kritik. Rezensionen aller Brecht Uraufführungen. Sowie ausgewählter deutsch- und fremdsprachiger Premieren* (Munich: Kindler, 1977), 51.

Helene Weigel

CHAPTER TEN

Helene Weigel

BERTOLT BRECHT
TRANSLATED BY ROMY FURSLAND

HELENE WEIGEL is one of Germany's most interesting actresses. She had her first spectacular successes at the age of seventeen in Frankfurt am Main which, after Berlin, is the most important city in Germany for theatre. She was then taken on at the *Staatstheater* in Berlin, where she acted in the classics. But she also performed at *Max Reinhardt's Deutsches Theater*. When *Brecht* was developing a completely new style of theatre at Berlin's *Schiffbauerdammtheater*, she (who had played almost exclusively classical roles up to that point) put her talents entirely in the service of this new theatre, the most modern in Germany.

What is special about her is her ability to blend stylised theatre and realistic theatre, and to portray the most ordinary working women (her most famous role was the *Mother* in a play based on Gorky's novel) so that they seem as graceful and noble as queens, and then again to play the queens of classical theatre (like Mary Stuart and Lady Macbeth) with great humour and the most unpretentious humanity.

In exile, she performed with unprecedented success in Paris and Copenhagen in Brecht's last two plays.

Brecht, 'Helene Weigel', in Brecht, *Schriften*, vol. 2 (Berlin and Frankfurt/Main: Aufbau and Suhrkamp, 1993), pp. 609–10.

CHAPTER ELEVEN

Weigel's Figuration and Defiguration in Brecht's Texts

PATRICK PRIMAVESI
TRANSLATED BY ROMY FURSLAND

In Bertolt Brecht's texts and poems Helene Weigel comes across as *the* actress of a new theatre which begins and develops with her. We find not only descriptions of the actress and her performances, but sketches of a figure between roles, silhouettes of a *persona* between the representation and the represented. The way the author portrayed the actress – and at the same time his work as a director – as a historic event, is calculated with an eye to posthumous fame in which everything human takes on phantom-like qualities. Thus Weigel's historicising acting style, which is built on showing and referencing and which, with the storehouse of symbols constituted by her props, masks and gestures, can already be understood as a scenic form of textualisation, has reached a paradoxical stage of survival in Brecht's 'documents'. The combination of praise, interpretation and defence sometimes renders the epic acting style ghostly, by dissolving the individual features of the actress and her interpretations of her roles, exposing them to a countermovement of *defiguration*. And Weigel in particular is frequently invested with 'profoundly human', animal-like and also asocial traits which associate her with a theatre of cruelty that runs counter to her self-image. This essay will explore such contradictions by outlining a (by no means comprehensive) series of role portraits and character masks. For Brecht, at any rate, there seems to have been more at stake in his portrayal of Weigel than an acknowledgement of his loyal partner in life and in work – her recurrence in his texts proves to be both a necessary and an impossible, utopian supplement to their joint theatre work.

Theatre deals with death, in that the actor's 'present' makes it possible for the audience to experience an intertwining of absence and presence. In a play with symbolic representation, which hides as much as it shows, the theatre retains something of the fascination we have with customs and ceremonies – even when it sees itself as criticising or overcoming these customs and ceremonies. A corresponding ambivalence, which shapes many modern conceptions of theatre in their attitudes to culture and ritual, can be found

---

Patrick Primavesi, 'Gestalt und Entstaltung der Weigel in Texten Brechts', *Brecht Yearbook*, 25 (2000), pp. 190–213.

in Brecht's work in particular. He often described the *Lehrstücke* and epic theatre in the age of science and technology as a secularisation of religious institutions, and thus rejected all kinds of magic, illusion and spells as fixtures of bourgeois artistic theatre. At the same time there are traces not only of Asiatic theatre but also of ancient tragedy in Brecht's work, and these frustrate the agenda of an expulsion of ritual or a 'total rationalisation' of mythical relics, if they do not obstruct it altogether. These traces of tragedy in Brecht coincide particularly with Weigel's performances – Weigel, the protagonist of epic and supposedly completely *untragic* theatre. Brecht almost seems to see her work as being strongly linked with the process of ancient theatre, which also goes one step beyond myth and can be seen as a challenge to ritual practices. At any rate, two of Weigel's roles that were particularly important to Brecht were from tragedies: from Sophocles' plays about Oedipus and Antigone. In both productions Brecht reflected on moments of enlightenment, and started working towards the idea of experiences of helplessness and pain not simply being attested by the theatrical performance but, on the contrary, being put up for discussion. This is also about the 'material value' of tragedies, which can only be released through new ways of staging and acting; about their realistic core and their inherent potential of gestures and ritual actions or behaviours. As his commentaries on these performances show, the appearance of Weigel in Brecht's texts documents his engagement with ceremonial structures in the theatre.

In the two essays written at the beginning of 1929, 'Latest Stage: Oedipus' and 'Dialogue on Acting', Brecht reacted to Leopold Jessner's production of *King Oedipus* and *Oedipus at Colonus* in a version by Heinz Lipmann at the Schauspielhaus in Berlin. (Fritz Kortner played Oedipus, Helene Weigel played Jocasta's maidservant, and Lotte Lenya played Ismene). Both texts were published in February 1929 in the *Berliner Börsen-Courier*, with the first one accompanied by a preliminary editorial note stating that Brecht would draw conclusions 'from Jessner's *Oedipus* production for an epic drama of the future'.[1] In fact Brecht describes this *Oedipus* work as the latest stage in a rapid revolution in drama and theatre. The main conclusion to be drawn, he claims, is that the new subjects of the age call for a new form of theatre: 'the traditional major form – the dramatic form – is not suitable for contemporary subject matter. To put it bluntly, for those in the business: today's subject matter cannot be expressed in the old "major" form' (BFA 22: 279). Brecht insists on the necessity of a *major form*, but says it must be epic, and must overcome empathy. Just as his text begins with a reference to philosophy ('The future of the theatre is a philosophical one'), it ends with a look at the techniques in the second half of Jessner's production, *Oedipus at Colonus*, concluding that the 'experience', if it comes from anywhere, comes from the philosophical realm. Thus the political interest of the text – Brecht also wants to be able to represent subjects as 'monstrous' as the wheat exchange – is embedded in a philosophical one. This points ahead to the role the Philosopher will play in *Buying Brass*: changing the function of the theatre, turning an institution focused solely on empathy into a place of enjoyable thinking (in this context too, the figure of Weigel will play an important role). In 'Dialogue on Acting', which appeared as a follow-up to the text about the major form, Brecht outlined acting styles which would convey to the public a new knowledge of human relationships, attitudes

---

[1] See Bertolt Brecht, *Werke. Große kommentierte Berliner und Frankfurter Ausgabe*, ed. Werner Hecht, Jan Knopf, Werner Mittenzwei and Klaus-Detlef Müller (Berlin and Weimar: Aufbau, Frankfurt am Main: Suhrkamp, 1988–99), cited hereinafter with volume number and page number. Here BFA 22: 710.

and capacities. Instead of the actors using 'hypnosis', putting both themselves and the audience into a trance, as they usually did, the performance should be accompanied by showing and recognising; the progress of the play should be characterised by distancing:

> Spiritual. Ceremonial. Ritualistic. Spectator and actor should not come close to each other but should distance themselves from each other. And each should be distanced from him- or herself. Otherwise the element of shock necessary for recognition is lacking.
>
> (BFA 22: 280)[2]

From this cursory answer to the question of what the new theatrical processes would look like, it is clear that Brecht wanted to counter the familiar praxis of empathy with spiritual, ceremonial and ritualistic moments. These, however, were to be thought of as replacing any belief in fate.[3]

No recognition without shock – this encapsulates the idea of *learning through suffering* which is put forward in Aeschylus's *Oresteia*. And *distancing oneself from oneself*, which is necessary for shock, corresponds to a technique of distancing which was central to ancient theatre: masks, stylised speech, demonstrative gestures. What Brecht outlines as a new technique is closer to ancient theatre, at any rate, than to the bourgeois theatre fixated on empathy and psychology. Brecht argues that it is not human beings themselves who are to be made comprehensible, but processes; and for this to happen it is necessary for the audience to experience the 'full strangeness and incomprehensibility' of actions and characters. This new technique, which is also supposed to liberate the actor from being dependent upon the tastes of the audience, cannot be introduced *gradually*, according to Brecht, because it amounts to 'adopting an entirely different purpose' for the theatre. Thus Weigel's acting had demonstrated the last stage of the major form to be the first stage of the new theatre, summarised in epic fashion in Brecht's report:

> When an actress of this new sort was playing the servant in *Oedipus*, she announced the death of her mistress by proclaiming 'dead, dead' in a completely emotionless, piercing voice, her cry of 'Jocasta is dead' was devoid of any sorrow, but pronounced so firmly and inexorably that the bare fact of her mistress's death created a more powerful impression at that precise moment than could have been generated by any grief of her own. Horror did not conquer her voice, then, although it did her face – she used white make-up to signify the impact a death makes on those who witness it. In her report of how the suicidal woman had collapsed as if before a slave-driver, there was not so much pity for the woman as there was a sense of the slave-driver's triumph, so that even the most sentimental spectators could not fail to realise that a decision had just been made that called for their consent. She described with astonishment, in a single lucid sentence, the dying woman's ravings and apparent irrationality, and though the unambiguous tone of her 'And how she ended we do not know', she signalled her

---

[2] Translation taken from *Brecht on Theatre*, ed. Marc Silberman, Steve Giles and Tom Kuhn (London: Bloomsbury Methuen Drama, 2015), 46.

[3] A similar view is put forward by Wolfgang Pasche who, with regard to Brecht's *Lehrstück* theory, arrives at the phrase 'liquidation of the ritualistic' precisely through a ritual acting style. This does, however, mask the individual and in many cases also particularly productive contradictions in favour of an overall concept, which Brecht dispensed with in this context, probably not by accident. See Pasche, 'Die Funktion des Rituellen in Brechts Lehrstücken *Der Jasager* und *Der Neinsager*', in *Acta Germanica* 13 (1980), 137–150.

refusal to give any further information about the death – a meagre yet unshakeable tribute. But she descended the few steps from the stage with such long strides that her slight figure seemed to cover an immense distance between the empty scene of the tragedy and the people below stage. And as she raised her arms in mechanical lamentation, she asked at the same time for pity for herself, the one who had witnessed the catastrophe, and with her loud '*now* you may lament' she seemed to deny the validity of any previous, less well-founded regrets.

(BFA 22: 281–2)[4]

This is the first time Weigel makes a major appearance in Brecht's texts, as a 'slight figure' in a report which itself underlines reporting as a formal principle. The actress's performance is historicised as an epoch-making event, demonstrating the servant's astonishment at her mistress's ravings and reporting the death in a voice completely free of emotion, whilst at the same time leaving room for enough of a sense of horror (using her face, make-up and posture) that the death could triumph as a 'bare fact' and the spectators could be asked to give their consent. The meaning of the scene was to show, in a very specific way which elicited agreement, the impact 'a death makes on those who witness it'. This reporting style, however, is achieved at the expense of a traditional aesthetic of character – the white make-up and the emotionless voice can be interpreted as the defiguration of the person, in accordance with Brecht's idea of a neutralisation or effacement of the individual. With this tendency, which is particularly associated with the *Lehrstücke*, the text follows Weigel's descent from the empty space of the atrocities to those beneath the stage – the People. Hardly anybody seems to have registered the moment, however, apart from Brecht, who worked with Weigel on this performance. What is so new about it is recognised only in his commentary, which establishes the significance of the moment as well as its lack of impact on the audience:

> What sort of a reception did she get? / A pretty modest one, from everyone except a few connoisseurs. Wrapped up in empathising with the characters' emotions, hardly anyone had participated in the intellectual decisions that make up the action. That terrible decision she had communicated had almost no effect on those people who saw it merely as an opportunity for new emotions.
>
> (BFA 22: 282)[5]

The new acting style is still dependent upon an as-yet-unattained art of spectating. Still, Weigel's report of the death of Jocasta makes it more difficult for the audience to empathise, so that 'even the most sentimental spectators could not fail to realise that a decision had just been made that called for their consent' (BFA 22: 282). The decision Brecht is interested in with regard to the portrayal of the death in *Oedipus*, as part of the last stage of the old major form, is a decision in favour of both a new kind of theatre and a new attitude on the part of the spectators, who must reflect on their involvement in the violence that has been reported to them.

The manuscript versions of the texts show that Brecht, with his reflections on the new major form of the theatre, already had the example of Weigel in mind and that without

---

[4]Translation taken from *Brecht on Theatre*, ed. Marc Silberman, Steve Giles and Tom Kuhn (London: Bloomsbury Methuen Drama, 2015), 47.
[5]Translation: ibid., 48.

her he would probably not have emphasised the importance of Jessner's production the way he did. An initial sketch for an addition to the first text describes the 'slight figure' in more detail:

> She is small in stature, well-proportioned and robust. Her head is large and well-formed. Her face narrow, soft, with a high, somewhat domed forehead and strong lips. Her voice is rich and dark and pleasant even in sharpness or in a shout. Her movements are precise and soft. / What is her character like? / She is good-natured, gruff, brave and dependable. She is unpopular.
>
> (BFA 22: 711f.)

This paragraph, written as a type of scene in response to the imperative 'Describe her!', falls midway between the role and the person, and lets each shine through in the other. Thus Brecht sculpts a portrait of Weigel which oscillates between the role of a messenger of death, her stage presence as an actor and her real being – the writing style accomplishes what the stage performance should have achieved. Not without irony, the comment 'even in sharpness or in a shout' alludes to the fact that Weigel stood out early on in her career thanks to her voice, which was both flexible and piercing.[6] The final sentence, 'She is unpopular', elevates the actress above the level of trying to curry favour with audiences, but also, as a postscript to the traits 'good-natured, gruff, brave and dependable', points primarily to the person as she appeared behind the scenes, in everyday life. Brecht, by giving his description a realistic slant, stylises himself as the creator of this Weigel figure. This matter-of-fact characterisation marks the way Brecht talks about Weigel in general – there is a tension between showing and being shown, figure and defiguration, especially with regard to success, shock and learning. Her individual physiognomy is so distorted that Weigel can seem like a surface for the author to project his self-portrayal onto,[7] and at the same time like the site of a new theatre. This tendency is also noticeable in the texts written in connection with Weigel's performance in Brecht's *Antigone Model*.

With the *Antigone* production in 1948 in the Swiss city of Chur, Brecht – newly returned from exile – was attempting to counter the 'techniques of the Göring-theatre' whose 'radiance' was so often admired, as well as a decline in the art of both acting and spectating (BFA 25: 73). Through its dialectic of specification and changeability, *Antigone Model* shows that the theatre can only be certain of the subject matter and texts of its tradition on a trial basis, at the moment of working on them, but not in the grip of what is supposedly timeless. The many interventions in the text of Hölderlin's translation focus the plot of the tragedy on an exploration of the problems caused by tyrannical abuses

---

[6] See the critiques in the volume *Helene Weigel zu ehren. Zum 70. Geburtstag von Helene Weigel am 12. Mai 1970*, ed. Werner Hecht and Siegfried Unseld (Frankfurt am Main, 1970), 101ff.

[7] Brecht's tendency to reflect himself 'physically' in actresses is described by Marieluise Fleißer in her biographically tinged story *Avantgarde*: 'The woman had to be an actress so that he could express himself directly through her. That was the true complement to a man like him, it was a vital need for him. That was what he could really do something with, and that helped him progress, because then he could see himself physically. [...] When a woman only wrote she was quickly brushed aside, that wasn't an eternal work. He could do that himself.' (*Gesammelte Werke* 3 [Frankfurt am Main, 1983], 136f.) This distinction is informative, even if it obscures the importance of Brecht's relationships with women. In Weigel's case we can assume that the possibility of expressing himself through her as a woman not only shaped the roles Brecht wrote for her but also his texts about her and about her acting (whereby her anticipated fame as an actress which he writes about in these texts was to contribute to the fame of Brecht's 'eternal work', which he had certainly not produced *in isolation*.)

of power. However, the chorus of old men paying homage to the 'god of pleasure' can hardly be interpreted as a resistance movement, and Antigone is complicit because she has endured subjugation by Creon for too long, and through her desperate act she actually helps the enemy while bringing down destruction upon her own people. Thus the text is not simply 'rationalised through and through' or 'purged of idols'. On the fundamental question of whether the actors should perform inside the circle of 'barbaric totem poles with horses skulls' or outside of it, Brecht and his set designer Caspar Neher were in agreement: 'We decided the action should take place between the poles – after all, we are still living in the totemic state of the class struggle!' (BFA 27: 261). Another entry in the *Journal* is even clearer; its criticism of classical trivialisation is also directed at Brecht's own version: '*Antigone* in its entirety belongs among the barbaric horses' skulls. The play is by no means entirely rationalised, only' (BFA 27: 265). Here the text breaks off; the extent of rationalisation that may or may not have been achieved is left open. The barbaric site of the old poem cannot simply be left behind, at any rate, and this decision made for the first performance is exemplary in that it manifests the indissolubility and at the same time the productivity of a conflict between theatre, myth and enlightenment.

If Brecht was forced to qualify the planned rationalisation of the play based on practical experiences, the same goes for the acting style. Again, Weigel was the model for this. The entire undertaking, including the text version, came about because Brecht, after Weigel's long break from acting during their time in exile, wanted to prepare for her fresh start in Berlin: 'Between 30/11 and 12/12 I finished an "Antigone" *adaptation*, because I want to prepare Courage for Berlin with *Weigel* and *Cas*, and I can do that in Chur, where Curjel is based, but to do it I need a second role for *Weigel*' (BFA 27: 255).

One very revealing comment about acting styles is Brecht's criticism (noted during the rehearsal period) of the 'homely moralistic tone' of the German Stanislavsky edition. In contrast to this, Brecht emphasises fun and an antisocial quality as necessary elements of acting: 'If actors are too decorous, how can they possibly summon up the dark stores of vitality (unsocialised life force) found in the realm of the antisocial?' (BFA 27: 261). This marks out a boundary which Brecht probably also tried to transcend as the director of the actress Weigel, by questioning and examining epic acting styles.[8] After a certain point, the construction of a stage role had to turn back into its dissolution in order to make the tensions of the figure productive (without letting the figure get lost in the individuality of the character or any kind of positive lesson). The extent to which this was possible during the work on *Antigone Model* can be roughly reconstructed from Brecht's own comments and from critiques. Despite rather makeshift working conditions, the play seems to have managed to create effects out of what were ostensibly mistakes – in the casting, for example (Weigel, who was really too old to play Antigone, was acting opposite Hans Gaugler, who was really too young to play Creon). The difficulties that arose during rehearsals, however, were to do with the fact that the staging concept – according to Hans Curjel, 'Weigel set the exemplary tone of the gestus for the actors'[9] – was not understood

---

[8]On the tension between epic and identificatory acting styles in Brecht's theatre work – a relationship based more on practice than on preconceived ideas – see also John Rouse, 'Brecht and the Contradictory Actor', in *Acting (Re)Considered*, ed. Phillip B. Zarrilli (London, 1995), 228–241.

[9]Hans Curjel, 'Brechts Antigone-Inszenierung in Chur 1948', reprinted in *Brechts Antigone des Sophokles*, ed. Werner Hecht (Frankfurt am Main, 1988), 189.

by all the actors and even Weigel herself was not able to do it consistently. Brecht himself highlighted this in a letter to Curjel on 7 February 1948:

> With Weigel it's like with Laughton; the epic style of acting can only defend itself against a surrounding dramatic style, it cannot go on the attack; and there is no middle ground for such an actor to fall back on – a moment of thoughtlessness and the curve is warped, irreparable for the performance and in need of more rehearsal.
>
> (BFA 29: 444)

In the confrontation between different acting styles, the epic style was isolated. As Brecht writes in his preface to *Antigone Model*, the play features 'much that is unintentional and provisional' because the actors, apart from Weigel, 'do their own thing, so to speak' – particularly in the field of gesture. The work was shaped by the consumer society in which it was performed: the actors were all acting 'with very different aims' (BFA 25: 80). The reference to possible mistakes by Weigel suggests that Brecht could not consider the intended overall effect to have been achieved so long as the play could only be 'repaired' from the outside. Thus the reliance on another rehearsal, and possibly a director who would have to reconstruct the 'curve', reveals further inadequacies of epic acting – the fact that it had to make 'mistakes' in order to be effective, but also that its effect could be unsuccessful and require intervention by the author and director Brecht. The parallels with Brecht's comments about Jessner's *Oedipus* production are evident. What the *Antigone* production was supposed to herald in the way of innovations, 'both for theatre people and for those who want to become spectators' (BFA 29: 444), are again mainly to be found in Brecht's statements about Weigel's acting. The Modelbook makes reference to the fact that Weigel was the only person who, when playing tragedy, could perform the gestus of showing and changeability with the necessary naturalness. Here too, however, audiences failed to pick up on Weigel's technique of exhibiting her own acting as a model, as the generally sympathetic reviews show: 'In accordance with the intentions of the creator and director, she perfectly embodied this heroic woman whose heroism was based on her quiet majesty and simple insistence on her perceived duty'[10] or the similarly cliché-ridden: 'Simple, human, with almost prosaic diction, she played Antigone as a passionate but also a heroic and dignified woman. A character among many villainous characters.'[11] The 'mask-like nature of the Antigone actress' was remarked upon, at least;[12] but otherwise the innovations of Weigel's acting style seem to have gone largely unnoticed.[13] While the work was still going on, Brecht – who was used to critics misunderstanding him – came to the sceptical conclusion with regard to his plays that the author could only save himself by 'giving up the substance or (and) providing his own programme notes' (*Journal*, 7.1.1948,

---

[10] Andreas Brügger, 'Gelungene Aufführung der *Antigone*', *Bündner Tageblatt*, Chur, 18 and 19 February 1948, in *Brechts Antigone des Sophokles*, 201.

[11] C.S., 'Eine Antigone Bert Brechts (Zur Uraufführung im Stadttheater Chur)', *Tagesanzeiger*, Zurich, 19 February 1948, in *Brechts Antigone des Sophokles*, 205.

[12] Be., 'Antigone, ein Trauerspiel von Sophokles. Uraufgeführt zu Athen im Jahre 442 B.C.', *Neue Bündner Zeitung*, 18 February 1948, in *Brechts Antigone des Sophokles*, 195.

[13] See also Weigel's own assessment of the performance as a preparation for Berlin: 'As far as I was concerned it was an experiment, and Brecht created it for that purpose too. [...] The experiment turned out well for me. We discovered we could still stage plays. You can't take something like that for granted after a long break! But of course Chur was not the right place for a popular success.' From an interview with Werner Hecht in November 1969, in *Brechts Antigone des Sophokles*, 182.

BFA 27: 263). This, he declared, was due to the ability of the bourgeois acting style to assimilate everything that was foreign to it ('everything from antiquity, the Asiatic realm, the Middle Ages'). An anti-bourgeois and also anti-moralistic engagement with tradition must therefore remain ambiguous.[14] This was even more true of an acting style which, in a new version of the tragedy which was ostensibly aiming to update it, dispensed with *immediacy*. As Brecht explains in the dialogues in the Modelbook, what Weigel's acting generated above all was distance from herself: 'Like everything else, Weigel played Antigone going to her death as if it was a famous scene, both as a historical event and as a theatrical one; indeed, she played it almost as if her own acting in this scene was famous' (BFA 25: 132). With the chronological perspective of fame as a future past, Weigel's portrayal of Antigone is assimilated into Brecht's writing process just like her performance as the maidservant in the *Oedipus* production. This is not just to do with the anticipation of an as-yet-unachieved success, but is also about playing with absences: the text reveals that the centre around which the ceremony revolves is actually empty and that the divide between person and role can also be interpreted as a defiguration insofar as it symbolically represents a person going to her death, and refrains from actually depicting it. By visibly stepping outside the horses' skull shrine, Weigel portrayed dying as a scenic process and as a dissolution of the role-fiction. Even more so than the report of Jocasta's death in *Oedipus*, which led Weigel to 'the people beneath the stage', 'Antigone going to her death' is portrayed as 'going the way of all flesh', *ad plures ire*. Again, Brecht's writing style mainly brings out Weigel's handling of the ceremonial potential of tragedy: instead of exhausting itself in the pathos of the scene, as in the bourgeois conception of tragic acting, the shock of recognition should also apply to the framework of the performance, and involve the spectator in an 'analytical' form of empathy.

The reference to the spiritual, ceremonial and ritual quality of the new acting style with its intended effect ('each should be distanced from him- or herself') describes nothing other than the ability to die. Thus Brecht's reflections on Weigel's portrayal of Antigone show acting to be an anticipation of death in the sense of the loss of any ability to play a figure. Based on the text about the major form as the last 'stage' (which has by no means yet been overcome), Weigel's acting also stands for the ceremonial function of a new theatre, demonstrating the charged relationship between figuration and defiguration. This is also evident in the transition from performing tragedy as a 'tester' or 'preview', to the performance of *Mother Courage and her Children* in Berlin. This transition can be seen from two poems in which the act of showing keeps the figure in limbo:

> Come out of the twilight and walk
> Before us a while
> Friendly one, with the light step
> Of the determined, terrible
> To the terrible.
>
> You who turn away, I know
> How you feared death, but

---

[14]See the entry in Brecht's *Work Journal* on 10 April 1948: 'Everything in me resists hearing the new version of *Antigone* called a moral play. [...] It is dangerous to want to enforce a moral mission upon art, unless you are in a position to see the morals that are practical for a particular period of time in all their relativity – and who could do that?' (BFA 27: 267).

Even more did you fear
Unworthy life.

And you did not let the powerful
Do as they wished, and did not reconcile yourself
To the obfuscators, nor did you ever
Forget dishonour, and the grass did not grow
Over their crimes.
I salute you!

(BFA 15: 191)

The poem was written in Chur, and first appeared in the programme for the premiere of *Antigone Model* on 15 February 1948. It is titled 'Antigone' and contains allusions to the subject matter of the play which, however, could also refer to the 'Fate of Weigel in Exile'.[15] The first stanza opens up this perspective, once again oscillating between role and person, with the scene of the performance itself, which the author as director and representative of the audience demands of the actress – for a brief moment before death, for the limited time of the performance. The stepping out of the twilight would be the moment in which the figures overlap each other. It almost seems as though the attitude of the Brecht actress Weigel becomes the model for Antigone and not the other way around. The third stanza goes so far as to edit out Antigone's involvement in the injustice of power, which is implied in the text of the new version, and to celebrate the consequence of her defiance with a kind of final acknowledgement in the form of a military salute. If the poem alludes to the plot of the play, it aims above all – in the tone of an obituary for a tragic heroine – to reintroduce the actress. This gestus is resumed in the poem below (which is in many ways related to the 'Antigone' poem). This second poem takes the portrayal of Mother Courage as an opportunity to let the actress show 'what is right' and 'her good face':

And now step in your easy way
Onto the old stage of this ruined city
Full of patience but also implacable
Showing what is right.

Show what is foolish with wisdom
Show hatred with kindness
Where the house has collapsed
Show that the plans were flawed.

But show the unteachable
With a little hope
Your good face.

(BFA 15: 203)

This poem too, which was dedicated to Helene Weigel on the occasion of the premiere of *Mother Courage and her Children* on 11 January 1949, lets the actress appear as an actress. Again the author/director's invitation proves to be a mode of realisation or visualisation – he wants to see his figure before him and the audience *now*, on the stage of the ruined city, implacably kind. The task of showing the unteachable person her 'good face' is related

---

[15] See the note in the editor's comment on this poem (BFA 15: 426).

to the cliché of the permanently good-natured woman, which Brecht explored in various permutations. Thus the actress stands for the 'little hope' that acting can change things. The complementarity of the good and the bad face, which is also found in *The Good Person of Szechuan*, does not lead much further here, however. Where Brecht concerns himself with the actress as an actress, it is more a question of the reverse side of the mask, a non-face, which remains as far away from the real person as from the rounded figure of a dramatic character.

What the poems explicitly devoted to Weigel and her roles frequently disguise, due to their ideological focus, comes across much more overtly in Brecht's comments on his plays (where Brecht himself is not spared either). Several other texts about *Courage* make this particularly clear: the perspective undergoes a large-scale revision in the process of being updated. The elevation of Weigel to an icon not only for a theatre of the new age but also for a workers' state committed to peace is famously embodied in the following poem:

> The theatre of the new age
> Was established when, onto the stage
> Of a ruined Berlin,
> Rolled Mother Courage's wagon.
> A year and a half later
> At the 1st of May demonstration
> Mothers showed Weigel to their children
> And praised peace.
>
> (BFA 15: 226)

The inspiration for this poem was the experience of the 1 May celebrations in Berlin in 1950. As Brecht initially noted in his *Journal*, on that 'radiant day' he was able to watch the demonstration from a platform in the Lustgarten. He writes that there were also 'an astonishing number of districts from West Berlin' taking part. 'The Berliner Ensemble goes by on its float, Barbara is sitting on Courage's wagon waving a red flag. Helli is greeted all the way along the route. Women actually hold their children up for a better view: "It's Mother Courage!"' (BFA 27: 311f.) The delight at Weigel's success seems to segue seamlessly into the praising of peace, as if Courage's wagon had played a part in securing the peace of the new age. A different assessment appears in the review Brecht wrote in 1953 (on the occasion of a new production in Copenhagen), entitled 'Courage Learns Nothing', which reflects on certain misunderstandings. At the time of its creation at the beginning of the Second World War, writes Brecht, the play had come too late even to Scandinavia, and by the time it arrived on the Berlin stage it merely confirmed the 'disaster' of the lost war without really being able to question it:

> When Courage's wagon rolled onto the German stage in 1949, the play explained the immense destruction that Hitler's war had inflicted. The ragged clothes on the stage resembled the ragged clothes in the auditorium. [...] Weigel played Courage harshly and angrily; that is to say, her Courage was not angry but she, the actress, was. She depicted a trader, strong and cunning, who loses her children one after the other to the war and still believes there is profit to be made from the war. [...] The success of the play, i.e. the impression it made, was undoubtedly great. People pointed to Weigel in the street and said: That's Courage! But I do not believe and I did not believe at the time that Berlin – and all the other cities that saw the play – understood the play. They were all convinced they had learned from the war; they did not understand that

Courage had learnt nothing from her war, in the playwright's opinion. They did not see what the playwright believed: that people learn nothing from war.

(BFA 24: 272f.)

The playwright sees his prophecies confirmed: 'The war would not only bring them suffering, but also the inability to learn from it.' In an almost word-for-word repetition of certain lines of the poem, the excitement of the people in the street when they see Weigel is mentioned, but now in the context of doubting whether they have learnt anything. The audience, too, learns nothing – a bitter realisation to which Brecht, in the (posthumously published) Modelbook of the production, can only respond with a repeated call for a new acting style: 'for the spectators to learn something, the theatre must develop an acting style which does not aim to make the spectator identify with the main character (heroine)' (BFA 25: 241). It would be necessary to learn 'non-learning', however. The altered acting style would have to reflect its own failure and give it back to the audience. This would mean that Weigel's anger could be interpreted thus: 'her Courage was not angry but she, the actress, was'. As stated in the Modelbook, the distancing of the actor from the role should also demonstrate the role's own dialectic. Thus Weigel's face, even when she was portraying Courage's wickedness, had shown 'a glimmer of wisdom and even nobility' to make clear that her attitude was the result of her circumstances: 'by doing this, she herself at least stays aloof to some extent from the fact that she is giving an insight into this weakness, indeed showing anger about it' (BFA 25: 206). Yet this somewhat watered-down interpretation of the anger suggests that the real problem of the play can only become apparent in a dissolution of the figure, by means of the exposed contradiction between empathy and showing. Ultimately Brecht had to admit the danger of identification with acting that was too successful: 'The audience will only reinforce its own tendencies to resignation and capitulation – and will allow itself the pleasure of standing above itself into the bargain' (BFA 25: 207). This comfortable self-affirmation could not really be prevented – at most it could be disrupted by exposing the character as a concrete scenic manifestation of that anger:

DENIAL

Courage sits with her daughter standing beside her, holding her hand. When the soldiers come in with the dead man and she is asked to look at him she stands up, goes over to him, looks at him, shakes her head and goes to sit back down again. All the while she has a grimly determined look: her lower lip juts out. Weigel's boldness in exposing the character reached its peak here. (The actor playing the Sergeant can invoke the astonishment of the spectators by turning to his men with a look of astonishment at such harshness.)

(BFA 25: 203)

At the point in the play where Courage denies her dead son, Brecht claims that Weigel 'exposes' her character. This double 'denial' is played out on her face. Thus Courage's mask has been defigured by the actress's tension, and astonishment at this technical 'boldness' is important. In this way the text portrays Weigel's acting as a ceremony of defiguration – the suffering in the depicted situation is deconstructed, sometimes carried over into a *dismantling* of the role.

In this context, Brecht's attempt to compare his play with the tradition of tragic theatre is also very revealing. Although he rejected the numerous interpretations of the play as a modern Niobe tragedy, it is striking that he himself gave the title 'Finnish Niobe' to his early notes on the material (BFA 24: 258). In contrast to the mother whose children are killed by a jealous goddess, however, Courage is prepared to risk the deaths of her children due to her stubborn belief in the economy of war. The character is thus far more reminiscent of Medea than Niobe; Medea kills her children in an act of hatred, revenge and self-destruction. As early as 1939, the suggestion that Courage is 'no Antigone' aims to prevent the character being seen as heroic. In the post-war era too, it was important to Brecht to dismantle the cliché of the mother figure who overcomes the unjust blows of fate. And yet: in the reflection 'Mother Courage Played in Two Ways',[16] which he wrote in 1951, Brecht contrasted the popular 'triumph over the indestructibility of a vigorous person who has been beset by the trials of war' with Weigel's technique, which had prevented total empathy precisely by demonstrating the tragic nature of the character.

> Here too, trade was a natural source of income, but a polluted one from which Courage drank death. The trader-mother became a great living contradiction, and it was this contradiction which disfigured and deformed her beyond recognition. [...] The tragic nature of Courage and her life, which was profoundly perceptible to the audience, consisted in the fact that here was a horrifying contradiction which was destroying a human being, a contradiction which could be resolved but only by society itself and in long, terrible battles.
>
> (BFA 23: 409f.)

Exposing the contradiction no longer allows for any kind of unifying figure (e.g. that of a suffering mother or that of a mercenary trader) – on the contrary, the tension which Brecht describes here as being a 'profoundly perceptible' tragedy leads to the destruction of the figure, a disfigurement and deformation 'beyond recognition'. The learning of non-learning is realised therein in a contradictory and thoroughly inhumane way. At least as important as the reference to the tragic as the defiguration of the character is the observation of Weigel's animalistic traits; the fact that, in the scene on the battlefield, she was 'every inch the hyena' and that she pounced on the soldiers with the coat, cursing, 'like a tigress' (BFA 23: 409). Or one of the most remarkable details from the Modelbook: 'In one of the later performances, as she set off again, Weigel threw up her head and shook it, like a tired old war horse getting ready to move on. The gesture is almost impossible to imitate' (BFA 25: 228). The imitation of the animal becomes *almost* impossible to imitate through the gesture with which once again the inhuman is shown in an exposing of the character, through a defiguration of the figure. Brecht subsequently interpreted Weigel's other roles in a similar way, as being shaped by a technique which, precisely in its intimate relationship with death, had to go beyond mastering an epic, distancing acting style. Thus these comments can be understood as a critical reflection on his earlier plans for an epic theatre and a theatre of *Lehrstücke*. It is significant that Brecht's theatre work, for all his interest in secularisation, remained reliant on 'unsocialised drives' and on a tragic logic of the split subject. Inherent in the plays that are most important for Weigel is a dynamic of self-sacrifice whereby the various mother roles remain ambiguous and contradictory:

---

[16]From the collection *Dialectics in the Theatre*, which appeared in 1956 as the 37th issue of the *Versuche*. A preliminary note on the application of materialist dialectics references the fact that the term 'epic theatre' 'is ever more in need of such elaboration of its substance' (BFA 23: 603).

as well as Courage, they include Pelegea Vlassova in *The Mother* and the fisherwoman in *Señora Carrar's Rifles*. But particularly where Brecht describes Weigel's acting in the brutal scenes these figures are given, the transitional function of the old major form becomes visible as the matrix of every new form; an idealistic logic of victimhood and the associated aesthetic of the figure must be replaced by the process of defiguration which affects both the role and the appearance of the actress. Brecht's comments become the site of this process by reflecting the provisional nature of all theatrical solutions.

The fact that Weigel's commitment to acting in Brecht's plays not only improved her acting but saved her from a career in traditional theatre is hardly in doubt. In *Buying Brass*, Brecht summed up this development again by historicising representation, starting with Weigel's magical power to make the spectators 'cry when she laughed and laugh when she cried.' At this point her real achievement becomes clear: 'Weigel's Descent into Fame': 'For once she had mastered her art and wanted to appear before the biggest audience – the people – and apply her art to the biggest themes – the ones which concerned the people – she completely lost her standing and her descent began' (BFA 22: 796). Thus this sharp decline in Weigel's career appears as the traversing of a symbolic death. Again, the descent – like the descent of the maidservant in *Oedipus*, or Antigone going to her death – led to those below the stage, to the people. As Brecht emphasises, however, Weigel's art was not met with any great fanfare: 'The workers, who flocked to see her, welcomed her warmly and thought she was excellent, but didn't make a fuss about it because they were preoccupied with the subject matter.' By renouncing the illusion that she *was* the working-class mother instead of just an actress playing her, she had – at the expense of her own fame as an actress – turned her acting into a historical moment and thus at the same time demonstrated the political cause. To that effect Brecht epicizes his description of the actress during the rise of Fascism, when Weigel put herself at great risk every time she performed ('After the performances she now often found herself in a police cell') and had almost no audience left:

> She continued to perfect her art; she took her ever more significant art to ever deeper depths. In this way, once she had completely renounced and lost her former fame, her second period of fame began: a lowly fame, existing in the thoughts of a few persecuted people at a time when very many people were being persecuted. She was quite content, because her goal was to be famous among the less fortunate – among as many of them as possible, but also just among these few, if nothing else was possible.

(BFA 22: 798)

This description, which aims to highlight Weigel's political impact, makes her descent appear a necessary process; the increasing significance of her art is linked with resistance to the totalitarian regime. This justification of the simultaneously highest and lowest perfection, impact and ineffectiveness hardly admits of the idea of greater fame – as if Weigel's international success in the post-war era could never be more perfect or more significant than it already was among the 'less fortunate'. The paradoxical logic of this other fame, which is closely linked to her roles but does not apply to her art, can be seen as a precondition of all the texts that Brecht wrote with the aim of reintroducing Weigel as an actress on the stages of the war-ravaged cities. The perspective here, however, has shifted from the person back to the theatrical praxis which calls for its own commemoration.

Under the title 'Weigel's Props', Brecht drafted two different pieces of writing for a future commemoration of the actress. In the later version, written in 1952, the reminder of resistance and exile (which had already solidified into one of the enduring myths of the Socialist state) is absent. However, the series of roles Weigel has played and props she has used is not only updated but also distinguished by the sensory concreteness of individual moments as a memory of highlights in the theatre. The earlier poem (around 1940) explores, with a deictic and museum-like gestus ('See, here'), an ossified collection of props: 'See the make-up pencil, the tiny pot of face paint / And here the net she wove as a fisherwoman! // But see, too, from the time of her exile, the chipped fivepence piece and the worn-out shoe' (BFA 15: 11). In the end this rather conventional version with its alternate rhymes and strophic form lapses into the tone of a hymn, with almost comic pathos: 'O great treasure, who did not adorn yourself! Actor and refugee, maid and wife!' Here we find praise for the unique figure who proved herself in all her roles on the stage and her roles in real life too. By contrast, the later poem (which features in *Buying Brass*) actually brings 'Weigel's Props' to the fore. Only now do the things 'themselves' get their chance to speak, and the moralising tone (largely) recedes. Thus the balladesque quality of the first poem is set against a materialist and emblematic poetics of remembrance, in which an emphatic portrayal of the figure is almost completely dispensed with. What remains of the person are only her things, a symbolic testament:

> Just as the millet planter picks out the heaviest seeds
> For his trial field and the poet
> The most apposite words for his poem, so
> She selects the things which will accompany
> Her characters across the stage. The tin spoon
> Which Courage tucks into the buttonhole
> Of her Mongolian jacket, the party membership card
> Of kind Vlassova and the fishing net
> Of the other mother, the Spanish one; or the bronze bowl
> Of dust-gathering Antigone. Impossible to confuse
> the working woman's tattered bag where she keeps
> Her son's leaflets, with the moneybag
> Of the spirited camp follower. Every item
> In her collection is carefully chosen: straps and belts
> Tin boxes and ammunition pouches; carefully chosen too
> Are the capon and the stick which at the end
> The old woman twists through the draw-rope
> The Basque woman's board for baking bread
> And the Greek woman's stocks, carried on her back
> With holes for her hands to poke through, the Russian woman's
> Jar of lard, tiny in the policeman's hand; all
> Carefully chosen for their age, function and beauty
> By the eyes of the expert
> The hands of the bread-baking, net-weaving
> Soup-cooking connoisseur
> Of reality.
>
> (BFA 22: 869)

This ending too is laden with pathos to the point of being comical, but it retains a vestige of irony. The beginning of the poem makes clear the ironic distance of the poet, who situates himself somewhere between the planter experimenting with heavy millet[17] and the actress working with carefully selected props. His position as both mediator and 'witness' is hidden behind the props, which seem to speak for themselves. These are not just the little things one needs for acting, however, but decisions which document the process of theatre work. The objects which 'accompany her characters across the stage' are described like pieces of kit that are essential for survival on dangerous expeditions, or like possessions buried with the dead. As if it were a great achievement on Weigel's part to have applied her knowledge of reality to the props she selected for her scenes. The fact that, according to Weigel's knowledge of her craft, age is what counts most, followed by function and beauty, underlines the interest in a memory of things, particularly for the theatre. It is not so much their original appearance as the physical experience which lingers in the objects that makes them into useable props. Thus the poem, by using the quality of the objects to highlight the distinctiveness of the different roles, sees the actress migrate to the world of things – a phantom image of the figures who are accompanied across the stage by the props and are in this sense the objects' own shadow. What remains, with the 'soup-cooking connoisseur of reality', is the grotesque formulation of a practical wisdom whereby Weigel's art of living is again linked with her acting style and ultimately both are reduced to a poetic gestus of selection ('as [...] the poet the most apposite words'). Weigel's acting work is preserved in a double sense, not only enshrined in memory but deconstructed and updated. Where they set the model in motion without fixing it in place, where they inscribe the figure with the movement of a defiguration, Brecht's writing styles have their own theatrical and at the same time utopian quality. This is highlighted by the way Brecht abruptly breaks off his 1938 'Letter from the Dialectician to the Actress Weigel Regarding a Change in her Acting Style' (BFA 14: 389), which encourages her to keep thinking and distancing herself from herself:

> For over a decade
> Of tireless work
> With your talent for portraying people
> For feeling keenly and making feelings clear
> And also for arousing those feelings
> In the people watching you
> You have made a name for yourself. Now
> I urge you to [...]

---

[17]See also the poem 'Tschaganak Bersijew or the Cultivation of Millet', particularly the 13th line, 'During the day he pulled the earliest ears from the field / And sat brooding over them at home at night. / Separated the heaviest seeds from the earliest ears / And sowed them the next year.' (BFA 15: 230).

Karl Korsch

CHAPTER TWELVE

Brecht's Marxist Aesthetic: The Korsch Connection

DOUGLAS KELLNER

In the voluminous literature on Bertolt Brecht, the impact of the version of materialist dialectic advocated by Brecht's Marxian 'teacher' Karl Korsch on Brecht's work has not been adequately clarified.[1] Not only did Korsch strongly influence Brecht's conception of Marxian dialectics, but the Marxian ideas that were most fruitful for Brecht's aesthetic practice were precisely the ideas shared by Brecht and Korsch in their conception of materialist dialectics and revolutionary practice. Brecht used the Korschian version of the Marxian dialectic in both his aesthetic theory and practice, in a way that is central to his work, and not incidental as it is sometimes claimed to be.[2]

KORSCH AND BRECHT

In the 1920s Brecht began serious study of Marxism while attempting to write a play on the stock market (the fragmentary *Joe Fleischhacker*) and shortly before working on *St. Joan of the Stockyards*. When he could not find anyone to explain the workings of the capitalist economy, he began to read Marx's *Das Kapital* and became increasingly interested in both the Marxian theory of society and the dialectical method of analyzing

---

Douglas Kellner, 'Brecht's Marxist Aesthetic: The Korsch Connection', in Betty Nance Weber, Hubert Heinen, Iring Fetscher and Frank Trommler, *Bertolt Brecht: Political Theory and Literary Practice* (Athens: U of Georgia P, 1980), pp. 29–42.

Thanks to Steve Bronner and Betty Weber for stimulating discussions of topics in this paper and help with revisions.

[1] The theme was first discussed in Wolfdietrich Rasch, 'Bertolt Brechts marxistischer Lehrer' *in Merkur* 188 (1963): 94–99. Other contributions to the discussion include the material in *Alternative* 41 (1965); Klaus-Detlef Müller, *Die Funktion der Geschichte im Werk Bertolt Brechts* (Tübingen: Niemeyer, 1967; 2d ed. 1972); Ingeborg Muenz-Koenen, 'Brecht in westdeutschen Publikationen', *Weimarer Beiträge* 15(1969): 123–47; Reiner Steinweg, *Das Lehrstück* (Stuttgart: Metzler, 1972); Heinz Brüggemann, 'Bertolt Brecht und Karl Korsch', *Über Karl Korsch* (Frankfurt: Suhrkamp, 1973), pp. 177–88, and *Literarische Technik und soziale Revolution* (Reinbek: Rowohlt, 1973); Franco Buono, *Zur Prosa Brechts* (Frankfurt: Suhrkamp, 1973); and Werner Mittenzwei, 'Nachwort' to the DDR version of *Me-ti* (Berlin: Henssel, 1975). *Alternative* 105 (1975) contains a Korsch-Brecht issue that summarizes the discussion of the Korsch-Brecht relationship.
[2] See *Alternative* 91 (1973) and 93 (1973). Interpreters who downplay or denigrate Brecht's Marxism include Martin Esslin, *Brecht – The Man and His Work* (Garden City, N.Y.: Anchor, 1961), and Eric Bentley, who tries to disassociate Brecht from Marxism and to associate him with Beckett; see 'Brecht Was a Lover, Too', *The Village Voice*, May 3, 1976.

society and history.³ To help him in his study of Marxism, Brecht sought the acquaintance of people who could teach him its fundamental ideas and method. At the time, Karl Korsch was one of the leading Marx scholars in Germany and was also one of the most active militants in the communist movement.⁴ After serving on the ill-fated socialization commission following the November revolution, Korsch joined the Independent Socialist party (USPD) and then the Communist party (KPD) in 1920. He served as justice minister in a short-lived left coalition in Thuringia in 1923, became editor of the communist journal *Internationale*, was on the Central Committee of the German Communist party, and represented the communists in the Reichstag. In 1926 Korsch was one of the first victims of Stalinism and was expelled from the movement to which he was deeply committed and which he had loyally served. Thereafter he moved into the forefront of the Left Opposition and developed one of the sharpest critiques of the Stalinization of the Soviet Union, the Comintern, and the German Communist party. He worked with a variety of left oppositional groups and taught courses on Marxism at the Karl Marx School and in small study groups in Berlin. Brecht joined these courses and Korsch's study group and from then on titled Korsch 'my teacher' of Marxism.⁵

From the beginning of his involvement with the communist movement in the early twenties, Korsch saw the Marxian dialectic as the theoretical core of Marxism. He characterized the Marxian dialectic by the principles of historical specification, critique, and revolutionary practice. The principle of historical specification articulates Marx's practice of comprehending 'all things social in terms of a definite historical epoch'.⁶ For Korsch, Marx's achievement was his analysis of historically distinct and specific features of capitalism and bourgeois society, and his development of a method that enabled one to analyze distinct social formations critically and to transform them radically. Bourgeois political economy and theory, on the other hand, dealt with the forms of bourgeois society as if they were universal, eternal, and unchanging relationships, rather than historical forms of a system that was full of contradictions and subject to radical transformation.

---

³See Brecht, 20: 46 and 15: 129, where he states 'when I read Marx's *Kapital*, I understood my plays' and describes Marx as 'the only spectator for my plays'.
⁴For a detailed reconstruction of Korsch's political activity and theory see my introduction to *Karl Korsch: Revolutionary Theory*, ed. Douglas Kellner (Austin: University of Texas Press, 1977).
⁵See Brecht, 20: 65, and his letter to Korsch, end of March 1945, 'You know that you are a teacher for life, so take it easy', cited in *Alternative* 41: 45. Concerning Brecht's relation to Korsch, Hedda Korsch has written me:

> K.K. met B.B. in the early twenties, I think through the mediation of Felix Weil and the Frankfurt people who introduced him also to the Malik Verlag, George Grosz, etc. K. was greatly interested in the modern literary and artistic movements and followed them eagerly although his personal taste and direct enjoyment remained mostly with Goethe. An exception, you might say, were the works of B.B. We saw *The Threepenny Opera* at its first night or shortly after and were immediately and totally captivated by it. We met B.B. not there but at the same time. K. admired him and was also attracted by his original personality. B.B. attended K.'s private courses pretty regularly and joined in the discussions after courses in a cafe at the Alexanderplatz. He never agreed with K.'s criticisms of the Soviet developments. To discuss it all more in depth he organized meetings between himself and some friends with K.K. and some friends of his; those were held at B.B.'s apartment about 1930 and were discontinued when such meetings became dangerous for the participants. By then K.K. and B.B. were friends. K.K. never thought much of Pollock, not too much of Horkheirner as a philosopher, but liked and esteemed Walter Benjamin. We admired the works of Döblin who also attended Karl's courses and discussions.

⁶See Karl Korsch, *Marxism and Philosophy* (London: NLB, 1970); 'The Marxian Dialectic' and 'On Materialist Dialectic', *Karl Korsch: Revolutionary Theory*, Kart Korsch, 'Why I Am a Marxist', *Three Essays on Marxism* (New York: Monthly Review, 1972); and Karl Korsch, *Karl Marx* (London: Chapman and Hall, 1938), p. 24.

Problems or economy, politics, and culture cannot be solved through a general abstract description of 'economics as such', but requires 'a detailed description of the definite relations which exist between definite economic phenomena on a definite historical level of development and definite phenomena which appear simultaneously or subsequently in every other field of political, juristic, and intellectual development'.[7]

For Korsch, the Marxian dialectic is a *critical dialectic* that aims at the critique and transformation of the existing bourgeois order. The Marxian dialectic sees reality as a process of continual change and is interested in those contradictions and antagonisms that make radical transformation possible. Above all, Marxian dialectic integrates critical theory with *revolutionary practice* which would emancipate the working class and construct socialism. Korsch summarizes his description of the basic principles of Marxism in *Karl Marx*, a book written in part while Korsch was a guest of the Brecht family in exile:

> Marxian theory, viewed in its general character, is a new science of bourgeois society. It appears at a time when within bourgeois society itself an independent movement of a new social class is opposing the ruling bourgeois class. In opposition to the bourgeois principles, it represents the new views and claims of the class oppressed in bourgeois society. It is, so far, not a positive but a critical science. It 'specifies' bourgeois society and investigates the tendencies visible in the present development of society, and the way to its imminent practical transformation. Thus, it is not only a theory of bourgeois society but, at the same time, a theory of the proletarian revolution.[8]

Brecht's theoretical writings show that he agreed with Korsch on these issues and that he developed his conception of dialectics while working in Korsch's seminars and discussion groups.

EPIC THEATER: MATERIALIST DIALECTICS, THE V-EFFECT, AND THE POLITICS OF SEPARATION

In his epic theater built on the principles of historical specification and critique. Brecht sought to illuminate the historically specific features of an environment in order to show how that environment influenced shaped, and often battered and destroyed the characters. Unlike dramatists who focused on the universal elements of the human situation and fate, Brecht was interested in the attitudes and behavior people adopted toward each other in specific historical situations. Thus, in *Mahagonny* and *The Threepenny Opera* he was interested in how people related to each other in capitalist society; in *Mother Courage*, how tradespeople related to soldiers and civilians during war in an emerging market society; in *The Measures Taken*, he depicted revolutionary relationships in the struggle in China. Brecht called this practice 'historicization' and believed that one could best adopt a critical attitude toward one's society if the present social arrangements and institutions

---

[7] Korsch, 'Why I Am a Marxist', pp. 64–65.
[8] Korsch, *Karl Marx*, p. 86. Brecht also consulted with Korsch on theoretical and aesthetic issues throughout the exile period. See the Korsch-Brecht correspondence published in *Alternative* 41 (1965) and 105(1975). Much of Brecht's 'Marxian Studies' is a dialogue with Korsch: see the passages that summarize Korsch's works and set out theses developed in Korsch's seminars, e.g. 20: 68–72.

were viewed as historical, transitory, and subject to change.⁹ Brecht intended that epic theater show emotions, ideas, and behavior as products of, or responses to, specific social situations and not as the unfolding of the human essence.

The primary theatrical device of epic theater, the *Verfremdungseffekt* was intended to 'estrange' or 'distance' the spectator and thus prevent empathy and identification with the situation and characters and allow the adoption of a critical attitude toward the actions in the play.¹⁰ By preventing empathetic illusion or a mimesis of reality, epic theater would expose the workings of societal processes and human behavior, and would thus show the audience how and why people behaved a certain way in their society. For example, the greed in *Mahagonny* and *The Threepenny Opera*, Mother Courage's sufferings, or Galileo's persecution were to be understood as historically specific constituents of a social environment. As Walter Benjamin stressed, the response to epic theater should be: 'Things can happen this way, but they can also happen a quite different way.'¹¹ The strategy was to produce an experience of curiosity, astonishment, and shock: 'Is that the way things are? What produced this? It's terrible! How can we change things?' This attitude was also fostered by a 'montage of images' and series of typical social tableaux that Brecht called 'gests'.¹² He wanted his spectators to work through these examples, to participate in an active process of critical thought that would provide insights into the workings of society, and to see the need for and to implement radical social change.

Brecht's epic theater broke with the 'culinary theater' that provided the spectator with a pleasant experience or moral for easy digestion. He rejected theater that tried to produce an illusion of reality and that reproduced the dominant ideology, just as Korsch rejected the identification of bourgeois ideologies with reality. Brecht appropriated Korsch's theory that ideology was a material force that served as an important tool of domination; they both saw ideology as a deluding force from which people should be emancipated.¹³ Hence Brecht's practice of ideology-demolition and intervening thought is an application of Korsch's principle of ideology critique and intellectual action.¹⁴ Thus both Korsch and Brecht viewed intellectual action as well as aesthetic theory as important moments in revolutionary practice (along with economic and political action).

In order to produce a revolutionary theater, Brecht argued for a 'separation of the elements' or a 'politics of separation'.¹⁵ In the important *Mahagonny* notes, Brecht distinguished his separation of words, music, and scene from the Wagnerian *Gesamtkunstwerk*, which fused the elements into one seductive and overpowering whole in which word, music, and scene work together to engulf the spectator in the aesthetic totality.¹⁶ In his 'radical separation of the elements', each aesthetic component retains its autonomy and 'comments' on the others, often in contradiction, to provoke thought and insight. For instance, in *The Threepenny Opera*, first Mac and Polly, and then Mac and Jenny sing of love and romance, but the scene is first a warehouse full of stolen goods

---

⁹*Brecht on Theater*, ed. and trans. John Willet (New York: New Directions, 1964), p. 140.
¹⁰E.g. *Brecht on Theater*, pp. 91–99, 136–47, 191–96.
¹¹Walter Benjamin, *Understanding Brecht* (London: NLB, 1973), p. 8.
¹²*Brecht on Theater*, pp. 42, 86–87, 104, 134, 139, 198–205.
¹³Korsch, *Marxism and Philosophy*, pp. 70–73; and Brecht, 13: 156–58, and 20: 156–58.
¹⁴Korsch, *Marxism and Philosophy*, pp. 95–98; and Brecht 18: 156–58,
¹⁵See Betty Nance Weber, 'Marxismus, Brecht, Gesamtkunstwerk', in *Brecht Jahrbuch* (1976): 120–27, and Colin MacCabe, 'The Politics of Separation', *Screen* 16, no. 4 (1975–76): 46–61.
¹⁶*Brecht on Theater*, pp. 33–36.

and then a brothel, and the plot is one of deception and betrayal, thus shocking one into reflecting on the bourgeois ideology of love. In Brecht's film *Kuhle Wampe*, romantic organ music is played as a young unemployed youth returns home after another futile search for work, evoking a poignant contrast between music and image. Contradiction between the elements, Brecht believed, would prevent identification and passive immersion and would provoke critical reflection. Each aesthetic medium retains its separate identity, and the product is an 'aggregate of independent arts' in provocative tension.

Brecht's theory of aesthetic production is congruent with Korsch's model of the workers' councils as the authentic organs of socialist practice.[17] For just as Korsch urged a democratic, participatory activity of coproduction in the spheres of labor and politics, Brecht urges the same sort of coparticipation in his aesthetic production. Brecht worked whenever possible in collectives in which a team of co-workers collaborated on production. He was especially attracted to radio and film as exemplary of the highest development of the forces of production and as involving a new kind of collective work.[18] He saw his co-workers as important participants in the creative process, all of whom were encouraged to contribute to the production of the work of art. Such a revolution in the concept of creation, rejecting the notion of the creator as the solitary genius, was intended to alter aesthetic production radically, much as the workers' councils were intended to revolutionize industrial and political organization, thus providing a model for socialist cultural organization.

Both Brecht and Korsch stress the primary importance of production in social life and see socialism as a constant revolutionizing of the forces and relations of production. Thus, in opposition to such critics as Georg Lukács, Brecht defended the need to innovate, experiment, and produce new aesthetic forms. He argued that since the apparatus of aesthetic production was not yet controlled by artists and did not work for the general good, revolutionary artists should strive to change the apparatus. One had to develop 'the means of pleasure into an object of instruction, and to convert certain institutions from places of entertainment into organs of mass communication'.[19] Brecht's art aimed at a *radical pedagogy* that would provide political education, cultivate political instincts, and provoke revolutionary political practice.

THE LEARNING PLAYS AS THE MODEL OF BRECHTIAN REVOLUTIONARY THEATER

Parallel to his work on epic theater, which he feared might be as 'culinary as ever',[20] Brecht developed a new type of play, the 'learning play'. Here, too, Korsch's influence is pronounced, for, as Hans Eisler has noted, these plays resemble political seminars.[21] Brecht described them as 'a collective political meeting' in which the audience is to participate actively (18:132). One sees in this model a rejection of the concept of the

---

[17]See Karl Korsch, 'What Is Socialization?' *New German Critique* 6 (1975): 60–81, and 'Fundamentals of Socialization', *Karl Korsch: Revolutionary Theory*, pp. 124–34.

[18]Brecht, 19: 119–34, 137–216. For discussions of Brecht and film see the two issues of *Screen*, 15, no. 2 (1975) and 16, no. 4(1975–76), and the book by Wolfgang Gersch, *Film bei Brecht* (München: Hanser, 1975).

[19]*Brecht on Theater*, pp. 33–36, 42. For Brecht's attack on Lukács and argument that the revolutionary artist should revolutionize form as well as content, see 'Against Georg Lukács', *New Left Review* 84 (March–April 1974): 36–38.

[20]*Brecht on Theater*, p. 41.

[21]Hans Eisler, *Alternative* 78/79 (1971): 132.

bureaucratic elite party where the theorists and functionaries are to issue directives and control the activities of the masses. In these plays, correct doctrine and practice would be discovered and carried out through a participatory, collective practice rather than through hierarchical manipulation and domination; that is, they were to function as Korsch had envisioned the operation of the workers' councils.

The 'learning plays' were conceived by Brecht as the model for the 'theater of the future'. They exemplified materialist aesthetics, whereas his epic dramas were seen as 'compromise forms'. The 'technical regression' of the latter (*Galileo*) was necessitated by conditions of production in exile and then in the early years of the DDR.[22] The learning plays were his most explicitly political plays and his most radical attempt to politicize art. In his 'theory of pedagogy' for a socialist future, he wrote:

> Pleasure in observation alone is harmful for the state just as pleasure in action alone. Insofar as young people while playing perform actions that are derived from their own observations, they will be educated for the state. This sort of playing must be invented and performed in such a way that it is useful for the state. It is not beauty that is decisive for the value of a sentence or a gesture or an action, but whether it is useful for the state when the players speak a sentence, perform a gesture, or carry out an action.
>
> (17: 1023)

The learning plays were superior to epic theater, in Brecht's view, because they were more effective pedagogically, both for the artistic producers and for the audience who were to participate in more direct and creative ways in the aesthetic experience. The actors and audience were to distinguish social from asocial behavior by imitating ways of behaving, thinking, talking, and relating. Within a single play the actors frequently exchanged roles so that they could experience situations from different points of view. The learning plays confronted them with situations such as sacrificing oneself for the good of the public (*Lindbergh's Flight, The Baden Learning Play of Consent*) or egotistically putting oneself above all else (*Fatzer, Baal the Asocial*). There would often be contradictory models of service or exploitation (*The Exception and the Rule*), social consent or refusal (*The Yes-sayer and the No-sayer*), and effective or ineffective revolutionary practice (*The Measures Taken*). Brecht called this practice the 'grand pedagogy' which would turn actors/audience into statesmen and philosophers. Whereas the 'lesser pedagogy' of the epic theater merely 'democratized the theater in the pre-revolutionary period', the 'grand pedagogy' completely transforms the role of the producers and 'abolishes the system of performer and spectator'.[23] Brecht intended his learning plays for schools, factories, or political groups; actors and audiences could read, improvise, and alter the plays at will as Brecht himself had done with many groups.

Thus, in Brecht's concept of emancipatory pedagogy and revolutionary theater, the learning plays are not concerned with advocating specific doctrines, handing down a

---

[22] See Brecht's *Arbeitsjournal* (Frankfurt: Suhrkamp, 1973), entry for 25 February 1939, where he calls *Galileo* a 'technical regression' and praises the learning plays *Fatzer* and the *Bakery* as technical models. My interpretation of the learning plays is much indebted to Reiner Steinweg's scholarship and the issues of *Alternative* (78/79, 91, and 107) dedicated to Brecht's learning plays.

[23] Brecht, 'Die Grosse und die Kleine Pädogogik', *Alternative* 78/79(1971): 126, and 'Theorie der Pädogogien', 17: 1022–24.

teaching for easy consumption, functioning as propaganda. Rather, the plays are to engage a small audience in a process of learning.

For example, *The Measures Taken* confronts the audience with basic questions of revolution: violence, discipline, the structure of the party, the relation to the masses, revolutionary justice, and so on. There is no 'correct doctrine' set forth; the actors are to present a scene and then discuss it with the audience. Like Korsch's model of the workers' councils there is to be no established hierarchy; rather there is to be democratic participation in coproduction. The people are to establish the principles of revolutionary practice, strategy, and tactics, and not the party elite theoreticians or bureaucrats. Moreover, the task of the revolutionary artist here is not to make palatable party doctrine for easy assimilation, but to encourage revolutionary thought and critique. This stance was clearly a threat to bureaucratic party functionaries, and they have consistently opposed Brecht's work.

Brecht saw his learning plays as a series of 'sociological experiments', as 'limbering-up exercises' or 'mental gymnastics' for dialecticians.[24] He thought that the learning plays would radically revolutionize the theater apparatus. Thus they should not be seen as minor works as many critics have suggested. Brecht did in fact return to epic theater with the advent of fascism and conditions of exile, for the learning plays were viable only in contexts where there were political groups who could perform them and an audience who could relate them to revolutionary practice. In his last years he again turned his attention to the learning play and suggested that *The Measures Taken* should be considered as the model for a revolutionary theater of the future.[25]

ME-TI: MATERIALIST DIALECTICS IN LITERATURE AND BRECHT'S POLITICAL CONTRADICTIONS

During the exile period, Brecht was forced to develop new aesthetic forms. One such experiment, the *Me-ti* novel, embodies the principles of his materialist aesthetics in the prose domain, while articulating the political conflicts of the times and unfolding the contradictions and ambiguities in Brecht's political position. Brecht was drawn at once to the ideas of democratic socialism espoused by Luxemburg and Korsch and to the authoritarian communism of Lenin and Stalin.[26] A tension between Brecht's work and orthodox Leninism in both politics and aesthetics surfaced in the hostility of the German Communist party to his work, and in the polemics with Lukács over the official aesthetic doctrine of Socialist Realism.[27] Although Brecht had an ambivalent position within the communist movement, he presented himself as an orthodox Marxist, a

---

[24]Cf. 'Gespräch über *Die Maßnahme*' and Reiner Steinweg, 'Das Lehrstück' and 'Die Lehrstücke als Versuchsreihe', *Alternative* 78/79 (1971).
[25]Steinweg, 'Das Lehrstück', pp. 102–3.
[26]Brecht admired the left-communists Korsch and Rosa Luxemburg because of their activism and the workers' councils. In Lenin he respected the ability to translate revolutionary theory into practice. Stalin, as *Me-ti*, the *Work Journal*, and unpublished manuscripts and clippings in the Brecht archives attest, elicited an ambivalence that has prevented consensus among critics on the subject of Brecht and Stalin. There is little evidence of his attitude toward Trotsky. In the *Work Journal* during the period when Trotsky was heatedly debated within the international communist movement, Brecht offered no substantive discussion of the issues.
[27]Many commentators have stressed the tension between Brecht's communism and his aesthetic practice; however, most fail to see the tension and the ambiguities within the former. Esslin's biased interpretations of attacks on

fervent devotee of Lenin, and publicly defended communist orthodoxy in the Stalin period. The private Brecht was torn by ambivalences and doubts concerning Stalinism and developments in the Soviet Union. These doubts, which Brecht confided to Marxian heretics such as Korsch and Benjamin, found literary expression in *Me-ti*, one of the most important sources for measuring Karl Korsch's influence on Brecht and Brecht's political contradictions.

There are formal similarities between the *Me-ti* novel and Brecht's learning plays. Both provoke thought and discussion of revolutionary theory and practice, rather than simply promulgate ossified doctrines or a party line. The main topics of *Me-ti*, 'the grand method' (dialectics) and 'the grand order' and 'the grand production' (socialism), are presented in the form of aphoristic debates in which Leninism, Stalinism, and the construction of socialism in the Soviet Union are measured against the ideas of Marx and Engels, Korsch, Luxemburg, and Trotsky. The reader is forced to think through the opposing positions of the Marxian classics and contemporary Marxian theorists and to evaluate events in the Soviet Union. Although Brecht inserts himself in the aphoristic dialogues, he does not represent a privileged point of view, nor does Me-ti, Mi-en-leh (Lenin), Meister Ko (Korsch), or any of the other participants. The readers of this literary experiment are thus co-workers who contribute their own thought to produce revolutionary critique and reflection on Marxian theory and practice.

Throughout *Me-ti*, Brecht applies the materialist concept of history to the history of historical materialism, as Korsch did earlier.[28] Like Korsch, Brecht analyzes how later Marxian theories and practice realized or failed to realize Marx's ideas, which in turn were critically appraised in terms of the results they produced (or failed to produce). A single passage, 'The Opinion of Philosopher Ko Concerning the Construction of the Order in Su' (12: 537), reveals the complexity of the situation Brecht was analyzing when he related Marxism to the developments in the Soviet Union. He indicates that Lenin 'created a powerful state apparatus for the construction of the *grand order*, which must necessarily become a hindrance for the grand order in the foreseeable future'. Here Brecht is referring to Marx's doctrine of the withering away of the state in the transition to a higher stage of socialism. He then refers to Korsch's critique that 'the orderer would be a hindrance to the order', in reference to Korsch's belief that the Stalinist bureaucracy would prevent the development of an emancipatory socialism. Brecht also advanced Korsch's position that 'actually the apparatus always functioned very badly and continually putrified, throwing off a sharp stink'. Further, Brecht cites Korsch's position that the power struggle between Stalin and Trotsky portended a surrender of Leninism, and that Trotsky merely 'proposed rather doubtful reforms'. The conclusion that 'those principles proposed by Ko showed a clear weakness where Mi-en-leh's principles were strongest, but Ko characterized excellently the weaknesses of the principles of Mi-en-leh'

Brecht by communists should not obscure the provocative material he presents. For Brecht's debate with Lukács, see 'Against Georg Lukács' (n. 19) and Helga Gallas, *Marxistische Literaturtheorie* (Neuwied: Luchterhand, 1971).
[28]Regarding Brecht's acceptance of Korsch's position that the workers' councils were indispensable to the construction of socialism, see Brecht's theses 'On the Model R [*Räte* = workers' councils] as a Moment of the Proletarian Dictatorship' in 20: 119 and Brecht's letter to Korsch in 1941 where he asks Korsch to write a historical account of the relationship of the councils to the party explaining the suppression of the councils system, *Alternative* 105 (1975): 252.

indicates that there are serious weaknesses in Leninism and suggests that there were sharp tensions in Brecht's political views.

While Brecht did not accept all of Korsch's sharp attacks on the Soviet Union, Leninism, and Stalinism, he continually reflected on Korsch's views and frequently incorporated them in *Me-ti*:

The Trials of Ni-En [Stalin]

Me-ti expressed his disapproval of Ni-en because in his trials against his enemies in the association he demanded too much confidence from the people. He said: When someone asks me to believe something which can be proven (without furnishing me the proof), it is tantamount to my being asked to believe something which cannot be proven. I will not do it. Ni-en might have benefited the people by removing his enemies inside the association, but he did not prove it. By conducting trials without proof he has done damage to the people. He ought to have taught the people to demand proof, especially from a man who in general is so useful. (12: 538)

Autocratic Rule of Ni-en

Me-ti spoke with Kin-jeh [Brecht] about Ni-en, who exercised autocratic rule. Me-ti said: Mi-en-leh, whose student one must consider Ni-en, believed before the great revolution that the workers would have to support the bourgeoisie in their struggle to free themselves from the rule of the Emperor. ... Later the workers, under his leadership, obtained power; but his successor, Ni-en, acted exactly like an Emperor. The backwardness of the country Su [Soviet Union], of which Mi-en-leh had always spoken, continued to manifest itself in this phenomenon. The great machinery was constructed not by the citizens under people's rule, but by workers under the rule of an Emperor. (12: 538)

Construction and Regression under Ni-en

Under Ni-en's leadership industry without exploiters was being constructed in Su and agriculture collectivized and furnished with machines. But the associations [Communist parties] outside Su decayed. It was no longer the members who elected the secretaries, but the secretaries who elected the members. The guidelines were issued by Su and the secretaries were paid by Su. When mistakes were made, those who had criticized the mistakes were punished; but those who had made the mistakes remained in office. Soon the office holders were no longer the best members but merely the most servile. ... Those who issued the orders in Su no longer learned any facts, because the secretaries no longer reported facts that might not have pleased them. In view of these conditions the best members were in despair. Me-ti deplored the decay of the grand method. Master Ko turned away from it. ... In Su all wisdom was directed toward the construction and chased out of politics. Outside Su all those who praised Ni-en's merits, even those which were undeniable, became suspect of corruption; inside Su all those who uncovered his mistakes, even those from which he himself suffered, became suspect of treason. (12: 539)

These are aphorisms in a literary experiment and one might argue that they were points of view Brecht was proposing for discussion and did not express his own position. He never published *Me-ti*, which indicates a reluctance to attack Stalin and the Soviet Union openly. The same ambivalences toward Stalin and the Soviet Union, however, are found in his *Work Journal*, where he considered Korsch's critiques with the utmost seriousness.[29] *Me-ti* represents Brecht's most comprehensive juxtaposition of Korsch's positions with 'official' Marxian doctrines and shows that throughout the exile period he pondered questions of practical and theoretical Marxism. *Me-ti*, Brecht's letters, and his *Work Journal* show that he continued to reflect upon, and to contrast his own views with, the ideas of his teacher and friend Karl Korsch, the theorist who helped provide the foundation for Brecht's Marxist aesthetic.

---

[29]For a fuller discussion of these problems see Helmut Dahmer, 'Brecht and Stalin', *Telos* 22 (1974–75): 96–105. Dahmer, however, neglects many passages in *Me-ti* and wrongly says that Korsch's views on the development of the Soviet Union are missing (p. 67).

Walter Benjamin

CHAPTER THIRTEEN

Walter Benjamin and Bertolt Brecht: Account of a Constellation[1]

ERDMUT WIZISLA
TRANSLATED BY ROMY FURSLAND

The relationship between Walter Benjamin and Bertolt Brecht is one of the most important artist friendships of the last century. Their influence in literature, theatre and political thinking is still felt to this day. Benjamin's friends, especially Adorno and Scholem, did not approve of his meetings with Brecht. This paper presents material from the author's book Benjamin und Brecht *(Suhrkamp 2004/Libris 2007). Several episodes illustrate the cooperation between Benjamin and Brecht: the project* Krise und Kritik *[Crisis and Criticism]; Benjamin's Paris speech on the German avant-garde in 1934; chess in Danish exile; and the impact of Brecht's poem 'Legende von der Entstehung des Buches Taoteking auf dem Weg des Laotse in die Emigration' ['Legend of the Origin of the Book Tao Te Ching on Lao Tzu's Way into Exile'].*

In February 1937, Walter Benjamin sent Margarete Steffin an excerpt from Chesterton's book on Dickens. This passage, he wrote, 'says the best things about the *Threepenny Novel* that it is possible to say'.[2] So just what does it say? Dickens, claims Chesterton, shows us the wildest monstrosities walking about the Strand and Lincoln's Inn. Dickens was an immoderate jester because he possessed moderation in his thinking. His riotous imagination had its source in the moderate rationality of his thought.

London is part of the topography of the relationship between Benjamin and Brecht. Only recently, in the spring of 2005, the draft of a telegram turned up in Moscow

---

Erdmut Wizisla, 'Walter Benjamin und Bertolt Brecht: Bericht über eine Konstellation', in Robert Gillett and Godela Weiss-Sussex (eds.), *'Verwisch die Spuren!'. Bertolt Brecht's Work and Legacy. A Reassessment* (Amsterdam: Rodopi, 2008), pp. 127–40.

[1]This essay presents theses and material from my book *Benjamin und Brecht. Die Geschichte einer Freundschaft* (Frankfurt am Main: Suhrkamp, 1994 [English translation: *Walter Benjamin and Bertolt Brecht: The Story of a Friendship*, tr. Christine Shuttleworth. London: Libris, 2009]). My thanks go to Godela Weiss-Sussex, Robert Gillett and Hamish Ritchie for the excellent conference in London.
[2]Walter Benjamin, letter to Margarete Steffin, 26.4.1937, WBGB V: 521.

which had been composed by Benjamin in June or July 1936 and addressed to Brecht, Hampstead, Abbey Road: 'Wire when definitely in Svendborg/Benjamin'.[3]

In April 1936 Brecht, then in London, had praised Benjamin's essay *Problems of the Sociology of Language*, saying: 'That's just how a new encyclopaedia should be written'. The letter – one of the few to have survived – ends with an invitation to Svendborg: 'So, what's happening this summer? I'm back in June. Will we see each other? I doubt we'll be able to play chess under the apple trees for many more summers.'[4]

The relationship between Benjamin and Brecht is here referred to as a 'constellation', which at first glance may not adequately express its importance, for Benjamin and Brecht's friendship was more than just a note in their biographies. My title is inspired by the beginning of Max Kommerell's essay 'Jean Paul in Weimar'. Jean Paul's stay in Weimar, writes Kommerell, can only be described using the word 'constellation'; in a constellation, the coincidental and the statutory are almost indistinguishable. The term expresses 'where every person stands in relation to every other person, and all in relation to all', 'in this age of heightened awareness and keenest reflection'.[5] This type of constellation has various things in common with constellations of celestial bodies: the concurrence of non-coincidental, specific – in this case opportune – circumstances, the combination of uniqueness and predictability and the expectation that the particular experiences and attitudes resulting from it are not limited to the desires and actions of individuals.

Benjamin and Brecht's friendship was a meeting of divergent experiences, interests and positions on politics and art history. These differences never went away, but they did give rise to a relationship that was both productive and fraught with tension and which, strangely, made many people uneasy. 'You have got into bad company: Brecht plus Benjamin', Johannes R. Becher warned Asja Lacis.[6]

Many years ago when I first started studying this relationship, I was surprised by how many testimonies had been overlooked or wilfully misinterpreted. This is mainly due to the hostility with which Benjamin's circle reacted to the friendship. Theodor W. Adorno's reservations about 'Berta' [i.e. Brecht] and her collective' are just as relevant as his claim that Benjamin had written the 'work of art' essay 'in order to outdo Brecht (whom he was afraid of) in radicalism'.[7] Gershom Scholem, like Adorno, was critical of the relationship: 'I would actually say that Brecht's influence on Benjamin's output in the thirties was harmful, and in some respects disastrous.'[8] The impact of these prejudices is astonishing. This even applies to the edition of Benjamin's *Collected Works*, which – particularly where his writing on Brecht is concerned – is full of errors.

---

[3]Russian State Military Archive ('Special Archive'), Walter Benjamin materials, Folder 48. See also Reinhard Müller and Erdmut Wizisla: 'Kritik der freien Intelligenz'. Walter-Benjamin-Funde im Moskauer "Sonderarchiv"', in *Mittelweg* 36. 14 (2005), Issue 5., 61–76.
[4]Bertolt Brecht, letter to Walter Benjamin, April 1936, BFA 28: 550–551.
[5]Max Kommerell, 'Jean Paul in Weimar', in Max Kommerell: *Dichterische Welterfahrung. Essays* (Frankfurt am Main: Klostermann, 1952), 53–82. Here 53 and 55.
[6]Asja Lacis, *Revolutionär im Beruf. Berichte über proletarisches Theater, über Meyerhold, Brecht, Benjamin und Piscator*, ed. Hildegard Brenner (Munich: Rogner & Bernhard, 1971), 59.
[7]Rolf Tiedemann, *Studien zur Philosophie Walter Benjamins* [1965] (Frankfurt am Main: Suhrkamp, 1973), 112.
[8]Gershom Scholem, 'Walter Benjamin' [1965], in Gershom Scholem, *Walter Benjamin und sein Engel. Vierzehn Aufsätze und kleine Beiträge*, ed. Rolf Tiedemann (Frankfurt am Main: Suhrkamp, 1983), 9–34. Here 26.

Of the dissenting voices who had positive things to say – including Günter Anders, Elisabeth Hauptmann and Ruth Berlau, among others – I shall cite only the most emphatic: Hannah Arendt. She believed the relationship with Brecht was a 'stroke of luck' for Benjamin, and that Brecht had been, 'in the last decade of his life, especially during the period of exile in Paris, the most important person' in Benjamin's life. She also wrote:

> The friendship between Benjamin and Brecht is unique, because it brought together the greatest living German poet with the most important critic of the day. [...] [I]t is strange and sad that their old friends never realised the uniqueness of this encounter, even after both, Brecht and Benjamin, were dead.[9]

Elisabeth Hauptmann spoke about the friendship in an interview in 1972. I quote her here because she tempers Hannah Arendt's enthusiasm a little. Her judgement, as someone who was directly involved, also carries particular weight. Benjamin and Brecht never tested their different attitudes in a joint work, she says (not entirely accurately), but their influence on each other was enormous. Benjamin as a partner for Brecht had been 'one of the best things there was'.[10]

The term 'constellation' plays a central role in Benjamin's reaction to the distrust. In May 1934 Gretel Karplus, later Adorno's wife, wrote to Benjamin that she was awaiting his move to Denmark 'with some anxiety' because she had severe misgivings about Brecht. Sometimes, she wrote, she had the feeling that Benjamin was somehow under Brecht's influence, and that Brecht posed a very real danger to him (see WBGB IV: 442–443).

Benjamin's reply illustrates a key characteristic of his thinking:

> What you say about his influence over me reminds me of an important and recurring constellation in my life. [...] In the economy of my existence there are a few specific relationships which enable me to maintain one which is the polar opposite of my primary being. [...] In such a case I can do little more than ask my friends to trust that the fruitful nature of these relationships, whose dangers are obvious, will ultimately become clear. You of all people cannot have failed to realise that my life, as well as my thinking, is moving towards extreme positions.
>
> (WBGB IV: 440–441)

This essay will describe some of the elements of the constellation. These are testimonials, fragments, which are intended as representatives of the whole.

Methodologically speaking, this essay might perhaps claim a rapport with Brecht's montage technique and Benjamin's understanding of allegory. To create an allegory, says Benjamin, is to join together what has been broken apart.

---

[9] Hannah Arendt, 'Walter Benjamin', in Hannah Arendt, *Walter Benjamin, Bertolt Brecht. Zwei Essays* (Munich: Piper, 1971), 7–62. Here 21.
[10] Elisabeth Hauptmann in conversation with Wolfgang Gersch, Rolf Liebmann and Karlheinz Mund for the film *Die Mit-Arbeiterin* (1972), archives of the Akademie der Künste, Elisabeth Hauptmann Archive (CD selection by Karlheinz Mund, CD 2). – I did not access this statement until after the publication of my book *Benjamin und Brecht*.

KRISE UND KRITIK

A key component of my book are the minutes of conversations about the setting-up of a journal called *Krise und Kritik*, which Benjamin and Brecht – together with Bernard von Brentano and Herbert Ihering and with the help of Bloch, Kracauer, Kurella and Lukács – wanted to bring out with Rowohlt Verlag in 1930/31. They envisaged an organ 'in which the bourgeois intelligentsia would take account of the demands and insights which uniquely enable it, under the present circumstances, to engage in interventionist production with real consequences, as opposed to the usual arbitrary production without consequences'.[11]

The minutes of these conversations indicate an unusual diversity of themes and methodological approaches. They centre around reflections on the position of the artist and intellectual, and on the relationship of form and content in art. A good example is the particularly rich conversation described below, which can be roughly dated to September 1930. The people involved in the project are intellectuals and artists who are preoccupied with the function of thought. Brecht proposes, with his typical pragmatism: 'any other thought than that which is realisable within a society is to be eliminated'.[12] Benjamin responds to this with a very significant contribution to the conversation. It is one of those fragments which encapsulate more than some entire systems of thought manage to do: 'there have always been movements – primarily religious ones, in the past – which, like marx [sic], wanted to see a radical destruction of imagery. /2 research methods: 1. Theology, 2. materialist dialectics'.[13]

Benjamin viewed theological and materialist methods as complementary because for him, the criterion for judging an approach was not its tradition or ideological position but its 'utility'. Thus he found philological potential in theological historical criticism which he felt was lacking in the humanities. An article Benjamin published in 1931 in the review 'Literaturgeschichte und Literaturwissenschaft' suggested that works of art should be portrayed 'in the era in which they came into being' in order to 'portray the era perceiving them – that is, our era' (WBGS III: 290). It owed some of its ideas to the historical-critical method, even if no direct link can be identified. Above all, however, Benjamin was interested in theological thinking in terms of its method and aspirations, because it took the totality into account, whereas every other view was based on objective facts. Benjamin's openness to seemingly contrary positions arose from his determination to prise apart entrenched problems and face social reality head-on, in a radical way.

But the way in which Benjamin's thinking brought together theology and materialist dialectics, messianism and Marxism, cannot be reduced solely to methodological questions. For Benjamin, theology had an *experimental character* (as did Benjamin's Marxism, according to Adorno). Benjamin's interest in directing his thinking 'towards those subjects most densely inhabited by truth' (WBGB IV: 19) led to a highly original fusion of contradictory traditions of thought.

During the period of *Krise und Kritik*, the range of Benjamin's thought is illustrated in a programmatic letter to Max Rychner of 7 March 1931: in it, Benjamin urged Rychner not to see in him 'a proponent of dialectical materialism as a dogma but a scholar to

---

[11]Walter Benjamin, 'Memorandum zu der Zeitschrift *Krisis [sic] und Kritik*', WBGS VI: 619.
[12]BBA 217/06.
[13]Ibid.

whom the *attitude* of the materialist seems, both scientifically and humanely, to be more productive in terms of everything that moves us than that of the idealist' (WBGB IV: 19–20). Almost a decade later, this unusual confrontation between philosophical models would be fully fleshed out in the theses 'Über den Begriff der Geschichte' ['On the Concept of History']. Brecht said of this text that it was 'lucid and clarifying (despite all the metaphor and Jewish-isms)'.[14]

AVANT-GARDE

The initial impulse for Benjamin's extensive engagement with Brecht's work came from the first issue of the *Versuche*, which appeared in April 1930. Benjamin was the first of Brecht's critics to take a theoretical approach to his work. The influence of Benjamin's readings is felt to this day; Heiner Müller's view of Brecht is a case in point.

Benjamin understood Brecht's work as a way out of an impasse which he described in 1932 as the 'stubborn insistence on contrasting writing and literature'. No great literature can be understood, Benjamin argued, without taking into account technique, which is a writerly concept.[15] The old polarity between the 'true' poet and his creative works, which cannot be grasped on a rational level, and the writer or man of letters with his profane, unartistic efforts, seemed questionable to Benjamin. Brecht, in connection with the journal project, also rejected 'the way "great literature" is set apart and treated as the only "true literature"'; this had, he claimed, 'turned literary history into a stomping ground of tastes'.[16]

Under the completely altered conditions of exile, Brecht's work retained its exemplary significance for Benjamin. This is evident from Benjamin's plan for a series of lectures he was to give at the home of the Parisian doctor Jean Dalsace in April 1934. He informed Brecht on 5 March 1934:

> I am advertising a series of talks on 'l'avantgarde allemande' among the French circles to which I have access and several others. It will be a cycle of five lectures – people will have to buy tickets for the whole series. In each of the different fields, I single out one figure whom I feel definitively reflects the current state of the art.
>
> 1) le roman (Kafka)
> 2) l'essay (Bloch)
> 3) théâtre (Brecht)
> 4) journalisme (Kraus)
>
> Preceded by an introductory lecture 'Le public allemand'.
>
> (WBGB IV: 362)

For the purposes of his lectures, Benjamin created (with remarkably sound judgement) a group which did not actually exist. Only the headings have survived, but Detlev Schöttker reconstructs the relationship as a contribution to a 'theory of literary constructivism'. Benjamin's statements on Kraus, Kafka, Bloch and Brecht are united by an interest in

---

[14]Bertolt Brecht, *Journal*, 9.8.1941, BFA 27: 12.
[15]Walter Benjamin, 'Jemand meint', WBGS: 360-363. Here 362.
[16]Bertolt Brecht, 'Über neue Kritik', BFA 21: 402-404. Here 402.

constructions and artistic techniques, in different forms of sparsity of style and reduction to the essentials, as amalgamated in the term 'poverty of experience' from the Kraus essay.

Apart from in Brecht's case, the relationships between the figures and their fields can only be explained with a healthy dose of *Verfremdung*: Kafka – novel / Bloch – essay / Kraus – journalism are all relationships which go against the grain. Methodologically, this is a continuation of the *Crisis and Criticism* journal project; the key to Benjamin's reading is the term 'criticism'. His chosen representatives of the avant-garde all engaged with their genres in a critical way – they revolutionized them.

HOUSES OF CARDS, AND CHESS

Houses of cards in exile: in January 1934, Benjamin sends Brecht a reproduction of a painting in the Louvre: *Le Château des cartes*, by the French painter Jean-Baptiste Siméon Chardin. The picture was painted in the mid-eighteenth century. 'Dear Brecht,' he began, 'I am sending you a blueprint to help with your training, which I, as a master builder, take a benevolent interest in.'

The painting is evidence of the closeness that developed between Benjamin and Brecht in exile, which we will now examine further. In the late autumn of 1933 Brecht invited Benjamin to Denmark for the first time, and in the years that followed he, Steffin and Weigel rarely wrote to Benjamin without issuing an invitation for him to come and stay. As soon as he got back from Paris, on 22 December 1933, Brecht was singing the island's praises:

> It is pleasant here. Not cold at all, much warmer than in Paris. Helli thinks you could get by here on 100 Kr (60 Reichsmark, 360 francs) a month. And the library in Svendborg can get you *any* book. – We have radio, newspapers, playing cards, your books soon, stoves, little cafés, an exceptionally easy language, and the world is falling apart more quietly here.

(BFA 28: 395)

Benjamin too appreciated the fact that the house on the sound seemed far removed from the field of battle. Of his second stay there in summer 1936 he wrote: 'It is a very agreeable life and such a friendly one that we wonder daily how much longer it can continue, with Europe the way it is.'[17] And two years later, clearly in reference to Brecht's phrase about the world falling apart more quietly here: 'the newspapers arrive so late here that it is easier to muster up the courage to open them'.[18]

Their time together in Skovsbostrand during the summers of 1934, 1936 and 1938 was marked by an 'atmosphere of intimacy', to quote a description by Ruth Berlau.[19] The activities over which Brecht and Benjamin bonded included conversations, working in the garden, reading the paper and listening to the news on the radio, and occasional trips to nearby Svendborg. The little exile community threw itself enthusiastically into card games and board games. They mainly played chess, but also games of dice like Monopoly (which was patented in 1935), billiards, poker and Sixty-Six (a card game). 'Eisler is

---

[17] Walter Benjamin, letter to Bryher [?] around mid-August 1936. Draft. WBGB V: 362.
[18] Walter Benjamin, letter to Kitty Marx-Steinschneider, 20.7.1938, WBGB VI: 142.
[19] *Brechts Lai-tu. Erinnerungen und Notate von Ruth Berlau*, ed. Hans Bunge (Darmstadt and Neuwied: Luchterhand, 1985), 105.

the uncrowned king of "66"'[20] reported Margarete Steffin, and Helene Weigel wrote to Benjamin:

> I want to know how you are feeling and whether you are able to play 66 with anyone, with all your unfriendly idiosyncrasies which I rather miss. I have started learning to play chess, so there would be an opportunity for you to annoy me to death. When would you like to do it?[21]

Benjamin noted Brecht's 'behaviour when playing poker' (WBGS II.3: 1371). Tournaments were organised and prizes offered – they once played chess for a double whiskey (Eisler lost 2:3) and on another occasion there was a bitter poker battle over a piece of Lebkuchen, which Brecht did not want to hand over. New games were in demand. 'Do you know Go?' Benjamin asked Brecht on 21 May 1934, before his first trip, 'a very old Chinese board game? It is at least as interesting as chess – we should introduce it to Svendborg. You don't move any pieces in Go, you just place them on the board, which is empty at the start of the game' (WBGB IV: 427).

In order to ward off boredom Brecht suggested, following a game of chess in July 1934, that they develop a new game. Benjamin noted down the proposition:

> So when Korsch comes, we should get together with him and develop a new game. A game where the positions don't always stay the same, where the function of the pieces changes after they have stood in the same place for a while: they either get weaker or more powerful. As it is the game doesn't develop; it stays the same for too long.
>
> (WBGS IV: 526)

Chess, in particular, became the embodiment of the peaceful and intimate communication at Skovsbostrand which Brecht hoped would motivate Benjamin to make 'the journey north': 'The chess board lies orphaned, every half hour a tremor of remembrance runs through it: that was when you would have made your moves.' The games reflected Benjamin's mood, which was dependent upon the progress of his work: 'A couple of games of chess, which ought to serve as a distraction, take on the colour and monotony of the grey sound, for I very rarely win.'[22] Once the family had fled Denmark, Benjamin mourned the loss in a letter to Margarete Steffin in Skovsbostrand on 18 April 1939: 'the games of chess in the garden are over now too' (WBGB VI: 267).

In fact, the chess game is not only a part of but also a model for Brecht and Benjamin's communication or constellation: chess pieces are placed and moved – in other words there is predictability (chessboard, pieces with predetermined possibilities, rules) and variability (every game is different). Composure and presence of mind are the sources of an effective strategy. The opposition inherent in the game cannot unfold without a partner. Competition invites comparison. The defeated player has the chance of a new game. Closeness and distance, consensus and independence correspond in

---

[20]Margarete Steffin, letter to Walter Benjamin, 20.7.1937, in Margarete Steffin: *Briefe an berühmte Männer. Walter Benjamin, Bertolt Brecht, Arnold Zweig*, ed. with a preface and notes by Stefan Hauck (Hamburg: Europäische Verlagsanstalt, 1999), 247.
[21]Helene Weigel, letter to Walter Benjamin, 20.1.1935, in *'Wir sind zu berühmt, um überall hinzugehen'. Helene Weigel. Briefwechsel 1935-1971*, ed. Stefan Mahlke (Berlin: Theater der Zeit/Literaturforum im Brecht-Haus Berlin, 2000), 12.
[22]Walter Benjamin, letter to Gretel Adorno, 20.7.1938, WBGB VI: 139.

a productive exchange. It is no coincidence that the first of Benjamin's theses 'On the Concept of History' uses the game of chess as a model for a philosophical constellation.

TALISMAN LAO TZU POEM

The last fragment we will look at here is a note written by Brecht following a conversation with Hans Sahl in New York in 1945:

> B explains the Lao Tzu poem to French officers in the camp –
> B takes out telephone when Sahl asks how Brecht is – in Paris
> B wants to sit on a café terrace twiddling his thumbs. – [23]

It is clear that Brecht, in using the initial B, can only mean Benjamin: the desire to sit on a café terrace features as a remark by Benjamin in the novel *Die Wenigen und die Vielen* [*The Few and the Many*] and in a diary written by Hans Sahl. In the version recorded in the diary, Benjamin says: 'If I get out of this alive, I shall never ask for anything more than to sit on a café terrace – in the sun – twiddling my thumbs!'[24]

The 'Lao Tzu Poem' is Brecht's 'Legend of the Origin of the Book Tao Te Ching on Lao Tzu's Road into Exile', to which Benjamin devoted one of his 'Commentaries on Poems by Brecht'. This commentary focuses on hope and friendliness. It deals with the 'minimum programme for humanity' encountered again in the phrase 'You see, hardness[25] must succumb in the end'. The poem, wrote Benjamin, 'was written at a time when this phrase sounded to the human ear like a promise that was nothing short of messianic'.[26]

Benjamin's commentary – as its writer had wished – had a direct impact which, astonishingly, first made itself felt in French internment camps. The poem and the commentary had both appeared on 23 April 1939 in the newspaper *Schweizer Zeitung am Sonntag*, a politically charged publication. The *Schweizer Zeitung am Sonntag* took a stridently antifascist line and was against appeasement; from its position on neutral ground, it called for armed resistance. Fritz Lieb, the Swiss theologian and student of Karl Barth who had arranged for the poem and commentary to be printed, published an article in the same issue entitled 'Warum wir schießen müssen' ['Why we have to shoot']. The idea of pre-emptively arming the population met with Benjamin's explicit approval.

Benjamin had been impatient for the publication of the issue featuring the poem and commentary. Now he himself helped to disseminate it; on 3 May 1939, with a conspiratorial undertone, he asked Lieb for some sample copies: 'one of the main purposes of such a publication is that one can make sure the right people get hold of it; that's my intention' (WBGB VI: 275).

When the internments began in September 1939, Heinrich Blücher, Hannah Arendt's husband, used Brecht's poem 'as a talisman with magic powers' – 'Those of his fellow

---

[23] BBA 1157/68.
[24] Hans Sahl, *Tagebuch* (Deutsches Literaturarchiv Marbach am Neckar).
[25] Although 'harshness' may sound like a more natural translation, the reference in the poem is to a hard rock being worn away by soft water (current Editor's note).
[26] Walter Benjamin, 'Zu der "Legende von der Entstehung des Buches Taoteking auf dem Weg des Laotse in die Emigration"', WBGS II.2: 568–572. Here 572.

prisoners who read *and* understood it were identified as potential friends.'[27] And Arendt recalled: 'The poem spread through the camps like wildfire, it was passed from mouth to mouth like glad tidings.'[28]

Benjamin's experience was similar to Blücher's. In autumn 1939, when he was in the camp at Nièvre, he introduced Brecht's poem and his commentary to the internees and – as is evident from Brecht's note – to their guards. The lesson of the water's triumph over the rock which earned Lao Tzu his exile now gave hope to the displaced people in the camp. Brecht will have taken encouragement from the evidence of the mediating role played by his most important commentator in his lifetime. In a recently discovered letter to the theologian Karl Thieme, written in April 1948, Brecht alluded to his friend's tragic end in the Spanish border town of Portbou. He drew a parallel between Lao Tzu and Benjamin that is more powerful than many an obituary:

> As for the Lao Tzu poem you quoted: I heard that Benjamin, in the French camp where he was last, recited it from memory several times. But he himself found no border guard who would let him pass.[29]

---

[27] Elisabeth Young-Bruehl, *Hannah Arendt. Leben, Werk und Zeit* (Frankfurt am Main: S. Fischer, 1986), 221.
[28] Hannah Arendt, 'Bertolt Brecht', in Arendt: *Walter Benjamin. Bertolt Brecht* (see footnote 9), 63–107. Here 102.
[29] Wizisla, *Benjamin und Brecht* (see footnote 1), 221 and 114.

Kurt Weill

CHAPTER FOURTEEN

'Suiting the Action to the Word': Some Observations on *Gestus* and *Gestische Musik*

MICHAEL MORLEY

In surveying the literature on the relationship between words and music, it is relatively easy to find discussions of what is *not* an effective marriage of poet and composer. It is more difficult to find analyses of how and why particular songs are effective in their combination of word and music, especially in a dramatic or, to use the Weill/Brecht term, 'gestic' context. Nor, understandably enough, can one find anything that could be seen as a normative program for writing an effective song, and it is far from the intention of this article to propose that one can derive such an algorithm from Brecht's or Weill's statements.

The rather nebulous concepts of *Gestus* and *gestische Musik*, defined neither systematically nor succinctly by either Weill or Brecht, describe nothing more than a technique for writing pointedly and economically within a dramatic context. In Weill's case, it evolved by gradually stripping away the compositional excesses that Wagnerian and Straussian music drama had led to (even in some of Weill's own works) and concentrating on concise melodic and rhythmic cells to convey musically the underlying dramatic kernel of a scene. This is clear from his own remarks concerning *Aufstieg und Fall der Stadt Mahagonny* and *Die Dreigroschenoper*, but perhaps even clearer in the models of gestische Musik by earlier composers that he selected: scenes from *Die Zauberflöte* and *Fidelio*.[1] The situations in these two scenes are musically and dramatically analogous: one character or pair of characters is discharging a task and commenting on it while the other is reacting to both the situation and the other's words by stating his or her own position. In Brecht/Weil terms, the Gestus of the temple guardians in *Die Zauberflöte* (act 2 finale, no. 21: 'Der, welcher wandert diese Strasse') could be seen as both instructional and

---

Michael Morley, '"Suiting the Action to the Word": Some Observations on Gestus and Gestische Musik', in Kim H. Kowalke (ed.), *A New Orpheus: Essays on Kurt Weill* (New Haven: Yale UP, 1986), pp. 183–201.

[1] See Kurt Weill, 'Über den gestischen Charakter der Musik', *Die Musik* 21 (March 1929): 419–23; reprinted in Kurt Weill. *Ausgewählte Schriften* (Frankfurt, 1975), pp. 40–45. For a discussion of the historical derivation of the term *Gestus* and a survey of various interpretations of its meaning, see Kim H. Kowalke, *Kurt Weill in Europe* (Ann Arbor, 1979), pp. 495–96.

cautionary, while Tamino's is assertive and deliberately confident. In *Fidelio* (Act 2, no. 12: 'Nur hurtig fort, nur frisch gegraben'), Rocco's is work activity, the need to complete a task in time, while Leonora's is mastering her own emotional and physical resources for *other* purposes while at the same time outwardly assisting Rocco in his.

Stanislavski might have found much to respond to in the latter scene, for it stands as a neat example of one character's major action crossing another's without any verbal exchange between the participants.[2] While one might argue that the note values given to Rocco's words are eighth notes and hence brisker and more appropriate to activity than the quarter notes and dotted quarters of Leonora's line of internalized questioning, there is another aspect to the scene which removes it from the realm of the purely illustrative. It would perhaps have been more obvious for Beethoven to have suggested the activity with scurrying and bustling figures in the orchestra and occasional emphatic accents. But the scene is given a stylized, almost 'distanced' quality by the musical delivery and dynamic level, which do not allow the singers and the music to rely on easy emotional associations by the audience, but rather impart to the scene a clearly defined tableau- or frieze-like character. The action is thereby suspended. While the previous scene has set up in dialogue the situation and provided the narrative detail, the duet now carries the scene forward in a different way by focusing on the *idea* of activity expressed with deceptively simple musical means. And it is these which, precisely because they *are* so simple, do not allow for excesses of emotional delivery or a soaring and overly dramatized declamation of the vocal line.

The concept of Gestus, both historically and critically, also encompasses the style of performance. If Gestus was, for Brecht, the clear and stylized presentation of the social behavior of human beings, a main concern must always be the question of *communication* and *delivery,* the *transmission* to an audience of an action, an emotion, a state of mind in gestic terms. For the librettist, this meant that the words as spoken had to convey the direction in which the speaker was aiming; they were not merely a vehicle for elegant expression of ideas and images. For the composer, it meant that the music required a rhythmic shape that embodied the ebb and flow of both speech patterns and the gist of thought itself. Once established, this shape should not be obscured by an overly ornate deployment of melodic devices which, though pleasing to the ear and sensibilities, might have little to do with the sense of the words.

To approach the topic from another angle, I now turn to two examples of unsuccessful (in gestic terms) marriages of word and music. The first example approaches the question from the composer's point of view, the second from the audience's and performers'; both represent, albeit in slightly exaggerated form, the sort of response that a performance of any of the works of Brecht and Weill is *not* calculated to produce. The first example by Dryden/Handel was cited by V. C. Clinton-Baddeley:

In Handel's setting of Dryden's *Ode on St. Cecilia's Day,* the lines

The TRUMPET shall be heard on high,
The dead shall live, the living die,
And Musick shall untune the Sky

---

[2] The idea of a character's 'major action' is a fundamental one for Stanislavski's approach to scene analysis. In this connection, another of his directorial concepts – that of the 'subtext' to the written text – has prompted the drawing of parallels in the relationship between words and music in Weill's compositions. For further details, see Kirn Kowalke's discussion of this point in *Kurt Weill in Europe,* pp. 130–31.

are prolonged throughout fourteen pages of an ordinary Novello score. Dryden's poem was deliberately written for musk, but by the time Handel had finished with it he might just as well have set the words backwards.³

The second strikes a cautionary note for all – not only music critics; be assured that your Bernard Levinish sins will find you out:

> The other day I attended a concert consisting mainly of the Song Cycles of Debussy, setting the words of Verlaine. They were sung by an Armenian lady who had escaped from a Turkish harem and had had no musical training. She was a barbaric creature who uttered loud howls, and the effect was to me disagreeable in the extreme; all the same, the audience was large and enthusiastic and the most enlightened organ of musical opinion today spoke of the performance with a chastened enthusiasm. I happened to meet the writer of the notice in the course of the following afternoon, and I asked him what he really got for himself out of that singular collocation of sounds. He said airily: 'Well, you see, one gets emotions!' I said: 'Good God! What sort of emotions?' He answered, 'Well, you see, if one shuts one's eyes one can imagine that one is eating strawberry jam and oysters in a house of ill-fame, and a cat is rushing violently up and down the keyboard of the piano with a cracker tied to its tail.'⁴

Notwithstanding the above, a major problem facing both the historian and the critic is the question, beyond that of origin and evolution, of the meaning and significance of the terms *Gestus* and *gestische Musik* for performers. Although it is to Weill that we owe the first extended analysis of the terms, I think it more likely that Brecht introduced the term *Gestus* to Weill rather than vice versa.⁵ Given the former's fondness throughout his life for developing a quasi-scientific approach to the theater (and the vocabulary to go with it), together with his classical background – *Gestus* in Latin means both gesture *and* attitude/mien – it seems more feasible that Brecht, who was concerned from the beginning with developing a theater and a dramaturgy of gestures which expressed relationships between characters rather than a drama of psychological investigation, prompted Weill to his own application of the term to the language of music.

As early as September 1920, Brecht, in an important note, toyed with two notions which became characteristic of his mature drama and which are, in fact, essential to any discussion of Gestus: the idea of contradiction and opposition and the need to find a visible and theatrically effective way of expressing both opposites and the unity of these opposites:

> I'm beginning to feel a faint prejudice against binary divisions (strong-weak, big-small, happy-unhappy, ideal-not ideal). It only happens because people are unable to think of more than two things at once. That's all that will fit into a sparrow-sized brain. But the soundest policy is just to keep on tacking.

---

³V. C. Clinton-Baddeley, *Words for Music* (Cambridge, 1941), p. 17. This brief study still stands as one of the clearest and most judicious examinations of the relationship between music and poetry.
⁴*The Bodley Head Ford Madox Ford* (London, 1962). 1:351.
⁵This contention is speculative. As far as can be ascertained at present, the first published use of the term occurs in Weill's essay of March 1929. For a discussion of this and related matters, see Susan Borwick, 'Weill's and Brecht's Theories on Music in Drama', *Journal of Musicological Research* 4 (October 1982): 39–67. The reader should be cautioned, however, about Borwick's oversimplification of Weill's notion of Gestus.

... Doing everything with all one's body and soul. Never mind exactly what. Small or great: both. Not just politics, hope for the future, sunshine all the time. See that rain? drink it.

... I want a gesture for all that, visible from the gallery, strong enough to smell and be carried away by, for Act 4 of *Drums*.[6] Where a man does something, then does something else (– but does it). Stirs up a whole city, drives deluded people to attack the newspaper offices, makes poor people drunk, fills them with speeches, decks them out with weapons, then goes home.

Let them go to the newspaper offices, not him. He's no longer deluded, no longer poor. The main thing is the gesture with which he goes home, removes his tunic, tears off his tie, grips his throat with his hands, breathes deeply, says 'It's all a bore' and goes off to bed with his woman.[7]

These are essentially primary dramatic ingredients, and what Brecht is looking for is the simple yet stylized rendition of these for an audience. Of course, at this stage the politicizing of these intrapersonal pieces of behavior was not part of his aim; that was to come with the commitment to Marxism after 1926. But social behavior was, from the beginning, a major concern of Brecht's drama, together with the search for its theatrical embodiment. Some impetus in this direction was provided first by the interest of the expressionist theater in gesture (one has only to look at expressionist cinema to find examples of this) and second by the interest that behaviorism had sparked among many writers at the time.

Weill's own writings prior to and subsequent to his first contact with Brecht also evince his interest in arriving at a simplified yet expressive musical language which would be dramatic without resorting to conventional and overly emotional poses and formulas. But whereas Brecht arrived at his ideas through his own practice and his fondness for the 'lower' forms of theater – circuses, music hall, the cabaret – Weill seems to have come at it from another angle: through his own studies of and experiments with opera and the influence of his teacher, Busoni. Many of Weill's views on opera and on the relationship between music and theater echo some of Busoni's pronouncements on these issues. Both men saw in Mozart and Bach the ideal models of the composer in whose works theatrical and absolute music were indivisible – though oddly Busoni is less convincing in analyzing this paradox than Weill.[8] Busoni draws attention to some fairly self-evident points: the dramatic quality of the Evangelist's passages in the *St. Matthew Passion* and the notion of interchangeability in Mozart's works (how 'every one of his operas is a pure symphonic score and there is something of an opera score in each quartet'[9] – a point he seeks to prove by adding words to an unidentified phrase, which turns out to be from the Piano Concerto in C major, K. 467; see ex. 1). Can one really maintain that this illustration helps in understanding what is theatrical about such moments? One might equally well suggest any number of alternative texts to ensure that what Busoni called Mozart's 'exuberant

---

[6]Brecht is speaking of his 1919 'comedy' centered on the Spartacist uprisings, *Trommeln in der Nacht* (Drums in the Night).
[7]Bertolt Brecht, *Diaries 1920–1922*. trans. John Willett (London, 1979). pp. 34–35.
[8]In this connection, see Busoni's observations in *The Essence of Music and Other Papers,* trans. Rosamund Ley (London, 1957), pp. 35–44.
[9]Ibid., p. 3.

interval of a sixth' attains its latent 'dramatic completion'.[10] What about 'If you come tomorrow, we can go and have a meal'; or 'Now we know the grim truth, let us string the villain up' (which has a rather Gilbertian ring to it); or 'When you look into my eyes, my heart begins to beat?' What Busoni's example does show, however, is how even a fleeting phrase of Mozart's music takes on a shape which readily accommodates words, precisely because the rise and fall of the melodic line are close to the rise and fall of speech rhythms and even of breathing itself.

But aside from these musical models, Busoni also drew attention to another aspect of the dramaturgy of opera which has direct bearing on Weill's later analysis of Gestus. This is his concept of the *Schlagwort,* the catchword or abridgment. Busoni's discussion of the term and his application of it to opera display some similarities with Weill's comments on the nature and function of Gestus and gestische Musik:

> Just as the abridgement can sum up the inner part of the text of an opera, it can be transferred in a changed form to the action in general. In relation to the music it serves to create a situation rather than to give the reasons for it logically. ... Therefore the audience's counterpoint of attention should be simplified by allowing speech and music to retire where action has the chief role; ... by putting music and action in the background when a thought is being communicated.[11]

But whereas Busoni's comments explore the question from a theoretical standpoint, Weill is more concerned with both the nature and the function of gestic music: how the composer can *assist* the performer to convey the appropriate attitude to any particular incident at any particular moment.

The concern with performance and delivery is common to both Weill's and Brecht's notions of Gestus, as is the conviction that it must articulate social behavior rather than internalized, personal psychological states. Needless to say, social and political thrust is integral to Brecht's later pronouncements; but the concern for capturing human behavior, for concentrating on interaction between individuals, is there in Weill's essay when he notes: 'We find gestic music wherever an incident involving human interaction is depicted through a naive kind of musical language.'[12] Compare this with Brecht's much later remark: 'A *Gestus* delineates the relationships of human beings to one another.'[13] Of course, solutions to the problem of conveying this Gestus then had to be sought by both men in different areas – Weill through music, Brecht through language, scenic effect, and character. But what is important is that initially at least – and in Brecht's case throughout

---

[10]Ibid., pp. 73–74.
[11]Ibid, p. 13.
[12]Weill, 'Über den gestischen Charakter der Musik', p. 421. In Heinrich Strubel, 'Situation der Oper: Gespräch mit Kurt Weill', *Melos* 10 (February 1931): 43–45, Weill articulated his own sociological bases for his aesthetic path: 'Today, when a grand form of theater is once again emerging, a form that seeks with elevated language and heightened reality to incorporate ideas of the present with timeless ones, opera must then also find its sociological sphere. What is more, it can be assumed that this form of theater can by no means do without the gestic effect and stylizing power of music' (translated in Kowalke, p. 535).
[13]Bertolt Brecht, 'Gestik' (undated note, 194–?) in *Gesammelte Werke* 16:753. In two essays from 1932 Weill wrote of a theatrical form that recaptures the original purpose of theater: 'representation of types of human behavior'. See Kowalke, pp. 541–44.

his life – they approach the problem from the same standpoint: from the point of view of performance, delivery, and the clarification of human behavior for the audience.

Two of Brecht's observations are relevant here. Looking back on his own early attempts to write both text and music, he stated, 'It must be remembered that my main work was in the field of the theater: I was always thinking of actual delivery.'[14] And from the 1940s comes the following interesting, if somewhat choleric, diary entry:

> A musician to whom I gave the *Courage* texts to compose, along with a few guidelines, did three settings, played them to his friends, heard that he was copying Weill and pulled out. In vain I explained to him that he had just retained a principle – a principle Weill hadn't discovered. (I told him how I'd come across Weill when he was a pupil of Schreker and Busoni, as the composer of atonal psychological operas, and how I'd whistled things to him bar by bar and above all performed them for him.)[15]

The most important point here is not the undoubtedly exaggerated picture of Brecht giving Weill musical dictation, but the emphasis on *actual delivery*. And it does tie in with Weill's own remarks – closer to the time – that Brecht's primitive setting of the 'Alabama Song' was an attempt to fix both the rhythm and his own inimitable manner of delivery.[16]

This manner of delivery requires some description, since it is fundamental to any understanding of Gestus and how it functions. Brecht's own delivery has often been described as aggressive, even savage – a characterization that is not quite apt. Of course, his voice never prompted description as 'cream poured over purple velvet'. Rather than brutal or aggressive, however, it is more accurately characterized as exaggeratedly harsh and clear. It is this clarity and directness which also distinguish early, authentic performances by other singers – as in the selections from *Die Dreigroschenoper* recorded by members of the original cast. All these performers used a vocal and dramatic technique appropriate to Brecht's call for textual clarity and nonemotional delivery, yet in keeping with Weill's melodic lines: that is, a very 'forward' type of voice production linked with a style of performance in which the singer does not immerse him- or herself in the character or in the emotions of the song. Indeed, a fondness for this performing style led both Brecht and Weigel to admire Ethel Merman's – and, in Weigel's case, even to borrow a gesture from her for *Mother Courage*.

This manner of performance has become almost a paradigm of Brecht/Weill performance practice; insisted upon by Brecht and also by Eisler, it is not as revolutionary as it may appear, for it has a definite tradition. The neuroses of the operatic tenor had been cleverly satirized in Gilbert and Sullivan's 'A tenor, all singers above', which opens Act 2 of *Utopia Limited*. At the same time, interpreters of Weill and Brecht might also use Fitzbattleaxe's complaints as a primer for performance:

---

[14]Bertolt Brecht, 'Über reimlose Lyrik mit unregelmässigen Rhythmen', *Das Wort* 3 (March 1939): reprinted in *Gesammelte Werke* 19:395–403.

[15]*Bertolt Brechts Arbeitsjournal* (Frankfurt, 1973), p. 188. The implications of this later, somewhat colored account of Brecht's and Weill's working methods have been discussed by Kowalke in his study and in my own article 'New Tunes for Old: Brecht, Weill and the Language of Music in Four Unpublished Songs', *German Life and Letters* (April 1982): 241–52. Weill never studied with Franz Schreker – he only considered doing so. [Editor's note: In an interview with Arnold Sundgaard on 14 September 1984 in Los Angeles, the librettist of *Down in the Valley* told me that when he and Weill worked together, he tried to hum for the composer certain tunes he'd envisioned for his lyrics. Weill cut him off: 'I don't want to hear them. Brecht used to whistle his horrible tunes to me, and it just threw me off.' K. K.]

[16]See Weill, 'Über den gestischen Charakter der Musik', p. 422.

You can't do chromatics
With proper emphatics
When anguish your bosom is ringing. ...
One ought to be firm as a rock
To venture a shake in *vibrato*
When fervor's expected
Keep cool and collected
Or never attempt *agitato*.

More immediately relevant, however, is the following: 'Moreover, he never permitted violent expression in a performance. The singer, as a rule, only relates the experiences and feelings of others and does not himself impersonate the characters whose emotions he describes.' Not, as one might think, a report of guidelines Brecht, Weill, or Eisler gave to performers, but Sonnleithner's account of Schubert's suggestion for the correct delivery of his songs.[17]

It is, alas, all too easy to list famous opera singers with marvelous voices who deliver the text of a song or aria as if they were reading the telephone directory in Tibetan or as if they'd just emerged from a daydream and were unclear as to where to begin. (A famous Australian example immediately springs to mind.) At the same time, such singers manage to imply to the audience that any attempt to clarify the meaning through gesture – let alone acting – would be an insult. This is *not* the emotional detachment that Brecht and Weill sought; as Brecht put it in a fragmentary poem:

The operating with definitive gestures
Can alter your character
Change it.
If the feet are higher than the behind
The speech itself is different and the way of speaking
Changes the thought.
A certain violent
Movement of the hand with the back facing downwards
While the upper arm stays close to the body convinces
Not only others, but also you who are making the movement.
Leafing back while you read, literally drawing up a
scheme –[18]

Weill also implies some rudimentary, stylized gestural underlining in his comments on Tamino's aria from *Die Zauberflöte,* 'Dies Bildnis ist bezaubernd schön', when he says that Tamino can hold the portrait in his left or his right hand, but it makes no difference because

---

[17]Quoted in Otto Erich Deutsch, *Schubert: Memoirs by His Friends,* trans. R. Ley and J. Nowell (London, 1958), p. 116.

[18]Brecht, *Gesammelte Werke* 8:377. A similar view is expressed in the anecdote recounting the exchange between Keuner (an alter ego of Brecht's) and the professor of philosophy, who makes great play to Mr. Keuner of his wisdom: 'After a time, Mr. Keuner said to him: "You're uncomfortable sitting, you're uncomfortable speaking, you're uncomfortable thinking." The Professor of Philosophy became angry and said: "I did not want to learn something about myself, but about the content of what I was saying." "It has none," said Mr. Keuner. "I see you walking clumsily, and there is no goal for you to reach while I watch you walking. You speak obscurely and there is no brightness created by you while you speak. Seeing your attitude, I'm not interested in your goal"' (*Gesammelte Werke* 12:375).

the Gestus is dictated by the music itself.[19] In this case, the Gestus establishes a certain quizzical response to the attractiveness of the unknown subject of the painting and combines this with reflection on his own reactions and an awareness of the resurgence of emotion.

Application to the present case of Brecht's dictum on the proof of the pudding being in the eating may be dangerous, but we leave this series of recipes to look at several songs as illustrations of some of the points already raised. The first thing to remember about all of them – whether set by Weill, Eisler, or Brecht himself – is that they present a dramatic situation *in nuce*. We must see and hear the singer as *singer* and as *persona* telling a story, commenting on it, and inviting the listener to share or to step back from the persona's attitudes. This sounds somewhat complicated and text-oriented, but music has an essential role to play in the process.

Take the 'Barbarasong' from *Die Dreigroschenoper,* for example. The text of the stanza on the page might suggest that Brecht intended one attitude to be sustained until the refrain – an attitude which might be described as a performer taking a tough line saying: 'You can't pull the wool over my eyes; I was starry-eyed once but I soon saw through life's illusions.' Of course, this attitude is very much to the fore, but it is not the only one that needs to be presented. Rather than playing only that attitude, the performer is guided by Weill's musical setting to show attitudes *in stages*. This procedure is very close to the notion of finding the 'beats' in a character's speech that articulate a change in mood or intent. Thus, the song's opening section establishes the Gestus of the storyteller and with it an attitude of (perhaps forced) naiveté, which the audience is invited to share, not only through the 'einst so wie du' but through the jaunty bounce of the music. This is offset by Weill's choice of the minor key, which in itself is an ironic comment. In this opening we can find a lucid illustration of what Weill meant when he wrote that 'the gestic means are expressed first of all in a rhythmic fixing of the text'.[20] It seems likely that this emphasis on rhythm dates from Weill's collaboration with Brecht – after all, he provided Weill with the texts – but rather than the question of who had the greater say, more interesting is the readiness on Weill's part to see the logic of this approach and to work with it. In the earlier setting of the song that Brecht worked on with Franz S. Bruinier, the rhythmic shape is similar to Weill's in many respects (see ex. 2).[21]

To return to the earlier point about 'beats', it is significant that these are actually reflected in the musical settings – somewhat primitively and directly in the Brecht/Bruinier version, more subtly and, if you like, more gestically in Weill's. One of the most distinctive features of a Weill/Brecht song (but, to be sure, not only of theirs) is the fact that the text and music, rather than simply evolving organically, proceed in stages or episodes. One distinct section follows another rather than a whole emerging gradually from the flow of music and text together. (In some cases, of course, this structure corresponds to the verse/refrain pattern or a simple A +B+C+refrain form.) In the Brecht/Bruinier setting of the 'Barbarasong', there are four clear episodes (marked A, B, C, D in example 2), although the sudden musical hiatuses are sometimes ill contrived. Weill's version manages to be more adroit with its juxtaposition of C- and F-minor and at the same time to catch the Gestus more faithfully. In this case, note the matter-of-fact sharing of a confidence

---

[19] Weill, 'Über den gestischen Charakter der Musik'. p. 422.
[20] Ibid., p. 421.
[21] Bertolt Brecht-Archiv 249/60. Permission to reproduce material from Mrs. Barbara Brecht-Schall for the Brecht Estate, and Suhrkamp Verlag, Frankfurt.

with the audience and the suggestion that they and the singer have the same values – a suggestion, of course, shockingly dispelled by the sudden 'No' and the sense of flying in the face of accepted attitudes and moving on to better things.

The refrain proper provides another illustration of how Weill could deploy the wide range of harmonic and melodic means at a genuine composer's disposal to develop what is present in only embryonic form in the original setting. Weill constructs an overly languid and 'emotional' melodic line to comment ironically on the unromantic, almost aggressive words in such a way that – just as in the 'Alabama Song' – one responds both to the effectiveness of the melody and to the implied ironic comment on its banality. Or, as Brecht put it:

> [The performer] must perform everything, especially something dreadful, with enjoyment and show his enjoyment.[22]

> The manageability [it is significant that Brecht prefers this term to *intelligibility* or something analogous] of a description depends on whether it contains yes and no in it and whether the yes or no is sufficiently established in it.[23]

Unlike the Brecht/Bruinier setting, Weill's music does not merely chug along beside or beneath the text. His setting manages to be simple, even trivial, and at the same time a perfect example of musical irony. (This same approach, incidentally, is followed in the 'Liebeslied' from *Die Dreigroschenoper*, where Weill combines a deliberately saccharine melody with the stilted rhythm of the hesitation waltz or 'Boston'.) In such cases the rhythm and the melody are simple, interdependent *musical* gests which indicate to the perceptive performer the way in which he or she might externalize through character-attitudes and physical behavior the *social* gests of the scenes.

It might be argued that thus far the attempt to give a concrete example of Gestus has adopted a rather tangential approach. The reasons are simple. Weill's analysis of the term is extremely compressed and refers to but one example from his own work. Brecht, rather than providing a series of notes for the performer, prefers to draw his or her attention to something analogous or to an example drawn from another work. Most annoying of all is Brecht's failure, in a commentary on *Aufstieg und Fall der Stadt Mahagonny*, to provide some precise negative reference points which might have helped the reader or critic to arrive by inference at the positive: 'I should not like to leave unmentioned the fact that in my opinion Weill's music for this opera is not purely gestic: it does, however, contain many gestic sections, at least enough to seriously endanger the usual type of opera.'[24] Which ones are and which ones are not? one asks with impatience, although an informed guess might single out 'Herr Jakob Schmidt' (in the version for the 1931 Berlin production), 'The Maiden's Prayer' scene, and 'Moon of Alabama' as decidedly gestic.

Given Weill's and Brecht's concurrence that the rhythmic fixing of a text is the starting point for a gestic setting, one of the more ambiguous arguments that Weill advanced in his essay on gestic music must be his comment that 'one can interpret a sentence rhythmically in various ways and yet express the same *Gestus*'.[25] If one compares Weill's

---

[22]Brecht, 'Anweisung an den Schauspieler' (undated notes, 1935–41?), reprinted in *Gesammelte Werke* 15:411.
[23]Brecht, 'Das Ja-Nein', reprinted in *Gesammelte Werke* 15:413.
[24]Brecht, 'Über die Verwendung von Musik für ein episches Theater' (1935?), reprinted in *Gesammelte Werke* 15:476.
[25]Weill, 'Über den gestischen Charakter der Musik', p. 421.

two settings of 'Lasst euch nicht verführen'[26] from *Aufstieg und Fall der Stadt Mahagonny* with Brecht's own early setting – where it was still entitled 'Luzifers Abendlied'[27] – two points are immediately clear: the rhythm and meter (Brecht's 6/8 versus Weill's alla breve) are different, and the singers' attitudes are quite different. (See ex. 3.) Weill opts for the mock-solemn, portentous, somewhat threatening; Brecht aims at a combination of the insistent and the encouraging. But both subvert familiar expectations. After the E-minor opening and the arresting leap of an octave onto the significant word 'euch' in Brecht's setting, one expects the exhortation to continue, but the shift to A major (on the words 'Der Tag steht vor den Türen') provides a wry sweetness to offset the negative thrust of the lines. Presumably this is a Lucifer with a honeyed tongue and an engaging manner. Whereas Brecht finds this way of bringing out the Gestus of the anti-Christian credo, Weill's settings take the shape of an anti-chorale in which the usual diatonic progressions are replaced by more widely spaced melodic intervals and harsher harmonies. Weill's specifically *musical* parody is certainly more obvious, and it is used to comment in its way on the religious attitudes parodied in the text.

The difficulty in discussing the Brecht/Weill collaborations is the very difficulty over which they later fell out: the territorial imperative. There is little doubt that because of his own musical leanings and concern with the question of delivery, Brecht was of help to Weill. At the same time Weill was no unthinking 'setter of words'. As a composer with an understanding of theater, he shaped the form and content of Brecht's librettos according to musical precepts while still adhering to Brecht's attitudes – attitudes similar in their way to those expressed by William Butler Yeats when he wrote: 'Music that wants of us nothing but images – that suggest sound cannot be our music. ... Such music can but dislocate wherever there is syntax and elaborate rhythm. The poet ... hears with derision most settings of his work. ... And yet there are old songs which melt him into tears.'[28] Although one must accept that Weill could not have continued to collaborate with Brecht without even more room for independent or interdependent development, his settings of Brecht's texts written in the United States without consultation with the poet, 'Nannas Lied' (1939) and 'Und was bekam des Soldaten Weib?' (1943),[29] are a curious mélange of styles and approaches. They raise three somewhat contentious points of criticism:

1. These two songs aspire to the concert platform. Indeed, they come very close to a German equivalent of the much-maligned English art song. Not that the music is trite: 'Nannas Lied' in particular, with its haunting melody and flowing line, might almost persuade the listener that the words and the music really *ought* to melt on the ear.

2. Linked with this, the rhythmic outline is much less determinate than in Weill's earlier settings of Brecht's texts. Of course there is a funeral march suggested by the punctuated quarter notes of the 'Soldier's Wife', but this becomes hypnotic, almost numbing, rather than disturbing,

---

[26]The two versions of the number appear in the piano-vocal score *of Aufstieg und Fall der Stadt Mahagonny* (UE #9851, ed. David Drew) on pp. 234–35 and 292–93.
[27]Brecht's setting is in private hands, along with a number of early songs and simple guitar accompaniments. I am grateful to Walter Brecht for his permission to reproduce the setting.
[28]Quoted in Clinton-Baddeley, p. 11.
[29]Both are published in *The Unknown Kurt Weill,* ed. Lys Symonette (European American Music Corp., 1982), pp. 1–4, 16–19, as recorded by Teresa Stratas *(The Unknown Kurt Weill),* Nonesuch D-79019.

3. Perhaps because of his Broadway work and the need to take on the idiom of American popular music, Weill reacted by returning not to the German cabaret song for a model, but to a style midway between the French ballad and the German lied.

Both songs are 'occasional pieces': 'Nannas Lied' was a Christmas present for Lenya in 1939, and 'Und was bekam des Soldaten Weib?' was intended for propagandistic use during the war. Weill had no hand in shaping the text of either song, as he often did during his direct collaborations with Brecht. Although neither of these settings was written with a theatrical production in mind, Weill's approach to Brecht's texts – which nevertheless can be seen as self-contained theatrical moments that embody the social and personal Gestus of a character and situation – is less obviously theatrical or 'gestic' than his earlier settings of similar texts. Whereas many of Weill's earlier songs based on Brecht's poetry (and indeed Eisler's settings of the same texts) present characters in stages with an episodic juxtaposition and alternation of attitude and behavior that are reflected in the music, in these two later songs the words and attitudes of the singer become blurred by, and are absorbed into, the music itself. It seems that Weill returned to a more conventional approach to songwriting with mood settings concerned more with capturing in the music an overall, generalized attitude (in 'Nannas Lied', a reflective, bittersweet melancholy) than with the contradictory aspects of the persona expressed in the words. Moreover, the overall musical shape is more regular and predictable; 'Nannas Lied' is built on a periodic phrase structure, with the verse and refrain falling into a predictable 12+12 bar pattern.

Echoes of the German lied tradition are evident: the introductory figure of 'Nannas Lied' suggests Schubert or perhaps Schumann, and where the earlier Weill might have pointed this ironically, these chords are, arguably, less ambiguous. One might suggest that the counter-melody, doubled at the octave, which spices the accompaniment to the third stanza, is an ironic echo of the Liszt 'Liebestraum' (which Weill played as a youth). But when the left-hand chords are related to the ascending Lisztian progressions in the right hand and the rather bland harmonic palette, it seems that we have a case of a musician in search of an idiom rather than a composer juxtaposing the new with the old in such a way that one comments on the other. Eisler's setting – composed with a stage production of *Die Rundköpfe und die Spitzköpfe* in mind and far simpler, apart from the arresting jagged opening notes – comes closer to the implicit Gestus of the text in its theatrical context, which, from the poet's viewpoint, *must* be both social and psychological.[30]

Whereas Weill's flowing melodic line smoothes out the irregularities in Brecht's text and evolves continuously throughout the song, Eisler's primitive setting pays closer attention to speech inflections, draws attention to the episodic shape of the singer's account, and almost approaches montage. Rather than aspiring to the homogeneous texture adopted by Weill within each strophe, Eisler's song corresponds more to a recitative and aria pattern in its verse/refrain opposition for each stanza. The irregular speech inflections are reflected in the changing meter (4/4, 2/4, 3/4), and the vocal line of the verse is kept deliberately unadorned, following a basic chord progression of 9ths and 7ths. Weill's refrain effects a smooth transition from the verse and moves logically and inevitably toward its musical culmination on the word 'Tränen', but Eisler's refrain, in keeping with the text, comes as more of a disruption, in which the prostitute's moment of reflection is offset by emotional detachment. Although Eisler allows Nanna human dimensions in the

---

[30] Eisler's setting is readily accessible in the *Brecht-Eisler Songbook* ed. Eric Bentley (New York, 1967), pp. 156–58.

refrain (in contrast to the Blues of the verse in which the merchandization – or reification – is presented), the music is not emotionally charged. It has something of the naiveté and directness of a folk song, and this unsophisticated musical language is used to express by implication the singer's real feelings, which, far from being emphasized and heightened by the music, are kept, as it were, at arm's length. It is only in the last bars of Eisler's refrain, with its final falling phrase in the vocal line (which mirrors the 7th-chord and falling phrase immediately before the refrain) and in the unresolved piano postlude that the listener is allowed to sense the gap between the matter-of-fact recital and the reality of the character's past and present situation.

Brecht's other text set by both Weill and Eisler allows similar comparisons to be drawn. Although not wishing to use Eisler as a stick with which to beat Weill, I would suggest that, although 'more gestic' is not synonymous with 'more effective' or 'better composed', in this case Eisler's setting again may be more in keeping with the poet's intentions.[31] Weill's setting of 'Und was bekam des Soldaten Weib?' opens with emphatic chords, characteristically vacillating between the major and the minor, to establish the mood of ominous foreboding which will dominate the song. This might be seen as revealing the outcome too early – even allowing for the paradoxical change to pure B major at the end to accompany the receipt of the widow's veil. The text suggests a simple folk song or round, and its recurrent linking of the names of cities with the gifts received suggests an up-tempo, briskly moving setting rather than the more deliberate and musically sophisticated idiom chosen by Weill. It might also be argued that he distorts the speech rhythms by choosing to emphasize the '-kam' of 'bekam' at the expense of the more important 'Was', which, when stressed, establishes the rhetorical and attention-grabbing Gestus which is so crucial to the song's opening – as if a salesman were displaying his wares or a *Bänkelsänger* drawing the crowd's attention to the various objects depicted on his screen.

The text's gestic elements are of the most basic theatrical type – question/answer/commentary – and they allow the performer the opportunity, in Brecht's terms, to show *and* to be. This linking of performance modes (the performer as both narrator and mime) is presented throughout the text: 'Und was bekam des Soldaten Weib aus der Lichterstadt Paris? Aus Paris bekam sie das seidene Kleid, (narrator) zu der Nachbarin Neid das seidene Kleid' (which suggests an elementary piece of character portrayal/mimicry). Weill's setting, although it does differentiate in musical terms between question and answer, still follows the periodic phrase structure noted in 'Nannas Lied'. And rather than providing opposition and contradiction through gestic elements, it establishes from the beginning a type of generalized *Grundgestus* (which might be described as 'it'll turn out bad in the end') that is simply reiterated throughout the song. Once again we find traces of an uneasy combination of lied elements with echoes of Broadway: in particular, the Schumannesque opening with its reminder of 'Die beiden Grenadiere' and the ending with the typical Broadway melodic unit which can be found in any number of songs from the period.[32] Moreover, it is difficult to argue for the presence of any of that characteristic Weillian irony in this setting – irony which is so distinctive an element in earlier songs and which depends on the dialectic of word and music linked with what David Drew accurately summarizes as 'ambiguities of structure and expression together with apparent

---

[31]Ibid., pp. 183–85.
[32]The closing figure has become almost a cliche in popular song. For other examples, see 'The Kid's Last Fight' and 'It's Harry I'm Planning to Marry' from *Calamity Jane*.

anomalies of tone and idiom [which are] exploited with such merciless accuracy that no formal or emotional expectations are secure'.[33]

Eisler's setting finds a more convincing musical equivalent for the episodic structure of the text, although it might be said that the shift to the minor and to extended note-values in the final stanza could be seen as merely reinforcing in musical terms the implied attitude of the text. Yet even the bleak close of the song provides a good example of how a basic Gestus of sadness is filled out by the addition of a call to witness and an implicit accusation. A song of lamentation is simply not enough; the sadness and horror of the final section leave a stronger impact precisely because they have been preceded by the jangling, bouncing, cheap, and even humorous music of the opening (although one might get into some difficulties with any attempt at a complicated explanation in gestic terms of the opening bars, which conform to a fairly common folk-song pattern of tonic-dominant progression). Finally, one might argue that Weill's rhythmic fixing of the text is not as responsive to the metrical pattern as Eisler's, especially given the breaks after 'Weib'; perhaps he was simply unwilling to usurp blatantly – as Eisler did – Stephen Foster's 'Camptown Races' for his opening idea! In both songs, Eisler seems to be more willing than Weill to sacrifice musical sophistication and compositional prerogatives for the 'naive', gestic quality that Brecht probably envisioned.

Through comparisons such as these we can perhaps comprehend the admittedly nebulous notion of gestic music. But in the second section of one of his most extended and complex poems, 'The Shoe of Empedocles',[34] Brecht reflects on the question of how subsequent generations of scholars tended to mystify their teacher's disappearance, seeing his shoe – left behind before his leap into Mount Aetna – as an objective correlative for anything ranging from immortality and transcendent mystery to the intangible proof of their opposites. And the poet strikes a cautionary note which could well apply to any overly confident interpretations of Gestus:

> We hasten to make obscurity
> More obscure and prefer to believe the absurd
> Rather than to seek for a sufficient cause.

and

> Scholars are busy scenting a mystery
> Developing profound metaphysics, in fact all too busy.

Any discussion of the meaning of this term prompts such thoughts, and I would not claim that the preceding comments are the honorable exception. Perhaps one or two of the illustrations might serve to clarify the issues, though ultimately we may still end up holding the Greek philosopher's leather sandal in some confusion, finding our elaborate interpretations gainsaid by its worn, unremarkable appearance. But at least in *that* case the Gestus will be appropriate.[35]

---

[33]David Drew, 'Kurt Weill and His Critics', *Times Literary Supplement*, 3 October 1975, p. 1144.
[34]Brecht, *Poems 1913–1956*, pp. 253–55.
[35]John Willett's discussion of Brecht's musical collaborators ('Brecht and the Musicians', in *Brecht in Context* [London, 1984], pp. 151–77) also addresses some of the questions raised in this article. In particular, his comments on Brecht's attitudes toward the relationship between words and music and toward vocal delivery (pp. 173–77) are a valuable complement to the above discussion.

174 MICHAEL MORLEY

EXAMPLES

EXAMPLE 1: Busoni's addition of words to Mozart's Concerto for Piano and Orchestra in C major, K. 467, mvt. I, mm. 128–29.

EXAMPLE 2: Brecht/Bruinier: 'Barbarasong'.

EXAMPLE 3: Brecht, 'Luzifers Abendlied'.

Because no early draft of the song's text has survived, the underlay of text for the Brecht/Bruinier melody is conjectural in places. In some cases, the reconstruction suggests itself (e.g., the repetition of 'dann sage' at mm. 21–24, although even here one might argue in favor of 'dann sag' ich' followed by 'dann sage ich'.); in other cases, it is more problematic to arrive at a convincing underlay of text (e.g., mm. 18–21).

Hanns Eisler

CHAPTER FIFTEEN

Eisler/Brecht or Brecht/Eisler? Perspectives, Forms and Limits of their Collaboration

ALBRECHT DÜMLING
TRANSLATED BY ROMY FURSLAND

I.

In an article published in 1931 in the journal *Melos*, entitled 'Die neue Musik und ihre Texte' ['The new music and its lyrics'], Hans Mersmann singled out one particular author as defining the direction of contemporary music: 'modern music in Germany had found its poet. That poet was Bertolt Brecht'. With Brecht, new forms had emerged that were 'only attainable through music: the *Lehrstück*, with its "activating" effect on the listener; the cantata and later the opera (*Mahagonny*) as part of the existing social order; *Lindbergh's Flight* and *He Said Yes* (cantata-style plays designed, with varying explicitness, to be performed by amateurs); the *Threepenny Opera* – which stands apart from previous forms and represents a renewal of the concept of opera itself – and *The Decision*, as the foundation of an oratorical choral music based on the workers' choir'. Following this overview of the new genres, the Berlin-based pedagogue and critic touched upon the new relationship between text and music: 'Brecht's texts exist in a decidedly new relationship to music. In contrast to the self-destruction of the word in Stravinsky, here the word rules supreme. Behind the word there is always the idea, tangible and powerful in its expression, sometimes heightened to the point of didactic rationalism. Brecht completely refrains from "literary" style, in the old sense. He is ruthless, frank, cynical, brutal and often borders on aggressive. He has presented music with entirely new challenges. Brecht's lyrics could not be "set to music", they could not be melted down and remoulded; all music could do was to subordinate itself to them in order to fully realise them.'[1]

Mersmann identified in Brecht's lyrics a powerful eloquence which cast its spell over the musician. At the same time, he wrote, there was in this writer's work such a thorough

---

Albrecht Dümling, 'Eisler/Brecht oder Brecht/Eisler?', in Albrecht Riethmüller (ed.), *Brecht und seine Komponisten* (Laaber: Laaber, 2000), pp. 93–110.

[1] Hans Mersmann, 'Die neue Musik und ihre Texte', in *Melos* 10 (1931), 171f.

reflection on the use of music that the only option left to the composer was that of adaptation, subordination. Mersmann went on: 'It is no longer the case that music seeks out a finished text to be composed to; both music and text are now dependent upon each other and exist *through* each other to a greater degree than ever before. This is a source of limitless possibility.'

Composers like Kurt Weill, Paul Hindemith, Hanns Eisler and Paul Dessau were all drawn to Brecht, for here was a writer whose lyrics were created out of rhythmical impulses and unmistakeably designed with music in mind.[2] His poems, ballads and dramas were built upon functional frameworks as well as their thematic, rhythmical and formal structures. Unlike the authors once favoured by musicians – such as Goethe, Heine, Hofmannsthal – Brecht's influence on music went beyond mere stylistic questions. It affected the structures of entire musical genres. The reason this young writer, so recently arrived in Berlin from Munich, was able to play such an key role in the development of music in the 1920s was that the issue of musical genres and thus the search for new social functions had become a subject of intense debate at the time (as evidenced by the Baden-Baden Chamber Music Festival). Like some of the writers of the day, many influential musicians also felt that questions of genre anticipated social changes.

II.

As Mersmann points out, Eisler (like Hindemith and Weill) initially went along with an approach dictated by Brecht. Although he dated his first encounter with Brecht to the year 1922 – he claimed to have seen Brecht singing at the Ukrainian Embassy in Berlin during his time as a student under Schönberg – they did not actually work together until 1928. This was in connection with the Feuchtwanger play *Kalkutta, 4. Mai*, for which Brecht wrote the song lyrics and Eisler the stage music. It is clear that the 'Ballad of the Woman and the Soldier', which was created for this production, was heavily influenced by the writer both textually and musically.[3] After this singular start, Brecht and Eisler entered into a period of intensive and ongoing collaboration, beginning in 1930 with their work on *The Decision*. The special quality of their partnership was already evident at this stage, as Eisler attests: 'Brecht was not just a great teacher but a learner, too. Brecht's genius lies in his ability to learn from everyone – for example, he was able to produce work in the midst of heated debates about what he was doing. For half a year I spent every day from half past nine in the morning till one in the afternoon at his flat, working on *The Decision*. Brecht wrote, and I criticised every line.'[4] Eisler's textual criticism, which will have touched upon thematic and political issues as well as linguistic and musical ones, was perceived by Brecht not as an irritation but as motivation. 'Anyone else would either have thrown me out or told me "Look, I can't work like this!" But with Brecht, it motivated him to work. The amazing thing was that having these debates, having this contradiction

---

[2]On the interaction of sound and typography, see the author's article 'Hearing, Speaking, Singing, Writing: The Meaning of Oral Tradition for Bert Brecht', in *Music and German Literature. Their Relationship Since the Middle Ages*, ed. J. M. McGlathery (Columbia, South Carolina, 1992), 316–326.
[3]See Albrecht Dümling, *Laßt euch nicht verführen. Brecht und die Musik* (Munich, 1985), 280.
[4]Nathan Notowicz, *Wir reden hier nicht von Napoleon! Wir reden von Ihnen! Gespräche mit Hanns Eisler und Gerhart Eisler*, transcribed and edited by J. Elsner (Berlin, 1971), 189.

in human form sitting there in his living room, actually motivated him.'[5] One of the key phrases in the *Lehrstück The Decision* is a quotation from Lenin: 'The intelligent person is not the one who makes no mistakes, but the one who can quickly put them right.' Brecht and Eisler applied this idea both to politics and to their own work. Multiple redrafts and revised versions testify to their learning process.[6] Brecht benefited above all from Eisler's experience in the workers' music movement, and from his credibility among the workers. As one young Communist put it: 'It's a shame Brecht doesn't want to know anything at all about the KPD. The ambiguities in *The Decision* stem from his ignorance of the working class, and he'll never really be able to create anything for us if he carries on like this. If he hadn't had Eisler by his side, he'd have been finished before he'd even begun.'[7] The writer of these lines, Margarete Steffin, would soon become a close collaborator of Brecht's. The playwright who had made a name for himself writing for a bourgeois audience had Eisler to thank for gaining him access to the labour movement. From the point of view of the working class it was Eisler who was the driving force, not Brecht.

III.

The *Lehrstück The Decision* warns against the temptation of isolated, 'pure' emotion and thus against the ideological element of politics; against sentiment, rhetoric and 'intoxicating' pathos. As in Brecht's *Domestic Breviary*, ideology is again criticised through the secularisation of religious models. Brecht adopted the form of the oratorio as a medium, but replaced suggestion with discussion. Biblical associations came naturally to Brecht, who had grown up in Catholic Augsburg but been brought up a Protestant. Eisler, on the other hand, came from an atheist family: his education at a Jesuit school in Vienna served primarily as a catalyst for critical and rebellious thinking. For him, religion was merely a social phenomenon. Where he does engage with the Church in his early works, it is always from an ironic distance. His growing interest in church music from 1930 onwards, particularly the music of Johann Sebastian Bach, is largely down to Brecht. Eisler had once been firmly of the opinion that Beethoven was the most important composer of all time; from 1930 onwards, however, the tables increasingly began to turn in favour of Bach. Under the playwright's influence, Eisler reinterpreted the religious themes in the Bach oratorios as secular ones. 'The prevailing mood in Bach's vocal works (St Matthew Passion, St John Passion, Mass in B minor, Christmas Oratorio, etc.) can only be understood by considering the terrible impact of the Thirty Years War on Germany, and by seeing these works as expressions of the suffering among the devastated population,' he explained in 1935.[8] Shortly before his death, he said: 'They are quite simply magnificent things, and the religious element in them is not important to me. The "St John Passion" is all about the fate of a suffering and martyred human being. You could

---

[5] Ibid.
[6] On the multiple reworkings of stage scores see also the author's article '"Im Stil der Lehrstücke". Zu Entstehung und Edition von Eislers Musik für Brechts Gorki-Bearbeitung *Die Mutter*', in *Der Text im musikalischen Werk. Editionsprobleme aus musikwissenschaftlicher und literaturwissenschaftlicher Sicht*, ed. W. Dürr, H. Lühning, N. Oellers, H. Steinecke (Berlin, 1998), 361–381 (= supplements to the *Zeitschrift für Deutsche Philologie*, Vol. 8).
[7] Cited from Dümling (1985), 313.
[8] Eisler, 'Einiges über das Verhalten der Arbeitersänger und -musiker in Deutschland', in *Musik und Politik, Schriften 1924–1948,* critical edition by G. Mayer (Leipzig, 1973), 249.

just as well perform it for the victims of Fascism in the Second World War.'[9] But Eisler was also influenced by strictly musical criteria. The same Eisler who declared himself to be one of the most irreligious people in the history of music also considered Bach's *Mass in B minor* to be the most brilliant piece in the history of music. Brecht was instrumental in this re-evaluation.

The two men were largely united in their scepticism towards Romanticism and towards emotions, which were dismissed at the time as 'bourgeois'. The postcard Brecht wrote to Eisler from Ammersee in July 1930 is typical. Beneath a photograph of himself sitting in a director's chair, Brecht had written: 'Lord, more soul ... more expression.' On the back he had written: 'Dear Eisler, please permit the undersigned to make this no-longer-unusual request or demand of you too.'[10] The card was signed by Brecht, the director Slatan Dudow, Helene Weigel and her son Stefan. The music for *The Decision*, which Eisler wrote in Berlin in the summer of 1930, followed this request to the letter with its sparse linearity and its lack of strings.

IV.

Composing is usually a solitary art. Gustav Mahler, for example, used to withdraw to his little wooden hut to compose, listening to his inner voice before writing down the sounds he had imagined. Hanns Eisler, too, spent hours in solitary concentration testing out sequence structures. While he was doing this he did not like to be disturbed. However, important elements of his 'applied music' (compositions for practical purposes such as the stage, films or workers' choirs) emerged from collective work, from conversations in a group. Surprisingly, he did not perceive noise as a disruption in these cases. Brecht once told Elias Canetti he worked best when the telephone kept ringing all the time.[11] Likewise, even very loud noises did not seem to distract Eisler from his creative activity in those days. While Eisler was working on *The Decision*, Theo Roth was pounding away with a hammer putting up shelves in the same room. This music was not created in a quiet little chamber but in a loud and busy room. For Eisler, composing was not at odds with physical work.

Ruth Berlau observed the two artist friends working together in Danish exile: 'When they were working, it was like they were playing ping-pong with their thoughts. Eisler soon got used to me, and sometimes I'd sit there watching them and just marvelling. A phrase grew out of a melody – a melody out of a phrase. I'd go so far as to say that such a close collaboration is more than rare, it's unique. They were two masters of their art unafflicted by the scourges of jealousy, inferiority complexes or oversensitivity.'[12] According to Ruth Berlau neither Brecht nor Eisler, text nor music, took priority over the other. Musical ideas could therefore give rise to phrases and lyrics. This called for openness and an ability to learn on both sides – as did chess, which both men played with great enthusiasm (Eisler usually won). To outsiders this collaboration was mysterious at

---

[9]Eisler, 'Inhalt und Form', in *Musik und Politik, Schriften 1948–1962*, critical edition by G. Mayer (Leipzig, 1982), 523.
[10]Cited from Dümling (1985), 296.
[11]Elias Canetti, *Die Fackel im Ohr. Lebensgeschichte 1921–1931* (Frankfurt am Main, 1982), 257.
[12]Ruth Berlau, in *Wer war Eisler. Auffassungen aus sechs Jahrzenten*, selected and introduced by M. Grabs (Berlin, 1983), 258.

first, for the rules of the game were difficult to understand. Hints and allusions often sufficed to describe an entire system of thought. As Ruth Berlau put it: 'At first it was hard to follow because they could get their meaning across to each other in just a few words – they were such kindred spirits in their mission. The great propositions I had studied so laboriously were thrown around like everyday chit-chat. Stick to the subject, I learned. At the beginning I concentrated very hard, thought almost gleefully: Now they've lost the thread, but they always found their way back to the subject. Later on they might have been oceans apart, but as soon as they met they were immediately back on the subject.'

The fact that Eisler also influenced Brecht's stage scripts is evident from another account by Ruth Berlau: 'Eisler made suggestions for *Fear and Misery of the Third Reich*. Brecht rarely reads anything aloud – he gives it to Eisler to read. Eisler goes into the garden and reads it straight away. He says Brecht expects it of him, he's not allowed to be lazy. Then he comes back into Brecht's study. "Brilliant, excellent" – but then come changes and suggestions. Brecht notes them down immediately on tiny little slips of paper which he promptly loses. They are of one mind: they will never be able to come up with such a sentence again, and they go hunting for the slip of paper. Brecht feels guilty. Eisler comforts him and comes up with a replica of the lost phrase. But Brecht is not satisfied – they must find the slip of paper! The whole house searches for it. Then Brecht fishes it out of one of his innumerable pockets. Now they get to work. They pace in circles around each other, up and down. Brecht reads aloud what is still in the typewriter. I don't understand a word, and he laughs, cigar in mouth. Eisler, however, understands everything.'[13] According to this account, which is confirmed by findings in the Brecht Archive, Eisler had a significant influence on Brecht's texts. He suggested changes, improvements and new forms of words, and even underlying ideas. Berlau reiterates this: 'Many of the best parts of Brecht's work wouldn't exist without that close collaboration with Eisler, that true friendship throughout all those years, all those difficulties. Just as many of Eisler's best works wouldn't exist without Brecht's lyrics.'

Eisler's function, then, was not limited to the usual role of a composer (i.e., selecting lyrics and then setting them to music). He was not only Brecht's musical collaborator but also his dramaturg and editor. Brecht saw Eisler's contribution as a genuinely integral part of the whole. As Ruth Berlau notes, the writer sometimes even changed his own lyrics to fit his friend's music. She gives the example of the translation of *Life of Galileo* from the original English into German. 'Now, Eisler could have altered the music, but Brecht wanted to avoid that at all costs, because he loved that music. It took forever to translate: tam ta tam – tam tam; Brecht was very musical, it's true, but it still took a lot of patience.'

Today, when Brecht is accused of violating copyright and intellectual property rights and of exploiting his collaborators, we forget that in the 1920s teamwork or collective work was seen as a desirable, sometimes even idealised counterpoint to personal style, which was felt to be 'Romantic' and outdated. We might think of collectives like the conductorless 'Persimfans' orchestra in Moscow or the form of collective music criticism introduced by the journal *Melos*. Brecht's talent for teamwork had been evident ever since his youth in Augsburg. He liked to keep hold of tried-and-tested groups of collaborators. *The Decision* team including Slatan Dudow and Eisler subsequently worked together on the film *Kuhle Wampe*. A particularly successful result of this collaboration is a song which embodies the principle of collectivity in its title: the 'Solidaritätslied' ['Solidarity Song'].

---

[13]Berlau, ibid., 262.

It was created as a public response to the question of how a popular song can be transmitted to a wide audience. The step-by-step development of this song, which can be seen from the surviving drafts, is a particularly compelling example of collaboration.[14]

Brecht and Eisler were also involved in other collective projects, such as the revue *Wir sind ja sooo zufrieden* [*We are just sooo happy*] which the Junge Volksbühne created together with the writers Brecht, Ernst Ottwald, Ludwig Renn, David Weber, Erich Weinert and Günther Weisenborn and the composers Eisler, Friedrich Hollaender and Kurt Weill. Brecht and Eisler contributed the 'Ballade vom Paragraphen 218' ['The Ballad of Paragraph 218'] and the 'Lied vom SA-Mann' ['Song of the SA Man']. As Theodor W. Adorno also confirmed, the composer's ability to work collectively was on a par with the playwright's. 'The only experiments with collectivist music which really represented something genuinely new, and went beyond empty affirmations of solidarity, were the works of Hanns Eisler.'[15]

The collaboration between Brecht and Eisler gave rise to such important works as *The Decision* and the play with music *The Mother*. Another joint project was the volume *Lieder Gedichte Chöre* [*Songs Poems Choruses*], which was developed in exile in Denmark and printed in Paris, and from which the *Deutsche Symphonie* [*German Symphony*] later emerged. We might also mention popular songs for the masses like the 'Einheitsfrontlied' ['The United Front Song'] or the 'Saarlied' ['Saarland Song']. The less well-known results of Brecht and Eisler's collaboration in exile in Hollywood include *Die Gesichte der Simone Machard* [*The Visions of Simone Machard*] and *Life of Galileo*, still the most successful collaborative stage project in the USA.

V.

When it came to *Galileo*, as had also been the case with *Round Heads and Pointed Heads*, Eisler's views sometimes differed from Brecht's. Although Eisler wrote his stage music for the second version of the play, he always preferred the first version of the text which he had received in 1939 in Mexico City. For him, it was essentially historical material. The real subject of the play was not physics but 'the new human being in an old society'. Eisler had little involvement in the work on the second version, which Brecht modernised to take account of what had happened at Hiroshima. Eisler left this work to Brecht and the actor Charles Laughton. Eisler's stage music, with its stripped-down sound composed of flute, clarinet and harpsichord parts and treble voices, and its Palestrina harmonies, comes across as historicising rather than modernising, as if it had been written for the first version of the play.

For the balladeer who appears in a marketplace in the tenth scene reporting Galileo's 'shocking' discoveries, Brecht draws on the tradition of the town crier, whose modern-day counterparts he was familiar with from the Augsburg fairs. To Eisler, this form (consisting of recited verses) was musically unattractive, and he set the balladeer's song to music in his own, more melodious way. But this called for a proper singer rather than an actor, which led to a clash between the collaborators. Eisler's student Serge Hovey, who had taken on the role of musical director for the premiere in Beverly Hills in 1947, recalls:

---

[14]On the process of its creation, see Dümling (1985), 320ff.
[15]Theodor W. Adorno, 'Neunzehn Beiträge über neue Musik', in *Gesammelte Schriften*, Vol. 18 (Frankfurt am Main, 1984), 67.

'Eisler insisted on a tenor and thought the singer who had been engaged had a dreadful voice; Brecht demanded that the role be played by an actor who was to more or less chant his lines, in the style of a recitative. The two of them got into a big argument about it. When I went to see him in the evenings, Eisler became more and more annoyed with me because he said I wasn't fighting his corner enough. He said: "Tomorrow I'm going into that theatre and I'm going to kick up a right stink at the rehearsal." I'd never seen him so worked up.'[16] The 'stink' never came to pass, although Brecht did everything he could to unsettle the tenor.

Brecht's vision won through in the end, and this was accelerated by something that happened in Eisler's absence. Hovey comments: 'This tenor wasn't very bright, but he had a powerful voice. He asked: "How would you like me to stand?" Brecht stroked his chin, and everyone in the theatre waited a long time – almost a whole minute. At last Brecht looked up and said: "Like a machine."' Brecht's command achieved its aim: the terrified singer never came back and at the performance he was replaced by an actor. Aside from his fundamental distrust of musicians and especially tenors, Brecht had ideas about the performance of the ballad which Eisler had not taken into account. His composition lacked the mechanically droning balladeer-style tone Brecht was looking for. If it was Eisler's mistake to have failed to strike the right tone and to have composed the ballad for a singer rather than an actor, it was Brecht's mistake to have still insisted on an actor for the performance. For a while, this affected Eisler's willingness to compose any more music for Brecht's plays. In American exile especially, he was anxious to maintain his musical independence.

VI.

In the years 1937–1942, the two friends had been separated from each other. Brecht suffered from this separation, whereas Eisler simply carried on composing music for Brecht's texts independently. He continued work on the *German Symphony*, the *Lenin Requiem*, the choral variations *Gegen den Krieg* [*Against War*] and the songs *Über die Dauer des Exils* [*On the Duration of Exile*]. When setting these texts of Brecht's to music, he reverted to a modified twelve-tone technique which at the time he was testing out as a universal method of composition. Brecht showed little understanding of this technique, but tolerated it as something that was part of Eisler's field and not his. Once Eisler moved from New York to Los Angeles in April 1942, the two men could at last start working together again. Brecht had eagerly awaited his friend's arrival. In his *Journal*, he noted: 'When I see Eisler it's almost as if I'm stumbling around in some crowd with my brain in a fog and then suddenly somebody calls me by my old name.'

Now it was often Eisler who was the initiator. He changed some of the titles of Brecht's texts, for example, for his *Hollywooder Liederbuch* [*Hollywood Songbook*]: 'Finnische Landschaft' ['Finnish Landscape'] became 'Frühling' ['Spring'], and 'Die Pfeifen' ['The Pipes'] became 'Auf der Flucht' ['On the Run']. Eisler's distillations made many of the poems pithier. Here is one of Brecht's original poems:

> The village of Hollywood is designed to look like
> What the people here think Heaven looks like. Here

---

[16]Serge Hovey, '"Zeit zum Aufstehen!" Erinnerungen an Hanns Eisler im USA-Exil' in *Notate*, Berlin 5 (1982).

> They have decided that God,
> Requiring both Heaven and Hell, saw no need
> To design two establishments, but
> Just the one, namely Heaven – which serves
> For the poor and unsuccessful
> As Hell.

Eisler shortened and improved this prototype before setting it to music:

> This city has taught me that
> Paradise and Hell can be one city.
> For the poor
> Paradise is Hell.

Brecht recognised Eisler's literary abilities, which were demonstrated most clearly a decade later by Eisler's self-penned libretto for the *Johann Faustus* opera.[17] He affirmed the close relationship between his words and Eisler's music through commentaries on key works such as *The Mother* and *The Decision*. But despite plans for several volumes in which the musical score was to be printed alongside the text, the only work for which this idea ever materialised was *Songs Poems Choruses*. Brecht was at his most egocentric, however, when it came to the contractual division of royalties. He would not hear of equality between the writer and the composer in this respect.

Eisler, for his part, maintained his independence from his revered writer friend: he refused (unlike Paul Dessau) to go along with Brecht's 'misuc' [sic] ideas, for example, and he persisted in his admiration for Beethoven, Wagner, Schönberg, Hölderlin and Thomas Mann.[18] Firm proof of his artistic autonomy can be seen not least in his last composition, the *Ernsten Gesänge* [*Serious Songs*], which are based on Hölderlin and Hermlin, not on Brecht. In the end, however, Eisler was buried close to his friend in the Dorotheenstadt Cemetery.

VII.

Only rarely did Eisler give up his own language and adopt Brecht's. One occasion when this did happen was in the *Notes on The Decision*, written together with Brecht and Slatan Dudow. The three men were interested in the use of music after an interruption. The music remained unchanged, and thus was not aligned with the changed situation. 'When the music, which on the whole constitutes a tradition, does not change the attitude of the Control Chorus, it is retrospectively subjecting its initial praise to its general function of fixing a procedural attitude as a heroic one. So if the overall process is portrayed as one which develops from a) to b), with a) signifying praise and b) a procedural attitude,

---

[17]See Irmgard Schartner, *Hanns Eisler, Johann Faustus. Das Werk und seine Aufführungsgeschichte* (Frankfurt am Main, Berlin, Bern, 1998 [= *Musikleben. Studien zur Musikgeschichte Österreichs*, ed. Fr. C. Heller, Vol. 7]). Unfortunately, in the new edition issued by the Leipzig publisher Faber & Faber in 1996, the blank verse is turned into prose. The documentation edited by Hans Bunge (*Die Debatte um Hanns Eislers 'Johann Faustus'*, Berlin, 1991), on the other hand, is still indispensable.

[18]See Lynn Matheson, "'Ein Thema hat ungefähr so viele Möglichkeiten wie ein Mensch'. Zur Beethoven-Rezeption Hanns Eislers', in *Hanns Eisler. Es müßt dem Himmel Höllenangst werden*, on behalf of the Stiftung Archiv der Akademie der Künste, ed. M. Köster (Hofheim, 1998), 107–119.

the fact that the music preserves its heroicising attitude in b), which is taken from a), means that the initial praising attitude retrospectively gains a procedural character and the procedural attitude gains a heroic character.'[19] This attempt to consider an emotional phenomenon in a scientifically detached way is signed by Brecht, Dudow and Eisler but uses Brecht's language, not Eisler's. This is an analysis not of musical forms but of attitudes, whereby the attitude of the chorus is set apart from that of the music; they are not supposed to merge, but are to be perceived independently of each other.

In some cases, Eisler was prepared to significantly modify his approach even in musical matters. When Brecht came down with viral influenza in April 1956 and had to leave the *Galileo* rehearsals at the Berliner Ensemble to be admitted to Berlin's historic Charité Hospital, Eisler composed a short 'Charité Circular Canon' for him featuring the words 'The illness will pass, Brecht will last'. Next to the title he noted: 'repetio ad infinitum'. Like a perpetual chime of bells, this canon was designed as light-hearted 'misuc' to cheer up the sick poet.

His friend's early death came as a shock to Eisler. The last time he visited him was on a Sunday; the mood was cheerful, even though Brecht was having trouble speaking. As they were saying goodbye, Brecht said: 'I'm sorry I didn't do enough for your great music.' Eisler was surprised. Only afterwards did he realise that these were Brecht's last words to him. 'I wonder: did he already know how ill he was that Sunday? Otherwise why would he have said those words?' In hindsight Eisler regretted not having taken Brecht up on his repeated suggestion that he move closer to his house on Chausseestraße.

The composer was 'completely floored' by Brecht's death on 14 August 1956. He worked through his grief in a way Brecht would have approved of, however, using it as an impetus to create something new. In the style of the *Lenin Requiem*, for example, he wrote the text for a (not composed) 'Kantate auf den Tod Bertolt Brechts' ['Cantata on the Death of Bertolt Brecht']. Although the composer was by now in poor health himself, the death of his friend spurred him on to new activity, to pleasurable productivity. He busied himself composing the music for premieres of Brecht's plays, which were now coming thick and fast: the premiere of *The Days of the Commune* took place on 17 November 1956 in Karl-Marx-Stadt (now Chemnitz), the premiere of *Schweyk in the Second World War* on 15 January 1957 in Warsaw, the East German premiere of *Life of Galileo* in Berlin on the same day and the premiere of *The Visions of Simone Machard* on 6 March 1957 in Frankfurt am Main. He planned to adapt Brecht's last play *Turandot or The Whitewashers' Congress* as an opera.

In his non-theatrical compositions, too, Eisler tried to put Brecht's musical aims into practice – particularly in the Lenin cantata *Die Teppichweber von Kujan-Bulak* [*The Carpet Weavers of Kujan-Bulak*] for soprano and orchestra, which was completed on 4 June 1957. Eisler prefaced the musical score with one of Brecht's mottos: 'It is particularly necessary to take a light-hearted approach to profound subjects and to greet authorities with friendly benevolence.' Like the carpet weavers in Brecht's poem, Eisler also paid his homage in a productive way. Just a few days after the *Kujan-Bulak Cantata*, he had completed a new Brecht cantata: the *Legend of the Origin of the Book Tao Te Ching on Lao Tzu's Road into Exile*, his most successful response to his friend's call to reinvigorate the art of music-making through epic poems. In autumn 1957 he produced another

---

[19]Brecht/Dudow/Eisler, 'Anmerkungen zur *Maßnahme*', cited from Hanns Eisler, *Musik und Politik. Schriften 1924-1948*, 131.

Brecht cantata, *Bilder aus dem Kriegsfibel* [*Images from the War Primer*], in which text and music functioned as commentary on projected newspaper photographs. Initially a song called 'Zu Brechts Tod (Die Wälder atmen noch)' ['On Brecht's Death (The Forests are Still Breathing)'] was envisaged as a prelude and postlude to this piece. Eisler had written and composed the song in August 1956, based on a poem by his old friend. Thus the cooperation between the two men continued even after the writer's death. It almost seems as though, in his approach to composition, Eisler was never *more* aligned with Brecht than in those years after 1956.

VIII.

Brecht/Eisler or Eisler/Brecht? The shifting of the balance within this partnership was the result of shifts in historical and social conditions. Whilst Brecht maintained his links with the world of bourgeois culture where he had first made a name for himself, Eisler had definitively broken with the avant-garde cultural scene in 1928. Throughout his life he remained the more prominent and popular figure among politically organised workers. This was the case not only in the Weimar Republic but also in exile in the USA. Brecht had never experienced anything like the kind of solidarity Eisler was shown by various luminaries – ranging from Albert Einstein, Picasso and Thomas Mann to Chaplin and Stravinsky – when he was forced by the authorities to leave New York in 1948. Soon afterwards, however, their positions would be reversed. Long after the Brecht boycott in West Germany had subsided, Eisler's connection to the East German national anthem proved a serious blemish on his reputation. Now, all of a sudden, the composer could only be evoked using the restrictive 'Brecht-Eisler' label. This was why Eisler was only rediscovered in West Germany via a book with the title *Ask Me More About Brecht*.[20]

In many political but also literary and dramaturgical respects, Eisler might be said to be the more influential figure. As a materialist dialectician and an advocate of productive debate, fitting his work into traditional genres or functions was not enough for him. His collaboration with Brecht gave rise to works which set new trends in terms of style and function. With the *Lehrstück The Decision* – a combination of oratorio and drama, opera and agitprop – the two men developed a new musical-theatrical genre which at the time was hailed as the future of proletarian art. The use of music as a dramaturgical counterpoint in the film *Kuhle Wampe* – putting the learning process on a parallel track via the step-by-step development of the final melody – was also completely new. There were hardly any existing models for the cantata-like number sequence of the *German Symphony* or for the fluent transitions between the stage music and the opera in *Schweyk in the Second World War*.

Ruth Berlau often got the chance to watch Brecht and Eisler playing chess. 'The two friends did not play chess the way I've seen other people play it. No: when Brecht got into difficulties, Eisler would simply turn the board around and take up Brecht's position. They weren't playing chess to win. It made an unforgettable impression on me: had either of these two masters ever done anything in order to win something for himself? As in work, so in play – and therefore "everything must be fun", both in work and play alike.'[21]

---

[20]Hans Bunge, *Fragen Sie mehr über Brecht. Hanns Eisler im Gespräch* (Munich, 1970).
[21]Berlau, 258.

As in their games of chess, in Brecht and Eisler's collaboration there was no dichotomy between play and seriousness, between work and entertainment, between daily routine and relaxation. They relaxed by working, and enjoyed themselves by being productive. This is evident from their joint stage works such as *Schweyk in the Second World War* and *Galileo*. Just as Brecht, in his 1954 poem 'Pleasures', does not distinguish between 'high' and 'low' pleasures, Eisler did not accept that there was any difference in status between 'serious' and 'entertaining' music. The director Manfred Wekwerth, who worked with Brecht until his death, had a very high opinion of the composer's influence on the writer: 'Eisler took thought in the moment of thinking and turned it immediately into pleasure. With him there was no division between emotion and reason.' For Wekwerth, therefore, Eisler was 'one of the greatest teachers of practical, elementary thinking and the pleasure of thinking. And that, I think, made him a necessary complement to Brecht.'

The fact that pleasure and thought can form a single unit became clear to Brecht not least through Eisler's music. In one of his most important texts on the aesthetics of music – the preface he wrote in 1955 to Eisler's *Lieder und Kantaten* [*Songs and Cantatas*] – Brecht remarked that his friend's vocal music changed 'both the singer and the listener in a positive way'.[22] Here he was voicing one of the basic premises of his work: art should be measured by its effect; it should not simply be consumed without consequences, but should intervene in people's lives. In Eisler's music, Brecht was able to see this active effect in action. The educational process was not an ordeal but a pleasure – for the listeners and the musicians alike.

---

[22]Brecht, 'Zum Geleit', in *Gesammelte Werke* in 20 Bänden, Vol. 17, 771.

Paul Dessau

CHAPTER SIXTEEN

Composing for BB: Some Comments

PAUL DESSAU
TRANSLATED BY HELLA FREUD BERNAYS

I had already heard a good deal about Brecht as far back as the twenties, and *Der Jasager*, Brecht and Weill's school opera, made a tremendous impression on me when it was performed at the Karl Marx School in Berlin. Not long after, in the Kroll Opera House under the direction of Otto Klemperer, I went to a concert performance of Brecht and Weill's (and Hindemith's) *Der Flug der Lindberghs*. And, of course, there was the *Dreigroschenoper*. But I knew at that time it was too early for me to talk to Brecht about collaborating- the libretto for my *Children's Cantata*, which I had written myself, demonstrated both my lack of independent ideas and the great influence Brecht then had on me.

The first text of Brecht's for which I did the music was the series of scenes later called *Fear and Misery of the Third Reich*; I wrote 99% of the songs. Brecht himself considered the work relatively 'Aristotelean' (and to my mind it is uncharacteristic, *Mother Courage* being characteristic). We used only seven musicians, and the *gestus* of the music was purely political. The first performance using my songs was in Paris in 1938. Helene Weigel was in the cast, Slatan Dudow directed.

Our close work together began after we had both emigrated to America, during World War II. At 'An Evening with Brecht', in a large auditorium in New York City, 1942 (Elizabeth Bergner and Peter Lorre were there), a young Italian singer was to sing the music I had written for the 'Song of the Black Straw Hats', from *St. Joan of the Stockyards*. At the very last minute, the singer didn't appear. Brecht, who particularly liked the song, urged me to take her place – 'Eisler sometimes sings his own songs himself, too!' Later that evening we set a date for our first working conference, and he suggested that I set to music his poem, 'Oh, Germany, pale mother', which later became the introduction to the choral work, *German Miserere*; we worked on the *Miserere* for a long time, and it wasn't completed until shortly before we returned to Germany.

I recall that Brecht would give me texts almost as an aside, as though he was somewhat embarrassed. For example, he handed me the poem 'Song of a German Mother' one day as we were walking on Broadway, with the words, 'I've already composed one line myself'. He then sang for me the few notes which he had composed, right then and there, loudly:

'Had I known then what now I know'

Obviously, it's hard to incorporate into your own song a phrase by someone else, with nothing preceding or following it, but I liked these two bars very much and was especially pleased with the way Brecht sang them, so I put a lot of effort into it, and thought and hummed continuously to myself, trying to make eight bars out of Brecht's two (for the lines called for eight bars). Pretty soon I was able to play the whole song for Brecht, and he was very happy about it.

Before he left New York, Brecht said to me, 'Why don't you come along to Hollywood too? We'd be able to work together better there.' Easier said than done. Where would I get the money for the trip? What would I live on once I got there? Fortunately, a solution came out of the blue: a young director, with whom I had already worked in Paris, commissioned me to write some music for a film short. At that time I was earning my living as a worker on a chicken farm in New Jersey, but I had enough spare time for composing. So my work on the movie score provided travel funds to California.

I visited Brecht in his little white house in Santa Monica, and our work proceeded as though there had been no interruption. One day he said, 'Here's a play that you really ought to read one of these days, because there's got to be some music in it.' He immediately began to read the verses aloud to me, quietly, delicately, and in a manner wholly dedicated to the meaning, as musically as any poet had ever read aloud before. Then he gave me the little book, bound in black – an offset copy of the text of *Mother Courage*.

Earlier, Brecht had showed me a melody which was printed among the songs appended to *Hauspostille*. It was called the 'Ballad of the Pirates', and the melody supposedly stemmed from the French, 'L'Etandard de Ia Pitié'. [See p. 259 of Eric Bentley's translation of *Hauspostille*, Grove Press, 1966 – ed.]

I was quite taken aback by the banality of this melody, and by Brecht's suggestion, which he made quite politely, that he would like to use it as the model for the opening song of *Mother Courage*. I told him, 'It would require a great deal to enable such a theme to carry an important song,' and he agreed. That is how the song came into being in its present form:

This sort of plagiarism was quite unknown, and somewhat shocking, to me at that time. Today it seems not only perfectly legitimate, but natural and productive.

It was always a great delight to observe Brecht when he listened to music, and I learned from watching him. So he wouldn't be diverted by anything extraneous, he used to close his eyes, and he never was satisfied by listening to something just once. Brecht always first acquainted himself thoroughly with the vocal line alone; only then would he listen to a song with its accompaniment. He had the memory of an elephant. He was very sparing in his judgments, and sometimes I'd learn only months later what his opinion was: a happy contrast to the general run of professional critics. He took his time, which is just as important for prescribing as for producing.

Brecht had the highest regard for Bach and Mozart. As for Beethoven, Hanns Eisler had reported Brecht's opinion: he thought it insulting to have to listen to Napoleon's lost battles set to music. Oddly enough, he most liked music in which nothing counts but the sounds themselves, and despised program music. The music in his plays does not illustrate the text, though it may comment on it. Incidentally, we never used the real music of a period as direct source material. Though the songs in *Mother Courage* have a folk, archaic feeling, they, like the language he used, create Brecht's world of the 30-years-war, not history's.

Most modern composers aroused Brecht's scepticism, and he particularly disliked Strauss, Hindemith, and Honegger. As for Schoenberg, the kind of poetry he used in his vocal work disturbed Brecht. Stravinsky, however, was asked by Brecht in California to work in making an opera from *The Trial of Lucullus*, but Stravinsky said he was overwhelmed with work and wouldn't be able to get to the project for two years, so the idea was dropped.

As for me, I found that the limitations imposed by writing for actors rather than trained singers were a positive advantage because of the discipline imposed. Also, the dialectic between the actor/song and accompaniment/ comment was a pleasure – for example, in *The Trial of Lucullus* (which I composed for Brecht finally), when the general sings about the famous family he comes from, the accompanying music caricatures him, and, as he goes on and on, the orchestra ends up making a fool of him. The direct involvement with stagecraft and Brecht's meticulous rehearsing was also helpful and fascinating for me; to take just one case, the Eilif Song in *Mother Courage* was entirely developed during the 1948 rehearsals at the Deutsches Theatre, finally going through five or six versions.

ABOUT THE MUSIC FOR THE CHALK CIRCLE

The richness and diversity of *The Caucasian Chalk Circle*'s music were created at Brecht's direction. The importance he attached to the music for this particular play is indicated by that fact that at the very beginning he calls for a 'singer' who is further assisted by two 'musicians'. There are nine instrumentalists called for ideally – an unusually large number for what is not, after all, an opera. If necessary, the piano part can be taken by the gong player; if one does without guitar, mandolin, and accordion, the music can be, for better or worse, performed by five players. It will be very much for the worse. Yet Brecht always happily reminded us that we must think of performances at schools, colleges, and other small theatres.

There are several versions of the score, and I would like to emphasize that one should not shrink from varying a piece of stage music; it *must* be adaptable to the specific performers. When I look at the score today, it is imaginable, for example, that the first passages of the singer could be done *a capella* (without accompaniment). In the Berlin performance, #6 (Singer: 'Forever, my great lord!') was omitted – since there is a total of 45 musical numbers, a few can be left out.

In #8 ('As she stood between the door and the gate'), the pantomime of Gruscha with the child is portrayed by the singer. This very important number has its difficulties, and, if it cannot be handled either instrumentally or vocally, it must at least be spoken, with Gruscha performing what the singer describes. This is an adaptation from the Chinese theatre of which Brecht made frequent use. An ambitious and talented player can learn an enormous amount about how to do this pantomime through studying the polyrhythms of the music.

From #10 on, alternating songs begin between the male singer and his two assistants. In our original Berlin production, the short duets (score, p. 37) were done by two female voices. In Cracow, however, they followed my original directions and used two male singers – which convinced me of the correctness and beauty of my original idea. What's more, much of the music in Cracow was done by heart – a pleasant surprise, which I mention only to say that there is nothing wrong with having the singer and his assistants sing from notes.

To illustrate the contradictory relation that often is present between the music and the text, on page 37 of the score – at a point when the Ironshirts are just about to take over the Palace – there is a place where the guitars are gently overtaken by the piano. The duet is to be rendered (despite the indicated 'Cantabile') very lightly, in contrast to the text, not the least bit hurried or anxiously, but with a veritably bewildering cheerfulness, that is, a 'quasi leggiero con anima'.

#17 (Gruscha: 'As one wants to take you', score, page 55) should be sung *a capella*. For #19 (Gruscha: 'Those that go together will hang together') I would like to suggest a new version. The words 'Mitgegangen' to 'nicht unsern Weg' are to be spoken, then (one bar before #20) begin with the male singer. #20 itself (Gruscha: 'Your father is a robber') could if necessary be sung *a capella*.

Beginning with #22 ('In the northern mountains') the quality of the music changes. The source was a book of Azerbaijanian folk dances, though for the most part I took only segments of the melodies, and did not always adhere strictly to the notes. Only one piece is directly and entirely 'quoted' – an Agachanym folk tune which Katchaturian also used, in his ballet *Gajaneh*.

In the original, there is an additional section, from which I took only one item, a four-part tune in 16th notes, and transplanted it:

This motif, with its intervals changed but the characteristic four-part time preserved, is carried through all the story-telling songs, which form a commentary, as a rhythmic ostinato. In these songs the folk tune also appears, partly in its original form, partly in variations – for example, this one, which is in songs #23, #25, and #28:

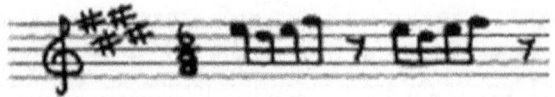

Through the thematic relationship a complete entity is formed, linking words, music, and the play's over-all structure.

The final dance (#45) is in eight sections, the basis of which is a reminiscence of the Agachanym folk dance which recurs throughout. Unfortunately, Brecht never put this final dance on the stage, and a 'Polonaise', in which the principal characters in the play, as well as the little horse and its 'little apples', appear once more, the way they would in a revue, was omitted. The original intention was that the music of the final dance would be played, and danced, until the public leaves the theatre. It would get softer and softer, and would stop only when the lights in the auditorium were lowered.

Brecht's Female Collaborators

CHAPTER SEVENTEEN

Victimhood or Camouflage? The Modesty of Elisabeth Hauptmann

SABINE KEBIR
TRANSLATED BY ROMY FURSLAND

Every so often, there is a rekindling of the ongoing debate in Augsburg about whether or not the university should bear Bertolt Brecht's name. On 25 May 1996, the following argument from a woman's perspective against naming the university after Brecht was published in the *Augsburger Allgemeine Zeitung*: '[...] because he fought for the equality of the classes but not of the sexes. Because every woman who fell in love with him ended up working for him; because he never helped Helene Weigel around the house [...] Such a macho man should not be allowed to oppress even one more woman, least of all his alma mater. His lovers may have forgiven him, but the women of Augsburg stand firm.'[1] Hopefully, I thought, the women of Augsburg stand just as firm when it comes to their husbands, lovers and sons!

In this statement we see a significant breakthrough for feminist positions arrived at in a seemingly evidence-based way. The apotheosis of such positions was the claim, made by John Fuegi in 1994 and circulated internationally in the press, that Brecht's work was in fact produced by his female collaborators and resulted from an exchange of 'sex for text'.[2]

The core of the theory that Brecht demeaned and exploited women, and made them dependent upon him is not new. But taking this stern feminist view of Brecht has been a surprisingly male-dominated sport, from left-wingers like Peter Weiss and Klaus Theweleit, to liberals like Fritz Raddatz and Carl Pitzker,[3] all the way through to the neoliberal puritan Fuegi. In my book *An Acceptable Man?* I was able, as far back as 1987,

---

Sabine Kebir, 'Opferhaltung oder Tarnung? Die Bescheidenheit der Elisabeth Hauptmann', in Kebir, *Ich fragte nicht nach meinem Anteil. Elisabeth Hauptmanns Arbeit mit Bertolt Brecht* (Berlin: Aufbau, 1997), pp. 5–17.

[1] Angela Bachmeier, cited from the editorial article 'Brecht in Augsburg', in *Dreigroschenheft* (Augsburg, 4/1996), 20.
[2] John Fuegi, *Brecht & Company. Sex, Politics, and the Making of the Modern Drama* (New York, 1994). The same version appeared in the UK under the title *The Life and Lies of Bertolt Brecht* (London: HarperCollins, 1994). A forthcoming 'authorized, extended and emended German edition' under the title *Brecht & Co.* has been announced by the Europäische Verlagsanstalt (1997).
[3] Peter Weiss, *Ästhetik des Widerstands* (Frankfurt am Main, 1983). Klaus Theweleit, *Buch der Könige*, Vol. 1 (Basel, Frankfurt am Main, 1988). Fritz Raddatz, 'Bertolt Brecht', in *Männerängste der Kunst* (Hamburg, 1993), 165ff.

to list a whole phalanx of male interpreters[4] who had tried to divert the sympathies of the female public away from Brecht and onto themselves. I cannot see any other explanation for this continued male interest in the women's rights supposedly violated by Brecht.

Fuegi, however – founder of the International Brecht Society, long-time managing editor of the *Brecht Yearbook* and currently a professor of literature in Maryland – estimates the extent and importance of women's contributions to Brecht's work to be much higher than his predecessors did. He claims that large parts of the texts were written by the women. And in terms of their material remuneration, too, he concludes that Brecht robbed his female collaborators. According to Fuegi, for example, Elisabeth Hauptmann was responsible for 80 per cent of the text of the *Threepenny Opera*, and as much as 90 per cent of other works that had become internationally famous under Brecht's name. Hauptmann's share of the royalties, however, was inversely proportional to her actual input.

Of course, the fact that Brecht's plays, and in some cases also his prose, were indeed produced 'collectively' is not a new idea for Brecht scholarship. And since American professors with high-circulation books are obliged to promote themselves, they might well be tempted to capitalise on familiar information by sensationalising it. In Germany the situation is different; to a great extent, the discipline of German Studies leaves the edification of the general public to the mass media. One of the few scholars to publicly oppose Fuegi was Jan Knopf, one of the editors of Brecht's works in the *Große kommentierte Berliner und Frankfurter Ausgabe*. He shows, by reference to a letter written by Ruth Berlau[5] (in which her grammar is appalling), that she at least could not have been responsible for the final versions of any of Brecht's texts.[6] But *Konkret* magazine does not, of course, have anything like the same reach as the popular daily newspaper, the *Bildzeitung*, which promptly asked: 'Was Bertolt Brecht a fraud? Suspicion: His lovers wrote his works. [...] Women love to surrender.'[7] Jörg von Uthmann declared in the more high-brow *Frankfurter Allgemeine Zeitung*: 'Particularly when it came to money, the high priest of Communism was as hard-nosed as any capitalist robber baron. Kurt Weill only received a third of the royalties for the *Threepenny Opera*. The real author Elisabeth Hauptmann was fobbed off with an eighth.'[8] Hellmuth Karasek, however, set the record straight by diagnosing in Fuegi's attitude 'the fervour of a narrow-minded, bourgeois political correctness' and the 'desire of a keyhole voyeur to see dirty linen'.[9]

In relation to Elisabeth Hauptmann, however, Fuegi's book is just the culmination of an image already formed by other interpretations. It was heavily influenced by Marieluise

---

Carl Pitzker, *Ich kommandiere mein Herz. Brechts Herzneurose, ein Schlüssel zu seinem Leben und Schreiben* (Würzburg, 1988).

[4] Sabine Kebir, *Ein akzeptabler Mann? Streit um Bertolt Brechts Partnerbeziehungen* (Berlin, 1987) 160f. (As of January 1988 a revised and extended edition with Aufbau Taschenbuch Verlag.)

[5] Ruth Berlau (1904–1974) was a Danish actress and left-wing journalist married to the doctor Robert Lund when she first met Brecht in Skovsbostrand in 1933. She immediately put Brecht in contact with workers' theatres, and published the *Svendborg Poems* on a subscription basis. From 1935 onwards she was Brecht's lover, and she collaborated with him until his death. She was also a theatre director.

[6] Jan Knopf, 'Sex for text. Anleitung zur Firmengründung oder Wie der amerikanische Literaturwissenschaftler John Fuegi einmal die Laken des Dichters Bertolt Brecht entzifferte', in *Konkret* (Hamburg, 10/1994), 53–55.

[7] *Bildzeitung* (Berlin, 11 July 1994).

[8] Jörg von Uthmann, 'Vom reichen B.B. und seinen Opfern', in the *Frankfurter Allgemeine Zeitung* (Frankfurt am Main, 5 August 1994).

[9] Hellmuth Karasek, 'Von Brecht vollbracht?' in *Der Spiegel* (Hamburg, 38/1994), 210-215.

Fleißer's story *Avantgarde*, which appeared at the beginning of the 1960s.[10] The story depicts the encounter between an author, whose real-life model was undoubtedly the young Brecht, and a female character into whom Fleißer incorporates both her own and Elisabeth Hauptmann's experiences with Brecht. The writer positions himself as the woman's lover and literary champion, but takes it upon himself to make sweeping changes to her work. By the end, the woman no longer recognises her work or herself. Her only options are to take refuge in death or return to the provincial town she once so optimistically left behind. This story was interpreted as autobiographical or biographical depending on whether the critic identified the female protagonist as Fleißer herself or as Hauptmann. The only really important thing seemed to be the negative portrayal of Brecht. The literary nature of the story, and Fleißer's own self-critical statements regarding her quarrel with Brecht, went unnoticed. When Fleißer sent Hauptmann the story in 1963, she wrote that 'something of the bitterness of the second half of my life has overflowed into' this very critical view of Brecht. 'Even so, I hope it will also bring back memories of the good years.' Elisabeth Hauptmann replied: 'I read the two memoir sections very quickly and intently. [...] The story of self-denial over the course of many years, and its dreadful consequences, is unforgettable.' Hauptmann was evidently affected by the story, then, but prudently left unsaid whether she had recognised herself in the female character or not.[11]

Ute Wedel translated the literary picture painted in *Avantgarde* into theoretical certainty: '(Potential) women of letters were assigned the role of "co"-workers by Brecht, who was in this respect acting in accordance with a patriarchal social order and its allocation of roles to women. Those of their own ideas which these women, now his collaborators, *could have exchanged with him*, were nipped in the bud by Brecht.'[12]

The same arguments are put forward in two more recent works by Astrid Horst[13] and Paula Hanssen,[14] specifically with regard to Elisabeth Hauptmann. These works, however, have the merit of highlighting (with the aid of archive materials) specific sections of

---

[10]Marieluise Fleißer (1901–1974), dramatist, writer; encouraged by Feuchtwanger and then mainly by Brecht, who helped stage two of her early plays. She criticised Brecht's collective method in the play *Der Tiefseefisch* [*The Deep-Sea Fish*], which, like *Avantgarde*, is published in *Ausgewählte Werke* (Berlin and Weimar, 1979).

[11]Marieluise Fleißer's letter is dated 29 October 1963 and Elisabeth Hauptmann's 21 February 1966. Both are located in the Elisabeth Hauptmann Archive in Folder 332. In the interviews carried out for the purposes of the 1972 documentary about Hauptmann (see footnote 28, p. 242), the conversation turned to Marieluise Fleißer's conflict with Brecht who, when staging her play *Pioneers in Ingolstadt*, had changed the text in a way Fleißer was unhappy with. The fact that directors do sometimes make major changes to plays they are staging is a common conflict in theatrical practice. Elisabeth Hauptmann felt that in this case the two positions had been irreconcilable, and that it was therefore legitimate for Fleißer to have undone the changes Brecht had made: '[...] I can understand that. Because it was something completely different. But Brecht could only help to stage the play if the plot made sense [...] for this particular production. I remember it well.' She suggested that there were also personal reasons behind the conflict that had not been mentioned in *Avantgarde*: '[...] I don't want to be indiscreet. She was very friendly with a man who was the complete opposite of Brecht, whom Brecht hated. He belittled her in every way he could think of. And this man was a very posh man from the Baltic. She travelled around France with him. And she admired his slim feet which he had stretched out on the seat opposite, etc. I remember those days very well, and also the quarrel with Brecht, particularly in relation to *Pioneers of Ingolstadt*. But it was a fascinating production in the end [...]'.

[12]Ute Wedel, *Die Rolle der Frau bei Bertolt Brecht* (Frankfurt am Main, Bern, New York, 1983), 101.

[13]Astrid Horst, *Prima inter pares. Elisabeth Hauptmann. Die Mitarbeitein Bertolt Brechts* (Würzburg, 1992).

[14]Paula Hanssen, *Elisabeth Hauptmann. Brecht's Silent Collaborator* (Bern, Berlin, Frankfurt am Main, New York, Paris, Vienna, 1995).

Brecht's texts which were contributed by Hauptmann. Contrasted with Fuegi's claims, the outcomes of Hanssen and Horst's investigations look rather tame. In their enquiries they quickly come up against the limits of what can be reliably determined, due to the working methods of the Brecht collective. Translations, ideas and jointly produced texts were often typed up immediately – sometimes by Brecht himself – and the resulting sheets of paper were promptly cut up again and stuck down in a different order, sometimes photographed, to be typed out again a few minutes later. As a result, personal copyright (as defined in the German Civil Code) did lose some of its discriminatory power.

The most astonishing thing about the works cited thus far seems to me to be the way they purport to paint a clear picture of Hauptmann's state of mind at the time, but base this picture on very little (or no) autobiographical documentary evidence. It is not only Fuegi who assumes that the women were internalising some kind of patriarchal dominance on Brecht's part. With his magical male charisma Brecht is supposed to have been able to ruthlessly exploit Hauptmann's artistic creativity and that of his other female collaborators. The problematic elements of the relationship – and they did exist – are presumed to reside only in the private sphere, and are analysed like some sort of chamber play; Fuegi even poses the question of whether the people affected were able to achieve their dreams of happiness (which he defines at a level worthy of the tabloid press). This automatically sweeps another important question under the carpet: for Elisabeth Hauptmann, Margarete Steffin[15] and Ruth Berlau, as politically left-wing artists, were there actually any alternative routes to greater self-fulfilment, in a world that was increasingly turning towards Fascism? Or later on, as exiles in foreign countries?

The fact that feminist-oriented literary studies should set a feminist standard against which to measure things is only natural. But what is this standard? Is there only one? Fuegi elevates the rights and duties of bourgeois marriage (whereby the husband is traditionally seen as being largely responsible for his wife's material and sexual welfare) to the ultimate measure of happiness for Brecht's female collaborators. The values against which Horst and Hanssen judge Brecht's behaviour, on the other hand, are those of a feminism based on gender equality, shaped by the modern ideas of intellectual women. But can we really take an ideal which even today has not been realised anywhere in the world, and project it onto an already historical situation? Can we really judge that situation against such a benchmark? If we only view Elisabeth Hauptmann's experience through this particular lens, all we can hope to establish is whether she was the victim of a patriarchal society or of a patriarchal individual. More recent feminist approaches – such as Judith Butler's[16] – take the view that emancipation can mean something very different in different eras, different cultures and different social classes. From a historically differentiating point of view, Elisabeth Hauptmann can be seen as a pioneer of that post-First World War generation of women who, having won the right to vote as well as new opportunities in terms of their careers and political engagement, wanted to experience sexual and artistic emancipation too. Such a completely new kind of life for women was never going to

---

[15]Margarete Steffin (1908–1941) came from a proletarian family and was active in the labour movement. She was Brecht's lover and collaborator from 1932 onwards, and accompanied him into exile. In 1941 she died in Moscow from tuberculosis.

[16]Judith Butler, *Das Unbehagen der Geschlechter* (Frankfurt am Main, 1991) [English original: *Gender Trouble*, 1990].

be free of pain and disappointment. But it was certainly neither unhappier nor more frustrating than the life of a woman who conformed to the bourgeois value system.

The thing that disturbs me about the approaches of Wedel, Horst, Hanssen and Fuegi is that they view avant-gardist women like Elisabeth Hauptmann as passive objects, as mere victims of a personal relationship. The barriers these women quickly encountered in their quest for self-expression owed far more to unfavourable social conditions than to the power of one individual man.

Elisabeth Hauptmann's reserved and seemingly modest personality is another explanation for her subjugation by Brecht – or so the title of Hanssen's work *Brecht's Silent Collaborator* suggests. The fact that her attitude was also influenced by the specific conditions of the society in which she – without abandoning her ideals – spent her life, is barely taken into account. But before I attempt to define this historical terrain in more detail, it is important to note that in Hauptmann's case, her life was shaped not only by her relationship with Brecht but also by her relationships with a number of other men, and they too must bear some responsibility – if we see responsibility as an entirely personal phenomenon.

It was not only female socialisation, however, that led Elisabeth Hauptmann to make herself as small and invisible as possible. With the rise of Fascism in Germany – and also later on in American exile – she was forced to conceal certain fundamental elements of her personality behind the ladylike persona of an 'unassuming secretary and teacher' in order to survive. Under the pretence of this diminished identity she was able to escape imprisonment by the Nazis and find employment at a college in the USA. Her role as Brecht's editor in both Germanys was politically sensitive too, and she was only able to sustain it by continuing to submit to the discipline of an outwardly perfect opportunism. Here too, the role of an 'unassuming administrator' was called for – and it was not Brecht, incidentally, but the publishers who expressly requested it.

So far the only balanced assessment of Elisabeth Hauptmann that I have come across is the short section which Gerda Marko devotes to her: 'As a woman, her chances of making a living from writing – at the time when she would have had to make the decision to do so – were extremely slim. But there is nothing in her life to indicate that she reluctantly abandoned her dreams of a writing career or that she was prevented by Brecht from realising her own goals. This clever, confident woman clearly understood the difference between genius and talent, and preferred being indispensable to Brecht's working process over trying to make a name for herself through her own works, possibly without achieving the same standard of quality she had learnt from Brecht. To suspect that she did not freely choose her position would be to trivialize her self-aware subordination.'[17]

Elisabeth Hauptmann was known for her extreme reserve in talking about her contribution to Brecht's work and her relationship with Brecht himself. The huge volume of work required of her right up until the end of her life, in her role as Brecht's editor, put paid to any hopes of pursuing her own literary ambitions. She never took Suhrkamp Verlag up on their frequent offers to publish her recollections of Brecht, and refused to

---

[17]Gerda Marko, 'So erwirbt der Apfel seinen Ruhm, indem er gegessen wird ... Bert Brecht und Marieluise Fleißer, Elisabeth Hauptmann, Margarete Steffin, Ruth Berlau' in *Schreibende Paare. Liebe, Freundschaft, Konkurrenz* (Zurich, Düsseldorf, 1995), 181.

make use of the dictation machine she had been provided with for this purpose.[18] Her colleague Werner Hecht[19] reports that she could become quite angry if you tried to coax an overly personal detail out of her. And she even insisted that he remove her name from the edition of Brecht's *Journals* – during her lifetime it stayed removed. Another colleague, Hans Bunge,[20] who recorded his detailed conversations with Ruth Berlau,[21] never managed to persuade Elisabeth Hauptmann to agree to the same. It is hard to imagine, therefore, that she would have told Fuegi (whom she spoke to often after 1966)[22] about her alleged exploitation by Brecht or said anything that would have justified the conclusions he came to. Elisabeth Hauptmann was extremely distrustful of political and even artistic adversaries, an attitude she developed as a covertly oppositional figure in Nazi Germany but also in the USA. Eric Bentley writes: '"She can't say, 'It's raining', without looking over her shoulder to check whether J. Edgar Hoover[23] is listening." [...] A statement which no longer amounts to an aspersion on Elisabeth Hauptmann's character since we [...] know that J. Edgar Hoover usually *was* listening. But paranoia is still paranoia, even if it is justified.'[24]

Due to her heavy workload, particularly towards the end of her life, she was no longer able or willing to receive the many Brecht scholars who flocked to her from all over the world as an authentic source. On 18 June 1970 she told Siegfried Unseld[25] that at the end of the month she would be retiring to her little country house in Eggersdorf: '[...] there is no telephone there and I won't have tourists "dropping in", especially from the USA, which is supplying a constant stream of Germanists again this summer'.[26]

The most important reason why Elisabeth Hauptmann, even in old age, did not want to talk about Brecht except within the narrow parameters she herself had set, was surely of a political nature. Nobody knew better than she did that the most important pages of Brecht's art had found only an ambivalent home in the GDR. And in the official Federal Republic – despite the impressive sales figures – they were not exactly welcome either. Editing Brecht's work, therefore, was an exercise in dispensing politically controversial aspects in doses that would be just about acceptable in each of the Germanys. To be able to continue with her editing work at all, Elisabeth Hauptmann felt the need to shut herself off from certain political problems, and above all personal ones.

It is true that by 1972, Brecht was an accepted member of the official East German canon – but this only applied to a very small portion of his work which could be interpreted

---

[18] In her estate there is a contract with Suhrkamp for *Mein Leben und die Arbeit mit Bertolt Brecht* [My Life and Work with Bertolt Brecht], EHA 19.
[19] Werner Hecht (born 1926), dramaturg and director at the Berliner Ensemble 1959–1971, head of the Brecht-Zentrum 1977–1991. Hecht edited and published many original editions of Brecht's works and several documentary volumes about him. See 'Bescheidenheit und Leistung der Elisabeth Hauptmann', in *Notate* (May 1987), 16.
[20] Hans Bunge joined the Berliner Ensemble in the 1950s as an assistant to Brecht. After Brecht's death, Bunge was the first director of the Brecht Archive.
[21] *Brechts Lai-tu. Erinnerungen und Notate von Ruth Berlau*, ed. Hans Bunge (Darmstadt, Neuwied, 1985), 324.
[22] John Fuegi, *The Life and Lies of Bertolt Brecht*, 617.
[23] As director of the FBI, J. Edgar Hoover organised extensive intelligence-gathering operations, e.g. with regard to German emigrés during and after the Nazi era.
[24] The phrase Eric Bentley is referring to and commenting on here is attributed to Paul Dessau's daughter Therese Pol. In Eric Bently, *Erinnerungen an Brecht* (Berlin, 1995), 26.
[25] Siegfried Unseld, head of Suhrkamp Verlag since 1959.
[26] EHA 25.

as relatively conformist. The fact that Brecht's work also contained some elements – many, even – that were *not* conformist, was something which intellectuals with an interest in Brecht were well aware of. Werner Mittenzwei[27] in particular pursued a strategy of using Brecht's official prestige to bring hitherto neglected artistic, philosophical and political elements of his work to public attention. This was not only to do with Brecht himself but with the reformist attempt to bring about a relaxation – i.e. a liberalisation – of the cultural policies regulated by the Party machine. One important goal (which was ultimately achieved) was the rejection of the artistic dogma of a 'positive hero' as a supposedly necessary role model for the public to identify with. Brecht's aesthetics allowed for this rejection.

When the media hype around Fuegi had reached its peak, the director Karlheinz Mund drew my attention to a series of interviews with Elisabeth Hauptmann which Mund and his fellow film-makers Rolf Liebmann and Wolfgang Gersch had carried out as part of a documentary they had made about Hauptmann in 1972 (entitled *Die Mit-Arbeiterin*).[28] Mund encouraged me to analyse the recordings, only parts of which were familiar to the public, from a journalistic perspective.

When I listened to the tapes I was immediately struck by Elisabeth Hauptmann's voice. The calm authority she radiated did not belong to that embittered – because hard-done-by – woman so often portrayed by the literature that is written about her. By 1972, taking stock of her sometimes symbiotic closeness to Brecht, she was naturally able to take a more positive view than had always been possible during the direct experience of it. The publication of their partially joint work had undoubtedly given her a feeling of power in relation to this work and its former organiser, Brecht.

But I was also fascinated by the content of the interviews. The fact that there were personal details on the tapes which had been lacking from the film was one of the lesser surprises. It was inexplicable to me that the (deficient) transcripts of the tapes had been used by various Brecht biographers but nobody had ever thought to publish the tapes themselves. For they represent no more and no less than the most authentic and detailed source we have about Brecht's collective working method.

But how to explain Hauptmann's willingness to be interviewed by Liebmann, Gersch and Mund in 1972 when she had refused so many others? In a letter to Siegfried Unseld on 30 May 1972, she writes: 'Unfortunately – without realising that it would take up a lot of *my* time and energy and not only that of the DEFA/television crew – I have agreed to have a documentary made about me. It is already a burden to me. It won't be broadcast until the autumn, thank God.'[29]

Her willingness to be interviewed at this time may have had something to do with the fact that she was suffering from cancer and knew she would not live much longer, so this might be her last opportunity to break her silence. She had also realised that the Brecht 'terrain' was increasingly occupied by people who had little to no experience of working with him directly. In answer to the question of why she had never published any memoirs

---

[27] Werner Mittenzwei (born 1927), literary scholar, dramaturg. He has published numerous works on Brecht since 1962.
[28] The film *Die Mit-Arbeiterin. Gespräche mit Elisabeth Hauptmann* was produced for East German television in 1972 by the DEFA-Dokumentarfilmstudio Berlin. Director: Karlheinz Mund; scenario and commentary: Rolf Liebmann, Wolfgang Gersch.
[29] EHA 27–28.

about Brecht, she told the filmmakers: 'Yes, yes – it would have been, yes perhaps it would have been very important to do that. But I didn't manage it. Now and again I did jot something down that interested me. But to put it all together in a suitable form – I just didn't get round to it. Yes, yes, people did ask me to do it. And some of it would have been very important and a lot of things which I then spoke about with other people. And then I see that other people have written about it and sometimes I think, that's not exactly how it was. And then I think, God – you ought to have written it yourself! [...] It was just that while I still had Brecht's work on my mind – and I still do – I had to give up on any serious attempt to write anything myself, to create anything myself. It calls for a kind of concentration and energy [...] that I haven't always had, over the past ten years [...].'

The tapes of the 1972 interviews belong to Hauptmann's estate, which she left to the Akademie der Künste der DDR [GDR Academy of the Arts] (now managed by the Stiftung Archiv der Akademie der Künste, Berlin). The tapes have yet to attract the interest of scholars or a publisher. Even Fuegi, Hanssen and Horst, who used part of this estate and interpreted it in their own ways, did not take the tapes into account. It seems to me, however, that in order to shed light on the relationships between Brecht and his female collaborators, their own accounts should be the first thing we look at.

Although no other author has deliberately elevated collective working methods to the status of a fundamental principle the way Brecht did, collective authorship and intertextuality – i.e. textual references to the texts of other authors – have long been considered within the field of literary studies to be perfectly common practice, and not in any way ignominious. When Fuegi declares them to be a scandal, then, he is not trying to make a scholarly contribution to the discipline; he is pursuing an ideological agenda as part of a neoliberal values offensive. His arguments need to be competently addressed, a task which until now has mainly fallen to literary scholars from the USA. One intervention which seemed to me particularly noteworthy was the call by Angelika Führich (University of Iowa) for the contributions to Brecht's work made by Elisabeth Hauptmann and the other female collaborators not to be simply calculated in percentages; in future, argues Führich, they should be taken seriously as independent authors as well as co-authors, and should finally be given their own public profiles.[30] Here Führich touches on another weakness of all previous considerations of the female collaborator problem in the context of a Brecht reception: until the end of the 1980s, not only scholars but also publishers and the media largely refused to work on or even publish the collaborators' own works. My search for publication opportunities for the Hauptmann audio documents once again underlined the fact that Brecht's female collaborators are not welcome in the book market as independent authors. In the wake of this rejection, they become blank canvases onto which fanciful interpretations are projected – interpretations based on the now famous sexual power with which Brecht is supposed to have appropriated women's creative abilities. Up to now, the names Hauptmann, Steffin and Berlau have been almost exclusively marketed in this way.

It is interesting to note Elisabeth Hauptmann's stipulation in her will that her estate should be left not to the Brecht Archive but to the Akademie der Künste. However generously she had devoted her time and energy to Brecht's work, she clearly wanted her own contributions to it to remain visible. She knew that posterity would initially

---

[30]See Michael Erber, 'Niemand baut ein Haus allein. Notizen zur Debatte über Brechts kollektiver Autorschaft von der Tagung der International Brecht Society 1995 in Augsburg', in *Dreigroschenheft* (3/1995), 12.

have no interest in acknowledging the collective nature of Brecht's work, because for all kinds of instrumentalizations it was more practical to cast him in the tradition of the lone genius. But the transfer of her estate to the Brecht Archive has long been under discussion. Her letters to Walter Benjamin have already been sold to the Adorno Archive. This is evidence of the same patriarchal administrative and utilisation principles which, during her lifetime, probably hampered Hauptmann's creative autonomy considerably more than Brecht did. It is reasonable to want to consolidate archives, but this would only be justified, particularly in the case of the Brecht Archive, if the collective nature of the work was made clearer (including to the public).

In this book [for which this is the introductory chapter], my aim is to make the collective form of production which characterised Brecht's works comprehensible from the point of view of Elisabeth Hauptmann. I will focus in particular on Hauptmann's own statements. My sources are the tape recordings of the interviews with the film-makers in 1972, as well as letters and records from Hauptmann's estate. Diary-style notes she made in 1926, during her second year with Brecht, are published in full for the first time. The value judgements on which this work is based are those of a feminism of gendered difference founded on historical and sociological arguments. This means looking at the conditions in which texts are produced – not only the interpersonal conditions but the universal ones too (in other words, those which are socially constructed). Since Brecht himself openly publicised the collective nature of his work, we need to look at the mechanisms which prevented this fact from being perceived by the public.

I view the collectively produced work not merely from the legal perspective of contemporary copyright law and its consequences for the collaborators, which are imagined by Fuegi with such astonishing specificity. We might counter this view with the argument that the currents of ideas and of money that flowed or did not flow between Brecht and his collaborators cannot be precisely determined from the surviving contracts and accounts. It is also important to note that, for long stretches of time, Brecht's work was not commodified. Performances and publications were extremely dependent upon the political climate, even after his death. If their shared political engagement was a reason to work together, everybody involved also had to understand from the outset that this collaboration represented a risk from which something other than material benefits were to be reaped. In this context, is it conceivable that it was all just about sex? Political parties and religious organisations wanting to change the world as they found it have always been motivated by ideological concerns.

The main focus of this book, however, is neither Brecht's Communism nor the rather different Communism of Elisabeth Hauptmann. The things Hauptmann personally strived for and failed to achieve were not solely linked to her Communist utopia. Today, more women than before – women of all cultures and social systems – strive for very similar things. Hauptmann's case, however, is an example of the fact that political correctness in personal relationships between the sexes is not enough to ensure the presence of women in public life and culture as a matter of course.

CHAPTER EIGHTEEN

'... Now I've Gone and Put Ideas in His Head Again': Notes on Margarete Steffin, Brecht's 'Personal Editor'

WOLFGANG JESKE
TRANSLATED BY ROMY FURSLAND

In descriptions of Margarete Steffin's work for Brecht after 1933, the word 'collaborator' is often used. Steffin helped Brecht by recopying manuscripts and collecting material, by translating foreign sources and contributing ideas to texts on which he was working, and by exercising her linguistic sensitivity in pointing out imprecise expressions. Not only was she thorough, reliable and diligent; she was also one of Brecht's most careful readers. In a close analysis of the editing notations on Brecht's original manuscripts, it becomes apparent to what extent Steffin's work went beyond copy-editing and represented a real creative contribution.

Writers in exile have always needed someone to make their works 'legible to the world'. This, at least, is how Thomas Mann described his collaborator's role in the presentation copy of *Doctor Faustus* (1947) which he gave to Hilde Kahn.[1]

This statement need not be confined to the period of exile; Lion Feuchtwanger's collaborators, for example, were Lola Sernau and Hilde Waldo, while Brecht worked with Elisabeth Hauptmann in the 1920s and with Ruth Berlau during the exile years in Denmark – although Berlau, being Danish, could not contribute as much linguistically in this regard as Berlin-born-and-bred Margarete Steffin. Because they were frequently in different places from 1933 onwards, Steffin's communication with Brecht often takes the form of letters, meaning that the new role she takes on in the summer of 1933 (at the latest) is well documented. Her role has been described as that of a 'secretary' or 'collaborator', but in fact it goes far beyond this.

Wolfgang Jeske, '"... jetzt habe ich ihm wieder Flöhe ins Ohr gesetzt": Anmerkungen zu Margarete Steffin, "Hauslektorin" bei Brecht', *Brecht Yearbook*, 19 (1994), pp. 118–39.

[1] Hilde Kahn in an interview in *'Hilde, bitte schreiben Sie ...!' Als Sekretärin bei Thomas Mann und Lion Feuchtwanger*, a film by Ulrich and Klaus von Dobschütz and Elisabeth Wehmann, WDR/MDR 1993.

Thanks to Steffin's linguistic sensitivity, diligence and thoroughness, as well as her excellent foreign language skills (she speaks English and Russian and learns the languages of all the countries they spend time in: French, Danish, later Swedish and even Finnish), Brecht relies on her to carry out all kinds of work on longer texts, as well as preparing anthologies. She plays an important role in almost all Brecht's projects from 1933 to mid-1941: she reads newly written texts, issues general criticism, points out specific inaccuracies, and criticises individual passages and descriptions that are too sparse or too long-winded; she refines and she standardises. She becomes Brecht's 'personal editor'.

In addition to this, she stays in contact (both on Brecht's behalf and her own) with friends like Walter Benjamin and Karl Korsch, keeping them up-to-date on what she and Brecht are working on. She forges new links with translators, publishing houses etc. Her sense of order leads her to note the date of receipt on any undated letters she is sent and to write the (sometimes provisional) date of completion on other texts, as well as sorting out the huge piles of manuscripts and keeping them in a manageable form (manageable for herself, at least). In May 1940, when Brecht is trying to get a US visa for Steffin, he writes to Erwin Piscator (who is to help with the arrangements to make it easier for Brecht to give lectures at Piscator's 'Dramatic Workshop' at the New York School for Social Research): 'In fact she is the only one who has a handle on my thousands of manuscript pages, and without her there would be an enormous delay in me delivering any lectures.'[2]

Steffin is involved in work on the first version of the play *Round Heads and Pointed Heads*, but it does not appear straight away because the planned publication of the eighth volume of the *Versuche* (in 1933) is prevented by the Nazis. That summer, in Paris, she edits the texts for *The Seven Deadly Sins of the Petty Bourgeoisie*.[3] She also reviews Brecht's poems, some past (1918–1933), some present, and some from his two most recent plays (*The Mother* and *The Decision*, BFA 3), then puts together an initial selection for the volume *Songs Poems Choruses* (BFA 11) which appears the following year with Willy Münzenberg's publishing house, Editions du Carrefour, in Paris. She is involved in selecting the content of this collection of existing material but also in creating a manuscript for print. And she continues to be involved during the next stages of the book's genesis; she reads the proofs, checks the completed corrections and helps with issues relating to the wrap.

At the end of July 1933 Brecht starts work on the *Threepenny Novel*; Steffin gets involved with the project soon afterwards. Around six months later, at the beginning of 1934, she writes to Walter Benjamin: 'Brecht's novel is going to be wonderful. He was finished, poor thing, but now I've gone and put ideas into his head again – he picked up the last few chapters, which he was going to get me to copy out, and silently packed them away again.'[4] All writers set down on paper both initial ideas and then drafts of what they want to say or write: some do this by hand and some on a typewriter, like Brecht (from the 1930s onwards he almost always typed his work). Brecht was never or very rarely satisfied with himself and his texts the first time around. And he did not have the option of using a computer – fortunately, one might say. It has meant that many variants and

---

[2] Bertolt Brecht, *Briefe*, ed. Günter Glaeser (Frankfurt am Main, 1981), 415 (number 409).
[3] See Bertolt Brecht, *Werke. Große kommentierte Berliner und Frankfurter Ausgabe*, ed. Werner Hecht, Jan Knopf, Werner Mittenzwei and Klaus-Detlef Müller (Berlin, Weimar, Frankfurt am Main, 1988-1995); here 4: 495f. (Cited hereinafter as BFA with volume and page number, in some cases also line number; for evidence referring to the comments, I use: See BFA).
[4] Margarete Steffin to Walter Benjamin, undated letter from early 1934. Partial estate of Walter Benjamin, Akademie der Künste in Berlin, 23/102-103. See also Ludwig Hoffmann et al., 'Mitarbeiter: M. Steffin' in *Exil in der Tschechoslowakei, in Großbritannien, Skandinavien und in Palästina* (Frankfurt am Main, 1981), 482–506; here 487.

versions have survived, showing how a text developed with Steffin's input until it became the final printed version that was (and is) available to the public.

In an age without computers, then, one of Margarete Steffin's tasks is to retype various texts to produce (provisionally) 'clean' versions – usually with the 'successful' outcome that Brecht can return to them and make handwritten changes, cut up passages of text and stick them back together in a different order, etc. This retyping is understood to be part of the drafting stage before the final version is achieved: the idea is to create a clean version so that the writer himself can read what he has written with fresh eyes and be inspired to make changes and improvements.

These tasks which Steffin (and Helene Weigel) carried out are described by Ruth Berlau, whom Brecht meets in Denmark in 1933:

> Helli was very keen to learn to type and be Brecht's secretary ... Margarete Steffin couldn't be replaced as Brecht's secretary, not by anyone. Once Brecht had made changes to a version, he would find freshly retyped manuscripts on his desk the next morning without him even having to say a word. And the manuscripts were beautifully clean, the way Brecht needed them to be in order to carry on working.[5]

Margarete Steffin's retyping takes a very different form once a text reaches a more advanced stage. For convenience, Brecht tends to write everything in lower case and without punctuation marks: they are not important to him at this stage. Instead of typing a full stop he prefers to press the space key twice, and commas do not interest him at all. His primary concern is the content (and he can hear everything he is writing, everything he is putting into the mouths of his characters, with all its nuances and undertones etc.).

A task which Steffin, in her role as editor, increasingly takes responsibility for over time is typesetting Brecht's texts for printing – in other words, aligning them with the rules of the Duden dictionary and inserting standard punctuation. Full stops – generally signified by a double space in Brecht's original – are relatively unproblematic. But Steffin is well aware of all the ways in which a sentence can be changed, derailed and distorted by the insertion or omission of a comma. (Brecht himself gave a drastic example of the importance of punctuation. He knew the phrase from the Sayings of Solomon, Proverbs 16, 9: 'Man thinks, God guides.' He adapted it to: 'Man thinks: God guides'. By changing a punctuation mark, the phrase changes from a list into an assertion or an observation.[6] In such cases, of course, he was obliged to press the shift key on the typewriter himself in order to type the colon.)

Steffin taking on the role of Brecht's secretary is only one side of the story. She is not being entirely untruthful when she tells the Danish immigration authorities (she moves to Copenhagen in December 1933 and to Svendborg in February 1934) that she is not carrying out 'secretarial work' for Brecht – something she is forbidden to do under Danish law – but working for herself.[7] This is confirmed by her translations and by new texts she writes herself (even if she has no opportunity to publish them during this period), as well as the additional work she undertakes to Brecht's texts. What this looked like in practice can be illustrated by the example of the *Threepenny Novel*. First, however, it is important to note that this was not the only text she contributed to.

---

[5]*Brechts Lai-tu: Erinnerungen und Notate von Ruth Berlau*, ed. Hans Bunge (Darmstadt and Neuwied, 1985), 110.
[6]In the chorus of 'The Song of the Great Capitulation' in *Mother Courage and her Children*, BFA 6: 49f.
[7]Hans Christian Nörregaard, 'UDL. Nr. 36316-57120: Bertolt Brecht und die dänischen Behörden 1933-41' in *Deutschsprachiges Exil in Dänemark nach 1933* (Copenhagen, 1986), 100f.

In 1935, when Brecht drafts a new scene for his play *The Mother* in connection with the New York production, Steffin adds by hand the title 'Railway scene' (BFA 3: 391–398, 499). In the second version of *Round Heads and Pointed Heads*, which was published in 1938 in the second volume of the *Collected Works*, she is named alongside others as a collaborator (BFA 4: 148), and even before the work appears, her contribution to it is documented by several letters she writes to friends (see BFA 4: 463, 469, 479, 480). In this context she mentions instances of linguistic carelessness: Brecht has the characters in the play alternate between saying 'horse' and 'nag'. She is convinced it would be better if only the peasants were to talk about 'nags' and the landowners and officials about 'horses' (see BFA 4: 482).[8] In the first edition of *The Horatians and the Curiatians*, Steffin is named as the only collaborator (BFA 4: 280) and the same is true for *Señora Carrar's Rifles* (BFA 4: 306), both of which also appeared in the second volume of the *Collected Works* (1938).

After contributing as previously mentioned to the volume *Songs Poems Choruses* in 1934 (by selecting the poems and composing the collection), she prepares these same poems for another volume of the *Collected Works* in 1938 (although it does not materialise due to outside circumstances). She makes changes to the texts themselves and the order in which they appear (see BFA 11: 364, 367). In 1937, when Brecht is revising his poetry collection *Domestic Breviary* to be printed in this additional volume of the *Collected Works*, Steffin is called upon again for various tasks including checking the proofs. In 1938 she is once again busy with proofreading work for the separate edition of the *Svendborg Poems* (see BFA 12: 352, 356); in this as in many other cases, it is only Steffin's records which make it possible to date the poems. The volume which Brecht later calls the *Steffin Collection* (BFA 12: 93–112) is given this title because it was Steffin who selected the poems and copied them out consecutively (see BFA 12: 389–391). She would have been credited in the series *Fear and Misery of the Third Reich* (BFA 4: 340), as the wrap for the separate edition shows, but in 1938 it was no longer possible to publish this either. Since 1934/5, she had been helping collect material from newspapers and magazines on the subject of daily life in Germany, which forms the basis of the scenes in the series.[9]

After finishing the first version of *Life of Galileo* (1938/39), Brecht describes Steffin in a letter to Erwin Piscator as a collaborator on the play (see BFA 5: 335f.). From Steffin's correspondence, various details about the development of this version are available to us; in this case too she does more than just type out the text (see BFA 5: 354, 356 and other places). The same goes for the fragment *The Business Affairs of Mr Julius Caesar*, for which she initially seeks out literature in libraries, reads source material (particularly foreign-language sources)[10] and helps in other ways with the acquisition of material – by

---

[8] See Steffin's letter to Walter Benjamin, 15 March 1934, in Steffin, *Konfutse versteht nichts von Frauen*, ed. Inge Gellert (Berlin, 1991), 320f.

[9] See BFA 4: 523. She may have been the one who read a report from Dresden in the *Deutschland-Berichte der Sopade* [that informed the scene 'The Chalk Cross']: 'The workers and above all the unemployed are showing their discontent very clearly. [...] SA members in plain clothes mingle with the groups of workers who are deep in discussion. Each of these SA men has a cross drawn in chalk on the palm of his hand, which he then *imprints on the ringleader's back*. If any man with a chalk mark on his back then walks past an SA billet, he will be dragged inside and beaten up.' 1.1 (1934), 109. My thanks go to Lars Bardram, Nästved/Denkmark, for bringing this to my attention.

[10] See Georg Brandes, *Cajus Julius Caesar*, two volumes (Kóvenhavn og Kristiania, 1921; the copy in the Brecht estate library contains numerous marginalia by Steffin), or Jérôme Carcopino, *César* (Paris, 1936).

reading the papers attentively, for instance, in order to identify parallels with the present day. She then goes on to help with fundamental elements of the text, stylistic refinements etc. She is named as a collaborator on the radio play *The Trial of Lucullus* (1940; BFA 6: 88) and the 1951 version of the same name (BFA 6: 116), which appears ten years after her death, and she is also credited in *The Good Person of Szechuan*.[11]

The genesis of *Mother Courage and her Children* is well documented by Steffin (see BFA 6: 377) and for *Mr Puntila and his Man Matti*, Steffin works with Hella Wuolijoki to produce a translation of Wuolijoki's original, the play *Sahanpuruprinsessa [The Sawdust Princess]* (see BFA 6: 456). Steffin is able to refine certain aspects of the text when it comes to the women's conversations at the table, cooking, etc. The first complete version of *The Rise of Arturo Ui*, entitled *The Resistible Rise of Arturo Ui*, is marked by Brecht: 'Helsingsfors, 29.3.41, collaborator: Steffin' (see BFA 7: 354). In the first manuscript, under the title *Arturo Ui (Dramatic Poem) by K. Keuner* (one of Steffin's fair copies), there are handwritten corrections by her alone, relating to stylistic and metrical details (see BFA 7: 363). As Brecht's 'editor' she points out the inadequate verses in this play in particular. Brecht admits: 'I was very sloppy with the iambic'[12] and revises the text, but Steffin is still not satisfied and insists doggedly on further improvements.[13] And the list goes on: there are many other individual poems, stories and theoretical texts which benefit from Steffin's input.

In retrospect, Margarete Steffin's importance to Brecht is very clear. After her death in 1941 Brecht is mourning the loss of his lover on the one hand and missing his collaborator on the other; in the unfamiliar surroundings of California, he feels her absence in many ways.[14] He suffers a kind of paralysis in his work – big projects like the novel *The Business Affairs of Mr Julius Caesar* and the *Tui Novel* (BFA 17) are abandoned unfinished, for example, as are *Buying Brass* (BFA 22) and *The Book of Interventions in the Flow of Things (Me-ti)* (BFA 18). When it comes to these larger projects in particular, Brecht lacks the patience and the stamina to see them through to the end. We can only speculate as to whether, if he had been able to carry on working with Steffin, some of these projects which we know only as fragments would actually have been completed.

Brecht's most ambitious and only completed novel project, the *Threepenny Novel* (BFA 16), owes a great deal to Margarete Steffin (possibly including its ending). This is a prime example of what 'collaboration' looks like. Brecht starts working on the project in summer 1933; once large portions of the text are already written and with Brecht keen to finish the novel off quickly, Margarete Steffin is asked to give her opinion on the content. 'Next week I'm going to send you a third of the *Threepenny Novel*. I hope you won't pick it to pieces straight away,' writes the author suspiciously.[15] A few days after this letter, Steffin receives the impatient enquiry:

> I'm curious to see what you're going to say about the novel. I want to get it finished soon and start work on something else, something more important. Anyway, when I get near the end (the book isn't going to be very long) and at the proofreading stage

---

[11] BFA 6: 176; along with Ruth Berlau.
[12] Bertolt Brecht, *Arbeitsjournal*, ed. Werner Hecht (Frankfurt am Main, 1973), 252 (2 April 1941).
[13] Brecht, *Arbeitsjournal*, 254 (7 April 1941).
[14] See Brecht, *Arbeitsjournal*, 291 (1 August 1941).
[15] Brecht to Steffin; received by Steffin on 5 August 1933. Part of the correspondence is located in the Central State Archive for Literature and Art in Moscow (hereinafter: ZGALI), section 631/14; here: 631/14/394/3.

I'll need your help, and not just with typing. I've got the contract, incidentally, a very decent one in the end; I refused to haggle. – So we won't starve just yet ... [16]

But in the event Steffin gets involved with the project at an earlier stage, well before the proofreading and the typesetting and even before Brecht is getting 'near the end' of the novel. Brecht types up the first version of the text (written between June and August 1933), all in lower case as usual; it is 137 pages long.[17] The handwritten alterations are mainly Brecht's (Mr Beckett was originally a 'wool merchant' but in the handwritten edit becomes a 'timber merchant'). At this stage Steffin is already making changes to the text, bringing her stylistic abilities to bear: she changes 'The timber merchant was no novice when it came to women – his various marriages were proof of that. He had little time for adventures ...' to 'The timber merchant was no novice when it came to women. He had already had several wives – often simultaneously. He had little time for adventures ...'.[18] The 'rust buckets' which the profiteers call cargo ships are initially given English names by Brecht – 'Beautyfull Ann' and 'Young Cheapman' – Steffin changes them to 'Schöne Anna' and 'Junger Schiffersmann'.[19] Aside from Brecht's handwritten corrections, insertions and crossings-out, there are longer passages of text added in. Some of these are typed up by Brecht himself, with the resulting strips of paper glued to the relevant page, but Steffin makes similar additions – at least in outline.[20] She does not completely 'pick to pieces' the original text, but in many places she makes eminently sensible suggestions, which Brecht acts upon.

At this stage of the work on the text, Steffin is still living in Paris while the Brechts, in early August 1933, have just managed to buy their 'Danish thatched cottage' on Skovsbostrand in Svendborg using the advance from the publisher. It is during this time that Brecht sends the following letter (in which he does not complain of a lack of solidarity with what he has written but calls for solidity, from himself and his editor):

The criticism is good, but too short and not detailed enough. (And, like the novel, it lacks a certain solidity). You still need to answer all my questions. Also: don't copy out anything you don't like! Instead send everything back, in batches, and mark anything that is carelessly worded, any strong language or deliberate witticisms. The best thing would be for you to insert slips of paper, which can be in the form of very brief notes, just to give a rough idea. And you only need to send pages where you've marked something, if that isn't all of them. You should send them in batches so that they reach me sooner and I can start looking through them. Then I'll send them straight back to you, altered or – stubbornly left as they are ...

The accidental, crude, abrupt nature of the moral considerations is intentional. Perhaps that won't come out properly until later in the book!

I don't know, do you want to show it to Borchardt? ...[21]

---

[16] Brecht to Steffin; received by Steffin on 18 August 1933. ZGALI 631/14/394/5.
[17] BBA 269-271.
[18] BBA 269/14; see BFA 16: 33, 38-34, 1.
[19] E.g. BBA 269/22; see BFA 16: 40, 34 f.
[20] E.g. BBA 270/40; corresponds to BFA 16: 202, 26-203, 16.
[21] Brecht to Steffin; received by Steffin on 22 August 1933. ZGALI 631/14/388/24.

The latter part of this quote relates to the italicised passages which come later in the novel, whose significance Steffin has evidently not understood at first. This leads Brecht to wonder about asking Hermann Borchardt (who was also involved in *Saint Joan of the Stockyards*) for his opinion and impressions.

Particularly in this early phase, the editor does have some fundamental questions about the plot. The author remarks:

> ... the comment about the somewhat unfortunate distribution of weight at the beginning of the story (Fewkoombey's experiences with the beggars' trust) is quite correct. Perhaps together we can put it right. So keep writing to me with criticisms like that – I find them extremely useful.[22]

Steffin does as Brecht asks and continues to send her criticisms (which do not only relate to the beginning of the novel) from Paris to Svendborg. In August Brecht declares, without yet having seen all the criticisms: 'I now have 95 pages of the *Threepenny Novel*, which is almost two-thirds of the whole thing (total length 150 pages).'[23] In September he travels to Paris to work with Steffin directly there (and also in Sanary-sur-Mer in the south of France, where they stay for a month with Lion Feuchtwanger). During this time Brecht reports to his wife Helene Weigel in Denmark, rather more circumspectly: 'The novel is almost finished (the bare bones, at least).'[24]

In December 1933 Steffin accompanies Brecht to Copenhagen, where she stays with Ruth Berlau for a few weeks (she translates Berlau's novel, *Videre* [*Onward*], in order to practise her Danish, and writes stories). She also continues work on the *Threepenny Novel*. Once the first phase is complete, a second version of the novel emerges in December 1933 and January 1934, provisionally beginning with the introductory chapter 'The Residence'.[25] Initially this version consists of a manuscript typed by Steffin in upper and lower case, incorporating the additions to the first version and further supplementary material. Unsurprisingly, Brecht is not yet finished with the text and makes more handwritten changes to this fair copy. Here he clearly marks for the first time the sections which will be italicised in the printed version, indicating them via lines in the margin.[26] How important this is to him is evident from his many letters to the publisher at the proofreading and typesetting stages.)[27] There are also traces of Margarete Steffin's editing of the typescript: she takes out the product placement by replacing 'Gilette razors' with 'razor blades'.[28] She also adds, specifies and refines: 'He was not quite sure ...' becomes 'Just like on the way home from the picnic, he was not quite sure ...';[29] 'Polly was happy too and forgave Mac not only his professional past as a burglar, which he had told her about over the bottle of Burgundy in the hall, but also his love affairs ...' becomes 'Polly was happy too and forgave Mac his professional past as a burglar, which he had told her about over the bottle of wine in the hall – he let her feel that she was,

---

[22]Brecht to Steffin; received by Steffin on 28 August 1933. ZGALI 631/14/394/7.
[23]Brecht to Steffin; received by Steffin on 30 August 1933. ZGALI 631/14/394/8.
[24]Brecht to Helene Weigel, October/November 1933, in Brecht, *Briefe* (number 189), 183.
[25]BBA 272–273.
[26]BBA 272/06; BFA 16: 13, 21–30. BBA 272/08–09; BFA 16: 15, 35–16, 26. BBA 272/21–22; BFA 16: 30, 23–31, 16, etc.
[27]Brecht, *Briefe* (numbers 217–225), 214–221.
[28]BBA 272/42; BFA 16: 50, 18.
[29]BBA 272/49; GBA 16: 56, 18f.

to an extent, in charge. She even forgave him his love affairs ...';[30] '... and thus several murders in the winter of '95 were ascribed to the "Knife" which certainly could not have been committed by the man who put his name to them, i.e. claimed responsibility for them' becomes '... and thus several murders in the winter of '95 were ascribed to the "Knife" which certainly could not have been committed by the dead man in the cemetery at Dartmoor, and could hardly have been perpetrated by the man who had adopted his nickname and thereby claimed responsibility for these murders';[31] and so on.

In mid-January 1934, Brecht writes to her from Svendborg about further additions he has made thanks to the ideas Steffin 'put into his head' ('I'll have to type up the extra bits myself') and about the laborious work on the final chapter. 'I'm putting 1 duplicate sheet underneath, any more than that is too time-consuming for a first draft! Is it *very* bad?'[32] Brecht is referring to the chapter he is writing at this point, which is numbered '12', the first formulation of the later sections 'Work and Do Not Despair', 'Slaughter at the West India Docks', 'The Pitcher Goes to the Well', 'A National Catastrophe', 'Uneasy Days', 'The Alibi', 'A Victory for Common Sense' and 'Fog'.

This second version is initially comprised of 145 continuously typed pages with the aforementioned alterations as well as many others, and further additional text in the form of strips of paper glued to the manuscript; it ends with the concluding part of the eighth chapter.[33] The third phase in February/March 1934 sees the creation of the subsequent 62 typescript pages, all in lower case (meaning they were typed up by Brecht), featuring the main incidents of the later chapters 14 and 15.[34] Here Steffin's involvement can be seen in the addition of chapter numbers and titles such as 'Work and Do Not Despair' (later: 'The Strong Man Fights'),[35] 'The Pitcher Goes to the Well' (later: 'Clean-up Operation'),[36] 'Uneasy Days',[37] and 'A Victory for Common Sense':[38] 'And send me the *Threepenny Novel* a bit at a time. You must write to me about it chapter by chapter, too!'[39]

After this third phase, Steffin once again has a great deal of text to type up (or duplicate) in order to make more edits to this new version and refine the content further:[40] '10 pennies' or '5 pennies', for example, become 'a tuppence piece' and 'a ha'penny'.[41] In many places she also simply copies out Brecht's handwritten amendments, which are not always easy to decipher, for her own use and for the next copy of the novel, i.e. the final typewritten manuscript (for the publisher).[42] The figure and role of the narrator does not initially feature in the episode where Polly and Mrs Peachum watch the film *Mother, Your Child is Calling!* To illustrate what going to the cinema was like in the days of silent films, Brecht has evidently dictated these additions, and Steffin has transcribed them in

---

[30] BBA 272/87; BFA 16: 94, 1–5.
[31] BBA 274/04; BFA 16: 128, 20–25.
[32] Brecht to Steffin; received by Steffin on 13 January 1934. ZGALI 631/14/400/1-2.
[33] BFA 16: 162–166.
[34] BBA 273/47–108; see BFA 16: 306–374.
[35] BBA 272/47; see BFA 16: 306.
[36] BBA 273/60; see BBA 16: 327.
[37] BBA 273/67; see BFA 16: 332.
[38] BBA 273/86; see BFA 16: 354.
[39] Brecht to Steffin; received by Steffin on 13 January 1934 (see footnote 32). ZGALI 631/14/400/1-2.
[40] BBA 291-293.
[41] BBA 291/15; see BFA 16: 23, 34 and 23,35 f.
[42] This manuscript itself has not survived, but is documented by the proofs (without the corrections) (BBA 288–290).

shorthand,[43] numbered them and added the numbers to the typescript of this version[44] once she has moved to the Svendborg guesthouse 'Stella Maris' at the end of February 1934 and is therefore 'on the spot'.

Aside from such changes to the individual versions, there are various notes by Steffin about individual passages or ongoing storylines which she feels do not work.[45] These are the 'slips of paper, which can be in the form of very brief notes, just to give a rough idea'.[46] They include comments such as 'Peachum's reasons for leaving his business' and 'Smiles [English in the original] / Polly too short'[47] or notes like 'Closing speeches Machieth [sic] initiative' and 'patriotic movement'.[48] These are all examples of the ideas Steffin 'puts into Brecht's head' during the work on the text. Among the materials for the *Threepenny Novel* there are also several notepads of Steffin's in which the former office clerk notes down the figures for the shipping deals, for example (prices, repair costs, commission fees, etc.), and carries out various calculations.[49]

The fact that the author can sometimes react 'stubbornly' is also documented by just such a 'slip of paper':[50] the typewritten question '?????????????? / Should agreement to a divorce be given in return for gaining access to the National?' is probably Steffin's – Brecht writes 'no!' straight across it.[51] But this is more the exception than the rule.

The points summarised under the heading 'Criticism' are probably all attributable to Steffin, and not just the first one which is marked with a G (for Grete):

1–9 too broad, main purpose, Peachum organisation not there. (G)

11 Introduction of Beckett too weak. Need references to his inconspicuousness and big role for Polly.

12 Mac's basic motive: money?

13 Account of the grinding conversation on the way home.[52]

The ways in which Steffin helped with the proofreading from July to September 1934[53] can be seen from those of the proofs that have survived intact.[54] Most of the corrections, particularly relating to spelling and punctuation, are hers (easily identifiable by her handwriting, which uses Latin letters in contrast to Brecht's German script or a mixture of that and the older Sütterlin script).

---

[43]BBA 293/19. The following sections in BFA 16: 287, 30–34; 287, 38f.; 288, 6f.; 288, 12f.; 288, 25–27; 288, 30f., 288, 37–39. See also BBA 293/50 and 29364 with further shorthand notes.
[44]BBA 293/20–21.
[45]E.g. BBA 293/160.
[46]Brecht to Steffin; received by Steffin on 22 August 1933 (see footnote 21). ZGALI 631/14/388/24.
[47]BBA 294/30.
[48]BBA 294/119.
[49]BBA 294/29.
[50]See Brecht to Steffin; received by Steffin on 22 August 1933 (see footnote 21). ZGALI 631/14/388/24.
[51]BBA 294/100.
[52]BBA 295/18.
[53]The original German for 'with the proofreading' reads 'beir Korrektur'. 'Beir' is a made-up word, an abbreviation of 'bei der'. Brecht was keen on this word, and it was another of the things Steffin had to correct in order to make the text 'legible to the world' (see footnote 1).
[54]BBA 288–290.

And in this regard Steffin has a great deal of work to do correcting the errors made by the Dutch publishers (the *Threepenny Novel* is to form part of the German-language list of the publisher Allert de Lange in Amsterdam). Not only does she have to ensure consistency in the case of common 'traps' like 'selbstständig'/'Selbstständigkeit'[55] and 'das'/'dass'/'daß'; she also has to correct 'heete' to 'heute', 'unf' to 'und' and 'Mämnern' to 'Männern', etc. She corrects word divisions, marks instances of letters being the wrong way round ('fp' instead of 'pf') and picks up on the spelling of 'Fotographie' (it must either be written 'Fotografie' or 'Photographie', she decrees, but it cannot use both 'f' and 'ph'). She does all this very thoroughly, if somewhat unconventionally: she crosses out the relevant word and writes a little 'd' (for deletion) in the margin; she writes missing letters between the lines and usually copies out the whole word again in full in the margin; she rewrites incorrect letters next to the line, then crosses them out and writes the correct ones instead.

Of course, the 'solidity' which the typesetter promptly changes to 'solidarity' – perhaps he knows the author, who wrote the 'Solidarity Song' in 1931 for the film *Kuhle Wampe* (BFA 14: 116–118, 512–518) – has to be changed back to 'solidity' before the book goes to print.[56] And Steffin prefers 'Schlagzeile' ['headline'] to 'Schlachtzeile' ['battle-line'/'slaughter-line'],[57] even though the latter may initially have been intentional on Brecht's part. After all, she has been asked to mark all the parts which are 'carelessly worded' or contain 'strong language or deliberate witticisms'.[58] She has to make sure that the 'Triumpf' so beloved of Brecht is corrected throughout, and that some of his other writerly idiosyncrasies like 'Preiss' (instead of 'Preis') do not make it into print. The 'Mahagonny furniture', however, along with the 'Mahagonny table' and the panelling made from 'Mahagonny wood', are allowed to stay.[59]

Steffin also checks the completed version of the novel manuscript or typescript produced by the typesetters, who occasionally miss out half a sentence here and there. This is easy to spot when one reads: 'He invited more than ever on Coax'. After 'invited', Steffin adds: 'He invited him to his house for dinner with the family. Now everything depended [on Coax]'.[60] It is less easy to spot omissions when a word is used twice in quick succession, resulting in a phrase being missed out. This will only be spotted by someone who knows the text inside out and is checking very meticulously. The typesetter has: 'We sell a hundredweight of potatoes to anyone, irrespective of the person ...' whereas the text is supposed to read: 'We sell our goods to rich and poor. We sell a hundredweight of potatoes to anyone, irrespective of the person ...'[61]

Steffin refines English terms, turning 'pennies' into 'pence',[62] for example, and 'pfennigweise' into 'pennyweise';[63] she changes place names – correcting 'Turnbridge' in

---

[55] See BBA 288/139; see BFA 16: 114,4; BBA 290/17 and other places.
[56] BBA 288/107; see BFA 16: 89, 12.
[57] BBA 289/159; see BFA 16: 243, 18.
[58] See Brecht to Steffin; received by Steffin on 22 August 1933 (see footnote 21). ZGALI 631/14/388/24.
[59] BFA 16: 117, 22f.; 136, 2 and 215, 25; 166, 8.
[60] BBA 288/52; see BFA 16: 49, 2f. (again varied).
[61] BBA 290/91; see BFA 16: 340, 10–12.
[62] See BBA 288/83; see BFA 16: 72, 25.
[63] See BBA 288/84; see BFA 16: 72, 32.

the proofs to 'Tunbridge'[64] and substituting 'Plymouth' for 'Manchester',[65] 'Limehouse' for 'Soho',[66] 'Nunhead' for 'Kensington'[67] and 'Whitechapel' for 'Withechapel'[68] – and makes sure that Brecht's correction of 'Maveking' to 'Mafeking'[69] the first time it appears is implemented throughout.[70] She changes and standardises character names: Lord 'Bloomsbury' was originally called 'Lansbury', which still appears in places in the typesetter's document[71] (as does the misspelling 'Blumsburry', especially in the chapters 'Napoleonic Plans'[72] and 'Mr X.'[73]). She remembers that English currency is not based on the decimal system, so '1 shilling and 95 pennies' needs to become '1 shilling and eleven pence ha'penny'.[74] She realises that if the 'retail trade' features in the novel,[75] it needs to be referred to as such throughout and not sometimes called 'the wholesale trade',[76] which is exactly the opposite. The text must not refer to 'wholesalers' when 'chain stores' are meant.[77]

Steffin standardises the general capitalisation at the beginnings of verses in the mottos for individual chapters, deletes the full stops after the chapter numbers and chapter headings, and standardises the spelling of 'Macheath', which in some places is still spelt 'Machieth'[78] (a hangover from the earlier phases of the novel's development). She also writes out abbreviations such as 'e.g.' in full. Other stylistic changes can be traced back to Steffin too: thus 'you're not really looking at it' eventually becomes 'you're not looking at it properly',[79] 'Mr Beckett listened to her' becomes 'Mr Beckett listened to her gloomily',[80] 'picked out furniture' becomes 'selected furniture',[81] 'Since the search for a suitable house had not worked out' becomes 'Since the search for a suitable house had hitherto proved unsuccessful',[82] 'improvers of people' becomes 'improvers of humanity',[83] 'deferral of payment' becomes 'allowances'[84] and 'They went' becomes 'They betook themselves' (which fits better here).[85] Steffin changes the original 'He went off with Blumsbury' to 'Macheath did not dare look Bloomsbury in the eye'.[86] 'The deal

---

[64] E.g. BBA 288/97; see BFA 16: 83, 17 and 83, 20.
[65] BBA 288/119; see BFA 16: 98, 26.
[66] BBA 289/4; see BFA 16: 127, 16.
[67] BBA 289/53; see BFA 16: 163, 39-164, 1. Also BBA 289/82; see BFA 16: 186, 8 and other places.
[68] BBA 289/133; see BFA 16: 224, 23.
[69] BBA 288/38; see BFA 16: 38, 15. They both overlook it at 38, 19 but clearly the typesetter was on form and corrected it him- or herself, as the first edition shows (Amsterdam: Allert de Lange, 1934, 40).
[70] See e.g. BBA 288/113; see BFA 16: 94, 18 and 94, 21.
[71] See BBA 288/107; see BFA 16: 89, 23.
[72] BBA 289/37–56; BFA 16: 152–166. And 'Lansbury' appears there too (BBA 189/44; BFA 16: 157, 30).
[73] BBA 289/92–97; BFA 16: 194–197.
[74] BBA 289/18; see BFA 16: 137, 21 f.
[75] BBA 289/42; see BFA 16: 156, 1 and 156,9.
[76] BBA 289/42; see BFA 16: 156, 5. Also BBA 289/47; see BFA 16: 159, 34.
[77] BBA 289/46; see BFA 16; 158, 34.
[78] E.g. BBA 288/111; see BFA 16: 93, 2.
[79] BBA 288/87; see BFA 16: 75, 33.
[80] BBA 288/89; see BFA 16: 76, 32.
[81] BBA 288/102; see BFA 16: 86, 10.
[82] BBA 288/103-104; see BFA 16: 87, 30f.
[83] BBA 288/116; see BFA 16: 96, 9f.
[84] BBA 289/122; see BFA 16: 100, 14.
[85] BBA 289/46; see BFA 16: 159, 23.
[86] BBA 289/48; see BFA 16: 160, 33.

came off' becomes 'He made good deals on his linen, and on wool'.[87] In the episode with the funeral service for the drowned soldiers, 'the clergy' was originally represented by a 'provost'; in the proofs, Steffin changes this to a 'bishop' throughout.[88] In Aaron's subsequent speech she refines the address, changing 'Ladies and gentlemen' to 'Dear Sirs and Madam', for Polly Macheath is the only woman present among the bankers and union men.[89]

In the chapter introducing the Knife's gang, Steffin also deletes the following phrases: 'They [the murders] strengthened the gang inwardly and outwardly',[90] and 'Their speciality was breaking and entering',[91] and '"Travellers" who simply looked out for opportunities, receivers of stolen goods and other specialists. The members worked independently, in small units',[92] and 'The gang was divided into small, mobile units which worked in tandem with each other',[93] and the instruction 'The cigar box is already on the table. When they sit down, dignity goes out of the window. Then they start arguing all over again over the goods which other people have to go out and get!'[94]

Steffin marks rearrangements of passages of text[95] and she changes the position of mottos which, in the proofs, begin on the preceding page instead of on a new page at the start of the associated chapter.[96] Not least, she types up ten long additions which have to be newly typeset and inserted.[97] Instead of the last three paragraphs of the tenth book,[98] the proofs initially read: 'The next morning, when the lawyer Walley came on behalf of Mr Peachum to speak to him about divorce, and hinted that if he agreed to one then certain exonerating material might perhaps come to light, Macheath brusquely dismissed the idea. He insisted that his marriage had been a love match.'[99] The three new paragraphs inserted here are initially located just before the final section of 'Mr Peachum Sees a Way Out'.[100] Instead of the two final paragraphs of the third book (BFA 16: 374, 37–40), the proofs originally read: 'He met with general approval. He had spoken from the heart to those present.'[101]

Once the general criticisms have been taken into account, once the text has been further corrected, altered, standardised and extended right into the final phase when it has already been typeset, once the German first edition has finally appeared in Amsterdam in November 1934, and once Brecht has read the first reviews in newspapers and magazines

---

[87] BBA 289/88; see BFA 16: 191, 6f.
[88] BBA 290/126–129; see BFA 16: 368, 9-371, 34. Also in BBA 290/142; see BFA 16: 381, 5.
[89] BBA 290/131; see BFA 16: 372, 6.
[90] BBA 289/10; in the first set of proofs this comes after '... went out'. (BFA 16: 130, 35).
[91] BBA 289/10; in the first set of proofs this comes after '... face'. (BFA 16: 131, 3).
[92] BBA 289/10; in the first set of proofs this comes after '... lawyers'. (BFA 16: 131, 3). However, she corrects 'but also lawyers' to: 'smugglers, receivers and lawyers'.
[93] BBA 289/32; in the first set of proofs this comes after '... carts'. (BFA 16: 148, 9).
[94] BBA 290/114; in the first set of proofs this comes before '... What disgusts me ...' (BFA 16: 358, 17).
[95] E.g. BBA 290/39–40; see BFA 16: 300, 26–29: the paragraph was initially typeset after 300, 38.
[96] BBA 288/57-58; see BFA 16: 315.
[97] These are the sections BFA 16: 53, 30–54, 6 (BBA 288/59), 65, 32–66, 4 ('... idiocies'; BBA 288/74), 169, 10–25 (BBA 289/60), 185, 10–22 (BBA 289/81), 230, 11–26 (BBA 289/142), 232, 20–33 (BBA 289/144), 241, 21–31 (BBA 289/157), 251, 25–33 (BBA 289/171), 318, 37–319, 7 ('The hostility ...'; BBA 290/63), 325, 12–23 (BBA 290/72).
[98] BFA 16: 227, 3–13.
[99] BBA 289/136.
[100] BBA 289/112–113; BFA 16: before 209, 21.
[101] BBA 290/135.

and is trying to interest foreign-language publishers in translations of the novel, he writes a letter from Denmark to Steffin, who has gone to the Caucasus for further treatment for her tuberculosis:

> There have been offers for foreign-language editions: a Czech one, a Polish one, a Danish one and a French one (by Grasset, via Wolff). They only come with small advances, but it's better than nothing. (The advance from Grasset is 3000 francs, for example). Something of a struggle in England, not because novel is set in England (as we thought) but because English public cannot understand(!). On the occasion of the recent marriage of an English prince to a Balkan princess, which gripped the English nation for three weeks, unemployed people sent wedding presents! Reviews so far: *Pariser Tageblatt*, by Lania – glowing, obviously. Then by Schlamm in the *Europäische Hefte* (the competitor of the *Weltbühne*) – great, *Baseler Nationalzeitung* – likewise eulogistic (even if printed very small). In general you seem to have written a masterpiece, genie of the lamp. Your clean, clear language comes in for particularly high praise. In all seriousness: it's good to have one's most discerning reader *at home!*[102]

When she leaves the Caucasus in early 1935 and travels to Moscow, one of the things she is working on is the second German-language edition of the *Threepenny Novel*, which is prepared by the Publishing Cooperative of Foreign Workers in the USSR (Moscow-Leningrad), and delivered in the first few days of 1936. And the novel is not the only thing occupying her time.

Steffin, who has been in Moscow again since January 1936, reports:

> The *Horatians* is printed, you'll receive a copy soon. They are coming out in about two weeks, as is the novel. On the cover of the novel is a fish and three wavy lines. At first I didn't know what it meant, but ... 'Oh, the shark has ...'[103]
>
> So the *Threepenny Novel* is finished. It will be in the shops in the next few days (the German edition – and Stenitsch has delivered the Russian one). A copy costs 7.75 roubles, quite expensive. The publisher is sending you ten complimentary copies, but I'll buy some more. Now please write and tell me how many copies you want sent to Svendborg, and who shall I send hard copies to directly from here? (From here it's cheaper, and easier for you?)[104]

All of this shows that Steffin has become increasingly important to Brecht in terms of his work on the texts, as a necessary (and welcome) corrective – a role which had been fulfilled before 1933 by Elisabeth Hauptman. Like Hauptmann, Steffin is not merely tolerated as an editor but accepted, even after Ruth Berlau comes on the scene.

'Total length 150' manuscript pages, was Brecht's original plan for the *Threepenny Novel*; but thanks in large part to Steffin's comments and suggestions – both general and specific – the novel ends up being 494 pages long. The author is pleased: 'I can live well, I've written a 500-page novel and, more importantly, I have a good contract

---

[102]Brecht to Steffin; received by Steffin on 19/20 December 1934. ZGALI 631/14/388/7. The reviews Brecht mentions can also be found in *Brechts Romane*, ed. Wolfgang Jeske (Frankfurt am Main, 1984), 152–157, 157f., 161 f.
[103]Steffin to Brecht, 20 February 1936. ZGALI 631/14/415/6-9.
[104]Steffin to Brecht, 4 March 1936. ZGALI 631/14/415/18-19.

with a Dutch publisher,' he writes to George Grosz on 2 September 1934.[105] With hindsight, given the (low) sales figures for the Amsterdam edition of the novel, Brecht proves to have made the right decision in asking for a sizeable advance. Without a good text, however, it is unlikely that the many other German-language editions and numerous translations of the novel would have come about. Today we know that Steffin contributed to a long-seller.

---

[105]Brecht, *Briefe* (number 226), 221.

CHAPTER NINETEEN

Berlau Photographs Brecht's Life and Work – a Collaboration (More or Less)

GRISCHA MEYER
TRANSLATED BY ROMY FURSLAND

Ruth Berlau came to photography somewhat by chance, and relatively late in her career compared to her other endeavours. It was not the only activity to which she tried to apply her wide-ranging talents and inclinations – with limited success, however, and with many failures along the way. As a girl she initially tried her hand at journalistic writing, but then changed career to become an actress and got the opportunity – rather by chance – to work with an amateur theatre group where she had her first experience of directing. On returning to Copenhagen from an amateur theatre conference in the Soviet Union in 1930, successful and brimming with naïve impressions, she made a grand gesture and joined the Danish Communist Party at the age of 24.

Her lifelong and indissoluble bond with Brecht and his work sprang from a similarly spirited enthusiasm on the part of this young woman who was searching both for her vocation and for a political home, and who met Brecht – newly arrived in Danish exile – at just the right moment in her life. He was her 'way in' to the committed struggle for the cause she was so passionate about: the revolutionary transformation of the world. As Brecht's accomplice, she was willing and able to become a 'co-conspirator' to great deeds – this meant so much to her that she was prepared to give up her homeland, the security of a bourgeois marriage, and a burgeoning career. In a vicious circle of devotion and discord, constantly alternating between periods of solitary and collaborative work, she followed Brecht and his ever-renewed promises all the way around the world and ended up in East Berlin where, as an exile returning to a country that was not her own, she was left in limbo right up until the end, and was never able to find her place.

The scope and substance of Brecht and Berlau's collaboration is a much-debated and often controversial subject. The positions people have espoused over the years range from

---

Grischa Meyer, 'Berlau fotografiert bei Brecht – eine Zusammenarbeit (mehr oder weniger)', *Brecht Yearbook*, 30 (2005), pp. 183–201.

the view that Brecht did not write any of his plays himself, at least never 'on his own', but consistently preyed upon and exploited his (male and female) collaborators – of whom Berlau was one, and was frequently called upon as 'chief witness for the prosecution' – through to the confidently voiced opinion that Ruth Berlau was only of marginal importance to Brecht's work, and carried out nothing more than auxiliary services. Her own works, on the other hand – where they are published at all – are all attributed to Brecht's artistic talents. According to this view, Brecht is behind everything Berlau ever published, as a supplier of ideas, writer or editor: in a central role, at any rate.

Berlau herself more or less deliberately laid the groundwork for both these skewed views of her work. For one thing, she called herself (almost revelling in her self-abasement) a mere 'scribe', thereby giving the impression that she had no 'merits' of her own – neither in her contribution to Brecht's texts nor in her own work. This exaggerated modesty was an inevitable counterpart to the strident and uncontrolled behaviour with which she provoked those around her and completely and permanently destroyed her credibility.

With both these strategies, she placed herself in deliberate(?) opposition to the activities of everyone else in Brecht's circle in Berlin.

Berlau always prostrated herself a little too devoutly before Brecht's 'genius', and her enthusiasm was always a little too laden with pathos: she was parodying the behaviour she saw daily in Brecht's collaborators during their time in Berlin. She could not help measuring the 'later Brecht' with his slick self-stylisation, in his seemingly unassailable position of power within the cultural scene of East Berlin, against the powerless Brecht of fifteen years before, who had relied upon her help during their shared period of exile. A 'guilty conscience' personified (like Banquo's ghost at Macbeth's banquet),[1] Berlau stumbled around the Berlin landscape of compromises and partisan feuding like a shadow of disappointed hopes. Nobody could forgive her this recklessness.

In the long run, Berlau's temperament meant she could not make peace with the part she was expected to play: that of an outsider and 'Girl Friday' for special tasks. The traditional role of the patient martyr or selfless heroine of the 'communist'[2] cause was one she could and would not adopt. Her self-destructive outbursts and desperate quest for attention and recognition were the result of her personality and of her illness, which increasingly caused her to lose touch with reality. The working relationship between Brecht and Berlau was affected by a love affair which atrophied and decayed as the years went on, but the nature and length of which eclipsed many of Brecht's other 'relationships'.

How should we describe the nature of the collaboration between Brecht and Berlau today, almost sixty years on? The idea of dealing with Brecht – the poet who has long been taught in every German school, the classic writer of the modern age, the analytical theorist of Marxist aesthetics – on the same level as the perpetually disorganised, sentimental 'car crash' Berlau, seems contrived, presumptuous and disproportionate. Berlau is remembered – if at all – as the archetypal loser, a woman who was beyond help and was destroyed by illness, alcohol and the mercilessness of a cold male world. This has made her easy prey for psychologising interpretations and fashionable gender studies approaches which make little effort to examine Ruth Berlau's political and artistic

---

[1] It is also worth noting that she gave herself the name 'Ruth Hamlet' as a pseudonym. Why did she choose the name of the Danish prince who was incapable of avenging his father and who drove himself and his lover into madness and death?

[2] i.e. unpaid.

motives. Brecht, on the other hand, appears to us today as the product of a canonisation in which he himself played an influential role. The writer has transformed himself into a literary figure, a branded product with a clearly outlined brand identity and a 'product range' which, at least for the theatre, has concentrated on the 'saleable goods' (under current market conditions) of his literary production. When we look at the exceptionally lively and beautiful portrait Josef Breitenbach took of Brecht in Paris in 1937,[3] however, we see something quite different: the face of a poet. A man in exile, with a rather birdlike demeanour, undernourished and not particularly well-groomed, in whose thin-lipped face the yearning for security after five years abroad is undimmed, and to whom it is difficult to attribute the revolutionary pathos of 'Workers Farmers Take up your Rifles', and the cold gaze of *The Decision*.

* * *

One area in which the nature of Brecht and Berlau's collaboration is almost indisputable is photography. This is what I want to concentrate on in this article. For in photography (unlike in the supposedly collaborative writing of a play or – even more complicated – the development of a production or its conception), tasks are clearly separated from each other. The 'technical' process can be distinguished in a reasonably comprehensible way from the 'artistic' element.

It will be useful initially to note a few preliminary technical points about the way in which photographs are developed and delivered.

Most of the surviving photographs taken by Ruth Berlau are held in the Bertolt Brecht Archive,[4] where they were initially divided into two groups: the purely theatrical photographs (documentary images of scenic processes during rehearsals and performances, portraits of actors in costumes and masks, props etc.) and photographs featuring a) Brecht, b) Brecht with other people and c) Helene Weigel.

There are also 235 35mm rolls of film held in the BBA,[5] which are neither dated nor annotated by Berlau and which depict (alongside a few familiar faces) a great many unfamiliar people, occasions and places: these have formed the principal basis of my research thus far.[6]

Further material is held in the Ruth Berlau Archive,[7] whose photographs have been archived from her estate. Parts of the estate are still in the hands of Ruth Berlau's heirs, the family of Johannes Hoffmann, who died in autumn 2004. A few photographs (but important ones) are on film rolls in possession of private individuals to whom Berlau gave negatives or who had access to negatives she produced for the Berliner Ensemble or which were developed or enlarged in the laboratory there.

---

[3] In Josef Breitenbach, *Photographien*, ed. V. T. O. Immisch, U. Pohlmann and K. E. Göltz (Munich: Schirmer & Mosel, 1996) and displayed in 2004 in the CAMERA WORKS gallery in Berlin. Brecht wrote to Breitenbach: 'the picture of me [...] is the best one I have ever had of myself [...] I would also like another couple of copies – would that be possible?' (Brecht and Weigel to Breitenbach, Svendborg, 10.01.1938), in: K. Holtz/W Schopf, *Im Auge des Exils* (Berlin, 2001).
[4] Under BBA FA in the Bertolt Brecht Archive of the Stiftung Archive der Akademie der Künste, Berlin.
[5] Under B 1 – 235.
[6] Grischa Meyer, Ruth Berlau – *Fotografin an Brechts Seite* (Berlin: Propyläen, 2003) (RBF).
[7] Ruth Berlau Archive of the Stiftung Archive der Akademie der Künste, Berlin (RBA).

In the photo archive of the Berliner Ensemble – the last place Ruth Berlau worked – it is documented that in addition to her surviving negatives, there were many film rolls which disintegrated after fifty years due to her improper handling of them, and were disposed of. The whereabouts of her camera (a Leica, which may have been purchased by Brecht) is unknown. In the RBA there is a document stating that she received a Contax single-lens reflex camera as a bonus for work she did on the *Modelbooks*. The whereabouts of this camera is also unknown.

Whilst Ruth Berlau, as is evident from the sources, only became seriously interested in photography after she went to America, Brecht had his own camera long before she did. Many of the 'personal photos' of the Brecht/Weigel family from the first years of their exile will have been taken with this camera. It was probably a 6 x 9 cm roll-film camera with an extendable bellows, a popular gadget for amateurs in the early 1930s. Perhaps in Sweden or later Brecht must have bought a Leica,[8] which Ruth Berlau used for a long time. In all the photographs taken by Berlau until well into the 1950s, the same traces of a sub-optimal film transport can be seen on the negative strips, indicating the consistent use of a single camera.

Photographs were always important to Brecht.[9] He took some photos of productions of his plays from the 1920s and 1930s into exile with him. Brecht paid close attention to Josef Breitenbach's documentation of the Paris productions of *Señora Carrar's Rifles* and scenes from *Fear and Misery of the Third Reich*.[10] Evidently he often sat patiently for portraits of himself, and criticised the results at length later on.[11]

While Brecht was one of the most photographed writers of his day, there are relatively few portrait photos of Ruth Berlau. Some of the best from the period before 1940 were taken by Mogens Voltelen.[12] But Brecht clearly used the camera himself several times to take photos of Ruth Berlau. During one of his longer stays at Berlau's New York flat he shot a lovely portrait of her, showing a young woman with lightly ironic charm, seen in profile wearing a headscarf.

For a long time Berlau was what people called the sporty type of the *Neue Sachlichkeit* movement. She drove a convertible and rode a motorbike and a bicycle; she wore tight

---

[8] In a photo it is clear to see that it must be a Leica Model A, which was produced from the end of the 1920s onwards.

[9] Brecht's 'faith in pictures' is illustrated by a letter to Ruth Berlau, who in April 1950 is on a trip abroad: 'and if a theatre wants to put on one of my plays, take photographs of one or two of the scenes for me so I can see how it is doing!' Bertolt Brecht, *Werke. Große kommentierte Berliner und Frankfurter Ausgabe*, ed. Werner Hecht, Jan Knopf, Werner Mittenzwei and Klaus-Detlef Müller (Frankfurt and Berlin: Suhrkamp and Aufbau, 1987–2000) (BFA), Vol. 30, 21.

[10] Holz/Schopf, p. 73: 'describing the new performance/representational style is almost impossible without such photos [...] What's more, I lost most of the photos of performances – I systematically photographed the performances – in Germany. They were never as beautiful/good as yours, though.' Brecht to Breitenbach, Svendborg, Nov. 1937.

[11] Gerda Goedhart, *Brecht Porträts* (Zurich, 1964), 106: 'Brecht was a great lover of photos. But he was camera-shy, and did not allow many people to photograph him.'

[12] The Danish architect M.V. was one of Ruth Berlau's Copenhagen friends. He often accompanied her on visits to Brecht and his family in Skovsbostrand, and was commissioned by Helene Weigel to convert the farmhouse she had bought in order to make it suitable for Brecht's needs. Two leather sofas, which are now located at Brecht's house in Chausseestraße in Berlin, were designed by him. The photos taken on these and other occasions during the period from 1933 to 1939 – evidently with his camera, and possibly by M.V. himself – later came into Berlau's possession. Most of them are now held in the BBA.

skirts, white stripy socks and silk blouses, but could also don an elegant suit with a fur collar and borrowed jewellery if the occasion demanded it.

Her outward appearance was increasingly shaped by Brecht's very specific preferences with regard to the clothing, underwear and hairstyles of his 'creatures'. This only becomes evident to some extent in later photographs of Berlau. In matters of love and lifestyle Berlau was a much more modern person than Brecht; she allowed herself to be guided by her passions, cared little about the effect she had on others, did not set much store by etiquette and made far fewer concessions to the bourgeois code than he did. She, after all – a married woman – was capable of following her lover abroad and then, with the help of that lover's wife, negotiating a 'bespoke' divorce that would give her a certain amount of independence (from which Brecht also benefited, incidentally).

* * *

When Berlau wrote to Brecht in April 1944 that she wanted to learn photography, he replied immediately and enthusiastically and in his next few letters began to develop initial ideas of how her photographic activities could be useful to him.

Evidently Brecht had not forgotten what he had read in *Life* magazine in 1940:[13] the library of the University of Chicago was reproducing newspaper pages in such small sizes that you could fit four months' worth of issues of *Life* magazine (i.e. over 1,600 pages) into a cigarette packet(!) The article had also said that microfilm, which had been invented during the previous decade, was the biggest revolution in the recording of the written word since Gutenberg had invented movable type. Thick books could now be cheaply(!) recorded, permanently saved and conveniently stored on 16 or 35 mm film, and easily viewed using a small projector. It was also reported that in London, books which had been destroyed in the bombing could now be reproduced because they had previously been microfilmed. Two pieces of evidence point to the fact that Brecht read this article in *Life* and took careful note of what it said. In a letter on 18 May 1944[14] he asks Ruth Berlau whether one needed special apparatus 'to photograph things very very small, to be read with a microscope? Then you'd be able to duplicate manuscripts and it wouldn't cost much ...' He also picks up on the illustrative phrase about the cigarette packet. Günther Weisenborn recalls: 'He brought his works with him on microfilm. They all fit inside a little packet, he says.'[15]

Thus, thanks to the tip in *Life* and Berlau's willingness to take up photography, Brecht had found an easy way of making as many copies of texts as he wanted without having to rely on the services of a secretary to type them up. The death of Margarete Steffin who, alongside many others, had taken on this time-consuming and arduous work, had posed a technical production problem for some time: now that problem could be solved. Berlau had no more talent as a typist than Helene Weigel, who had tried it for a time but soon gave up in despair and turned her attention to the more calming and creative activity of bookbinding.

---

[13]*Life* magazine, 16 December 1940, 78.
[14]BFA: 29, 337.
[15]G. Weisenborn, 'Zürcher Tagebuch', in *Erinnerungen an Brecht*, compiled by Hubert Witt (Leipzig: Reclam, 1964), 148. (The cigar-smoking Brecht could not bring himself to use the term 'cigarette packet'!)

Ruth Berlau, however, threw herself into photography partly in the hope that it might enable her to work more autonomously as an author and a journalist in a foreign language[16] and thus to find another job independently of Brecht after her work at the OWI[17] came to an end in 1943.

But right up until the end of their American exile, the task of photographing all the existing manuscripts and printed editions of Brecht's texts took up more and more of Ruth Berlau's time. In 1945 there was already a temporary photo lab technician working in the darkroom which Berlau had installed in her New York flat specifically for this purpose. As it started to look as though Brecht and Berlau's exile in America would soon be coming to an end, this amount of manpower was no longer sufficient to get the project finished. External photography companies were tasked with creating reproductions of pages of text. In 1947, before Brecht left for Europe, a copy of the film rolls was handed over to the New York Public Library for safekeeping, and is still there to this day.

The practice of reprographic 'filming' was also used in the creation of the 'official' Brecht Archive. Today, those taking advantage of the little grey folders at 125 Chausseestraße in Berlin should spare a thought for Ruth Berlau and the closet in Santa Monica where it all began.[18]

One of Ruth Berlau's character traits was her oft-cited 'Chinese' industriousness and the restlessness with which she sought to put her plans into action (and other people's, too). This restlessness often led to careless mistakes and a lack of consistency in completing and making use of the results of her work. In New York in the spring of 1944 she took photography lessons from Josef Breitenbach, the German photographer whose work for Brecht she was already familiar with. From Breitenbach Berlau learned, over the course of several months, the basics of how to work the camera and how to use the darkroom; but her teacher's influence clearly went much further than this. Breitenbach had taken his work for Brecht very seriously and, in addition to the stills he had been asked to take, had produced a large number of pictures depicting the rehearsal process and the conditions under which the production was created. This resulted in a unique testimony to the humble circumstances in which theatre history was being made.

Breitenbach knew how to be both documentarist and reporter at the same time, and how to link photography with writing. Thus his work also served to produce a photo reportage on the *Carrar* production which could appear with accompanying text. He offered this as an article for *Life* magazine, but it was rejected. It appeared later in a German-language magazine in Prague.[19] This kind of 'second-order usage' undoubtedly served as a model for Ruth Berlau. But her encounter with the 'straight photography' which was becoming very popular in New York in the 1940s will also have been a source of inspiration for her. Numerous photos testify to her explorations of the city streets, during which she produces portraits of striking workers, of sailors on Danish ships in New York Harbour, of passers-by in the streets and walkers in Central Park.

---

[16]'I write down what I see and hear, but often people only believe me when I am able to provide concrete proof of what I write: THROUGH PICTURES.' (RBA N 152)

[17]OWI – Office of War Information, an American government agency which was responsible for all activities relating to war propaganda. Ruth Berlau worked at the agency's overseas broadcaster in New York in 1942 and 1943.

[18]The archive is a 'legitimate child' of German exile and the American film industry, since the 'Ansco' 35 mm films that were used were obtained cheaply from the unexposed remnants of the big Hollywood film rolls.

[19]*Volksillustrierte*, Prague, November 1973; see K. Holz/W Schopf, 90.

On the drives she took with Brecht across the USA she photographed the vast expanses of the American Midwest, which had only entered the public consciousness a few years before thanks to the work of the FSA photographers.[20] This work was undoubtedly familiar to her and Brecht, for it appeared regularly in the pages of *Life* magazine, which they both read.

* * *

In summer 1945, Brecht and Charles Laughton had completed the first version of an English translation and adaptation of the play *Life of Galileo*. After the atom bomb was dropped on Hiroshima and Nagasaki, there was an even greater need to stage the play in New York. Brecht writes about this to Berlau: 'it is important in many respects.'[21] He wrote to her from Santa Monica to keep her up-to-date on what he was doing, and expected her to carry out a series of assignments for him – he saw her as his 'liaison officer' in New York. The work on *Galileo*, as the English version of the play was now called, was progressing rather slowly and taking a very long time. In 1946 there was a model of the stage set, which Ruth Berlau photographed in glaring sunlight beside a Californian swimming pool. But it was not until June 1947 that rehearsals for a planned production at the Coronet Theatre in Beverly Hills could begin.[22] Brecht's time in the USA was coming to an end and there were many demands on his attention. Preparations for his departure were in progress. When the rehearsals began, Brecht wrote in a letter that this production was his 'only theatrical undertaking in the States; it seems apt to me to stage this particular play in the land of advanced nuclear physics.' Brecht's actual interest in the progress of rehearsals, however, seems to have been variable to say the least. On the one hand Charles Laughton, who was a central figure in this production, was a difficult character to direct. His contribution to the creation of the text gave him an incontestable right to be involved in decision-making, and in this situation Brecht could not afford to engage in open warfare over questions of taste. The co-director Joseph Losey was present and could step into the role of director at any time. This made Berlau's presence at the rehearsals as Brecht's representative all the more important. This time too – like in 1936/37 in Paris – the photographic documentation of the production was a priority for Brecht. His return to Europe was imminent, and he was keen to have documentary evidence of his work to take back with him. Thus Berlau was tasked with documenting the production in as much detail as possible. She photographed not only the rehearsals but also Brecht and Laughton's visits to stage hands and a work meeting with the choreographer Lotte Goslar, in whom Brecht was so interested[23] that he wrote a pantomime script for her.[24] A rare insight into the work on the *Galileo* production is provided by the reminiscences

---

[20]FSA – Farm Security Administration, a government agency which, as part of the 'New Deal' policy, worked to improve living conditions for the rural population in the USA. The FSA operated a photographic documentation department headed by Roy F. Stryker, and its work became one of the most remarkable projects in the history of photography. It also – like *Life* magazine, which was founded in 1936 – offered lucrative job opportunities for freelance women photographers.
[21]BFA: 29, 362f.
[22]Premiere (first performance of the English-language version) on 30 July 1947.
[23]RBF, 63. Or: H. Bunge, *Brechts Lai Tu* (Neuwied: Luchterhand, 1987), 178f. Here RB talks about Brecht's encounter with Goslar.
[24]From Zirkusleben (Circus Scene) in BFA: 20, 184.

of actress Shelley Winters, who was present at the rehearsals as a spectator. There she met a relatively disinterested and unshaven little man with a strong German accent, and introduced him to her parents, who were German-speaking Jewish immigrants.[25]

Berlau, who had already met Laughton while working with Brecht, found that her presence was not always appreciated by those involved in the production. This made it difficult for her to carry out Brecht's instructions. Laughton became increasingly annoyed, feeling as though he were 'under surveillance' by this woman who was always hanging around taking pictures. Several times Berlau found herself on the receiving end of angry outbursts and was ejected from rehearsals, making her task almost impossible. Eventually, as a last resort, she switched to a small and unobtrusive film camera in order to fulfil her duties as a documentarist.[26] She documented the production from beginning to end, and on the night of the premiere she photographed the audience, which included several celebrities – among them Charles Spencer Chaplin and his wife Oona, Hanns Eisler and Charles Boyer.

The planned New York production of *Galileo*, which was to take place in the winter of 1947, ran into even greater difficulties. Brecht, after his hearing at the HUAC, had left the United States. In the run-up to the play's Broadway premiere, the *New York Times* was already speculating about this production's chances of success, insinuating that it was only happening at all because the Experimental Theatre, which produced the play for Maxine Elliott's Theatre, did not want to pass up such a big name as Charles Laughton. The play was not considered to be particularly important.[27] Laughton, ahead of his long-awaited return to the New York stage, was under enormous pressure to succeed. At the same time Laughton took advantage of the weaknesses of the young Joseph Losey (which had become apparent in Brecht's absence) to make his performances more 'palatable'.

Brecht, who was regularly getting little piles of *Galileo* photographs sent to him in Switzerland, was nevertheless delighted. He was full of praise, and wrote: 'The photos are so brilliant! You're an expert now.' And in the next sentence he was already making more plans, thinking about where next to deploy his much-missed expert: 'I think I'll do something at the end of January here in Switzerland, and you must be the first person in Europe to photograph it'.[28]

At the end of 1947, with this express invitation to Berlau to come and photograph *Antigone* in Chur, Brecht resumed his collaboration with her for the third time. In this letter, as well as his enthusiastic comments and concern about the expensive photos, he issues the dubious praise: 'You're a good soldier'. In the midst of this period of general 'demobilisation', Brecht is reminding his recruit of her rank.

The foundations of a secure existence were not available to Berlau in a Europe of displaced persons. She could just as easily have stayed in New York, returned to Denmark or gone to California, where she still had several friends who might have been able to help her. Over the previous five – existentially very unstable – years, she had learned enough typical New York survival strategies to stay in the city if she wanted to.[29]

---

[25] S. Winters, *Shelly, Also Known as Shirley* (New York: Morrow, 1980), 310–312.
[26] Brecht writes to RB of this film: 'I am very happy to have it, the result of two years' work!' BFA: 29, 425.
[27] The premiere was on 7 December 1947 in Maxine Elliott's Theatre on 39th St.
[28] Mid-December 1947 from Zurich, BFA: 29, 439.
[29] E.g. Ruth Berlau, 'My Time as a Barmaid in New York' (Min Tid som Barpige i NY), RBA 90.

In contrast to her former rather spontaneous and impulsive decision-making, this time Berlau had prepared in a more provident way for the coming uncertainties. With the same concern about the future which had motivated Brecht to leave behind copies of his photographed manuscripts at the Public Library, shortly before her departure Ruth Berlau made enquiries about journalistic assignments for the Danish press. A letter dated 10 December 1947[30] (three days after the *Galileo* premiere!) from her long-time friend Ole Cavling, editor-in-chief of the newspaper *Ekstra Bladet*, identified her – not entirely truthfully – as the newspaper's representative in the USA, thus enabling her to enter Germany and work with the press offices of the American occupation force. From this development too, Brecht would ultimately benefit more than Berlau herself.

Underlying Brecht's urgent summons to Berlau was his desire to surround himself once more with a circle of collaborators whom he could trust and who were used to his ways (he was not always an easy person to be around). Now that he had been reunited with Caspar Neher in Zurich, now that Fritz Kortner had returned and it looked likely that Lorre, Piscator, Lenya and other colleagues from the pre-exile days might be coming home too, opportunities seemed to be opening up for Brecht and Helene Weigel in the theatre world. In a letter to Berlau he tells her about the advice given to him by Anna Seghers (whom Brecht had met in Paris while she was visiting her children): 'As far as Berlin is concerned, [...] it's vital to form a strong group. Alone, or almost alone, it's impossible to exist there [...] I'm going to need you.'[31] For himself and Ruth Berlau he concludes from Seghers' report: 'It's clear that one needs to have a residence outside Germany. [...] You will be enormously necessary in Berlin, judging by everything Seghers told me!'[32]

It was by no means essential that Ruth Berlau should be the one to photograph *Antigone*. There were theatre photographers in Switzerland. But Ruth Berlau's many years of professional experience with Brecht and the productions of his plays, and the very different roles she had played – actress, director, photographer – made her almost indispensable. For Brecht's first piece of work after his return to Germany, no risks could be taken with any element of the production, for it was of an entirely experimental nature. Its primary purpose was to serve as Brecht's 'homecoming': to his native language as well as the language of the theatre. It was the revival of his collaboration with his friend Caspar Neher and – most importantly of all – it was Helene Weigel's first stage role in fifteen years. On Brecht's instructions, therefore, Berlau produced huge numbers of detailed shots of the production's development over the course of the rehearsals, as well as 'role portraits' of the actors and pictures of props and scenery. This laid the detailed material foundations for *Antigone Model 1948*, which had been planned from the outset.

In the exhibition 'Neues vom Herrn Keuner' ['New Material from Mr Keuner'], which was put together to mark the arrival of the Mertens-Bertozzi collection in the Bertolt Brecht Archive and was dedicated to the subject of 'Brecht in Switzerland', a hitherto unknown series of colour photographs taken by Ruth Berlau at the rehearsals went on public display for the first time. The Eastman colour slides, which had been sitting tucked away in a box and forgotten about in the Helene Weigel Archive, give

---

[30] RBF, 146.
[31] 5 November 1947, BFA: 29, 427. In a letter to Hanns Eisler (BFA: 29, 430) he sums up Seghers' descriptions rather more drastically: 'It seems Berlin is becoming more and more like Shanghai.'
[32] 3/4 November 1947, BFA: 29, 424/425.

a vivid impression of Caspar Neher's stage set, the draft drawings for which are only available in poor-quality reproductions.

Hardly any other production up to that point had been so thoroughly photographed and so rarely shown – only twice in total!

If in Chur Brecht had managed to insist on Berlau being allowed to take the photographs – which had clearly entailed extra rehearsals with 'photo light' and a great deal of additional effort – for the next production[33] at the Zurich Schauspielhaus he could not prevent the theatre from using its own stage photographer to carry out this work. How 'enormously necessary' Ruth Berlau really was in Berlin was about to become clear.

* * *

The publication of the modelbook *Antigone Model 1948* signalled the beginning of efforts (coordinated from Switzerland) to produce a new series of book editions, which would continue over the course of the 1950s and 1960s in Berlin/GDR. For Ruth Berlau, this once again heralded a change of direction in her professional life. She became a 'publisher'. She was not inexperienced when it came to publishing, and had dealt with all kinds of assignments for Brecht in the preceding years in various different countries. Now she was tasked with the publication of the Berliner Ensemble's theatre books – alongside her work as 'head of the photographic laboratory and archive, and theatre director'.[34] This somewhat confusing job title was an (inadequate) attempt to solve one of the main problems inherent in the Ensemble's relationship with its new member of staff: Berlau struggled to find her place in this new environment. She was unable to define her role within the 'business' of the theatre, and unwilling to clearly identify with any of the available job descriptions.[35] The day-to-day routine of a 'secure' job had caught up with her after so many years of itinerant unpredictability, and it threatened to overwhelm her. The language barrier, but also generational differences and divergent personal experiences, led to problems between her and many members of the Ensemble – problems she was unable to confront. Furthermore, it quickly became clear that she was unsuited to the job of running a photo lab. For the first time there were now 'experts' available to do this work, just as there were 'experts' available to photograph productions. Given the condition of Berlau's negatives and what it suggests about the way she handled them, it is probably safe to assume that archiving was not her forte.

From now on the collaboration with Berlau became increasingly difficult for Brecht, and involved clashes which were painful to both parties. But even he had to admit that his relationships with the people around him had changed. Remembering his working collective in days gone by, his resignation is palpable in the sentence: 'I don't have students, I have employees.'[36]

Can Brecht and Berlau's working relationship in the last few years still be described as collaboration? There was plenty of work going on, but something had definitely changed.

---

[33]*Mr Puntila and his Man Matti*, first performance, premiere: 5 July 1948, Schauspielhaus Zurich.
[34]According to the entry in the 'workbook replacement card' from 8 October 1949 (RBA N 248).
[35]"Chief archivist! […] I am a director and a writer […] it's like someone asking Brecht to become an acrobat!' RBF, 164.
[36]See BBA 2166/52.

As well as working directly for the Berliner Ensemble, Berlau also took on dramaturgical assignments, directed her own productions[37] and did lots of travelling. Based on the available data about her output,[38] we have to assume that in the first half of the 1950s her workload was not reduced even though it was punctuated by multiple absences, stays in hospital and periods of convalescence.

With a few exceptions, however, Brecht and Berlau never again engaged in the kind of collaboration that had characterised their relationship during the exile years. This was partly due to the fact that Brecht's working conditions – given the need to oversee the day-to-day running of a theatre and deal with the GDR's unpredictable cultural and Party bureaucracy – had changed dramatically.

Despite many disappointments, Brecht continued to have a fundamental confidence in Berlau's work, and on this basis the relationship survived; but the nature of it had changed considerably. There were certain habits neither of them could shake. Brecht too was anxious and clingy, plagued by a fear of abandonment and full of sentimental emotion, as is evident from many of his letters. Aside from Elisabeth Hauptmann, Berlau was Brecht's longest-standing and most faithful female friend (though in a harrowingly desperate way). She seldom gave him cause for warranted jealousy, but inflicted her own upon him all the more persistently for that.

In 1952 Berlau wrote to Brecht: 'Through my involvement with work at the theatre I've realised that my poor spelling bothers not only you but also our co-director [...] I actually stopped writing to you this past year because I could see that now you're here in your own country and you have German collaborators, my bad German not only bothers you but makes my opinions incomprehensible to you. Ruth'.[39]

Her constant quest for approval, recognition and affection sometimes took on grotesque forms, but was essentially characterised by an astonishing lucidity about her own situation.

It is this lucidity which can tip a sensitive, spirited person who is also experiencing the first signs of ageing and infirmity (deafness, pain in her hips, an increasingly serious drinking problem) over the edge into despair. Having spent decades being reminded by Brecht of the 'third thing' to which all selfish emotions must apparently be subordinated, she now had very valid doubts. She observed forlornly: 'We who believe there is no heart and no soul do not quite know how to describe where it hurts, when it hurts and if it hurts.'[40]

But Brecht, too, in a letter he sends from the Charité hospital to her flat just a few metres away at Charitéstraße 3, asks of both Berlau and himself: 'We have sadly lost sight of the third thing,[41] haven't we?' And this 'we' is clearly not just the 'we' of a private consensus: in Brecht's words we can hear his sorrow at the loss of a grand utopia and a concept of living built on generosity and selflessness, which in the very next sentence must

---

[37]E.g. in late 1949, *The Mother* in Leipzig. A letter from the Berliner Ensemble dated 10 January 1951, which is presented to her along with a Contax camera as a bonus, says: 'For excellent work for the Berliner Ensemble, particularly for the Modelbooks and the model production of *The Mother* in Leipzig, from which the Berlin production has borrowed many ideas [...] Signed Helene Weigel' (RBA N 169).
[38]E.g. in W. Hecht, *Brecht Chronik 1898-1956* (Frankfurt am Main: Suhrkamp, 1997) (BC).
[39]14 April 1952 (RBA).
[40]RB on 10 April 1952 (RBA).
[41]'The *Third Thing* is Socialism, and what is important is what we can do for Socialism at this stage and in these times, in a concrete sense.' Letter to Ruth Berlau, 10 March 1950. BFA: 30, 19.

be chased away like a ghost. For he immediately adds that the work on the Modelbooks must once again be done in a 'political, communist[42] way – that is now the main thing – for in our country everything is quickly becoming formal, superficial, mechanical.'[43]

* * *

Brecht had had plenty of experience of the formal, mechanical nature of the GDR's cultural bureaucracy over the preceding years. One particular example of this is the publishing history of Brecht's last big project, which Berlau played an important role in bringing about: the *War Primer*.

When the book edition of this work finally appeared in 1955, it was the belated culmination of almost twenty years of preparatory work.

In 1934 Brecht started writing his *Journals*,[44] which were comprised of a mixture of essays, reports on his work, diary entries and a montage of annotated newspaper cuttings. Over the years there arose from this project (which he continued working on intermittently until 1955) a series of four-line epigrams which he composed as comments on photographs in newspaper cuttings. They initially formed the group of works entitled 'Photo Epigrams', of which only a few were provisionally published.[45]

In several respects Berlau made a clearly definable contribution to the development of this work. First of all, she supplied Brecht in Denmark and Sweden with newspaper cuttings from the national and international press, which were initially collected in folders and some of which appeared in the *Journal* as early as the 1930s. The first picture Brecht pastes into the *Journal* is a portrait of himself,[46] which had appeared as a print in an unknown newspaper. This is a clear indication of how closely he felt himself and his destiny to be entwined with geopolitical events, which were represented in the *Journals* in subsequent years mainly by newspaper cuttings pasted in by Brecht.

In the *War Primer*, as in the *Journals*, many of the newspaper cuttings from those early years are taken from German – as well as Swedish and Danish – publications. Brecht would not have been able to translate the captions and articles attached to these photos without Berlau's help.

The substantial increase in the number of pasted-in newspaper cuttings after Brecht's arrival in the USA is striking.[47] They are the direct precursor to the *War Primer*, verses from which are made public for the first time under the title *Contemporary Picture Book* at the mass gathering in New York's Madison Square Garden on 3 April 1943. Piscator has put together a selection of verses, and they are recited as an accompaniment to the photo projections. By July 1944 the collection contains almost 60 four-liners, of which

---

[42] i.e. selflessly and without insisting on appropriate payment.
[43] End of April 1956 during a stay in hospital, BFA: 30, 450.
[44] BFA: 26 and 27.
[45] For a detailed account of this and the publishing history, see Jan Knopf (ed.), *Brecht-Handbuch* (Stuttgart and Weimar: Metzler, 2001), Vol. 2, 383ff. (BHB).
[46] In between the entries on 16 August and 18 August 1938. BFA: 26, 319-320. The form of the reproduction in the printed version does not enable us to clearly identify what the picture relates to. It would be good to know whether the portrait shot is included in reference to the reflective thoughts on Shelley's poems ('even back then ...') on 16 August.
[47] BHB, Vol. 4, 424f.

Brecht remarks in his journal that they are a 'satisfactory literary report on the exile period'.[48]

On 18 December 1944 Ruth Berlau, who is living in Santa Monica at this point, borrows an enlarger from Venice High School[49] over the Christmas holidays (she had done a photography course there to help her with her work in the dark room). She starts making reproductions of the newspaper cuttings and the typewritten epigrams. She pastes these onto black pieces of card the size of playing cards. Several copies of the roughly sixty-six photo epigrams must have been produced in this form. Among the surviving copies is the one Brecht sent to Karl Korsch.[50] Korsch was delighted and wrote to Brecht, after he had looked at the cards several times with and without a magnifying glass (!), that he considered them to be 'the best thing ever written about this war.'[51]

Berlau was familiar with the development of the *War Primer* from the outset, and with her reprographic work she also paved the way for the realisation of Brecht's vision of a book publication. Once his time in exile was over, Brecht planned to publish the *War Primer* as one of his first books and as a 'primer' in the truest sense of the word, from which people could and should learn how to 'read' the pictures of the war that had been lost. The teacher Brecht presents his audience/students with this textbook as a contribution to their 're-education'. In this way, Brecht was seemingly complying with the expectations of the American occupation force, which openly discussed its plans and possible strategies in relation to a defeated Germany. These included a general re-education of the population and the bourgeois-democratic rebuilding of Germany during the post-war period.[52] Of course, Brecht had absolutely no desire to support the restoration of bourgeois conditions, but the idea of the 'Primer' with its lessons about the causes, background and effects of the war was an obvious one and, under the terms of the Allied censorship, would have called for the application of the fifth difficulty when writing the truth – cunning.

In 1948, the playing-card-sized epigrams were offered to Kurt Desch Verlag in Munich. The publisher did not express any interest in the project, so in November Brecht asked for the folder back, as he wanted to publish the *War Primer* in Berlin. He appointed Ruth Berlau to take receipt of the copy in Munich for him.

The difficulties with the GDR's cultural bureaucrats – who accused the work of almost everything it could possibly be accused of, from 'pacifism' to 'pornography' – lasted many years, during which Brecht made various changes and adjustments in order to get the book into print.

When the book finally appeared in 1955 with the East Berlin publisher Eulenspiegel Verlag, which specialised in humour and satire, Ruth Berlau was given the role of editor. She wrote a text for the preface explaining the intentions behind the book, but made a veiled reference to the 'delay' in its publication: 'Why are we presenting the workers in our people's-owned industries, the members of our agricultural cooperatives, our forward-looking intellectuals, our young people enjoying their first rations of happiness –

---

[48]BFA 27: 196.
[49]The school is still there in Santa Monica, at 13000 Venice Boulevard.
[50]Harvard University, Cambridge Mass. call # bMS Ger 130,2.
[51]BBA 1185/57-64 (as per BC, 748).
[52]E.g. L. Nizer, *What to Do with Germany* (Chicago and New York: Ziff-Davis, 1944) and H. Mosberg, *Reeducation: Umerziehung und Lizenzpresse im Nachkriegsdeutschland* (Munich: Universitas, 1991).

why are we presenting them with these sombre pictures of the past *now*?' [italics GM]. In the rhetorical style of the day, she answers her own question: 'We do not escape the past by forgetting it. The aim of this book is to teach people to read pictures [...] The great ignorance about social conditions which capitalism carefully and brutally maintains, turns the thousands of photos in the glossy magazines into veritable hieroglyphic tablets, indecipherable to the unsuspecting reader.'[53]

Even if there is good reason to believe that Brecht and Peter Palitzsch, who designed and generally supervised the *War Primer* edition, had a considerable impact on the form of the preface which was ultimately published,[54] and decided that the longer part should be printed as a blurb, Berlau's contribution is still significant. It contains the first account of Brecht's working method while he was developing the *War Primer* (and the *Journal*) and descriptions of his life in Danish exile. She explains Brecht's attitude and the gestus of the epigrams as that of one who is 'observing' and 'waiting'. As a 'non-German' she wonders at Brecht's affection for his fellow Germans who have driven him out, deprived him of his citizenship and rendered him homeless. 'A great German writer is surprised and ashamed at the way his compatriots are being misled, and yet he begs: *Warm them, they are cold.*'

In October 1954, Brecht writes a serious letter to Berlau in which he again talks about how her drunkenness is affecting the work of the Ensemble and her own position. He exhorts her to give up drinking, especially now 'when you have been given the responsibility *and the opportunity* [italics GM] to edit the *Modelbooks*, which only you can do!'[55] In this sentence, the dilemma now inherent in their working relationship is made very plain. We can discern the generous gesture of Berlau's employer, the Berliner Ensemble, in entrusting her with an editing job which could easily have been done by somebody else. At the same time we hear Brecht's conciliatory tone – he knew that Berlau, despite all her absences, would be able to get this work done more quickly than anyone else. He also understood the need to find a role for Berlau, and her 'moral' right to such a role.

* * *

Even if nothing had survived of Berlau's work other than the *Modelbooks*, the *War Primer* and the huge number of theatre photographs which were published for many decades without any specific mention of her name – even without her own stories, her reports and other texts, and the many photos she took during the years in American exile and her residence in Switzerland – this creative contribution to Brecht's theatre alone ought to secure her legacy.

It would be a long-overdue gift for her 100th birthday on 24 August 2006 if we were to view her life's work with the respect which is its due, for: 'We do not escape the past by forgetting it.'

---

[53]Cited from Brecht, *War Primer* (Berlin: Eulenspiegel, 1955), 5. (1st extended edition 1994).
[54]As with the new edition of *Antigone-Model 1948*, published as *Modellbuch 1* [*Modelbook 1*] (Berlin: Henschel, 1955), here too, in Palitzsch's design, 'an extract' will have been produced. (BFA 30: 368).
[55]BFA: 30, 273f.

Brecht's Assistants
in the Theatre

CHAPTER TWENTY

Notice [3]: *To the Members of the Berliner Ensemble*

BERTOLT BRECHT
TRANSLATED BY ROMY FURSLAND

Not for the first time I get the impression that the work of our young directors at the Ensemble is being misjudged. My contribution to their productions shouldn't be discounted entirely, but it shouldn't be overestimated either. These young directors have not only learnt their 'trade' with us, so to speak; they also learn about a very special type of theatre which is still being developed, and which causes me plenty of difficulties myself. This means that every performance is still an experiment, and hopefully will be for some time to come. I will *not* let the backward-looking attitudes of certain actors deter me from participating in the Berliner Ensemble's experiments, whoever they are undertaken by. This cannot be laid at the door of the lead director, whoever he or she happens to be.

Brecht, 'Aushang [3]', in Brecht, *Schriften*, vol. 3 (Berlin and Frankfurt/Main: Aufbau and Suhrkamp, 1993), p. 359

CHAPTER TWENTY-ONE

Interviews with Claus and Wera Küchenmeister and with Egon Monk

JOACHIM LANG AND JÜRGEN HILLESHEIM
TRANSLATED BY ROMY FURSLAND

CLAUS AND WERA KÜCHENMEISTER

The interview took place on 19 August 1997 in Siethen.

Claus Küchenmeister was born in Berlin on 7 September 1930. His father and brother were active resistance fighters against the Nazi regime. To avoid being arrested, Claus Küchenmeister attended a boarding school in Switzerland from 1942 onwards. Only later did he learn that his parents and many of his loved ones in Germany had been arrested and murdered. In May 1946 Küchenmeister returned to Germany, and in 1947 he moved back to Berlin. From 1949 to 1950 he studied at the Theatre Institute in Weimar where he also met his future wife, Wera Skupin.

He spent a short time at the DEFA's 'young talent' studio,[1] and from 1951 he was one of Brecht's *Meisterschüler*[2] and an actor and assistant director at the Berliner Ensemble. The most important project he was involved in while working with Brecht was the *Urfaust* production in 1952, for which he was assistant director. In 1955 Küchenmeister went to work for the DEFA. In his letter of recommendation, Brecht described him as follows: 'He is talented, erudite and progressive, and he is good at working with actors. I can recommend him as a director. The Berliner Ensemble would gladly welcome him back at any time.'

In the following years, Claus Küchenmeister became one of the most highly regarded directors and authors in the GDR. The films *Sie nannten ihn Amigo* [*They Called Him Amigo*] (1958), *Wer bürgt für Deutschland* [*Who Will Vouch for Germany*] (1962) and *Die rote Kapelle* [*The Red Orchestra*] (1971) attracted a great deal of interest. He collaborated with his wife Wera on most projects. Küchenmeister has won many prizes, including the

---

Interviews with Claus and Wera Küchenmeister and with Egon Monk, in Joachim Lang and Jürgen Hillesheim (eds), *'Denken heißt verändern...'. Erinnerungen an Brecht* (Augsburg: Maro, 1997), pp. 57–75 and 93–111.

[1] The DEFA (Deutsche Film-Aktiengesellschaft) was the state-owned film studio of the GDR.
[2] *Meisterschüler* is an untranslatable term denoting a talented apprentice under the tutelage of a significant master of a trade (current Editor's note).

Ministry of Culture Prize for Children's and Young Adult Literature in 1958 and 1959, the Heinrich Greif Prize and the Ernst Zinna Prize of the city of Berlin in 1959, the Erich Weinert Prize in 1965, the Art Prize of the FDGB [Free German Trade Union Federation] in 1971, the Film and Television Critics' Prize in 1981, and the Critics' Prize in 1987. In 1965 and 1971, Küchenmeister was awarded the National Prize of the GDR.

Wera Küchenmeister, née Skupin, was born in Berlin on 18 October 1929. She developed a love of literature at a young age, and tried her hand at short pieces of creative writing. After taking her *Abitur* [school leavers exam] she studied at the Theatre Institute in Weimar from 1949 to 1950. By this point she was already a member of the SED [Socialist Unity Party of Germany] and appeared for them at public events. In 1950 she became an assistant director to Brecht, and as one of Brecht's *Meisterschüler* she received a bursary from the Akademie der Künste until 1955. The most important project she worked on with Brecht was the production of his play *The Mother*, as assistant director. She also carried on working on her own writing. One notable piece was the 'Waldfest der Tiere' ['The Woodland Festival of the Animals'] which was initially intended as a Christmas performance for the children of members of the Berliner Ensemble, and was created in 1952 in collaboration with Wera Küchenmeister's husband Claus, Martin Pohl and Brecht.

Following her time as Brecht's *Meisterschülerin*, Wera Küchenmeister quickly established herself as one of the most respected dramaturgs and directors in the GDR and as a writer of dramas, novellas and poetry as well as films and radio plays. Political issues and children's literature are central to her work, which she produced in close collaboration with her husband Claus. His best-known works (as listed above) are also hers, therefore; and the accolades she was awarded by the GDR are almost identical to his. She won the Ernst Zinna Prize of the city of Berlin and the Heinrich Greif Prize in 1959, the Ministry of Culture Prize for Children's and Young Adult Literature in 1958 and 1959, the Critics' Prize in 1966, the Erich Weinert Prize in 1967, the Art Prize of the FDGB and the National Prize in 1971, and the Film and Television Critics' Prize in 1981 and 1987.

– Wera and Claus Küchenmeister, you were both Meisterschüler of Brecht's. Can you tell us how you came to work with him?

WERA: My name was still Wera Skupin at the time, and I'd come from the new Institute for the Renewal of German Theatre in Weimar, where I'd taken a theatre studies course. The head of this institute was Maxim Vallentin, who before 1933 had been an exponent of agitprop theatre and had gone into exile in the Soviet Union. He brought the Stanislavksy method back with him when he returned, but I was disappointed with how it was applied at the Institute. Then a friend wrote to me and said Brecht had also returned from exile and was looking for young people who wanted to work with him. So I left the confines of Weimar and went off to introduce myself to Brecht.

Suddenly I realised that although I was aware of him as a major figure in the literary world, I didn't actually know much about him. So I got hold of the *Short Organon for the Theatre*, in which he develops his theories on theatre, and read it in preparation for my interview with him.

But in the end it all turned out quite differently from how I'd expected. I was waiting for him in a little room when a man came in, very simply dressed, like a workman who had a job to do there. I should mention that at the time I had never seen a photo of Brecht.

This man struck up a conversation with me. Then he introduced himself and asked if I would like to come and work with him. It gave me a hell of a shock. Later he told me he'd already read some of my work, poems and other things, but he wanted to have a simple conversation with me to find out about my attitude to life. And so I was taken on.

CLAUS: I returned to Germany from Switzerland in 1946. What I really wanted was to get into film – I was a big film buff. But then I started studying theatre in Weimar. My experience was similar to Wera's. Eventually I'd had enough and I left the Institute. I applied to the DEFA's young talent studio, which was unfortunately shut down soon afterwards. Then Wera said: 'Come and work with Brecht.' I'd heard of him, because I come from a 'red family'. I knew the *Threepenny Opera*, for example.

So I just went along. Sitting by the rehearsal stage was a grey little man in a grey suit. He looked at me with his searching, piercing eyes. After I'd introduced myself, I said what I really wanted was to work in film, which was stupid really. Anyone else would have said 'Well go and work in film then!' Brecht, however, found it very interesting. The next day I was back. A week later I had to borrow five marks from Helene Weigel because I was supposed to be getting a bursary and I needed a bank account for it to be paid into, but the minimum deposit for opening an account was five marks. About three weeks later Brecht told me I was going to work with Egon Monk on the *Urfaust* production. That's how quickly and easily it all happened.

– It's interesting that Brecht surrounded himself with lots of young people who had hardly any theatrical experience. Why was that?

CLAUS: He worked with young people because everyone else was tainted by association with the Nazi era. It wasn't that the theatre in those days was perpetuating Fascist ideology, but the style of the theatre was that of the Nazi era. That's what I thought. As children or young teenagers we'd lived through what had happened in Europe and in the world in Germany's name, and we were profoundly horrified by it. And so when a man comes along and counters this traditional theatre with a play like *Mother Courage and her Children*, in a powerful, impressive production that's like nothing you've ever seen before, then any halfway sensitive and committed person is going to want to work with him. Brecht also believed that young people are still willing to 'kick against the pricks'.

WERA: But Brecht also worked with experienced people who had been in exile. There was Erwin Geschonneck, who'd been in a concentration camp, John Heartfield, the composers Hanns Eisler and Paul Dessau whom he'd worked with before, Ernst Busch, of course, and many others. It was a successful mixture of young and old, which was enriched even more by young people from Switzerland like Benno Besson and Regine Lutz. This work with international artists and others who had been in exile naturally had a big impact on us. But those who had been in exile never acted like know-it-alls – there was no feeling of 'us-and-them' between the different generations. There was a sense of togetherness in our artistic production as well as our interpersonal relationships. Of course there were also misunderstandings and disagreements, but that didn't stop it from feeling like a family.

– Mother Courage and her Children was Brecht's first production in Berlin. The German premiere of the play took place on 11 January 1949 at the Deutsches Theater, directed by Brecht and Erich Engels. Helene Weigel played the lead role. This performance has

gone down in history as a legendary success. You both saw the production. What was so innovative about it, in your view?

CLAUS: That production took my breath away with its lightness and its precision. There was no pulling of faces, no huffing and puffing and stamping of feet. It simply presented something. Something that was very important from an aesthetic point of view was the fact that everything was brightly lit. You could see everything, even the flies.

WERA: Processes were demonstrated in a powerful and precise way, so that the scales fell from people's eyes. 'Yes, it's true, little people shouldn't get involved in the war!' The war had only ended four years earlier.

Everything was transparent, startlingly open. 'Glasnost' in the theatre, to use a modern term.

– Brecht assigned independent work to the younger members of the Ensemble very quickly. Did you feel as though you'd been thrown in at the deep end?

WERA: There were two things I was 'thrown into', so to speak. The first was the dramaturgical collaboration on the adaptation of Gerhart Hauptmann's *The Beaver Coat and Conflagration*. Brecht wanted to merge the two plays into one and thereby say something about the history of the SPD [Social Democratic Party]. It was around the time when comrades from the Communist Party and the Social Democratic Party were joining together to form the Socialist Unity Party, the SED. Brecht felt it was important to make people more aware of the origins of the Social Democratic Party. A difficult task, which was not crowned with success. Egon Monk was the director. The premiere was on 24 March 1951. Georg Lukács wrote that it must be very difficult to make the splendours of Hauptmann's Naturalism compatible with Brecht's method. He was probably right. My bigger role was as assistant director on the production of Brecht's *The Mother*, an adaptation of the novel of the same name by Maxim Gorky. Brecht himself was the lead director, and the set was designed by Caspar Neher. The premiere was on 12 January 1951. This work represented something entirely new for me – I had hardly any theatrical experience.

Among other things, I had to take notes – I had to note down everything that happened on stage.

– This process has been described by the other assistants too: 'noting down what happened on stage.' It sounds like a painstaking task. What did you learn from it?

WERA: We learned to look very closely. We realised how blocking could be used to make a process transparent, how at every stage, in every individual scene, a little bit more of the plot became visible.

CLAUS: For us, of course, working on the Modelbooks was a bit of a crappy job. We sat there in a little cubbyhole, pasting things down. And whoever pasted most industriously would be in Brecht's good books. If we stopped pasting we got called lazy. And lazy was sometimes a dirty word. Sometimes the worst possible word. 'Lazy' or 'bohemian', 'artist' or 'time-server': those were damning judgements for Brecht.

His aim in putting together the Modelbooks was to record the results of his work. It wasn't vanity – he wasn't vain, in any case. He just wanted everything to be meticulously recorded. These Modelbooks, if they were done properly, included details of the scene, the sentence from the scene which the actor was speaking, and the corresponding annotation. That's excellent, of course, for illustrating and identifying things.

– You both wrote a book together: the title is a quote from Brecht, something he once said to you: 'A talent has to be discouraged'. What did he mean by that?

CLAUS: I didn't understand it at first, but I wrote it down because I thought it was tremendous. Later I realised it's dialectics – he's turning something on its head. You have to discourage a talent, because if it lets itself be discouraged it's not really a talent. Not allowing yourself to be discouraged – being obsessed with succeeding – is all part of the talent. It's a fantastic phrase, although a lot of people do struggle with it at first.

WERA: He put these maxims into practice in our day-to-day work together, too: this discouragement. Once I had to write a text for the programme of *Mother Courage and her Children*, and I ended up having to rewrite it seven times. I couldn't have done it more than three times before I started bawling, and I wanted to give the whole thing up as a bad job. But the text was gradually being made more and more succinct, more and more precise. Brecht said: 'Look carefully at it again, Wera. Think about whether you really need every word.' That was typical of Brecht. He encouraged you to look carefully and to describe the things you could see, not the things you wanted to see.

– Frau Küchenmeister, you were already a member of the SED at that time. What was your role in the Party in relation to the theatre?

WERA: I was twenty years old and Secretary of the BE Party Group in Berlin Mitte, where the Theater am Schiffbauerdamm is. In my youthful naivety I felt revolutionary and great.

I tried to create a balance in our group between the different views held by the younger people and those who had been in exile. As a younger person myself. Brecht was highly amused by my revolutionary zeal. When he directed *The Mother*, in which Helene Weigel played the lead role, I was the assistant director. Some of my comrades asked me, wasn't I going to try and get Helene Weigel to become a member of the Party; after all, she was playing the Mother in a revolutionary play? So eventually I did ask her. She was very nice about it, smiled at me and said: 'You know, I've done everything for the Party. I've always fought for the working class, I've even betrayed my own class. That's enough, I think. I don't have to become a member of the Party too.' And that was that! My suggestion was not taken up...

– There were attempts by the Party to influence the work of the Berliner Ensemble and Brecht's art.

CLAUS: I could never understand the vehemence with which politicians – politicians who didn't even know anything about art – used to attack artists who'd already come under attack by the Nazis. There was bad blood there. We lost very good people because of it – they were positively driven away. On the other hand, the debates were sometimes reasonable and understandable: the debate about Brecht and Paul Dessau's opera *The Trial of Lucullus*, for example. The first version rejects any kind of war whatsoever – as per Brecht's intention. Only a few years earlier, however, the Soviet Union and the Western Allies had waged a just war. So one cannot be completely anti-war. Brecht was able to accept this, at least partially. Hence the praise of those who defended the towns.

We should try to understand the debate about *Lucullus* from the perspective of its specific historical situation.

WERA: Many of the altercations with the people in charge of cultural policy dated back to the time before the Nazis came to power; they were 'old habits', as it were. To give one example: the writer Alfred Kurella, who lived in the USSR from 1934 to 1954 and then in the GDR after 1954, had considerable influence over cultural policy. He'd never approved of Brecht, even in the 1920s. Disputes like that were put on pause by what happened in 1933, but later, in the GDR, people tried to stir them up again.

– *One of the first things you worked on for Brecht, Frau Küchenmeister, was the cantata 'Appell'. It led to problems with the cultural bureaucracy.*

WERA: Yes, that's right. Brecht (as the advocate of the work) and Paul Dessau and I had to go and explain ourselves to a number of people including Herrnstadt, the editor-in-chief of *Neue Deutschland*. We were told the text was biblical and the music formalistic.

CLAUS: Because there are syncopations in it.

WERA: Exactly, because there were syncopations in it. I was very shy and completely flustered by this discussion. I'd tried so hard to write a really lovely text that spoke to people's feelings at the time, and then it was rejected and disparaged. Brecht defended the work vigorously. And so did Paul. In the middle of the conversation Brecht stood up. Dessau too. They left the room, and I went trotting after them. We got the feeling that was the end of the discussion. But the cantata did end up being performed later on, in Leipzig.

– *Herr Küchenmeister, you worked on the* Urfaust *production. There was fierce criticism of that production.*

CLAUS: Yes, the production caused concern in some quarters. Brecht had formulated the plot in rather an extreme way: aging professor seduces minor and then abandons her. A character almost like Professor Unrath [from the 1930 film starring Marlene Dietrich, *The Blue Angel*]. But you must remember, Brecht was a provocateur who wanted the work to be productive. This interpretation of the plot was only a stage in his process, and was not to be taken literally. Taken literally, in its 'neat' form, it was of course – for the official view of realistic art at the time – a disaster. I had no preconceptions back then and approached the thing in a naïve way. Brecht was trying to take the classic out of the 'classical', in order to get people to see the social aspect. He didn't like the idea of anyone being intimidated by a classic text. I was struck by the harsh criticism we received after the premiere; this confrontation with realistic theatre was also a profound experience, somehow.

It was great fun to belong to a collective in which we engaged in a collaboration focused on the work itself.

– *But there was often heavy criticism from the Party. What was Brecht's relationship with the Party leadership like?*

WERA: There were different people within the Party leadership, so Brecht had different relationships with each of them. He had a good relationship with Wilhelm Pieck, for example, the President of the SED. The Berliner Ensemble performed a German folk play which Brecht and I had adapted together as a Christmas surprise for Pieck. As a thank-you, he gave some money to Helli to give to everyone who had been involved in the performance. There were other people, however, with whom Brecht did not have such a good relationship. The feeling was certainly mutual. But we have to judge certain debates in light of the realities we were dealing with. Brecht basically believed the GDR represented the only option for realising a humane socialism. He certainly believed that the GDR had its idiots, and he would openly call them 'idiots'. He stuck with the 'GDR experiment', which unfortunately went awry. Fortunately Brecht was spared the knowledge of this.

– There were debates about the Stanislavsky method, which was officially legitimised and applied. The Berliner Ensemble's work took it in quite a different direction.

WERA: There was definitely a contrast, even a confrontation between the two theatrical methods. But Brecht wasn't to blame for that.

There was also no hardening of attitudes on Brecht's side, as is often assumed. On the contrary. He showed great interest and asked me, for example, what we'd done at the Institute in Weimar and what it had been like. Looking back at the debates about the Stanislavsky method and Brecht's method I'd say, with hindsight, that both methods could have learned something from each other. Many a psychological moment in Stanislavsky would have fitted quite well into many a production by the Berliner Ensemble and even enriched them.

– Can you describe the events of the uprising of 17 June 1953?

CLAUS: We were living in Weißensee at the time, near Brecht. On 17 June, when the unrest began, I met Brecht outside his house on the way to the theatre. Because so many people had taken to the streets, including workers, he told me no government could survive this.

The next day there was a staff meeting at the Berliner Ensemble, during which Brecht stated unequivocally that there was no alternative to the GDR. We then voted on a resolution, and everyone voted in favour, even Regine Lutz, who was Swiss. There was only one stagehand who didn't – I don't know why. Then Brecht asked us assistant directors to go out among the people.

We could see things gradually escalating, the atmosphere growing more and more febrile. We realised that elements from the past were up to their old tricks again, to put it mildly: we suddenly saw that a kiosk had been set alight on Unter den Linden! And in Germany, when people start burning the printed word, that's a very bad sign. But on the whole things remained relatively peaceful. Suddenly we heard the sound of approaching tanks. I was terribly frightened because I thought war had broken out and the Americans were coming with tanks. But in fact they were Soviet tanks. They drove very carefully – as carefully as you can do in a tank. They didn't shoot. Didn't react to people throwing stones at them. Then there was a heavy downpour, and it was all over. The demonstration also broke up because a state of emergency had been declared. I didn't find out about the other things until later.

WERA: We never knew what Brecht wrote about all this in his journal. He certainly viewed the events in a more nuanced way than us young people. The government's demands to increase productivity genuinely were a bad thing. But they were withdrawn, and still things escalated. At any rate, the assumption that it was a popular uprising was just as ridiculous as the myth of a Fascist *putsch*. The fact is that a perfectly understandable feeling of discontent on the part of the people was exploited by certain groups.

– Can you remember the specific arguments Brecht put forward at the staff meeting? What was his attitude to what was going on?

CLAUS: As I said: he made clear that there was no alternative to the GDR. I noted in my jotter at the time: 'bb. An alternative to what is being done here in the GDR does not exist. It would only be a step backwards.'

We formed a brigade, we wanted to go to the State radio station and broadcast revolutionary songs and texts. Enlighten the population. This clearly didn't meet with the bosses' approval, however, and was vetoed. And soon after that came the period when Brecht basically started to give up hope.

WERA: I had an encounter with Brecht once where he seemed very despondent. But that was later, in 1954, when the Berliner Ensemble was on tour in Paris – Claus was there too. Brecht was back in Berlin. He wanted to talk to me about something to do with a radio programme. The house was empty and quiet, and Brecht had opened a book of poetry by Baudelaire. He read me the poem about the albatross, a very reflective poem, and I believe he felt himself to be just such an albatross, whose wings are too heavy and who feels oppressed when he is sitting on solid ground. Only when he can soar through the air does he feel free. But he can't. Brecht read me this poem and there was such a strange, sad atmosphere. We went into the tiny garden at Chausseestraße, where I picked a rose from a branch. During our conversation there, he told me: 'Wera, I have lived my life.' I couldn't understand why Brecht would say something like that to me and later, when Claus got back, I told him about it. I tried to process my thoughts at the time in a poem:

MEMORY

I picked a rose
in my teacher's garden. Above
the plumy green shone
the flower.
At the tip of the twig
a bud promised
renewed delight. In austere November
I remember joys

– Why do you think Brecht was having thoughts like that at this time? He wasn't particularly old.

CLAUS: After the events of 17 June 1953, a great weariness seemed to come over Brecht. I think he was hoping there would be a big democratic debate. He had concrete ideas. But this hope was disappointed. This disillusionment was accompanied by a physical and artistic weariness. As an artist, as far as literary production was concerned, I felt he was spent. He was 'all written out'. He'd said what he had to say. I'm glad he wasn't there to see what happened later on in Hungary and Czechoslovakia, and the reaction of the Soviet Union. It was a clear illustration of the attitude, later dubbed the Brezhnev doctrine, whereby the right of all Socialist states to self-determination is defined by Party ideologues as 'limited'. That would have finished Brecht off.

– Particularly in the last years of his life, Brecht received a lot of recognition. Not only through his Stalin Peace Prize, but also in the West. The Berliner Ensemble's tours to Paris led to an international breakthrough.

CLAUS: It was intoxicating. The French were wildly enthusiastic about us. Not that we'd been invisible in the GDR; but now we were abroad, and people looked up to us. The dressers and the other theatre staff in particular were very well-disposed towards us because they thought we were all Communists. Most of them were members of left-wing organisations themselves.

– How did Brecht react to this success?

CLAUS: At premieres and similar events I always thought he seemed very agitated and anxious. Apparently he was the same in the 1920s – didn't even go to premieres, just went for a beer somewhere nearby and waited to hear whether people clapped or not.

After the success in Paris he was cheerful and relaxed – after all, it was a great accolade for his work.

WERA: I think he really was living between two poles in those days. On the one hand he was still able to take pleasure in his international success. But on the other hand, he already felt empty.

– How did you hear about Brecht's death?

WERA: We'd just come back from a holiday we'd spent with Iva and Benno Besson and some other people at Benno's parents' home. It was my first trip abroad. When we got home, Isot Kilian rang and told us Brecht had died. We were completely blindsided – it came totally out of the blue for us. We'd had no idea how ill he was.

CLAUS: On the Weidendammer Bridge there was a newspaper kiosk. The seller had stuck up a copy of the *BZ am Abend* featuring the news of Brecht's death and a photograph. There were people standing around it. One of them said: 'Look, Brecht's died.' They were ordinary people. That meant more to us than any official obituary.

WERA: After the official funeral, which we didn't attend, we went to lay flowers on Brecht's grave. But as we stood there by his grave looking at all the flowers and wreaths, we were aware of that ceremonial atmosphere Brecht had disliked so much, so we took our bunch of roses and went and laid it on Hegel's grave.

– What did your time with Brecht mean to you?

WERA: It shaped our whole lives. Everything we did, and the way we tried to communicate it to others, wouldn't really have been possible if it wasn't for our time with Brecht. Not only through his art but also as a person, Brecht made a huge impression on us. The fundamental attitude of being open, listening to people, bringing them together as a productive collective – we learned that from him.

CLAUS: He also taught us an important motto for life: that people and the world can be changed. I believe in that idea to this day.

– You said Brecht also made a huge impression on you 'as a person'. How would you describe his character?

WERA: He was a very friendly person. And he was someone who was simultaneously patient and impatient, rational and irrational, and who had the gift of reconciling both qualities.

He had a talent for introducing people to new ideas, new intellectual experiences. But to do that you have to be as erudite as he was. He was a very erudite man.

CLAUS: Brecht was a man who respected others. And he looked out for the people close to him. Wera had a difficult birth with our first child, and ended up with late rickets – it could only be treated with certain drugs that were not available in the GDR. Brecht went to great lengths to get hold of these drugs. We eventually got them from Israel, via West Berlin. Even though it was strictly forbidden to import medicines.

After our son was born, Brecht was very excited, he shook me by the collar and asked if everything was alright.

Of course he was also a cowardly, sly, sometimes even devious man. A human being, in other words. But he was a great writer and thinker, and I was lucky to have had the opportunity to work alongside such a man and to have experienced him 'at first hand'.

We used the familiar 'du' form when addressing Helli Weigel, incidentally, and the polite 'Sie' form to Brecht. We called him 'Brecht'. He addressed the women by their first names, and also used the 'Sie' form with them. I just got called by my surname. But our interactions with him were sometimes very informal. We also visited him at his house in Buckow. Rolf the German shepherd was always there. Once we sang him prostitute songs from our childhoods. He liked them very much. He promised to sing us prostitute songs from Augsburg one day, which we were to record. Songs from the Hasengasse, where the brothel was. It never happened, unfortunately.

– Brecht is regularly accused of having exploited his collaborators. What is your take on that? Did he exploit you?

WERA: Not at all. Brecht made people productive for him. That much is true. There were certainly moments when it annoyed us. But that's not important. In the end. Proof of the fact that Brecht wasn't exploiting anyone is found in a definitive statement by Brecht's long-time collaborator Elisabeth Hauptmann (who should know better than anyone). She said: 'The effort was fun.' He was a great inspirer, but no exploiter.

EGON MONK

The interview took place on 5 August 1997 in Hamburg.

Egon Monk was born in Berlin on 18 May 1927. In 1943 he became a member of the Luftwaffe auxiliary personnel, and in 1944 he entered the Reich Labour Service. Following the Second World War, after taking his *Abitur* at Berlin's Lessing-Gymnasium, he attended drama school in Berlin from 1945 to 1947. In 1949 he joined Brecht's newly formed Berliner Ensemble. As an assistant director to Brecht, Erich Engel and Berthold Viertel, he worked on productions including *Mr Puntila and his Man Matti*, Maxim Gorky's *Vassa Zheleznova* and Brecht's adaptation of Lenz's *The Tutor*. The production of Gerhart Hauptmann's comedies *The Beaver Coat* and *Conflagration* in Brecht's 1951 adaptation was the first play Monk directed by himself. In 1953 he filmed Brecht's *Señora Carrar's Rifles* for the DEFA; it was the first ever film version of a play on German television.

In 1953 Monk left the GDR and worked from 1955 to 1957 as a director of radio plays and author at RIAS Berlin, and then from 1957 to 1959 as a director at NDR [North German Broadcasting]. From 1960 to 1968 he was head of the main television drama department at NDR. During this time he also directed productions at the Staatsoper and the Hamburg Schauspielhaus, including Brecht's *Rise and Fall of the City of Mahagonny*. In 1968 Monk became artistic director of the Deutsches Schauspielhaus Hamburg, but left the job after 75 days.

After 1970, back at NDR, Monk continued to work as a television director and freelance author. His best-known television productions are the five-part series *Bauern, Bonzen und Bomben* [*Farmers, Big Wigs and Bombs*] (1973) and the two-part TV drama *Die Geschwister Oppermann* [*The Oppermanns*] (1983), which was awarded a gold Adolf Grimme Prize. Monk also turned Ralph Giordano's novel *Die Bertinis* [*The Bertinis*] into a TV series, which he worked on for five years and which was awarded the Critics Prize in the television category in 1989. He has won several other national and international awards.

– Herr Monk, you joined a group of young people who were already engaging with Brecht's writing long before he came back to Germany. How did people in Berlin come to be interested in Brecht at that time?

I was positively waiting for him. I read the few new books that were available in those post-war days, and I came to the conclusion that Brecht, of all the German writers who'd had to go into exile, was the one worth waiting for. I followed his progress from America to Switzerland, and then I heard he would soon be back in Germany. My colleagues and I were very keen to meet him – more out of appreciation for his work than any ulterior motive in terms of the theatre he might potentially set up. In my opinion, what Brecht had to say was exactly what young people in their early twenties, who had lived through the war, wanted to hear. Isot Kilian, Bruno Lorenz and I organised Brecht revues in Berlin factories which included anything of Brecht's that we could get our hands on. My job was to say a few words about what was to come and talk about Brecht's life. Isot Kilian was brave enough to speak to Helene Weigel on one occasion, and ask her advice about the items for our Brecht events. This resulted in a meeting, and I was summoned to the Hotel Adlon where Brecht was staying, in the one surviving wing.

– What happened at the first meeting?

He asked what I already knew, I told him what we'd included in our performances so far and then asked him to tell me about his life – how he'd become a Marxist, for example. In response, he told me about how he'd originally planned to write a play about the American wheat exchange. This had given rise to questions for which he'd found no answers in literature, but he *had* found them in Marx and Engels. He'd come to Marxism through self-study, through his own thirst for knowledge. The play about the wheat exchange, however, had never materialised.

– Did Brecht also tell you about his time in exile?

Not at all – nor did he say anything about it later on, after we started working together at the theatre in September 1949. When it came to a theatre project you could talk and debate with Brecht for hours and days on end. But conversations of a more personal nature were out of the question; Brecht had no use for them at all. I don't know why that was. In the four years I worked with Brecht, we had perhaps ten such conversations – you could count them on your fingers. Besides, I had far too much respect for him to ask him why he emigrated to America instead of the Soviet Union, for example. I wouldn't have dreamt of it.

– So then you gave the lecture and organised the evening. Brecht himself was present on one occasion.

Even after I started working for him as an assistant director, he was still keen for these Brecht evenings to go ahead. He wanted our little troupe to carry on visiting schools, factories and adult education centres because he thought it would be good publicity for the nascent Berliner Ensemble. I remember the fright I got once when I was standing in a school assembly hall and I'd just started talking about his life when I saw Brecht himself sitting in the tenth row, listening with interest to my description of his life. In the moment it was rather an awkward situation, but I quickly got my head around it. He didn't say anything about it. He seemed to approve. I'd already recited the poem 'To those born later' to Brecht during my visit to the Hotel Adlon. He summoned me to the Deutsches Theater, where the Berliner Ensemble was originally based. Brecht was sitting in an armchair, and I stood right in front of him. It was strange performing such a difficult poem, which is a kind of key to Brecht's thinking and behaviour, to the man who wrote it, but it went all right. Brecht was very easy to get along with generally. He was shy, I was shy, so in a way we cancelled each other out. He said nothing about my performance, which I took as indirect criticism but which I didn't feel as a rebuke.

– You were one of several young collaborators. Why did Brecht mainly surround himself with young people? It's surprising, really, getting the opportunity to work with Brecht at the Berliner Ensemble in your early twenties.

I asked myself the same question at the time, and for a while I thought I knew the answer. I thought that on the one hand he was falling back on old, tried-and-tested collaborators from the pre-1933 days and on the other hand he wanted very young collaborators who had no 'biography', so to speak. According to this theory he wouldn't have had any use for the so-called 'middle generation', i.e. anyone aged between thirty and fifty, because they had spent their formative years in the Nazi period. But that wasn't actually the case. There were more and more exceptions, which eventually made me realise I was wrong to think Brecht was following any kind of principle. In this context it's important to note that the success of *Mother Courage and her Children* was seen as such an event on the German theatre scene that many people gravitated towards the Berliner Ensemble and towards Brecht – an event with a long-term impact, incidentally.

– What was so new and innovative about the production of Mother Courage and her Children *– what made it such an important event in theatrical history?*

I was present at one of the last rehearsals for *Mother Courage*, as a drama student. Lots of drama students from all over Berlin were invited, so I remember the auditorium being almost full. What I saw was completely different to anything I'd seen in the last years of the war and in the post-war period. I recall the overwhelming, almost dazzling brightness of the lights, and I can't remember now whether it was just a sensation or whether I properly thought about it. At any rate it signified brightness, clarity, lucidity. Gone were the days of that blurred, dim, indistinct stuff of the Nazi era. Darkness favours shady dealings, as the saying goes. In the Berlin production of *Mother Courage*, by contrast, shady dealings were completely out of the question. It was a call to look closely, to listen carefully and to engage your intellect as well as your feelings. Gone were the days of that strange mixture of excessive sentimentality and a declaratory tone. You often got the impression that something was being proclaimed, and the hostility of the previous form of theatre towards the intellect was still very palpable. Now, all of a sudden, we were being asked to join in with the process of making meaning. Before, you always used to get the feeling that there was a sign hanging above the stage saying 'Don't think! Don't think! Don't think!' This was one of the themes of my film *The Oppermanns*, based on Lion Feuchtwanger's novel. It's about a Nazi German teacher who comes to work at a Berlin grammar school in 1933 and teaches the students to perceive German history not with their rational minds but with the opposite: their feelings. But what feelings! This context is barely understood today. Today it is almost the other way round: the theatre may not be completely hostile to the intellect, but it has the reputation of being didactic, wagging its finger and even wanting to impart knowledge. All things which apparently shouldn't take place on the stage and will cause a play to fail. With Brecht's *Mother Courage* it was quite the reverse. The production would not have had the enormous impact it did, however, if it hadn't taken place at that particular moment in time. Much of Berlin lay in ruins. Everyone was still feeling the effects of the war that had just ended. In many cases, people's relationships with each other had been destroyed, and there was hardly anything to eat. I didn't know much about the context and I asked myself: 'How was such a thing even possible? How on earth could such a catastrophe come about?' Here in Brecht's *Mother Courage* there was an answer to many questions, presented not in a didactic way but in an illustrative one. When the recruiters talk about the war in an unwontedly cynical and humorous way before Mother Courage's wagon rolls up, for example. Or in the famous political conversation on Courage's wagon in which she claims the Poles should not have interfered in their own affairs. I realised that you can talk about such hallowed concepts as 'the nation' and 'the life of the nation' in a different way, and laugh about them too. I gained a completely different perspective on things, relationships, people. I adopted a new point of view. The war, as an event so recently past, became – as a result of this snapshot of the Thirty Years' War – current and transparent in a way it never was to me again. It was clear that this play had been written by a man who understood his era and was completely in tune with it. He was thoroughly contemporary. All these things taken together were truly electrifying. I said to myself: 'You've got to work with him!' And luckily that's what happened.

– *When you joined the Ensemble, Brecht was engaged on the production of* Mr Puntila and his Man Matti, *and you were able to see how he worked at close quarters. Was it 'epic theatre' – did you have to be conversant with the* 'Short Organon'? *Or how did Brecht go about things?*

Of course, everyone who worked there was familiar with the *Short Organon for the Theatre*. It had just appeared in the special Bertolt Brecht edition of the magazine *Sinn und Form*. It played no part in our day-to-day theatre work, however. Brecht must have realised that, with his rigorous (if witty) wording and his vision of the distant future of a Marxist aesthetic, he was expecting too much of his contemporaries. Brecht himself didn't speak about it at all. He never even mentioned the term 'epic theatre' while we were working. He knew that while he was setting up his new theatre he would not be able to implement everything he had in mind right from the start. As it turned out, it was very difficult to achieve a natural acting style, natural movements and natural speech in a way that differentiated them from the existing acting style. At the rehearsals for *Puntila* it became clear to me that Brecht, alongside all his other qualities, could also be seen as a 'custodian'. He wanted to pass on the high standard of 1920s Berlin theatre to the next generation by personifying this standard; he embodied tradition, as it were. He had not only shaped this period but had also come into contact with all the famous theatre people, like Kortner, Reinhardt etc. He knew exactly how good German theatre had once been. After his return, he felt that it had deteriorated and tried initially to restore and re-establish what had gone before. He tried to re-establish precisely this natural acting style. At the time of *Puntila*, he felt it was too early to go much beyond that.

– *What were your duties as Brecht's assistant director? Can you give an idea of what the rehearsals were like, and what your work entailed?*

When I started working with Brecht I wasn't even the fifth wheel – more like the seventh or the eighth wheel on the waggon. I was taken on as an employee for 600 marks a month, and I was expected to serve as a jack of all trades – although I'd been hoping they'd take me on as an actor, since that's what I was. When I read the cast list for *Mr Puntila and his Man Matti*, I saw I wasn't on it and asked Brecht whether I couldn't at least be involved in the production as his assistant director. He immediately agreed. When I went to the director's desk there were already six or seven other people sitting there, including Benno Besson and Peter Palitzsch, and I sat down with them. The really good jobs – noting down the blocking, keeping track of how the blocking developed – were already taken. So I was left with overseeing the props, which I found great fun but not very fulfilling. Then good fortune worked in my favour. All the assistant directors were struck down by a bout of flu, meaning I was the only one left and all the important jobs were assigned to me. One of these jobs was to closely observe what happened at the rehearsals and write everything down. I had shorthand pads in which I noted down everything that moved, the things Brecht changed and the comments he made – I still have those notepads today. Since Brecht refused to spend time deciphering other people's handwriting, I had to very quickly learn to type so I could copy up my notes on a typewriter. These typed notes would then be submitted to Brecht the next day. He used them to monitor what was going on, as a basis on which to proceed with our work. Brecht liked to act things out himself, and I had to record this as well as what the actors came up with after watching him. The aim was for whoever read the notes to be able to follow exactly what had happened on stage; we had to describe not only Brecht himself but also what resulted from his work. In short: a large part of the job of assistant director to Brecht involved recording clearly and concisely what went on at the director's desk and on the stage. The notes were supplemented by photos taken by Ruth Berlau. Because the theatre seasons were mainly in the winter, there were times when I didn't see daylight for weeks on end. When I went out in the morning it was still dark, and when I came home at night it was well after dark. Part of this daily routine consisted of preparations for the rehearsal, then sorting and laying out the written reports, and then the rehearsal itself, which usually went on until about 2 p.m. After a short break it was back to work compiling the Modelbooks: we had to sort through rehearsal photos, paste them in and annotate them, which was very complicated. On the days we weren't rehearsing, there were performances. So we were busy all week, including Saturday which was a working day like any other.

– The Berliner Ensemble staged many important productions. But the production of The Tutor *is mentioned again and again. What was so special about this work?*

The work on *The Tutor* was particularly felicitous, for various reasons. First of all it resulted in a great production. And the work in and of itself made us happy. We felt cheerful, we looked forward to coming to rehearsals every day. We didn't want the rehearsals to end, that's how much fun they were. As the day of the premiere approached, everyone felt sorry that the rehearsals would soon be over. Every day there was something new to discover; every day was happier, more cheerful. There wasn't a big crowd of assistant directors around Brecht, just Besson and me, and sometimes we were joined by [set designer] Caspar Neher, and it was very enjoyable chatting just the four of us. Brecht was very witty, he did less acting himself, he sometimes called out his observations loudly from the floor and was met with laughter from the stage. It was a wonderful time, even though it was by no means certain that it was going to result in a successful production. But this happy time did continue right up until the premiere. You can't ask for more than that.

– Brecht is sometimes accused of having exploited his collaborators. Did you feel as though your labour was being exploited, or is it all just speculation?

It's nonsense. Nobody felt exploited by Brecht. And Brecht would never have dreamt of exploiting anyone. Quite the reverse, in fact. A week before the premiere of *The Tutor*, he told Besson and me that we should both be named as directors. So the production would be under our names today if we hadn't told Brecht that we wouldn't hear of it, because it was his production. Brecht was very displeased. He didn't want to be the only named director, so in the end it was Brecht and Neher. And he was the same on other occasions too. He was increasingly inclined to give away the role of director; it wasn't at all important to him to be named as the director. Once he said to me and Besson: 'Stand on your own two feet, take over from me! I'm not a director and I need my time for other things!' That didn't change the fact that Brecht loved directing and was the ablest and most experienced director around at the time. But he set no store by it. Nobody was exploited by Brecht. Around him you became productive, you started working and thinking. You came up with things that never would have occurred to you otherwise. His presence was a constant spur to achieve things, but voluntarily, based on your own initiative. It was only after Brecht was gone that people started using the labels 'teacher' and 'pupil'. I was his assistant, he was indisputably my boss. But it would never have occurred to me to see myself as his pupil. He never gave instructions. Those who waited for instructions came away empty-handed, and were let go after a year as a 'dead weight'. That wasn't uncommon. To work with Brecht, you absolutely had to be able to use your own initiative. He expected actors to argue their own corner. He couldn't stand it when actors stood there waiting for him to play their role for them, so to speak. He said his aims as a director were completely different, and that the performance arose from the clash between the actors' goals and the director's. He once told somebody: 'I don't want to have to tell you to enjoy acting! That has to come from you.'

– *Another thing Brecht is accused of is having exploited the women in his life and treated them badly.*

Only someone who didn't know Brecht and who had deliberately misunderstood him could accuse him of that. Women became productive when they were around him too; they worked better and more intensively, even if in these cases the driving force was their affection for him. If I can put it that mildly. We who worked at the Berliner Ensemble took it for granted that Brecht was not only a writer and a director but also a man, who had several women he lived with. Apart from the usual canteen gossip – of which there was a certain amount, of course – nobody took exception to it. And nobody wondered about whether it might be to the women's detriment.

– *Following the initial successes with* Mother Courage and her Children *and* Mr Puntila and his Man Matti, *there were debates with the Party leadership about the opera* The Trial of Lucullus. *What did you witness of these debates and Brecht's reaction to them?*

Since I was working on another theatre project at the same time, I can't tell you much about it. After the dispute, I watched one of the rehearsals and it seemed to me that almost nothing had been changed, apart from the title and the ending.

– *Did the Party often intervene directly in the work of the Berliner Ensemble?*

We never had delegates from the Party Group at the BE coming to speak to us in that regard, no. The Berliner Ensemble worked completely independently. If the Party did express its wishes and demands to Brecht, then this happened on another level which we were not privy to – especially in my case as I wasn't a Party member. I can't remember any direct interventions in the running of the theatre in the years between 1949 and 1953. There were some petty annoyances as a result of the Party's oversensitivity. But I just found them laughable. The heavy criticism levelled at the *Urfaust* later on was less of a laughing matter, but in the early years there was nothing like that.

– *What sort of a relationship did Brecht have with the Party leadership?*

I know from hearsay that his relationship with Wilhelm Pieck is supposed to have been very good. And Pieck, as far as I know, came to all our productions and was genuinely pleased about our successes. Brecht's relationship with Ulbricht, on the other hand, was not good. Brecht accepted that the Party leadership would have its own opinions, just as he accepted it of everybody else. And this included opinions about his theatre. In this respect, the reactions in West Germany to the debates around *Lucullus* seemed to me to be rather over the top. When Brecht couldn't understand the reasons behind a particular criticism, that was when he put up a fight. When Honecker deleted Ernst Busch's name from the 'Herrnberger Bericht' ['Herrnburger Report'], Brecht telegraphed to ask the 'Right Honourable Comrade Honecker' why this measure had been taken. Without specific reasons he did not want to delete Busch, and in the end the name was left in. But the production was punished for it: the work was performed only once and then never again. In his telegram, incidentally, Brecht spelt Honecker's name 'Honegger', which shows that at the time he didn't have any relationship at all with the Central Council of the FDJ [Free German Youth]. Brecht could understand the objections to *Lucullus*, and it was for that reason (not for tactical reasons) that he made the changes. If he thought someone was an idiot, he said so outright. I once had a long conversation with him in his car. Brecht loved driving and wanted me to learn too. I said I couldn't afford a car on my small salary, so I didn't need to learn to drive. He disagreed and told me how his poems had enabled him to buy his first Steyr, and he said the government gave Johannes R. Becher even nicer cars for his poems. In the same conversation he also got onto the subject of the Russians, and voiced his opinion that their competence in and knowledge of Marxist thinking were very immature and that they often didn't understand anything at all. Brecht called an idiot an idiot, even if he or she was a Communist idiot in a position of authority. He wasn't afraid of reprisals.

– You've already mentioned that the Party's strongest criticism was reserved for the Urfaust *production, which you directed.*

That was very surprising for me, even though we didn't live 'beyond good and evil' and we'd followed the formalism debate closely. Moscow dictated how Socialist Realism was to be understood. Everything that deviated from this model was dismissed as formalistic, including Brecht's treatment of the *Urfaust*. The criticism directed against the *Urfaust* entailed a clear danger: an 'administrative solution' was mentioned, and that meant nothing less than arrest if the Party and the State didn't get anywhere with friendly persuasion. The Party's dealings with Brecht and the Berliner Ensemble had suddenly been placed on another level entirely. It was suggested that Brecht's relationship with his pupils was similar to Socrates' relationship with *his* pupils in ancient times. I, at least, interpreted this as a threat, for we all knew what had happened to Socrates. I thought they'd gone too far.

– Before you left the Berliner Ensemble, you directed the television production of Brecht's Señora Carrar's Rifles. *It was the first time a stage play had been adapted for television. How did you go about it?*

It was a challenge for me, because I'd always wanted to be a film director. I only joined the Berliner Ensemble because of Brecht as an individual. I thought I would now be able to use what I'd learned at the DEFA, and Peter Palitzsch and I wrote a screenplay with over a hundred takes. We had to film it in about four days, which was practically impossible. As I left the Berliner Ensemble on 1 May 1953, I didn't see the film in its entirety on television until about ten years later, and I was actually very happy with it.

– At the rehearsals, Brecht and Helene Weigel argued about how the role of Señora Carrar should be played. Do you remember that?

There were no arguments – Brecht wouldn't allow arguments – but there were differences of opinion. Weigel, as a well-known and important actress, was in some ways too independent a person for Brecht. That was the case not only with *Señora Carrar's Rifles*, incidentally, but with *Mother Courage* and *The Mother* too. In *Señora Carrar's Rifles*, she was openly moved by the wider context, along with the spectators. She knew the circumstances from which the play had arisen, and in some scenes she did shed tears. More often than not it was during rehearsals; it very rarely happened during performances. On these occasions Brecht reminded her – sometimes forcefully, sometimes very gently – that this was to the detriment of the role. Such disagreements did occur from time to time, but they weren't arguments as such. Elsewhere Brecht declared that this kind of empathy was a mistake which epic theatre (if it were ever to be properly realized) would have to deal with.

– Why did you leave the GDR?

I decided to leave the GDR for two reasons: firstly because the state was increasingly interfering in my private affairs in order to get to Brecht. It was already clear at the time that the country was on its way to becoming a police state. One example: I lived with my wife and my mother close to the sector border, near where the Wall was built later on. It was customary in those days to change GDR marks at a rate of 1:5, to cross over to the West and buy a quarter of a pound of butter, for example. No more than that, because people were poor on both sides of the border. The *Volkspolizei* [People's Police], when they were checking the women, regularly went into their bags and confiscated the little food they had there. I witnessed such incidents myself. It happened to my wife and my mother too. And there were increasingly serious consequences if you got caught buying the [West German magazine] *Der Spiegel*. I didn't want to live in a state that dictated to me what I was allowed to read and what I was allowed to say. There were two arrests within the Ensemble, too. Two of Brecht's pupils, Martin Pohl and Horst Bieneck, disappeared; all of a sudden they were just gone. We never found out what had happened to them. Things like that were commonplace under Stalinism. Later on GDR society became a little more liberal, and people who drew attention to themselves had files kept on them. During Stalin's lifetime, however, the response to any suspicion was quicker and more brutal: people disappeared and in some cases were never seen again. What was more, the Party group was becoming increasingly visible within the Berliner Ensemble. This didn't have an impact on our work, but it was already foreseeable that the Ensemble would not always remain the refuge or the island it had been before.

Secondly, I was keen to get away from Brecht anyway. Prior to this I'd already had an offer to go and work as a senior director in Halle. Brecht had reacted with enthusiasm and said, 'Ah, wonderful!' He had the idea that his productions could then be staged in Halle too, and the plays performed in Halle could be put on in Berlin. He was planning to absorb the theatre in Halle straight into the consortium of Brechtian theatres. But the job in Halle didn't come to anything in the end. I stayed at the Berliner Ensemble for a while. But I still felt the desire to leave. By that time I wanted to be able to make my own mistakes and pay for them myself. That's the only way to learn. Working alongside an authority like Brecht – in the truest sense of the word, because his opinions and judgements were almost always right, and I was happy to admit it – was no longer an option for me. Brecht said that in order to be a director I also had to be in tune with the times from a philosophical point of view – to master the dialectical method, in other words. He said he wanted to teach me about it. But he didn't get the chance. In April 1953, after the *Urfaust*, I left the GDR. I told Brecht in person beforehand, but I didn't write him a letter. Because it was a criminal offence to know somebody wanted to leave the GDR and not to report it. It's unlikely anything would have happened to Brecht; but the fact was that his knowledge of my intentions would have been punishable by law. That's why I didn't write to him.

– How did Brecht react to you leaving?

He tried to get me to come back. After a few months he sent Isot Kilian to see me in West Berlin, as a messenger. I stayed friends with her right up until her death a few years ago. She told me Brecht was very keen for me to come back. At the time I didn't know Brecht was now in love with her. But I stuck by my decision and said that under no circumstances would I be returning to the GDR and the conditions there, and Isot Kilian accepted that.

– Did you hear anything more from Brecht after that?

Not directly. Johannes R. Becher invited me via telegram to go to the funeral and I went. There was a certain amount of risk involved – after all, I had committed a criminal offence under GDR law. So I could have been arrested and imprisoned. But I wasn't really afraid of being detained on this occasion. I took Becher's telegram with me, though, just to be on the safe side.

– Brecht was also subject to these restrictions, this interference. He too was monitored – when he took his typewriter to Buckow, for example, he had to submit a permit for it. Was leaving the GDR not an option for him?

I think it was. In the time leading up to his death he toyed with the idea of settling in Switzerland. That undoubtedly had something to do with the living and working conditions in the GDR. Brecht would never have allowed himself to be walled in. His personal freedom was extremely important to him. He wouldn't allow himself to be straitjacketed. He certainly didn't like constantly having to show his passport and things like that.

– Did you or Brecht ever feel threatened in the GDR?

I'm sure Brecht didn't feel threatened, but for less prominent figures the risk of being arrested by the security service was very real. Brecht and others at the Berliner Ensemble were always saying subversive things. We would often get together in Caspar Neher's room and improvise individual scenes for which the dialogues had not yet been written. There were some hilarious role plays – like when Brecht played Gustchen from *The Tutor*. During these improvisations it was inevitable that parallels would be drawn between past and present, between the historical material and the current social conditions. Allusions were made. Subversive comments were par for the course. And the closer you got to Brecht the more subversive it became – like when we made fun of the officials' pomposity and their hollow pathos. If something like that had happened outside the buffer zone of the Berliner Ensemble, or if it had reached the ears of the Party group, it would undoubtedly have posed a significant risk.

– What did Brecht mean to you personally?

He was my most important teacher. Nothing else in my career has made such a strong impression on me as my time with Brecht and the Berliner Ensemble.

– What was Brecht like as a person?

The friendliest person I have ever met, and one of the most thoughtful. In his dealings with other people he was extremely considerate, he would never have wanted to offend anybody. He showed the most perfect courtesy to everybody. He was a person one might describe as a role model, if that hadn't gone out of fashion.

PART THREE

GLOBAL BRECHT

Europe

CHAPTER TWENTY-TWO

The Politics of the Body: Pina Bausch's *Tanztheater*

DAVID W. PRICE

Pina Bausch has been a dominant force in the dance world for many years, but her unique conception of *Tanztheater* has often been overlooked by drama critics writing about theories of the stage. Although Bausch's works have attracted the attention of dance enthusiasts and critics, her later productions often leave these same critics frustrated, confused, or disappointed because the current vocabulary of dance theory cannot address the multifariousness of Bausch's productions adequately. Even those few drama critics who have been attracted to Bausch limit their theoretical approach to *Tanztheater* and chiefly rely upon a Brechtian vocabulary.[1] Bausch has been repeatedly characterized as a feminist performance artist and dramatist who consciously uses Brechtian 'epic' techniques.[2] What distinguishes Bausch, however, is her development of an art form based upon a binary opposition that does not reproduce an either/or dichotomy; instead, Bausch's productions are *both* dance *and* theater. Hers is an art form that rejects a totalizing Wagnerian vision in favor of a dialectical theatricality.[3]

Bausch's *Tanztheater* quite literally sets in motion a dialectic between two conservative components: the performance part, which, according to Josette Féral, 'is made up of the *realities of the imaginary*', and the theatrical part, which is 'made up of *specific symbolic structures*'.[4] On Bausch's stage the dialectic between the performance and the theatrical

---

David W. Price, 'The Politics of the Body: Pina Bausch's *Tanztheater*', *Theatre Journal*, 42: 3 (1990), pp. 322–31.

[1] For example, in the only full-length treatment of Bausch's works in English, Norbert Servos wrote that Bausch's productions begin with the 'daily social experiences of the body', which she 'translates and alienates' onstage. See Norbert Servos and Kurt Weigelt, *Pina Bausch Wuppertal Dance Theater or the Art of Training a Goldfish: Excursions into Dance* (Cologne: Ballet-Bühnen Verlag, 1984), 21.
[2] Janelle Reinelt discussed how other feminist dramatists have used Brechtian techniques in order to examine the 'material conditions of gender behavior' in 'Beyond Brecht: Britain's New Feminist Drama', *Theatre Journal*, 38:2 (1986): 154.
[3] Sue-Ellen Case has described both a radical feminist theatrical group and a materialist feminist theatrical group who use Brechtian techniques in order to explore the issues of gender construction in her book, *Feminism and Theater* (London: Macmillan, 1988), 67, 92–93. Bausch is different in that her works express both radical and materialist feminist perspectives on gender construction and do not rely solely on Brechtian methods of performance.
[4] Josette Féral, 'Performance and Theatricality: The Subject Demystified', trans. Térèse Lyons, *Modern Drama* 25:1 (1982): 178.

is played out upon the body, or, more specifically, upon the bodies of the dancers/ performers. In each of her productions Bausch stages the social inscription of the body affected by cultural symbolic structures in opposition to and sometimes in collusion with a somatic imaginary. In other words, Bausch's *Tanztheater* examines gender construction and explores the possibility that gender attributes are both expressive and performative.

Assessing Bausch's dialectical theater necessitates a theoretical combinatory method of sorts. Because Bausch makes the body the focal point of her work, it is natural to turn to Antonin Artaud. As Susie J. Tharu has noted, 'Artaud's "Theatre of Cruelty" is perhaps the earliest and certainly the most explicit attempt to establish an aesthetic of performance based entirely on bodily perception and expression.'[5] And because Bausch draws attention to bodily gestures by alienating those gestures through performative acts of decontextualization, it is logical to refer to Brecht. But combining the theories of Artaud and Brecht requires that those theories be discussed no longer in modernist terms; rather, it is necessary to speak of Artaud and Brecht in a postmodern context.

In *The Sense of Performance: Post-Artaud Theatre*, Tharu argued against the modernist Artaud and championed what she called 'the other Artaud', in whom 'the political and epistemological implications of his idea of the body as medium and his sense of performance as radical act' can be discovered.[6] This other, 'postmodern', Artaud presents the frenzied body, which becomes a sign 'that reveals, through its transformation of the act into the spectacular, the *sense* or the lived meaning of that gesture'.[7] Brecht, too, exhibits a postmodern dimension. As Elizabeth Wright has argued, Brecht qualifies as 'a deconstructionist *avant la lettre*'.[8] In this discussion I am going to maintain that Bausch's works *combine* the theoretical approaches of Brecht and Artaud and that the use of their respective theories will disclose Bausch's unresolved dialectical examination of the politics of the body – that is, how gender is constructed. Bausch's dance theater reveals the body as the site of a social inscription – the body on which the writing of the politics of gender reveals itself in performative acts – and the body as the nexus of the nonlogocentric imaginary, which reveals itself through expressive acts.[9] In this respect I follow Rainer Nägele in that I reject the familiar modernist view that contrasts Artaud and Brecht. Nägele argued that 'Artaud's rebellion' provides for the 'reintroduction of the body in theatrical space' and 'Brecht's theatrical revolution points in the same direction'.[10] Nägele wrote:

> Brecht's *Gestus* paradigmatically shows the difference in the body: *Gestus* is the sum of concrete bodily gestures, facial expressions, tones of voice, and rhythm and figures

---

[5] Susie J. Tharu, *The Sense of Performance: Post-Artaud Theatre* (Atlantic Highlands: Humanities Press, 1984), 82.
[6] Ibid., 11.
[7] Ibid., 60. It is precisely this expression of the body as a sign, whose gestures comprise the significatory act and whose very materiality serves as the locus of inscription, which makes Artaud's theories central to any discussion of Pina Bausch's works.
[8] Elizabeth Wright, *Postmodern Brecht: A Re-Presentation* (London: Routledge, 1989), 1. Wright has argued that Brecht's *Lehrstücke* and the early plays contain his postmodern dimension. These 'dialectical works' employ a method of representation that 'continually reveals the contradictions in the incidents and the objects it singles out' (36).
[9] I borrow the oppositional terms expressive and performative as used by Judith Butler in her excellent essay, 'Performative Acts and Gender Constitution: An Essay in Phenomenology and Feminist Theory', *Theatre Journal* 40:4 (1988): 519–31.
[10] Rainer Nägele, *Reading After Freud: Essays on Goethe, Hölderlin, Habermas, Nietzsche, Brecht, Celan, and Freud* (New York: Columbia University Press, 1987), 112.

of speech, but it is not identical with any of these. It contains the *relation* to another body and *Gestus*. It is structured by the symbolic code of a specific social situation. The body does not have the identity of its wholeness in itself. It provides the ideal and the idol, the *Gestalt*, of wholeness, which it only finds in the distribution along a symbolic chain.[11]

I hope to show that by combining the theories of Brecht and Artaud it is possible to perceive Bausch's stage productions as political performances that explore the question of gender from radical feminist *and* materialist feminist perspectives.

What follows, therefore, is an attempt to position Bausch at the crossroads of two approaches to theater – first by identifying the elements of Brechtian and Artaudian theories that are commonly revealed in various Bausch productions and then by providing a detailed examination of a specific work – *Cafe Müller* – in which the theories of Brecht and Artaud are combined in order to examine critically Bausch's dramatic exploration of the dialectics of gender. Bausch, like other dramatists (for example, Peter Weiss, Heiner Müller, Edward Bond, and others), combines the techniques of Brecht and Artaud. But the tension produced by these modes of theatrical presentation in her works reveals the unresolved ideological debate which underscores her recurrent theme of the constitution of gender and its role in relationships between men and women. For if the Brechtian elements in Bausch's work serve as a feminist critique of the patriarchal social structure extant in the West, the aspects of her theater that echo Artaud's theories suggest an essentialist feminism which views men and women as fundamentally different and inherently irreconcilable.

I. (NON)CONTRADICTORY COMBINATION: BRECHT AND ARTAUD IN BAUSCH'S WORKS

It is clear that if the viewers of Bausch's theater agree on nothing else, they are in accord in their recognition of Brecht's presence in her works. Brecht defined the alienation effect as 'turning the object of which one is to be made aware, to which one's attention is to be drawn, into something ordinary, familiar, immediately accessible, into something peculiar, striking and unexpected'.[12] Dance critic Anna Kisselgoff practically echoed Brecht's words when she analyzed a Bausch performance and wrote, 'She can make the commonplace unimaginable. Just as obviously she renders the absurd commonplace.'[13] Johannes Birringer observed that 'in Bausch's works we are confronted directly with the gestures of conventions and internalized norms we no longer see'.[14] Hilton Als described a scene in *1980* in which a woman repeatedly and mechanically kisses a man such that his face becomes a map of lipstick prints. Als pointed out that with this kissing gesture, Bausch penetrated 'the meaning of gesture as gesture and how that gesture is utilized in defining one's role'.[15] Raimund Hoghe discussed the final scene from *Kontakthof*, in

---

[11]Ibid., 113.
[12]Bertolt Brecht, *Brecht on Theater: The Development of an Aesthetic*, trans. John Willett (London: Methuen, 1964), 143.
[13]Anna Kisselgoff, 'Dance: Pina Bausch Presents Mountain', *New York Times*, 10 October 1985, sec. C.
[14]Johannes Birringer, 'Pina Bausch: Dancing Across Borders', *The Drama Review* 30:2 (1986): 86–87.
[15]Hilton Als, 'Pina und Kinder', *Ballet Review* 12:4 (1985): 79.

which several men surround a woman and 'cover her body with touches'. These 'tender gestures become blows' as the woman collapses beneath the male acts of tenderness.[16]

The ramified elements of alienation effect and *Gestus* which lie beyond characterization also exist in Bausch's theater. It is necessary to look no further than the formulation of epic theater, which, Brecht said, 'is chiefly interested in the attitudes which people adopt towards one another'[17] to find the essence of Bausch's recurrent theme, which always has 'to do with man-woman relationships'.[18] 'The work', Bausch said, ' – like everything I do – is about relationships, childhood, fear of death, and how much we all want to be loved'.[19] In addition to similar thematic foundations, Bausch shares with Brecht an enthusiasm for making elements of the theater stand out independently from the 'narrative' of the performance. Servos pointed out that for Bausch 'the various theatrical elements do not combine into a harmonious whole, but instead retain their independence'.[20] Thus, in *Kontakthof* a dancer with a tape recorder and microphone amplifies the dialogues and monologues of the men and women onstage.[21] Similarly, in *Legend of Chastity* a woman reads passages from Ovid's *Ars Amatoria*, one man sings the Rühmann song 'Ich brech die Herzen der stolzesten Fraun', and fragments of Rudolf G. Binding's novel, *Legend of Chastity*, are roared onstage.[22]

Bausch also produces alienation effects through repetition. Servos wrote that 'word patterns and sentence fragments sound alien through monotonous, arbitrary repetition',[23] and repetitiveness is something Bausch defends, claiming, quite simply, 'We must look again and again'.[24] In *Bluebeard*, for example, the Bluebeard character onstage listens to Bela Bartok's opera, 'Duke Bluebeard's Castle', on a tape recorder. He listens to the opera and rewinds the tape so as to replay certain sections again and again for nearly four hours. The repetition of the beautiful music of the opera makes it sound alien, and the music becomes alienated further when compared to the savage violence inflicted upon women depicted onstage.

Bausch, like Brecht, takes pleasure in shattering the illusion of theater. Unlike performers in classical ballet, Bausch's dancers do not attempt to make their movements appear effortless. Bausch's dancers are physically pushed to the limit, and they exhibit their exhaustion and pain quite openly onstage. Bausch also discards the notion of the fourth wall. In *Bluebeard* she turns on the houselights. 'In doing this', according to Jack Anderson, 'she implies that we who watch inhabit the same world as her characters'.[25] In *Come Dance with Me* the performers mingle with the audience, and in *Bandoneon* part of the set is dismantled in the middle of the performance right before the audience. Servos contended that in Bausch's effort to break down barriers between audience and performers in *Kontakthof* she succeeds in metaphorically pulling the audience onstage

---

[16]Raimund Hoghe, 'The Theater of Pina Bausch', *The Drama Review* 24:1 (1980): 66.
[17]Brecht, *Brecht on Theater*, 86.
[18]Servos and Weigelt, *Pina Bausch Wuppertal Dance Theater*, 227.
[19]Quoted in Stephen Holden, 'When Avant-Garde Meets Mainstream', *New York Times*, 29 September 1985, sec. II.
[20]Servos and Weigelt, *Pina Bausch Wuppertal Dance Theater*, 55.
[21]Hoghe, 'The Theater of Pina Bausch', 68.
[22]Servos and Weigelt, *Pina Bausch Wuppertal Dance Theater*, 146.
[23]Ibid., 55.
[24]Quoted in Birringer, 'Pina Bausch: Dancing Across Borders', 91.
[25]Jack Anderson, 'Plotless Dance-Drama that Deals in Emotions', *New York Times*, 26 August 1984, sec. II.

when the dancers seat themselves with their backs to the audience and everyone watches a film about the mating habits of pochards.²⁶

The catalogue of Brechtian techniques could continue. What is essential, however, is seeing how Bausch uses these techniques. When Bausch stages the acts of foreplay between men and women and alienates these acts, she emphasizes the politics of the exchange, the violent nature of the acts, and the social context from which they emerge. In short, Bausch demonstrates how sexual behaviors are learned and how the body submits to cultural inscription. In *Renate Emigrates*, for example, a stage full of 'men and women stand opposite each other and are instructed by two teachers ... as to how to raise the eyes innocently, emit sighs and kisses'.²⁷ That the teachers' efforts end in failure suggests Bausch's rejection of cultural models of behavior. However, Bausch clearly recognizes the myriad forms of cultural inscriptions of the body – forms which include artistic representations of love in classical poetry and popular novels and the recurrent misogynist thematics in high cultural forms such as opera. By shattering the illusion of the effortlessness of dance, Bausch draws attention to her dancers' physicality and in so doing stresses the illusion of a socially constructed subject encased within a body that has been formed by and conforms to a given cultural norm.²⁸ In other words, when Bausch uses Brechtian techniques, she demonstrates that the gendered female subject is the confluence of cultural codes and practices that are socially reinforced.

But to interpret Bausch's *Tanztheater* as Brechtian drama is to balance only half the equation. There are elements in Bausch's productions which cannot be explained as types of *Gestus* or alienated effects. Bausch crowds her stage with so many images, movements, and objects that some critics find it exasperating. Dance critic Marcia Siegel has listed the Bausch trademarks – 'fascination with costume, ... accumulation of objects, ... the eclectic and nonlinear choice of music, verbal text, visual reference'²⁹ – and rejected them outright. She asserted that the *mises en scène* are 'gigantic' and 'irrelevant' and 'completely overtake the production' and that Bausch's works 'are action based and essentially formless' and have 'no plots, progressions, developments or denouements'.³⁰ The theater, according to Bausch, is in many ways a dreamscape, a place where the fantastic, the mundane, and the absurd all occur simultaneously. For example, in *Arien* the stage is flooded with water and at one point a huge hippopotamus lumbers out among the performers. In *Legend of Chastity*, however, the dancers find themselves confronted by huge crocodiles. The stage is literally a field full of flowers in *Carnation*, whereas in *Come Dance With Me* the back of the theater is a huge concave slide that spills out onto a stage littered with birch branches. As is readily apparent, the *mise en scène* plays an important role in Bausch's theater, and she couples this with a willingness to subordinate speech and text. In many of her productions characters speak and recite texts, but at no time does she allow the words onstage to dictate the action nor does she feel constrained by librettos or staging directions found in source material.

---

²⁶Servos and Weigelt, *Pina Bausch Wuppertal Dance Theater*, 118.
²⁷Ibid., 80.
²⁸See Wright, *Postmodern Brecht*, 138–39, for a more detailed discussion of the illusion of the self in the works of Bausch.
²⁹Marcia B. Siegel, 'Carabosse in a Cocktail Dress', *The Hudson Review*, 39 (1986): 111–12.
³⁰Ibid., 108.

Bausch's emphasis on the *mise en scène* and her subordination of language are two aspects of her theater that align her with Artaud's theories of the stage. Artaud, the logophobe *par excellence*, called for 'the substitution, for the poetry of language, of a poetry in space'.[31] He declared flatly, 'the possibilities for realization in the theater relate entirely to the *mise en scène* considered as a language in space and in movement' (45). For Artaud, the stage had to be purged of psychologisms and social critique. The plastic and the physical, not the psychological, were the true domain of the theater (71). It should not be a surprise that Pina Bausch, a trained dancer and choreographer, would produce work that has affinities with Artaud's vision of the stage. It is not dance alone, however, that links Bausch's work to Artaud. His stage was 'indeed a theater of dreams',[32] crowded with objects and bodies seen as signs, open to interpretation, bereft of a narrative text. If language exists at all, declared Artaud, it must have the same importance that it possesses in dreams (94). Artaud wrote of actors who were 'animated hieroglyphs' (54) – bodies that moved about like living ciphers in a type of choreographed cryptography. Artaud's theatrical writing is what Derrida terms nonphonetic writing, a writing that does not transcribe speech, a 'writing of the body itself'.[33]

Perhaps there is no better way to describe Bausch's *Tanztheater* than through the very terms that have just been used to describe Artaud's theatrical vision. Hers too is a hieroglyphic theater, which is quite literally a writing of the body, a choreographed cryptography. The montage effect produced by the combination of operetta, film, and cartoons in a piece like *Renate Emigrates* reminds the viewer of some of the bizarre combinations encountered in dreams. The hippopotamus and crocodiles previously mentioned also recall the dreamworld and the absurd creatures often seen there. Nearly every Bausch work contains dream-like elements. Observers of Bausch's works admit that there often appears to be an excess of signs on the stage, a surplus of signifiers which puzzle, disturb, and, in many instances, remain indecipherable. Bausch, it seems, would agree with Artaud: the theater is 'a kind of organized anarchy', (51) a confluence of disparate images, objects, and signs.

There is also a fourth similarity between Bausch and Artaud. In his 'First Manifesto on The Theater of Cruelty' Artaud wrote, 'we shall not act a written play, but we shall make attempts at direct staging around themes, facts, or known works' (98). Artaud eschewed dramatic texts and only considered developing themes taken from well-known works. In a similar fashion, Bausch rarely works with a dramatic text. Her *Macbeth* piece – *He Takes Her by the Hand and Leads Her into the Castle, the Others Follow* – reflects none of the play's dramatic or narrative structures. Her piece, *On a Mountain a Cry was Heard*, which refers to the slaughter of the innocents described in *Matthew*, contains nothing about the story of the Christ child or the flight into Egypt. Even in two works that constitute notable exceptions, one in which Bausch choreographed Stravinsky's *Rite of Spring* and another in which she staged Brecht's *Seven Deadly Sins*, her *mises en scène* departed from established norms.

By using Artaud's techniques in her productions Bausch necessarily criticizes the logocentrism of the West, and by writing the body in the context of man/woman

---

[31] Antonin Artaud, *The Theater and its Double*, trans. Mary Caroline Richards (New York: Grove Press, 1958), 38. All references to Artaud's writings will be to this translation and will appear in parentheses in the text.
[32] Jacques Derrida, *Writing and Difference*, trans. Alan Bass (Chicago: University of Chicago Press, 1978), 242.
[33] Derrida, *Writing and Difference*, 191.

relationships she rejects the phallogocentrism of her culture. In a certain sense she produces works that exemplify Luce Irigaray's notion of the female imaginary – an imaginary which brings into play 'scraps' and 'uncollected debris' and is not 'too narrowly focused on sameness'.[34] Bausch's productions are a riot of diversity; her form of creativity challenges the notions of linearity and reasoned discursive practice and offers in their stead an expansive, fluid, multiple, and diffuse form of expression. Her use of the body, particularly the female body as the site of performative acts, suggests not only gender as a culturally inscripted artifact but also gender as irreducible difference which discloses itself through the imaginary.

II. EXEMPLUM: *CAFE MÜLLER*

Cafe Müller may be the most suitable of Bausch's works to illustrate her concept of Tanztheater as a point of juncture between Brecht's and Artaud's theories of the stage because it contains in a nascent form Bausch's examination of the gendered body, which becomes increasingly problematized in later productions. In *Cafe Müller* men and women attempt to establish relationships with one another, but all their attempts end in failure. The Brechtian elements in the piece are easy to discern. The first figure seen is a female dancer who walks with a faltering gait, which makes her appear crippled; she presses her body flat against the wall. Anna Kisselgoff noted that such physical maneuvers are 'textbook examples of movements performed by schizophrenics'.[35] The bodily movement suggests isolation, despair, and mental illness, but these movements take place in a social setting. In *Cafe Müller* the tables and chairs onstage serve as a metonymic expression of all public spaces in which men and women meet. But, as Anne Ubersfeld has stated, metonymy can be re-metaphorized.[36] When a woman wearing a red wig and a fur coat skips nervously about among the furniture, the audience begins to see the chairs as a type of maze, and when the 'waiter' charges onto the scene and literally clears tables, the audience understands that social structures hinder individual freedom of movement and obstruct the development of human contact. In *Cafe Müller* there is a stunning moment of stillness in which two men and a woman sit at a table overlooking the body of a second woman lying in a heap on the floor. This living tableau perhaps best conveys the idea of alienation and estrangement between the sexes. As the performance progresses, the audience begins to wonder how much the public forum inhibits exchanges between men and women because it requires women to adopt schizoid behaviors so that they are divided against themselves and must in some sense disfigure themselves in order to be on public display.

Another sequence shows a man and a woman being trained by a second man to go through a series of movements which seem to be aimed at having the man carry the woman. The couple receives instruction eight consecutive times, but each time the woman slides out of the man's arms and onto the floor. Even without guidance, the man and woman cannot succeed in maintaining the correct position. The couple's frantic movements and repeated attempts constitute what Patrice Pavis called a *gestualité* or way

---

[34]Luce Irigaray, *This Sex Which Is Not One*, trans. Catherine Porter (Ithaca: Cornell University Press, 1985), 28–30.
[35]Anna Kisselgoff, 'Dance: Premiere of "1980" a Piece by Pina Bausch', *New York Times*, 22 June 1984, sec. C.
[36]Anne Ubersfeld, *L'école du spectateur: Lire le théâtre 2* (Paris: Éditions Sociales, 1982), 161.

of behaving.[37] These repeated movements signify that behavior between men and women is learned, culturally coded and determined, and just as inadequate as it is inept.

Seen from this perspective, *Cafe Müller* articulates a form of materialist feminism that emphasizes the social and cultural conditions that shape women's experience. Yet, despite the catalogue of Brechtian techniques already noted, *Cafe Müller* cannot be neatly circumscribed within a Brechtian horizon of interpretation because elements of another theory of theater can be seen in the performance. A man lifts a woman, spins her body in a half arc, and gently lowers her to the floor, whereupon she rises, slips off her dress, and slumps over a table. This movement occurs several times in the background while other dancers perform in the foreground. The unusual nature of the movement and its repetition suggest dream imagery, as does the moment when the half-nude female figure walks somnambulistically off the stage clutching a dress to her breasts. Anne Ubersfeld has observed that 'The scenic space can also appear as a vast psychic field where the psychic forces of the self-confront one another'.[38] Artaud, who forcefully described the theater in terms of a dream, who, as Derrida wrote, 'traces the form of theatrical writing from the model of unconscious writing',[39] reinforced the concept of the theater as a psychic battlefield on which the symbolic representation of the unconscious is realized. The oneiric images capture the audience's imagination in *Cafe Müller* no less than the alienation effects. The man and woman curled up together onstage in a fetal wrap not only emulate a typical dream image but also suggest a primal union of man and woman before sexual differentiation. Perhaps the most haunting sequence in the entire work is that of a woman walking in slow motion over a man. This image, which appears to spring directly from the unconscious, remains with the viewer and cannot be explained away as wish fulfillment.

The dream-like sequences in *Cafe Müller* all include actions of terror and cruelty. The object of the theater, for Artaud, is 'not to resolve social and psychological conflicts ... but to express objectively certain secret truths, to bring into the light of day by means of active gestures certain aspects of truth that have been buried under forms in their encounters with Becoming' (70). According to Artaud, there are immutable truths lurking beneath the surface flux of phenomena, and it is these truths which must be presented onstage. In *Cafe Müller* the buried truth is revealed in the production's most disturbing sequence. A man and woman begin an awkward duet, which culminates in the two alternately slamming one another into the wall. The sequence is painful, almost unbearable to watch, but it should be noted that unlike the rehearsed sequence, in which the man receives instructions on how to hold the woman, the slamming movements occur without prompting or provocation. It might even be said that they evolve naturally during the course of events. Bausch is suggesting that certain conditions cannot be changed and that certain fundamental laws exist. Seen in this light, *Cafe Müller* becomes a theater piece of molecular movement, in which 'characters' succumb to an ineluctable entropy. One character executes the same frenetic movements eleven times in a row before finally dissipating all his energy and collapsing on the floor. A second character briefly appears bouncing back and forth in the environment and then quickly disappears. By offering

---

[37]Patrice Pavis, *Languages of the Stage: Essays in the Semiology of Theater* (New York: Performing Arts Journal, 1982), 41.
[38]Ubersfeld, *Lire le théâtre*, 170. My translation.
[39]Derrida, *Writing and Difference*, 192.

Cafe Müller as a representation of inevitability, Bausch appears to agree with Artaud that 'We are not free. And the sky can still fall on our heads. And the theater has been created to teach us this first of all' (79).

But to wrest a single meaning from *Cafe Müller* or any Bausch production that shows the influence of both Brecht and Artaud by denying one of these constituent elements is to overlook the true tension in her productions. If Bausch is to be taken at her word, and it is assumed that in her work 'the themes are always to do with man-woman relationships',[40] then it is necessary to ask what determines the nature of those relationships. Brechtian theory suggests that the nature of man-woman relationships is socially conditioned and can – indeed must – change. On the other hand, Bausch's work – imbued with the theories of Artaud – seems saturated with an essentialist feminism: men and women are fundamentally different and can never be reconciled. This latter point of view has received some critical attention. Jay L. Kaplan noted with chagrin that 'Bausch's feminism is a grim world-view which proclaims biology is destiny. It is male nature to dominate women, and love is a continuation by other means of the battle of the sexes.'[41] Essentialist feminism can even be dimly perceived in Bausch's very first production of the *Rite of Spring*, in which a virgin girl is brutally sacrificed. To Horst Koegler's mind, the production 'emerged as a vision of the blackest terror and despair rather than as a purifying rite of hope and rebirth'.[42] What is clear is that both kinds of feminism exist simultaneously on Bausch's stage; there is no need to overlook the one or suppress the other.

In *Tanztheater* there is no resolution. The audience is left to contemplate the opposing points of view. The final scene in *Cafe Müller* captures the essence of Bausch's theoretical paradox. The solo female dancer allows the red wig and the fur coat to be placed upon her. Up to this point the solo female dancer's actions and responses have appeared to occur outside a social context, but when she dons the garments of cafe society, the audience must ask, Is her pain and anguish a natural response or is it socially determined? Bausch offers no answers; instead she prefers to depict the dialectic of opposing theories of gender artistically encoded in her *Tanztheater*.

There are two paths to be taken from the present overview of Bausch's work. The first would examine *Tanztheater* in the social and historical context of German feminism of the 1980s. Bausch's works could be explained as an artistic representation of the debate between essentialist and Marxist feminists. The second path would lead to a detailed analysis of Bausch's works as a form of feminine writing of the body as described by advocates of *écriture féminine*. Clearly, both paths emerge from an understanding of *Tanztheater* as situated between the writings of Brecht and Artaud, and any future examination of Bausch should acknowledge these contending elements in her work.

---

[40]Servos and Weigelt, *Pina Bausch Wuppertal Dance Theater*, 227.
[41]Jay L. Kaplan, 'Pina Bausch: Dancing Around the Issue', *Ballet Review*, 15:1 (1986): 76.
[42]Horst Koegler, 'Exponent of the Avant-Garde: Pina Bausch', *Dance Magazine*, 53:2 (1979): 53.

CHAPTER TWENTY-THREE

Theatre for the People: The Impact of Brechtian Theory on the Production and Performance of *1789* by Ariane Mnouchkine's Théâtre du Soleil

AGNIESZKA KARCH

Ariane Mnouchkine is a contemporary French theatre director, associated with the Théâtre du Soleil, known for its 'activism, formalism and cosmopolitanism' (Singleton 2010, 29). Her theatre, made by the people and for the people, breaks with the traditional perception of theatre as elitist. Her revolutionary status in the profession can be explained through her belief in the power of collaborative theatre (*création collective*) as the most democratic art form, capable of dealing with political questions. The redistribution of the power of decision-making in the process of production and staging can be seen as a metaphor of a political system based on civic participation. Mnouchkine's theatre teaches the audience how to react critically to what is being observed, and to translate this reaction into political activism and participation, in shaping their community. One of the central elements of her philosophy is to make the spectators aware of their potential to participate in the process of change. Instead of passively witnessing the unfolding of political and social events, citizens should feel encouraged to act and to note their personal impact on history. Such an approach is almost certainly inspired by the work of an earlier artist whose creation also falls into the category of political theatre – that of Bertolt Brecht. Brecht was known for having coined the term *Verfremdung*, crucial in achieving a critical response, and which can be described as the opposite of the suspension of disbelief, commonly cited as a requirement for most forms of entertainment.[1] In the Brechtian epic theatre, the spectator must be aware of the fictional character of the play.

Agnieszka Karch, 'Theatre for the People: The Impact of Brechtian Theory on the Production and Performance of *1789* by Ariane Mnouchkine's Theatre du Soleil', *Opticon1826*, 10 (2011), online.

Only then can the characters' actions be judged in an objective way. The motivations behind these actions are explained by the actors, often through another device typical of Brecht's style – *gestus*, defined in his own words as 'convey[ing] particular attitudes adopted by the speaker towards other men' and 'allow[ing] conclusions to be drawn about the social circumstances' (Brecht 1978, 104–5).

Bernard Dort likens Mnouchkine's method to 'the Brechtian paradigm' (Dort 1990, 100). Though the two directors' works share a number of common features and objectives, such a statement underestimates Mnouchkine's contribution to the development of political theatre. In a statement reflecting her attitude to Brechtian theory, she says that 'Brecht is not a form; it's a vision of theatre' (Williams 1999, 56). Rather than using his work as a pattern to be imitated, she reinterprets his ideas and applies them to her own artistic strategies. This is the reason why Mnouchkine calls Brecht a vision rather than a form – Bertolt Brecht is an ubiquitous artistic spirit. One could argue that the resemblance of the two is accidental, with both artists' work falling into the category of people's theatre. It is therefore not surprising that they both use similar tools to address their audiences. Given that Brecht preceded Mnouchkine, his influence on the French director is a natural consequence of the evolution of theatre.

Presenting a problem is not sufficient; the Théâtre du Soleil must engage the audience in a dialogue. Brechtian techniques play an important part in facilitating the task of speaking to the spectator. However, the difference between the two directors lies in the fact that Brecht is more text-based and Mnouchkine is better known for her use of improvisation. This is perhaps one reason why the term 'paradigm' becomes problematic. This essay will analyse the different methods, inspired by Brechtian theory, which enabled Mnouchkine to advance her own model of political theatre rather than relying on the reproduction of Brecht's techniques. In order to do so, it will focus on the performance and the staging of *1789: La révolution doit s'arrêter à la perfection du bonheur* (*1789: Revolution Must Stop When Complete Happiness is Achieved*).

As a starting point of this investigation, it is useful to note that the works of the two artists share a political link undeniably shaped by the events taking place in their lives. For Brecht this is the fascist ideology of the 1930s together with its consequences, and for Mnouchkine it is the climate of the 1968 movement. Viewing history as a dialectical class struggle and aware of the threat posed by capitalism, their work emanates the philosophy of change. Their Marxist approach makes them devoted to opposing bourgeois domination. Within the context of their profession, this essentially means fighting against the exclusive character of theatre. Rendering theatre-going a mass activity was a priority for Brecht: 'Anything less than two hundred at a time is not worth mentioning' (Brecht, trans. Willet and Manheim, 1970, 31).

Only by demonstrating exceptional force could Brecht and Mnouchkine counteract the bourgeois domination. Their approach required, therefore, revolutionising the concept of theatre; this was achieved by introducing a political dimension into their works. As a committed Marxist, Brecht believed that theatre must be a vehicle for political ideas. Such an attitude appealed to Mnouchkine and soon became her artistic driving force. Theatre had to be adapted to social needs arising from political circumstances, with entertainment no longer being its primary focus. Brecht's and Mnouchkine's works are therefore often referred to as social experiments rather than plays, with the success of

---

[1]The term *Verfremdung* is often deliberately mistranslated as 'the alienation effect' or 'the distancing effect' due to the lack of an accurate English equivalent of the German word. This translation will be used here along with another term – the V-effect.

these experiments measured according to the reaction of the audience. Brecht once wrote that the effectiveness of theatre lies in its capacity to lead people into believing that they too can act upon their reflections and actively participate in the process of change as '[t]he present-day world can only be described to present-day people if it is described as capable of transformation' (2001, 274).

Brecht's and Mnouchkine's socialist ideals are clearly visible in their working methods. Opposed to bourgeois domination, state despotism and the fascist idea of the personality cult, they support an even redistribution of power among the members of the troupe – *la création collective* (the collective creation). The political significance of this concept was particularly critical for Brecht, to whom it was clear that collectivism must be reborn after it was destroyed by fascism. The concept of an omniscient director is therefore eliminated from his works. Performances are a result of members' collaboration, discussions and conflicts. There is no hierarchy, every member of the troupe is encouraged to share her or his ideas and thus becomes a source of knowledge for the others. Therefore, such an approach does not only favour an egalitarian mode of creation but is also beneficial due to its didactic value. Mnouchkine describes the method of collective creation this way: 'They know that they must watch. They know that it is valuable for them to watch the others. To watch the others properly' (Kiernander 1993, 15). Collective creation is as beneficial to the performers as it is to the audience. By empowering the actors and by letting them have an impact on their work, spectators are led to believe that they too can have a say in their community and thus influence the process of change.

Developed by Brecht, collective creation as a means of extracting performers' creativity is a perfect tool for experimentation – it is also the approach favoured by Mnouchkine. Actors are encouraged to make contributions at any stage of the production, even during an actual performance. There is therefore no single formula for a successful performance because it constantly evolves due to improvisation. Since they usually cannot predict the final outcome of their work, the Théâtre du Soleil performers often refer to their acting as 'a journey into the unknown' (Kiernander 1993, 22). The idea of change is engraved into the three-year long evolution of the play *1789*, just as it is inherent in the course of history.

The use of collective creation techniques is only one way of showing the audience their potential to provoke social change. More importantly, both Brecht and the Théâtre du Soleil attempt to awaken the spectators' critical thinking, which they see as a more direct incentive to action. Brecht, and subsequently Mnouchkine, wanted their audiences to produce logically-deduced judgements on presented ideas and to subsequently act upon them. In order to pursue this project, new performative devices became necessary. Brecht and Mnouchkine could no longer rely on traditional theatre forms, too often faithful to the Aristotelian concept of the catharsis. Their refusal to comply with the device of the *Ausbruch*[2] can be explained by its tendency to hypnotise the audience and thus weaken their logical reasoning abilities. Brecht himself was, for instance, opposed to the concept of traditional opera, which makes wide use of the technique. Yet he collaborated with the socialist composer Kurt Weill to produce an opera, its distinction lying in their attempt to challenge the very concept of theatre while simultaneously offering a critique of the capitalist system. Music is therefore not used to provoke a purely emotional response, which is one of the objectives of bourgeois theatre. Instead, it is meant to create emotional detachment.

---

[2]'The sudden, devastating cry from the depth of the soul that in their terms constituted the climactic moments of drama' (Esslin 1990, 137).

This way it acts as a tool for educating the audience and encouraging them to question the reality they live in. This is also achieved through the use of *gestus* – a way of presenting social interactions between contradictory characters and allowing the audience to critically assess their behaviour and choose the right attitude. Such an approach appeals to Mnouchkine, who aims to educate more than she seeks to entertain.

Another way in which both directors challenge the notion of traditional theatre is by refusing any kind of expressionist devices which they perceive to be irrelevant to their aims; dramatic theatre does not appeal to them. They are, equally, against the other end of the stylistic spectrum – naturalism. According to Mnouchkine, imitating reality 'turns actors into living pieces of furniture' (Kiernander 1993, 26). A naturalistic approach encourages observation rather than critical inquiry on the part of the audience. Reproducing the status quo creates the impression of an inescapable reality and does not leave any room for potential change. Illusion, which leaves the spectator passive, is therefore renounced. In pursuit of the awakening of the audience's critical thinking, Brecht's most influential device – the *Verfremdung* effect – comes into play.

Before answering the question of how the V-effect is adapted by the Théâtre du Soleil, it is necessary to focus on its original meaning, as devised by Brecht. Its main principle is the process of creating distance between the characters and the audience, the distance being not physical but emotional. The audience move away from the inner reality of the play; they do not suspend their disbelief. They must be aware of the distinction between their reality and the reality of the play. Martin Esslin calls the V-effect 'non-emphatic distancing' (1990, 140). The consciousness of the spectator renders her or him capable of passing objective, unbiased judgement on presented problems. Brecht was not the first to employ the technique – it was previously used by East Asian, Indian and Elizabethan theatre. However, his application of it within a European context may be seen as revolutionary. Not only did he detach his audience from the events presented, but he also encouraged them to act upon their reflections. The success of the V-effect depends on the synchronisation of various theatrical devices.

The process is evident in the techniques employed by the Théâtre du Soleil. Mnouchkine's choice of a historical setting for the play is the first aspect of the V-effect, as one of the most important Brechtian influences on the production of *1789* is the idea of historical distancing. By contradicting the concepts of timelessness and universalism perpetuated in bourgeois theatre, Brecht presented history as a closed chapter to which public access was denied. Revolutionary personages from Mnouchkine's play guard their historical reality by making sure that the audience is not immersed in it by identifying with the characters. Watching historical events from a temporally conscious perspective allows the spectator to adapt a critical approach. The characters' reality is analysed by the audience and the consequences of this analysis applied to their political outlook.

The task of the actor in Mnouchkine's theatre is to facilitate the transformation of a humble spectator into an active participant. The Théâtre du Soleil actor stands in opposition to the dramatic actor. Here, the performer is more of a craftsman who presents his skill and knowledge. Inspired by cabaret and circus performances, Brecht writes that 'the beauty of nature is a quality which gives the human senses an opportunity to show skill' (Hauptmann 1967, 645–6). The actor's constant self-observation, later defined and described by Barthes,[3] shows him as aware of a permanent subjection to judgement.

---

[3] In *The Death of the Author*.

This internal detachment of the actor is also visible in his alienation from the character played, which can be observed in the chapter entitled *Le Lit de Justice* (*The Bed of Justice*): '*Le bateleur se moque de son propre personnage en le rendant larmoyant, suppliant et dérisoire*' (The juggler ridicules his own character making him look tearful, wishful and pathetic), or: '*Le bateleur qui va jouer ce rôle [...] se présente en ironisant sur son personnage*' (The juggler who is going to play this part [...] introduces himself and makes ironic comments concerning his character) (Théâtre du Soleil 1971, 18–19).[4] The separation between the personage and the craftsman who masters it is clear. Mnouchkine's actors create characters, who are not a given, but who appear in the intellectual space between the performer and their audience. It is left to the spectator to read these characters.

This technique of acting can be defined in opposition to realistic presentation. Mnouchkine says that 'for a long time Europeans have not represented anything. Europeans present everything' (Kiernander 1993, 89). She wants therefore to exercise the art of the parable, to present ideas rather than people and events. The presence of the Brechtian concept of *gestus* is clearly visible here. Mnouchkine adapts it by juxtaposing contradictory social situations and relying on the capacity of the audience to read between the lines and to identify, by means of logical reasoning, the behaviour that she means to represent. This is the case during the performance of the chapter *La Réunion des États Généraux* (*The Meeting of The Estates-General*), when actors use marionettes to present in a mocking fashion the pre-Revolution class conflict.

To intensify the effect of detachment by further convincing the audience that they are merely watching a play, all processes, which normally belong behind the scenes, become visible: props are carried around during the performance, actors dress and put make-up on in front of the spectators' eyes: '*pendant le discours du roi, l'autre bateleur maquille son compagnon qui va jouer Mirabeau*' (during the king's speech, the other juggler does the make-up of his fellow actor who is going to play Mirabeau) (TdS 1971, 18). What is more, Mnouchkine introduces third-person narration to her performances. As a consequence, the audience not only watches the actors but is also told what is being presented.

The reality of the play no longer belongs to the present, but to the past – through the use of verbs conjugated in the past historic – and the future – when Crieur, Conteur and Presentateur announce the stage directions and describe what is about to happen before it is acted out: '*Mesdames et Messieurs, nous allons vous jouer la célèbre comédie: La réunion des États-Généraux*' (Ladies and gentlemen, we are going to perform in front of you the famous comedy: The Meeting of the Estates-General) (TdS 1971, 14). Chapelier, following Presentateur, says: '*Et maintenant, mesdames et messieurs, vous allez assister à un authentique débat parlementaire sur la question des droits de l'homme et du citoyen*' (And now, ladies and gentlemen, you are going to witness an authentic parliamentary debate on the issue of the rights of man and of the citizen) (TdS 1971, 34). The audience is not only presented with the content of these scenes, but also their emotional aspect – the jugglers say: '*c'est cette colère que nous allons jouer*' (it is this anger that we are going to perform) and '*nous allons vous jouer dans le mode barbaresque "le roi aux deux visages"*' (we are going to perform in front of you in a Barbary fashion 'the two-faced king') (TdS 1971, 18, 20).

---

[4] All extracts from the play have been translated by myself. Further references to this edition of the play are given as 'TdS' within the body of the text.

This is aptly described by John Willett as 'quoting the character played' (2001, 94). By addressing the audience directly, the actor engages in a dialogue regarding the character that he plays. A close relationship is established between the performer and the spectator. One can recognise here the influence of environmental theatre, which favours the rapprochement of actors and audiences. The *1789* performers make full use of this device. The scene of the parliamentary debate engages the spectators in a discussion by transforming the theatre space into an arena for democratic participation. One of the *députés castellanes* (Castillian delegates) acknowledges the close link between the people in the theatre hall when he says: '*Je suis certain que la majorité de ceux qui m'écoutent pensera comme moi*' (I am convinced that the majority of those listening to me will agree with me) (TdS 1971, 36). By recognising the presence and the active involvement of the audience, the actor makes them aware of their political potential and encourages them to participate in the life of their community or their country, and to have their personal input into the process of change.

The V-effect is not only achieved through acting techniques; it is equally visible in the physical structure of the play. The structural fragmentation and discontinuity of the performance allows the spectators to see presented problems clearly and logically, preventing them from suspending their disbelief. Brecht writes:

> As we cannot invite the audience to fling itself into the story as if it were a river and let itself be carried vaguely hither and thither, the individual episodes have to be knotted together in such a way that the knots are easily noticed. The episodes must not succeed one another indistinguishably but must give us a chance to interpose our judgement.
>
> (2001, 201)

The fragmented character of *1789* is clearly visible through the presence of its distinguishable parts. Similarly, consecutive scenes in Mnouchkine's play are not logically connected. Each of them is a separate chapter that must be appreciated as an individual entity. The idea of giving names to scenes in *1789* conveys a strong Brechtian influence, as during the staging of some of his plays, titles and numbers of scenes were projected onto screens at the back of the stage. Mnouchkine also uses music which is incompatible with the atmosphere of presented events in order to mark this discontinuity. The aim of such devices is to challenge the bourgeois tendency to perform plays in a smooth and hypnotic way. Thus, the audience are constantly reminded that what they are watching is merely a staged act, which can be seen in Bateleur-Magicien's words: '*Si vous le voulez bien, nous allons laisser là l'imaginaire et revenir à notre réalité!*' (If you wish, we are going to leave the imaginary world behind and go back to our reality) (TdS 1971, 21).

The source of Brecht's penchant for the technique of fragmentation can be found in the Dada movement, which flourished in the years following World War I. This aesthetic style favoured the spontaneous combining of arbitrary elements rather than harmony. Brecht's preference for multiplication is clear in his reproach to film: 'the camera gives us only one eye' (Van Dijk 1990, 126). He used, therefore, what Franco Ruffini calls 'vertical montage' (1986, 33), which involved operating on several different levels of fiction simultaneously. Mnouchkine builds on this technique in *1789* by the use of *mise en abîme* and thus develops her own distinctive style. Actors play fairground performers, who, in turn, play participants of the Revolution. Another example of theatre-within-theatre in her play is the appearance of actors of the Comédie-Française who are in fact actors of the Théâtre du Soleil performing the roles of actors of

Comédie-Française. Levels of characterisation are multiplied; theatrical space is also subject to multiplication. Actors appear and disappear from different spots in the audience: 'Un homme sort de la foule, il porte dans ses bras une jeune fille évanouie' (A man comes out of the crowd holding in his arms a young girl, who has just fainted) (TdS 1971, 32). During the performance they remain both at the centre and at the periphery of events. Mnouchkine achieves this effect by the use of *tréteaux* (multiple platforms located around the theatre hall). As a consequence, the spectators' gaze is directed at a subject of their choice. They are even verbally encouraged to move around the theatre space: '*les spectateurs debout sont invites à se déplacer librement tandis que ceux qui souhaitent plus de confort peuvent s'asseoir sur des gradins*' (The standing audience are invited to circulate freely whilst those wishing to be more comfortable can sit down on the steps) (TdS 1971, 7). Due to the availability of this choice, they become aware of their potential to choose their perspective (here physical, but elsewhere political) and to play an active part in the life of their community.

The idea of change is inherent to Ariane Mnouchkine's artistic creation. According to the philosophy embraced by her Théâtre du Soleil, changing the world should start with the challenging of traditional theatrical techniques established over the centuries. The ideal consequence of this would be rendering theatre-going a more popular activity and engraving a political message into theatre performances. By means of the Brechtian revolutionary concept of *gestus* the actor of the Théâtre du Soleil speaks to the audience and establishes a dialogue, which would have been unacceptable in bourgeois theatre. The purpose of this dialogue is paradoxically not to immerse the audience in the inner reality of the play, but the opposite – to keep them behind an imaginary wall of reason. Eliminating the distance between the stage and the audience serves therefore not to invite the spectator to a fictional world but to encourage them to reflect upon presented events. This makes the audience aware of their potential to participate in the real social and political world. *Gestus* became for Mnouchkine a basic pattern which enabled her to develop other concepts such as theatre for the people and collective creation – all this to achieve greater audience participation. All of these strategies, developed by Brecht but later adapted by Mnouchkine, are a reflection of the peculiar character of the Théâtre du Soleil. They are marked by a strong Brechtian influence but their originality cannot be denied. Brecht is indeed a vision – an ideology to which Mnouchkine added her original technical elements. Calling Mnouchkine a Brechtian paradigm seems therefore to be an oversimplification.

Mnouchkine was not spared criticism even from within her own troupe. Her intention to give the masses an interest in theatre undeniably deserves acclaim. In the spirit of May 1968, the transformation of working conditions should be accompanied by the widening of access of the working class to lifestyle choices traditionally associated with upper classes. However, the insignificant working class participation in the performances of the Théâtre du Soleil suggests that her impact on the central problem of the exclusive character of theatre has been overestimated. What is more, the very concept of *création collective* has also been put into question. In the article 'Ariane Mnouchkine: démiurge et tyran' Philippe Léotard, a member of the Théâtre du Soleil, states:

> One must not be utopian. If there has been a small collectivist phenomenon at the Théâtre du Soleil it is due to the authority, to the tyranny even, of Ariane. [...] If we had wanted to direct collectively we would still be in the process of thinking about our first production, and we would never have got around to performing.
>
> (Salino 1981)

Mnouchkine developed some of the most important concepts that have since transformed theatre. Her own influence is undeniable. The Brechtian influences, rather than overshadowing her genius, added to it and improved the overall appearance of her work. Despite Léotard's criticism, the work of the French director, regardless of its overall social impact, should be seen as a significant step on the way to permanently changing the face of theatre. Since change is continuous, the audience should be full of hope for the future as others see Mnouchkine as an inspiration for their work, just as she viewed Brecht when adapting his techniques to her original work.

REFERENCES

Brecht, Bertolt. *Bertolt Brecht: Collected Plays*. Trans. and eds. John Willett and Ralph Manheim. London: Methuen, 1970.

———. *Brecht on Theatre: The Development of an Aesthetic*. Trans. and ed. John Willett. London: Methuen, 2001.

———. *Brecht on Theatre: The Development of an Aesthetic*. Trans. and ed. John Willett. London: Methuen, 1978.

Dijk, Maarten van, 'Blocking Brecht', *Re-Interpreting Brecht: His Influence on Contemporary Drama and Film*. Eds. Pia Kleber and Colin Visser. Cambridge: Cambridge University Press, 1990. 117–134.

Dort, Bernard, 'Crossing the Desert: Brecht in France in the Eighties', Trans. Colin Visser. *Re- Interpreting Brecht: His Influence on Contemporary Drama and Film*. Eds. Pia Kleber and Colin Visser. Cambridge: Cambridge University Press, 1990. 90–103.

Esslin, Martin, 'Some Reflections on Brecht and Acting', *Re-Interpreting Brecht: His Influence on Contemporary Drama and Film*. Eds. Pia Kleber and Colin Visser. Cambridge: Cambridge University Press, 1990. 135–146.

Hauptmann, Elissabeth, ed. *Gesammelte Werke*. Frankfurt-on-Main: Suhrkamp Verlag, 1967.

Kiernander, Adrian. *Ariane Mnouchkine and the Théâtre du Soleil*. Cambridge: Cambridge University Press, 1993.

Ruffini, Franco, 'Horizontal and Vertical Montage in the Theatre', *New Theatre Quarterly*, 11.5 (Feb. 1986): 29–37.

Salino, Brigitte, 'Ariane Mnouchkine: démiurge et tyran', *Les Nouvelles Littéraires*, 10 December 1981.

Singleton, Brian, 'Ariane Mnouchkine: Activism, Formalism and Cosmopolitanism', *Contemporary European Theatre Directors*. London: Routledge, 2010.

Théâtre du Soleil. 1789: *La révolution doit s'arrêter à la perfection du bonheur*. Paris: Stock, 1971.

Williams, David, ed. *Collaborative Theatre: The Theatre du Soleil Sourcebook*. London: Routledge, 1999.

Asia

Asia

CHAPTER TWENTY-FOUR

Brecht's East Asia: A Conspectus

ANTONY TATLOW

A wrap-up is supposed to draw everything together.[1] In my experience, that usually misfires. Anyone left out is offended, everyone mentioned feels misunderstood. I will try something different, more like unpacking: topics not explored, misunderstandings not clarified, futures not addressed. I will stay with Brecht's East Asia, with discussions I had and the pre-postdramatic stress disorder productions I saw by people I knew.

But first, to an event outside our remit: the 2008 King's College Cambridge *Festival of Nine Lessons & Carols*. Brecht was part of it, not one of the lessons, but in Dominic Muldowney's setting of his poem 'Maria' (1922).[2] In Asia he is almost exclusively a dramatist, so listen to this Christmas Carol text:

> The night when she first gave birth
> Had been cold. But in later years
> She quite forgot
> The frost in the dingy beams and the smoking stove
> And the spasms of the afterbirth towards morning.
> But above all she forgot the bitter shame
> Common among the poor
> Of having no privacy.
> That was the main reason
> Why in later years it became a holiday for all
> To take part in.
> The shepherds' coarse chatter fell silent.
> Later they turned into the Kings of the story.
> The wind, which was very cold
> Turned into the singing of angels.
> Of the hole in the roof that let in the frost nothing remained
> But the star that looked through it.

Antony Tatlow, 'Brecht's East Asia', *Brecht Yearbook*, 36 (2011), pp. 353–68.

[1] Invited to 'wrap-up' the International Brecht Society's 13th Symposium in Honolulu 2010, I here retain the direct address of that event.
[2] Bertolt Brecht, *Werke: Große kommentierte Berliner und Frankfurter Ausgabe*, Vol. 13, ed. Werner Hecht et al. (Berlin, Frankfurt/Main: Aufbau and Suhrkamp, 1987–2000), p. 243.

> All this was due to the vision of her son, who was easy
> Fond of singing
> Surrounded himself with poor folk
> And was in the habit of mixing with kings
> And of seeing a star above his head at night-time.[3]

Thousands heard this on the BBC World Service and TV. In *Christmas Legend* (1923)[4] it's the voice of the social unconscious, which permeates his work: 'Come in dear wind and be our guest / You too have neither home nor rest.'

There's a special charge in this writing. Philosophers have called Brecht 'a philosopher among the poets', even that 'daring poet-philosopher' Friedrich Nietzsche dreamt of.[5] Distrusting abstractions, Brecht was attracted to practical Chinese thought, in the spirit of Wang Yangming's saying: 'Knowledge is the beginning of action and action the completion of knowledge.'[6] Knowledge is only acquired through practice. If action fails, what does that say about your knowledge?

The 1968-generation idolized Brecht, but their faith in the political efficacy of his work diminished when the social system did not collapse. Three responses were possible: abandon, situate, and/or re-read it. The Heirs forbade deviations from their view of his intention. Rehearsing *The Threepenny Opera* in the Berliner Ensemble, Dario Fo heard a voice in the stalls: 'But where is Papa's text?' Pretending to throw it over his shoulder, he replied: 'Papa's text?' They fired him. Productions beyond Europe and America were not beholden to this writ.

The narrowly interpreted plays, hardly performable in Germany, have a certain cachet elsewhere. The poetry still astonishes. His innovative dramatic theory was faithfully misunderstood. Brecht's views on language – for example, *Fetischismus der Begriffe* – scarcely registered.[7] Some re-reading fantasizes, like Stephan Bock's onomantic, kabbalistic chinoiserie, in which *The Good Person of Szechwan* encodes virtually all East Asian culture and the future of international theater. But productive re-reading must uncover a neglected responsibility *in* the text.

Brecht read the *Daodejing* in 1920. His work reached Japan in 1932. The dancer Ito Michio's younger brother, Ito Kunio (1904–1994), returned from Berlin in 1931, where he had seen *Man is Man* and *The Measures Taken* as well as *The Threepenny Opera*. After seeing Alexander Tairow's Moscow production on the way home, he thought he could do better.[8] Said to have constructed the text from memory, he told me he had G. W. Pabst's film scenario. Playing Macheath, he called it *Beggars' Theater*, set in Tokyo at the start of

---

[3] Bertolt Brecht, *Poems 1913–1956*, Michael Hamburger, trans. (London: Methuen, 1976), p. 98, modified.
[4] BFA 13, p. 271.
[5] The first comment I heard from Gerd Irrlitz, Humboldt University Professor of Philosophy, during a Berlin Seminar. The second is by Wolfgang Fritz Haug, Free University, Berlin Professor of Philosophy and editor of the *Historical-Critical Marxism Dictionary*, in Wolfgang Fritz Haug, ed., *Philosophieren mit Brecht und Gramsci* (Berlin: Argument Verlag, 1966), p. 10. The quotation comes from Friedrich Nietzsche, *Sämtliche Werke. Kritische Studien-Ausgabe*, Vol. 12 (Berlin: de Gruyter, 1988), p. 240.
[6] Wing-Tsit Chan, comp. and trans., *A Source Book in Chinese Philosophy* (Princeton: Princeton University Press, 1963), pp. 669–670.
[7] BFA 21, pp. 761–762.
[8] Koreya Senda, *Wanderjahre* (Berlin: Henschelverlag, 1985), p. 145. In 1930 *Drums in the Night* was translated, see Antony Tatlow and Tak-Wai Wong, eds., *Brecht and East Asian Theatre* (Hong Kong: Hong Kong University Press, 1982), p. 111.

Meiji Era. The artist's name he took describes him: Senda Korea. Koreans were blamed for causing the 1923 earthquake. Mistaken for one, he was chased and beaten up in Sendagaya, a district of Tokyo.

After prison and the War, Senda, helped by Iwabuchi Tatsuji, performed and published virtually all of Brecht, the outstanding Asian achievement. His model productions provoked the experimental 'Black Tent' reaction, but I found some among the very best: his 1980 *Caucasian Chalk Circle*, and *The Good Person of Szechwan* in 1986 with Komaki Kurihara's subtle narrative acting and credible *doubleness* of voice, speaking *through* – not instead of – the other self, interweaving – not separating – identities, as no Western production I've seen ever quite managed.

Huang Zuolin's six-hour lecture introduced Brecht to China in 1951. Stimulated by Senda, his 1959 anti-war *Mother Courage* in Shanghai 'failed', he told me, after eleven performances, though I don't really believe in failure. Many left, but Ba Jin stayed to the end.[9] But *Life of Galileo*, staged with Chen Rong en suite for six weeks in 1979, sold out in the large China Youth Arts Theater in Beijing, now symptomatically replaced by a larger shopping mall. This was the longest run of any Western play, translated by Ding Yangzhong on paper given him to write his confession in detention during the Cultural Revolution. When a prelate waved his little black book, everyone knew what was meant.

Brecht was seriously discussed in China in the early 1980s, just as German directors abandoned him. They said the problem was not the model, which could be changed, but the figures, who can't. They were too constructed and can't be questioned.[10] That became the default response. Roland Barthes linked Brecht's social gestus with Denis Diderot's tableau, as an ideal meaning is 'contained under a single point of view'.[11] However, Jean-Paul Sartre suggested a more striking analogy in the 1950s. He argued that Brecht's plays were like Jean Racine's, not on account of a comparable distancing but, as its consequence, of the reverse, namely a more intense engagement between audience and characters, for 'we find ourselves in them without diminishing our stupefaction'.[12] Brecht's audience was like a group of ethnographers approaching a foreign tribe, and exclaiming in astonishment: 'those savages, that's us!'[13]

---

[9]Forced to kneel on broken glass during the Cultural Revolution, Ba Jin cried out to his tormentors: 'No matter what you do to me, it will not change the truth.' When I met him in 1984 (22 October), he was most interested to hear about Brecht's painting by Gao Qipei.

[10]Jürgen Flimm said this to me in Cologne (8 September 1980). Likewise, Volker Hesse (Düsseldorf) told me he couldn't direct the late plays. *The Good Person of Szechwan* was unperformable (30 June 1984). Directing *The Caucasian Chalk Circle* in Singapore in 1989, Markwart Müller-Elmau (Ulm) spoke of Brecht's 'ideological puppet theater', whose final act must take place outside the theater. He put 'simplicity on stage'. His 'typified characters' particularly appealed to Asian actors and directors because they expect first of all 'clear unambiguous statements that do not require reading between the lines' (16 December 1989). For Peter von Becker, Brecht could *only* be performed in Asia, where the fairy-tale quality of his work could be realized. Von Becker, 'Wo Märchen wieder wahr werden', *Theater Heute* 2 (1987): pp. 15–19.

[11]Roland Barthes, 'Diderot, Brecht, Eisenstein', in Roland Barthes, *Image, Music, Text* (London: Fontana, 1977), p. 71.

[12]Jean-Paul Sartre, 'Brecht et les classiques', in Jean-Paul Sartre, *Un théâtre de situations* (Paris: Gallimard, 1973), pp. 90–91. This first appeared in a brochure, 'Hommage international à Bertolt Brecht', in April 1957 in a programme of the *Théâtre des Nations* for which the Berliner Ensemble performed *Life of Galileo* and *Mother Courage*.

[13]Ibid., p. 110.

The audience then *produces itself*, if shocked into an auto-ethnographic experience more complex than either current extreme, scientific certainty or empathetic identification, can furnish since both, though differently, inhibit self-examination. Without some empathy – 'that's us' – there is no impulse to question the self. But only then do we realize that 'we are victims and accomplices at the same time'.[14]

In 1941 Brecht described the traps within two instrumentalizing social theories: Behaviorism and Marxism. If Behaviorism encouraged the subject to believe in its freedom to choose between material goods, Marxism justified political control, because the ultimate subject of history was still creating the conditions for an as yet imperfectly realized universal freedom. He remarked: 'the demolition, explosion, atomization of the individual psyche is a fact, so it's not a false, conventional observation if one discerns in individuals a strange lack of center. But lack of center does not mean lack of substance.'[15]

We think of substance as centering, so what does this unusual distinction imply? The most quoted line of modern German poetry – 'Erst kommt das Fressen, dann kommt die Moral' (Food comes first, then comes morality) – echoes Alfred Forke's paraphrase of Mencius (Mengzi).[16]

Mengzi distinguished between a *desire* for action and the possibility of *realizing* it. Conditions permitting, ordinary people will do what is right. So it is incumbent upon the ruler to create those conditions. He discusses this situational morality in the vivid anecdotal manner Brecht admired. A philosopher says 'man's nature is indifferent to good and evil, just as water is indifferent to east and west'. Mengzi replies it is not indifferent to up and down. If you use force, water will go uphill, and when men do what is not good, their nature is treated in this way.[17]

That is perhaps one source, though not the only basis, for the distinction between absence of center and presence of substance. Here substance is the precipitate of desire, a somatically discernible psychological phenomenon and moral possibility, at times only visible by its absence, in depression and, sometimes, in rage. It can't create the world to its liking. Centerlessness is the lack of focus or ability, not just a matter of individual choice, to realize what is substantial. That this can be achieved by an exercise of will, or by declaring it should be so, is the illusion of every orthodox moral system, philosophical or religious, Eastern or Western, as it was the illusory hope of the expressionists in Brecht's generation.[18] In Erich Fromm's analytic social psychology, necessary conformity to *social character* also forms the *social unconscious*, the repository of unrealized substantial

---

[14]Ibid., p. 91.

[15]BFA 26, p. 476.

[16]'Hunger und Durst ... sind Feinde jeder Moral.' Alfred Forke, *Geschichte der alten chinesischen Philosophie* (Hamburg: Kommissionsverlag L. Friederichsen & Co., 1927), p. 212. Brecht had this book as well as Richard Wilhelm's Mencius translation, Richard Wilhelm, *Mong Dsi* (Jena: Eugen Dietrichs, 1916).

[17]See James Legge, *The Chinese Classics*, Vol. 2 (Hong Kong: University of Hong Kong Press, 1960), pp. 395–396. This theme recurs in Brecht's writing. See Antony Tatlow, *The Mask of Evil* (Bern, Frankfurt/Main, Las Vegas: Peter Lang, 1977), pp. 469–475.

[18]The questions raised by this distinction between 'substance' and 'center' occur throughout Brecht's work. Their formulation depends on the socio-political context. A later version of this dilemma appears around 1945, connected with an unfinished poem, 'Lehrgedicht von der Natur der Menschen', itself related to *De rerum natura* by Lucretius: 'So auch der tapfere Mensch ist nicht ganz tapfer: manchmal versagt er. / In ihm liegt Feigheit und Mut und der Mut triumphiert, doch nicht immer. / Und wenn er einmal versagt, dann listet ihn nicht bei den Feigen' (BFA 15, p. 172).

desire, hence the divergence between 'substance' and 'center', as Chinese social and moral philosophy supposed.[19]

Brecht avoided the language of psychoanalysis. Emotions are deemed distractions from the main event: we should rather watch what the characters do, or what is done to them. But marginalizing, or decentering, the emotions increases their force. Any putative rejection of psychology needs situating. Brecht refused ego-psychology, not the unconscious, which is pivotal to his work. When asking in 1938 whether he really wanted 'to do away with the space where the unconscious, half conscious, uncontrolled, ambiguous, multipurposed could play itself out' the unstated answer is obviously: No![20]

Ego-psychology encourages the individual to accept normative social character. But if society has gone mad, deviation may signify sanity. An assumed normalization operates well in a naturalist aesthetic, *even* where the audience sympathizes with the resisting character, since the *frame* of normality remains unquestioned. Turning away from naturalism or forestalling empathy in order to inhibit identification seems to de-psychologize and thereby to de-*problematize* the subject. But the reverse is true.

Because de-psychologizing *re*-problematizes the subject, since it creates the conditions for formulating a halfway adequate theory of subjectivity upon the stage. The audience are not confirmed in their possession of a *certain* truth or, alternatively, justified in its rejection, but must rather question the relationship between ego and other, self and certainty, practice and theory, and confront the problematic nature of their *own* identity. This is what energizes Brecht's theater.[21]

It does not, of course, reject emotions, but enquires into their origin. It abandons an emotional style, since identificatory presuppositions determine the response. In anthropological distancing, strangers estrange us from ourselves. If not somehow distanced, they offer psychological escape through an empathy, which *appears* to share their burden, but in reality amounts to self-exculpation, sustaining a repression, as we project onto others what we hide from ourselves. The moment we 'identify' with them, secretly pleased by our own sensitivity, we paradoxically both lose our self and sever ourselves from them. We effectively scapegoat them and they suffer for us. Then the actual *inter*relationship between audience and character, reader and read, remains opaque.

Brecht did not always manage to inhibit this escape. One reason may have been a way of talking about *the* alienation effect. Singularized, it created the expectation of a recognizable method, an applicable technique, enabling the audience to see through whatever estrangement has singled out for observation. Not only Barthes equated this with a correct perspective. Simplifications are easier to remember.

But estranging may have divergent consequences. All estrangements depend on realizing that, for whatever reason, a conventional response is no longer adequate. An imperfectly known reveals a lack of understanding, which lies either inside or outside us. Separating them distinguishes between alienating to clarify and explain, or to question and explore. Either ignorance is replaced by knowledge, or superficial understanding points to a deeper

---

[19]Erich Fromm, *The Erich Fromm Reader*, ed. Rainer Funk (New Jersey: Humanities Press, 1994), p. 9; originally in Erich Fromm, *The Crisis of Psychoanalysis* (New York: Henry Holt, 1955).
[20]BFA 22/1, p. 468.
[21]Anyone doubting that Brecht's theater is still equated with the rationalizations of an instructional style, might look at some responses during the Brecht Centennial. See *Brecht 100 <=> 2000, The Brecht Yearbook* 24 (1999): pp. 1–3.

ignorance. One offers knowledge, the other confronts us with uncertainty. Theory either explains estrangement, or estrangement reveals an insufficient theory. The effect of this distinction is far reaching, since the consequences are psychologically, epistemologically, and politically different.

The alienation effect is mostly equated with instruction. The other estrangement, less discussed, or even discounted, perhaps because 'self'-questioning seems to turn towards the so-called 'Aristotelian' theater and needless self-preoccupation, offers nothing instructional, and draws us into a more troubling analysis. If we recognize our doubleness as victim and accomplice, we both participate and separate from ourselves. What matters is to interrupt any *self-retraction* or, as Brecht remarked, the audience's tendency to believe in its *own* indestructibility, to assume 'this could never happen to me'.[22] The solution for what looks like a dilemma – to both identify and not identify – is not to simplify but to complicate the figure. The emphasis is not on the certainty of the observed but on awakening uncertainty in the observer. What matters is not that the character learns, and we too should mark and inwardly digest this, but that 'the spectator should see', or confront his own repressions.[23]

Brecht became an expert in counter-discourses: philosophical, ethical, political, psychological, metaphorical, linguistic, and dramaturgical. Not only East Asia helped formulate them, but there are numerous echoes. The less proof positivist for such echoes, the more interesting they are. Herr Keuner remarks: whoever boasts of writing long books all by themselves has lost the mental ability of Zhuangzi, nine-tenths of whom consists of quotations.[24] We have heard the *ethical* counter-discourse in *The Threepenny Opera*, mediating Mencius, and the *psychological* counter-discourse about substance and center.

Brecht's early diaries allude to Chinese thought: 'A Chinese sentence: If the grains of sand turn against people, people must go away' (September 1920).[25] The encounter with Laozi occurred in the same month. Richard Wilhelm's translation adjusted the *Daodejing* to salvationist expectations, even including the forgiveness of sins.[26] Unlike Alfred Döblin or Klabund, Brecht reflected none of this. A comment in July 1921 suggests how he then read it: 'I am too lazy for childish battles and too Asiatic to perish at the stake for truth.'[27] His central metaphor, the flux of things, feeds on this Daoist tributary, on Nietzsche and, later, on Karl Marx's 'flow of movement'.[28] Daoism expresses the Chinese social unconscious, A *pro memoria* note I found in the Archives interprets this *integrative* metaphor from Heraclitus to Marx: 'their teaching of the flow of things / not just that

---

[22]BFA 25, p. 241.
[23]BFA 24, p. 264.
[24]BFA 18, p. 441.
[25]BFA 26, p. 167.
[26]Laotse, *Tao Te King. Das Buch vom Sinn und Leben* (München: Eugen Dietrichs Verlag, 1996), p. 105.
[27]BFA 26, p. 232.
[28]'In ihrer mystifizierten Form ward die Dialektik deutsche Mode, weil sie das Bestehende zu verklären schien. In ihrer rationalen Gestalt ist sie dem Bürgertum und seinen doktrinären Wortführern ein Ärgernis und ein Greuel, weil sie in dem positiven Verständnis des Bestehenden zugleich auch das Verständnis seiner Negation, seines notwendigen Untergangs einschließt, jede gewordene Form im Flusse der Bewegung, also auch nach ihrer vergänglichen Seite auffasst, sich durch nichts imponieren lässt, ihrem Wesen nach kritisch und revolutionär ist.' Karl Marx, Friedrich Engels, *Werke* (Berlin: Dietz Verlag, 1972), p. 28, dated 24 January 1873 in the *Afterword* to the 2nd edition of *Das Kapital*.

everything flows / but how it flows / and can be made to flow.'[29] In his Laotse poem hope is possible when it appears least justified. The Dao and Marxist thought, far from opposing each other, in fact interpenetrate.

The *philosophical* counter-discourse stretches across cultures, theories and religions and though the object of attention changes, there are constants in the questioning. Brecht complains in 1929 about 'world systematizers', who pretend to conduct their politics entirely for the working classes: when they 'refer to the proletariat, it's only customer service'. His German words now sound impeccably Neu-Deutsch: 'Dass diese Weltbildhauer sich auf das Proletariat berufen, das ist nur Service (Kundendienst).'[30] He adds: 'There are some people who are suspected of only wanting to make revolution in order to bring about dialectical materialism.' In other words, they are idealists without regard for real people or practical consequences. At the time he was reading Mozi (Me Ti), a contemporary of Socrates, who furnished his Me-ti persona and says virtually the same about the Confucian scholars.[31]

Brecht's Me-ti was 'against constructing too complete images of the world'.[32] Transferred into *aesthetic* counter-discourse, this explains his admiration for Chinese painting, whose empty spaces remind us of nature's irreducibility, never submitting everything to one single point of view or accomplishing 'the thorough subjugation of the viewer'.[33] 'This order', he remarked, 'requires no force'. The same attitude guides in 1955 his *critical* response, another counter-discourse, to Ernst Schumacher's reading of the early plays. Brecht tells him: 'You could drop some evaluations and instead leave some questions open. That's always productive. Why put everything into one category, even if it's the most attractive?'[34]

In his study, Brecht hung two pictures of Confucius.[35] We shouldn't sentimentalize this, for the respected teacher served as a warning that you may cease to learn. V. I. Lenin argued that matter is independent of consciousness, and historical materialism independent of social consciousness.[36] Josef Stalin administered this as 'revolution from above'. Brecht invokes the silence of Buddha, who refused metaphysical disputes with his students about the nature of nirvana instead of getting out of the burning house.[37] Buddhism criticized the effect of concepts, and anti-essentialism links Brecht with a philosophy of practice: 'The theory of knowledge must above all be a critique of language', and 'philosophy should be more concerned with the language of people than with the language of philosophers'.[38] That could be Ludwig Wittgenstein. Brecht pasted

---

[29]Bertolt Brecht Archiv (BBA) 328/10.
[30]BFA 21, p. 349.
[31]*Mê Ti des Sozialethikers und seiner Schüler philosophische Werke*, Alfred Forke, trans. (Berlin: Kommissionsverlag der Vereinigung wissenschaftlicher Verleger, 1922).
[32]BFA 18, p. 60.
[33]BFA 22, pp. 133–134.
[34]BFA 30, p. 329.
[35]The text above one of these portraits reads: xiān shī kǒng zǐ xíng jiāo xiàng (a picture of the first teacher Confucius on his way to educate).
[36]V. I. Lenin, 'Materialism and Empirio-criticism', *Collected Works*, Vol. 14 (Moscow: Progress Publishers, 1968), p. 326.
[37]BFA 12, p. 36.
[38]BFA 21, pp. 413, 402.

a 'Song Guanyin Boddhisatva' opposite the title page of his own Lutheran Bible, turning its back on the written word, on absolutes and dreams of transcendence.[39]

The *metaphorical* counter-discourse in *Terzinen über die Liebe* (also called *Die Liebenden / The Lovers*, or *Song of the Cranes*)[40] rejects transcendence, and counters metaphysical longings with East Asian metaphors of life's flight through time.[41] Among the early *Psalms* are what one might call Schopenhauerian haiku.[42] Other poems remind critics of tanka, though I am more struck by the differences. A tanka version of *Die Maske des Bösen*[43] would imply everything in half as many words.[44] But when his Chinese poems differ from their source, they often resonate with the originals he did not know.[45]

As for dramaturgical counter-discourse, Brecht adopted Japanese and Chinese plots, and learnt from their acting. The evidence is incontrovertible, but there is disagreement about the consequences. Elizabeth Hauptmann told me he read Arthur Waley's Introduction to the *Noh* plays. Seami describes how representing a state or emotion involves its opposite, something Brecht also noted in Chinese technique. As Seami said: 'in matter there is also emptiness, in emptiness there is also matter.'[46] Due to this commonality, I called a section in *Brechts Ost Asien* 'Alienation Effects in Japanese Acting'. Of course they were very different, though there is a visual analogy in *Man is Man*, but he was stimulated by their practices.

Though it also looks, sounds, and seems different, Chinese theater had a conscious social component and sometimes even a political effect, and Brecht was also impressed by its aesthetic quality. Reading one through the other is perhaps not as unproductive as it may first seem to Western and Eastern scholars.[47] It is said that Chinese theater expresses a character's emotional life, which Brecht's actor critiques. Brecht says of Chinese acting:

> The performer's self-observation, an artful and artistic act of self-alienation, stopped the spectator from losing himself in the character completely, *i.e. to the point of giving up his own identity*, and lent a splendid remoteness to the events. *Yet the spectator's empathy was not entirely rejected.* The audience identifies itself with the actor as being an observer, and accordingly develops his attitude of observing or looking on.[48]

That Mei Lanfang demonstrated acting techniques is thought to explain why Brecht missed the full evocation of the character's emotions. Self-observation is considered more obviously a consequence of demonstration than of performance and it cannot be

---

[39]This figure is sometimes described as a water-moon type, gazing on the moon's reflection.
[40]BFA 14, p. 15.
[41]See Jan Knopf, *Brecht-Handbuch*, Vol. 2 (Stuttgart: Metzler Verlag, 2001), pp. 168–172.
[42]BFA 11, p. 30.
[43]BFA 12, p. 124.
[44]See Antony Tatlow, *Brechts Ost Asien* (Berlin: Parthas-Verlag, 1998), p. 36.
[45]Ibid., pp. 30–35.
[46]Ibid., pp. 17–22.
[47]For Min Tian, Brecht's response is an orientalizing imposition and an example of 'prescribed superiority'. Min Tian, '"Alienation-Effect" for Whom? Brecht's (Mis) interpretation of the Classical Chinese Theatre' *Asian Theatre Journal*, 14.2 (Fall 1997): pp. 200–222. Ronnie Bai gives a more differentiated reading, but stresses Brecht's words and not the practice that followed. He sets out to prove the sole impulse from Chinese theater. Ronnie Bai, 'Dances with Mei Lanfang: Brecht and the Alienation Effect', *Comparative Drama* 32 (1998): p. 3.
[48]BFA 22, p. 202, I quote John Willett's version in Bertolt Brecht, *Brecht on Theater*, John Willett, trans. (New York: Hill & Wang, 1964), p. 93. I have italicized what Min Tian omits from this passage in presenting Brecht's views.

extended to suggest the *self-alienation* Brecht advocates. But Mei Lanfang corroborates Brecht's admiration for what demonstrating can achieve, recording his own astonishment at the dramatic and psychological effect of watching another actor's 'mere' demonstration without costume. Demonstration heightens the distancing, which in Chinese aesthetics brings things closer, creating, on another level, as Brecht understood, a more powerful and penetrating, hence memorable, effect of reality.[49] By 'self-alienation' (*Selbstentfremdung*) Brecht meant a contrary effect, both *preventing* a *complete* loss of spectatorial identity and *encouraging* a degree of empathy through the skillfully represented complexity of the character's position, which is too subtle for easy identification.

Brecht's essay on Chinese acting is often read in translation with consequences for its interpretation.[50] Where John Willett's version speaks of the *coldness* with which the Chinese actor 'holds himself remote from the character portrayed', Brecht says *Durchkältung*. Willett says that gestures representing emotions are 'decorously expressed', though Brecht meant and also wrote *sparsam dargestellt*,[51] which means 'sparingly' represented, not overdone. *Durchkältung* refers to a style that chills, cools down, understates or underplays, in the sense of 'less is more'. The consequence, however, is something like the opposite, not freezing, but rather increasing emotional effect. At issue is *how* emotions are shown.

Brecht does not say Chinese acting is cold, only that it seems so when measured by Western conventions. He says:

> To the Western actor the Chinese artist's playing appears in many respects cold. That does not mean the Chinese theater does without the representation of emotions. The artist performs events of great passion but his presentation is unheated. At moments of intense excitation for the character the artist takes a strand of hair between his lips and bites it in two.[52]

When Brecht speaks of the actor 'quoting the character played', the evidence for many critics of Brecht's misrepresentation, he adds: 'But with what art he does this!'[53] At issue is not the style as such, but what that style achieves: the clarity of an aesthetically satisfying externalized representation of intense emotions and complex, contradictory situations that took Brecht's breath away. As for the style, which of course he never copied but whose effect he wished to emulate, he was still talking about it twenty years later to the doubtlessly bemused actors in the Berliner Ensemble.

Some critics argue that the sophisticated Chinese audience holds back, not simply identifying with the character but taking in the whole sequence of events. That is why Brecht wanted to develop the art of spectating (*Zuschaukunst*), adequate to the art of acting (*Schauspielkunst*) in Chinese theater. If Chinese actors stress and Brecht downplays emotions, that does not mean he misunderstood Chinese theater or that the effect is essentially different. In some respects it may be, but I am arguing one central point.

---

[49] Mei Lanfang, 'Reflections on my stage life', in Wu Zuguang, Huang Zuolin, Mei Shaowu, eds., *Peking Opera and Mei Lanfang* (Beijing: New World Press, 1980), p. 44.
[50] Brecht, *Brecht on Theater*, pp. 91–99. The cited quotations are on p. 93.
[51] BFA 22, p. 203.
[52] Ibid., pp. 202–203.
[53] Ibid., p. 204.

He was struck by the difference between comparatively crude Western and sophisticated Chinese acting. Apart from taste or preference, the Chinese method distances or stylizes in order to intensify. Emotional excitation in conventional Western theater was directly expressed by yelling and waving your arms. In Chinese theater it is *symbolized* as the actor bites through an imagined hair (though Willett says 'chews' it), one of the imaginative externalizations Brecht mentions.

The effect is so powerful because, while apparently doing less, it *shows* the discerning spectator more: we *see* a figure driven by passion and frustration, *and* we *see* the repression that is still in command. Aware of this doubleness when playing Yang Guifei in *The Drunken Concubine*, Mei Lanfang offered a contradictory emotional engagement, not release. Brecht saw a style that clarified his intentions by externalizing complex events gesture by gesture, step by step, sentence by sentence with a gracefulness that affected his later aesthetic, the opposite of the German uncorporeal lack of clarity he criticizes in the *Short Organon*.

As for events in East Asia, a Hong Kong Seminar in 1981 brought first accounts of East Asian productions from those directly involved, also from Indian practitioners and Westerners.[54] The discussion centered on whether traditional forms would evolve or Marxism change. I specially remember Huang Zuolin's observation of a gap between emotion and gesture in traditional Chinese acting, denied by some critics. The challenge, he said, was to show the drunk Li Bai on a sober horse.

Encouraged in 1983 to organize an International Brecht Society (IBS) Symposium in Beijing, I was asked not to mention Marxism. But it was frustrated anyway by the *Campaign against Spiritual Pollution*. *The People's Daily* had published an article in March 1983 by Central Committee member Zhou Yang suggesting that 'alienation', not only a capitalist phenomenon, was also possible under Communism: not the best time to discuss the A-Effect!

During the 1985 *Brecht in China* Conference in Beijing and Shanghai there were notable productions, including a shortened version of *The Good Person of Szechwan* in the Central Academy of Drama, distanced into the old Chinese society and developing a Chinese style, played very fast with clever pantomime, especially from the scroungers and hangers-on, who lost that phoney strangeness they can have in Europe or America. An Academy Shakespeare expert said to me: 'I didn't realize how well Brecht understood China. That's what China was like!' Many said: only after the Cultural Revolution could they really understand Brecht. In comparison, the visually innovative Sichuan opera adaptation of the play seemed abstract and unsure of itself. In Lin Zhaohua's *Schweyk*, a huge rope net hung over Schweyk's encounter with Bullinger. Lin and Gao Xingjian were both working in the People's Art Theater, and in *The Other Shore* Gao uses a rope to suggest various human relationships including an enmeshing spider's web. At the Beijing Brecht conference Gao said: 'Brecht was the first to make me understand ... that the rules of this art could be reconstructed completely anew ... So my own dramatic writing, all that I know, and all that I've written from my knowledge, has drawn a lot of courage from his work on this point.'[55]

---

[54] Tatlow and Wong, *Brecht and East Asian Theatre* and *Communications from the International Brecht Society*, Vol. 10, No. 3 (July 1982), pp. 3–14.
[55] Gao Xingjian, *Wo yu Bulaixite* (Me and Brecht), *Qingyi* (1985), pp. 52–56.

Of the performances presented at the 7th IBS Symposium in Hong Kong (1986), these re-readings of Brecht's plays deserve special mention:

a) The Haiyuza Theater's *Der Jasager/Neinsager*, in which *He said Yes*, but *She said No!* In this imaginative and literally high-wire production, the chorus of men and women in both plays wore dark green jackets and black trousers, but the all male performers in *Jasager* wore blue and white horizontally striped smocks over blue trousers and leggings and carried grey rucksacks, while the *Neinsager* were all female, wearing similar but now red and white striped smocks, with red rucksacks and red leggings, vividly stressing the interpretively significant gender difference.

b) The Philippine Educational Theater Association's *The Caucasian Chalk Circle*, set in Mindanao, adapted to an indigenous style, soldiers with machine guns among the spectators, the child taken from the crowd, an example of vibrant community theater acting out their daily experience.

c) The Hong Kong Academy of Performing Arts' *The Visions of Simone Machard*. A Brecht Handbook spoke of its 'very strange, unrealistic dream sequences' and 'absolutely puzzling dream scenes'.[56] But they are central to the play. The director, Fredric Mao, set it in China during the 1930s Japanese invasion, drawing on the heritage of the Chinese imagination. Ah Sei (Simone) dreams that she is one of the well-known women generals of the Yang Family, who resisted the 13th century Mongol invasion. As her daydreams begin, the acting gradually moves towards Chinese opera style. The pictures show three stages: the inn during the occupation; the transition to the dream sequences when her brother appears as a messenger; the counter world in the social unconscious unfolding as a dream of opera.

I mentioned Ba Jin's interest in Brecht's Gao Qipei (1672–1734) painting, which hung behind his bed. His programmatic 1937 poem, *The Doubter*, describes the consequences of looking at this blue-black ink picture in the vigorous finger-painting style, depicting a man on a bench whose shoulders are hunched in thought.[57] The painting itself contains a poem, which explores in a Buddhist context the relationship between mind and universe, and the problem of distinguishing between good and evil men. The ontological vision in the words is offset by the earthiness of the portrait. Text and picture qualify and contradict each other, suggesting fissures within the text and in the portrait. No dignified visionary in the tradition of Buddhist iconography, this man wrestles with a problem, as can be seen from the positioning of the feet and the tension between them and the hunched shoulders.

The gap between practice and theory is a very Chinese theme, and his picture-poem suggests the inevitable ambiguity of all practice. Both poem and painting are in some sense self-portraits. There is no record of how much Brecht knew about the Chinese painting: the less, the better. But the analogies do not come from nowhere. The other resonates within ourselves, and we then glimpse the unconscious of a culture. Like the

---

[56] Jan Knopf, *Brecht-Handbuch*, Vol. 1 (Stuttgart: Metzler Verlag, 1980), pp. 240–241.
[57] I have discussed in detail this fascinating relationship in German in Tatlow, *Brechts Ost Asien*, pp. 13–16, and in English in Antony Tatlow, 'Unconscious Documents. Brecht and East Asia', in Paolo Amalfitano, *L'Oriente. Storia di una figura nelle arti occidentali (1700-2000)*, Vol. 2 (Roma: Bulzoni Editore, 2007), pp. 215–232.

painting, Brecht's poetic self-portrait questions the 'ontological' vision, the theory that is never, as contemporary convention decreed, scientifically correct, that cannot be taken for granted and must always be tested and changed through practice.

Our problem now is not how to realize the future but how to avoid it. Western culture has been defined by teleological models, whether religious, metaphysical, or economic: the Day of Judgment, absorption into some Absolute, the realization of Communism, or so-called globalization. If Marx turned G. W. F. Hegel upside-down to stand him on his feet, Arthur Schopenhauer transformed Hegel's ultimately benevolent World Spirit into a malevolent Will. His equally metaphysical model now seems a better way of concentrating minds. What we now need is a relational, cybernetic, anti-teleological catastrophe avoidance theory. Vital to Brecht's legacy is what he called 'interventionary thought'.[58]

In Forke's *Me Ti* translation, Brecht marked this passage: 'If you tell bad people that Heaven acts justly, their character, even if capable of improvement, will not be changed. You must cheerfully announce to them that Heaven behaves badly.'[59] Friedrich Engels once remarked that we should not 'flatter ourselves overmuch on account of our human conquest over nature. For each such conquest nature takes its revenge upon us ... Thus at every step we are reminded that we by no means rule over nature like a conqueror over a foreign people.'[60]

And that may well be the ultimate, self-alienating anthropological encounter.

---

[58] BFA 21, p. 524.

[59] 'Wenn man zu schlechten Menschen sagt, dass der Himmel gerecht handelt, so lässt sich ihr Charakter, auch wenn er verbesserungsfähig, nicht ändern. Man muß ihnen frohlockend verkünden, dass der Himmel schlecht handelt.' Me Ti, p. 505. Brecht also marked this short sentence – 'Generosität schließt das eigene Selbst nicht aus.' (p. 510) – whose doubleness resonates throughout his work and corroborates what is so succinctly formulated, and problematized, in this last poem: 'Dauerten wir unendlich / So wandelt sich alles. / Da wir aber endlich sind, / Bleibt vieles beim Alten' (BFA 15, p. 294).

[60] Karl Marx and Friedrich Engels, *Selected Works* (London: Lawrence & Wishart, 1968), p. 365, from *The Dialectics of Nature*, first published in 1925 in German in the USSR.

CHAPTER TWENTY-FIVE

Brecht: A Participant in the Process of Nation-Building

AMAL ALLANA

After Brecht's death in 1956, his work became extremely well known internationally, especially in countries where great changes were taking place: Latin America, Egypt, Africa, India, and many parts of South East Asia. Most of these countries had been colonized and had gained their freedom after fighting fascism in its imperialist garb. As newly emerging postcolonial cultures, they were searching for their own, indigenous identities. In this context India's reception of Bertolt Brecht is an interesting and significant phenomenon, particularly with regard to the development of contemporary Indian theater during the post-independence period.

Among the first Indians to see Brecht's work in Berlin a few years before his death in August 1956 was the eminent Punjabi playwright and director Balwant Gargi. He describes a memorable evening in February 1955, when the famous curtain of the Berliner Ensemble, painted with the Picasso dove, rose on Brecht's powerful anti-war play, *Mother Courage.*

> On the revolving stage, two young men yoked to a wagon walked with heavy steps. Mother Courage (Helene Weigel) in a full-length skirt and padded grey jacket, a pewter spoon tucked in her pocket, stands in a wagon singing a marching song in her bugle-like voice ... Some scenes still stand out in my memory: Mother flirts with the soldiers to hide her identity, refusing to recognize the body of her son. As the soldiers bend forward to examine the face of her son, Mother lets out a silent cry, a dumb wail ... Finally, as the soldiers shoot [her daughter] down, she gives one final beat with her limp hand, and collapses ... Mother – dehumanized, stubborn, mean, foolish, a beast – learns nothing from the experience. She reminded me of my own mother. I continued to sit in my chair, overpowered by emotion. [My interpreter] Kitty tapped my shoulder. 'Get up, it's over.'[1]

The following year, in 1956, Habib Tanvir, a young director at the time, was returning to India after studying theater at RADA, in England. He writes about his experience in Berlin:

> From Prague I finally went to Berlin ... but the thing is, when I arrived in Berlin, Brecht had died a few weeks before. That was very disappointing. But his productions

---

Amal Allana, 'Brecht: A Participant in the Process of Nation-Building', *Brecht Yearbook*, 36 (2011), pp. 27–43.

[1] Balwant Gargi, 'Meeting Brecht in Person', in Nissar Allana, ed., *A Tribute to Bertolt Brecht 1993* (Delhi: Theatre and Television Associates, 1993), p. 25.

were all there, and I saw them all ... I saw the rehearsals done by two very eminent directors who directed together, special disciples of Brecht. I was in Berlin for eight months, met all the actors and actresses, sat in their canteen, discussed many things, saw *Caucasian Chalk Circle*, some Chinese one-act plays, *Mother Courage*, the whole gamut ... Of course, I did meet Elisabeth Hauptmann and also Helene Weigel. She was doing the role of the Mother. I made lots of friends and traveled all over East Germany. At that time there was no division, no wall, many people were working in the East and living in the West.[2]

In India, the 1950s were a time when the trauma and bloodbath of the Partition of the country into India and Pakistan, which had caused the displacement of hundreds of thousands of people, was still vivid in the memory. This was followed by the most tragic loss of all time for Indians, the assassination of the Father of the Nation, Mahatma Gandhi, by fundamentalist right-wing forces. Communal strife between Hindus and Muslims continued for some time, all of which left India's first Prime Minister, Jawaharlal Nehru, with a truly disturbing legacy.

Nehru took on the problem of binding India together with missionary zeal. His slogan became 'unity in diversity', and he made the notion of one state, as one indivisible whole, a national agenda to be realized. To achieve this goal, Nehru propagated a pan-Indian identity – that is, a single, unified cultural identity – for a basically diverse people whose languages, religions and ethnic differences were already beginning to manifest themselves in different ways. But Nehru was a dreamer and idealist who believed that a strong, unified India was not a distant or impossible dream, and he quickly embarked on several projects of nation-building. One of the key areas he tackled was culture. He recognized the crucial role artists could play in cultivating an integrated identity for a new India. For this massive enterprise he began to draw on the support of the most eminent musicians, dancers, painters, cinema directors, writers and theater persons of the day.

A wave of euphoria swept the newly liberated, post-independence generation of artists such as Tanvir and Gargi, who willingly committed themselves to supporting Nehru and his grand plans. They were confident and proud to be part of the nation-building process he advocated through creating a pan-Indian as well as 'modern Indian' culture by linking city to village, past to present, and by attempting to synthesize India's vast storehouse of traditions with a contemporary artistic sensibility.

A playwright/director like Balwant Gargi, for example, was energized to undertake a massive journey across the country, in an effort to have a first-hand experience of all the existing folk performing traditions of the country. Documenting traditional performances through photographs and making copious notes and sketches in his diary, Gargi compiled material for what came to be regarded as the first comprehensive book on the subject, *The Folk Theatre of India*.[3]

Equally fervent and committed was Habib Tanvir, who at this time in the late 1950s was a member of the Hindustani Theater, a theater group set up in Delhi under the guiding spirit of Begum Qudsia Zaidi. Driven by a strong desire to stage a Sanskrit classic

---

[2]Anjum Katyal and Biren De, 'It Must Flow: A Life in Theatre' [Interview with Habib Tanvir], *Seagull Theatre Quarterly*, 10 (1996), p. 15.
[3]Balwant Gargi, *Folk Theatre of India* (Seattle: University of Washington Press, 1966).

in a *new* way, Habib chose *The Little Clay Cart* for his first production after his return to India from England and Europe.

The choice of Shudraka's Sanskrit classic was not merely an aesthetic one. It was part of the creed of the postcolonial artist to do Indian plays in an attempt to reforge his identity in relation to his own culture. However, at this juncture the problem was that no guidelines were available on how to stage a classic, other than those set out in the *Natya Shastra*. After looking for other performative sources of inspiration, Tanvir ultimately turned to our existing folk traditions:

> I have come to this conclusion, that if you want to interpret Sanskrit drama you must go back to your folk theater traditions and draw from them, even take folk actors to introduce these techniques, and you'll get somewhere. The two together, the folk and the classical, are going to give to our modern type of Indian producers lots of ideas, lots of inspiration. Everything new, and yet Indian, can, in my belief, flow from this kind of a background.[4]

Seeing Brecht's plays during his travels in Europe, Tanvir recognized the influence of popular theater as well as Eastern performance traditions on Brecht:

> If you analyze it, I should think there is this distinguishing feature in Brecht that he has assimilated influences from all periods of dramatic history, also from all countries ... [T]he folk elements are very strong in Brecht. Then he received influences from American jazz and Negro blues, the Chinese theater, Indian and Burmese (theater) ... Now the amalgamation of these and the reaction against what was going on in Germany and Europe ... he was fed up with it ... which resulted in him and his collaborators experimenting and developing the theory of epic theater.[5]

Seeing how Brecht himself had used and synthesized diverse folk elements and popular traditions into a modern/post-modern aesthetic, Tanvir was excited and stimulated enough to extend his stay in Berlin. What he saw was the emergence of a new dramaturgy, derived from international traditions and physicalized into an entirely new mode of theatrical expression. Brecht's 'epic' theater took realism to a new level, challenging the naturalistic mode that had so far held sway internationally. Even for Indian theater practitioners like Tanvir, naturalism as a genre had outlived its efficacy.

> Strangely enough, in a fundamental sense what my observation of the European theater did to me, was precisely to turn me back to India even more intensely and much more vigilantly. I concentrated mostly on Bertolt Brecht's dramas at the Berliner Ensemble. As you are aware, Brecht already had imbibed so much from the Eastern theater traditions, including the Indian. So it made me look back at Indian traditions in a new light.[6]

---

[4]Habib Tanvir, 'The Crisis of Identity and the Question of Authenticity in Theatre', paper presented at a symposium on *Perspectives of Contemporary Indian Theatre* by the Sangeet Natak Academy, December 1984 (reprinted in Pratibha Aggarwal and Natya Shodh Sansthan, eds., *Habib Tanvir ek Vyaktitva* [Kolkata: Natya Shodh Sansthan]), p. 210.
[5]Amal Allana, interview with Habib Tanvir (TV documentary), Door Darshan, 1998.
[6]Rajinder Paul, interview with Habib Tanvir, *Enact*, 1974 (reprinted in Pratibha and Sansthan, p. 179).

M. S. Sathyu, who later became the well-known filmmaker of *Garam Hawa* and was a young member of Hindustani Theater at the time, notes:

> I think it was way back in the late 50's when Habib Tanvir returned from Germany after his training at Royal Academy of Dramatic Arts, that he spent some time in Germany, in Berlin. He saw some of Brecht's plays and he was quite enthused about them. When he came back, we were going to stage *Mitti ki Gadi / The Little Clay Cart*, the Sanskrit classic of Shudraka. It was in this production that he wanted to use Brechtian techniques. Whatever he explained to us about Brecht seemed very interesting. So we did *Mitti ki Gadi* as our first Brecht-style play.[7]

Eventually Hindustani Theater in Delhi produced *Mitti ki Gadi* in 1958 in Hindi. The production was conceived of as a blend of folk forms and Brechtian modes of narrative dramaturgy. Using folk artists from Chhattisgarh for the proletarian characters such as the gambler and the thief, the influence of Brecht on this production basically lay in the manner in which Tanvir structured the central love story to be set against the political uprising. Sharvilak the rogue, like Brecht's Azdak, cunningly agitates for a better world. At the end of the play the hostile masses, which have hovered in the background so far, take center stage, becoming the focal and climactic point of the narrative. Masks were used for certain characters in order to distance them. Songs, using melodies from Chhattisgarh, were sung both by the Narrator and the characters in the play, as a means to interpret the fable as well as a comment on the action.[8] Some of Tanvir's experiments in this production of *Mitti ki Gadi* were, perhaps, carried out for the first time: the presentation of a classical Sanskrit text using conventions and techniques of folk traditions; the combination of classical and folk traditions using Brechtian narrative devices; the reorganization and reshaping of the text so as to focus on its political dimensions, compelling the audience to make social choices (again a fallout of the Brechtian encounter); the updating of an older text to make it more contemporary and relevant to the present; and the blending of folk and urban actors in the same production. Forging the contemporary through classical and folk traditions, aided by a Brechtian approach, this production of *The Little Clay Cart* very much served as a template, or module, for other directors and playwrights to follow and develop over the decades to come.

INDIAN ENCOUNTERS WITH BRECHT

From the mid 1960s Brecht's Asian aspects began to be discussed at seminars and symposiums, especially in New Delhi. For example, Dr. Lothar Lutze from Heidelberg University gave a talk on 'Indian Classical Drama in the Light of Bertolt Brecht's Dramatic Theory and Practice' at the Max Mueller Bhavan in Delhi.

In the early 1960s the International Theater Institute (ITI) and the Bharatiya Natya Sangh organized an East/West Theater Seminar in Delhi, which was attended by an authority on contemporary German theater, Dr. Käthe Rülicke-Weiler. The international delegates also included Joan Littlewood of *Oh! What A Lovely War* fame. A student at the National School of Drama (NSD) at the time, I vividly remember this seminar where she

---

[7] Amal Allana, interview with M. S. Satyu, *Brecht in India* (TV documentary), Door Darshan, 1998.
[8] See Vasudha Dalmia, *Poetics, Plays and Performances: The Politics of Modern Indian Theatre* (Oxford and New York: Oxford University Press, 2008), p. 261.

graphically demonstrated Brechtian acting techniques, generously sharing her experiences of adopting Brechtian techniques into her own work. Important seminar participants from India included Ebrahim Alkazi, then Director of the NSD, Dr. Kapila Vatsyayan, Kamaladevi Chattopadyay and others. The discussions at the seminar concluded in a series of contractual agreements between the Indian and the GDR governments, leading to the establishment of cultural exchange programs.

BRECHT IN BENGAL

Bengali theater practitioners with leftist leanings were excited by Brecht early on. Brecht enthusiasts in Bengal were comprised of the most progressive elements of contemporary Bengali theater; many had been erstwhile members of the Indian People's Theater Association (IPTA), the cultural wing of the Communist Party in India that had done pioneering work in the 1940s during the fight against British imperialism and international fascism.

IPTA's efforts had helped establish theater as a platform for political debate, giving modern Bengali theater its strong political orientation. Summing up the impact of Brecht in Bengal, the critic Samik Bandyopadhyay writes that although the early years of IPTA's work were not affected by Brecht, translations of Brecht published in Moscow had begun to circulate in Calcutta. After a hiatus of nearly two decades, that is, by the early 1960s, information regarding Brecht began to be available in India in English through, for example, *Brecht on Theatre* and *The Messingkauf Dialogues*, both translated by John Willett.

From 1961 onwards translations of Brecht's plays into Bengali also began to appear on the scene. One of the earliest Brecht plays to be staged in Bengal was *The Life of Galileo* in 1964 at the University of Burdwan, translated by the well-known film director Ritwik Ghatak, who followed this up with a translation of *The Caucasian Chalk Circle*. The same year saw the establishment of the Brecht Society of India, founded in Calcutta with Satyajit Ray as the President and Shova Sen, the brilliant actress/wife of Utpal Dutt, as its Secretary. Dutt himself, who spoke and wrote fluent German, edited the magazine of the Brecht Society of India, aptly calling it *Epic Theatre*, with the cover designed by Ray himself. From 1967 onwards the magazine began to serialize *Himmatbai*, Dutt's adaptation of *Mother Courage* into Bengali. All this led to a growing critical interest in Brecht in Bengal.

One of the first landmark productions was Ajitesh Bannerjee's adaptation of *The Threepenny Opera* in 1969, which transported the action to Calcutta in 1876. Speaking at a seminar on Brecht in Calcutta in 1978, Banerjee recounted his desperate and mainly futile efforts in the early 1960s to learn more about Brecht and his theater. A new methodology seemed to be required in approaching a Brecht text:

> Half-educated people told us there was no scenery in Brecht, that the acting was stylized, the same gesture was repeated continuously, the same music was used throughout.[9]

However, when he saw *Mother Courage* on film, it proved they were wrong. Production stills of Brecht's own productions as well as Brecht's own theoretical writings clarified

---

[9] Ajitesh Banerjee quoted in *Bertolt Brecht '80, 1898–1978*, Samik Bandyopadhaya's account of a seminar held in Kolkatta and organized by Max Mueller Bhawan and ICCR, p. 41.

doubts further. Finally, Satyajit Ray, who had recently returned from abroad, physically acted out a scene from *Arturo Ui* that he had seen, followed by Utpal Dutt who acted out the same scene even better! All of this was very helpful to Banerjee, who has made the following salient point about handling Brecht as an Indian director:

> When I came to do *The Threepenny Opera* in 1969, I tried to bring it *as close* to the Bengali experience as possible. Adaptation is only possible if one knows one's own country. I would like to know Brecht through my *own* tradition. I am not interested in a *German* presentation of Brecht.[10]

BRECHT AT THE NATIONAL SCHOOL OF DRAMA

These were individual responses of receptive Indian directors. However, further north, in Delhi, there was an *institutional* response to Brecht's teachings and practice by the NSD, India's premier institution for theater training, which led to the methodical study, understanding, and absorption of Brecht into Indian mainstream thinking and, eventually, theater practice. The participation of NSD director Alkazi in the Brecht-Dialog in East Berlin in 1968, organized by the ITI and the Brecht-Zentrum, now facilitated the Indian reception of Brecht on a larger institutional level.

At the NSD Brecht was initially performed under the direction of German experts, in *Modellbuch* productions, which closely followed the original Brecht productions of the Berliner Ensemble. In 1968 Carl Weber, whose visit was supported by the Goethe Institute and who stood out because he had been a first-generation assistant to Brecht at the Berliner Ensemble, directed *The Caucasian Chalk Circle* at the NSD, with a new Indian score composed by Vanraj Bhatia. This was followed in 1970 by *The Threepenny Opera*, directed by Fritz Bennewitz, a second-generation student of Brecht and, at the time, artistic director of the National Theater at Weimar, GDR. Both productions were in Hindi, the former translated by Razia Sajjad Zaheer, the latter by Surekha Sikri. Earlier the same year I had met Bennewitz in Weimar, where I was studying Brecht, and he had asked me to be the assistant director and costume designer on *Threepenny Opera*, to which I readily agreed. Under the guidance of these Brechtian experts, Brecht began to be taught systematically at the NSD, allowing student actors to gain a direct insight and experience of how to approach a Brechtian role, using techniques of alienation. Weber gave a series of lectures on Brechtian drama, while Bennewitz, concurrently with his rehearsals of *Threepenny Opera*, taught an eight-week course on Brecht to the students.

The incorporation of Brecht into the syllabus of the NSD was not arbitrary on the part of the NSD director Alkazi. Even though he was laying the foundations of a national institution based on both traditional and contemporary Indian theater, it was quite clear to him that the students also required an international dimension. Alkazi sums up Brecht's relevance to Indian theater in an interview with Nissim Ezekiel:

> Of all Western playwrights we believe that Brecht has the greatest relevance to the Indian theater today, not only on account of the content of his plays but particularly because of their form. He has broken away from the closed three-act play and, chiefly as a result of his intense study of the classical Indian, the Chinese and the Japanese

---

[10]Ibid.

theaters, he has evolved the loose epic style. He has used such devices of our own ancient theaters as the narrator, the chorus, song, music and poetry, to bring back color and vitality to the insipid prose theater of today.[11]

To Alkazi the Brecht connection was contiguous with his own interest in developing a cultural relationship between Indian and other traditional forms of Asian Theater. He felt that an exposure to various international legacies could provide a springboard that would propel contemporary practice into exciting directions of creating a new Indian modernism, contextualized within Asia. Therefore, at the NSD Brecht began to be taught in conjunction with Kabuki and Noh traditions. Shozo Sato was invited to do *Ibaragi*, while Alkazi himself directed the students in a new version of Dharamvir Bharati's *Andha Yug* (The Age of Blindness) in 1976, a contemporary take on the *Mahabharata*, in a spectacular production mounted against the historic ruins of the Old Fort/Purana Quila, in Delhi.

Culling many elements of his presentational style from Kabuki, Noh and Brechtian theater, Alkazi introduced a formal Kabuki-like chorus, painted the faces of the characters with Kabuki and Kathakali-inspired makeup, and dressed the characters in costumes that were an eclectic mix of traditional Indian and Japanese styles.

It was during these very years that the study of Indian folk theater was also introduced into the NSD curriculum. Yakshagana gurus like Kota Shivaram Karanth were invited to direct the students in traditional productions, while Shanta Gandhi, an ex-IPTA person herself and teacher of Sanskrit drama, staged a landmark production of *Jasma Odan* with the NSD students. Using the Bhavai tradition of Gujarat, Gandhi reinvented an old folk play, contemporizing the choices made by Jasma, the central woman character.

Between 1968 and 1977, the NSD was a veritable cauldron, a laboratory where an extraordinary amount of study, research and practical experimentation was underway with folk theater, Brechtian and Asian theater all being explored for contemporary use. In this way Alkazi, while compiling a canon for a national/Hindi theater, was simultaneously allowing and preparing the ground for a new movement in Indian modernism to take shape.

BRECHT IN MAHARASHTRA

The phenomenal success of both *The Threepenny Opera* and *The Caucasian Chalk Circle* in Delhi prompted Alkazi to travel with these productions to Mumbai, Pune, Hyderabad and Bangalore. Using straight translations, and following the *Modellbuch* treatments, these productions went a long way in acquainting both theater practitioners and audiences alike with an 'authentic' rendition of the Brechtian performance style. As theatrical experiences they opened doors to a new dimension of, and approach to, contemporary theater per se.

In Mumbai Vijaya Mehta, responsible for nurturing a new wave of Marathi experimental theater, had just directed Venkatesh Madgulkar's adaptation of *The Good Person of Szechwan* as *Devajeena Karuna Keli*, in Marathi. She describes why Indian theater practitioners like herself were responding favorably to Brecht:

> I felt that was the period when all of us, the directors, were trying to know what is Indian theater's identity in terms of world theater. Whatever we were doing, it was

---

[11] Nissim Ezekiel, interview with Ebrahim Alkazi, *Indian Express*, 17 Jan. 1971.

tailored on British heritage, which stayed with us. And we all were in search of trying to belong to the Indian soil. We were all *urban* people. We separately tried to understand what our roots were. What we did at that time was not folk theater, it was an urban mind exposing itself to the various traditions, which were rooted in the soil, and having those traditions reflect in our work. Sorry to say, but at that time Brecht came in very handy, because he talked of Asian theater, he talked of *Total* Theater, something that our researchers were also leading us towards. Here was a European mind talking of a very contemporary idiom of Total Theater, that's why I feel we found Brecht attractive.[12]

However, Bennewitz, the director of *The Threepenny Opera* at the NSD, was not completely satisfied with his maiden venture. As he wrote in his article 'How the Story of the Indian Chalk Circle Happened': 'The results of this work remain limited, because to a large extent it has remained a production transmitted to the Indian stage from *our* theatrical traditions and *our* habits of play.'[13]

However, the cultural agreement between India and the GDR allowed for yet another opportunity in 1973. This time Bennewitz's venture was a collaborative one, namely to co-direct, along with veteran Vijaya Mehta, C. T. Khanolkar's *Ajab Nyaya Vartulacha/The Caucasian Chalk Circle*, in Marathi, in Mumbai, for the Mumbai Marathi Sahitya Sangha. Bennewitz felt that,

> [i]n order for Brecht to be fully absorbed into the fabric of India, it is necessary for us to have more comprehension of their history and culture in theater, an experience of the vitality of grass roots Indian theater is necessary ... It is my conviction that our knowledge and experience can be communicated more profitably on both sides by a certain amount of *adaptation* of the text to the Indian context and traditions.[14]

Mehta has commented on her collaboration with Bennewitz:

> We worked, to start with, on the basis that it will be an adaptation. We got a person, who was the greatest poet Maharashtra ever had, to do the translation, Khanolkar, He did not read a word of English. There were seven or eight drafts ... I used to go to Germany, get it looked at by Bennewitz. The division of work was basically that he will watch out for the content and allow me the freedom to go to town as far as actors and the whole form was concerned ... He would be my guru and I would be the director. And he would work with me on each scene and he would attend rehearsals every four to five days to see whether those ideas were reflected in the performance or not. Working with an equally talented mind like Khanolkar's, a man who did not read English – forget German – he was able to capture even the meter of Brecht! ... There were no cypress trees, there was 'champa ki dali!'[15] There were mango groves! If there was christening there, it was 'Ganga Tirth'[16] in our version, but the whole thing blended so beautifully that I think, without our having to believe in Brechtian ideology and thought, we delivered the goods.[17]

---

[12]Amal Allana, interview with Vijaya Mehta, *Brecht in India* (TV documentary), Door Darshan, 1998.
[13]Fritz Bennewitz, 'The Story of Indian Chalk Circle', *Rangavarta* 55 (Nov. 1994), p. 21.
[14]Ibid., p. 22.
[15]Branches of the *champa* tree.
[16]Ritual bathing in the River Ganga on auspicious occasions.
[17]Amal Allana, interview with Vijaya Mehta, *Brecht in India* (TV documentary), Door Darshan, 1998. (The interview was conducted in English.)

Although Indian audiences were becoming familiar with Brecht, there was trenchant criticism regarding the 'Indianization' of this and other productions of Brecht's plays. D. G. Nadkarni,[18] a well-respected critic, argued that the productions were 'formal exercises that had lost interest in Brecht's radical politics', while Arun Naik, a young playwright, complained in *Enact* that by 'Indigenizing the content of Brecht we had made him too familiar, so that the element of alienation or "estrangement", so intrinsic to Brecht, had vanished'.[19]

NEW WRITING

Throughout this period from the mid-1960s until the mid-1970s, when the Brechtian impact was consolidating itself, a remarkable spate of plays by Indian writers like Dharamvir Bharati, Mohan Rakesh, Girish Karnad, Vijay Tendulkar, and Adya Rangacharya exploded onto the scene, giving voice, for the first time, to the volatile and unstable conditions that began to prevail, especially in the urban metropolises. What linked these plays together was that they were peopled by alienated, disturbed, practically schizophrenic characters living in the grand, new megapolises built by Nehru. Urban reality with all its uncertainties registered an angst and existential questioning that found unparalleled expression in the explicit violence characterizing this new writing, all of which disturbed and shocked spectators.

Writing in their own mother tongue, these playwrights were still highly influenced by the Euro/American tradition of realistic playwriting. However, with the growing number of Brecht translations and performances, as well as in-depth research into folk performing traditions, writers were becoming increasingly familiar with various aspects of epic dramaturgy and were tentatively beginning to explore non-linear narrative modes.

THE EMERGENCY

By the mid 1970s, it was clear that the honeymoon with Nehruvian ideals and dreams of a strong unified nation under a powerful and centrally controlled Congress Government were over. Massive migrations to the cities, unemployment, a shift in the equations of caste, class and gender politics, together with growing regional aspirations, reflected a society in transition. Events took a turn for the worse with widespread unrest among students and workers, which ultimately provoked the Socialist leader, Jayprakash Narayan, to call for a total revolution. The mounting pressure forced the next Prime Minister, Indira Gandhi, to declare a national state of Emergency in 1975. Opposition leaders were arrested, civil liberties suspended, censorship of the press and mass media enforced, with the Prime Minister assuming the executive authority to overrule the law.

Alarmed and seized by a sense of betrayal and loss of idealism, all kinds of artists found themselves in a similar predicament and in a sense began to produce work that could be considered a part of independent India's first self-conscious and dissenting subculture. Playwrights like Badal Sirkar, Mahesh Elkunchwar and Satish Alekar, filmmakers like Mani Kaul, Shyam Benegal, Govind Nihilani, Adoor Gopalakrishnan, Mrinal Sen, painters

---

[18] D. G. Nadkarni, 'The Search for Form', *Enact* 118/119 (Oct./Nov. 1976), p. 16.
[19] Arun Naik, 'Brechtian Experiment in Marathi', *Enact* 145/146 (Jan./Feb. 1979), p. 13.

like Bhupen Khakkar, Gulam Mohammad Sheikh, Sudhir Patwardhan, Gieve Patel were radical in their political views and broadly postmodernist in their aesthetic. Their work bore testimony to an India that was shaping itself within the horizons of the present.

Asserting their Third World status and location, they imported the local environment, its look, feel, its explicit and encoded histories, onto the stage, screen, and canvas. Discarding myth, history or folklore as a peg to talk about contemporary issues, dramatists now turned their attention to their local environment, in plays like *Aadhe Adhure, Khamosh! Adalat Jari Hai, Giddhare, Wada Chirebandi, Kamala*, and others.

The implications of this maneuver were momentous. Characters began to lose their significance as symbols with universal qualities and began to acquire a specificity of class, occupation, region, and ethnicity. Described in this way, the characters spoke viscerally of situations of dominance and enslavement, presenting themselves in their everyday *avtars* as ordinary, middleclass women, clerks, and lawyers. These characters carried their habitats with them into the new theatrical space; the metropolis, the suburbs, satellite townships, and small towns began to be drawn into the orbit of scrutiny. Ordinary characters and locations had never been memorialized on the modern Indian stage before. They now took center stage. More importantly, these playwrights redefined their roles of poets and seers to those of social agents and participants in the process of self-definition, constructing for themselves through their practice a vantage point from which to relate to their own social and political realities.

At this juncture, when there was a complete disillusionment with the idea that the new cities of India represented a hope for the future, when they had been revealed instead to be veritable jungles of corruption and dung heaps of dirty politics, the city plays of Brecht became particularly meaningful and powerful. Productions of such plays as *The Good Person of Szechwan* or *Threepenny Opera* were staged in a number of regional languages, making this perhaps the most intensive period of Brecht appropriations in India, in the form of full-scale cultural adaptations.

It was against this background of feverishly pitched avant-garde work that P. L. Deshpande, an eminent Marathi writer/actor, and Jabbar Patel, a young director from the Progressive Dramatic Association (PDA) in Pune, collaborated on a production of *The Threepenny Opera*, adapted as *Teen Paishacha Tamasha*. An established satirist, Deshpande saw the pursuit of money as a dehumanizing and corrupting force and made this the central thematic impulse of the play. Combining presentational elements of Tamasha, the secular folk performing tradition of Maharashtra, with Brechtian dramaturgy, Deshpande created a new text that bristled with social critique, political satire, while contextualizing the play within the framework of India's Emergency, a fact that got the play instant attention and publicity. As Aparna Dharwadker writes:

> With the event of the Emergency as his immediate referent, Deshpande launched into a multipronged attack on politics and nationhood, spheres that are still idealized in India ... The experience of the Emergency with its suspension of constitutional rights and the large number of secret arrests had given the already menacing figure of the policeman, for example, an entirely new dimension in Indian political and public life. The Sutradhar/Narrator in the play, therefore, emphasizes the predatory connotations of Police Chief Tiger Bhandare/Brown's nickname and reacts with exaggerated terror whenever Bhandare and his men appear. The complicity of spies and informants during the Emergency also gives new meaning to Tiger's betrayal of his old friend, Macheath. When the men in Mackie's gang object to a business like theirs being conducted by

a woman, Polly/Malan strong-arms them into agreeing that *only* a woman can carry on such a business! In the following scenes Polly/Malan begins to mimic the physical appearance and mannerisms of Indira Gandhi, with the distinctive white streak in the hair, and the habit of covering her head with her *sari*. Her metamorphosis and draconian control over the gang become a satiric re-enactment of the Emergency.[20]

The eclectic musical score by Bhaskar Chandavarkar was a pastiche of semi-classical and popular Indian musical traditions ranging from *gazals* and Natya Sangeet to Bollywood and western pop music; the casting of a young pop singer in the role of Macheath and the highly politicized landscape of the Emergency against which the play was set gave a cutting-edge quality to this dissonant production that utilized Brecht to describe a frantic and displaced urban Indian landscape. In my view all these aspects catapulted Brecht out of the practically pastoral prettiness of some earlier folk-inspired Brecht productions, truly reinventing him as our contemporary.

MY WORK

This paper would not be complete without my sharing the deep and abiding impact that Brecht has had on my own directorial work, both in relation to the plays of his that I have staged as to his ideas that have shaped the fundamental philosophy of my work.

Born after Independence, I, too, was searching for an identity but, unlike the generation of Tanvir, Mehta, Alkazi, B. V. Karanth and others before me, it was not a *pan-Indian* identity on 'behalf' of the whole nation nor a *national* identity of any kind that I was looking for, but one more personal and close to me, the more autobiographical identity of being a postcolonial at this point. In a 1998-interview I said:

> Brecht was indeed one of the first inter-culturists, an approach which is the core of our postmodern culture, a fact that both interests me and pertains to my context. By virtue of the fact that I am a postcolonial, a product of two cultures, both Indian and Western, I don't and cannot lay claim or subscribe to a single, monolithic, 'Indian' identity, as those before me in the 60's felt compelled to do in order to reassert their identity as Indians. I am no true, blue, 'traditional' Indian, I don't hail from some remote village in India. I am of mixed parentage. Arab and Indian. I was born and brought up in Mumbai. I went to a Protestant School and I speak English at home. So ... I have a hybrid, bastardized identity! Like millions of other urbanized Indians, I have plural identities because I respond to and interact with more than one tradition, more than one culture, a phenomenon which is being experienced increasingly by India's diaspora, all over the world, as greater migrations occur, as technology makes the world a smaller and smaller place, etc. These are facts of my birth and my circumstances. So am I not to be regarded as a true 'Indian'?[21]

As a postcolonial director then, what I needed to construct for myself was a performance language that would reflect my cultural *instability*, the instability of the postcolonial, my in-betweenness, my *lack* of belonging to any culture/language/ethnic group specifically. In

---

[20] Aparna Bhargava Dharwadker, *Theatres of Independence: Drama, Theory, and Urban Performance in India since 1947* (Iowa City: University of Iowa Press, 2005), pp. 379, 380.
[21] Interview by Amal Allana, *Brecht in India* (TV documentary), Door Darshan, 1998.

theatrical terms this ultimately translated into my attempt to create a constantly *shifting, vacillating identity* on stage, one that would dynamically reflect my constant state of *uprootedness*. So, unlike those before me who were searching for rootedness, I needed to assert my *lack* of it. And although my very first play on my return to India after two years of studying Brecht in the GDR was about the identity of Galy Gay in *Man Is Man* and how it was blotted out, it was not until much later that I realized that there were autobiographical connotations in my choice of this play.

What I found compelling and intriguing about *Man Is Man* was that besides the powerful political statement we were made to witness the transformation of an individual's identity. Here the character had not been conceived of as a fixed psychological entity, with unalterable traits, but as something that could be taken apart and remodeled at will. This struck me as an entirely new formulation of character. It was the death of character in the old sense.

The lack of fixity of character was a theme I was to take up two years later, again with a play by Brecht, *The Good Person of Szechwan* (produced in 1973 and 1982). Here the transformation of identity is treated in a more complex manner. Unlike Brecht's earlier play, where Galy Gay moves categorically from point A to B, here Shen Te, the central character, moves continuously back and forth between performing female and male. There is no respite for Shen Te if she wishes to survive, except to be in a constant state of flux between male and female genders. It has become her permanent state of being, her condition.

AN ANDROGYNOUS BEING: *HIMMAT MAI*

Eleven years later, in 1993, I was to return to the same theme, the paradox of dual gender which finds its most powerful and mature formulation in the central protagonist of Brecht's best known play, a chronicle of the 30-years war that ravaged Europe, *Mother Courage*. Brecht's contention can be simply stated – the female (Mother), if she wants to survive (in this case, the condition of war), requires a degree of maleness (Courage) to protect herself and her children. Here Brecht crystallizes the male and female into a single identity. Mother Courage does not suffer the schizophrenia of Shen Te, rather, in her the disparate identities have grown into one another so that the sharp demarcations of gender are no longer visible. The split is not evident. Mother Courage is both male and female at once and simultaneously. The warring identities have congealed, as blood into stone, which results in a character of savage and brutal mien. The dynamics of her ambivalent split gender have given rise to a character who is both repulsive as well as one to whom we are compassionately drawn. Mother Courage's sexuality, then, is an expression of her toughened will to survive. Brecht's concern is with the havoc war can play with human nature, brutalizing and desensitizing the human being to the point where he begins to resemble a grotesque creature, half man/half woman, a practically deformed androgynous being. It is this 'unnatural' mother that the casting of a man in a woman's role sought to represent in my production.[22]

---

[22] Amal Allana, 'Gender Relations and Self Identity', in Lakshmi Subramanyam, ed., *Muffled Voices: Women in Modern Indian Theatre* (Delhi: Har-Anand Publications, 2002), p. 301.

Another reason why Brecht appealed to me and my condition as a postcolonial subject was the manner in which he treated his material. Breaking the linearity of the narrative through several means, Brecht applied the treatment of collage, assemblage and bricolage by combining fragments of texts or statistics with songs or clowning routines, thereby coupling multiple media with the performative skills of the actor and creating out of the material a complex web of dynamically imparted information that energized the audience into what he called alert, *complex seeing*.

Despite applying, modifying and reinventing many of his strategies to the treatment of all my following work, I was never really concerned with recreating any particularly 'Brechtian' style, but Brecht's ideas propelled me to construct and explore for myself new methods of approaching any material, any text. My effort is to always construct a performative dramaturgy through which I can dynamically perform the narrative, on multiple levels, through multiple means. Of late this has been expressed through creating, for example, a continuously shifting stage picture that becomes a continuously moving, fluid, unstable vantage point, through which the spectator is required to read/view the drama. I believe that my work achieves its energy and rhythm from the creation of such fluid, shifting registers, through which the performance, in a sense, is filtered.

CONCLUSION

As a woman director, one of the problematic areas for me has been the fact that most plays, whether western or Indian, have been written by men. Although male playwrights can give us a profound and sympathetic insight into a woman's psyche and world, their works are often, albeit unwittingly, dominated by the male gaze. Suffice to say here that Brecht's 'Verfremdung' has helped me gain a neutral perspective and vantage point into drama. Such a vantage point constantly shuttles between the polarities of the subjective and objective, between character and actor, between the emotional and the distanced, which in terms of gender could be read as the male and female. This is the liminal space I have chosen to explore, that twilight zone between sleep and waking, the thin dividing line that separates the conscious from the unconscious, illusion from reality, where experiences of both may overlap, and where moments of clarity as well as ill-definition co-exist.

In my search to evolve my own language of theatrical articulation, I have been constantly drawn to study and explore older performance traditions of India and other parts of Asia, in conjunction with the theoretical premises on which Brecht formulated a new theater for the scientific age. These, as well as cinema, are invaluable storehouses of possible narrative modes through which stories and characters can travel along several trajectories simultaneously. I would like to describe my work, then, as 'experiential'. My attempt is to relate directly to the senses, without the mediation of the mind, so that colors, sounds and images 'evoke' meanings, rather than use words to describe them. What is important to me is to 'experience' theater, both as thought and feeling. This undoubtedly relates to my experience of being both an Indian and a woman.

Africa

CHAPTER TWENTY-SIX

African Brecht

BRIAN CROW

I

That Brecht has been an iconic figure in much postcolonial drama and theater – and nowhere more so than in Africa – is well known. When the Nigerian dramatist and director Bode Sowande hailed Brecht as 'my brother', a German who 'could have put on an "agbada" in the Yoruba story-telling theatre' (Sowande 131), he was merely articulating the widespread creative and critical perception in Africa of the close affinities between Brechtian Epic Theater and indigenous performance traditions that have profoundly influenced modern African literary drama.¹ In her recent book on 'postimperial' Brecht Loren Kruger explores and extends the theoretical perspective of this perceived affinity by offering a stimulating account of his impact and the debates around his work and influence within what she calls 'a field of multilateral lines of force' in which the Cold War axis between West and East intersects with the postcolonial axis of North and South. Against the prevalent Western critical habit of treating Brecht's method as 'a timeless set of tools' (Kruger 16), Kruger argues for the necessity of understanding the institutional and more broadly sociohistorical settings within which Brecht's ideas and practices were originally forged and later developed, as well as their subsequent modification in a variety

---

Brian Crow, 'African Brecht', *Research in African Literatures*, 40: 2 (2009), pp. 190–207.

¹While agreeing that playwrights like Soyinka and Osofisan 'are attracted to the German playwright's dramaturgy in large measure because it parallels certain aesthetic structures found within their own indigenous culture' and that they are employing techniques 'analogous' to Brecht's, Sandra Richards nevertheless cautions against 'the automatic assumption of influence and imitation' and insists that their creative source is stylistically indigenous (see Richards). Muyiwa Awodiya concurs, following Ola Rotimi in arguing that '[a]ll of the salient determinants of Brecht's epic theatre were already in vogue in traditional African theatre practice' (Awodiya 210). He approvingly quotes Rotimi in his 'Much Ado about Brecht' to the effect that 'the features which define epic theatre are not singularly of Brecht's genius, as they are being glibly made to appear in the African world. Rather, it is clear that those features had existed in our African theatre tradition long before Brecht was born in 1898' (259). The Nigerian critic Sam Ukala goes further in asserting the primacy of traditional African dramaturgy, proposing that to ascribe Brechtian influence to Osofisan's dramaturgy is to overlook the playwright's 'artistic patrimony'. Arguing that there are significant differences between the aesthetics of traditional African folktale performance and Brecht's epic theatre, especially in relation to the *Verfremdungseffekt* (the so-called 'alienation effect'), Ukala's conclusion is striking: 'Osofisan's dramaturgy is, therefore, not a perpetuation, but a subversion of the European or Brechtian aesthetic hegemony in Africa. Subversion is the cornerstone of the politics of aesthetics required to totally free the African mind from the cultural shackles of colonialism' (39). In an ironic twist of critical reception, then, Ukala asserts that the European practitioner/theorist whose name is synonymous with the subversion of bourgeois aesthetic practice must in turn be rejected/subverted so that African artists and audiences can gain their full liberation from European (or 'Brechtian', in a curious polemical elision) cultural hegemony.

of global contexts. More specifically, she investigates Brecht's impact on a variety of South African theater practices and practitioners during the apartheid period and after to give substance to her assertion that Brecht's influence in Africa is not just a peripheral supplement to his European after-life but can be seen as a genuine point of intersection between North-South and East-West political and cultural axes.

As well as helping to establish in greater detail Brecht's global – and specifically African – significance, Kruger's study is part of a wider exploration and reassessment of this most complex and resonant theatre theorist and practitioner in the light of ongoing research based on writings that have only recently been made available, first in German and subsequently, at least in part, in English translation.[2] A feature of the more recent scholarly and critical commentary has been a reconsideration of the rather stark earlier formulations of Brecht's dramaturgy, stage-audience relationships, and so forth (pioneered notably by John Willett's seminal *Brecht on Theatre*) that have characterized our understanding of Epic Theater. The main outlines of Brecht's conception of Epic spectatorship have long been clear: an intellectually (and even emotionally) alert audience, which is enabled through the drama's formal devices or techniques to see anew by a process of 'estranging' what has become familiar and taken for granted, thus provoking audience awareness that character and action is always embedded in, and in large measure produced by, causal socioeconomic structures. While this established understanding of Epic Theater remains basically undisturbed, there has nevertheless been a growing sense in recent commentary of the complexity involved in the development of his conception of Epic Theater during his career and, with it, his changing, increasingly layered ideas about spectatorship and audience behaviour. The *Mahagonny* schema, as presented by Willet, has been hugely influential, at least in the English-speaking world, in establishing a clear and perhaps exaggerated contrast between 'dramatic' or 'Aristotelean' theater and Brecht's rival conception of Epic Theater and, with it, the polarized representation of audience response – empathy on the one hand, critical distance on the other. From the mid-1930s onwards, as for instance John J. White argues in his recent scholarly account of the development of Brecht's dramatic theory, Brecht's theoretical formulations became less fixed, his writings tending to complicate this polarization as his view of desirable audience response increasingly emphasizes the idea of enjoyable audience 'productivity' (*Produktivität*) and the role of feelings as well as thought in Epic Theater (White 206–09, 231–34).

My particular reflections here take up Susan Bennett's invitation, in her seminal study of Western audiences, to see Brecht as a theorist and practitioner whose work 'sets up a number of starting points for the study of audiences in theatres' (Bennett 30) and makes manifest 'the productive role of theatre audiences and positions that role ideologically' (33). More particularly, I want to argue that the common critical and creative assumption that African spectatorship and much of the dramaturgy associated with it is intrinsically

---

[2]Seminal in this process has been the publication of the *Werke: Grosse kommentierte Berliner und Frankfurter Ausgabe* (30 volumes with *Registerband*), edited by Werner Hecht, Jan Knopf, Werner Mittenzwei, and Klaus-Detlef Müller. For an authoritative examination and analysis in English of Brecht's dramatic theory in the light of this newly available material, see White. For a vital body of Brecht's theoretical writings not hitherto available in English, see Kuhn and Giles. Their volume both complements and interrogates some of the perspectives on Brecht established by John Willet's pioneering and foundational *Brecht on Theatre*. For a stimulating example of how poststructuralist critical thinking applied to more recently available theoretical material can affect critical perspectives on Brecht's drama, see Wright.

'Brechtian' – unquestioned even by Kruger in her discussion of South African theater – is problematic and at least requires more rigorous critical scrutiny. The gist of my argument, illustrated both by personal experience as a director and audience member of some Brecht productions in Nigeria and by reference to several published African adaptations of Brecht, is that a broadly 'Brechtian' impulse in the characteristic activity of African audiences of popular and literary theater is typically in complex and uneasy tension with other characteristic features of their responses and behavior. Apparent affinities, in short, conceal quite deep-seated differences in characteristic expectation and response. This, I will argue, is also true of the dramaturgy of at least two of the three Brecht adaptations I will refer to in my discussion – the Ghanaian Mohammed ben Abdallah's *Land of a Million Magicians* (first produced in 1991), based on *The Good Person of Szechwan*; and two versions of *The Threepenny Opera* – the Nigerian Wole Soyinka's *Opera Wonyosi* (first performed in 1977) and the South African Junction Avenue Theatre Company's *Love, Crime and Johannesburg*, which premiered in 1999. My conclusion will suggest why it may be that *Love, Crime and Johannesburg* differs from the other two adaptations in its absorption of Brecht's influence and the kind of spectatorship it seems to invite, and proposes the need to reassess the Brechtian legacy in Africa.

II

While Susan Bennett's work helped to inaugurate a burgeoning interest in audiences and theatrical reception in English-language scholarship in recent years, attention to African spectatorship has been largely limited to the study of popular theater in West Africa. The available scholarship certainly suggests that popular audiences in Africa have been in certain respects Brechtian *avant la lettre*, even if it is in ways that Brecht himself might not have envisaged. Take Karin Barber's description of the typical audience behaviour of West African popular theater:

> The concert party audiences weep, jeer, sing, and mount the stage to give presents to the characters they sympathize with or to the performers they admire. Yoruba popular theatre audiences are frequently so rowdily responsive that they have to be quelled with microphones attached to a powerful sound system. Their participation in the creation of the play – intervening to make suggestions, complete proverbs, pass comments, shout warnings – is hard to miss. (Barber et al. xv)

At least in relation to his desire for a theater audience that does not sit silently in the dark, transfixed by illusion, but behaves more like a crowd at a football or boxing match – relaxed but alert, able and willing to participate actively as they watch – the audience behavior Barber describes seems to fulfil Brecht's prescription. Though more 'middle class', generally more educated African audiences in 'art theaters' may be somewhat less volatile in their responses than the 'popular' audiences described by Barber, there is normally no less a sense of continuous and lively participation in the performance, of an audience almost rapacious in its hunger for stimulation and response. As much in a theater on a university campus as in the kind of large open space that, in its heyday, was often the venue of Yoruba traveling theater, the audience members are likely at crucial moments to directly address the characters on the stage (and sometimes, quite specifically, the actors), to give advice or offer warnings or condemnation and to maintain a steady flow of comment between themselves based on their perceptions and judgments of what they are witnessing.

In other respects too theater spectators in Africa seem instinctively to fulfill some of Brecht's aspirations towards a new kind of audience. In his time, the German dramatist was concerned not only to revolutionize the consciousness and behavior of European audiences but the fundamental relationship between them and the performances they witnessed. Historically, this had to do with his desire to create a new kind of proletarian audience in Germany and was intimately tied up with his development in the early 1930s of the *Lehrstück* as a form and his work with amateur working-class performers belonging to or affiliated with the Communist Party. In short, he wished to alter radically the nature of property relations in the theater, as in society at large, so that the working class audience would *own* the theater as a means of production, and would be able to *use* the theatrical representation of reality for their own, revolutionary purposes. Commenting on a South African township audience's interruption of an early performance of the Brechtian *Sizwe Bansi Is Dead* devised by Athol Fugard, John Kani, and Winston Ntshona, Loren Kruger observes that by appropriating the play as they do, the spectators in New Brighton were transcending 'the system of player/spectator', in line with Brecht's notion of the learning play: 'By intervening in the play, the members of the audience do not abandon the fiction; they *use* it' (Kruger 251; emphasis in original).

In a quite different theatrical context, that of the Yoruba popular theater, Barber has noted how audiences construed the dramatic narrative as a kind of ethical model, less a representation of things as they are than 'a demonstration of the consequences of certain courses of action' (*Generation of Plays* 222). In the process, audience members typically located what was most interesting and important in the play in the normative lessons to be derived from it, rather than from the exploration of complexities of character and motivation. Barber argues that the audience, presented with vivid and concrete exempla of truths already known, typically 'normalizes them still further by fitting them into a larger picture of received opinion about the world "nowadays", a picture that corroborates and is corroborated by the events shown in the play' (224). Of particular interest is a characteristic audience maneuver 'whereby characters in the play were held to embody moral messages specifically for spectators of the same gender or occupying the same social role' – a form of identification that involves individual audience members in drawing a moral lesson applying specifically to themselves and that thus permits considerable variability in the lessons picked out. The process of interpretation is also, then, for this kind of audience too, a series of *useful* acts of self-recognition, with the potential for very personal application. The most recent and comprehensive study of the relatively educated and 'elite' audiences of West African literary theater endorses Barber's findings (Asiedu 2003). Arguing that the audiences of literary drama as much as any other 'fill the "gaps" in the performance' by drawing on their own individual experiences, Awo Asiedu concludes: 'Above all else, they seek to gain lessons to use in their own lives. Pavis's statement that in the theatre "meaning is *the use made of the stage*" (1982:81 his emphasis) is an apt description of the West African audience's interpretation process. They "make use" of the theatrical production, applying the ideas or messages presented to their own contexts' (298–99).

My personal observation of the behavior and reactions of audiences for university-based literary drama in Nigeria over several years both confirms Asiedu's conclusions as to the similarities between 'literary' audience responses and those of popular theater analyzed by Barber (and others) and, at the same time, suggests in what ways African 'audiencing' departs quite radically from the affinities thus far adduced with the Brechtian ideal of an active, enquiring, commentating audience that uses the stage for its own ends.

Particularly relevant to this discussion were the responses and reactions of audiences comprised mainly of university staff and students to a series of productions of Brecht's plays, adapted and translated to suit their new environment, performed at the Studio Theatre at Ahmadu Bello University, Zaria, Nigeria, during the late 1970s and 1980s. These included a freely adapted version of *The Threepenny Opera* entitled *The Five Kobo Opera*, and three plays that were translated into Pidgin but were otherwise unadapted – *The Good Person of Szechwan*, *The Caucasian Chalk Circle*, and *The Rise and Fall of the City of Mahagonny*. The underlying aim of this series of Africanized productions of Brecht was to introduce both drama students and an 'elite' university audience to the plays of a European playwright whose work at that time was still relatively little known even to campus-based audiences but which seemed to offer much that was immediately interesting, as well as a style of dramaturgy and performance of relevance to the developing literary drama in Africa. In particular, there was a desire to see how the kind of audience that frequented the Studio Theatre would respond to a sustained attempt to put into effect in an African context Brecht's ideas on Epic Theater, including a calculatedly 'gestic' style of performance that refused to invite familiar forms of empathy and audience identification and that sought to externalize the socioeconomic contradictions within the characters' behavior. Those responsible for the productions – African and Western lecturers in drama at the University, working with their largely Nigerian students – discovered that their expectation that Brecht's plays would be popular with their usual audiences was well founded. The often identified affinities between features of Brecht's epic theater and elements traditionally found in African performance – such things as the 'presentational' quality of performance, the enjoyment of narrative and of music and song for choric comment, the presence of a narrator/presenter, the use of typicality and stereotypes in characterization – together with the evident ethical focus of the issues and relations dramatized, and the distinctively dry and earthy quality of Brechtian humor and comedy – all of these were not too surprisingly appreciated by many in our audiences, at least in part because of their recognizability. Less predictable was what Nigerian audiences made of Brecht, not just in the sense of what specific meanings audience members might take from, or impose upon, the plays, but also in terms of how their interactions with the performances might generate particular kinds of theatrical events. In this respect, what was most striking, at least to me, was the extent to which Brecht's dramaturgy and our attempts at presenting his plays according to the precepts of epic theatre failed to deter audiences from 'melodramatizing' what they witnessed and siding emotionally and ethically with what they perceived as the forces of good.

Considerable attention was paid in the productions – and in the overall teaching of Brecht of which the productions were a part – to the theatrical possibilities implied by his theory's skepticism about Western realist mimesis and its ideological implications for the presentation of subjectivity. A significant part of the excitement and enthusiasm for doing Brecht for Nigerian audiences was the recognition that an essential feature of traditional African performance aesthetics has been the privileging of a social perspective that does not encourage the conventional Western insistence on the transcendent, irreducible individuality of the dramatic protagonist. As Antony Tatlow puts it, writing of what he sees as the deep-rooted compatibility between the Brechtian aesthetic and that of East Asian traditional performances from which Brecht drew so much of his inspiration, both theaters 'question the authenticity of the mimetically constructed subject, by allowing us to see the field of forces in which that subject inescapably stands and whose articulation it must be. Yet this subject remains at the center of attention. Only thus do we understand the forces that constitute it' (Tatlow 56). Much the same could be said of African traditional and popular forms of theater, with their insistence on a socially focused dramaturgy and their characteristic 'externalized' ways of demonstrating emotion. A major reason for staging Brecht for Nigerian audiences, then, was to see how far and to what effect the apparent affinities between performance modes that were recognizably and congenially African and the ideological and aesthetic intentions of the Brechtian project would work in practice.

Part of Brecht's desire in revolutionizing stage-audience relationships was to make what he regarded as inert, passive spectators into active, judging moral communities. We have already noted that theater audiences in Africa are, at least by most Western standards, unusually active participants in the theatre event – and active not only in their interjections, running commentaries, satirical jibes, and so forth, but more generally in the sense that its members typically constitute themselves as a collective moral force that evaluates, judges, approves, and sometimes denounces the proceedings on stage. It was precisely in this area – on the face of it, one where there is so much in common between Brecht's epic theater and African performance – that Nigerian audiences proved deeply resistant to the 'complex seeing' central to Brecht's theory and practice. For while both kinds of theater are committed to the promotion of ethically educative experience, they are at variance, indeed in almost total opposition, in their understandings of what that entails.

Criticism has identified features of melodrama that Brecht, like other dramatists before him but in his own distinctive way, exploited and adapted to suit his dramatic and ideological purposes (Heilmann 171–85). Clearly enough, Shen Teh in *The Good Person* and Grusha in *The Caucasian Chalk Circle* are intended to invite audiences' emotional investment as poor, kind-hearted women who wish to do good to others. While Grusha retains that straightforward emotional appeal in a play that seems to operate on the basis of a definite division between 'good' or at least sympathetic characters (Grusha, Simon, Azdak) and 'bad' ones (Natella Abashvili and her lawyers, the peasant who cheats Grusha) – and therefore justifiably invites a 'melodramatic' response – Shen Teh does not. Her inability to remain unproblematically good in a harsh and far from good world forces her, however involuntarily, to resort to her alter ego, her ruthless 'cousin' Shui Ta. Brecht subverts the moral polarities of melodrama and its characteristic responses by forcing his audience to recognize the *dialectical* relationship between the heroine and her supposed cousin. The 'message', of course, is that what the audience perceives as the 'evil' that is Shui Ta is as much a part of the same personality, the same human nature, as is the 'good' Shen Teh. What we perceive as morally right or wrong, good or bad, are not, for Brecht, fixed essences but aspects of one and the same entity that exist in dynamic relationship, as responses to intolerable social conditions. Any effective production of the play must strive to make that dialectical relationship as powerfully clear as possible, by intervening in and catching out the audience in its initial 'melodramatic' empathic investment in Shen Teh.

No doubt there were members of the audience for the Nigerian production of the play in 1982 who left the performance understanding this dialectical relationship perfectly well. But my impression, both at performances and in discussion with audience members (including drama students), was that the point of Brecht's dramaturgical conceit in *The Good Person* was resisted by many in the audience, not because of any lack of clarity in the production but mainly, I suspect, because it was so much at odds with the prevalent and deeply ingrained conviction that morality is precisely a matter of permanent truths, of fixed essences rather than, in Brecht's Marxist formulation, of dialectical relationships. For audiences sustained by such a conviction there seemed to be a real problem in fully absorbing, or at least accepting, the idea that the qualities associated with Shui Ta can be produced by the same human nature that has earlier and simultaneously demonstrated the impulse to generosity and altruism. And for much the same reason an ending that leaves the 'good' Shen Teh's moral and existential dilemma so resolutely unresolved goes against the grain of an ethical worldview that expects, and demands, the restoration of moral order.

In other ways too, received moral opinion could and, I believe, did interfere with some audience members' capacity to interpret *The Good Person* in an appropriately Brechtian way. As several writers have observed, the character stereotype, together with such allied linguistic devices as the cliché and the proverb, have prominent and important functions in African popular literature and theater (Barber et al.; Newell). Brecht wrote Shen Teh as the tart with a heart of gold, the woman who in the eyes of bourgeois society is 'fallen' but who has a capacity for love and generosity that would shame the average bourgeois. Or so at least this particular stereotype would be understood among most Western audiences. But for an African audience that is largely male, and that finds it hard to interrogate its own patriarchal assumptions, the stereotype of the kindly prostitute brings with it some ideological baggage that for most informed Western audiences distorts perception of the play. For the typical audience of Brecht in the West there is nothing in Shen Teh's status as a prostitute that seriously affects the perception of her essential goodness; if anything, empathy is enhanced by the understanding that her poverty has forced her to sell her body. But in a culture where, though prostitutes are frequently used, a combination of puritanical religious conviction and patriarchal ideology makes it impossible for some people to see them as anything other than 'wicked' or 'degraded' or 'irredeemably corrupt'. The perception of the reprehensibility of Shen Teh's profession overwhelms the perception of her and her vocation as a dramatic device, and may thus proceed to distort an audience member's entire reading of her role within the play. (Apart from anything else, it may be no easy matter for a respectable female to play such a character on the stage, at the risk of being associated, as actresses in African as in other cultures have traditionally been, with 'loose' or otherwise 'bad' women – especially when faced with a young, noisy, largely male audience that on a bad night can be merciless in its taunting.) This can produce such wayward but nevertheless predictable and understandable interpretations as that being a prostitute, she was a bad person all along, even if she said she wanted to do good, and that her taking in of the gods was really always a ploy to get money. An inappropriate moralism, in short, can play havoc with interpretative strategies.

It needs to be stressed that neither with this particular production nor with other productions were 'misreadings' of this kind a unitary response. On the contrary, the combination of the tendency towards the imposition of one or another moralistic interpretation on a play with the proclivity, noted above by both Barber and Asiedu, to pick out a 'lesson', or make a meaning, consonant with the individual's particular context and self-identification contributes to a multiplicity of readings rather than necessarily a single dominant one. I was frequently surprised, as a director and audience member, not just by what seemed at the time so often to be the perversity of Nigerian audiences and students in not understanding plays more or less the same way that I did but, even more alarmingly, in discovering that Nigerian playgoers and readers could generate so many quite distinct and conflicting interpretations among themselves.

III

Literary playmaking in Africa depends, just like any other kind of theater, on its practitioners' sense of their possible audiences, of their assumptions and deep-seated perceptions of how things are, of what they expect or at least are willing to tolerate in a theater space. An important aspect of the under-researched topic of African theater audiences is how patterns of dramaturgy may have been influenced by particular kinds of audience and the playwrights' conceptions of, and relationships with, them.[3] How far do dramatists' sense of their audience and what its characteristic expectations and assumptions are affect not just what they write about but how they write and the horizon of possible meaning thus generated? I have suggested that Nigerian university audiences were acutely concerned with the ethical implications of the characters and action of Nigerianized versions of Brecht' s plays but in ways that radically departed from the Brechtian notion of complex seeing, with its capacity for juxtaposing perspectives and critically interrogating predictable reactions. Instead, audiences of the series of Brecht productions typically operated within a fundamentally conservative moral framework in the sense that their interpretations of character and action and the 'lessons' they drew from them tended to be already imbedded within received ethical opinion, even when their perceptions perhaps articulated or complemented 'radical' popular criticism of the status quo. I now turn to the three published African adaptations of Brecht to investigate whether, and in what ways, they may be seen as influenced by what is posited here as African (not just Nigerian) audiences' proclivity to assume a distinctively moralistic stance in their reception even of 'élite' literary theater. Among other things, such a discussion must be alert to the possibility of differences of typical audience behavior and response across sub-Saharan Africa, as well as individual playwrights' deployment of a variety of dramaturgical strategies in their interactions with their audiences.

Ben Abdallah's *Land of a Million Magicians* was commissioned and first performed as part of the entertainment for the heads of state of nonaligned countries meeting in Accra in August 1991. As well as allowing him a much bigger budget than usual for this production, which included members of the resident company of the Ghana National Theatre, the special nature of its première and first audience clearly had a considerable impact on ben Abdallah's reshaping of *The Good Person*. Significantly, as we shall see, the published text of the play (and presumably subsequent productions) departs in at least one major respect from what was performed for the visiting heads of state.

Ben Abdallah broadly follows the story of *The Good Person*: having been rewarded by the three gods with a suitcase full of cash for providing shelter for the night, the good Hasana, like the 'angel of the slums' Shen Teh, makes altruistic use of her good fortune only to become disillusioned in her efforts. Hasana invents, or rather resurrects, her dead twin brother Fuseni to come to the rescue, though unlike Shen Teh's hard-hearted cousin Shui Ta, he comes to stay (Hasana having supposedly traveled) rather than making at first occasional short-lived and, on Shen Teh's part, reluctant interventions. Though his tough, profit-oriented approach soon has the buses running again and the

---

[3] Another under-researched topic is the nature of African acting, especially in the literary theater. Even more attention has been paid in recent Western theater studies to techniques of acting, rehearsal methods, etc., than to the study of audiences. Reasons of space preclude consideration here of performance styles in African theater in relation to Brecht's theory and practice of epic acting, much as I would have liked to comment on this important aspect of 'African Brecht'.

farms producing, the gods return in response to the many prayers for help they have received from the losers in the new order. Whereas in Brecht Shui Ta is arraigned before the judge/gods because of rumors that he has murdered Shen Teh – which of course metaphorically he has – in ben Abdallah's version the gods decide to set up 'a tribunal of the people' to determine Fuseni's fate and 'the fate of your land and people' (67). As in Brecht, the defendant reveals that he is both the compassionate altruist *and* the ruthless businessman. *The Good Person* ends on a note of deep uncertainty about how to resolve the dilemma embodied in the split between Shen Teh and Shui Ta: *Land of a Million Magicians* also ends with the withdrawal of the gods and a large question mark, but in a way that departs significantly from Brecht. Before their departure Hasana's friend and collaborator, the former queen of the prostitutes Magajiya (corresponding roughly to Mrs. Shen in Brecht's original), asks the gods why they chose to place such a heavy burden on Hasana rather than giving the money to the authorities. The god disguised as a cardinal responds in turn with a series of questions: 'Who are the authorities? ... What is authority? ... Where does the power of the authorities come from?' (77). Nothing will change in their lives, he asserts, until the people wake up to the fact that 'you are the source of all authority. The power of authority must flow from you' (77). Hasana takes up the challenge, proclaiming, 'We must bring change into our land ... but we don't need the gods or their money to do it. We need to organise ourselves to be the source of all the power of authority' (78). Her words are at first greeted with loud cheers from the crowd but when she turns down Mummuni's public proposal of marriage, the people lose interest, leaving one by one until no one at all is left on stage except Hasana and her urgent but unanswered question: 'How do we change the land, Magajiya? How? How? How, Magajiy ... !' (80).

As well as borrowing his dramatic material from *The Good Person*, ben Abdallah is genuinely Brechtian in the way he seeks to defamiliarize and complicate moralistic instincts and expectations. Not only the on-stage audience but the real audience of *Land of a Million Magicians* is compelled (or at least invited) to recognize that the decisive vote in favor of the one's 'goodness' against the other's 'badness' that happened only moments ago has been rendered deeply problematic by the public revelation that Hasana and Fuseni are one and the same. The 'message' of the parable, in the logic of ben Abdallah's version, is that since Hasana quite deliberately transforms herself into Fuseni to initiate a different economic and social system, the genuine *desire* to change society for the better can be associated with the profit motive and market forces as well as with African socialism, though both fail to have much effect on the prevailing moral stagnation of the general public and the former, no less than the latter, brings large numbers of casualties in its wake. Rendered in terms of social systems as well as individual personality, the polarity of 'good' and 'bad' is presented as inadequate, a moralistic illusion from which the audience in the theater as well as on the stage needs to be estranged. However, what is presented at the play's conclusion as not being illusory or problematic, at least in its formulation, is the political *principle* by which society can change for the better – the people's conscious organization of itself into the source of all authority and the power it wields. But in ben Abdallah's bleakly pessimistic (published) ending, the call to organize is rejected in practice by those who acclaim it rhetorically, presumably because it requires too great a shift out of their habitual preoccupation with the demands of the moment. (It is arguably a major dramaturgical weakness of the play that the crowd lose interest in Hasana's summons to organize for no more plausible reason than that they are disappointed by her rejection of Mummuni's proposal of marriage, which leaves unexplored the precise reason for their indifference to the way forward, and seems to make ben Abdallah vulnerable to the accusation of political fatalism.)

What is striking, when we compare ben Abdallah's reworking of the story with Brecht's original, is both the explicitly sociopolitical emphasis of the parable and its residual moralism. In *The Good Person*, the gods' gift to Shen Te allows her to move up the social ladder from common prostitute, who sells herself, to petit-bourgeois trader, the owner of a small tobacco shop. But she cannot fulfill her altruistic instincts and at the same time stay in business, since the laws of capitalist exchange demand that she make a profit. Hence a split inevitably develops between the private self, with its moral sensitivity to the plight of others, and the public self, which engages in the laws of capitalist exchange and which comes to the fore as the 'good' private self becomes increasingly isolated. Brecht's demonstration of the contradictions that open up within the self in capitalist society is replaced, in *Land of a Million Magicians*, by an explicitly socio-political parable about the relative merits of African socialism and a market-driven economy, and the related issue of the fate of the land and its people. Ben Abdallah has relatively little interest in the dialectical relationship between public and private selves; instead, he focuses attention on how a viable political system that can eradicate poverty, corruption, and 'badness' in its many forms can be constructed. Significantly, the operative principle for this is first enunciated by one of the gods, who in *The Good Person* are dismissed as so much worthless ideological baggage. Even more significant, the principle is presented as a clear and valid precept, an uncontentious recipe for necessary change proclaimed by an unproblematic Hasana – even if the people cannot match up to its, and her, challenge.

The conclusion of the published text of *Land of a Million Magicians* offers, then, an opposition between ethical and political clarity, on the one hand, and the failure of the people to take the lead offered them, on the other. Brecht's dialectical clash of accumulating contradictions, the necessary absence of clarity in a time when 'the relations of people ... are unclear' (cited by Wright 44) is replaced by a starkly undialectical conflict between 'good' and 'bad'. But there is a significant difference between the ending of the original production for an audience of nonaligned dignitaries and that of the published text. In the original version, the ending has Hasana making an uplifting appeal to the people to organize to be the source of authority – a speech greeted, according to the original stage direction, by the crowd cheering loudly. The last few moments witness Mummuni's proposal of marriage and rejection on the grounds that 'we have work to do', followed as a finale by celebratory music and general cries of jubilation as she is carried off shoulder-high. The fact that the playwright could, and did, change his ending so radically between the première in 1991 and the text published in 1993 underlines, to my mind, the rhetorical, undialectical nature of his undertaking, as well as the influence of different kinds of audience. Presumably, ben Abdallah, both as an artist and a political figure himself in Ghana at that time, wished to make a positive political statement about the possibility of a democratic politics in the nonaligned world to suit the specific nature of the occasion and the audience. Later, less influenced by a particular event and more attuned to everyday Ghanaian realities, he offers the diametrically opposed conclusion, in which the people signally fail to rise to the challenge thrown down by his protagonist. But the revised ending is in no way more Brechtian, in the sense that it offers, as *The Good Person* does, a genuine, unresolved complexity, a sense of the unavoidable perplexity of a dark and intrinsically dialectical reality.

The enduring popularity of Brecht's *Threepenny Opera* (1928), itself based on John Gay's *Beggars' Opera* (1728), has, not surprisingly, guaranteed that there have been more

African adaptations of this than of any other Brecht play.⁴ Famously, that popularity with bourgeois audiences, both in Germany in the late 1920s and subsequently elsewhere, contradicts Brecht's critique of 'culinary' theater, a theater that in his pejorative formulation 'theatres it all down' ('Notes to the *Threepenny Opera*' in Willett 43). One of the first experiments in constructing 'epic' theater, *The Threepenny Opera*'s appealing music and lyrics, on which Brecht collaborated with Kurt Weill, and its entertainingly humorous and farcical elements have persistently undermined in practice Brecht's aim of ensuring that the bourgeois audience member 'sees his wishes not merely fulfilled but also criticized' thus theoretically positioning him 'to appoint a new function for the theatre' (43). More particularly, the play's concern with 'bourgeois conceptions' (43) centers on the essential identity of 'respectable' business and criminality in the unspecified capitalist but clearly in many respects Weimar-esque system presented in the play. In this society, everyone and everything is commodified, their value determined by the economic dictates of the system: the bourgeois businessman is functionally no different than the gangster, and the gangster aspires to bourgeois gentility.

For all their differences, *Opera Wonyosi* and *Love, Crime and Johannesburg* share an enthusiastic relish for topical political and social satire that is much more reminiscent of Gay's original than of Brecht's adaptation. In the former, the setting of the action in the supposedly Nigerian quarter of Bangui, capital of the then Central African 'Empire', permits Soyinka to highlight and condemn the abuses and excesses of oil-boom Nigeria's social elite and its military rulers alongside his ridicule of the brutality and corruption of current African tyrants, notably the egregiously absurd and horrific 'Emperor' Bokassa. Junction Avenue's version, co-written by Malcolm Purkey and Carol Steinberg, focuses on the bizarre and sometimes surrealistic contradictions of the transition to democracy in post-apartheid Johannesburg, in which former heroes of the anti-apartheid resistance movement are convicted of bank robberies, while their former comrades enjoy their new élite positions as owners of banks and other lucrative businesses, often in partnership with the former 'enemy'. Though both – and especially *Love, Crime and Johannesburg* – deal like Brecht with the ways in which the overtly criminal and the apparently legitimate, in business and politics, rub together and fuse in their respective social locations, the African versions are much more concerned with doing so in ways that, like ben Abdallah's adaptation of *The Good Person*, foreground the contemporary political plight of, and prospects for, the nation-state. Though he was living through a crucial moment in German history, on the eve of the triumph of fascism, Brecht's play is devoid of specific and topical political or social references and was not primarily engaged in satirical analysis of the body politic. It is capitalism as system that is the object of ironic enquiry in *The Three penny Opera*, not the contradictions and prospects of a particular capitalist society in crisis. In contrast, both Soyinka and the creators of *Love, Crime and Johannesburg* are centrally concerned, as we have seen *The Land of a Million Magicians* also is, with power – with who has it, how it is used, and what it does to both those who wield it and those who are its subjects – and both have their origin in specific events (Bokassa'a

---

⁴As well as Soyinka's *Opera Wonyosi* and Junction Avenue's *Love, Crime and Johannesburg*, there were also an unpublished version of Brecht's play *The Five Kobo Opera*, devised by students of the Drama Department of Ahmadu Bello University, Nigeria, a few months before the first production of Soyinka's version at the University of Ife in 1977; and the South African Pioneer Theatre's *Beggars Consolidated* in 1980 (see Kruger, 'Theatre, Crime').

self-styled coronation, the arrests of Mzwakhe Mbuli and later of Robert McBride and Colin Chauke) that engage issues of power.

The satirical dissection of the deformations of power and wealth in young African nation-states involves, in a way that Brecht's perspective in *The Threepenny Opera* did not, an implied moral stance on the part of both creators and audiences. However deeply concerned Brecht was with the moral effects of capitalism, his position in the *Opera* was that bourgeois rhetoric about morality is merely an ideological illusion, moralistic assertion an irrelevance, when other, more fundamental needs have not been satisfied ('Eats first, morals later'). Not so Soyinka. Especially in the context of *Opera Wonyosi*'s première – attended by a state military governor and his retinue as well as the 'lace madams' and other representatives of the élite that is so savagely attacked in the play – Soyinka offers a vision of social degeneracy that does not explicitly refer to but is nevertheless constructed on the common recognition of right and wrong. When the playwright was criticized in a review of the first production in the Ife-based *Positive Review* for the absence in his play of a class-based analysis of the deformations presented, Soyinka's response, published in a foreword to the Methuen volume including *Opera Wonyosi*, was to insist that the writer's role is complementary to others, such as the sociopolitical analyst, and 'not one which can usurp one or all of these roles in entirety without forfeiting its own claim to a distinctive vocation' (297). Pointing to the failures of his Marxist or neo-Marxist critics in explaining such elements of the Nigerian *malaise* as public executions and ritual murder for the magical attainment of wealth, or in evolving 'an effective idiom for their own active social alternatives' (299), Soyinka insists on his confidence that sooner or later, and with or without the benefit of academic social analysis, society will recognize itself in the artistic portrayal of 'the preponderant obscenities that daily assail our lives' and that it will 'be moved to act in its own overall self-interest' (299–300). He points as evidence of his play's efficacy to the tangible response of the socially diverse audience, crossing all class divisions, at its première at the University of Ife. For him at least, 'the social impact of that experience' clearly included a collective act of moral recognition induced by the play's angry humanist critique of contemporary Nigerian society.

Where *Opera Wonyosi* is predominantly bitterly angry in tone, Junction Avenue's *Love, Crime and Johannesburg* is much more ambivalent, dissecting the ironic complexities of power in the new, postapartheid South Africa no less trenchantly than Soyinka's satire but largely in an irreverently playful and celebratory mode. In both its playfulness and its emphasis on the structural links between the new capitalism and crime in post-apartheid South Africa, *Love, Crime and Johannesburg* has much more in common with Brecht's play than does *Opera Wonyosi*. There is also a more Brechtian opacity, a more genuinely dialectical sense of social and political open-endedness, in Junction Avenue's representation of what may really be going on at the heart of the new power structure in the Republic. In the shocking, sometimes frankly surrealistic, postapartheid transformations of wealth and power, even the apparently absurd notion of a 'secret' secret service, which Jimmy 'Long Legs' Mangane, the Macheath figure, claims to be working for, cannot be discounted. Scene 16 is emblematic of the shadowy, uncertain world about which it seems impossible 'to say who is right and who is wrong', as the Company sings in its final song (54). Queenie Dlamini and Lewis Matome, former comrades in the struggle against the apartheid régime, now uneasy allies as respectively chief of police and business tycoon, stand in 'sinister pools of light' amid an otherwise shadowy stage, trying to communicate with each other on their cellphones. The vagaries of cellphone conversation – 'you're breaking up', 'I've lost you completely now' – ostensibly explain the difficulties they encounter in communication. But even when they can hear what each other is saying, there is the deeper problem of what they mean, or how to act. The scene is dominated by unanswered questions: To keep Jimmy in jail or to let him out? Is he innocent or guilty? What is really going on? Even the question of what's the question is at issue. At the end they are back were they began. 'So. Do we let him out or do we keep him in?' Queenie again asks. 'I just don't know' is Lewis's response (40).

The ambivalence and moral relativism of the murky, deceptive world evoked in *Love, Crime and Johannesburg* seems to extend to its own moral stance. There are several different 'takes' on morality represented in the play, ranging from Queenie's frustrated desire to uphold the principle of law and order to the opportunistic pragmatism of the businessmen, Bokkie and Lewis, and – arguably the closest it comes to a compelling moral commentator – the exhausted, angrily disgusted old criminal Bones who nostalgically recalls the good old days when gangsters were proper gangsters and had honor, style, 'a set of rules, a code of conduct!' (28). But just as we never discover the true nature of what Jimmy Mangane has been doing or why, so the play itself seems reluctant to settle on a definitive moral position, caught as it is between condemnation and celebration, transfixed by 'the stagy glamour of "love and crime"'.[5] Some of this, as the authors indicate, has to do with their desire for a product that would exhibit 'an ease, a lightness and a celebratory quality' (xii) that is certainly sanctioned by Brecht's emphasis on the importance of *Spass* (fun) in epic theater, nowhere more so than in *The Threepenny Opera*. And the celebratory mood, in turn, is explained by the playmakers' love-hate relationship with Johannesburg itself, which is so central to their play, but even more significantly, by the release from apartheid and the birth of democracy (however flawed) that was also an artistic liberation from what Purkey and Steinberg describe as 'the intense moral burden that playmaking in apartheid South Africa imposed' (xiv). In this newfound sense of freedom not just the company but the audience too seem to have engaged.

IV

According to its authors, the audiences of *Love, Crime and Johannesburg* were 'young, diverse and clearly engaged' and made the play very much their own property – especially, apparently, in making it much funnier than the company had expected (xiii–xiv).[6] As Martin Orkin has pointed out in a discussion of the term 'popular' in relation to South African theater, very little information exists on the size or composition of township audiences, though the audience composition of what he terms 'contestatory theatre', in venues such as the Market Theatre complex, the Baxter Theatre, or the People's Space Theatre of the late '70s, is more easily conjectured or measured (Orkin 56). Such audiences are usually viewed as being 'made up of, probably, liberal-minded or dissident members of the ruling middle classes, together with those township people able to afford

---

[5] Kruger complains that having raised audience expectations for pointed satire of South Africa's *comprador* capitalism, the play fails to take the opportunity to make 'a timely critique of the much more sinister normalization of white-collar crime, corruption, and patronage schemes in which funds from government departments, international donors and non-government foundations have been squandered for the pet projects of the well-connected rather than the truly disadvantaged ...' ('Theatre, Crime' 278–79).

[6] Its premiere was at the Standard Bank National Festival of the Arts in Grahamstown, followed by a season at the Market Theatre in Johannesburg.

the price of tickets and a journey into the city. Again, these are usually described by commentators as likely to be predominantly members of the township middle- or petit-bourgeois classes only' (56). It would not be unreasonable to assume that the audiences of *Love, Crime and Johannesburg* both at the Grahamstown Festival and during its run at the Market conformed to this general description. We are therefore talking about an audience that is quite different in composition and in behavior than characteristic African audiences described earlier in this essay. Such audiences in South Africa, as already noted, are likely to receive and respond in ways familiar to Western, or at least Anglo-Saxon, playgoers, unlike the township audiences whose characteristic patterns of reception and response seem to have much more in common with typical audiences in, say, Ghana and Nigeria. This seems particularly likely to be the case when what Purkey and Steinberg call the 'intense moral burden' of theater production and reception, especially art or literary theater production and reception, has been lifted, minimizing the onus on directly ethical response and permitting 'a wonderful freedom to be critical, to be dissident, to be irreverent, to be playful' (xiv).

The particular composition of the South African audiences for *Love, Crime and Johannesburg*, as well as the specific postapartheid celebratory context of its creation and reception, underlines how far practitioners' sense of their audience and its characteristic behavior and expectations may affect both what they create and how they create it. It also underlines, by contrast, how far the Brechtian legacy in African literary theater has been influenced by the impulse to ethical gratification and the enunciation of moral wisdom shared by both élite and popular African audiences. Brecht, we know, was concerned to re-create the German (and more generally Western) audiences of his time as judging, moral communities. For all the inflections of emphasis over time in his own writings, central to Brecht's notion of epic theater have been the twin notions of 'complex seeing' and the *Verfremdungseffekt* – the need for audiences to think 'above' as well as 'within' the flow of the play, and at the same time, to 'estrange' the spectators from their routine, embedded perceptions and assumptions, including of course their habitual moral assumptions. Though his own practice as a dramatist was uneven, some of his plays being more ethically interrogative, ambivalent, and open-ended than others, surely what the best of Brecht and the Brechtian legacy teaches us is that it is possible to be both morally serious and at the same time sensitive to the opaque complexities and perplexities of current reality when 'the relations of people ... are unclear'. What may be broadly delineated as the 'Brechtian tradition' in Africa, and more specifically the published African adaptations of Brecht's plays, demonstrate a commitment to moral seriousness generally and, in a particular inflection, to sociopolitical topicality and sharp, often satirical analysis of the nation-state and its governance in particular. But in two versions out of the three considered, the adaptations largely eschew Brecht's dialectical, open-ended dramaturgical perspective for something more affirmatively homiletic, explicitly in ben Abdallah's case, more subtly and implicitly in Soyinka's. Extrapolating from this we may suggest that much African literary drama, while pursuing the thoroughly Brechtian aim of being morally serious and purposeful and often having affinities with Brecht in dramatic technique and presentation, is often too prone to adopt the rhetorical expression of what is perceived as commonly grounded, self-evident truth, thus ultimately negating both complex seeing and de-familiarizing effects. This is true, I would argue, even of some of the output of one of the most genuinely Brechtian of African dramatists, Femi Osofisan – for example, *The Chattering and the Song*. The same applies, I believe, to that most vibrant and distinctive African offshoot of the Brechtian tradition, the body of work that has come to be known as Theater for Development. In my personal experience of it, and in much of what I have read about recent work in that area, the homiletic impulse too often prevails over the open-ended critical interrogation of embedded perceptions and habitual moral assumptions. Writing serious drama without an appreciation of the tastes and expectations of one's audience is of course likely to be calamitously unproductive. But by the same token, writing drama that is constrained in its impulse to question and criticize, especially in ways that may be profoundly uncomfortable, by the established ethical parameters of its intended audience is equally likely to prove unsatisfactory. In the context of one of the Brechtian tradition's most distinguished exponents in Africa entitling a recent essay – 'Is the Theatre Dying in Africa?' – it may be timely for commentators and practitioners to address the whole issue of spectatorship and to revisit the strengths and weaknesses of the Brechtian legacy on the continent.

WORKS CITED

Asiedu, Awo Mana. 'West African Theatre Audiences: A Study of Ghanaian and Nigerian Audiences of Literature Theatre in English.' PhD thesis. U of Birmingham, 2003. Print.

Awodiya, Muyiwa P. *The Drama of Femi Osofisan: A Critical Perspective*. Ibadan: Kraft, 1995. Print.

Barber, Karin. *The Generation of Plays: Yoruba Popular Life in Theatre*. Bloomington: Indiana UP, 2000. Print.

Barber, Karin, John Collins, and Alain Ricard. *West African Popular Theatre*. Bloomington: Indiana UP; Oxford: James Currey, 1997. Print.

Ben Abdallah, Mohammed. *Land of a Million Magicians: An Abibigoro*. Accra: Woeli, 1993. Print.

Bennett, Susan. *Theatre Audiences: A Theory of Production and Reception*. London: Routledge, 1997. Print.

Brecht, Bertolt. *The Good Person of Szechwan. Brecht Collected Plays 6*. Ed. Ralph Manheim and John Willett. New York: Random House, 1976. Print.

———. *The Threepenny Opera. Brecht Collected Plays 2*. Ed. John Willett and Ralph Manheim. London: Methuen, 1994. Print.

———. *Werke: Grosse kommentierte Berliner und Frankfurter Ausgabe* (30 vols. with *Registerband*). Ed. Werner Hecht, Jan Knopf, Werner Mittenzwei, and Klaus-Detlef Müller. Berlin-Weimar: Aufbau; Frankfurt a. M.: Suhrkamp. 1988–2000. Paperback ed. 2003. Print.

Gay, John. *The Beggar's Opera. The Beggar's Opera and Other Eighteenth Century Plays*. Selected by John Hampden. Intro. by David W. Lindsay. London: Dent, 1974. Print.

Heilman, Robert Bechtold. *The Iceman, the Arsonist, and the Troubled Agent: Tragedy and Melodrama on the Modern Stage*. London: Allen and Unwin, 1973. Print.

Junction Avenue Theatre Company. *Love, Crime and Johannesburg*. Johannesburg: Witwatersrand UP, 2000. Print.

Kruger, Loren. *Post-Imperial Brecht: Politics and Performance, East and South*. Cambridge: Cambridge UP, 2004. Print.

———. 'Theatre, Crime and the Edgy City in Post-Apartheid Johannesburg.' *Theatre Journal* 53.2 (2001): 223–52.

Kuhn, Tom, and Steve Giles, ed. *Brecht on Art and Politics*. London: Methuen, 2003. Print.

Newell, Stephanie. *Ghanaian Popular Fiction*: *'Thrilling Discoveries in Conjugal Life' and Other Tales*. Oxford: James Currey, 2000. Print.

Orkin, Martin. 'Whose Popular Theatre and Performance?' *Theatre and Change in South Africa*. Ed. Geoffrey V. Davis and Anne Fuchs. Amsterdam: Harwood Academic, 1996. 49–64. Print.

Osofisan, Femi. 'Stirbt das Theater in Afrika? Überlegungen aus nigerianischer Perspektive.' *Kreatives Afrika*. Ed. Susan Arndt and Katrin Berndt. Wuppertal: Peter Hammer, 2005. 35–51. Print.

——. 'Yoruba Theatre in Crisis: Death or Transition?' *Interfaces between the Oral and the Written: Versions and Subversions in African Literatures* 2. Ed. Alain Ricard and Flora Veit-Wild. *Matatu* 31–32. Amsterdam: Rodopi, 2005. Print.

Richards, Sandra. 'Wasn't Brecht an African Writer?' *Brecht in Asia and Africa: The Brecht Yearbook XIV*. Hong Kong: U of Hong Kong, 1989. 168–83. Print.

Rotimi, Ola. 'Much Ado about Brecht.' *The Dramatic Touch of Difference*. Ed. Erika Fischer-Lichte et al. Tübingen: Gunter Narr, 1990. Print.

Sowande, Bode. *Flamingo and Other Plays*. Harlow: Longman, 1986. Print.

Soyinka, Wole. *Opera Wonyosi*. *Soyinka: Six Plays*. London: Methuen, 1984. Print.

Tatlow, Antony. *Shakespeare, Brecht, and the Intercultural Sign*. Durham: Duke UP, 2001. Print.

Ukala, Sam. 'Politics of Aesthetics.' *African Theatre: Playwrights and Politics*. Ed. Martin Banham, James Gibbs, and Femi Osofisan. Oxford: James Currey/Witwatersrand UP/Indiana UP, 2001. 29–41. Print.

White, John J. *Bertolt Brecht*'s *Dramatic Theory*. Rochester, NY: Camden House, 2004. Print.

Willett, John, ed. and trans. *Brecht on Theatre*. London: Methuen, 1964. Print.

Wright, Elizabeth. *Postmodern Brecht: A Re-Presentation*. London: Routledge, 1989. Print.

North America

CHAPTER TWENTY-SEVEN

New Measures for Brecht in America

PETER W. FERRAN

Roughly 30 years ago, while the Berlin Wall, just erected, was stimulating West German theaters to renew their call for a Brecht boycott across 'free' Europe, America was generating an enthusiasm for Brecht's plays and ideas that burgeoned into near worship and almost brought about a revolution in its theater. Today, only five years after the unpredictably abrupt collapse of that infamous Wall, the American theater appears to have given up on Brecht, and a new biography paints him as a criminal expropriator of his collaborators' work.

America's somewhat belated embrace of Brecht in the early 1960s was no doubt stimulated by the combination of his premature death in 1956, the long (1954-59) Off-Broadway run of *The Threepenny Opera* in Marc Blitzstein's adaptation, and the liberal climate that arrived with John F. Kennedy. Martin Esslin and John Willett's books had started the swelling of popular Brechtiania after their 1959 and 1960 paperback appearances, and there was also Bentley's championing, steadfast since the mid-40s, which issued in his *Seven Plays by Bertolt Brecht* in 1961. Grove Press followed this with its rapid publication of more Bentley versions and other translations in the next few years, and a rash of productions broke out everywhere. *The Tulane Drama Review* brought out its first special Brecht issue in 1961, with three of his own essays, the poem 'To Those Born Afterwards', the libretto for Weill's ballet 'The Seven Deadly Sins', Werner Hecht's synopsis of epic theory before 1933, and several other enlightening pieces. The American Brecht mania expanded through the 1960s into an outsized assortment of artistic projects, critical exercises, and academic businesses. By the time the first volume of the joint British-American translation project by Random House appeared in 1970, Brecht and the idea 'Brechtian' had become a significant part of what we now think of as a revolution in American culture.

But during the next two decades Brecht fell into a weirdly constructed disregard. His initial slide from the liberal favor of the radical 60s was due in part to America's political regression into conservatism; but it also owed something to the theatrical avant-garde's shift away from Brecht's articulated aesthetic aims, however they were understood. Although leading experimental groups such as the Living Theatre, Chaikin's Open Theater, and Schechner's Performance Group at first pursued what they understood to be Brechtian values, the main force in this American avant-garde theater turned out to be Artaud, not Brecht. Soon the 'holy' and 'immediate' theatrical impulses (of Peter Brook's catalog) supplanted the 'rough' ones. And all the while, the rational adamancy of radical Marxism was being ground down by the depredations of Vietnam, the sociology of 'turn-on-drop-out', rock, dope, and sex, and the relentless political oppressiveness that set in with Nixon.

This transition from 60s uproar to 70s and 80s retrenchment, in which the mainstream American theater resumed its former habit of avoiding anything politically discomforting in favor of the commercially successful, torpedoed Brecht. His last decent Broadway production was the 1976 Papp-Foreman *Threepenny Opera* at Lincoln Center. But even that production, advertised by Papp as authentically Brechtian in its aggressiveness, convinced many Broadway theatergoers that Brecht was finally not their cup of tea. Meanwhile, there came news about European playwrights such as Handke who claimed to have gone beyond Brecht, about new theaters and directors in England who had abandoned Brechtians such as Arden and Bond, and about boldly different artistic versions of Marxism in East Germany. And developments at home included fashionable postmodernist skepticism about authorial authority, the fresh vitality of feminist theory and criticism, and growing educational pressures to accommodate programmatic multiculturalism (which soon led to a reflexive spurning of European male authors). Brecht began to develop a bad odor, especially among the increased numbers of Americans who had come to believe they knew a thing or two about 'Brechtian'.

Brecht-bashing increased noticeably about the time Ronald Hayman's new biography was published in 1983. Earlier admiration for the exile's cunning evasion of HUAC'S questions about Marxist ideology in his plays now turned into accusations of cowardice and lying. Indignation was expressed more and more frequently about his Stalinist sympathies, his casuistical accommodation of the Ulbricht regime in East Berlin, and some of his high-handed personal conduct in the Berliner Ensemble. The 1986 Toronto conference 'Brecht: Thirty Years After' featured much renunciation of influence and re-estimating of significance. Some critics pursued the question of his moral character as if all questions about his dramatic and theatrical achievements had been settled. Their writing showed a perverse satisfaction taken in his personal failings. We began to hear, routinely repeated, that Brecht had always exploited his mistresses and collaborators for both sexual and creative pleasure, not to mention financial gain.

The end of 1989 brought an absurdly hyperbolically publicized Broadway production of *The Threepenny Opera*, touting Sting (the millionaire celebrity with a social conscience) as a would-be 'Macheath for the 90s', a brand new translation by the *Village Voice's* Michael Feingold, and John Dexter directing a promising cast that included Maureen McGovern, Georgia Brown, Ethyl Eichelberger, and Alvin Epstein. Dexter's Brechtian idea was to load the stage with flocks of homeless, thereby making relevant the 'social criticism' embedded in the text's beggars. This laughably misconceived project, with its gratuitous musical-comedy prancing and prating, validated for good the Brechtian proposition that the all-devouring theater institution resists any change in its apparatus, 'theater-izing' everything it touches.

It now seems just too ironic to be true that this cynically commercialized appropriation of Brecht and Weill coincided with the collapse of the Berlin Wall and the German Democratic Republic – a reversal of the paradoxical situation of Brecht's American popularity just after 1961, and a metaphor for what West German free-marketeers were simultaneously rehearsing as they prepared to enter the stage of Brecht's former country.

Not only could we read in the failure of the Sting-Dexter *3 Penny Opera* [sic] a verification that the American theater had never really got Brecht right, but we could also glimpse in the collapse of East European Communism the portentous certainty that it probably never would, because now *all* Communists had proven to be failures. With the removal of the Red Menace, it would never again seem necessary to do Brecht right, if at all.

Sure enough, four years later only one production of Brecht was scheduled in the entire combined season of America's regional theaters (according to *American Theatre's* listing, October 1993). And a year later we would see the even more dismaying publication of Fuegi's biography. Beyond the likely fact that this book will nail Brecht's English-language coffin shut, it also gives us ample evidence that disparaging Brecht personally has more appeal than mounting productions of his plays or conducting responsible critical studies of them. Soon we shall be able to avoid his disturbing influence altogether.

America's present image of Brecht encapsulates all its own contradictory ideas about artists, theater, politics, and theory. He is acknowledged as a great artistic talent; he is known as a didactic Marxist whose plays deliver Communist (or at least socialist) lectures; he is recognized as an influential theorist of modern theater; and he is admitted to be someone who experienced an arduous middle period of his life, in exile from his native country, deprived of a German-language theater, but still engaged in constant combat with the tyrant Hitler. But his didacticism is unacceptable because of its Communist politics; his theory is untenable because it flouts essential laws of the theater; and his person is insupportable because he was devious, unscrupulous, and exploitative. However, his plays transcend his political ideology, his aesthetic biases, and his personal short-comings, because he was a greater artist than anything else. He is therefore significant. But that doesn't matter a great deal either, because we have seen the error of making too much of artists.

DIE MASSNAHME: CULPRIT *LEHRSTÜCK*

The one play everyone thinks of in connection with Brecht's unacceptable ideology is *Die Massnahme – The Measures Taken*. The best known of the 'learning plays' (*Lehrstücke*) written between 1928 and 1930, its obvious difficulty is its content. That Brecht ratifies the Agitators' killing of the Young Comrade because it is done, in accord with Communist doctrine, for the higher good of fulfilling the Party's political ends is widely accepted. Eric Bentley pointed out long ago that civilians in Western countries where human rights have been guaranteed 'may well be shocked by Bertolt Brecht's *Measures Taken* because of its clearcut defense of the right of the group to liquidate the individual in the group interest' (*The Brecht Commentaries*, 278). Because the play represents a group's liquidation of an individual, Brecht is assumed to condone it. 'Brecht's most doctrinal play', declares Karl H. Schoeps (*Bertolt Brecht*, 175), 'it expresses his first frank and unreserved profession of communism, and his only attempt to present the extreme sacrifice required by the class struggle'.

This view originates with early critics like Reinhold Grimm and Martin Esslin, who read the play in the most conventional critical manner. Esslin famously called it 'the only great tragedy on the moral dilemma of Soviet Communism' (*Brecht: The Man and His Work*, 156). But where these scholars endeavored to rationalize the apparent teaching of the play with what they understood as Brecht's quest for a political faith, some more recent commentators have found it easy to use this presumed Marxist morality play to construct their negative personal criticism of Brecht. *The Measures Taken* has become a vehicle for articulating an animus towards Brecht the scoundrel.

Timothy Garton Ash, for example, uses his *TLS* review of Hayman's biography ('The Poet and the Butcher', 9 December 1983) to present Brecht as one of that breed of artist whose life had to be bad in order that his poetry might be valuable to us. Anchoring his attack in *The Measures Taken*, he proceeds to repeat the common, received interpretation of it and spell out Brecht's culpability for having engendered it:

> Having embraced communism [Brecht] rushed to spell out its most radical moral implications in *Die Massnahme*. ... [It] argues precisely those ethical conclusions from Marx-ism ... and Leninism ... which would be used to justify all the atrocities of Stalinism in Brecht's lifetime. It uncannily anticipates the Moscow trials.

This is exactly what Esslin had said in 1961. But unlike Esslin, Ash insinuates a negative moral judgment upon Brecht, using the rhetorical trick of drawing a damning conclusion from a non-occurrence. 'It is a remarkable fact that Brecht never explicitly disowned the morality of "The Measures Taken".' And then he defines that unacceptable morality at the same time as he unwarrantedly imputes it to Brecht: 'To the end of his life he would maintain that *in principle* the end – communism – justified the means – killing, lies, injustice – being used by the governments he supported.'

Ash, an influential social critic, not only makes free with unsupported assertions and unjustified assumptions, he also practices astonishingly fallacious reasoning. 'Brecht's political life matters for at least two reasons', he tells us. 'First, our knowledge of it may affect our reading of his work.' A moment later he concedes: 'Perhaps our knowledge of the man's compromises should not affect our judgment of the work; but in practice it does.' But notice how Brecht's 'political life' has turned into his 'compromises'. To clinch his point, Ash offers this dubious proof: 'We are less impressed by a sermon on fidelity, if we know the minister for a philanderer; by a call to heroism, if we know the writer for a coward.' So: Brecht is assumed to be a preacher, then convicted of hypocrisy; supposed a courageous revolutionary, then condemned for faint-heartedness.

The most disgraceful thing about these moralizing critics is not their relying on *ad hominem* innuendo, but their failing to appreciate the salient *structural* fact of *The Measures Taken*, the one feature that distinguishes it from the other musical *Lehrstücke*, and also from every other play of Brecht's: the presumed dramatic action is not being rendered in a theatrical 'present tense' at all, but is literally being re-presented by one group of people to another on the stage. This means that the killing of a young comrade by Communist agitators working in China does not 'happen'. It is not the dramatic action. There is no dramatis persona of 'Young Comrade'. Therefore, he cannot be a 'tragic protagonist', or any other kind of customarily defined 'character'. Neither, for that matter, can the other 'characters' usually listed in English translations. Ostensibly, the dramatis personae of this piece are 'Control Chorus' and 'Agitators'.

A lot of the interpretive hysteria about *Die Massnahme* could have been avoided if its critics had proceeded from this formal feature instead of from the moral content. And if they had then studied Brecht's comments on the *Lehrstück* form in general and on *Die Massnahme* in particular, and had also analyzed how Hanns Eisler's music works as part of the text-to-be-performed, they would have seen from the start that this experimental piece is no doctrinal political lesson. In fact, all this evidence combines to persuade us that *The Measures Taken* is not a play at all, but just what Brecht called it – an 'exercise' (*eine Einübung*). As such, it is the most hypothetical work in Brecht's entire output, the one pure example of his theory in practice. It is the definitive experiment in Epic Theater. 'The *Lehrstück* teaches by being played, not by being seen', wrote Brecht.

> Theoretically, no spectators are necessary for the *Lehrstück*, although they naturally could come in handy. What is basic to the *Lehrstück* is the expectation that the players, through the carrying out of certain kinds of behavior, the adopting of certain attitudes, the reproducing of certain speeches, and so forth can be socially influenced.[1]

These remarks 'On the Theory of the Learning Play' emphasize the distinction between aesthetic criteria used for playing 'stage plays' (*Schaustücke*) and those that apply to these *Lehrstücke*. For example: 'Particularly individualized, unique characters are irrelevant, unless individuality and uniqueness are the subject of the learning.' And: 'The form of the *Lehrstücke* is austere, but only in order that segments of original invention and of topical character can more easily be inserted.' And: 'For the playing style, *epic theater's* directions apply. Study of the *Verfremdungseffekt* is indispensable.'

Brecht declared: 'Conceptual mastery of the whole play is absolutely necessary. But it is not advisable to make conclusions about the learning therein before the actual playing.' And in connection with this thought, he offered a corrective to 'Misunderstandings About the *Lehrstück*'. However useful the 'blackboard' might be to instruction, he said, it is not the main thing about learning. 'It was not our plan to place a dramatic and theatrical form at the disposal of the individual dogmatism and opinion-mongering of the literati' (*GW* 17, 1026).

For the 'exercise' of *The Measures Taken*, he offered these guides:

> The dramatic presentation must be simple and sober; exceptional energy and particularly 'expressive' playing are superfluous. The players have simply to show the existing behavior of the four, which must be known for an understanding and a judgment about the case. ... Each of the four players should have the opportunity to show the behavior of the Young Comrade once; thus each player should play one of the Young Comrade's four main scenes. The presenters (singers and players) have the assignment to teach by learning.
>
> (*GW* 17, 1032)[2]

But, he warned, 'efforts to extract from *The Measures Taken* prescriptions for political action should not be undertaken without an understanding of the abc's of dialectical materialism' (1032-33).

From his numerous remarks about the piece over the 25 years after its first performance in December 1930, the following, from a 1956 interview with a French critic, sum up Brecht's ideas most provocatively:

> This play is not made to be read. This play is not made to be seen ... [but] to be played. For people to play among themselves. ... Each of them must change from one role to the next and assume, one after another, the place of the accused, the accusers, the witnesses, the judges. Under this condition each will be able to submit himself

---

[1] Bertolt Brecht, *Gesammelte Werke* 17 (Frankfurt/Main: Suhrkamp, 1967), 1024.
[2] The last sentence: 'Die Vorführenden (Sänger und Spieler) haben die Aufgabe, lernend zu lehren.'

to the exercises of discussion and ultimately gain the understanding – the practical understanding – of what dialectics is.[3]

He says he means to write a general introduction to this play and others like it, to explain his special purpose in writing them.

> The reader would be warned away from looking in them for a thesis or counter-thesis, arguments for or against opinions, defenses, or accusations that clarify their own particular way of seeing things – but simply [find] exercises in suppleness designed for that type of intellectual athlete who would be a good dialectician. The right or wrong justification for the judgment is another matter entirely, which aims at things I have not introduced into the debating.

THE MASSNAHME EXERCISE

In Brecht's described *Einübung* of this piece – a *practicing* activity not aimed at an audience – the chief thing the players must 'conceptually master' is *Verhalten*, meaning conduct that reveals attitude (*Haltung*).[4] Not only the figure of the Young Comrade, but also those of the other re-presented figures exhibit clearly defined dispositions in each presented incident of the text, and so does the Control Chorus. The text and the music together define them. This domain of *Verhalten* defines the matter that the players must practice. Let us examine some of its detail.

Collaborating composer Hanns Eisler pointed out that the introduction contains a *Situationsänderung* – a change of situation: 'The Agitators interrupt the praise that is being bestowed upon them with a request to initiate an investigation into their work' (Steinweg KA, 240).[5] Eisler also called the Control Chorus a 'mass reporter' – 'it reports a certain political content to the masses' (248-49)[6] – and the music he wrote for their opening text has a broadly marked 4/4 meter, expressing 'elevated dimension and iron assurance' (216).[7]

This introductory 'change of situation' presents the first behavioral pattern that the players are to practice. The particulars of this pattern include the following: the singers of the Control Chorus *report*, using a text that *praises* and music that *assures and elevates in broad terms*; the activity being praised and reported, with broadly marked musical assurance and elevation, has been accomplished by the four Agitators *in the past*; the particular 'crisis' of this accomplished activity is the killing of a Comrade; the immediate demand is for *a judgment* about this action. The final directive in this changed situation is *to show* the how and why of what happened. Summarizing in Brechtian terms: the given situation changes *gestically*, from one in which a judging body bestows (by singing) routine praise and approval upon a reporting body, to one in which the judging body commands

---

[3] Bertolt Brecht, *Die Massnuhme: Kritische Ausgube*, ed. Reiner Steinweg (Frankfurt/Main: Suhrkamp, 1972), 261–62.
[4] This is the basis for Rainer Naegele's reassessment of the Lehrstücke. See his *Reading After Freud* (New York: Columbia University Press, 1987), Chapter 5, 'Brecht's Theater of Cruelty'. This first appeared as 'Brechts Theater der Grausamkeit: Lehrstücke und Stückwerke', in *Brechts Dramen: Neue Interpretationen*, ed. Walter Hinderer (Stuttgart: Philipp Reclam jun., 1984).
[5] This and similar remarks reprinted in Steinweg pp. 239–43 come originally from published 'Notes' to the 1931 *Versuche, Heft 4* edition.
[6] Also in Eisler, *Materialien zu einer Dialektik der Musik* (Leipzig: Reclam, 1976), pp. 80 ff.
[7] This is Manfred Grabs's descriptive analysis: '... drückt erhabene Grösse und eherne Festigkeit aus'.

its activist-subordinates to furnish a performance, by means of which a judgment may be determined about an example of their past behavior.

The first numbered scene, 'The Classical Teachings', has a synoptic introduction that functions like a scene title, although spoken by one of the Agitators. It thoroughly 'covers' the past situation into which the Agitators entered:

> We came as agitators from Moscow. We were supposed to travel to the city of Mukden in order to make propaganda and support the Chinese party in the factories. We were supposed to announce ourselves at the last party headquarters before the border and demand a guide. In the anteroom a young comrade stepped towards us, and we spoke of the nature of our assignment. We shall repeat the conversation.

More than simply reporting their particular reason for going on this journey, the synopsis states the Agitators' whole reason for being. When they present their reproduced conversation with the Young Comrade in the anteroom, they repeat, 'We come from Moscow', thereby reinforcing the fact that they have this mission and no other. Their text also carefully establishes that their mission contained these, and only these, requirements – what *'we were supposed to do'*.

But the feature of this first scene that marks the entire practicing method is the schematically formal (some might say 'stilted') nature of the conversation that is being re-presented. This resembles no ordinary conversation in life as we know it. 'We shall repeat the conversation', say the Agitators. And they re-enact what they have just summarized. First they form a configuration of three facing a fourth ('a young comrade stepped towards us'). The 'Young Comrade' is introduced by the actor as 'secretary at the last party headquarters before the border'; this repeating of what the Agitators have already explained by way of narrative location suggests that this line may thus be addressed by Agitator to Control Chorus for the purpose of indicating which 'character' he is playing at this juncture. And then this Young Comrade is re-presented as a person whose 'heart beats for the revolution', who 'was driven by the sign of injustice into the ranks of the fighters', who believes that 'human beings must help one another', who 'is for freedom', who 'believes in humanity', and who 'is for the measures taken by the Communist Party, which fights against exploitation and ignorance for the classless society'.

Thus reproduced, the Young Comrade (not a 'present dramatic character') articulates clichéd sentiments; these, rather than 'characterizing' him in the customary way, define him starkly in attitudinal terms of revolutionary fervor. The Agitator who is here *playing* the Young Comrade must present a *gestical* definition of the character: *'how he was in this first conversation where we were to announce ourselves and demand a guide'*. The reason for presenting the character in this gestical way is antinomical to the theater's usual objective: not to portray an individual who may be liked or disliked, admired or scorned, feared for, cheered on, or sympathized with, but to show a persona who exhibited *this* attitudinal behavior on *this* particular occasion, so that an eventual judgment may be rendered about action taken concerning this character. But we are not yet in a position to make such a judgment ourselves; we are still examining the details of the *Einübung*.

Eisler's music is indispensable to this examination. Described as a 'recitative' by Hans Heinz Stuckenschmidt, the music critic who reviewed the first production, this section consisted of 'spoken words, set off by triads from the winds' (Steinweg *KA*, 346).[8] In his

---

[8] Stuckenschmidt's lengthy description of the Eisler score appeared in the journal *Der Anbruch*, Volume XIII, Number 1, Berlin, 1931, pp. 5–8.

more detailed analysis, Manfred Grabs relates that this section is taken 'fast', that 'the unaccompanied questions and answers are punctuated by unvarying phrygian-aeolian cadences from the orchestra', that these are 'heavy chordal attacks which each time die away with a tom-tom stroke', and that the last sentence of the Young Comrade ('Marching forward, spreading the teachings of the communist classics: World Revolution') 'is underlined by a crescendo roll on the snare drum' (Steinweg *KA*, 217).

Thus the total *gestical* definition of the Young Comrade. From the beginning of his re-presentation by these apprentices acting as Agitators, this 'reproducible' Young Comrade is the same fervently humanistic and ideologically determined persona as is *cumulatively* re-presented by the entire musico-dramatic text. No need to look further than his textually demonstrated utterances and activities to find the schematic 'victim' of those 'given circumstances' – i.e., a sentimental humanist trying to carry out Communist agitational propaganda in China. But 'he' is not 'here'. He is an idea of 'behavior under certain circumstances to be judged through re-presentation'.

The several other 'characters' whom the Agitators must re-present in the course of their *Darstellung* also fall into this category of gestically demonstrable specimens. The text consistently requires the Agitators to identify their represented personae in each new scene. 'I am the overseer. I must get the rice to the city of Mukden by evening.' Thus one Agitator identifies himself in the third scene, 'The Stone'. Two others announce: 'We are the coolies and pull the rice barge up the river.' Not only do the Agitators report their assumed personae for this scene, but they also summarize their characters' gestical essence. The overseer's function is simply defined: *he* is responsible for getting the rice delivered to the city. The coolies, self-evidently enough, *haul* (*schleppen*) the barge *up* the river. But they also sing 'beautiful songs' to cover their misery, something the Young Comrade is shown to find 'hateful'.

In the next scene, an Agitator portrays a Policeman who describes himself thus: 'I am a policeman and get my bread from the rulers by combatting dissatisfaction.' Too many actors have been tempted to play this Policeman as a caricature of an insensitive brute, complete with low-comic accent and swagger. But the more illuminating *Gestus* for this figure, who says that a policeman is *defined* as someone who receives his sustenance from the rulers for combatting dissatisfaction, is this: 'I understand what the definition of policeman is.' Thus the Agitator shows the figure of the Policeman not as an easily rejectable stereotype, but as a persona with a problematic social definition.

A similarly gestical challenge faces the actors in the fifth scene, 'What is a Human Being Anyway?' One must show the self-satisfied heartiness of a hateful exploiter of human beings, and do so by re-performing his very zesty song, cast in a jazz idiom. Eisler said, 'The brutality, stupidity, arrogance, and egotism of this type could not be "modeled" in any other musical form.' Neither, he said, could any other kind of music 'have such a provocative effect upon the young comrade'. But he stresses that this 'Song of Supply and Demand' is an *imitation* of the music that reflects the businessman's basic attitude, distinguishing between jazz as a technical musical matter and jazz as something commodified by the entertainment industry (*GW 17*, 1031).[9] Another actor must then show that the Young Comrade was *therefore* outraged enough to refuse to collaborate with this schematic capitalist, despite his having agreed to the Party strategy of exploiting the strife among the ruling factions in order to arm the coolies.

---

[9]The section headed 'Anmerkungen zur "Massnahme"' contains both Brecht's and Eisler's remarks, the latter's on 'Die Musik zur "Massnahme"' taking pages 1030–32.

In the discussion sections that follow each of the three scenes demonstrating the tests to which the Young Comrade was put, the instructive questions posed by the Control Chorus resemble the catechetical stimuli used in the earlier *Baden-Baden Learning Play on Consent*. Each time the Agitators give a rote reply, the Control Chorus repeats its formulaic 'Wir sind einverstanden' – 'We are in agreement.' In other words, the 'correct' answer has been given by the Agitators. In the first such discussion, following 'The Stone' scene, this choral reply leads directly into their spirited canon, 'Happy the Man', which rehearses instructively the text's two-line maxim: 'The wise man is not he who makes no mistakes, but he who knows how to correct them quickly.' And in the last of the three discussions, the choral reply introduces their hymnlike 'Change the World, It Needs It', which so many critics read as propaganda from Brecht's own mouth. After all, here is where we find that incontrovertibly tough paradox: 'Sink down in the slime / Embrace the butcher / But change the world: it needs it!' And Eisler's setting for this line – two difficult ascending intervals with a sudden crescendo – is appropriately shivering.[10]

But these Communist songs are also part of the exercise in re-presenting gestical behavior. Singing in the Control Chorus must lead the players to discover that the Chorus always expresses itself with a bureaucratic officialness. Throughout the text, their *Gestus* is a familiar one: they speak 'by the book'. In the last scene, they pose a familiar enough question to the Agitators' reported intention to 'shoot him and throw him into the lime pit': 'Didn't you find a way out?' The musical direction for this line is described by Grabs as 'softly, without expression' (Steinweg KA, 230). But the same features characterize the sung lines in which the Chorus reassures the Agitators of its sympathy. Finally, the Control Chorus's repetition of its initial agreement with the Agitators – 'Wir sind einverstanden mit euch' – has exactly the same musical character as it did in the introduction (Grabs: '... entspricht genau der entsprechenden Stelle in Nr. 1.' – Steinweg KA, 232). What is significant is that this judging body has not changed its habituated behavior in the course of the demonstration.

These examples illustrate how the text and music of *The Measures Taken* provide Epic Theater trainees the means to practice *gestical* performance of past behavior. Fundamental to this practice is *showing attitudes*, which implies *discovering* these attitudes in the written and musical text. This process – to summarize the guidelines of Brecht and Eisler – entails several kinds of activity: *technical* (learning tones, gestures, postures, movements, melodies, harmonies, dynamics, and so forth); *intellectual* (discussing, analyzing, arguing the facts and concepts that inform the given 'action'); and *artistic* (combining technique and understanding to fashion or execute something beautifully). The object of this process, the would-be 'action' contained in the text, is unlike that of conventional dramatic texts. It is schematic, illustrative, and abstract, more extruded from a patterned topical reality than imitatively rendering a structure of that reality. This structured dynamic, what we would normally call the 'plot', might better be termed a *parable*. Indeed, this is how Eisler referred to it in a 1958 interview:

> One must learn to see a parable as a parable, not as a 'natural event'. The young comrade is on the stage, he is certainly not being shot in reality. This is a completely uninteresting play ending, because what is supposed to be shown is political behavior.
>
> (Steinweg KA, 266-67)

---

[10] See Eric Bentley, *Songs of Bertolt Brecht and Hanns Eisler* (New York: Oak Publications, 1967).

The most critically rewarding insights about *The Measures Taken* proceed from the implications of not performing for an audience. Without an audience's perceptual experience and response – its *reception* – there is theoretically no true play, no 'dramatic event'. Nor is this practicing activity a rehearsal, for rehearsal also implies preparing a performance for an eventual audience. If the practicing players of this *Lehrstück* can accomplish their exercise with the intentionality described – i.e., to show the gestical behavior of past fictive personae to a body that will judge it – then they may indeed be able to *exhibit* their 'performance' to an audience. But it will be for the sake of showing a new theater method in operation. In fact, one of Brecht's numerous statements about *The Measures Taken*, supposedly included in the original presentation's program note, suggests just this:

> The *Lehrstück* 'The Measures Taken' is not a theatre play in the ordinary sense. It is an exhibition by a massed chorus and four players. In our performance today, which is supposed to be more like an event, the part of the players has been undertaken by four actors. But of course this part can also be carried out in a quite simple and primitive way, and that is precisely its chief object.
>
> (GW 17, 1033)

This only underscores Brecht's main *Lehrstück* principle: that the practicing is for the participants, who are not to concern themselves about an audience. *The Measures Taken* furnishes these learning actors an arena within which to inquire, through artistic and critical practice, into the *attitudes* that inform such behavior as constitutes the Agitators' reported *past* action. But all of this attitudinal behavior 'exists' only in the provisional realm of dramatic fiction, in that *parable* that furnishes the exercise its demonstrable action. *The Measures Taken* shows the usual drama's 'presence' of represented characters-in-action transformed into the practice of an 'epic present', i.e., a repetition, *by showing*, of *re*-presented characters-in-behavior. This encompasses the Agitators, too, who must show themselves as 'characters in the past', just as they do for the Policeman, the Leader of the Party Headquarters, the Merchant, and so on.

Here I would like to state what I believe is the only valid conclusion about *The Measures Taken*. Because there is no customary 'dramatic present' in it, there is no plot and no action. These have been replaced by the idea and activity of *Einübung*. What 'happens' in this exercise is: *demonstrating a past action for the purpose of eliciting a judgment about it*. Brecht's judgment about it cannot be discerned with certainty, either from the text or from the rest of his writings. There is no particular ethical lesson to be drawn, nor any certain significance to be interpreted, from the substance of the piece. The subject of Communist ideology and questions about its principles, practice, and morality – however inherently provocative – do not yield the 'meaning' of this work. *The Measures Taken* is not 'about' any of this, because it is not a 'play'.

THE MODEL OF EPIC THEATER

What it is, however, is a complex model of Epic Theater. In the same year of its first production, 1930, Brecht composed the poem 'On Everyday Theatre', which includes a provisional description of ordinary people 'showing' in their natural manners the behavior of other ordinary people around them.[11] Eight years later, at the time he

---

[11] See *Bertolt Brecht: Poems, 1913-1956*, ed. John Willett and Ralph Manheim with the cooperation of Erich Fried (New York: Methuen, 1976), 176–79.

was authorizing the newest version of *The Measures Taken*, Brecht fashioned another analogical description of the Epic Theater: 'The Street Scene', the subtitle of which is 'Basic Model of an Epic Theater' (*Grundmodell eines epischen Theaters*). In this essay, he elaborated upon one of the earlier poem's examples of 'epic acting': a witness to an accident consciously demonstrates what happened for a crowd that has gathered on a street corner. Brecht points out:

> The bystanders may not have observed what happened, or they may simply not agree with him, may 'see things a different way'; the point is that the demonstrator acts the behavior of driver or victim or both in such a way that the bystanders are able to form an opinion about the accident.[12]

In his summary Brecht says, 'the elements of natural and of artificial epic theatre are the same'. The 'natural' street corner theater is 'primitive', but it has methods that serve its aim 'to make it easier to give an opinion on the incident'. By contrast, the 'artificial' epic theater is 'a highly skilled theatre with complex contents and far-reaching social objectives'. He continues:

> In setting up the street scene as a basic model for it we pass on the clear social function and give the epic theater criteria by which to decide whether an incident is meaningful or not. The basic model has a practical significance. As director and actors work to build up a performance involving many difficult question – technical problems, social ones – it allows them to check whether the social function of the whole [theatrical] apparatus is still clearly intact.
>
> (128)

Besides possessing 'complex contents', *The Measures Taken* is an example of how this 'artificial' Epic Theater both decides on the meaningfulness of an incident and checks whether the social function of the whole apparatus is still clearly intact. The significant relevance of its chosen content was obviously proven by the responses of audiences near and far, immediate and long-term. In addition, however, its textual and performance pattern analogously checks the functioning of the theater's apparatus, by having the Agitators stand for actors and the Control Chorus for audience. In the conventional theater, the audience usually arrives with the attitude we see represented by the Control Chorus's first speeches: 'So, here you [actors] are. *We agree with what we already think you should be doing.*' However, the Agitators respond as consciously experimenting actors might: 'Wait a minute! *we do is going to be changed before your eyes, and then you are going to have to give us your judgment about what we show you.*' The Control Chorus, in constantly reiterating things it already believes – its Communist orthodoxy – behaves just like a conventional theater audience. The Agitator-actors, therefore, must strive to *teach* this Control Chorus-audience a new way to behave as perceiving spectators, even while they are themselves *learning* how to bring this about. Moreover, all the performers will be learning both sides of this process, being advised by Brecht to trade parts throughout the exercise. Now we may understand the full import of Brecht's charge to the *Lehrstück* apprentices: *lernend, zu lehren* – 'to teach by learning'.

The purpose of Epic Theater, as Brecht repeatedly characterized it, was to establish *the pleasure of the critical disposition* as a new aesthetic experience. To create this possibility

---

[12]*Brecht on Theatre*, ed. and transl. John Willett (New York: Hill and Wang, 1964), 121.

for theater audiences of the 20th century, plays would have to be written that showed contemporary reality as criticizable, and a theater-making method would have to be developed that would 'teach' the audience to see the performance critically. This method would have to start with a radical practice for training actors. Thus the *Lehrstücke*, Brecht's 'Epic Theater Laboratory', and *The Measures Taken*, the quintessential example of a composed and re-composed practice piece for apprentice 'epic' performers. Through it they were to learn a dialectical form of addressing topics of burning contemporary significance, in and by a highly skilled process of theatrical performance that was itself defined by those same topics, indeed by the very *idea* of topicality.

Because so many have misunderstood this definitive experiment in that 1928-30 group of musical and dramatic exercises, Brecht continues to be mistaken *essentially*. By underscoring 'essentially' I mean to emphasize that the object of Brecht's artistic practice and theory was not overtly political-ideological – i.e., to change the world from capitalist to socialist, by whatever means. Rather, it was covertly political-aesthetic *to change the way audiences conventionally enjoy the theater, by artistic means*. If his work could accomplish this alteration of theater pleasure from passive-culinary to active-critical, then his rationally *and* aesthetically revived spectators *might* be more likely to undertake what Brecht wanted to see undertaken: the changing of the world. But his plays do not *tell* people to make revolutions. Is it too late to take enjoyable lessons from the aesthetic Brecht? Certainly not. The disintegration of Communist Europe clears the ground, in a way. All we have to do is decide to regard Brecht's plays as the work, not of a Communist preacher or a moral scoundrel, but of a great artist whose dramatic challenge remains one of our most valuable necessities.

South America

CHAPTER TWENTY-EIGHT

Brecht and Latin America's 'Theatre of Revolution'

DIANA TAYLOR

Copy Brecht? Never, it would be poor and useless.
Imitate him? There's no point. Work with him? Yes.

Fernando Peixoto, 'Brecht, Nuestro Compañero'.[1]

The impact of Bertolt Brecht on Latin American theatre is enormous though perhaps difficult to assess in any straightforward way. Every theatre practitioner in the region, I would venture to guess, knows Brecht's theories, yet, few stage his plays. All of Brecht's works are translated into Spanish and Portuguese and are available in most academic bookstores. No other theatre artist, from Latin America or abroad, boasts a similar status or reach. But no one would claim to do 'Brechtian' theatre. This essay attempts to address this seeming paradox by looking at both the historical context within which Brecht gets introduced in Latin America, and at the way that theatre practitioners integrate 'Brechtian' elements in their own work.

Brecht fever caught on quickly and spread rapidly throughout Latin America around the time of his death in 1956. Coinciding with the waves of Marxist anti-capitalist struggle that swept through Latin America at the end of the 1950s, culminating in the Cuban Revolution of 1959, Brecht's theories of a socially responsible, critical, and historically grounded theatre, directed at the children of the scientific age, resonated throughout the region. The *Festival of the Nations* (Paris, 1954) had introduced Latin American practitioners to the theory, plays, and stagings that were to become the most decisive single influence on them during the next two decades.[2] Translations soon followed. By the mid-1960s Latin America's most renowned groups and directors (such as Santiago Garcia and Enrique Buenaventura, both from Colombia) were putting on their own versions of *Galileo* (1965) and *Seven Deadly Sins* (1969). Playwrights such as Enrique Buenaventura and Griselda Gambaro adapted the fragmented structure of *Fear and Misery of the Third Reich* to

---

Diane Taylor, 'Brecht and Latin America's "Theatre of Revolution"', in Carol Martin and Henry Bial (eds), *Brecht Sourcebook* (London: Routledge, 2000), pp. 172–84.

[1] Fernando Peixoto, 'Brecht, Nuestro Compañero', *Conjunto* 69 (July-Sept. 1986), pp. 104–6. All translations from Spanish are mine, unless otherwise noted. This essay is a reworking of an argument I first put forth in my study, *Theatre of Crisis: Drama and Politics in Latin America* (Lexington: Kentucky University Press, 1990).
[2] See Marina Pianca's overview of this period, 'De Brecht a Nueva York: Caminos del teatro latinoamericano', *Conjunto* 69 (July-Sept. 1986), pp. 93–103.

describe the political violence in their countries: *Documents from Hell* (Colombia, 1968) and *Information for Foreigners* (Argentina, 1972) respectively. Other major playwrights, such as Osvaldo Dragún and Ricardo Talesnik (Argentina), Luisa Josefina Hernández and Emilio Carballido (Mexico), started adapting or somehow engaging artistically with a 'Brechtian' epic structure.[3] Politically activist theatre groups (such as *Escambray* in Cuba and *Yuyachkani* in Peru) used 'Brechtian' methodology to train actors in the alienation techniques that would encourage critical participation from their audiences. Theatre schools and cultural centers hosted discussions on Brecht's dialectical theatre.[4] Terms such as epic, 'culinary' theatre, and *Gestus* became commonplace in discussions about art and society. Brecht's reflections on the '"popular" as intelligible to the broad masses'[5] sharpened the focus of popular (or 'New') theatre practitioners in the Americas who were dedicated to raising political awareness among disenfranchised populations.

The evidence of Brecht's impact, then, is overwhelming. But this was no mere 'borrowing', and nothing as simple as what we normally think of as literary or theatrical 'influence'. Brecht fever hit at the height of the Cold War for two main reasons. First, his way of infusing the epic form with Marxist ideology offered one more way of framing and making sense of Latin America's revolutionary praxis and aspirations. Participants and spectators could see in the escalating political events a kind of gestic political theatre. Second, Brecht's efforts to combine anti-capitalist ideology with aesthetic principles inspired Latin American theatre artists to do the same for themselves, and in their own way. How could artists who lived surrounded by extreme social inequity and brutal political violence justify being artists if that meant an 'art for art's sake' mentality or cooptation into state-sponsored programs favoring special interests? Latin American theatre artists, as opposed to the famous Latin American novelists, had few possibilities for working if they separated themselves from the intense struggles affecting their societies.[6] Enrique Buenaventura aptly summed up their predictment in 'Theatre and Culture': 'Many Latin Americans who belong to the international republic of arts and letters resolve [the] contradiction by making a radical separation between arts and politics [...] The best way to do this is to live in Europe and support Cuba.'[7] Brecht offered a contemporary model of a theatre practitioner who had successfully brought politics into immediate conversation

---

[3]The use of a 'Brechtian' epic structure, to my mind, was very idiosyncratic and at times parodic. In Carballido's *I, Too, Speak of the Rose*, Carballido pokes gentle fun at what he sees as the rigidity of Marxist ideology (as it was promoted in Mexico), and he softens the episodic framework associated with Brecht by transforming it into a heart-beat rhythm associated with oral traditions. However, in his book *Brecht en el teatro hispanoamericano* (Ottawa: Girol Books, 1984) Fernando de Toro argues that Latin American theatre practitioners utilized the 'Brechtian system' ('sistema Brecht'), p. 56. His work is an attempt to show how this is so. De Toro emphasizes that these practitioners do not imitate Brecht, but use his epic theatre as a way of bringing political (marxist) ideology into a congruent aesthetic mode that avoids the pitfalls for Aristotelian identification, catharsis and so on.
[4]Gilberto Martínez, 'Mi experiencia directa con la obra de Bertolt Brecht', *Conjunto* 20 (April-June 1974), pp. 106–26.
[5]Bertolt Brecht, 'The Popular and the Realistic', *Brecht on Theatre*, translated John Willett (New York: Hill and Wang, 1964), p. 108.
[6]While theatre people such as Griselda Gambaro, Eduardo Pavlovsky and Diana Raznovich from Argentina (to name a few), Denise Stoklos and Augusto Boal from Brazil, Ariel Dorfman from Chile, and others left their countries during the periods of extreme periods of military dictatorship, many theatre people in countries like Peru and Colombia that had suffered chronic political violence chose to stay.
[7]Enrique Buenavenura, 'Theatre & Culture', trans. Joanne Pottlitzer, *TDR* 14/2 (Winter 1970), pp. 151–6.

with aesthetics, challenging every political system from Nazism to the U.S. House on Un-American Activities Committee (HUAC). The theatre artist, Brecht suggested, was at the forefront of political conflict, not sitting somewhere with his back to it.

Let me start with what I see as the first reason why Brecht became so popular in Latin America. Brecht's epic theatre provided one kind of lens for looking at the intense political drama unfolding in the late 1950s. The Cuban revolution, aside from providing the hope of viable political alternatives for Latin America, also produced a riveting theatrical image. Here was a massive, epic drama if there ever was one – one that 'aroused the spectator's capacity for action' (Brecht 1964:37), that proposed that both human beings and social systems were 'alterable and able to alter' (ibid.), that begged for a public capable of making decisions and adopting heroic political stances. In other words, though the revolution worked primarily on the 'real' order, it had a significant symbolic component. Without reducing the revolution to a spectacle, it is important to notice that its spectacular components served a vital function. They captured worldwide attention; they rallied followers and admirers by ennobling the revolutionaries while delegitimizing their opposition. The compelling figure of Ché, and to a lesser degree the figure of Castro, dominated the imagination of a huge portion of the population of Latin America. The revolution generated images of epic proportions, which coincided with Brechtian terminology: the frozen frame of Ché in his beret; the green fatigue uniforms of the *Castristas*; the Brechtian *Gestus* as the revolutionary attitude of 'men' in action; the episodic plot described by Ché in his diary, his continuing struggle to move the revolution to Bolivia and then to other oppressed regions of Latin America; the enthralled popular audience. Ché's heroic quest embodied the continent's hopes for liberation. The entire sequence was highly spectacular: a new world was being created out of conflict, a new beginning, a new hero or 'revolutionary man'.[8] Events reactivated the 'revolutionary myth' envisioned by Latin American liberation thinkers such as José Carlos Mariátegui.[9] And just as scholars argue that theatre provides one means of forging a collective identity, the revolution too created a sense of national and international identity mediated through an image. Instead of twenty-five politically marginal, economically and culturally dependent countries, Latin America could envision itself as a united, coherent entity, a producer (rather than importer) of cultural images.

Notwithstanding its epic proportions, the theatre of revolution, cannot be 'read' according to any strict Brechtian terminology. Although it staged the uprising of the oppressed and tried to expose a bourgeois, capitalist, imperialist ideology, it also imposed its own myths. The contradictions underlying many discussions of 'new' or 'popular' or 'revolutionary' Latin American theatre reflect the paradox that lies at the heart of this and perhaps every revolution. If we continue to examine it according to theatrical terminology (discussions of 'revolutionary' theatre tend to conflate the two), we detect a significant overlap with Artaud's dramatic theory as expressed in his collection of essays *The Theater and Its Double*. Unlike the Brechtian dialectical theatre, which insists on space for critical distancing – 'Spectator and actor ought not to approach one another but to move apart' (Brecht 1964:26) – the theatricality of the Revolution encouraged an Artaudian identification, even a merging, with those heroic figures 'capable of imposing

---

[8] Freddy Artiles, 'Teatro popular: Nuevo heroe, nuevo conflicto', in Sonia Gutierrez (ed.), *Teatro populary cambio social en América Latina* (Costa Rica: EDUCA, 1979), p. 80.
[9] José Carlos Mariátegui, 7 *ensayos de interpretación de la realidad peruana* (Lima: Amauta, 1975).

this supreme notion of the theater, men who [would] restore to all of us the natural and magic equivalent of the dogmas in which we no longer believe'.[10] Artaud's theory calls for collective fusion in the name of metaphysical transcendence; the individual assumes the image and takes on the 'exterior attitudes of the desired condition' (Artaud 1958:80). Likewise, the revolution encouraged subsuming the personal to the collective ideal. The actor, committed to the process of creating a new real, 'makes a total gift of himself', as Jerzy Grotowski advocated, following Artaud's lead, and 'sacrifices the innermost part of himself'[11] But not only in theatre do people give themselves up like Artaud's 'victims burnt at the stake, signaling through the flames' (Artaud 1958: 13). The mythification of violence as a source of liberation, whether self-directed or other-directed, in Artaudian theories of a total, essential, and heroic theatre – the 'theatre of cruelty' – also forms part of revolutionary thinking, a factor as much in its discourse as in its military strategy. Images of self-sacrifice and surrender characterize works on revolution. Fernando Alegria, in *Literatura y revolución*, describes 'the bloody operation' of self-examination and recrimination through revolutionary literature, in which authors and their public undergo a painful and glorious striptease: they unmask, 'wash, scrub, fumigate themselves, burn their clothing and expose their flesh to merciless scrutiny'.[12] Moreover, revolutions themselves are almost synonymous with violence; though people do speak of 'nonviolent revolutions', the term seems contradictory. Hannah Arendt argues in *On Revolution* that revolutions 'are not even conceivable outside the domains of violence'.[13] This is a position the Cuban revolutionaries themselves, maintaining that the struggle for political power was inseparable from armed warfare, would have accepted.

This giving oneself up to the revolution, then, is not a Brechtian critical or dialectical position. A sudden linguistic shift occurs at the point where one would follow the Brechtian terminology to its logical conclusion, to critical awareness and emotional distancing. Here, the surrender to the revolution is described in natural rather than theatrical terminology: one *becomes* a revolutionary and creates a new reality by giving oneself up to the seemingly irresistible force or process. In this sense, 'revolution' means the steady motion of heavenly bodies in orbit, which follow laws of physics beyond human control. For one commentator on Latin American popular theatre, 'the new socialist hero' will be neither a pessimist nor a conflicted, tortured individual but 'a man caught up in the revolutionary whirlwind' (Artiles 1979:80).

Just as the Cuban revolution was theatrical, much of the so-called revolutionary theatre of this period incorporated and furthered revolutionary ideology, identity, and images. The theatre of revolution, while functioning primarily on the symbolic order, also aimed at real, political change and saw itself as an important instrument in the social struggle. During the 1960s, collective theatres began to reinforce the grassroots movements with their emphasis on leadership, unity, mass mobilization, and combined force. This theatre manifested the widespread preoccupation with war, either reaffirming or decoding military terminology. Augusto Boal, who acknowledges Piscator and Brecht as important influences, situates theatre firmly in the realm of political and social struggle. For him,

---

[10] Antonin Artaud, *The Theatre and Its Double*, trans Mary Caroline Richards (New York: Grove Press, 1958), p. 32.
[11] Jerzy Grotowski, *Towards a Poor Theatre* (New York: Simon and Schuster, 1968), p. 35.
[12] Fernando Alegria, *Literatura y revolución* (México: Fondo de Cultura Económica, 1976), p. 11.
[13] Hannah Arendt, *On Revolution* (Harmondsworth: Penguin, 1963), p. 18.

during the early 1960s, theatre was a 'weapon' in overthrowing systems of oppression. He describes theatrical 'raids' staged in 1963 during the Cuban crisis: 'A group of actors meet on a corner and begin arguing about politics to the point of threatening physical violence; people gather around them and the group suddenly begins an improvised performance that deals with the most urgent political issues. Only midway through the performance does the crowd realize that it is attending a play.'[14] In Cuba, theatrical groups such as the *Conjunto Dramatico de Oriente* (started in 1961) and the *Grupo Teatro Escambray* (1968) gradually moved away from scripted theatre and staged collective acts of group definition and affirmation. Revolutionary theatre was conceived as a pragmatic, educational, useful theatre, a practical exercise in learning about the revolutionary process and encouraging 'public participation in [revolutionary] solutions. Theatre is an excellent vehicle to detect and combat problems', wrote the Cuban scholar, Rosa Ileana Boudet.[15] Theatrical performances also became acts of collective affirmation and group definition. This partial, or selective, use of Brechtian principles to think about localized socio-political conditions is noteworthy. Rather than a simple 'borrowing', what we see is the process of transculturation, analyzed by Cuban anthroplogist Fernando Ortiz in the 1940s to describe a tripartite process (acculturation, deculturation and transculturation) whereby one cultural system receives and ultimately transforms material from another.[16] Without dismissing the reality of cultural imperialism, transculturation allows for creativity and selection in the process of cultural transmission.

While the Brechtian epic model offered a lens for making sense of riveting political events, Brecht was also profoundly influential in pointing to ways in which Latin American theatre practitioners could combine anti-capitalist ideology with the aesthetic requirements posed by the theatrical form itself. But again, the question of impact is far more difficult to assess than has been acknowledged. Latin American theatre artists experimented enthusiastically with Brechtian theory and methodology. But Latin America was so different from Brecht's Europe in terms of race, language, levels of literacy, performance traditions and expectations, not to mention the socio-economic realities. The adaptation of a 'Brechtian' model to this new context was complicated to say the least.

The example of the renowned Peruvian collective theatre group, Yuyachkani, is a case in point. Members of Yuyachkani stress the importance of Brecht's theory, practice and life in their formation and development as a group;[17] when they began working in the early 1970s, they saw themselves as politically 'committed' popular theatre practitioners, doing much the same thing that other such groups were doing in the late 1960s and early 1970s. They challenged the hegemonic systems that placed 'Theatre' with a capital 'T' and 'Culture' with a capital 'C' in lofty, aesthetic realms, beyond the reach of working-class

---

[14]See Augusto Boal, *Theatre of the Oppressed* (New York: TCG, 1985), p. ix, and 'A Note on Brazilian Agitprop', *TDR* 14/2 (Winter 1970), p. 96.

[15]Rosa Ileana Boudet, *Teatro nuevo: Una respuesta* (Havana: Editorial Letras Cubanas, 1983), p. 12.

[16]Fernando Ortiz, *Contrapunteo cubano del tabaco y el azucar* (Caracas: Biblioteca Ayacucho, 1978).

[17]The program notes for 'Baladas del Bien-Estar' recognize that 'Bertolt Brecht constitutes a fundamental element that gave rise to Yuyachkani. His plays, his theoretical writings, his "Short Organum", his "five difficulties with telling the truth", are texts that we come back to in those moments in which we ask ourselves: how do we continue? Or simple, what should we do? But it's not just his work, it's his life too; it's a living testimony of an exemplary attitude and ethics at the time of rising fascism in Germany. His pilgrimage, persecution, and later exile, were a key motivation in developing his texts. ...' 1996.

people and racially marginalized communities. They worked as a collective, rejecting the playwright- and 'star'-driven theatrical models that dominated highbrow and commercial theatre. They took the theatre out of elite spaces, staging free performances that had to do with the real life economic and political conditions of working people. They toured their shows to rural communities with little access to theatre, and involved spectators in productions that focused on community issues. Working under the Brechtian influence, which in Latin America was closely linked to strikes and other class/labor struggles, Yuyachkani was a rough, unpolished theatre that came into being because of a strike. Their first play, 'Puño de Cobre' (1972), dealt with a miner's strike, and toured Peru's many mining camps to show solidarity with the anti-imperialist, anti-corporate movement.

What Yuyachkani found, however, was that their 'method' was totally incongruent with the context in which they found themselves. Because Marxism privileged class, anti-capitalist and anti-imperialist struggles at the expense of racial, ethnic, and gender conflict, popular theatre groups in Latin America ran the risk of reducing deep-seated cultural differences to class difference. In Peru, and other countries with large indigenous and mestizo communities, the 'proletariat' in fact consisted of indigenous and mestizo groups who lived on the margins of a capitalist society for various reasons – including linguistic, epistemic, cultural, and religious – not reducible (though bound into) economic disenfranchisement. A call for solidarity organized around anti-capitalism allowed for cultural trespassing on all sorts of other grounds. The less the practitioners knew the communities they were engaging, the more the discrepancies in power and the lack of reciprocity threatened to place them in positions of moral superiority reminiscent of political pamphleteers or religious proselytizers.

Yuyachkani began to understand that the marginalized groups they were addressing in their own country had their own languages, expressive cultures, and performance codes that the group knew nothing about. Miguel Rubio, the artistic director of Yuyachkani, recalls how during that first play which they performed for the miners, the actors dressed in jeans and played a variety of roles and characters. After the performance, one miner commented: 'Compañeros, that's a nice play. Too bad you forgot your costumes.'[18] 'Much later', Rubio continues, 'we understood why the miners thought what they did. We had forgotten something much more important than costumes. What they wanted to tell us was that we were forgetting the audience that we were addressing. We were not taking their artistic traditions into consideration. Not only that, we didn't know them!' Thus began the education of Yuyachkani regarding Peru's ethnic and cultural heterogeneity. They added members from these communities to their group; they learned quechua; they trained in indigenous and mestizo performance practices that included singing, playing instruments, dancing, movement and many other forms of popular expression. They expanded the notion of political theatre to include the popular fiesta that emphasized participation, thus blurring the distinction between actor and spectator. Performance, for Yuyachkani as for other popular theatre groups, became less about implementing 'Brechtian' practice than about opening up an arena for learning. But in an important reversal, here it was Yuyachkani learning 'our first huaylars, pasacalle, and huayno dance steps [;] between beers and warm food, we started to feel and maybe to understand the

---

[18]Miguel Rubio, 'Encuentro con el Hombre Andino', *Grupo Cultural Yuyachkani, Allpa Rayku: Una experencia de teatro popular* (Lima: Edición del 'Grupo Cultural Yuyachkani' y Escuelas Campesinas de la CCP, 2nd edn., 1985), p. 9.

complexity of the Andean spirit'.[19] Only after they made their own the many elements they had learned – from Brecht, from the Andean communities, and from the Eurocentric theatre training they received in Lima – did Yuyachkani finally offer their tribute to Brecht. In *Encuentro de zorros* (1985), a cart much like Mother Courage's comes onstage pushed by the beggars displaced by Peru's war into the sprawling urban centers. And in that same year, Teresa Ralli, one the group's actors, presented a solo performance, 'Baladas del Bien-Estar' in which she performs poems and songs by Brecht.

The impact of Brecht on playwrights is just as difficult to assess. Those of us who have access to the written works notice immediate similarities. And even though the influence seems transparent, this apparent transparency may make it more complicated to understand how the 'Brechtian' elements are being deployed and what they might mean to local audiences. It is commonplace to isolate certain Latin American playwrights from their context and analyze how they 'imitate' or borrow from foreign sources. While examples of this kind of misreading abound, I will focus on how this plays out in the scholarly interpretations of Enrique Buenaventura. Commentators cannot speak highly enough of Buenaventura or emphasize the importance of his dramatic production. They situate him next to Brecht and Piscator in the European tradition of political theatre and interpret his plays in accordance with Brechtian models. They emphasize his preoccupation with history, note his use of historical figures as central characters (Rey Christophe and Bartolomé de Las Casas), and his theatrical technique of 'documentation'. The words 'Brecht', 'history', and 'popular' appear in tandem in studies on Buenaventura.[20]

Buenaventura's theatre certainly deserves all the praise it receives, and all the usual observations are in some way 'true'. He repeatedly acknowledges his admiration of and indebtedness to Brecht. From his earliest pieces onward we can discern Brechtian motifs and techniques: *A la diestra de Dios Padre* (*On the Right Hand of God the Father*, 1960) recalls moments of *The Good Woman of Setzuan*; and his cycle of plays *Los papeles del infierno* (*Documents from Hell*, 1968) is based on Brecht's collection of short pieces, *Fears and Miseries of the Third Reich*. Buenaventura's concern with history, too, is evident throughout. *Documents*, as he announces explicitly in the prologue, 'is a testimony of twenty years of violence and undeclared civil war', the period in Colombian history known simply as *La Violencia*, which began in the mid-1940s. Furthermore, Buenaventura is certainly a 'popular' theatre practitioner. He is committed to social change, even revolutionary change. In 1962 he founded Colombia's first professional theatre and repertory company, the TEC (Teatro Escuela de Cali). Buenaventura's activist stance cost him his teaching position at the Escuela Departamental de Teatro del Valle and resulted in the loss of all governmental recognition and support for the TEC. The showdown with the government came after he staged *Seven Deadly Sins* in 1969. If theatre practitioners were going to criticize the government, he and other practitioners were informed, then they shouldn't expect to be supported by the government. The reply was simple – 'government' money did not belong to the government but to the people it was supposed to represent, and Buenaventura would not receive funding to shut his mouth and close his

---

[19]Brenda Luz Cotto-Escalera, 'Grupo Cultural Yuyachkaui: Group Work and Collective Creation in Contemporary Latin American Theatre'. (Unpublished diss., University of Texas, Austin, 1995) p. 8.
[20]The major studies on Buenaventura are Beatriz Risk's *El nuevo teatro latinoamericano: Una lectura histórica* (Minneapolis: Prisma Institute, 1987) and Marina Pianca's work (cited above, n. 2). See also de Toro (cited above, n. 3).

eyes.[21] Buenaventura continued to write plays for the newly named Teatro Experimental de Cali (the new TEC) and began experimenting with collaborative playwriting. The texts of collective pieces emerged after a rehearsal process in which he and other TEC members devised, researched, and shaped a topic. In addition to his Marxist political perspective, Buenaventura addresses a 'popular' audience, traveling with his shows to rural areas where people have never seen theatre before. Aesthetically, these activities imply radical departures from traditional and hegemonic concepts of 'text', 'author', and 'culture'.

All this information is important, as in the case of Yuyachkani, but the standard interpretation of it has resulted, inadvertently, in obscuring rather than illuminating Buenaventura's importance and his position vis-à-vis his country's crisis. A brief look at the assumptions behind the different critical postures will show why they have failed to touch on what is most innovative and radical about Buenaventura's theatrical practice.

The most obvious limitation of the view that Buenaventura is Brechtian, historical, and popular is that those particular terms are themselves problematic and essentialist; they mean different things to different people, and they suggest that there is one Brecht, one Buenaventura. The case for Brechtian 'influence', to be meaningful, would require a host of considerations, perhaps principally of periodization (early Brecht? late Brecht? early Buenaventura? late Buenaventura?), which are not addressed in these studies. What do we mean by Brechtian? Are we referring to a political, dialectical theatre? To theatrical techniques such as having women act men's roles and vice versa? To distanciation? To epic narration? Finding answers would involve an examination of trans-cultural trends, the process by means of which Buenaventura selects and adapts Brechtian themes and strategies to construct 'meaning' in relation to his own specific spectactors, many of whom have never heard of Brecht. The Brechtian elements are not popularly known 'pretexts' for spontaneous improvisation, as the *commedia dell'arte* plots and characters were for its audience; nor do they constitute a shared belief or tradition, as biblical stories do for some groups and mythological ones for others. What, then, is the point of introducing these elements? How do these adapted features 'read' or 'play' when Buenaventura's theatre, in turn, is transplanted to another culture? Moreover, to argue simultaneously that Buenaventura is a Brechtian and a 'collective' playwright poses the problem of what we mean by *author* and *oeuvre*.[22] Single-author 'works' are difficult enough to establish, let alone compare with texts by other authors. The issue becomes even more troublesome with reference either to Brecht or to Buenaventura as 'author': the former collaborated with Ruth Berlau, Elisabeth Hauptmann, and Margarete Steffin, for example, not to mention musicians such as Kurt Weill; the latter gradually became a collaborator in a collective creation. Which Brecht or which Buenaventura are we thinking of? Can we even think of Buenaventura's later works as part of his oeuvre in the same way as we do his single-author plays?

Clearly, too, an emphasis on the Brechtian elements clouds the many important Latin American components of his work. His *A la diestra de Dios Padre*, much like Brecht's *Good Woman*, represents multiple 'gods': Jesus and St. Peter try to find and help a good person. What are rarely discussed, however, are the other traditions feeding into this drama, from Spanish mystery plays or *autos sacramentales* to the grotesque humor of Ramón del Valle

---

[21]Martinez (cited above, n. 4) p. 110.
[22]See Michel Foucault, *The Archaeology of Knowledge*, trans. A.M. Sheridan Smith (New York: Panther, 1972), p. 24.

Inclán's (1866–1936) *esperpentos*, to the farcical, *masked festivales* such as the *mojiganga*. Moreover the different representation of the gods bespeaks different world views and hence radically different 'solutions' for surviving in the face of formidable odds.

We could argue that Buenaventura's appropriation of foreign cultural material is Brechtian in spirit. After all, Brecht was one of theatre's most avid borrowers. Even here, however, the emphasis on Brecht is misleading; what we should be looking at is the process of transculturation itself. Just as Brecht's specific use of the elements he borrows makes him Brechtian, so does Buenaventura's use of his make him a new original. Buenaventura himself, from *A la diestra de Dios Padre* onward, calls attention to the process of transculturation by means of which marginalized people absorb foreign models and use them for their liberation: Jesus and St. Peter are furious because their designated 'good man', Peralta, has misused his powers, but Jesus acknowledges that he has been outsmarted, that in fact Peralta 'has done nothing more than use the powers that I gave him'.[23] Peralta will not be easily defeated or excluded; in the final scene, using the very wishes Jesus granted him, he jumps into the right hand of God, determined, as William Oliver (1971: 174) puts it, to 'plague God's own creativity' for eternity.[24] This, then, is a counterhegemonic strategy that Buenaventura proposes for his audiences; they are directed not to imitate the West but rather to appropriate the weapons of the powerful and use them for their own decolonization. Moreover, he explicitly refers to this strategy in his theoretical papers; he explains that he and his group purposely chose for production foreign plays that illuminated their own specific problems, notably colonization and dependency: 'We knew that the colonizer that imposed his culture was also giving us the instruments of liberation. But we can only use those instruments if we apply them to our concrete reality.'

In short, to emphasize the Brechtian elements in this way is misleading. Though it is laudable on the part of the commentators to want to stress the quality and importance of Buenaventura's work by situating him next to Brecht, this emphasis leads us away from those characteristics (by and large non-Brechtian) that most contribute to Buenaventura's importance.

Similarly, we contribute to the critical obfuscation of Buenaventura's work by simply stating that he is one of Latin America's foremost 'popular' theatre practitioners, since no one quite agrees on what 'popular theatre' means. Rather than allowing for differentiation between many kinds of 'popular' or 'people's' theatre – Chicano theatre, Piscator's 'epic' theatre, Boal's theatre of the oppressed, and others – the term 'popular' tends to group them all together, despite their important differences. What does the label 'popular' tell us about Buenaventura's own production? That it is for the 'people'? Yes, if by that we mean rural and semiliterate audiences along with urban and literate (university student) ones. That it is by the 'people'? Buenaventura is a self-taught, highly knowledgeable, articulate intellectual, not a man of the semiliterate circles he wants to incorporate in theatrical activity. That this theatre privileges political over aesthetic effects – that is, focuses specifically on a given set of social problems? Buenaventura has adamantly denied that theatre must sacrifice aesthetics to politics, differing radically in this respect both from Piscator and from more dogmatic Latin American popular groups. '"Popular theatre", or a "theatre for the masses", a theatre for a fixed audience and about a specific

---

[23]Enrique Buenaventura, *Teatro* (Bogota: Ediciones Tercer Mundo, 1963), p. 140.
[24]William Oliver (ed.), *Voices of Change in Spanish American Theatre* (Austin: University of Texas Press, 1971), p. 174.

set of problems', he says, is 'just another trick of the system, as elementary as nationalism, folklore, or agitprop. Because the system has cast out the exploited, should you create a product for them that is no more nutritious than the food surpluses it leaves them? Some maintain that the exploited don't want anything else, that they don't have the capacity to participate in the full and complex diversion of a real theatrical production ... To accept that we must do lowquality theatre at the outset to 'elevate' the level of the people is to enter wholly into the system' ('Theater and Culture', 154). The issue of 'popular theatre', then, is disorienting; it draws attention away from what Buenaventura actually does, away from the artistic and technical strategies he devises to communicate with disparate audiences and to continue producing outstanding theatre in the face of overwhelming difficulties – traveling to rural areas that lack traditional theatre spaces, working with minimum financial and technical resources, dealing with political ostracism and harassment. His is truly a 'poor' theatre in the economic sense of the word.

More important, however, is the fact that Buenaventura does not follow the path of consciousness raising normally associated with popular theatre. Rather than propose a vision or communicate a message associated with a specific ideology, he subverts dominant ideology through a process he calls 'deconscientization' (deconcienciación) or 'demystification'. For Buenaventura, this means seeing through the concepts of 'tradition', 'history', and race, class, and gender 'difference' which sustain the power elite. He undermines the boundaries – social, political, economic, cultural, and historical – by means of which the system excludes a substantial portion of its population as grotesque, poor, dirty, infirm others. He does not simply propose overthrowing the oppressors and grabbing their power, however, perpetuating thus the binary system of oppressed and oppressor. He has no intention of substituting one form of violence for another, or 'one set of illusions for another' (Reyes 1963:22). Rather, Buenaventura is far more like Brecht in the way that he questions the entire system, including the role of the oppressed themselves within it. The sociopolitical demystification proposed by Buenaventura strives toward the same political ends as do consciousness-raising theatres, but the difference is an important one that accounts for the subtle, non-didactic nature of Buenaventura's drama. Like Brecht, Buenaventura seeks to expose, rather than impose, ideology.

While the impact of Brecht is profound on Latin American theatre practitioners, it needs to be understood in a less literal fashion. As I have suggested, different groups have tried, in their own ways, to reconcile the aesthetic and political demands of theatre in their own particular contexts. The convergence of concerns, rather than a specific methodology or practice, brings them together. Ironically, scholars who stress Brecht's influence on Latin American and other colonized regions of the world, fail to mention what I consider its single most important feature: Brecht was a common source of inspiration to dramatists from many colonized and marginalized societies, responsible, indirectly, for introducing them to each other. This larger network of activist theatre practitioners from Latin America, India, Africa, and elsewhere who learned of each other through their shared interest in Brecht remains to be explored.

REFERENCES

Artaud, Antonin (1958) *The Theatre and Its Double*. Trans. Mary Caroline Richards. New York: Grove Press.

Artiles, Freddy (1979) 'Teatro popular: Nuevo heroe, nuevo conflicto.' In Sonia Gutierrez (ed.), *Teatro populary cambio social en América Latina*. Costa Rica: EDUCA.

Brecht, Bertolt (1964) 'The Popular and the Realistic.' *Brecht on Theatre*, trans. John Willett. New York: Hill and Wang.

Oliver, William (1971) (ed.) *Voices of Change in Spanish American Theatre*. Austin: University of Texas Press.

Reyes, Carlos José (1963) 'Introducción: El teatro de Enrique Buenaventura.' In *Enrique Buenaventura*: Teatro. Bogota: Ediciones Tercer Mundo.

CHAPTER TWENTY-NINE

Activist Theater: From Brecht through Boal

STEVEN K. SMITH

Brecht was right: if the theatre's sole object were to be even a 'dialectical' commentary on ... eternal self-recognition and non-recognition – then the spectator would already know the tune, it is his own. If, on the contrary, the theatre's object is to destroy this intangible image, to set in motion the immobile, the eternal sphere of the illusory consciousness's mythical world, then the play is really the development, the production of a new consciousness in the spectator – incomplete, like any other consciousness, but moved by this incompletion itself, this distance achieved, this inexhaustible work of criticism in action; the play is really the production of a new spectator, an actor who starts where the performance ends, who only starts so as to complete it, but in life.[1]

Theatre cannot be imprisoned inside theatrical buildings, just as religion cannot be imprisoned inside churches; the language of theatre and its forms of expression cannot be the private property of actors, just as religious practice cannot be appropriated by priests as theirs alone![2]

The conception of theater as being about questions and problems is certainly not new, but the idea that theater can motivate people to go out into the world to solve problems is fairly recent. In the middle of the 20th Century, Jean-Paul Sartre still had to point out that *Les Mouches* was 'not intended to guide [people] toward [the] future, but to encourage them to strive toward it'.[3] This is what is meant by activist theater in the current context: a theater that impels spectators to action after the show.[4] Many major theater names – notably including Augusto Boal – have put a premium on spectator action, but the degree to which such action has been realized is debatable. According to Jan Cohen-Cruz, 'Contrary to

---

Steven K. Smith, 'Activist theater: from Brecht through Boal', *Brecht Yearbook*, 30 (2005), pp. 279–99.

[1] Louis Althusser, 'The "Piccolo Teatro": Bertolazzi and Brecht; Notes on a Materialist Theatre', in *For Marx*, Trans. Ben Brewster (London: Verso, 1977), pp. 129–151; here, p. 151.
[2] Auguste Boal, *Legislative Theatre: Using Performance to Make Politics*, Trans. Adrian Jackson (London: Routledge, 1998), p. 19.
[3] Jean-Paul Sartre, *Sartre on Theater*, Trans. Frank Jellinek (New York: Pantheon Books, 1976), p. 192.
[4] Obviously this is completely different from the Aristotelian meaning of 'action' (*praxis*), which relates to what happens on the stage. See Aristotle, *Aristotle's Poetics*, Trans. George Whalley (Montreal: McGill-Queen's University Press, 1997), p. 66, for example.

popular opinion, there *is* activist theatre in the US today'.[5] But if popular opinion doesn't recognize it, does it really exist, practically speaking?[6] Marvin Carlson's respected history of theater theory does admit that 'Probably no contemporary theorist has explored the political implications of the performance-audience relationship in so searching and original a manner' as Boal, but Carlson's treatment of Boal is limited to less than two pages.[7] Does this mean that Boal's project of rehearsing for the revolution has failed or just that it is happening below the academic radar? Is it even possible, as Boal has admitted desiring, to create 'some form of theatre which could channel all the creative energy ... eager to change the world ... and to use this energy beyond the immediate duration of the show'?[8]

Bertolt Brecht heavily influences Boal's activism. Boal's first statement of his theatrical beliefs, *Theatre of the Oppressed*, is clearly written against an Aristotelian-Hegelian interpretation of theater. Inasmuch as 'Brecht's whole poetics is basically an answer and a counterproposal to the idealist poetics of Hegel',[9] Boal's whole poetics is basically an extension of Brecht. Much talk in recent decades has centered on the continued importance and utility of Brecht. Certainly in Boal he still is useful. Fredric Jameson hypothesized that 'Brecht would have been delighted ... at an argument, not for his greatness, or his canonicity ... as rather for his *usefulness* – and that not only for some uncertain or merely possible future, but right now'.[10] Indeed, Brechtian references abound in modern American theater criticism and analysis.[11] While it is perhaps true that many of Brecht's ideas have been discarded, many others still inform our fundamental understanding of theater. No longer does anyone question that there is a place for theater where the spectators do not 'leave their brains with their hats upon entering'.[12]

DIDACTICISM

What kind of theater could be used to achieve this activist goal? According to Jameson, a 'useful' theater is at least in part didactic.[13] Since its earliest beginnings, theorists have

---

[5]Jan Cohen-Cruz, 'Mainstream or Margin? US activist performance and Theatre of the Oppressed' in *Playing Boal: Theatre, Therapy. Activism*, Ed. Mady Schutzman and Jan Cohen-Cruz (London: Routledge, 1994), pp. 110–123, here, p. 110.

[6]An example of activist theater's absence from theater study in the US is that Oscar Brockett's widely used textbook on the history of the theater doesn't even mention Boal or the Theater of the Oppressed. See Oscar G. Brockett with Franklin J. Hildy, *History of the Theater* (Boston: Allyn and Bacon, 1999).

[7]Marvin Carlson, *Theories of the Theatre: A Historical and Critical Survey from the Greeks to the Present* (Ithaca: Cornell University Press, 1993), p. 475.

[8]Boal, *LT*, p. 9. The three major texts by Boal are abbreviated throughout this paper as follows:

- TO = *Theatre of the Oppressed*, Trans. Charles A. and Maria-Odilia Leal McBride (New York: Theatre Communications Group, 1985).
- RD = *The Rainbow of Desire*: The Boal Method of Theatre and Therapy, Trans. Adrian Jackson (London: Routledge, 1995).
- LT= *Legislative Theatre*, cited above.

When the abbreviations are not italicized, they refer to the general theories rather than the specific book.

[9]*TO*, p. 84.

[10]Fredric Jameson, *Brecht and Method* (London: Verso, 1998), p. 1.

[11]As just one of many examples, Bruce Weber refers to a theater troupe's 'Brechtian aesthetic' with no explanation. See Bruce Weber, 'A "Who Was Who" Weighs in on Art', *New York Times* 8 May 2002, p. B5.

[12]*TO*, p. 104, glossing Bertolt Brecht, *Brecht on Theatre: The Development of an Aesthetic*, Ed. and Trans. John Willett (New York: Hill and Wang, 1999), p. 27.

[13]'"Useful" in this context would not only mean "didactic", although ... there are signs that the "present age", with its new-found taste for impure aesthetics of all kinds, has also become more tolerant of didactic elements

recognized that theater has a didactic or pedagogic element. For Aristotle, it led to purgation of negative elements; for Hegel, theater is pedagogic in that it reveals truth. According to Sartre, 'The theater's job is not demonstration or solution. It thrives on questions and problems',[14] that is, on the actual thinking process, rather than on the teaching of specific ideas or doctrine. Although still very much in *a* Hegelian mode of subject recognition, Sartre tried to move away from a theater that discussed ideas to one that solved problems: 'The most moving thing the theater can show is a character creating himself, the moment of choice.'[15] However, Sartre was still focusing on the recognition relation that the spectator has with what is onstage. No weight is given to the social context of the situation, much less to the totality of the spectator's world or to some action to be taken by the spectator after the show. Sartre's theater would 'talk to the audience about itself'[16] but not be very useful in preparing it for society-changing action.

Conversely, the goal of Brecht's theater was eminently useful in this regard: 'Human behaviour is shown as alterable; man himself as dependent on certain political and economic factors and at the same time as capable of altering them.'[17] In Louis Althusser's words, Brecht's profound thesis is that 'he wanted to make the spectator into an actor who would complete the unfinished play, but in real life'.[18] Brecht worried that the 'common tendency of art [was] to remove the social element of any gest'.[19] By reintroducing that element, he wanted to 'put living reality in the hands of living people in such a way that it can be mastered'.[20] Boal also clearly believed that theater could be used not only to understand but also to tackle problems off the stage; it could aid with literacy as well as train the spectator for 'real action'.[21] Brecht himself says that 'it is precisely theatre, art and literature which have to form the "ideological superstructure" for a solid, practical rearrangement of our age's way of life',[22] but this must be done by making spectators aware of the working of ideology. Aristotelian anagnorisis, Hegelian resolution, and Ibsenite discussion are all transferred by Brecht off the stage to the spectator. The illusion on stage – ultimately an image of the real – is put back at the service of the real. But in the end this kind of didactic or pedagogic theater did not lead to activism. The presenting of brutish reality, along with the assurance that change is possible, perhaps raised consciousnesses. But knowing that change is in the spectators' power and acting are quite different. Brecht asserts that the theater must appeal to spectators' reason in order for them to 'come to grips with things',[23] but his audience did not run into the streets to implement a blueprint for social change.

---

and attitude than the more purist high modernities that preceded it. ... Yet, ... Brechtian usefulness ... although it certainly involves teaching, is something a little more fundamental than mere didacticism' (Jameson, p. 2).
[14]Sartre, p. 209.
[15]Ibid, p. 4.
[16]Ibid, p. 48.
[17]Brecht, p. 86.
[18]Althusser, p. 146.
[19]Brecht, p. 104.
[20]Ibid, p. 109.
[21]Boal, *TO*, p. 122.
[22]Brecht, p. 23.
[23]Ibid.

As with so much of Brecht, Boal takes the didactic element another step. His learning is two-way, transitive,[24] as he points out in an interview referring to forum theater, perhaps the most common of the TO techniques:

> Some people use this phrase 'raise consciousness' to mean you have to grab people by the hair and insist that they look at the 'truth'. I am against that. All the participants in a forum session learn something, become more aware of some problems that they did not consider before, because a standard model is challenged and the idea that there are alternatives is clearly demonstrated. We never try to find which solution proposed is the 'correct' one. I am against dogmas. I am for people becoming more conscious of the other person's possibilities. What fascinates me about forum is the transitive character of its pedagogy.[25]

Boal learned early that didactic and activist theaters are not the same. In the 1960s, he took his didactic Teatro de Arena to poor areas of Brazil, where they staged plays that exhorted 'the oppressed to struggle against oppression'.[26] However, they were unprepared for the reaction of the peasants for whom they performed: requests to take up arms and join them. Boal and his troupe declined, but 'it was difficult to explain ... how we could be sincere and genuine and true even though our guns wouldn't fire and we didn't know how to shoot'.[27] Boal's first lesson about activist theater: never write 'plays that give advice ... [e]xcept on occasions when I was running the same risks as everyone else'.[28] Didactic theater may simply preach, without regard to offstage praxis, but activist theater acknowledges that neither side in a didactic relationship has all the answers and that both sides may confront different realities.

The Theater of the Oppressed set out to address this. Boal describes the early phases of 'simultaneous dramaturgy', which later evolved into forum theater:

> we would present a play that chronicled a problem to which we wanted to find a solution. The play would run its course up to the moment of crisis – the crucial point at which the protagonist had to make a decision. At this point, we would stop performing and ask the audience what the protagonist should do. Everyone would

---

[24]The concept of 'transitiveness' is crucial throughout the evolution of Boal's project. It comes from Paulo Freire's pedagogy of the oppressed (as, obviously, does the name Theatre of the Oppressed). Along with Brecht, Freire was the second great influence on Boal. Space considerations prevent delving further into this connection than the following acknowledgement from *LT* which sums up thoughts which underlie the entire Boalian oeuvre:

> Paulo Freire talks about the transitivity of true teaching: the teacher is not a person who unloads knowledge, like you unload a lorry, and heaps it up in the head of another person – the bank vault where the money-knowledge is kept: the teacher is a person who has a particular area of knowledge, transmits it to the pupil and, at the same time, receives other knowledge in return, since the pupil also has his or her own area of knowledge. The least a teacher has to learn from his pupil is how his pupil learns. Pupils are different from each other; they learn differently. Teaching is transitivity. Democracy. Dialogue. (p. 19)

[25]Michael Taussig and Richard Schechner, 'Boal in Brazil, France, the USA: An Interview with Augusto Boal', in Schutzman and Cohen-Cruz, eds., *Playing Boal, etc.*, pp. 17–32; here, pp. 28–29.
[26]Boal, *RD*, p. 1.
[27]Ibid, p. 2.
[28]Ibid, p. 3. Boal recounts this and other lessons in many places. For the greatest detail, see Augusto Boal, *Augusto Boal, Coleção Palestras* (Rio de Janeiro: minC-Ministério da Cultura, INACEN- Instituto Nacional de Artes Cênicas; Biblioteca Edmundo Moniz, do CENACEN, [1986]).

make their own suggestions. And on stage the performer would improvise each of these suggestions, till all had been exhausted.[29]

With minor variations, this is the backbone of all of Boal's theater that followed. It is novel – if not revolutionary – not just with respect to audience participation, but also as regards what is being performed and who is 'writing' the play. Although Boal's theater to this point was perhaps useful in some regards, it was not activist: 'Continuei a fazer um teatro que acho, sempre achei, é um teatro útil.'[30] With the creation of TO, Boal began what he referred to as the pedagogic aspect of his work. He saw this as separate from his more traditional theatrical work; the pedagogic and the explicitly artistic were distinct spheres. What made TO pedagogic was that it 'ensina aos espectadores que eles são artistas também, que todo mundo é artista, queira ou não queira, porque é assim que os homens e as mulheres se exprimem'.[31] Even with Boal's broader, transitive interpretation of pedagogy, this separation of the artistic and pedagogic and his emphasis on 'teaching' seem to underline the fact that TO, especially the early stages of forum theater, were didactic – not activist – theater.

FUN

Traditional theater ('culinary' in Brecht's words, 'bourgeois' in Sartre's) has a social function: entertainment. While Sartre perhaps saw no need for an enjoyment aspect, both Boal and Brecht believed that entertainment – fun – was a necessary part of theater. The danger was in letting the entertainment aspect become stupefying, a substitute for life.[32] However, challenging the existing theater apparatus was not easy:

> We are free to discuss any innovation which doesn't threaten its social function – that of providing an evening's entertainment. We are not free to discuss those which threaten to change its function, possibly by fusing it with the educational system or with the organs of mass communication.[33]

But it is exactly this that Brecht and Boal wanted to do.

For Brecht, it was not difficult to maintain at least some of theater's traditional social function, because for him the didactic element is tied inextricably to entertainment: 'science and knowledge are not grim and dreary duties, but first and foremost sources of pleasure'.[34] Brecht constantly strove to answer the question, 'How can theatre be both instructive and entertaining?'[35] As a matter of fact, he believed the latter more important than the former:

> From the first it has been the theatre's business to entertain people ... It is this business which always gives it its particular dignity; it needs no other passport than fun, but this

---

[29]Boal, *RD*, p. 3.
[30]Boal, *Palestras,* p. 10: 'I continued to produce a theater that I think, I always thought, is a useful theater.' (My translation.)
[31]Ibid., p. 12: 'teaches the spectators that they are artists, too, that everyone is an artist, like it or not, because this is the way that men and women express themselves'. (My translation.)
[32]Brecht distinguished between necessary palliatives that help us not be overwhelmed by life and overpowering distractions and drugs which simply numb (see Brecht, p. 41).
[33]Ibid, p. 34.
[34]Jameson, p. 2.
[35]Brecht, p. 135.

it has to have. We should not by any means be giving it a higher status if we were to turn it e.g. into a purveyor of morality: it would on the contrary run the risk of being debased, and this would occur at once if it failed to make the moral lesson enjoyable, and enjoyable to the senses at that.[36]

Only a theater that can entertain is able to convey the pleasure of learning. It is exactly this pleasure, combined with the knowledge that action is possible, that facilitates the motivation of action in the spectator:

> our representations must take second place to what is represented, men's life together in society; and the pleasure felt in their perfection must be converted into the higher pleasure felt when the rules emerging from this life in society are treated as imperfect and provisional. In this way the theatre leaves its spectators productively disposed even after the spectacle is over.[37]

Brecht was certainly not trying to oust 'fun' from the process. As with all of his innovations, he was not after 'absolute antitheses but mere shifts of accent'.[38]

Boal also talks of fun in his books, perhaps most noticeably in the very tone of his prose. The sheer pleasure of his project pervades all of his writing, which is replete with interjections, exclamations, asides, and winks to the reader. It is surely no coincidence that for his manual of TO techniques, *Games for Actors and Non-Actors,* Boal chose such a playful word to describe the nuggets of performance that make up his project. Importantly, underlying this whole project is an effort to *take* theater back to a time before the ruling classes appropriated it and return it to its original party-like form: 'free people singing in the open air. The carnival. The feast'.[39]

EVOLUTION

Activist theater certainly does not begin with Boal, or even with Brecht. It grows out of a long historical tradition, into which both men seem to feel it is important to fit themselves. Brecht frequently points out the historical context within which he works.[40] In *TO*, Boal – before entering into his own 'story' – traces theater history from the dithyrambic celebration through Aristotelian oppression to Hegel's 'character as subject' and Brecht's 'character as object'. Boal lays out this history from an activist and politically aware perspective, starting from his first section title: 'Aristotle's Coercive System of Tragedy'. It is this activist perspective that unifies his evolution from TO into therapy (*RD*) and finally (or better, most recently) legislative theatre. He continued to use many of the same terms as he had in his earlier work,[41] but there was clearly an evolution.

---

[36]Ibid, p. 180.
[37]Ibid., p. 205.
[38]Ibid., p. 37.
[39]*TO*, p. 120.
[40]See, for example, 'On Experimental Theatre' (Brecht, pp. 130–135). This is related to but distinct from Brecht's insistence on the element of historicization *within* plays (Ibid, p. 140).
[41]For example, the following statement from *RD* echoes the original definition expressed in *TO*: 'The Theatre of the Oppressed is a system of physical exercises, aesthetic games, image techniques and special improvisations whose goal is to safeguard, develop and reshape this human vocation, by turning the practice of theatre into an effective tool for the comprehension of social and personal problems and the search for their solutions' (Boal,

The Arena project laid out so clearly in the last chapter of TO gave rise to plays that were overwhelming in their complexity and demands on the audience. As TO evolved, Boal's orientation turned toward working with the actors themselves (forum theater and the like) and eventually made an explicit link to therapy. Despite Boal's protests to the contrary, there are plenty of connections between his therapeutic work and the psychodrama of, among others, Jacob Moreno.[42] Perhaps the primary difference – at least in Boal's mind – is a continued focus on activism: 'I believe that sometimes the work of Moreno may differ from mine in that I favor the dynamization of people – making people do. I don't want people to use the theatre as a way of not doing in real life.'[43] This continued drive to get people to act eventually led to legislative theater, where theater is finally truly in the hands of the people to activist political ends. Given the strong popular conception of theater and law as separate,[44] Boal's success (even if limited) in bridging the gap between these two fields is perhaps the strongest sign of hope for an activist theater.

It should be noted that, despite a common motivation and other similarities, activist theater is not the same as agit-prop or guerrilla theater. Guerrilla theater is itself political action that uses 'a gathering or occasion to present unscheduled, brief, pithy, attention-getting skits as a means of arousing interest in some issue'.[45] A note attributed to Brecht makes the distinction:

> Whereas the agit-prop theatre's task was to stimulate immediate action (e.g. a strike against a wage-cut) and was liable to be overtaken by changes in the political situation, *Die Mutter* was meant to go further and teach the tactics of the class war. Moreover play and production showed real people together with a process of development, a genuine story running through the play, such as the agit-prop theatre normally lacks.[46]

Just as Brecht sometimes mixed features of agit-prop with 'legitimate' forms of theater, Boal also blended forms from time to time: 'Sometimes we do forum where what's important is not the theatrical event – not to show something to an audience – but to prepare for a real action a particular group is going to do.'[47]

SPECTATORS/ACTORS

Boal took both Brecht's 'new style of acting' and his theories on the actor's relation with the spectator to another level. Boal frequently acknowledges Brecht's importance in addressing spectator passivity, most notably in the middle section of TO, 'Hegel and Brecht: The Character as Subject or the Character as Object?' However, it is clear that Boal feels a need to go beyond what even Brecht suggested. In Brecht's *Lehrstücke*, the

---

RD, p. 15). As a matter of fact, a cursory reading of almost any two of Boal's books will quickly reveal that he has certain passages, definitions, anecdotes, and so on that he revisits regularly.
[42]See Daniel Feldhendler, 'Augusto Boal and Jacob L. Moreno: Theatre and Therapy', in Schutzman and Cohen-Cruz, eds., *Playing Boal, etc.*, pp. 87–109.
[43]Taussig, p. 27.
[44]Film director Sidney Lumet argues that there 'is a natural enmity between the artist and the legal profession, and it's mostly because of the law's rigidness and need for codification' (cited in Thane Rosenbaum, 'Where Lawyers With a Conscience Get to Win Cases' *New York Times* 12 May 2002: pp. 2–23).
[45]Brockett, p. 570.
[46]Brecht, pp. 61–62.
[47]Taussig, p. 24.

audience might become part of the stage world, interacting with the actors in something of a pupil-teacher relationship.[48] However, Boal tries to abolish the very idea of an audience that observes.[49]

Although he coined the term 'spect-actor' after *TO*, the concept is clearly laid out in that book and is worth quoting at length:

> In order to understand the *poetics of the oppressed* one must keep in mind its main objective: to change the people – 'spectators', passive beings in the theatrical phenomenon – into subjects, into actors, transformers of the dramatic action. ... Aristotle proposes a poetics in which the spectator delegates power to the dramatic character so that the latter may act and think for him. Brecht proposes a poetics in which the spectator delegates power to the character who thus acts in his place but the spectator reserves the right to think for himself, often in opposition to the character. In the first case, a 'catharsis' occurs; in the second, an awakening of critical consciousness. But the *poetics of the oppressed* focuses on the action itself: the spectator delegates no power to the character (or actor) either to act or to think in his place; on the contrary, he himself assumes the protagonic role, changes the dramatic action, tries out solutions, discusses plans for change – in short, trains himself for real action. In this case, perhaps the theater is not revolutionary in itself, but it is surely a rehearsal for the revolution.[50]

The ideal is attractive and clear: focus on the individual's capacity for action to address collective problems. In *RD*, where Boal is already using the term 'spect-actor', the importance of this collective is even clearer:

> In a Theatre of the Oppressed session, there are no *spectators*, only *active observers*. The centre of gravity is in the auditorium, not on the stage. An image or scene that does not reverberate for the observers cannot be worked on with these techniques, because it will be about a wholly personal, not pluralisable, case.[51]

The importance of pluralizing each case is repeated frequently throughout Boal's work. While taking care not to devalue the experience of any individual,[52] it is important that Theatre of the Oppressed not become 'theatre for one oppressed. The Theatre of the Oppressed is the theatre of the first person plural. It is absolutely vital to begin with an individual account, but if it does not pluralise of its own accord we must go beyond it.'[53]

While the goal is to address the collective, the focus is still on the individual:

> The Theatre of the Oppressed has two fundamental linked principles: it aims (a) to help the spect-actor transform himself into a protagonist of the dramatic action and rehearse alternatives for his situation, so that he may then be able (b) to extrapolate into his real life the actions he has rehearsed in the practice of theatre.

---

[48] See Brecht, p. 33, for example.
[49] In one of Boal's many lists of questions and answers, he begins a query as follows: 'Can people remain "spectators" in a Forum Theatre session? No! As a rule I never give peremptory answers, but in this case I answer blithely: No!' *Games for Actors and Non-Actors*, trans. Adrian Jackson (London: Routledge, 1992), p. 244.
[50] Boal, *TO*, p. 122.
[51] Boal, *RD*, p. 40.
[52] See Boal, *LT*, p. 46.
[53] Boal, *RD*, p. 45.

While Boal is talking about using theater for activist ends, his focus is the rehearsing actor. He is talking about demystifying that role, but he is not talking about staging plays as much as training actors. In fact, large portions of *RD* (and *Games for Actors and Non-Actors*) go on to provide many tools for tapping into inner beings in ways which certainly use theater (in the sense of repeated enactments for an audience) but where the activism is more personal than political, more individual than collective. One drawback to this approach is that the people who come to participate in this kind of activity are already probably predisposed to at least one sort of action: play-acting. There is little mention of 'average' spectators. For Boal action in general seems to come from becoming a spect-actor, but what about those who do not attend his workshops or speak up at a forum theater event, be it for lack of time, money, or courage?[54]

Up through *Rainbow of Desire,* Boal has created a type of activist theater, without a doubt. His focus is action and more importantly, motivating individuals for action:

> In conventional forms of theatre, the actors' (or characters') action is observed by spectators. In a Theatre of the Oppressed show, spectators do not exist in the simple '*spectare=to see*' sense; here to be a spectator means to prepare oneself for action, and *preparing oneself* is already in itself an action.[55]

But the level of commitment of time and intellect is not minimal. Brecht was accused of 'uncompromising intellectualism',[56] but Boal's games seem to have little to do with the day-to-day life of common people either. Brecht also transferred the sphere of action to the spectator, but not to the same extent. Whereas the traditional dramatic theater 'implicates the spectator in a stage situation' and 'wears down his capacity for action', Brecht's epic theater 'turns the spectator into an observer, but arouses his capacity for action' by forcing 'him to take decisions' in light of a bigger 'picture of the world'.[57] Boal follows Brecht, but with the spectator as agent, not observer. Walter Benjamin's statement about Brecht seems to apply even more to the Rainbow-of-Desire Boal: 'In every instance, the epic theater is meant for the actors as much as for the spectators.'[58]

This individualization of approach fuels criticism by, among others, David George, who argues that 'The simple truth is that much of Augusto Boal's theoretical legacy ... is a western academic fantasy'.[59] George is particularly interested in Boal's irrelevance in his native Brazil, but the question remains: does Boal's influence go beyond a narrow theoretical basis, applicable only to a few scholars and workshop-based games? Schutzman points out that in bourgeois environments, 'therapy apparently forfeits its potentially

---

[54] Boal does begin to address this issue in *LT.* See p. 42 ('They do theatre when they forget that they are doing theatre') and p. 46 ('The stage scares them') among other places.

[55] Boal, *RD*, p. 72.

[56] Brecht, p. 15.

[57] Ibid., p. 37. At times, Brecht's categorization of his own theater, not to mention the categories later applied to him by scholars in various disciplines, can be confusing. For the purposes of this paper, Brecht is being taken at his word when he says, 'Whatever was labelled "Zeitstück" or "Piscatorbühne" or "Lehrstück" belongs to the epic theater'. (Ibid, p. 70.)

[58] Walter Benjamin, 'What Is Epic Theater?' in *Illuminations,* Trans. Harry Zohn (New York: Schocken Books, 1969), pp. 147–154; here, p. 152.

[59] David S. George, 'Theatre of the Oppressed and Teatro de Arena: In and Out of Context', *Latin American Theatre Review* 28.2 (1995): pp. 39–54; here, pp. 29–40.

subversive edge and is reduced to a technique for coping rather than changing'.[60] Much interesting work could be done (and some already has) on the adaptations of Theatre of the Oppressed as it moves from Third World to First and back. What is already clear is TO's adaptability. The fact that it is criticized on one side as 'very nice for Latin America, but in other countries it will not work'[61] and on the other as 'a first-world phenomenon that now has little connection with Brazil'[62] probably means that it really falls somewhere in between. While Boal is certainly given to hyperbole and self-aggrandizement, even the critical George admits that Boal's strengths lie in his praxis: 'His skill lies not in his much-touted theoretical originality, but in his ability to adapt, synthesize, and codify.'[63] Scholars may or may not eventually sort out Boal's true place in the development of an activist theater, but there is no doubt that he indeed has one. Returning to the idea of usefulness, what interests us here is whether (Boal's) theater is useful for activism in a broader sense – getting spectators out of their chairs and into the streets, making them 'do' in Boal's terminology.

PARTICIPATION

At this point, it might be useful to distinguish between activist theater and community theater given that both relate to participation. On a simple level, the latter refers more to who participates while the former focuses on message and what the audience does after the show is over. Large numbers of people participating does not make activist theater. Similarly, just because lots of people are able to use forum theater techniques to tap into feelings of oppression[64] does not mean they are doing activist theater. That said, however, there are connections between community and activist theaters. One of the most successful modern community theater organizers – Ngugi wa Thiongo – believes that, 'Performance is representation of being',[65] which may appear closer to the classical idea of theater as a mirror of reality than as a statement of activist theater. However, Ngugi's recipe for theater clearly demonstrates an affinity with Boal: 'The main ingredients of performance are space, content, audience, and the goal, whose end, so to speak, could be instruction or pleasure, or a combination of both – in short, some sort of reformative effects on the audience.'[66] Ngugi's brand of participatory theater – both open rehearsals and open performances – often led to a situation where 'there was no longer any distinction between actors and the audience'.[67]

While activist theater is not, as noted, the same as community theater, nevertheless, an activist theater is of necessity participatory. Brecht's epic theater emphasized showing/

---

[60]Mady Schutzman, 'Brechtian Shamanism: The Political Therapy of Augusto Boal' in Schutzman and Cohen-Cruz, eds., *Playing Boal, etc.*, pp. 137–156; here p. 158.
[61]Boal, *LT*, p. 117.
[62]George, p. 49.
[63]Ibid.
[64]As well as to get more in touch with their bodies. The physicality of Boal's theater is also something that he shares with Brecht. See Philip Auslander, 'Boal, Blau, Brecht: The Body' in Schutzman and Cohen-Cruz, eds., *Playing Boal, etc.*, pp. 124–133.
[65]Ngugi wa Thiongo, *Penpoints, Gunpoints, and Dreams: Towards a Critical Theory of the Arts and the State of Africa* (Oxford: Clarendon Press, 1998), p. 37.
[66]Ibid, p. 39.
[67]Ibid, p. 51.

teaching over participation, but it was still a participatory activity, not merely passive entertainment.

> Epic theater's aim is to show us the individual's adventure insofar as it expressed the social gestus and also to show us, in what I would prefer not to call a didactic way – though Brecht did in fact write some didactic plays – but, shall we say, in a very ostensible way, the implications and reciprocal correlations of which a system is composed and which involve people in systems.[68]

The resulting intellectual demands on the spectator have already been mentioned and, indeed, this is something that Brecht would return to more than once. Yet in some ways Boal's theater, especially the therapy-oriented work went to the opposite extreme and risked favoring participation to the exclusion of showing/teaching.

SPACE

In many ways, the question of activist theater boils down to the very nature of the dramatic art. In addition to issues of theater's function (i.e., didacticism and/or entertainment) and questions of who participates (i.e., the actor-audience relationship), the physical location of theater is also important.[69] Certainly we can reject the idea that theater is limited to the proscenium stage and a passive audience, although this form obviously still exists. Conversely, while perhaps understandable from a theoretical point of view, there are decided practical limitations to Boal's answering 'Never' when asked when a TO session ends.[70] With language that shows how Brecht was dismantling all that came before, Benjamin points out that:

> The aims of the epic theater can be defined more easily in terms of the stage than of a new drama. Epic theater allows for a circumstance which has been too little noticed. It may be called the filling in of the orchestra pit. The abyss which separates the players from the audience as it does the dead from the living; the abyss whose silence in a play heightens the sublimity ... The stage is still raised, but it no longer rises from an unfathomable depth; it has become a dais. The didactic play and the epic theater are attempts to sit down on a dais.[71]

Boal – as always building on Brecht – changed the focus from the stage to the rehearsal hall and later, with legislative theater, to the public square. All theater deals directly with the idea of the implied fourth wall, which both Brecht and Boal explicitly address. Perhaps with regard to activist theater it would be helpful to think of a fifth wall – the one (or more) that separates the spectators from the outside world. When theater is isolated inside a building, it is not only easier to control, but is more cut off from the real world. Novel ideas on stage stand less chance of reaching the street if they are boxed in and can be 'easily pigeonholed as "just theatre" – that is, considered irrelevant because they take

---

[68]Sartre, p. 115.
[69]Cohen-Cruz has a coincidentally similar division of how activist theater has expanded the medium 'in terms of: (1) where it takes place; (2) what is considered the core of the theatrical event; and (3) how fully the actor and spectator are involved' (p. 110).
[70]*Games, etc.*, p. 245.
[71]Benjamin, p. 154.

place in spaces designated for 'art' and thus lack political clout'.[72] Ngugi points out that performance space is a class question and a political question par excellence given that it stands for openness while the state is defined by confinement.[73] A truly activist theater aspires to 'open space among the people [which] is the most dangerous area because the most vital'.[74] But the theater is not able to go anywhere it wants, at least not for Brecht, who says that epic theater 'demands not only a certain technological level but a powerful movement in society which is interested to see vital questions freely aired with a view to their solution, and can defend this interest against every contrary trend'.[75] Somewhat paradoxically then, at least for Brecht, an activist theater is only possible where, in some ways, it is already not needed.

Boal, on the other hand, does not seem to see any limitations to the space of activist theater. He did not limit himself to the stage, focusing rather on 'the collusion of politics, art, and therapy', creating a theater that 'blurs false boundaries between these disciplines' and whose 'philosophy and practices are in fact testimony to their inseparability when dealing with issues of change'.[76] Boal's TO crossed the proscenium to include the spectator in his definition of theater; in *Rainbow of Desire,* his conception of theater left the stage entirely in order to take on internal mechanisms of oppression; and with *Legislative Theater* he further expands the concept to include *actual* politics:

> the aim is to bring the theater back to the heart of the city, to produce not catharsis, but dynamisation ... to develop ... desire for change. The Theatre of the Oppressed seeks not only to develop this desire but to create a space in which it can be stimulated and experienced, and where future actions arising from it can be rehearsed. The Legislative Theatre seeks to further and to transform that desire into law.[77]

And in fact that is what it did. In 1992, Boal's Centre of the Theatre of the Oppressed (CTO) sought out Brazil's Worker's Party (PT) with an offer to use theater to help elect candidates that could change the country.[78] The PT's only requirement was that the CTO put forward its own candidate. Feeling it was an opportunity to publicize their project, with no chance of winning, the CTO nominated Boal. In fact, he did win and in 1993 joined five other PT members in the Rio de Janeiro municipal government.

In addition to creating a definition of theater that moves beyond the hall itself, activist conceptions of theater always problematize the space within the building as well.[79] Both Brecht and Boal constantly deal with the fundamental duality of the theater, both for spectator and actor:

---

[72]Cohen-Cruz, p. 111.
[73]Ngugi, p. 69.
[74]Ibid, p. 68.
[75]Brecht, p. 76.
[76]Mady Schutzman and Jan Cohen-Cruz, 'Introduction,' in Schutzman and Cohen-Cruz, eds., *Playing Boal, etc.,* pp. 1–16; here, p. 1.
[77]Boal, LT, p. 20,
[78]This was a critical year in Brazil's fledgling democracy, coming as it did on the heels of the popularly-led impeachment of the corrupt President Fernando Collor, the first democratically elected president since the 1964-1985 military dictatorship.
[79]Boal includes the human body in his discussion of aesthetic space (RD, p. 29ff), but deeper analysis of the role of the body in activist theater falls outside the scope of this paper.

> The aesthetic space is dichotomic and creates dichotomy, and all those who penetrate it become dichotomic there. On stage the actor is who he is and who he seems to be. He is here and now, in front of us, but he is also far away from us, in another place, in another time, where the story he is telling and experiencing is taking place ... [We] are here, seated in this very room, and at the same time we are in the castle of Elsinore.[80]

As Boal sees it, this dichotomy is ignored in classical theater; in Brechtian theater, it is acknowledged; and in Boalian theater, it is finally broken with the giving of voice to the audience. But if this dichotomy is completely destroyed, is it still theater? One can talk of degrees of transitivity between actor and spectator, of emphasizing sympathy over empathy, and of striving for ascesis and synthesis,[81] but the fundamental spectator-audience relationship must remain in some form or we are no longer talking about 'theater'. Thus, what Boal is trying to avoid is clear, but what he is striving for is less so:

> This phenomenon does not appear in the conventional theatre, since the intransitive relation which holds sway there does not allow the protagonist to respond to a spectator who challenges him. In such a circumstance, the spectator feels as if he is in front of phantoms to which he must surrender empathetically, since they are incapable of reacting to his interpellations. The only transmission is one-way, from stage to auditorium (empathy), without the reciprocal possibility of communion, of dialogue (sympathy).[82]

Just as it was for Brecht, the fundamental aspect of aesthetic space for Boal is the division between actors and audience:

> The mainstream theatre juxtaposes two worlds: the world of the audience and that of the stage. The conventional rituals of the theatre determine the roles to be played by the former and the latter. On stage images of social life are presented in an organic, autonomous fashion, in such a way that the audience may not alter them. During the show, the audience is de-activated, reduced to contemplation (even if this contemplation is sometimes critical) of the events unfolding on the stage.[83]

In contrast, the Theater of the Oppressed tries 'to invert ... *immobilisme*, to *make the dialogue between stage and audience totally transitive,* in both directions: the stage can try to transform the audience, but the audience can also transform everything, try anything'.[84] This is not, though, a destructive process: 'The Theatre of the Oppressed ... has as its first premise, the intention to democratise the stage space – not destroy it! – rendering the relationship between actor and spectator transitive, creating dialogue, activating the spectator.'[85]

Democratization of space is exactly what Boal was after with his most practical accomplishment: the transference of his theatrical ideas to a new arena with LT and the creation of 'transitive democracy'. While this project suffered a setback when Boal was

---

[80]Boal, *RD*, p. 23.
[81]See Boal, *LT*, p. 88 and on.
[82]Boal, *RD*, p. 27.
[83]Ibid, p. 41.
[84]Ibid, p. 42.
[85]Boal, *LT*, p. 67.

not reelected,[86] he and the CTO continue to work in such places as São Paulo and Munich to implement participatory legislative theater mechanisms. Even his single mandate in Rio led to concrete outputs, which Boal lists under 'Laws Promulgated During the Mandate'.[87] What is striking about this list is the mundane nature of the laws passed. They are eminently practical but not especially revolutionary. However, surely one aspect of activist theater is its grassroots nature and these laws reflect the day-to-day lives of average people. Whether these small steps show the limitations of this experiment or are just the first movement of a more wide-ranging activist theater remains to be seen. Perhaps a more impressive concrete result is the wide range of participants that Boal brought to legislative theatre. He worked with a variety of community groups (see pp. 106-113 of *LT* for an exhaustive list) because that was a way to truly give the people – all people – a voice.

DISCOURSE

As noted, for Boal, the communication between stage and audience must be two-way (transitive). An activist theater necessarily relies on each spectator's taking some message out of the experience. Yet Sartre points out that 'a play assumes an objective meaning which is assigned to it by an audience'.[88] Can a cohesive message be delivered? TO uses images and other theater 'languages' to approach difficult topics, but this complex process could lead to mixed messages. Boal says theater is discourse in and of itself, but more importantly, throughout all the phases of his project, his theater *leads* to discussion. In *TO*, '"Arena tells about Zumbi" was perhaps the greatest success – both artistically and in terms of its impacts on the audience – achieved by the Arena Theater. Successful in relation to the audience because of its polemical nature, its attempt to revive discussion.'[89] In *LT*, 'Little by little, ... we are able to go on to explain what certain words signify and the people begin to understand and take pleasure in increasing their vocabulary.'[90] Through images, through theater, the goal is discussion of political repression (*TO*), personal oppression (*RD*), and political potential (*LT*). At root, each of the games and exercises that take up so much of most Boal books is intended to lead to discussion, which will itself become not only the medium through which a revolutionary message will transmit, but part of the message itself.

CONCLUSION/BEGINNING

This paper has confined itself to theoretical questions. Much interesting fieldwork could be carried out in order to gauge the true level of activist theater. Hopefully, what has been demonstrated here is the continued usefulness of Brecht's ideas as a call to action and the continued adaptation and refinement of Boal's project as a tool for activism.

---

[86]Boal's first term ended in December 1996. Although he was favored to win re-election, his continual antagonism of the status quo in Rio, his insistence on giving voice to marginalized populations, and his general frustration with the lethargic processes of legislation all surely contributed to his loss.
[87]Ibid, pp. 102–105.
[88]Sartre, p. 212.
[89]Boal, *TO*, p. 167,
[90]Boal, *LT*, p. 45.

Boal's various phases of experimentation have led to concrete results and may finally (through LT) have overcome the individual focus that made them more therapeutic tool than a mechanism for political activism. While Boal appears to be redefining the very concept of theater, Brecht frequently reiterated that his theory was not a substitution, but a supplement: 'It must never be forgotten that *non-aristotelian theatre* is only *one* form of theatre; it furthers specific social aims and has no claims to monopoly as far as the theatre in general is concerned. I myself can use both aristotelian and non-aristotelian theatre in certain productions.'[91] Even Boal admits,

> I am not against any kind of theatre: I love them all. ... I would not like to hear any member of the audience shout 'Stop!' and come up on stage to take Hamlet's place and shoot Claudius. But the world of theatre is large enough to accommodate all theatrical forms ... In any case, all forms of theatre can interact.[92]

The success of activist theater then should not be measured by whether it does away with what came before.

Is there an activist theater? Certainly the theoretical groundwork has been laid. The ubiquity of Brecht and the fact that Boal's theories *are* used[93] and his workshops still command top dollar would suggest reason for hope. As Cohen-Cruz points out, 'It remains to be seen how far TO will go in the US', but 'TO's reception in the US is most promising. Like much contemporary US activist performance, TO finds political efficacy by inserting itself in social contexts. It necessitates new sites, draws on multiple phases of the theatrical process, and expands the roles of actor and spectator.'[94] In Brazil, Boal's continued support despite losing the last election is also a positive sign. Schutzman thinks that 'it might be more valuable to stop evaluating Boal's work solely on the basis of the quantifiable political activism it stimulates' given that the 'realm in which the work yields tangible results is mostly in the more personal arena – in one's sense of self, in one-to-one relationships'.[95] Indeed, consciousness-raising is certainly a necessary part of political action. But in light of the more practical aspects of LT, objective external results should not be discounted and Boal should not be judged solely on his therapeutic effects. Again to quote Schutzman, 'People will continue to question the political efficacy of his therapy and the therapeutic limitations of his politics'.[96] Although that very questioning already shows, to some degree, the success of Boal's project, it is surely an understatement. While still challenged by some, there is much to back up Richard Schechner's 'striking claim that Boal has "created the theatre Brecht only dreamed of"'.[97] Anthony Hozier once summed up the common belief in the limits of a Brechtian theater when he stated

---

[91] Brecht, p. 135.
[92] Boal, *LT,* p. 20.
[93] See David Diamond, 'Out of the Silence: Headlines Theatre and Power Plays' (pp. 35–52), Alistair Campbell, 'Re-inventing the Wheel; Breakout in Theatre-in-Education' (pp. 53–63) and Pam Schweitzer, 'Many Happy Retirements: An Interactive Theatre Project with Older People' (pp. 64–80), all in Schutzman and Cohen-Cruz, eds., *Playing Boal, etc.,* all of whom incorporate Boalian techniques, even though they may change the terminology.
[94] Cohen-Cruz, pp. 120–122.
[95] Schutzman, pp. 142–145.
[96] Ibid, p. 152.
[97] Paul Heritage, quoting from the back cover of Boal's own *Games for Actors and Non-Actors* in 'The Promise of Performance: True Love/Real Love,' in *Theatre Matters: Performance and Culture on the World Stage,* Eds. Richard Boon and Jane Plastow (Cambridge: Cambridge University Press, 1998), p. 156.

that 'Theatre does not change the world but it can operate at the points where change becomes apparent and where intervention is seen to be possible'.[98] In contrast, the laws, therapeutic results, and other outcomes of Boal's project demonstrate that the possibility inherent in such points of intersection between the world and the play is beginning to be actualized by theater. That is, not only can theater motivate audiences to activism, it can also create change itself.

---

[98]Anthony Hozier, 'Empathy and Dialectics – Brecht', *Red Letters* 13 (1982): pp. 13–23; here, p. 21

PERMISSIONS ACKNOWLEDGEMENTS

Edward Braun, 'Brecht's Formative Years', in Braun, *The Director and the Stage* (London: Methuen, 1982), pp. 162–79. Reprinted by permission of Methuen Drama.

Bruno C. Duarte, 'Rhythm and Structure: Brecht's *Antigone* in Performance', in *Performance Philosophy*, 2:2 (2017) online. Reprinted with permission of the author.

Excerpt from Bertolt Brecht, 1933–47. *Schriften zum Theater*. Band 3. © Suhrkamp Verlag Frankfurt am Main 1963. All rights reserved by and controlled through Suhrkamp Verlag Berlin.

David Barnett, 'Undogmatic Marxism: Brecht as Director at the Berliner Ensemble', from Laura Bradley and Karen Leeder (eds.), *Brecht and the GDR. Politics, Culture, Posterity*. Copyright © 2011 the Editors and Contributors. Reprinted by permission of Boydell & Brewer Inc.

Excerpt from Bertolt Brecht, 1918–33. *Schriften zum Theater*. Band 2. © Suhrkamp Verlag Frankfurt am Main 1963. All rights reserved by and controlled through Suhrkamp Verlag Berlin.

Rouse, John. 'Brecht and the Contradictory Actor', in *Theatre Journal*, 36:1 (1984), 25–42. © Johns Hopkins University Press. Reprinted with permission of Johns Hopkins University Press.

Kristopher Imbrigotta, 'Couragemodell: Detail and Arrangement of a Model Book', in *Framing Brecht: Photography and Experiment in the Modellbücher, 'Arbeitsjournale', and 'Kriegsfibel'*, unpublished PhD thesis, University of Madison, Wisconsin, pp. 100–11. Reprinted by permission of the author.

Tom Kuhn, 'Was besagt eine Fotografie?' Early Brechtian Perspectives on Photography', from *The Brecht Yearbook*, 31 (2006), pp. 260–83. Copyright 2006 by the International Brecht Society. All rights reserved.

Susanne de Ponte, 'Stilmittel einer Bühne in Caspar Nehers für das epische Theater von Brecht', in *Caspar Neher. Bertolt Brecht. Eine Bühne für das epische Theater*, pp. 48–53. © 2006 by Deutches Theatermuseum München und Henschel Verlag in der Seemann Henschel GmbH & Co. KG.

Excerpt from Bertolt Brecht, 1918–33. *Schriften zum Theater*. Band 2. © Suhrkamp Verlag Frankfurt am Main 1963. All rights reserved by and controlled through Suhrkamp Verlag Berlin.

Patrick Primavesi, 'Gestalt und Entstaltung der Weigel in Texten Brechts', from *The Brecht Yearbook*, 25 (2000), pp. 190–213. Copyright 2000 by the International Brecht Society. All rights reserved.

Douglas Kellner, 'Brecht's Marxist Aesthetic: The Korsch Connection', Betty Nance Weber, Hubert Heinen, Iring Fetscher, and Frank Trommler, *Bertolt Brecht: Political Theory and Literary Practice* (Athens; U of Georgia P; 1980), pp. 29–42. Copyright © 1980 by the University of Georgia Press.

Erdmut Wizisla, 'Walter Benjamin und Bertolt Brecht: Bericht über eine Konstellation', Robert Gillett and Godela Weiss-Sussex (eds.), *'Verwisch die Spuren!' Bertolt Brecht's Work and Legacy. A Reassessment.* (2008). Reprinted with permission of the publisher, Brill/Rodopi.

Michael Morley, 'Suiting the Action to the Word: Some Observations on Gestus and Gestische Musik', in Kim H. Kowalke (ed.), *A New Orpheus: Essays on Kurt Weill*, pp. 183–201. Reproduced with permission of the Licensor through PLSclear.

Albrecht Dümling, 'Eisler/Brecht oder Brecht/Eisler?' in Albrecht Riethmüller (ed.), *Brecht und seine Komponisten*, pp. 93–110. Reprinted with permission of the author.

Paul Dessau, Hella Freud Bernays, 'Composing for BB: Some Comments', *TDR/The Drama Review*, 12:2 (T38-Winter, 1968), pp. 152–55. © 1968 by New York University and the Massachusetts Institute of Technology. Reprinted by permission of MIT Press Journals.

Sabine Kebir, 'Opferhaltung oder Tarnung? Die Bescheidenheit der Elisabeth Hauptmann', in Sabine Kebir, *Ich fragte nicht nach meinem Anteil. Elisabeth Hauptmanns Arbeit mit Bertolt Brecht*, pp. 5–17. Copyright (c) 1997 Aufbau-Verlag Berlin. Reprinted with permission of the publisher.

Wolfgang Jeske, '"... jetzt habe ich ihm wieder Flöhe ins Ohr gesetzt": Anmerkungen zu Margarete Steffin, "Hauslektorin" bei Brecht', from *The Brecht Yearbook*, 19 (1994), pp. 118–39. Copyright 1994 by the International Brecht Society. All rights reserved.

Grischa Meyer, 'Berlau fotografiert bei Brecht – eine Zusammenarbeit (mehr oder weniger)', from *The Brecht Yearbook*, 30 (2005), pp. 183–201. Copyright 2005 by the International Brecht Society. All rights reserved.

Excerpt from Bertolt Brecht, 1933–47. *Schriften zum Theater*. Band 3. © Suhrkamp Verlag Frankfurt am Main 1963. All rights reserved by and controlled through Suhrkamp Verlag Berlin.

'Interviews with Claus and Wera Küchenmeister and with Egon Monk', in Joachim Lang and Jürgen Hillesheim (eds.), *Denken heißt verändern. Erinnerungen an Brecht*. Copyright © SWR.

Price, David W. 'The Politics of the Body: Pina Bausch's Tanztheater', in *Theatre Journal*, 42:3 (1990), 322–31. © Johns Hopkins University Press. Reprinted with permission of Johns Hopkins University Press.

Agnieszka Karch, 'Theatre for the People: The Impact of Brechtian Theory on the Production and Performance of 1789 by Ariane Mnouchkine's Theatre du Soleil', in *Opticon1826*, 10 (2011), online.

Antony Tatlow, 'Brecht's East Asia,' from *The Brecht Yearbook*, 36 (2011), pp. 353–68. Copyright 2011 by the International Brecht Society. All rights reserved.

Amal Allana, 'Brecht: A Participant in the Process of Nation-Building,' from *The Brecht Yearbook*, 36 (2011), pp. 27–43. Copyright 2011 by the International Brecht Society. All rights reserved.

Brian Crow, 'African Brecht', in *Research in African Literatures*, 40: 2 (2009), pp. 190–207. Reprinted with permission of Indiana University Press.

Peter Ferran, 'New Measures for Brecht in America', in *Theater*, Volume 25, no. 2, pp. 9–23. Copyright, 1994, Yale School of Drama/Yale Repertory Theatre. All rights reserved. Republished by permission of the copyrightholder, and the present publisher, Duke University Press. www.dukeupress.edu.

Diane Taylor, 'Brecht and Latin America's "Theatre of Revolution"', in Carol Martin and Henry Bial (eds.), *Brecht Sourcebook*, pp. 172–84. Reprinted by permission of the author.

Steven K. Smith, 'Activist theater: from Brecht through Boal,' from *The Brecht Yearbook*, 30 (2005), pp. 279–99. Copyright 2005 by the International Brecht Society. All rights reserved.

Every effort has been made to trace copyright holders and to obtain their permission for the use of copyright material. The publisher apologizes for any errors or omissions in the above list and would be grateful if notified of any corrections that should be incorporated in future reprints or editions of this book.

INDEX

Aadhe Adhure 308
abstraction 12, 102, 103, 110, 288
abstract photography 94
acting 10–11, 15, 19–20, 40, 65–6, 69,
 72–4, 76–7, 86, 88, 93, 120,
 121–7, 130–2, 134, 280–1, 294–6,
 302, 303, 343, 364
activist theatre 358–73, 371
actor and spectator 364–7
Adalat Jari Hai 308
Adorno, Theodor W. 149–51, 184
aesthetics 36, 41, 46, 48, 50, 55, 94, 96,
 102–3, 110, 111, 123, 137, 140–3,
 189, 207, 281, 301, 319–20, 337,
 344, 355–6, 370
African theatre 315 n.1, 317, 320–2
agitprop 188, 364
 style 17
 theatre 21, 243, 364
Ajab Nyaya Vartulacha (Khanolkar) 306
*A la diestra de Dios Padre/On the Right
 Hand of God the Father*
 (Buenaventura) 353–5
Alegria, Fernando 350
Alekar, Satish 307
alienation. See 'Verfremdung'
Alkazi, Ebrahim 303–5, 309
Allana, Amal 309–11
Als, Hilton 269
Althusser, Louis 360
American theatre 333, 335, 359
ancient theatre 39, 121–2, 305
Anders, Günter 151
Anderson, Jack 270
Andha Yug/The Age of Blindness
 (Bharati) 305
Antigone (Brecht) 23–4, 27–42, 70, 112,
 115, 124–6, 232
Antigonemodell/Antigone Model
 (Brecht) 27, 31–4, 36–7, 39, 41,
 124–7, 232–3
Antigone (Sophocles) 27, 32, 35, 41, 67 n.6
Arendt, Hannah 151, 156–7, 350

Arien (Bausch) 271
Aristotle 360, 363, 365
 'Aristotelian' theater 292, 316
Arrangement 70, 86–7
Ars Amatoria (Ovid) 270
Artaud, Antonin 268–75, 334, 349–50
Arturo Ui (Dramatic Poem) by K. Keuner
 (Brecht) 214
Ash, Timothy Garton 336
Asian theatre 305–6
Asiedu, Awo 318
Ask Me More About Brecht (Eisler) 188
Aufricht, Ernst Josef 15, 18, 20
*Aufstieg und Fall der Stadt Mahagonny/
 The Rise and Fall of the City of
 Mahagonny* (Brecht) 18, 97, 101,
 139–40, 161, 169–70, 179, 252,
 316, 319
avant garde 110, 153–4, 308
 abstract 96
 American 333–4
 culture 188
Avantgarde (Fleißer) 202–3

Baal/Life Story of the Man Baal (Brecht)
 9–10, 13, 142
Bab, Julius 12
Bach, Johann Sebastian 164, 181, 195
Baden-Baden Chamber Music Festival 14,
 180
Baden Learning Play of Consent, The
 (Brecht) 142
Ba Jin 289, 297
'Ballad of the Woman and the Soldier'
 (Brecht) 180
Bandoneon (Bausch) 270
Bandyopadhyay, Samik 303
Bannerjee, Ajitesh 303
Barber, Karin 317–18
Barth, Karl 156
Barthes, Roland 279, 289
*Bauern, Bonzen und Bomben/Farmers, Big
 Wigs and Bombs* (Monk) 252

Bausch, Pina   267–75
Beaver Coat and Conflagration, The
    (Hauptmann)   245, 252
Becher, Johannes R.   48, 54, 150, 258, 260
Beethoven, Ludwig van   162, 181, 186, 195
Beggar's Opera (Gay)   15, 324
Beggars' Theater   288
ben Abdallah, Mohammed   317, 322–5, 328
Benegal, Shyam   307
Benjamin, Walter   91, 93–6, 99, 103, 140,
    144, 149–57, 209, 211, 366
Bennett, Susan   316–17
Bennewitz, Fritz   304, 306
Bentley, Eric   206, 333
Bergner, Elizabeth   193
Berlau, Ruth   3, 36, 92, 151, 154, 182–3,
    188, 202, 204, 206, 208, 210, 212,
    216, 224–37, 256, 354
Berliner Ensemble (BE)   1–3, 23, 46–8,
    50–2, 58, 65, 66, 67 n.6, 72–4,
    76, 77 n.27, 84, 129, 187, 226–7,
    233–4, 237, 241–3, 247–50,
    252–7, 258–61, 288, 295, 299,
    304, 334
Besson, Benno   244, 250, 255–6
Besson, Iva   250
Bharati, Dharamvir   305, 307
Bharatiya Natya Sangh   302
Bhatia, Vanraj   304
Biberpelz und roter Hahn/The Beaver
    Coat and the Red Hen
    (Brecht)   48
Bieneck, Horst   259
Bilder aus dem Kriegsfibel/*Images from the
    War Primer* (Eisler)   188
Binding, Rudolf G.   270
Birringer, Johannes   269
Blau, Herbert   76
Blitzstein, Marc   333
Bloch, Ernst   152–4
Blossfeldt, Karl   95
Blücher, Heinrich   156–7
Bluebeard (Bausch)   270
Boal, Augusto   350, 355, 358–9, 361,
    361 n.24, 362–73
Bock, Stephan   288
Bois, Curt   58
Bond, Edward   269
*Book of Interventions in the Flow of Things,
    The. See Me-ti* (Brecht)
Borchardt, Hermann   215–16
Boudet, Rosa Ileana   351

bourgeois   22, 182
  acting style   127
  culture   188
  ideology   95, 140–1
  marriage   204, 224
  society   138–9, 321
  theatre   23, 121, 122, 279, 282, 362
  value system   205
Boyer, Charles   231
Bradley, Laura   50
Braunbock, Carola   57
Brecht, Bertolt
  in Bausch's works   269–73
  in Bengal   303–4
  bond with Berlau   224–37
  chorus handling   34–9
  collaboration with Eisler   179–89
  and East Asian theatre   287–98
  epic theatre   109–15, 121, 139–42, 276,
      301, 315, 315 n.1, 316, 319, 325,
      337, 349, 367–8 (*see also* epic
      theatre)
  exile   1, 23, 46, 142–3, 253
  exploitation of women   3, 201–4, 206–8,
      257
  friendship with Benjamin   149–57
  idea of performance   39–41
  impact on Latin American theatre
      347–56
  India's reception of   299, 302–3
  influence in Africa   315–29
  interest in photography   91–2, 95–101,
      103
  in Maharashtra   305–7
  Marxist aesthetics   137–46
  Mnouchkine's adaptation of
      techniques   276–83
  at National School of Drama   304–5
  original interpretations of plays   45
  poem   156–7, 171
  political contradictions   143–6
  production   10–11, 16, 20–1, 23,
      28, 47–9, 51, 53, 55, 57–8, 66,
      72–4, 76–7, 77 n.27, 84, 86, 142,
      304
  relationship with actors   65–77
  revolutionary theatre model   141–3
  roles as dramatist and director   9–11, 39,
      48–50, 53, 57, 65–7, 70
  Steffin's work for   210–23
  techniques   267, 271, 274, 283, 303,
      328

INDEX

theatre practice and theory   1–2, 19, 27,
    32, 40–1, 46–7, 50, 65–8, 91–2,
    109, 131, 134, 275, 277, 320, 344,
    347–8, 351–2, 360, 370
works
    Antigone   23–4, 27–42, 70, 112, 115,
        124–6, 231–2
    Antigonemodell/Antigone Model   27,
        31–4, 36–7, 39, 41, 124–7, 232–3
    Arturo Ui (Dramatic Poem) by
        K. Keuner   214
    Aufstieg und Fall der Stadt Mahagonny
        (The Rise and Fall of the City
        of Mahagonny)   18, 97, 101,
        139–40, 161, 169–70, 179, 252,
        316, 319
    Baal (Life Story of the Man Baal)
        9–10, 13, 142
    Baden Learning Play of Consent,
        The   142
    'Ballad of the Woman and the
        Soldier'   180
    Biberpelz und roter Hahn (The Beaver
        Coat and the Red Hen)   48
    Brecht on Theatre   303, 316
    Business Affairs of Mr Julius Caesar,
        The   213–14
    Caucasian Chalk Circle, The   195–7,
        289, 289 n.10, 297, 300, 303–6,
        319–20
    'Courage Learns Nothing'   129
    Couragemodell   83–8, 83 n.1
    Days of the Commune, The   187
    Der Flug der Lindberghs   193
    Der Hofmeister/The Tutor   58, 70,
        72, 74, 76, 77 n.27, 252, 256, 260
    Der Jasager   193, 297
    Deutsche Symphonie (German
        Symphony)   184, 188
    'Dialogue on Acting'   121
    Die Dreigroschenoper/The Threepenny
        Opera   15–18, 20, 48, 138 n.4,
        139–40, 149, 161, 166, 168–9,
        179, 193, 202, 244, 288, 292,
        303–6, 308, 317, 319, 324–7,
        333–5
    Die Gesichte der Simone Machard
        (The Visions of Simone
        Machard)   184, 187, 297
    Die Massnahme (The Measures Taken)
        3, 17–18, 139, 142–3, 179–84,
        186, 211, 226, 288, 335–44

    Die Mutter (The Mother)   20–3, 98,
        119, 132, 184, 186, 211, 213, 243,
        245–6, 259
    Die Rundköpfe und die Spitzköpfe
        (Round Heads and Pointed
        Heads)   93, 171, 184, 211, 213
    Die Teppichweber von Kujan-Bulak
        (The Carpet Weavers of Kujan-
        Bulak)   187
    Domestic Breviary   181, 213
    Doubter, The   297
    Dreigroschenprozeß   94, 98
    'Einheitsfrontlied'/'The United Front
        Song'   184
    Exception and the Rule, The   142
    Fatzer   142
    Fear and Misery of the Third Reich
        183, 193, 213, 227, 347, 353
    Fetischismus der Begriffe   288
    Good Person of Szechuan, The   129,
        214, 288–9, 296, 305, 308, 310,
        317, 319–25, 353–4
    Grundmodell eines epischen
        Theaters/'Basic Model of an Epic
        Theater'   343
    Happy End   18
    Hauspostille (Devotions for the
        Home)   14, 194
    Herr Puntila und sein Knecht Matti/
        Mr. Puntila and His Man Matti
        48, 51–4, 56, 58, 214, 252, 255,
        257
    He Said Yes   179, 297
    Hollywooder Liederbuch (Hollywood
        Songbook)   185
    Horatians and the Curiatians, The
        213
    'Hymn of Baal the Great'   13
    Im Dickicht der Städte (In the Jungle
        of Cities)   9–10, 13, 97, 103, 110,
        115
    Jae Fleischhack   97
    Joe P. Fleischhacker from
        Chicago   14–15, 137
    Kalkutta, 4. Mai   180
    Katzgraben Notes 1953   39
    Kriegsfibel   92–3, 99, 102–3
    Kuhle Wampe   141, 183, 188,
        219
    'Kurzer Bericht über vierhundert
        (400) junge Lyriker'   94, 103
    'Latest Stage: Oedipus'   121

Legend of the Origin of the Book Tao Te Ching on Lao Tzu's Road into Exile 156, 187
'Letter from the Dialectician to the Actress Weigel Regarding a Change in her Acting Style' 134
Lieder Gedichte Chöre (Songs Poems Choruses) 184, 186, 211, 213
'Lied vom SA-Mann'/'Song of the SA Man' 184
Life of Edward the Second of England, The 10–14, 47, 110, 112
Life of Galileo 23, 39, 47, 142, 183–4, 187, 189, 213, 230–1, 289, 303, 347
Lindbergh's Flight 142, 179
Mahagonny Songspiel 14
Mann ist Mann (Man equals Man) 13, 19–20, 103, 115, 288, 294, 310
Messingkauf Dialogues, The/Buying Brass 15, 40, 48, 66, 121, 132–3, 214, 303
Me-ti 143–6, 143 n.26, 214, 298
Modellbücher 92
Modellbuch/'Model book' 24, 73, 83–6, 126–7, 130–1, 227, 235, 237, 245, 256, 304–5
'More Good Sport' 13
Mutter Courage und ihre Kinder (Mother Courage and Her Children) 15, 39, 68, 72–4, 83–5, 87, 127–31, 139, 166, 193–5, 214, 244, 246, 254, 257, 259, 289, 299–300, 303, 310
'Notes on Plays and Performances' 114
Notes on The Decision 186
'Notes to *The Threepenny Opera*' 16, 325
'On Everyday Theatre' 342
'Pleasures' 189
Resistible Rise of Arturo Ui, The 214, 304
'Saarlied'/'Saarland Song' 184
Saint Joan of the Stockyards 137, 193, 216
Schweyk in the Second World War 14, 187–9
Señora Carrar's Rifles 132, 213, 227, 229, 252, 258–9

Seven Deadly Sins of the Petty Bourgeoisie, The 211, 272, 347, 353
'The Shoe of Empedocles' 173
Short Organon for the Theatre 65–6, 76, 243, 255
'Song of a German Mother' 193
Svendborg Poems 213
Threepenny Novel 211–12, 214, 216–22
Trommeln, in der Nacht (Drums in the Night) 9–10
Tui Novel 214
Turandot/The Whitewashers' Congress 187
'Und was bekam des Soldaten Weib?' 170–2
Urfaust 242, 244, 247, 257–8, 260
Versuche 153, 211
War Primer 235–7
Wedding, The (A Respectable Wedding) 14
'Weigel's Props' 133
Wir sind ja sooo zufrieden (We are just sooo happy) 184
Yes-sayer and the No-sayer, The 142
Brecht, Stefan 34
Breitenbach, Josef 226–7, 229
Brentano, Bernard von 152
Bronnen, Arnolt 9–10
Brook, Peter 66
Brown, Georgia 334
Bruinier, Franz S. 168, 175
Buddhism 293, 297
Buenaventura, Enrique 347–8, 353–6
Bunge, Hans 206
bureaucracy 142–4, 234–6, 235, 247, 341
Burian, Emil 54
Burri, Emil 20
Busch, Ernst 17, 20, 244, 258
Business Affairs of Mr Julius Caesar, The (Brecht) 213–14
Busoni, Ferruccio 164–6
Butler, Judith 204

cabaret 164, 171, 279
Cafe Müller 269, 273–5
'Camptown Races' (Foster) 173
Canetti, Elias 182
capitalism 14, 98, 100, 102, 137–9, 138, 202, 220, 237, 277–8, 296, 324–6, 325–6, 340, 344, 347–9, 352

Carballido, Emilio   348
Carlson, Marvin   359
Carnation (Bausch)   271
Caucasian Chalk Circle, The (Brecht)
    195–7, 289, 289 n.10, 297, 300,
    303–6, 319–20
Cavling, Ole   232
Centre of the Theatre of the Oppressed
    (CTO)   369, 371
Chandavarkar, Bhaskar   309
Chaplin, Charles Spencer   188, 231
Chardin, Jean-Baptiste Siméon   154
'Charité Circular Canon' (Eisler)   187
Chattering and the Song, The
    (Osofisan)   328
Chattopadyay,Kamaladevi   303
Chauke, Colin   326
Chen Rong   289
Chesterton, G. K.   149
Chicano theatre   355
Children's Cantata (Dessau)   193
Chinese theatre   294–6
chorus   34–9, 41, 115
Christmas Legend (1923)   288
Christmas Oratorio (Bach)   181
class consciousness   51–4
Clinton-Baddeley, V. C.   162
cognitive realism   91, 98, 103
Cohen-Cruz, Jan   358, 372
collectivism   278
Come Dance with Me (Bausch)   270–1
comic   23, 51–4, 59, 72, 133–4
'Commentaries on Poems by Brecht'
    (Benjamin)   156
communism   17, 22, 143, 202, 209, 296,
    298, 335–6, 342
Communist Party   16, 17–18, 23, 138, 143,
    245, 318, 339
    Danish   224
    in India   303
complex seeing   311, 322, 328
Confucius   293
Conjunto Dramatico de Oriente   351
constructivism   95, 153
Coronet Theatre   230
'Courage Learns Nothing' (Brecht)   129
Couragemodell (Brecht)   83–8, 83 n.1
Crisis and Criticism   154
Cuban Revolution (1959)   347, 349–50
'culinary' theatre   19, 140, 325, 348, 362
Cultural Revolution   289, 296
Curjel, Hans   70, 125–6

Dadaism   96, 281
Dalsace, Jean   153
Daodejing   288, 292
Daoism   292
Darstellung   37–8, 340
Das Kapital (Marx)   137
Days of the Commune, The (Brecht)   187
Decision, The. See Die Massnahme
    (The Measures Taken)
defamiliarization. *See 'Verfremdung'*
'Der Autor als Produzent' (Benjamin)   95
Der Flug der Lindberghs (Brecht and
    Weill)   193
Der Hofmeister/The Tutor (Brecht)   58,
    70, 72, 74, 76, 77 n.27, 252,
    256, 260
Der Jasager (Brecht and Weill)   193, 297
Der Kaufmann von Berlin (Mehring)   95
Derrida, Jacques   274
Deshpande, P. L.   308
Dessau, Paul   180, 186, 244, 246–7
Deutsches Theater (DT)   10, 13, 23, 46,
    119, 195, 244
Deutsche Symphonie/German Symphony
    (Brecht)   184, 188
Devajeena Karuna Keli   305
Dexter, John   334
Dharwadker, Aparna   308
dialectics/dialectical   58, 124, 130, 139,
    195, 246, 337–8
    of gender   269
    Marxian   137–9
    materialism   28, 31, 47, 49–50, 137,
        152, 293, 337 (*see also* materialist
        dialectics)
    method   137, 260
    performance   57–9
    process   3, 50
    relationship   55, 320–1
    theatre   67, 267–8, 348, 349, 354
'Dialogue on Acting' (Brecht) 121
Dickens, Charles   149
didacticism   179, 335, 359–62
Diderot, Denis   289
Die Bertinis/The Bertinis (Giordano)   252
Die Dreigroschenoper/The Threepenny Opera
    (Brecht)   15–18, 20, 48, 138 n.4,
    139–40, 149, 161, 166, 168–9,
    179, 193, 202, 244, 288, 292,
    303–6, 308, 317, 319, 324–7,
    333–5
Die Fabel (story)   11, 16

Die Geschwister Oppermann/The Oppermanns (Monk) 252, 254
Die Gesichte der Simone Machard/The Visions of Simone Machard (Brecht) 184, 187, 297
Die Liebenden. See Terzinen über die Liebe/ The Lovers/Song of the Cranes
Die Maske des Bösen 294
Die Massnahme/The Measures Taken (Brecht) 3, 17–18, 139, 142–3, 179–84, 186, 211, 226, 288, 335–44
Die Mit-Arbeiterin (Mund) 207
Die Mutter/The Mother (Brecht) 20–3, 98, 119, 132, 184, 186, 211, 213, 243, 245–6, 259
'Die neue Musik und ihre Texte'/'The new music and its lyrics' (Mersmann) 179
'Die Photographie' (Kracauer) 92, 103
Die rote Kapelle/The Red Orchestra (Küchenmeister) 242
Die Rundköpfe und die Spitzköpfe/Round Heads and Pointed Heads (Brecht) 93, 171, 184, 211, 213
Die Teppichweber von Kujan-Bulak/The Carpet Weavers of Kujan-Bulak (Brecht) 187
Die Welt ist schön (Renger-Ratzsch) 95
Die Wenigen und die Vielen/The Few and the Many (Sahl) 156
Die Zauberflöte (Mozart) 161, 167
Ding Yangzhong 289
directing 1–2, 10, 47, 50, 54, 70, 85, 152, 224, 256, 334
'distanciation'. *See 'Verfremdung'*
Döblin, Alfred 292
Doctor Faustus (Mann) 210
Domestic Breviary (Brecht) 181, 213
Dort, Bernard 277
Doubter, The (Brecht) 297
Dragún, Osvaldo 348
dramatic theatre 279, 316, 366
'Dramatic Workshop' (Piscator) 211
dramaturgy 10, 21, 31, 68–9, 75, 77, 163–5, 301–2, 307–8, 311, 316–17, 319–20, 322, 361
Dreigroschenprozeß (Brecht) 94, 98
Drew, David 172
Drunken Concubine, The (Mei Lanfang) 296
Dryden, John 162–3
Dudow, Slatan 20, 182–3, 187, 193
Dutt, Utpal 303–4

Ebert, Karl 97
economics 50, 68, 71–2, 100, 139–40, 161, 323, 325, 349, 352, 356, 360
Edward the Second (Marlowe) 10
Eichelberger, Ethyl 334
'Einheitsfrontlied'/'The United Front Song' (Brecht) 184
Einstein, Albert 188
Eisler, Hanns 17, 20, 22, 141, 154, 166–8, 171–3, 180–9, 195, 231, 244, 336, 338–9, 341
Ekstra Bladet 232
Elkunchwar, Mahesh 307
Elliott, Maxine 231
El, Lissitzky 95
emotions/feelings 22, 59, 72–4, 76, 85, 123, 140, 167–9, 171–3, 181–2, 187, 278, 291, 294–6, 320
empathy 40, 121–3, 127, 130–1, 140, 259, 290–1, 294–5, 316, 319, 321, 370
Encuentro de zorros 353
Engel, Erich 10, 15–16, 48, 53, 244, 252
Engels, Friedrich 50, 144, 253, 298
ensemble 58, 66, 77
epic drama 121, 142, 349
epic style 38, 126, 305
epic theatre 11–12, 14, 18, 20, 31, 85, 87, 109–15, 139–42, 255, 276, 301, 315, 316, 319, 325, 327, 337, 341–4, 349, 355, 366–9
Epstein, Alvin 334
Ernste Gesänge/Serious Songs (Eisler) 186
essentialist feminism 275
Esslin, Martin 279, 333, 335–6
estrangement 38, 95, 103, 140, 273, 291–2, 307, 316. *See also 'Verfremdung'*
Eulenspiegel Verlag 236
Exception and the Rule, The (Brecht) 142
Expressionism 12
expressionist theater 110, 164
Ezekiel, Nissim 304

Fabel 53, 57
Faber, Erwin 12
'fables' 67–70, 73–6
Fahnen (Piscator) 12
fascism 132, 143, 182, 204–5, 278, 299, 303, 325

Fatzer (Brecht)   142
Fear and Misery of the Third Reich (Brecht)
    183, 193, 213, 227, 347, 353
Feingold, Michael   334
Feininger, Andreas   95
feminism   204, 209, 269, 275, 334
Fetischismus der Begriffe (Brecht) 288
Feuchtwanger, Lion   10, 180, 210, 216, 254
Fidelio (Beethoven)   161–2
'First Manifesto on The Theater of Cruelty'
    (Artaud)   268, 272
First World War   95, 98, 281
Five Kobo Opera, The   319
Fleißer, Marieluise   124 n.7, 202–3,
    203 nn.10–11
Fo, Dario   288
folk song   172–3
folk theatre traditions   300–2, 305
Folk Theatre of India, The (Gargi)   300
Forke, Alfred   290, 298
Foster, Stephen   173
Friedrich, Ernst   98, 98 n.24, 102
Fromm, Erich   290
Fuegi, John   46–7, 66 n.3, 201–2, 204–5,
    207–8, 209
Fugard, Athol   318
Führich, Angelika   208

Gambaro, Griselda   347
Games for Actors and Non-Actors
    (Boal)   363, 366
Gandhi, Indira   307, 309
Gandhi, Shanta   305
Gao Xingjian   296
Garam Hawa (Sathyu)   302
Garcia, Santiago   347
Gargi, Balwant   299–300
Gaskill, William   66
Gaugler, Hans   70–1, 74, 125
Gay, John   15, 324–5
Gegen den Krieg/Against War (Eisler)   185
gender   204, 268–9, 273
genre   33, 48, 58, 77, 93, 99, 154, 179–80,
    188, 301
George, David   366–7
German Democratic Republic (GDR)   54,
    58, 142, 206, 233–6, 243, 247–9,
    252, 259–60, 303–4, 306, 310, 334
German Miserere (Dessau)   193
German Symphony (Eisler)   185
German theatre   10, 12, 73, 243, 254–5,
    302, 333

Gersch, Wolfgang   207
Gesamtkunstwerk   18, 140
Geschonneck, Erwin   52–3, 244
'gesellschaftliche'/'social' *Gestus. See gestus/geste*
gestic   51–2, 140, 168, 340–1, 348
    acting   86, 111
    style   319
Gestik   91
gestische Musik   161–75
gestures   11, 19, 27, 58, 70–3, 76, 93,
    111, 120, 121, 126, 131, 163–7,
    268–70, 295, 296, 303
gestus/geste   19, 46, 50, 52, 70–3, 93,
    103, 109, 111, 125–6, 133, 134,
    161–75, 193, 268–9, 270–1, 277,
    278, 282, 340, 348, 349
Ghana National Theatre   322
Ghatak, Ritwik   303
Giddhare   308
Gilbert, W. S.   166
Giordano, Ralph   252
Goethe, J. W. von   35, 180
Good Person of Szechuan, The (Brecht)   129,
    214, 288–9, 296, 305, 308, 310,
    317, 319–25, 353–4
Gopalakrishnan, Adoor   307
Gorky, Maxim   18, 20, 119, 245, 252
Grabs, Manfred   340
Gräff, Werner   95
Granach, Alexander   17
Greek tragedy   27, 29, 30, 33, 35, 37, 39,
    41, 52
Grimm, Reinhold   335
Grosz, George   95, 223
Grotowski, Jerzy   350
Grundarrangements   86–7
Grundgestus   70, 72, 172
Grundmodell eines epischen Theaters/'Basic
    Model of an Epic Theater'
    (Brecht)   343
guerrilla theatre   364

Haiyuza Theater   297
Haltung   338
Hamlet (Shakespeare)   115
Handel, G. F.   162–3
Handke, Peter   334
Happy End (Brecht)   18
Harnisch, Johannes   13
Hauptmann, Elisabeth   14, 151, 201–9,
    203 n.11, 210, 234, 251, 294,
    300, 354

Hauptmann, Gerhart   245, 252
Hauspostille/*Devotions for the Home*
  (Brecht)   14, 194
Hayman, Ronald   334, 336
Heartfield, John   95, 99, 244
Hecht, Werner   75, 206, 333
Hegel, G. W. F.   28, 49, 298, 359–60, 363
Heidelberg University   302
Heine, Heinrich   35, 180
Hellenism   32, 39
Heraclitus   292
Hermlin, Stephan   186
Hernández, Luisa Josefina   348
'Herrnberger Bericht'/'Herrnburger Report'   258
Herrnstadt, Rudolf   247
Herr Puntila und sein Knecht Matti/
  Mr. Puntila and His Man Matti
  (Brecht)   48, 51–4, 56, 58, 214, 252, 255, 257
He Said Yes (Brecht)   179, 297
Hess-Wyneken, Susanne   54
He Takes Her by the Hand and Leads Her into the Castle, the Others Follow (Bausch)   272
Himmatbai   303
Himmat Mai (Allana)   310–11
Hindemith, Paul   180, 193, 195
Hindustani Theater   300, 302
historical materialism   144, 293
historicization   32, 38–9, 54–7, 101, 120, 132, 139, 184
Hitler, Adolf   23, 29, 129
Höch, Hanna   95
Hoffmann, Johannes   226
Hofmannsthal, Hugo von   180
Hoghe, Raimund   269
Hölderlin, Friedrich   27–9, 32–7, 39, 124, 186
Hollaender, Friedrich   184
Hollywooder Liederbuch/*Hollywood Songbook* (Brecht)   185
Homolka, Oskar   12–13
Honecker, Erich   258
Honegger, Arthur   195
Hoover, J. Edgar   206
Horatians and the Curiatians, The (Brecht)   213
Horst, Astrid   203–5, 208
Hovey, Serge   184–5
'How the Story of the Indian Chalk Circle Happened' (Bennewitz)   306
Hozier, Anthony   372
Huang Zuolin   289, 296
'Hymn of Baal the Great' (Brecht)   13

Ibaragi   305
ideology   31, 35, 47, 55–6, 58, 67, 181, 319–20, 342, 348, 356
Ihering, Herbert   9–10, 12–13, 22, 152
Im Dickicht der Städte /*In the Jungle of Cities* (Brecht)   9–10, 13, 97, 103, 110, 115
Indian theatre   304–6
Information for Foreigners (Gambaro)   348
'In Praise of Dialectics' (Eisler)   22
'In Praise of Learning' (Eisler)   22
International Theater Institute (ITI)   302, 304
Irigaray, Luce   273
Ito Kunio   288
Ito Michio   288
Iwabuchi Tatsuji   289

Jae Fleischhack (Brecht)   97
Jameson, Fredric   359
Jasma Odan   305
'Jean Paul in Weimar' (Kommerell)   150
Jessner, Leopold   121, 124, 126
Joe P. Fleischhacker from Chicago (Brecht)   14–15, 137
Johann Faustus (Eisler)   186

Kabuki   305
Kafka, Franz   153–4
Kahlau, Heinz   55
Kahn, Hilde   210
Kalkutta, 4. Mai (Brecht)   180
Kamala   308
Kani, John   318
'Kantate auf den Tod Bertolt Brechts'/'Cantata on the Death of Bertolt Brecht' (Eisler)   187
Kaplan, Jay L.   275
Karanth, B. V.   309
Karanth, Kota Shivaram   305
Karasek, Hellmuth   202
Karl Marx (Korsch)   139
Karnad, Girish   307
Karplus, Gretel   151
Katzgraben Notes 1953 (Brecht)   39
Kaul, Mani   307
Kennedy, John F.   333
Khakkar, Bhupen   308
Khamosh!   308

Khanolkar, C. T. 306
Kilian, Isot 250, 252, 260
King Oedipus (Sophocles) 29, 121–3, 126–7, 132
Kisselgoff, Anna 269, 273
Klabund 292
'Kleine Geschichte der Photographie' (Benjamin) 93–5
Klemperer, Otto 193
Knopf, Jan 91, 202
Koegler, Horst 275
Komaki Kurihara 289
Kommerell, Max 150
Konjunktur (Lania) 14
Kontakthof (Bausch) 269–70
Korsch, Karl 137–41, 143–4, 143 n.26, 146, 155, 211, 236
Kortner, Fritz 121
Kracauer, Siegfried 91, 92, 94, 96, 152
Kraus, Karl 153–4
Krieg dem Kriege! (Friedrich) 98, 98 n.24, 102
Kriegsfibel (Brecht) 92–3, 99, 102–3
Kruger, Loren 315–18
Küchenmeister, Claus 2, 242–61
Küchenmeister, Wera 2, 242–61
Kuhle Wampe (Brecht) 20, 141, 183, 188, 219
Kurella, Alfred 152, 247
'Kurzer Bericht über vierhundert (400) junge Lyriker' (Brecht) 94, 103

Lacis, Asja 150
Land of a Million Magicians (ben Abdallah) 317, 322–5
Lang, Fritz 100
Lania, Léo 14
'Lao Tzu Poem' 156–7
Laozi 292
La Réunion des États Généraux/The Meeting of The Estates-General (Mnouchkine) 280
'Latest Stage: Oedipus' (Brecht) 121
Latin American theatre 349–51, 356
Laughton, Charles 23, 126, 184, 230–1
La Violencia 353
Le Château des cartes (Chardin) 154
Legend of Chastity (Binding) 270–1
Legend of the Origin of the Book Tao Te Ching on Lao Tzu's Road into Exile (Brecht) 156, 187
Legislative Theater (Boal) 369, 371–2

legislative theatre 363–4, 368–9, 371
Lehrstück 17–18, 20–1, 121, 122 n.3, 123, 131, 141–3, 179, 181, 188, 318, 335–8, 342–4, 364
Lenin, V. I. 143–4, 293
Leninism 143–5, 336
Lenin Requiem (Eisler) 185, 187
Lenya, Lotte 15, 121, 232
Lenz, J. M. R. 58, 70, 252
Léotard, Philippe 282–3
Lerski, Helmar 95
'Letter from the Dialectician to the Actress Weigel Regarding a Change in her Acting Style' (Brecht) 134
Lieb, Fritz 156
Liebmann, Rolf 207
Lieder Gedichte Chöre/Songs Poems Choruses (Brecht) 184, 186, 211, 213
'Lied vom SA-Mann'/'Song of the SA Man' (Brecht) 184
Life of Edward the Second of England, The (Brecht) 10–14, 47, 110, 112
Life of Galileo (Brecht) 23, 39, 47, 142, 183–4, 187, 189, 213, 230–1, 289, 303, 347
Lindbergh's Flight (Brecht) 142, 179
Lin Zhaohua 296
Literatura y revolución (Alegria) 350
'Literaturgeschichte und Literaturwissenschaft' (Benjamin) 152
Littlewood, Joan 302
Living Theatre 333
Lorenz, Bruno 252
Lorre, Peter 19, 193, 232
Losey, Joseph 230–1
Los papeles del infierno/Documents from Hell (Buenaventura) 348, 353
Love, Crime and Johannesburg 317, 325–8
Lukács, Georg 141, 143, 152, 245
Lutz, Regine 57, 244, 248
Lutze, Lothar 302
Luxemburg, Rosa 20, 143–4, 143 n.26

Macbeth (Bausch) 272
Macbeth (Shakespeare) 10
McBride, Robert 326
McDowell, W. Stuart 46
McGovern, Maureen 334
Madgulkar, Venkatesh 305
Mahagonny Songspiel (Brecht) 14

Mahatma Gandhi 300
Mahler, Gustav 182
'making the familiar strange.' See
    'Verfremdung'
Mann, Thomas 186, 188, 210
Mann ist Mann/Man equals Man
    (Brecht) 13, 19–20, 103, 115,
    288, 294, 310
Man Ray 95
Mao, Fredric 297
'Maria' (Muldowney) 287
Mariátegui, José Carlos 349
Marko, Gerda 205
Marlowe, Christopher 10
Marx, Karl 28, 137, 144, 292, 298
Marxism/Marxist/Marxian 14, 17, 30,
    49–51, 58, 138–9, 144, 146,
    152, 164, 253, 258, 277, 290,
    293, 296, 321, 326, 334–5, 347–8,
    352
  aesthetics 137–46, 225, 255
  feminism 275
  ideology 334–6, 348
  theory 47–9, 137, 139, 144
Mass in B minor (Bach) 181
materialist dialectics 137, 139–41, 143–6,
    152
materialist feminism 269, 274
Matthew (Bausch) 272
Mbuli, Mzwakhe 326
Mehring, Walter 95
Mehta, Vijaya 305–6, 309
Mei Lanfang 294–6
Melchinger, Siegfried 16
melodrama 319–20
Mencius (Mengzi) 290, 292
Mendelsohn, Erich 98–102, 98 n.24
Merman, Ethel 166
Mersmann, Hans 179–80
Messingkauf Dialogues, The/Buying Brass
    (Brecht) 15, 40, 48, 66, 121,
    132–3, 214, 303
metaphors 37, 56, 102, 153, 270, 276,
    292, 294, 334
Me-ti (Brecht) 143–6, 143 n.26, 214, 293,
    298
Metropolis (Lang) 100
Meyerhold, Vsevolod 19, 112
Mittenzwei, Werner 207
Mitti ki Gadi/The Little Clay Cart
    (Shudraka) 301–2
Mnouchkine, Ariane 276–83

Modellbuch/'Model book' (Brecht) 24, 73,
    83–5, 92, 126–7, 130–1, 227, 235,
    237, 245, 256, 304–5
modernism 305
Moholy-Nagy, László 95
Molderings, Herbert 97
Monk, Egon 2, 47, 242–61
montage 103, 140, 151, 171, 235, 272,
    281
'More Good Sport' (Brecht) 13
Moreno, Jacob 364
Mosse Verlagshaus 100
Mother, The (Gorky) 18
Mozart, Wolfgang Amadeus 164–5, 195
Mühsam, Erich 98
Muldowney, Dominic 287
Müller, Heiner 153, 269
Mumford, Lewis 101
Mumford, Meg 49
Mund, Karlheinz 207
Münzenberg, Willy 211
music 170–1, 173, 183, 187, 188, 189, 193
  and acrobatics 36–7
  Caucasian Chalk Circle, The 195–7
  contemporary 179
  drama 161
  genres 180
  history 182
  text and 179–80
  word and 161–2
*Mutter Courage und ihre Kinder/Mother
    Courage and Her Children*
    (Brecht) 15, 39, 68, 72–4, 83–5,
    87, 127–31, 139, 166, 193–5, 214,
    244, 246, 254, 257, 259, 289,
    299–300, 303, 310

Nadkarni, D. G. 307
Nägele, Rainer 268
Naik, Arun 307
Narayan, Jayprakash 307
naturalism/naturalistic 12, 40, 50, 55, 71,
    72, 75–6, 111, 245, 279, 291, 301
naturalist realism 102
Natya Shastra 301
Nazism 10, 20, 23, 29, 48, 54, 56, 205,
    246–7, 349
Neher, Caspar 10, 11–12, 14–16, 19–20,
    28, 97, 109–15, 125, 232, 233,
    245, 256, 260
Nehru, Jawaharlal 300
Ngugi wa Thiongo 367, 369

nicht/sondern (Not/But) 63, 84, 97
Nietzsche, Friedrich 288, 292
Nigerian audiences 319–21
Nihilani, Govind 307
Noh tradition 305
non-Aristotelian theatre 372
North German Broadcasting (NDR) 252
'Notes on Plays and Performances'
  (Brecht) 114
Notes on The Decision (Brecht and
  Dudow) 186
'Notes to *The Threepenny Opera*'
  (Brecht) 16, 325
Ntshona, Winston 318

October Revolution 22
Ode on St. Cecilia's Day (Dryden) 162
Oedipus at Colonus (Sophocles) 121
Oh! What A Lovely War (Littlewood) 302
Oliver, William 355
On a Mountain a Cry was Heard
  (Bausch) 272
'On Everyday Theatre' (Brecht) 342
On Revolution (Arendt) 350
'On the Theory of the Learning Play' 337
Opera Wonyosi (Soyinka) 317, 325–6
Orkin, Martin 327
Ortiz, Fernando 351
Osofisan, Femi 328
Other Shore, The (Gao Xingjian) 296
Otto Falkenberg 9–10
Ottwalt, Ernst 20, 184
Ovid 270

Pabst, G. W. 288
Palitzsch, Peter 66, 70, 77 n.27, 237, 255,
  258
Patel, Gieve 308
Patel, Jabbar 308
Patwardhan, Sudhir 308
Paul, Jean 150
Pavis, Patrice 273, 318
pedagogy 2, 32, 47, 84, 141–2, 179, 360–2
People's Daily, The 296
philosophy 41, 49–50, 121, 153, 293
photography 20, 31, 33, 36, 83–4,
  83 n.1, 86–8, 91–103, 96 n.19,
  226–30, 233
  art 94–6, 98, 102
  contemporary 97–8, 103
  experimental 94
  German 91

Picasso, Pablo 188
Pieck, Wilhelm 247–8, 257
Piscator, Erwin 9, 12, 14–15, 17, 21,
  112–13, 211, 213, 232, 235, 350,
  353, 355
Pitzker, Carl 201
Planchon, Roger 66
Playboy of the Western World
  (Synge) 67 n.6
'Pleasures' (Brecht) 189
Pohl, Martin 243, 259
popular theatre 114, 301, 317–18, 350–3,
  355–6
Problems of the Sociology of Language
  (Benjamin) 150
projections 92, 97, 110, 112–14
props 110–12, 120, 133–4
'Puño de Cobre' 352
Purkey, Malcolm 325

Racine, Jean 289
Raddatz, Fritz 201
Rainbow of Desire, The (Boal) 363, 365–6,
  369, 371
Rakesh, Mohan 307
Rangacharya, Adya 307
Rasputin (Piscator) 14
rational/rationality 22, 27, 30, 38, 40, 41,
  121–2, 125, 149, 179, 251, 254,
  334, 335, 344
Ray, Satyajit 303–4
realism 31, 35, 36, 50, 54, 76, 94, 96, 99,
  102–3, 301
rehearsal process 1, 10–11, 23, 47, 49, 52–5,
  57–8, 63, 69, 74–6, 77 n.27, 84, 93,
  109, 126, 187, 195, 229–30, 232,
  254–6, 342
Reich, Bernhard 10–11
Reinhardt, Max 13, 119
Remarks on Antigone (Hölderlin) 33
Remarks on Oedipus (Hölderlin) 33
Renate Emigrates (Bausch) 271–2
Renger-Ratzsch, Albert 95–6
Renn, Ludwig 184
Resistible Rise of Arturo Ui, The
  (Brecht) 214, 304
Reßler, Konrad 92–3
revolutionary theatre 141–3, 350–1
Revue Roter Rummel (Piscator) 14
rhythm and structure 27–8, 29, 33–4, 36
Rite of Spring (Stravinsky) 272, 275
Rodchenko, Alexander 95

Roh, Franz 91
Roth, Theo 182
Rubio, Miguel 352
Ruffini, Franco 281
Rülicke-Weiler, Käthe 302
Rychner, Max 152

'Saarlied'/'Saarland Song' (Brecht) 184
Sahanpuruprinsessa/The Sawdust Princess (Wuolijoki) 214
Sahl, Hans 156
Saint Joan of the Stockyards (Brecht) 137, 193, 216
St John Passion (Bach) 181
St. Matthew Passion (Bach) 164, 181
Salomon, Erich 92
Sander, August 92
Sartre, Jean-Paul 289, 358, 360, 362, 371
Sathyu, M. S. 302
Schall, Ekkehard 57
Schechner, Richard 372
Schiffbauerdammtheater 119
Schoenberg, Arnold 186, 195
Schoeps, Karl H. 335
Scholem, Gershom 149–50
'schöne Welt' (Renger-Patzsch) 96
Schopenhauer, Arthur 298
Schöttker, Detlev 153
Schreker, Franz 164
Schubert, Franz 167, 171
Schumacher, Ernst 293
Schumann, Robert 171–2
Schutzman, Mady 366, 372
Schweyk in the Second World War (Brecht) 14, 187–9
Schweyk (Lin Zhaohua) 296
Second World War 28, 54, 58, 129, 182, 193, 252
Seghers, Anna 232
Sen, Mrinal 307
Sen, Shova 303
Senda Korea 289
Señora Carrar's Rifles (Brecht) 132
Sernau, Lola 210
Seven Deadly Sins of the Petty Bourgeoisie, The (Brecht) 211, 272, 333, 347, 353
1789: La révolution doit s' arrêter à la perfection du bonheur/1789: Revolution Must Stop When Complete Happiness is Achieved (Mnouchkine) 277, 281
Shakespeare, William 10

Shaw, Bernard 45
Sheikh, Gulam Mohammad 308
'The Shoe of Empedocles' (Brecht) 173
Short Organon for the Theatre (Brecht) 65–6, 76, 243, 255
Shozo Sato 305
Shudraka 301–2
Siegel, Marcia 271
Sie nannten ihn Amigo/They Called Him Amigo (Küchenmeister) 242
Sikri, Surekha 304
Sirkar, Badal 307
Sizwe Bansi Is Dead (Fugard, Kani and Ntshona) 318
social classes 14, 48, 51–2, 54, 139, 204
Social Democratic Party (SPD) 245
socialism 58, 139, 141, 143–4, 324
Socialist Realism 143, 258
Socialist Unity Party (SED) 243, 245–6
Socrates 258, 293
'Solidaritätslied' ('Solidarity Song') 183
Song Cycles of Debussy 163
'Song Guanyin Boddhisatva' 294
'Song of a German Mother' (Brecht) 193
'Song of the Black Straw Hats' (Dessau) 193
Sonnleithner, Joseph 167
Sophocles 27, 30, 35, 41, 67 n.6, 121
South African theatre 316–17, 327
Sowande, Bode 315
Soyinka, Wole 317, 325–6, 328
'spect-actor' 365
stage set design 95, 109–14
Stalin, Josef 143–4, 143 n.26, 146, 293
Stalinism 144–5, 259, 336
Stanislavski, Konstantin 65–6, 65 n.1, 69, 162, 179, 243, 248
Steckel, Leonard 51–2, 58
Steffin, Margarete 149, 154–5, 181, 204, 208, 210–23, 228, 354
Steffin Collection. See Svendborg Poems (Brecht)
Steinberg, Carol 325
Sternberg, Fritz 94
Strauss, Johann 195
Stravinsky, Igor 179, 188, 195, 272
Strehler, Giorgio 66, 70, 72
Ströhm, Knut 115
Stuckenschmidt, Hans Heinz 339
Sturmflut (Piscator) 14
Sullivan, Arthur 166
Svendborg Poems (Brecht) 213

Tairov, Alexander 112, 288
Tai Yang erwacht (Piscator) 15, 21
Talesnik, Ricardo 348
Tanvir, Habib 299–302, 309
Tanztheater 267–75
Tatlow, Antony 319
Teatro de Arena 361, 364, 371
Teen Paishacha Tamasha (Deshpande and Patel) 308
Tendulkar, Vijay 307
Terzinen über die Liebe/The Lovers/Song of the Cranes 294
Tharu, Susie J. 268
Theater am Schiffbauerdamm 15, 18, 23, 46, 48, 246
Theater and Its Double, The (Artaud) 349
Théâtre du Soleil (Mnouchkine) 276–83
Theatre of the Oppressed (Boal) 359, 361–5, 367–72
Theweleit, Klaus 201
Thieme, Karl 157
Threepenny Novel (Brecht) 211–12, 214, 216–22
Toller, Ernst 98
tragedy 30–1, 32, 34, 35, 39, 41, 48–9, 56–7, 59, 121, 126–7, 130–1
tragic poetry 27, 29–31, 33–4, 38, 41
Tretyakov, Sergei 19
Trial of Lucullus, The (Dessau) 195, 214, 246–7, 257–8
Trommeln, in der Nacht/Drums in the Night (Brecht) 9–10
Trotsky, Leon 144
Trotz Alledem! (Piscator) 14
Tucholsky, Kurt 18
Tui Novel (Brecht) 214
Turandot/The Whitewashers' Congress (Brecht) 187

'Über den Begriff der Geschichte'/'On the Concept of History' (Benjamin) 153, 156
Über die Dauer des Exils/On the Duration of Exile (Eisler) 185
Ubersfeld, Anne 273–4
Ulbricht, Walter 258
'Und was bekam des Soldaten Weib?' (Brecht) 170–2
Unseld, Siegfried 206–7
Urfaust (Brecht) 242, 244, 247, 257–8, 260
U.S. House on Un-American Activities Committee (HUAC) 349

Uthmann, Jörg von 202
Utopia Limited (Sullivan) 166

Valentin, Karl 11
Valle Inclán, Ramón del 354–5
Vallentin, Maxim 243
Vassa Zheleznova (Gorky) 252
Vatermord/Patricide (Bronnen) 9
Vatsyayan, Kapila 303
V-effect 111–13, 139–41, 279, 281
Verfremdung 16, 20, 22, 29, 35, 40–1, 46, 46 n.3, 50–2, 71–2, 103, 111, 122, 131, 140, 154, 269–71, 273, 276, 279, 280, 291–2, 296, 304, 307, 328, 348, 354
Verfremdungseffekt 41, 140, 315 n.1, 328, 337
Versuche (Brecht) 153, 211
Videre/Onward (Berlau) 216
Viertel, Berthold 252
Voltelen, Mogens 227

Wada Chirebandi 308
Wagner, Richard 18, 186
'Waldfest der Tiere'/'The Woodland Festival of the Animals' (Küchenmeister) 243
Waldo, Hilde 210
Waley, Arthur 294
Wang Yangming 288
War Primer (Brecht) 99, 235–7
'Warum wir schießen müssen'/'Why we have to shoot' (Lieb) 156
Weber, Carl 23, 74, 304
Weber, David 184
Wedding, The/A Respectable Wedding (Brecht) 14
Wedekind, Frank 9
Wedel, Ute 203, 205
Weigel, Helene 1, 3, 17, 19–20, 23, 46, 72–4, 119, 120–34, 154–5, 182, 193, 201, 212, 216, 226, 228, 232, 244, 246, 251, 252, 259, 299, 300
'Weigel's Props' (Brecht) 133
Weill, Kurt 14–18, 161–73, 180, 184, 193, 202, 325, 333–4, 354
Weimar Republic 2, 95, 188
Weinert, Erich 184
Weisenborn, Günther 20, 184, 228
Weiss, Peter 201, 269
Wekwerth, Manfred 49, 56, 69, 189

Wer bürgt für Deutschland/Who Will Vouch
    for Germany (Küchenmeister)   242
West African literary theatre   318
White, John J.   316
Wilhelm, Richard   292
Willett, John   17, 19, 281, 295, 303, 316,
    333
Winds, Erich   84
Winters, Shelley   231
Winterschlacht/Battle in Winter
    (Becher)   48–9, 54–9
Wir sind ja sooo zufrieden/We are just sooo
    happy (Brecht)   184
Wittgenstein, Ludwig   293
working class   20, 22–3, 51, 56, 132, 139,
    181, 246, 282, 293, 318, 351

Wright, Elizabeth   268
Wright, Frank Lloyd   100
Wuolijoki, Hella   214

Yang Guifei   296
Yes-sayer and the No-sayer, The (Brecht)
    142
Yoruba popular theatre   315, 317–18
Yuyachkani   351–2, 354

Zaheer, Razia Sajjad   304
Zaidi, Begum Qudsia   300
Zhou Yang   296
'Zu Brechts Tod (Die Wälder atmen noch)'/
    'On Brecht's Death (The Forests
    are Still Breathing) (Eisler)   188